The Idea of Wilderness

MAX OELSCHLAEGER

The Idea of Wilderness

*From Prehistory to
the Age of Ecology*

YALE UNIVERSITY PRESS
New Haven and London

Designed by Barbara E. Williams.
Set in Sabon type by Tseng Information Systems, Inc.
Printed in the United States of America.

Library of Congress Cataloging-in-Publication Data

Oelschlaeger, Max.
  The idea of wilderness: from prehistory to the age of ecology /
  Max Oelschlaeger.
  p.   cm.
  Includes bibliographical references and index.

  ISBN 978-0-300-05370-8

  1. Human ecology—Philosophy.   2. Wilderness areas.   3. Man—
Influence on nature.   4. Philosophy of nature.   I. Title.
GF21.034   1991
333.78′2—dc20   90-46016
                      CIP

A catalogue record for this book is available from the British
Library.

The paper in this book meets the guidelines for permanence and
durability of the Committee on Production Guidelines for Book
Longevity of the Council on Library Resources.

10

For Clarence J. Glacken,
both example and inspiration

Contents

Preface   *ix*

Acknowledgments   *xi*

ONE   The Idea of Wilderness: From Paleolithic to Neolithic Culture   *1*

TWO   Ancient Mediterranean Ideas of Humankind and Nature: The Passage from Myth to History   *31*

THREE   The Alchemy of Modernism: The Transmutation of Wilderness into Nature   *68*

FOUR   Wild Nature: Critical Responses to Modernism   *97*

FIVE   Henry David Thoreau: Philosopher of the Wilderness   *133*

SIX   John Muir: Wilderness Sage   *172*

SEVEN   Aldo Leopold and the Age of Ecology   *205*

EIGHT   The Idea of Wilderness in the Poetry of Robinson Jeffers and Gary Snyder   *243*

NINE   Contemporary Wilderness Philosophy: From Resourcism to Deep Ecology   *281*

TEN   Cosmos and Wilderness: A Postmodern Wilderness Philosophy   *320*

Notes   *355*

Index   *461*

Preface

THIS BOOK IS ROOTED in my conviction that reason influences cultural outcomes. *The Idea of Wilderness: From Prehistory to the Age of Ecology* is therefore subversive, for I have assumed that what the members of a democratic society think ultimately makes a difference and that insofar as our ideals are warranted by evidence and argument, then the natural and cultural worlds can coexist harmoniously. Henry Thoreau and Aldo Leopold entertained similar presuppositions, and I have been influenced by them. Some will misunderstand this book as either romantic or unduly optimistic, even utopian; others will find it excessively dark and foreboding. Such assessments entail a tacit presupposition as to what I mean by "reason." Reason is ordinarily understood to eventuate in thoughts: a product of human cognition in social context. My position is different. I refer elliptically to Heidegger's observation that human beings never come to thoughts; thoughts happen—out of historical and linguistic inevitability—to us. To allow thought to be bounded by social context is not to think philosophically. And yet to be human is to be linguistically and historically enframed. Consequently, philosophical discourse must at some point affirm the presence of what can never be revealed through words. Skepticism of course rises at this juncture, and those with such misgivings are referred to the many explications throughout the text. Lest such readers prejudge the case, I simply affirm that I am neither Pangloss nor Cassandra.

A project such as *The Idea of Wilderness* is an immodest, almost hopelessly vast undertaking. Its scope compels reliance on authoritative opinion; my primary scholarship rests in the unifying perspective that integrates apparently disparate insights and frames a reinterpretation of matters many believe settled. Out of step with an age given to the methods of reduction and analysis as well as intense academic specialization, the argument will almost surely promote disagreement. Cultural geographers, historians of primitive religions, Bible scholars, ecologists, ethologists, archaeologists, natural historians, and so on ad infinitum will find shortcomings and oversights. Professors of literature will likely dismiss my reading of Thoreau as heresy, since even a tyro must know that he was, is, and will forever be a transcendentalist. Even within the philosophical camp the situation is unpromising. The enormous diversity of twentieth-century philosophy, a tendency countered only by various moments of fashion, makes attack inevitable, since no argument can through its own merits win uniform assent. And even within the wilderness genre itself resistance is sure to occur. There is variance, for example, between some of my conclusions and those of Roderick Nash in *Wilderness and the American Mind*.

I hasten to add, however, that Nash's study is important not only in a substantive sense but also in legitimating contemporary wilderness studies. His work is properly understood as a pioneering effort that remains a valuable reference and serves as a baseline to which other interpretations can be compared. Nash's agenda, I have discovered, helped to set my own, even if unconsciously. His steady vision of the importance of Thoreau, Muir, and Leopold, for example, is aimed in the right direction, even if our readings of these seminal thinkers are sometimes at odds. As many hermeneutists and critical rhetoricians suggest, the intellectual interprets in order not to be deceived, a process without end. My hermeneutic is one not of suspicion and deconstruction but of restoration and reconstruction.

A fundamental influence on my thought, one consciously acknowledged from the beginning, has been Clarence Glacken. No writer could legitimately claim to have emulated his monumental work, *Traces on the Rhodian Shore*. It was and remains sui generis, an inspiration to all who read it; this book does not aspire to such heights. So framed, my aims are threefold: to open up that Pandora's box of the Paleolithic, which *Traces* judiciously ignores; to extend the study in a similar yet different way that reflects both the rise of an evolutionary paradigm and nineteenth- and twentieth-century evolutionary thought; and to write what might be understood as a universal history organized around one steadfast theme—namely, the idea of wilderness, the study of an ever-changing yet constant relationship between humankind and nature.

Acknowledgments

I AM INDEBTED TO my readers, both collegial and anonymous, although the sins of commission and omission remain mine. Pete Gunter's criticism and lucid exegesis of many relevant ideas were essential, as were the timely support and suggestions of Gary Snyder and Paul Shepard. With their encouragement I have gone farther with this project than I first envisioned. Many chapters were improved by the criticism of scholars who have focused on figures or ideas I have incorporated. Among these individuals are Jim Baird, Joe Barnhart, Bob Bernard, Bob Bunge, J. Baird Callicott, Gene Hargrove, George James, Dolores LaChapelle, Curt Meine, Jack Weir, Bruce West, and Michael Zimmerman. I appreciate the assistance and encouragement of Charles Grench, executive editor at Yale University Press, and his associates Otto Bohlmann and Laura Jones Dooley. Ms. Dooley also deserves plaudits for polishing my sometimes unwieldy prose and for her useful suggestions. The trenchant commentary of anonymous reviewers was helpful in pushing the book into a form suitable for publication. And special thanks to Max and Carolyn Williams, Mark Parker, to the University of North Texas for a research leave, and to students who assisted me, particularly David Taylor and Robert Hood. Above all others I owe gratitude to Mary and Peter: for love, for companionship, for understanding the demands of scholarship, and most of all for making this project worthwhile.

I WISH TO THANK those individuals and publishers who authorized the reprinting of selected materials in this volume: John W. Bennett, *The Ecological Transition: Cultural Anthropology and Human Adaptation.* Copyright © 1976 by John W. Bennett. Reprinted with permission from Pergamon Press PLC. Susan Power Bratton, "The Original Desert Solitaire: Early Christian Monasticism and Wilderness." Copyright © 1988 by Environmental Ethics. Reprinted by permission of Environmental Ethics. Michael P. Cohen, *The Pathless Way: John Muir and American*

The Idea of Wilderness

CHAPTER ONE

The Idea of Wilderness
From Paleolithic to Neolithic Culture

*And we therefore remain faithful to the inspiration of the savage
mind when we recognize that, by an encounter it alone could have
foreseen, the scientific spirit in its most modern form will have
contributed to legitimize the principles of savage thought and reestablish it in its rightful place.*
— Claude Lévi-Strauss, *The Savage Mind*

A<small>S THE UNITED STATES OF AMERICA</small> nears the twenty-first century, relatively little of its land remains unhumanized. The past ten thousand years show such humanization to be the norm across the world. Driven by metabolism and reproduction, humans have pressed nature into its role as provider of the resources to sustain burgeoning populations.[1] An alternative idea of wild nature as a *source* of human existence is gaining a public hearing. This idea questions the long-entrenched civilized-primitive dichotomy, a bifurcation grounded in an assumption that the human story lies in our triumph over a hostile nature. The idea of nature as the source of human existence, rather than a mere re-source to fuel the economy, is the outcome of the second scientific revolution, initiated in the nineteenth century by Charles Darwin and Rudolf Clausius.

Like Thoreau, I need not speak of the virtues of civilization, for it has champions enough. Nor do I wish to speak harshly of it, for that would be radical ingratitude. I need not address factually the looming global eco-crisis, since that hoary potential now urgently presses itself on the earth's people. Instead, I wish to explore what remains for most—and has been for me—a terra incognita, a forbidden place, a heart of darkness that civilized people have long attempted to repress—that is, the wilderness within the human soul and without, in that living profusion that envelops all creation. Of course my thesis does involve the so-called environmen-

I

tal crisis, which reflects an underlying philosophy of nature. It also entails critical assessments of Western civilization, though I make no claim that my case is impervious to criticism in turn. Much about our culture encourages me to think that evolution in consciousness may yet forestall massive extinctions of natural species and calamitous disruption of global ecology. Humankind's apparent success in dominating and transforming wilderness into civilization not only endangers the web of life itself but fundamentally diminishes our humanity, our potential for a fuller and richer human beingness. And so, in the beginning, I can do no better than repeat Thoreau's admonition: "In wildness lies the preservation of the world."

IF WE BELIEVE nature enthusiasts and poets, humans still revel in the transhuman values experienced through wilderness encounters. Robinson Jeffers writes that the "beauty of things—Is in the beholder's brain—the human mind's translation of their transhuman/Intrinsic value."[2] Many of us experience this beauty in the outdoors, and find balm for our persons, stimulation for our imaginations. Sigurd Olson, who spent a lifetime guiding in the boundary waters of Minnesota, observes that once city folk are a day or two into the backcountry with everyday demands left behind, ancient rhythms again resonate with human spirits, and they are lifted up, renewed in body and soul.[3] Similarly, Colin Fletcher, perhaps the best known American backwoods trekker, finds backpacking's reason-to-be in its rekindling of his sense of unity with nature.[4] And John Muir, one of the giants of wilderness philosophy, catches the attractiveness of backcountry adventure in the first paragraph of *Our National Parks,* arguing that "going to the mountains is going home; that wildness is a necessity; and that mountain parks and reservations are useful not only as fountains of timber and irrigating rivers, but as fountains of life."[5]

Perhaps modern people cannot go home again, since at least ten thousand years of cultural history separate us from intuitive awareness of the *Magna Mater,* the natural, organic process including soil and sun that created *Homo sapiens* and all other life-forms on earth.[6] But wild nature still offers opportunity for contemplative encounters, occasions for human beings to reflect on life and cosmos, on meaning and significance that transcends the culturally relative categories of modern existence. Joseph Sax argues that providing such recreational occasions is the justification for, and should be the guiding consideration behind, the creation and management of national parks.[7] Yet the idea of wilderness is more than this, more than mere justification for preservation of wild lands so that backpackers and fishers, or hunters and romantics, might relax and ponder the meaning of existence, hunt game, or delight in unhumanized landscapes and mountain vistas.

Viewed retrospectively, the idea of wilderness represents a heightened awareness by the agrarian or Neolithic mind, as farming and herding supplanted hunting and gathering, of distinctions between humankind and nature. As understood today, it is a mélange of competing philosophies, ranging from resource conservation to so-called deep ecology. And prospectively the idea of wilderness may be understood as lying along a continuum where it is, on one end, little more than a romantic anachronism and, on the other, a category intrinsically bound up with the emergence of an evolutionary viewpoint on cosmological process. Understanding all these different, sometimes inconsistent, and even contradictory ideas of wilderness requires a long and careful consideration, itself caught up in the vagaries of history and thickets of detail. Yet, as the twentieth century careens toward the twenty-first, and an almost total humanizing of the earth's landscape looms on the horizon, the idea of wilderness paradoxically assumes a new importance in the stream of events.[8]

Henry David Thoreau found wilderness virtually on the edge of Concord, Massachusetts; a few decades later John Muir wandered freely in the backcountry, often without encountering even the smallest outpost of civilization. But in the fifty-two years between the deaths of Thoreau (1862) and Muir (1914) there occurred an almost simultaneous change in the American wilderness, construed broadly as including both animate and inanimate components of nature, and in the very concept of wild nature. The creation of America's national parks—Yellowstone, the first, was created in 1872—and conservation-minded, nature-preserving and protecting organizations—such as the Sierra Club, founded in 1892—testifies to this change. The idea of creating in perpetuity a wilderness enclave of land, plants, and animals would have been unthinkable at the beginning of the nineteenth century, akin to carrying coals to Newcastle.[9] Similarly, the need for an organization to educate Americans about the inherent values of wild lands and life, and to promote either conservation or preservation, would have been incomprehensible even a few decades earlier.

As the nineteenth century began, wilderness existed in abundance; even on the East Coast great expanses of land, timber, and water were yet to be encroached upon.[10] By 1900 demand for wilderness was beginning to outstrip supply. Frederick Jackson Turner's famous book, *The Frontier in American History* (1893), is a monument to the closing of the American frontier, the wildness Turner believed essential to American culture. Land use and the makeup of native plant and animal communities changed rapidly and widely in the nineteenth century. Propelled by a capitalistic political economy, wilderness areas were transformed into civilization.[11] Cities were built, canals dredged, forests cut and burned, grasslands fenced, and the land brought into use for crops and cattle; native animals like the bison were systematically hunted nearly to extinction, partly to promote farming and ranching, partly to facilitate "pacification" of the native children of the wilderness—the American "Indian."[12] The Republic was burgeoning demographically and economically, and wilderness was viewed almost exclusively as a natural resource to be exploited.

The nineteenth century also marked the beginning of an important change in the meaning of the idea of wilderness. Elliptically stated, a shift transpired from viewing wild nature as merely a valuable resource (as a means to economic ends) and obstacle (wilderness must be conquered for civilization to advance) toward a conception of wilderness as an end in its own right and an endangered species in need of preservation. This changing idea of wilderness, so vigorously set in motion by Thoreau and Muir and exhibited in the creation of national parks and organizations dedicated to protection of wilderness, is still evolving today.[13] Although history books begin and end, the processes that are the stuff of history continue. The idea of wilderness is no exception, and this book deals with past, present, and emerging ideas of wilderness. Ignoring the complexities and details of conceptual evolution, one can understand the category "wilderness" in terms of four phases or moments of history: Paleolithic (prehistoric), ancient, modern, and postmodern. As study turns to the workings of history—the paths winding from primal past to present day—the whole world, even the cosmos, becomes a stage on which this historical drama has been acted out.[14] Then the student of history realizes that some principle to guide selection of evidence and narrational organization must be introduced. To begin simply with species *Homo sapiens* is to neglect the immense journey that conditions all thought about the wilderness. A study of the idea of wilderness accordingly assumes the natural history of humankind.

Natural history bears directly on the thesis that the lines drawn between civilization and wilderness are not so firm as we characteristically think. In part this is because natural history leads to questions about the belief that Western civilization represents the human triumph over an inhospitable environment. If nature were so cruel, how could the human species have emerged and then flourished, becoming (at least for the moment) the dominant species on the planet? Natural history reminds us that even though culture apparently outweighs our genetic inheritance in determining the texture of existence, we yet have a human nature. This biological legacy is the consequence of tens of millions of years of evolution, whereas industrial culture is a recent phenomenon. The juxtaposition of these two time lines poses difficult questions about the respective roles of nature and nurture in determining human behavior and about the boundaries between wilderness and civilization.

An evolutionary perspective also helps resolve the enormous problem of selection and interpretation of evidence relevant to the idea of wilderness. The many transitions from Paleolithic to ancient, modern, and post-modern ideas of wilderness can be explained not as mere contingencies of existence but as events that gain cogency through location in an encompassing evolutionary framework. So viewed, the history of the idea of wilderness is not all sound and fury, signifying nothing, but intimately related to the evolving character of culture as human nature has articulated itself in particular places and times. In context, ideas of wilderness (Paleolithic, ancient, modern, and postmodern) appear as historically inevitable. If the hypothesis that the idea of wilderness is linked with the developing character of human existence is cogent, then contemporary wilderness philosophy represents more than an extolling of the recreational value of wild nature, retrograde romanticism, or mystical escape from an over-populated, industrialized, anxiety-ridden, polluted, and violent world.

Posthistoric Primitivism

Clearly, we are civilized human beings; of that there can be no doubt. Just as clearly, civilization makes comprehending the relevance of *the deep past* to our self-understanding difficult.[15] Even given the motivation to consider the implications of evolution and natural history for self-understanding, few have been capable of so doing. The problem is that we are through and through civilized human beings who have drawn rigid distinctions between ourselves and the wilderness. In the course of our study we shall see how this "fence" has been erected and how it has assumed different meanings.[16] Human beings have not always done so, and in this reality rest reasons for an optimistic outlook on the human prospect. Let us approach the question of the deep past and its relation to us from several directions, hoping to gain a convergence around the idea of posthistoric primitivism.

The modern mind typically believes that prehistoric humans wanted desperately to escape from the wilderness and dreamed of civilization.[17] I grew up in a world that fosters this view through relentless socialization.

I obstinately retained that conviction until overwhelmed by an avalanche of argument. This prejudice (or prejudgment) is often maintained by such arguments from common sense as, if the life of hunter-gatherers was so rosy, why did they leave it? The modern mind thereby confirms a failure to control the selection effect inherent in its own vantage point.[18] Just as the Schoolmen of Galileo's time believed that the cosmos revolved around the earth and could not conceive of an alternative framework to explain heavenly motion, so modernists cannot imagine any desirable form of existence or definition of human beingness save their own. So viewed, prehistory is little more than a story of degraded savages living lives that were nasty, brutish, and short.

Among a few thinkers the conception of prehistory has changed, perhaps to the extent of a paradigm shift. Natural history, paleo-anthropology, and forager research empirically validate the hypothesis that humankind is an unfinished project whose roots extend into a fertile soil far beneath ancient Sumeria and Egypt. The picture of Paleolithic culture is changing dramatically as a result.[19] Scholars are sketching an affirmative profile of Paleolithic humans, defining them in terms of positive, shared attributes rather than differences. Local variations aside (tools, geography, game), our prehistoric ancestors lived well by hunting and foraging; they buried human remains and were religious; they had an understanding of nature's ways that reflects an intelligence equal to our own; and their art reveals a rich imaginative life. In short, Paleolithic people were not the ignorant, fierce brutes that civilized humans imagine, a fact that places the onus upon us—especially on those who would grapple with the idea of wilderness—to reassess our self-concept. We come from that green world of the hunter-gatherers.

The emergence of a relatively adequate sense of prehistory may be among the more important twentieth-century changes in human consciousness. As Herbert Schneidau observes, "Perhaps someday it will be maintained that the most important development of consciousness in the twentieth century had to do not with moon walks or atomic bombs, but rather with the new availability of an adequate sense of prehistory."[20] The Paleolithic counterrevolution itself, however, is framed by the nineteenth-century idea of the Neolithic revolution, since before then the Western world lacked any notion of the deep past. But even upon realization that human history preceded the dawn of recorded history, it was inconceivable—from a nineteenth-century perspective—that European society could be anything less than its culmination. Through "the lens of history" European culture was the crowning human achievement, providing a yardstick by which cultures in other times and places might be judged.[21] Today this naive view of cultural evolution has been replaced by a new evolutionary synthesis. This theory recognizes each culture as unique and valuable in its own right, independently of comparison to any other.[22] Clearly, the ideas that "history begins at Sumer," that the modern age caps a human project started in antiquity, and that the story of humankind rests in triumph over the malevolent forces of nature cannot withstand critical scrutiny. Indeed, they beg for criticism, for deconstruction.

Of course, the Paleolithic counterrevolution is unfinished, an ongoing research project. No definitive paradigm for a posthistoric primitivism has yet to win consensus, and no decisive reading of the deep past is possible. Scholars are cautious in judging contemporaneous aborigines apart from the contexts in which they are studied.[23] And as inquiry turns to the deep, deeper, and deepest past, it seems to exceed the bounds of any legitimate research.[24] But if we recognize that our perception of prehistory has been conditioned by the accidents of history, a posthistoric primitivism becomes possible. From this perspective the basic cultural forms, from hunting-gathering to advanced industrial societies, form no linear sequence of evolution but rather are mosaics built over time and place by countless generations driven by the steadfast pressure of human metabolisms. Given an understanding that culture is a mosaic of ever-changing and yet recoverable parts that can be reintegrated into the present, it follows that humankind can recognize its many affinities with the Paleolithic past. By clearing away the undergrowth that obscures our connection with the archaic, we may discover vital relations between wildness and human beingness.[25] By putting aside our present view of ourselves as the norm for human existence, we can recognize affinities with the primitive while acknowledging differences. Paleolithic hunters and foragers, who lived in harmony with nature's economy, thus inspire us as we attempt to reform our own culture. This does not mean, however, that humankind can go back to the Paleolithic or to the old ways, for that is impossible. Rather, we might fashion an old-new way of being.

The boundaries between wilderness and civilization can be explored only obliquely.[26] If we look directly through the historical lens we see nothing. And the reason why we see nothing is clear: the *idea of history* itself precludes any understanding of a *Paleolithic idea of wilderness*.[27] The idea of history itself has a history, and we shall examine its origin and elaboration in chapter 2. What is crucial at this juncture is to recognize that through the lens of history human experience takes place entirely outside nature. The world becomes merely a stage upon which the human drama is enacted. The wild plants and animals, the web of life with which our humanity is bound, and without which the human drama could not be enacted, become bit players.[28] The modern viewpoint thus impels us to relentlessly subjugate the wilderness, since things wild and free are alien to sensibilities nurtured so carefully in the garden of civilization. Hence, the wild and spontaneous wonder of nature is translated into the convenient categories of culture. As Hans Peter Duerr writes, "Strangeness is alienated and resettled at home and thus neutralized. Things are understood as soon as it can be shown that we have always understood them, and they are arranged within what we consider the province of our culture."[29] Our prevailing definitions of "wildness" and "wilderness" preclude recognition of nature as a spontaneous and naturally organized system in which all parts are harmoniously interrelated; in consequence, humankind has believed itself compelled to impose order on nature.

The Paleolithic counterrevolutionary, however, actually sees the deep past. From such a perspective the relation between the human species and the "other"—that is, the wilderness itself—is not simply one of exploitation and domination. Instead, wild nature and culture are understood as organically related. So viewed, the destruction of things wild and free will entail the collapse of any civilization that rests upon them. Insofar as this thesis is correct, then the modern project, which has long promised the total humanization of the earth's surface, is paradoxically destined to fail through its own success. As Gary Snyder argues, "In a fixed universe there would be no freedom."[30] To enjoy the benefits of freedom human beings are obligated to practice good manners, and that etiquette begins with preservation of the natural grounds that underlie the cultural expression of our political and economical individuality. From the perspective of a posthistoric primitivism, wilderness is essential in revealing to us what it means to be *civilized* human beings, since only through the recognition of what we are not (the negative) can we understand what we are (the positive). Or, as Paul Shepard argues, even granted that we are culture-dwelling and thus socially intense creatures, "much of the unconscious life of the individual is rooted in interaction with otherness that goes beyond our own kind, interacting with it very early in personal growth, not as an alternative to human socialization, but as an adjunct to it. . . . Identity formation grows from the subjective separation of self from not-self, living from nonliving, human from nonhuman, and proceeds in speech to employ plant and animal taxonomy as a means of conceptual thought and as a model of relatedness."[31]

In sum, experience of the wilderness as an "other" is necessary to any grounded understanding of human beingness and articulation of individual identity. We can be what we are capable of being only if we also have some sense of what we are not. Duerr argues that we "should turn wild so as not to *surrender* to our own wildness, but rather to acquire in that way a consciousness of ourselves as tamed, as cultural beings."[32] Human beings are not pure thinking things ensconced within Euroculture but beings whose thoughts and feelings are embodied, centered, in an organic human nature fashioned in the web of life over the longueurs of space and time, internally related to nature.[33] Wilderness experience indelibly conveys the immediate reality of this natural universe of human experience. Of course, the urban dweller may be terror stricken by such an encounter, and the logical mind suspicious of any experience that cannot be measured. As Duerr points out, however, "At times, and whether this is more a psychological argument than an epistemological one we need not argue at the moment, we may even have to sacrifice the ability to *represent* such experiences in a generally intelligible way in return for achieving the ability to experience them."[34]

The Mythology of the Great Hunt

The fact that classical and totemistic myths have to refer to some version of translinguistic fact—to the Gods and Nature—proves not that there are Gods, but that our talents for interpreting our place in the world may be distinctly limited by the nature of language.
—Eric Gould, *Mythical Intentions in Modern Literature*

The modernist believes that Paleolithic people were a priori primitive because they believed in myth and practiced magic. Viewed directly through the lens of history, modern people are rational and therefore superior since they have achieved a factual and lawful scientific understanding of the world, dominated nature through technology, and abandoned mythological belief and magical practice. But posthistoric primitivism challenges the facile notion that belief in myth is a fortiori proof of irrationality, subjectivity, and even derangement. No longer can we dismiss the Paleolithic mind as a hopelessly retrograde form of consciousness held in the grip of magic and myth. Indeed, the human animal—prehistoric, archaic, or modern—must have its mythic beliefs. Myth reflects the lingering reverberations of the mysterious origins of speech and language. Modernism itself, as we shall see in chapters 2 and 3, is a fictive "mythicity" and, like all myth, is tied with language.[35] Our modern myths live on in our world: in the way we speak of the world, calling into being those meanings that define our existence. Eric Gould persuasively argues that when myth is taken seriously (that is, viewed positively rather than pejoratively, where myth equals silly superstitions and fables), "we confront the fact that somehow it has proven itself essential, or very close to essential, within the cultural and social scheme of things."[36] Leszek Kolakowski argues that "mythical consciousness is ubiquitous, although normally poorly revealed. If it is present in every understanding of the world as endowed with values, it is also present in every understanding of history as meaningful."[37] In other words, mythic consciousness is inescapable, and insofar as myths are successful, they make intelligible what would otherwise remain incomprehensible.

Mythic beliefs clearly are common to all people in all places at all times, representing the human attempt to struggle with ultimate mysteries in a narrative form. According to Joseph Campbell, "Myth is the secret opening through which the inexhaustible energies of the cosmos pour into human cultural manifestation. Religions, philosophies, arts, the social forms of primitive and historic man, prime discoveries in science and technology, the very dreams that blister sleep, boil up from the basic, magic ring of myth."[38] Eric Gould argues that myths likely "derive their universal significance from the way in which they try to reconstitute an original event or explain some fact about human nature and its worldly or cosmic context."[39] Myths are invariably reflected in language, beginning in an act of radical creativity that explains what is missing: an account of the origin, of the human place in the world. Schneidau argues that "language is the great original 'system of difference' which reaches and brings together all members of a culture; myth, a special kind of language, supports many other 'systems of difference' (kinship systems, geographics) which allow the culture to elaborate itself."[40] Since myth is language, then myth "is both hypothesis and compromise. Its meaning is perpetually open and universal only because once the absence of a final meaning is recognized, the gap itself demands interpretation which, in turn, must go on and on, for language is nothing if it is not a system of open meaning."[41]

Yet the modernist turns deaf ears and unseeing eyes to the evidence and arguments of the contemporary mythographer. Perhaps this is because grasping our own myths, at the level of self-conscious awareness, is both painful and difficult. As Albert Cooke observes, "Language is haunted by myth, and the act of defining myth is an act of something like exorcism."[42] The hermeneutic instruments of the mythographer cut deeply, for the modern mind believes in the reality of what is paradoxically only a world-in-force: a socially constructed reality enmeshed in linguisticality and historicity. Among other modernist articles of faith is belief in the myth of the technological fix; that myth, as we shall see in chapter 3, is grounded in a radical faith in the power of science to resurrect humankind from any and all travails—to build, in effect, a New Jerusalem. To the modernist, "primitive" people (lacking science and technology) had only their hunter mythology and magic, imaginative fabrications and superstitious practices ungrounded in reality, and thus they stood helpless before the forces of the world. Yet, as Lévi-Strauss reminds us,

> myths and rites are far from being, as has often been held, the product of . . . [Homo sapiens] "myth making faculty," turning its back on reality. Their principal value is indeed to preserve until the present time the remains of methods of observation and reflection which were (and no doubt still are) precisely adapted to discoveries of a certain type: those which nature authorised from the starting point of a speculative organization and exploitation of the sensible world in sensible terms. This science of the concrete was necessarily restricted by its essence to results other than those destined to be achieved by the exact natural sciences but it was no less scientific and its results no less genuine. They were secured ten thousand years earlier and still remain at the basis of our own civilization.[43]

From the perspective of a posthistoric primitivism, which sets aside the modern mind's assumption of an absolute vantage point, the broad outlines of mythological consciousness have been uncovered. Obviously, incomplete physical evidence complicates understanding of the Paleolithic mind, and since no record of Paleolithic language exists, the problem of interpreting the available evidence is enormous; further, alternative explications are possible. But the Paleolithic mind surely lacked any notion of wilderness akin to that which dominates the modern mind; for the Paleolithic mind was a mythic mode of consciousness, whereas the modern mind is historically conscious.[44] Several hypotheses about prehistoric ideas of wilderness are offered below (table 1). Although these hypotheses are conjectural, they are supported by an array of anthropological and mythographical studies. Perhaps enough evidence exists to warrant Joseph Campbell's judgment that the Paleolithic mind discovered "the *first* revelation of Nature-in-its-manner-of-operation."[45]

Because prehistoric human beings likely lacked reflective awareness of culture—that is, any conceptually clear realization that culture was a humanly initiated and sustained rather than an instinctive or natural mode of behavior—they thought of themselves as one with plants and animals,

Table 1. Conjectures on a Paleolithic Idea of Wilderness

PALEOLITHIC HUNTER-FORAGERS likely
  – believed that irrespective of place, nature was home
  – regarded nature as intrinsically feminine
  – thought of nature as alive
  – assumed that the entire world of plants and animals, even the land itself, was sacred
  – surmised that divinity could take many natural forms and that metaphor was the mode of divine access
  – believed that time was synchronous, folded into an eternal mythical present
  – supposed that ritual was essential to maintaining the natural and cyclical order of life and death

---

rivers and forests, as part of a larger, encompassing whole (which we would term a natural process or wild nature).[46] Most students of the deep past agree that no human thinking is entirely natural. "As soon as humans are aware of themselves in societies, they have already separated from nature. This entering wedge of alienation can be blocked in 'cold' [archaic] societies, which seek to inhibit further separation from nature by projecting back all their structures and folkways to natural sources and analogies."[47] Stated another way, the Paleolithic mind did not distinguish the human enterprise from the natural world, but it did wonder at the miracle of existence and created an elaborate hunter mythology to account for reality.[48]

Totemism, the identification of a hunting-gathering clan with a species of plant or animal, supports the conjecture that Paleolithic people believed themselves to be one with nature. Vestiges of a circumpolar Paleolithic cult of the bear have been found in widely scattered locations, suggesting that bear ceremonialism (and other kinds of rituals associated with bones) was practiced widely throughout the prehistoric world of hunter-gatherers.[49] "*Karhu—Bjorn—Braun—Bear,*" writes the poet Gary Snyder in *Turtle Island,* revivifying in this "saying" some sense of a pancultural ancient wisdom.[50] As a conceptual system, totemism is rooted in a concrete natural history. More specifically, totemism appears to arise from the human experience of interacting with the natural world for generations, stretching back into an obscure but remembered past—the point of origin. This temporal structure is sometimes called the *primeval* or *prehuman flux* and connotes the aboriginal belief in a "primeval kinship with all creatures of the living world and to the essential continuity among them all." The totem thus transcends the appearance of difference between various natural species; it refers to a more fundamental or basic reality where "all living beings existed in a state of flux—their external forms were interchangeable. This animate world includes all that grows and all that moves about in air and sky, on earth, below the earth, and in the sea; it includes even the gods and the everbearing earth in her totality." [51]

The totem also helps account for the emergence of human beings as distinct from other species while simultaneously maintaining an identity with the rest of creation. Totemic symbols—for example, the bear—represent the ancestral lineage of a clan, detailing the interrelations of clan and nature, mixed with either mythological or historical incident. For the Paleolithic mind the totem is a metaphorical link to or symbolic representation of both humankind's unity with the natural world and the vital interdependence (kinship) between humankind and nature. Paul Shepard argues that "plant and animal totems are not simply objects of reverence; they serve as codes for formulating and relating the conceptual systems of nature and of culture." [52] Totemic signs bound hunter-gatherers to the geographic locus of their clan. Home was wherever they happened to be within the domain where the band had always resided, hunting game and gathering foodstuffs. "For hunting-gathering people the natural environment is firm. The kin structure is stable because the individual is born or initiated into a group as durable as the plant or animal species taken by it as a totemic emblem. Given the reality of flux in all human society, this link to the natural throws people into closer intellectual and emotional recognition of the one constant in their lives, the terrain with its enduring natural community." [53] In such a world human beings could never be lost, for they were always among their kin, and the Paleolithic mind was therefore necessarily in its element wherever it happened to find itself.

The inhabited regions of earth—if prehistoric people had such a conception—were simply the location of a band within some traditionally determined hunting area.[54] The idea of wilderness with connotations of wasteland, badlands, or hinterlands was not conceivable, just as a "round earth" is not conceivable to people who believe in a "flat earth." Shepard argues that space for prehistoric people "is a society of named places—not categories such as 'river' or 'mountain' but proper names, marked in tribal memory and sometimes in myth. . . . Seeing all nature as a society may even have made possible the evolution of intelligence to that acute degree of awareness without which the vast physical universe would be found terrifying, even intolerable." [55] Home was a natural world of plants, animals, and land with which archaic people were bound. The idea of "being lost in the wilderness" logically necessitates a geographical referent conceptualized as home as distinct from all other places; but for Paleolithic people home was where they were and where they had always been. They could not become lost in the wilderness, since it did not exist. The conjecture that the conscious life of Paleolithic people was devoid of such ideas as "being away from home" or "in the wilderness away from the inhabited regions of earth" is thus plausible.[56]

Since human beings were at the top of the food chain (in spite of an occasional human loss to larger carnivores), hunting-gathering areas of some size were needed to sustain a group, depending on natural fertility, variations in weather, competition from other predators for game, and so on. Hunter-gatherers may have constructed semipermanent habitations, especially during periods of drought when animals concentrated around waterholes, but usually they wandered in search of game and other food-stuffs. Males and perhaps females without young might roam over protracted periods, as long as was required to track and kill game. Hunter-foragers typically hunted over vast areas since, as with any large carnivore, too much pressure on game rapidly depleted the supply. Given the sparsity of human population, the lack of permanent settlement, and the enormous areas hunters and gatherers ranged, the existence of such concepts as "property" or "trespass" is doubtful. Marshall Sahlins argues that "the first and decisive contingency of hunting-gathering" is continual movement. The value of anything therefore fell "quickly at the margin of portability. . . . Hence the hunter's very ascetic conceptions of material welfare: an interest only in minimal equipment, if that; a valuation of smaller things over bigger; a disinterest in acquiring two or more of most goods; and the like. Ecological pressure assumes a rare form of concreteness when it has to be shouldered."[57]

Paleolithic people lived comfortably in the wilderness, much as the Inuit on the polar ice or the Kalahari Bushmen in Africa, and they probably had plenty of nourishing food. There is no evidence of widespread malnutrition or death by starvation. Paleolithic people were not constantly living on the margin of survival. Poverty, as numerous inquiries make clear, is a condition of civilization. Paleolithic people lived in a world that, judged on its ability to meet the necessities of life, exceeded that of the high Neolithic civilizations and was devoid of economic exploitation of an underclass by an elite. Poverty "has grown with civilization, at once as an invidious distinction between classes and more importantly as a tributary relation—that can render agrarian peasants more susceptible to natural catastrophes than any winter camp of Alaskan Eskimo" or other archaic people living in prehistoric fashion.[58]

The claim that Paleolithic life was short is problematic and controversial. Modern medicine has increased the survival rate of infants and has made major strides in dealing with trauma (such as a head injury), thus creating an appearance, resting on statistical artifact, that the human life span has been increased. Medicine has not changed what has long been determined by biology—that is, the three-score-and-ten-year term of human life.[59] The modern mind is oblivious to the reality that starvation, malnutrition, warfare, and pestilence are post-Neolithic phenomena and therefore probably a consequence of urbanization, explosive population growth, and the socioeconomics of *agri*-culture. All these factors likely lowered life expectancies of human beings after the rise of agriculture. Modern medicine, by suppressing the diseases of civilization, has enabled more human beings to realize their genetically determined life span.[60]

Further, we have no reason to think that we have surpassed our prehistoric kin in cognitive powers and achievements. The intellectual life of hunter-gatherers was as rich as that of modern people, and the rate of intellectual innovation, as well as technological and artistic creativity, also appears to be roughly equivalent. Civilized people do have the legacy of the past to augment their efforts, but there is no evidence that the neocortex has evolved. Common sense alone suggests, as Lévi-Strauss points out, that minds of the caliber of a Plato or an Einstein cannot be assumed to exist only in the present epoch. "Already over two or three hundred thousand years ago, there were probably men [and women] of a similar capacity, who were of course not applying their intelligence to the solution of the same problems as these more recent thinkers; instead, they were probably more interested in kinship!"[61]

Clearly, the mythology of the Great Hunt and totemism are not stupid responses to the world but mirror the same level of intelligence—albeit one directed to an unmistakably different view of the world—as modern science. The modernist thinks of prehistoric humans as believing in myth, as identifying with totemic animals and plants, and as practicing magic, and therefore as being unscientific, superstitious ignoramuses or morons. Such a conclusion simply cannot be defended, since we have no evidence that our prehistoric ancestors were "prelogical." Different? Yes, clearly the content of their belief systems was unlike our own. As Lévi-Strauss argues, though modern science and magic are different modes of intelligence, both are intelligent.[62] The theoretical science of modern culture and the concrete science or magic of prehistoric culture are both at bottom an ordering of sensorial impressions that (though neurophysiologically classifiable as sights, sounds, and so on) do not array themselves into meaningful theoretical patterns of experience. In this characteristic, then, the sciences of Paleolithic and modern people are indistinguishable; indeed, to analyze the data in any other way leads to the assumption of radical, even miraculous, discontinuities in experience. Rather than contrasting magic and science, or evaluating magic in terms of modern science, a more accurate procedure is to compare them as alternative but parallel modes of knowledge. Although magic is often less successful than science in effecting practical consequence, it foreshadows its successor. Both "require the same sort of mental operations and they differ not so much in kind as in the different types of phenomena to which they are applied."[63]

The Paleolithic mind likely envisaged nature as alive and responsive, nurturing humankind much as a mother nourishes her baby at her breast.[64] Modern aborigines, such as the Lakota Sioux, still believe this.[65] Again, the modernist fallacy obstructs inquiry into the Paleolithic idea of wilderness. Civilized people perpetuate the presupposition that prehistoric humans longed for paradise, some luxurious garden of easy living that would free them from travail and hunger. Because it assumes the categories and values of the modern world—indeed, the psychological profile of the modern mind—as absolutes, this argument invites deconstruction. From a modern perspective, a binary opposition, which can be neither critically nor empirically sustained, appears between archaic and modern culture and underlies the claim that so-called primitive people wanted to gain control over land and animals, and nature more generally. Most if not all evidence contradicts such a reading, and indicates that Paleolithic people lacked a concept either of a wilderness to escape or a civilization to seek. Only by holding our own categories in abeyance can we possibly understand the Paleolithic mind. The assumption that Paleolithic people were mere children in comparison to us, a later, adult phase of humanity, is dubious. So is the belief that the modern mind is the culmination of human intellectuality. Indeed, given the grim realities of twentieth-century history, there is reason to think that the ancient aborigines were wiser than we in at least some regards and that we can learn much about how to live our lives from the study of prehistoric people and culture.[66]

Perhaps first among these lessons is the hypothesis that hunting-gathering culture was better adapted to the ecological realities of sustainable life on earth—far better adjusted than advanced industrial culture. Archaic culture existed in some form for at least 200,000 years, and obviously a small human population distributed sparsely across the prehistoric world caused minimal environmental damage. Pollution, extinction of species, uncontrolled population growth, the diseases of civilization, war, and the threat of nuclear Armageddon did not exist. Clearly, the relevant data are often difficult to assess, but to suggest that the run of Western civilization, and industrial culture, may be relatively short term is not far off the mark.[67] Integrity, stability, and beauty were facts of hunting-gathering culture rather than philosophical ideals.

Harmony with rather than *exploitation of* the natural world was a guiding principle for the Paleolithic mind and remains a cardinal commitment among modern aborigines. Rituals designed to maintain the cosmic order were central to such a belief system. Hunting-gathering people hunted and ate the bear; in so doing the Paleolithic mind likely experienced cognitive dissonance, for if hunter-gatherers identified with all of creation as children of a common ancestry, how was such behavior to be justified? Through rituals governing the preparation and disposal of the bear's remains, and through myths that explained the common lineage of bears and humans, the Paleolithic mind reconciled this tension. These ceremonies dealt with the mysteries of life and death, ensuring that the bear's spirit would return in the flesh since it had been treated reverently by those who killed and ate it.[68]

To assert that Paleolithic people lived in a reverential and complementary relationship with the environment and believed that the Magna Mater would provide for them does not imply that they lived by windfalls. The notion that early humans must have experienced boom or bust cycles, since populations of game animals fluctuate with the vagaries of weather and ravages of disease, and since insects destroy edible fruits and grains, has been shown to be improbable.[69] Food was generally plentiful, though specific items were seasonal. Because they were omnivores, hunting-gathering people could eat diverse foods. Attuned to the changing character of the location and availability of food stocks, hunger was for prehistoric—and remains for some aborigines—the exception rather than the rule.[70] Early humans did possess technologies, tools, and other human-made artifacts necessary for hunt and hearth: fire, such stone implements as scrapers and axe heads, bone needles, gourds for water, and hides for clothing and shelter. These were used, however, not to reconstruct the naturally given but to process what the Great Mother provided (for example, spears to kill game, knives to butcher the carcass, scrapers and needles to help prepare hides for wear). There is no evidence of attempts to dominate nature technologically, as in using fire to clear forest for cropland (although fire may have been used near the end of prehistory for driving game) or in diverting streams for irrigation.

After deconstructing the modernist view that prehistoric people longed to escape the wilderness condition, the Paleolithic mind can be reinterpreted. We have conjecturally established the idea that prehistoric hunting-gathering people were at home in the natural world (just as archaic people are today) and that they intuitively thought of their environment as alive and responsive to their needs. This idea coalesces around the Magna Mater metaphor, here distinguished from the fertility cults of agricultural people that centered around the Earth Mother.[71] The Paleolithic mind intuitively believed that the Magna Mater would provide for her children. Anthropologists note that some apparently incomprehensible behaviors characteristic of archaic people, such as apparent indifference to hunger, reflect a lore learned through countless generations of prehistory: nature will provide to those who know how to wait and where to look.

All aspects of the world, including humankind, were seen as interwoven, harmoniously coexisting in a mutually supporting system, symbolized by the Magna Mater. The Magna Mater was not an object for analysis and study, however. The myths of the hunter-gatherers were religio-poetic, intuitive expressions of sensibilities forged in the crucible of experience, of living—from our vantage point—almost totally within organic process.[72] The Magna Mater metaphorically represents an intuition, stabilized into a hunter mythology, that all life is mysteriously bound together in a benevolent and harmonious cycle of life, death, and birth. The metaphor rests on an obvious analogy to females generally, and the human female especially, in nurturing the young, and in the mysteries of menstruation, gestation, and lactation. Obviously, the metaphor varied from clan to clan, tribe to tribe, location to location. But the Paleolithic mind presumably conceived of the Magna Mater as providing for all the living world, including the human animal.[73]

More important, prehistoric hunter-gatherers almost surely viewed the Magna Mater as sacred.[74] This assertion has two difficulties, however. One is the challenge implicit within any attempt to outline prehistoric religion generally and upper Paleolithic religion specifically. Even assuming that cave art and burial sites are sources of relevant data, any number of divergent and even contradictory interpretations are possible. Further, the modernistic fallacy constantly intrudes, since interpretation of Paleolithic religion through later forms, such as the fertility cults of the Neolithic age or so-called primitive religions among contemporary aboriginal peoples, does not explain Paleolithic religion but is a methodological procedure that itself requires justification. Under the influence of early evolutionary thinking, the first students of prehistoric religion advanced an "up from darkness" hypothesis, believing that through time increasing refinement (progress) of religious sensibility led to the present—usually, the belief system held by the researcher.[75] Yet even comparing Paleolithic religion with Neolithic religion, which lies next in historical sequence, is highly problematic, and any comparison between prehistoric and contemporary primitive religions must be undertaken with reservation.[76] The modern mind too often *assumes* that Paleolithic religion is unproblematically comparable with other forms when that conjecture is difficult to support. In particular, any attempt to understand the Great Mother of the Paleolithic mind as an earlier and therefore primitive precursor to the Neolithic idea of the Earth Mother must be reconsidered.[77] Yet, to some extent we can comprehend Paleolithic religion. As Karl Narr points out, "A spiritual phenomenon such as religion does not develop in complete independence and isolation but depends to some degree on functional interrelations and limitations, including those of an economic and ecological kind."[78] If we are to do anything more than simply catalog Paleolithic relics, then philosophical interpretation must be undertaken within an ecological context.[79] Human beings can understand, if the problem of historical bias ("the lens of history") is controlled, the past (res gestae), the things done by human beings living in a determinate spatiotemporal context.

A second problem in interpreting Paleolithic religion is that modern people find virtually incomprehensible the notion that nature is sacred. We live in a secular world where the objective mode of knowledge enjoys cognitive hegemony, and thus any and all phenomena are increasingly brought within the rubric of (narrowly) scientific explanation.[80] As a result, among the vast majority of our coevals, the natural world is an object only, a standing reserve to be manipulated through technology, a stockpile of resources to fuel civilization. Those few in the modern age—such as Thoreau, Muir, and Leopold—who have suggested alternative perspectives have been at best understood as interesting men marching to the beat of different drummers and at worst as radicals out of step with the march of Modernism. Just as there is a radical contrast between the overwhelming majority and contemporary voices for the wilderness, so there is a radical contrast between modern people, who live in a desacralized nature, and Paleolithic humans, who lived in a sacralized cosmos. Mircea Eliade, among others, points out the challenges the modern mind has in understanding *Homo religiosus*. So different are the worldviews of modern and archaic people that the "*sacred* and *profane* are two modes of being in the world, two existential situations assumed by" human beings in the course of history.[81] This disparity pervades the fundamental ways of being of modern and aboriginal people. Eliade also contends that the study of species Homo religiosus is relevant to our self-edification, since the behavior of prehistoric and archaic people "forms part of the general behavior of [hu]mankind and hence is of concern to philosophical anthropology, to phenomenology, to psychology," and more generally to all the human sciences and humanities.[82] In chapter 10 we shall examine the question of the bounds of belief for a postmodern world as well as the implications of Eliade's thought apropos of a postmodern idea of wilderness.

The creation myths, or cosmology and cosmogony, to use modern terms, of the Paleolithic mind did not posit human beings as special children of creation separate from the rest of nature. This premise grounds a fundamental distinction between the Paleolithic and Neolithic. For hunter-gatherers humankind was not privileged over the rest of the world. Nature was alive and sacred, filled with spirits. Animals, plants, and even rocks, mountains and volcanoes, and rivers and oceans were viewed as animate entities that also filled a place in the Magna Mater's scheme. As Eliade argues, for Homo religiosus, "nature is never only 'natural'; it is always fraught with a religious value. . . . It is not simply a sacrality *communicated* by the gods, as is the case, for example, with a place or an object consecrated by the divine presence. The gods did more; *they manifested the different modalities of the sacred in the very structure of the world and of cosmic phenomena.*" Since divinity was in everything, the Paleolithic mind intuited its role to be that of living in harmony with life—that is, *nature in its order of operation.* "The cosmic rhythms manifest order, harmony, permanence, fecundity. The cosmos as a whole is an organism at once *real, living,* and *sacred;* it simultaneously reveals the modalities of being and of sacrality."[83]

Paleolithic mythology and magic served many functions, not the least of which was to maintain the harmony and order of creation. Religious ritual, dance, and art celebrated the sacred game and the divinely established bond between humankind and the rest of nature. Game animals, though hunted as a vital source of food, were sacred and worthy of veneration and emulation. Inherent in hunting lay the roots of cognitive dissonance, for mere humans were killing part of the divine. Thus, such ceremonies as the ritualistic piling of bones and other remains were conducted to preserve the natural order and to ensure that the animals would return. Other rites governed the manner in which game was stalked and killed. The ritualistic consumption of the heart or blood often consummated the kill. The hunter was thought to take on the animal's attributes—to become one with creation, however mystical and tenuous such a union seems to the modern mind. (Campbell points out that many of these practices are mirrored in Judeo-Christianity, as for example the communion.)

Just as the modern mind disparagingly reduces totemism to magic, since it is so clearly not experimental science, and thus misses the insights into nature at its heart, so Paleolithic religion is denigrated by reducing it to superstition. Yet there is no definitive vantage point from which some Olympian pronouncement might be made that God shall be personal and transcendent and that Paleolithic religion is thus retrograde, primitive, decadent, and naive. Indeed, it may be argued that in the egalitarian culture of the hunter-gatherers no justification for the hierarchization of either reality or society was required and that therefore divinity could be immanent. Since hunter-foragers were not organized hierarchically and shared nature's bounty equally among themselves, they lacked any need for a hierarchy of divinities to rationalize sociocultural inequalities. As Narr asks, "Is not the concrete and the personal more congenial to a simple mentality than abstractions of any kind? And if so, will not simple societies of hunters and gatherers, who are trying to achieve a basic understanding of things and processes for which they see no real explanation but on which they nonetheless depend, tend to think of personal supernatural beings (divinities) instead of more abstract powers and forces?"[84] The lens of history distorts our view of Paleolithic religion. Differences in the modes and forms of expression do not readily equate with differences in value.

Whereas the Neolithic mind clearly and quickly conceived of gods (and goddesses) as transcendent, though capable of revealing their presence in this world, there is no evidence that Paleolithic people so believed. Religions of transcendence sprang into existence with the agricultural revolution and its sociological and ideological effects. The accumulation and unequal distribution of wealth and property and the division of society into classes were not features of archaic culture. Further, post-Paleolithic religions are deeply anthropocentric, designed to placate divine beings to ensure fertility and to protect humankind against evil happenstance rather than to celebrate the sacrality of creation per se. Interpreted from a modernistic standpoint, Paleolithic burial sites *appear* to confirm belief in a transcendent deity and an eternal afterlife. More likely, Paleolithic people believed in timeless, repetitive cycles of life, a wheel of birth and rebirth, perhaps modeled on the analogy of the seasons, the withering away of autumn and winter followed by the rebirth of spring and summer.

The Paleolithic mind, from the imaginative reconstruction attempted here, seemed not to worship a transcendent deity but to celebrate the miracle of existence.

Nowhere is Paleolithic people's sense of the sacredness of existence more clearly manifest than in Paleolithic cave art—a prehistoric legacy discovered in approximately 150 sites in Western Europe that span two distinct but overlapping time periods of more than fifteen thousand years.[85] Today prehistoric art, if inadequately understood, is recognized as a magnificent affective-intellective achievement that symbolically expresses cosmological and metaphysical beliefs. Cave art illustrates, as more than one student of the deep past recognizes, that "under favourable ecological conditions, hunting was capable of sustaining an interesting, exciting and in some measure leisured life. The Garden of Eden had its own, very definite attractions."[86] Nonetheless, the why of cave art—that is, an imaginative reconstruction of its significance for the Paleolithic mind—is difficult to grasp. In part this is simply because in the modern age aesthetic consciousness itself is viewed as retrograde.

Cave art defined and reinforced the worldview, the metaphors of existence and reality, in which Paleolithic people believed. It gave shape to feelings that otherwise—as with all affective states of consciousness—remain evanescent.[87] Despite differences in interpretation, scholars of Paleolithic art uniformly agree that the paintings and statuary reflect a highly developed self-consciousness: the art is unmistakably intentional, and reveals perhaps more clearly than anything else the outlines of the Paleolithic mind. Cezanne reputedly said that "art is a harmony parallel to nature," and Paleolithic art clearly, almost unequivocally, discloses such a perception of harmony between human beings and the remainder of creation.[88] Lucy Lippard argues that prehistoric art is neither the imitation of nature nor its formalization but a perception of natural relationships between human beings and their environment. "Visual art, even today, even at its most ephemeral or neutralized, is rooted in matter. Transformation of and communication through matter—the primitive connection with the substance of life, or *prima materia*—is the rightful domain of all artists. Add to this the traditional, and ambivalent, connection between woman and nature, and there is a double bond for woman artists."[89] The crucial point in understanding Paleolithic cave art is to recognize in it the inescapable mark of sentience: surely the dawning of self-consciousness was the epochal event of prehistory. Cave artists were not simply imitating nature but celebrating the cosmic spectacle to which they were bearing self-aware witness.

The Paleolithic cave paintings primarily, though not exclusively, depict game animals, including the bear and wild bull of the Mediterranean region. Yet many animals are not represented, thus destroying any idea that the art is simply imitative. The cave paintings, especially considered from a perspective attentive to the kinds of animals and their arrangement, "do not reflect their perceptible relationships in the light world, but are of a symbolic order, significant of an intuited mythology of some kind, of which the entire cavern is a manifestation."[90] Many paintings depict a kind of bear ceremonialism, apparently designed to ensure that the bear's spirit reunites with the larger cosmic spirit of the Magna Mater and returns to live another day. Further, some of the creatures are clearly fantastical: most critically, the animal masters themselves. Human forms, when portrayed, are animal-human hybrids, again suggesting identification with the Magna Mater. A dominant theme of cave painting is the representation of animals, their characteristics, and their interrelations with humans.

> Central to this "animalism" are close relations between animals and humans and a heightened importance of the animal world even outside and above the natural realms. . . . Thus we often find the notion of the animal as tutelary spirit and *alter ego,* the idea that human and animal forms are easily and often interchanged, and the idea of a higher being who is thought to have an animal shape or to be capable of changing and combining shapes and who is regarded as a kind of lord of animals, hunters, and the hunting grounds, as well as of the spirits of game and of the bush.[91]

The cave can be interpreted as the vagina of the earth, or as "the containing space in the earth metaphor of the mother goddess." Its tunnel-like entrance represents a birth canal, and the larger rooms are the womb of the Magna Mater. The setting of cave, painting, and flickering fire provided a stage for a microcosmic reenactment of cosmic drama. "Cave art, . . . in conjunction with its religious use, was precisely a way of accepting reality [and of reaffirming the cultural view of reality]. Fidelity to a tradition and a sense of connectedness to a real outside world are related, for both rest on a conviction of order and participation."[92] We can empathetically reconstruct the overwhelming emotions of beauty and reverence experienced by Paleolithic people as they entered these sacred places and, through their religious rituals, reenacted sacred time. As Campbell argues, cave art "was magic. And its herds are the herds of eternity, not of time—yet even more vividly real and alive than the animals of time, because their ever-living source. At Altamira the great bulls—which are almost breathing, they are so alive—are on the ceiling, reminding us of their nature; for they are stars. . . . The hunter is identified with the sun, his javelin with its rays, and the herds of the field with the herds of the sky. The hunt itself is heavenly adventure, rendering in time eternal forms. And the ritual of the cave is, so to say, its transubstantiating element."[93]

To the modernist—the profane person of modern culture—such reconstructions of the meaning of cave art are fantasy. Nature is but a stockpile of resources, lifeless matter-in-motion, a standing reserve for human appropriation. From this perspective the Paleolithic mind's veneration of the Magna Mater as a living and sacred entity with which humankind was bound in an eternal, self-renewing cycle of existence is nonsense. To the modern mind time is not sacred, repeating in itself the mystery of creation and the cycle of life and death, but rather a succession of moments leading *ad seriatim* to the future.[94] But to Homo religiosus time is sacred, and cave art and ritual celebrates an eternal mythical present, reuniting humankind with creation. "This attitude in regard to time," as Eliade observes, "suffices to distinguish religious from nonreligious" humans. Homo religiosus "refuses to live solely in what, in modern terms, is called the historical present" and instead "attempts to regain a sacred time that, from one point of view, can be homologized to eternity."[95]

Mesolithic Transitions to Agri-Culture

No one knows for certain how long prehistoric people existed in an Edenlike condition of hunting-gathering, but 200,000 years or more is not an unreasonable estimate for the hegemony of the Great Hunt. Even while humankind lived the archaic life, clinging conceptually to the bosom of the Magna Mater, the course of cultural events contained the seeds of an agricultural revolution, since prehistoric peoples were practicing rudimentary farming and animal husbandry. The crucial question is that of cultural evolution itself. Why did the hunting-foraging way of life slowly give way to agrarian culture?[96] There is no absolute answer, no single variable that explains everything.

Circumscription theory, while predicated on the assumption that population growth is the primary factor, allows for multivariate causation in local contexts. (Interestingly, the end of the era of the Great Hunt in Europe is reflected in part by the end of the Great Art. Environmental crisis may have engendered a crisis of Paleolithic art.) One thing is clear: no longing for civilization and abhorrence of wild nature led to agri-culture. Such an explanation is a modernist gesture, usually accompanied by arguments that prehistoric cultures were mere "subsistence economies." To so categorize is to view the ancient aborigines through the lens of history, and thus to miss their significance from the standpoint of a posthistoric primitivism. Relative to us, and even to early agrarian culture, Paleolithic people had few wants yet lived an affluent and satisfying life in harmony with nature. The modern mind refuses to reconsider its basic assumption that we are *Homo oeconomicus,* and therefore naturally endowed with infinite wants and limited means. From the alternative standpoint of posthistoric primitivism we can see, however paradoxical to the modernist, that "people can enjoy an unparalleled material plenty—with a low standard of living." [97] In short, the posthistoric primitivist denies any explanation of the Neolithic revolution that is predicated on economic progress.

Although the ideological, economic, political, technological, and ecological changes that aggregated over time, literally thousands of years, were profound, revolutionary in sum, they developed slowly. Hunting-foraging and farming-herding at first existed side by side: the base of subsistence cannot be changed overnight. There is little significance to differences between gathering plants and killing animals whether these species be wild or domesticated. To judge one as progressive as compared to the other is extremely problematic. "What matters is . . . the knowledge and skill to exploit these resources. This does not alter the fact that the relationships established between men, animals and plants affect profoundly the size and density of human populations and the nature and potentialities of human societies." [98] Hunting-foraging culture was the dominant form of human organization from c. 200,000 B.C.E. until the end of the Ice Age, c. 10,000 B.C.E., but climatological changes at the end of the last period of glaciation adversely affected Paleolithic ecosystems.

Unquestionably, the onset and end of an ice age has significant, if poorly understood, effects on global climate and culture itself, but transformation from hunting-foraging to herding-farming cannot have taken place overnight, or even over a single generation. [99] The cultivation of grain likely preceded the domestication of ruminants (at least in the Near East), since sedentarism seems a necessary condition for the taming and breeding of animals. Significantly, the often associated activities of herding animals and cultivating grains started almost simultaneously in several areas of the world, implying that global climatic change was a relevant factor. The term *Neothermal environment* is sometimes used to designate the altered climatic condition at the end of the Ice Age. As the glaciers retreated, temperatures rose, and patterns of precipitation were transformed. The Pleistocene grasslands, which had supported vast herds of game, withered and died, and many species of animals became extinct (as for example, the saber-toothed tiger, the mammoth, and others bound up in grassland ecosystems). Charles Reed argues that in parts of southwestern Asia grasslands replaced forests, which in turn led to an increased use of seeds for food, especially barley and wheats.[100] In any case, the general worldwide warming trend at the end of the Ice Age cannot alone explain the origin of agriculture.

Circumspection theory implies that population pressure alone led to agriculture, yet prehistoric hunting-foraging groups likely had stable populations of twenty-five to fifty members. Common sense helps to resolve this apparent conundrum: decreased food supplies necessitate adaptation even for stable populations of hunter-gatherers. Once sedentary, further changes occur; as Reed puts it, "in evolution one thing can happen only after another."[101] Once the hunt is abandoned, dependency on crops makes a return to previous forms of subsistence difficult; only marginal agriculturists can forsake the field without suffering calamitous population losses (although group fission is possible). Further, sedentarism has physiological consequences on the human reproductive cycle, especially that of the female. A nomadic way of life combined with the demands of nursing lead to a natural form of birth control—infertility (secondary amenorrhea). Permanent settlement is accompanied by earlier menarche and shorter periods of lactation, thus contributing to a higher birth rate. Finally, ideological changes accompany agriculture: elites depend on surplus production, and people thus become increasingly valuable as labor to clear and till fields.

Besides climatological and population pressures, the role of serendipity in the Mesolithic transformation should not be underestimated. Intensely self-conscious as prehistory drew to a close, humankind was poised technologically (by mastering tool-making) and culturally (by developing germinal ideas of crops and tame animals) on the brink of agriculture. Climatological change adventitiously reinforced what must be recognized as a latent human potential to modify the environment.[102] Once the modernistic fallacy is overcome, and prehistoric people are recognized as possessing a concrete science, then the cultivation of grain and domestication of animals can be recognized as a legacy of archaic culture that enabled the Neolithic revolution. In addition, fortuitous happenstance likely played as significant a role in the agricultural revolution as human intelligence. Discovery of the seed's potential to provide predictable harvests may have been rooted in a return to former campsites where melons or tubers were now growing from waste piles; and discovery of the potential to domesticate animals may have occurred by gradually taming caninelike creatures that furtively skirted the edges of campsites looking for garbage and, ultimately, handouts.

Finally, human nature itself played a role in the agricultural revolution in several ways. The fires in the caves of our proto-humanoid ancestors presage the retort and internal combustion engine, just as wooden spears and rock knives portend spaceships and scalpels. The opposed thumbs on our hands, a unique adaptation, suggest a creature built to manipulate the environment. Further, all animals, including Homo sapiens, are opportunistic feeders. There is no reason not to think that hunter-gatherers might have abandoned traditional economic ways if circumstances allowed semipermanent settlement.[103] That humankind could turn to agriculturally based subsistence when necessary—if the end of the Ice Age did compel change—implies that transitional forms of living, including experimentation with grains and animals, had already been undertaken. Finally, some argue that the human animal is one of nature's mistakes, that we are "misfits" in the longer scheme of things, and that the "big brain" itself is defective.[104] From this point of view the agricultural revolution is simply a pathological manifestation of an inherently flawed human nature. However, the issue is empirical, and the data are not yet in. There is no guarantee that species Homo sapiens will either survive or fail. What is crucial is the recognition that our genes are fundamentally involved in determining our outcome.

Climatological change, population pressure, serendipity, and human nature are all, to some extent, involved in the agricultural revolution: no single explanation is cogent.[105] The consensus of informed opinion, however, is that the turn from hunting-gathering to herding-farming was not abrupt but occurred gradually. Since the notion of the Neolithic revolution was introduced in the nineteenth century (roughly in 1870, a short time after publication of Darwin's *Origin of Species*), we have learned to see that the transition from the Paleolithic to the Neolithic is a gradual process, where the prehistoric past remains evident in so-called Mesolithic cultural forms. This sequence is clearly manifest in the preservation of the idea that nature is sacred and feminine, although we must not infer that the Magna Mater of the Paleolithic mind is inferior to the Earth Mother of the Neolithic or agrarian mind.

Clearly, religious consciousness and institutions become more complicated in the post-Paleolithic period, a development consistent with circumscription theory. Just as clearly, since humankind is a culture-dwelling species, there can be no radical discontinuities. Eliade argues that "differences in religious experience [can be] explained by differences in economy, culture, and social organization—in short, by history. Nevertheless, between the nomadic hunters and the sedentary cultivators there is a similarity in behavior that seems to us infinitely more important than their differences: *both live in a sacralized cosmos,* both share in cosmic sacrality manifested equally in the animal world and in the vegetable world." [106] Although the settled agriculturists create new gods, no great break occurs until the Hebrews and the birth of historical consciousness, a saga we shall address in the next chapter.

The onset of Neolithic culture forever altered both intellectual and material culture: sweeping ideological, sociological, economical, and technological changes occurred, both cause and effect. Once humans became agriculturists, the almost paradisiacal character of prehistory was irretrievably lost. Although prehistoric people were relatively content in accepting the natural order and sought above all to maintain the integrity of their world, the agriculturists experienced an enormous quickening of the human potential to modify the naturally given. Rather than attempting to live in harmony with wild nature, as hunter-gatherers had done since time immemorial, farmers literally rose up and attempted to dominate the wilderness. Boundaries were drawn between the natural and the cultural, and conceptual restructuring was inevitable.

The agriculturist necessarily defines "fields" (areas cleared of natural vegetation), "weeds" (undesirable plants intruding upon fields), and "crops" (desirable plants suited to human purposes). In contrast, the hunter-gatherer lives on what is conceptually the "fruit of the earth" or Magna Mater's mana—fields, weeds, and crops simply do not exist. Furthermore, whereas the hunter-gatherer is at home anywhere in nature, the farmer creates a human settlement that is "home" as distinct from the "wilderness"; and "nature" or the "naturally existing" harbors threats to "home" and "field" as in the predations of "barbarians" or "wild men" who roam about nature, "wild animals" such as wolves and cats that prey on desirable domesticated animals such as sheep and goats, and "wild insects" such as locusts that eat grain. And, finally, the product of the agriculturist is no longer conceived as the fruit of the earth but rather won, at least in part, from nature through sweat and toil.

The hunting way of life—viewed either ideologically or materially—did not foster the accumulation of property. Unlike hunter-foragers, agricultural people accumulate material surpluses, more economic goods than can be immediately consumed. With agriculture came a settled way of life and the "land" itself. The agriculturist drives the environment for a net biological product by displacing naturally diverse wild plant and animal species with a few domesticated varieties. As a result, agrarian culture rapidly accumulated an unprecedented amplitude of material goods and the human population skyrocketed. But these two facts are not necessarily causally related; the Neolithic population explosion conceivably had more to do with the changing ideological orientation of agriculture and the method of economic production than the absolute supply of food. The point is important, since Paleolithic people had natural governors on population. The fertility mania of agriculture is a new ideological development. (With human beings crowded into urban environments, however, the opportunity for pestilence and plague was created, serving in effect as a natural governor on population.) Paleolithic culture was egalitarian and lacked a socioeconomic elite that profited from the labor of a peasantry; there was thus no ideological reason to be fruitful and multiply.

In the context of agriculture, war became conceivable and sometimes desirable. Archaeological evidence (for example, skulls with traumatic injury inflicted by an ax) confirms the existence of lethal violence during the Paleolithic. Hunter-gatherers episodically engaged in physical confrontations both within and between clans. Institutionalized warfare, however, seems unlikely for Paleolithic culture, since there was neither booty to be won, property to be protected, nor a central authority to organize an army. Hunter-foragers have a biological rationale not to fight among themselves, since injuries and mortalities would threaten group survival. Any contact with another band of human beings was likely to be fleeting, and even at such encounters, significant injury to either group could be grievous. Intra-group conflict was resolved usually by fission, not conflict. The Paleolithic era was thus devoid of ideological, economical, or political rationales for war. The only likely explanation for armed and therefore potentially lethal conflict is biological, given evidence of episodic cannibalism, yet that explanation founders on the survival of the human species.[107] With the Neolithic revolution, including the rise of central authority and increased population, the means and rationale for war appeared. Burgeoning populations supplied the humanpower necessary to fight battles without impairing group survival. And war was useful as a source of slaves and land.

PHILOSOPHY AND THEOLOGY, as the platitude goes, bake no bread; yet, once the agricultural turn was made, philosophy and theology sprang forth with a vengeance. The Neolithic mind no longer thought of itself as the child of Magna Mater, and wild nature increasingly loomed as an enemy, a foe opposed to human intentionality that must be conquered. From the agricultural revolution to the first great Near Eastern theological and philosophical outpourings is but a few millennia.[108] As philosophy and theology emerged, the crucial interaction between existential and conceptual materials—lying at the heart of cultural process and the ecological transition—increased in both frequency and pervasiveness. History, it has been said, begins at Sumer.[109] Clearly, the agricultural revolution provided the material precondition for the emergence of identifiably modern civilization by necessitating permanent settlement, producing an agricultural surplus, and starting a rippling process of social and technological change; ideological restructuring was inevitable. We must not overemphasize the rate of change, however; the pace of these events was slow.

Human beings are time binders and our ecological niche is time—bound into culture and history. The Paleolithic idea of wilderness, coalescing around the idea of the Magna Mater as a beneficent being who provided for all her children—humankind, plants, and animals—is so ancient and pervasive that the time and place of origin is unknown. Clearly, it existed before the beginnings of Egyptian and Sumerian civilization, for we can trace its presence among Mesolithic agriculturists. We can only speculate as to how long: fifty thousand years or longer is not an unreasonable estimate. Relatively considered, since the pace of change—conceptually, technologically, and, more generally, culturally—quickens after the Neolithic revolution, all other ideas of wilderness combined have lasted for only a fraction of that period.

Lying before us is a long and tangled history of the idea of wilderness that begins with the ancient Sumerians and Egyptians (c. 3000 B.C.E.), culminates in the modern idea of nature by the eighteenth century, and begins to encounter opposition, and thus evolve into a postmodern conception, almost immediately thereafter. Even so, accounting for the evolution of ancient Mediterranean ideas of wilderness is more complicated than it is for prehistoric ideas of wilderness. An explicit, self-conscious process of transition from Paleolithic to Neolithic ideas of wilderness begins with a dawning awareness that humankind, though part of nature, also differs in some ways and that nature is an orderly and purposive process. In his work of genius, *Traces on the Rhodian Shore*, Clarence Glacken argues that the belief that nature is orderly and purposive appears as early as 2500 B.C.E. in "The Theology of Memphis."[110] Thereafter, the pace of intellectual change quickens enormously. The task immediately ahead is to trace within reasonable compass the development of these ancient ideas of wilderness from inception to culmination.

CHAPTER TWO

Ancient Mediterranean Ideas
of Humankind and Nature
The Passage from Myth to History

We must stand apart from the conventions of history, even while using the record of the past, for the idea of history is itself a Western invention whose central theme is the rejection of habitat. It formulates experience outside of nature and tends to reduce place to . . . only a stage upon which the human drama is enacted. History conceives the past mainly in terms of biography and nations. It seeks casuality in the conscious, spiritual, ambitious character of men and memorializes them in writing. —Paul Shepard, Nature and Madness

THE PREHISTORIC MEDITERRANEAN world is sometimes characterized as "the first Eden" or "garden of God."[1] The roots of the word *Eden* include the Babylonian *eindu* and the Hebrew *Ēdhen*, translated variously as paradise, plain, and hunting ground. The transition from a hunting-foraging way of life to *agri*-culture has often been associated with or identified as the so-called Fall.[2] In leaving the Paleolithic world for the Neolithic, humankind likely encountered a host of woes and travails unknown in its collective experience, not the least of which was work itself. Paleolithic peoples, existing in traditional ways established over untold millennia, lived in a world where maintaining the timeless rhythms of nature was likely conceptualized as the overriding aim of life. If the thesis that agriculture underlies humankind's turn upon the environment, even if out of climatological exigency, is cogent, then the ancient Mediterranean theater is where the "fall from Paradise" was staged, for here began extensive humanization of the natural landscape.[3]

No absolute measure of humanization exists, but before the agricultural revolution humankind minimally altered the natural world, while afterward it became a relentless agent of ecological change. The cultivation of cereals and the domestication of animals are clearly positive accomplishments in the face of environmental crisis: the only apparent alternative was starvation. But the Near East was where humans first created an engine of pervasive environmental degradation; archaic hydraulic culture invited ecological ruin by modifying the landscape and watersheds, starting a process of ecological degradation that undercut the natural foundations of culture.[4] Yet no simple equation can be drawn between the agricultural revolution and environmental despoliation. Although they are associated, the road from there to here is winding.

The Mediterranean region spans a vast area, from Gibraltar on the west, along the northern terminus of the African continent, past Italy and Greece, to Turkey and the Holy Land of Western civilization—2,500 miles. Prehistoric Mediterranean culture probably split (c. 10000 B.C.E.) into an eastern sphere of influence, dominated increasingly by agriculturists, and a western sphere, where a hunting-gathering way of life lingered.[5] As a result, any attempt to generalize about the ideas of wilderness characteristic of the indigenous peoples of such a vast area of settlement, with its variety of culture, is inevitably subject to exception. And yet meaningful generalizations about ancient Mediterranean outlooks on wild nature are possible.[6] Evidence warrants the conjectures that (1) Mediterranean peoples became increasingly adept at and aggressive in their endeavors to humanize the landscape; (2) almost concomitantly, they became aware of themselves as beings partially dependent upon but distinct from nature; (3) they devised increasingly abstract and complicated explanatory schemes (mythologies, theologies) to account for their relation to, domination of, and separation from the natural world; (4) these schemes recognized a limited mastery over nature through technology, while preserving the idea that some forces were beyond human control; and, ultimately, (5) they conceived of the Mediterranean landscape as divinely designed for human habitation, cultivation, and modification.

This pattern is manifest throughout the process of cultural development, beginning with the ancient agriculturists and continuing through the patristic fathers of the early Christian church (c. 100–500 C.E.). The early agriculturists (10000–3500 B.C.E.) reveal a slowly dawning awareness of distinctions between culture and nature. Hunting mythologies, which did not explicitly distinguish between the human and animal worlds, were forsaken and replaced by religions that centered on the worship of gods, especially gods conceptualized as incarnate in such animals as the bull. These early religions tended to be polytheistic, idolatrous, and focused on fertility—plant, animal, and human. The pinnacle of polytheistic, animalistic worship occurred in ancient Egypt and Sumeria, where people first conceived of the natural world as an abode designed for the human species. Yet even in the very geographical and historical midst of the Egyptians and Sumerians (Canaan lies astride the travel routes between the Fertile Crescent and Egypt) arose a tradition avowing an ideology that rejected naturalistic polytheism and, after an internal struggle with lingering remnants of fertility cults, embraced a monotheistic supernaturalism. The Hebrews believed themselves to be Yahweh's chosen people living in a land expressly designed for them to civilize. The Pentateuch, as reflected in the many accreted layers of meaning that constitute the text, thus represents the grandest rationalization of an agriculturist mode of existence ever conceived.

Penultimately in chronology, but not in importance and subsequent influence on the idea of wilderness, was the rise of logocentrism in Attica. Greek rationalism abandoned mythopoetry for explicit theory and definition; it was later spread throughout the Mediterranean world by first-century B.C.E. Hellenistic culture and the Romans. Whereas the Hebrews remained content with the metaphorical, allegorical, and symbolic, the New Testament of Paul and the patristic fathers used the theoretical edifice of Platonism (as some one thousand years later Aquinas used Aristotle) to create the concept of humanity and nature that has ruled the West for nearly two thousand years. Yet Christianity did not contradict but rather redefined earlier conceptions of the earth as a designed abode for humankind. What was radical in both Hebrew and early Christian thought was its profound anthropocentrism and its abandonment of a cyclical for a linear conception of time. Hellenism and Judeo-Christianity in combination introduced an unprecedented direction to human intercourse with the earth, for *nature was conceived as valueless until humanized.*

Animal Idolatry, Polytheism, and the Rise of Fertility Cults

A transitional phase of some six thousand years stretches between the lower Neolithic and the advent of the hieratic city states in Mesopotamia and Egypt. Only an extended study could account for the many significant ideological, sociological, and technological modifications of this era. Tribes and villages replaced bands and campsites as the dominant forms of social organization; domesticated livestock supplanted wild animals as a food source; human knowledge proliferated, as in metallurgy, ceramics, architecture, and mathematics. Further, the agricultural revolution fundamentally transformed the relations between humankind and nature. To say that prehistoric people were passive in relation to nature is inaccurate, for hunting-gathering exemplifies the perpetuation of life through environmental transaction. In contrast to most agricultures, however, the exchange for hunter-foragers is balanced and harmonious.[7] Cynegetic (hunting-foraging) cultures alter neither the natural firmament nor the animals and plants that share the land with them. Agricultural people abandon the hunt and the spear, settle in villages, and take up the hoe and shepherd's staff. Animals are domesticated and herded, woodlands cleared, swamps and wetlands drained, the soil turned, planted, and tilled.

Materialists and idealists anguish over metaphysical priorities in this sequence, but most likely is simultaneous evolution in ideology, sociology, and technology—a rippling, interpenetrating process of cultural transition unknown to the early agriculturists who were living in medias res, living the agricultural revolution, perhaps as we are now living in an "age of ecology." Human beings were no longer tender carnivores in search of sacred game: domesticated livestock and planted crops were the focus of material life. Inevitably, the shaman of Paleolithic culture gave way to the priest. Religious life centered no longer on maintaining harmony and integrity but on fertility (although harmony with the eternal order was sometimes thought essential to fertility). Totemism, where the totem imaginatively mediated between humankind and the rest of nature, was supplanted by animal idolatry—the worship of icons fashioned in the image of animals, especially the Mediterranean bull.[8] The Magna Mater of Paleolithic culture became the Earth Mother, now a goddess of fertility rather than an all-embracing mother of creation.[9]

Slowly but inexorably, as centuries turned into millennia, change compounded upon change, and even the ways of the early agriculturists were modified. The village gave way to the city, and loose confederations of villages and cities to nation-states. Sociological changes were institutionalized, and politics and organized religion became a reality.[10] Priestly classes appeared, ensconced in the temples of new cities, part of a socioeconomic elite that increasingly controlled the surrounding countryside. Humankind became more and more conscious of itself as an agent of environmental change, and rationalizations of the new ways proliferated. Cultivated grains and domesticated livestock became familiar artifacts of culture, predictable supplies of food. Wild plant and animal species were increasingly devoid of mystery and unworthy of veneration; animal gods were replaced by gods with human forms.[11] Human beings became conscious of a mastery, however tenuous, over wild nature, and it occurred to them that the world was perhaps designed for their ends by divine forces.

Agriculturists initially (c. 10000 B.C.E.) retained mobility to the extent that camps or villages were semipermanent and could be relocated as rivers changed course and shifted the desirable crop and pasture lands; but permanent settlement was probably inevitable once the turn from hunting-gathering was made. Çatal-Hüyük (the ruins are located in Turkey approximately four hundred miles northwest of Jerusalem) is among the first permanent Mediterranean settlements of size, dating from 8400 B.C.E. Research at this site has added greatly to our understanding of the ecological transition from the Paleolithic to the Neolithic.[12] Situated at the foot of a mountain range, where each year run-off from melting snow replenished fields with silt and nutrients, permanent settlement was possible since relocation was not required to ensure fertility. In economic terms, Çatal-Hüyük represents a transitional form of life from hunting-foraging to agriculture, as indicated by abundant evidence of animal idolatry. Animal idolatry is arguably a transitional form of totemism; the clan no longer identifies itself with an animal but literally worships an animal statue as a god.

Archaic peoples the world over revere the animals and plants essential to survival: at Çatal-Hüyük this object was the great Mediterranean bull. About one-third of the rooms in the settlement are shrines, decorated with bull's heads carved into and clay heads built out from the walls. Inside these rooms are altars decorated with smaller bull's heads made of mud, and occasionally frontal portions of actual skulls. By all available evidence the bull itself was worshipped by these ancients, a veritable god incarnate, contrary to the thesis that the animal was sacrificed to transcendent gods. Repeating the apostasy of Paleolithic people, the cattle-gods were also consumed as food.[13] Smaller female-shaped figurines are also found, implying that a female Earth Mother image played prominently in the fertility cult, sustaining the thesis that the early agriculturists represent a zone of ecological transition from the Paleolithic to the Neolithic: the legacy of Paleolithic culture—artistic, religious, intellectual—cannot be denied. Marija Gimbutas argues that not only are Neolithic goddesses composites of agricultural and preagricultural images, but so, too, "the water bird, deer, bear, fish, snake, toad, turtle, and the notion of hybridization of animal and man, were inherited from the Palaeolithic era and continued to serve as avatars of goddesses and gods. There was no such thing as a religion or mythical imagery newly created by agriculturists at the beginning of the food-producing period." [14] And perhaps even more important, Merlin Stone suggests, "the most obvious fact may be of greatest interest to people of today—that in the lands that brought forth Judaism, Christianity, and Islam, God was once worshiped in the form of woman." [15]

The transition *from* totemic, hunter mythology and rituals, representing above all else the belief in the sacrality of existence and the endeavor to maintain cosmic harmony, *to* the animal idolatry and fertility cults of agriculture is a comprehensible development. Settled cultivators and herders, unlike wandering hunting-gatherers, depend on the everlasting fruitfulness of field and animal. Whereas hunting-foraging people accepted the bounty of the world as they found it and identified with this natural universe of being, agricultural people—through the very reality of an ecological transition—experienced a new phenomenal-existential field of meaning. [16] If the rains failed and the grass was stunted, the herds were imperiled; if insects descended in a plague, the crops were lost; and so on through myriad permutations of disaster. Such failings had serious consequences: starvation loomed continually. Little wonder the rise of fertility sects and the associated festivals, rituals, and other ceremonies, including plant and animal sacrifice. However barbaric such cultic fertility practices seem to the modern mind, such religions continued well into the Middle Ages. (Mithraism, for example, one of many Mediterranean bull cults, rivaled if not exceeded Christianity in popularity—that is, converts or believers— well into the third century C.E.) [17] All were part of a complex of behaviors and ideas intended to ensure fecundity and productivity. A religio-politico elite almost necessarily arose, serving the social functions of organization, control, and above all the rationalization of existence. The priest and chief supplanted the Paleolithic animal master, and society was slowly stratified. These new elites helped to explain the changing order of existence and thereby justify their own power.

By 4500 B.C.E. the stage was set for the emergence of civilization. Yet we must go slowly. Since *the history of Western civilization qua civilization* effectively begins with writing, there is a tendency to overvalue the written past and undervalue those eons of time that went before. When we pass from the upper Neolithic into the rich world of ancient Egypt and Sumeria it is as if these ancient people were yet alive, for they left writing that communicates through the millennia to us. History, in one sense, is intentional remembrance, whether oral or written, but there is a profound difference between the two. Many of the myths and narrative stories of ancient Egypt and Sumeria were doubtless inheritances from their past; yet, because their progenitors left no written records, ancient Mesopotamia and Egypt are the wellspring of our living sense of history. Examined more closely, the rise of civilization conceals fundamental continuities with the Paleolithic and Mesolithic past. The term *primitive survival* characterizes the relation of previous forms of existence to those that follow. We cannot simply abandon the past, for we are culture-dwelling creatures. It follows that lurking within modern forms of existence are relics of the past.[18]

Thus, although important changes occur with the rise of Egyptian and Sumerian culture, as for example the invention of writing (itself a necessity to pass from mythic to historic consciousness), these ancient peoples remained intent on understanding their relations with nature.[19] Geography certainly exerted an enormous influence on both Egyptian and Sumerian thought. The Egyptian sense of order, of mastery of its destiny, derives at least in part from a frontierlike spirit of adventure in developing a civilization. The floodplain of the Nile, blessed with fertile soils, ample moisture, and natural barriers to fend off invaders, was ideal for agriculture. The Egyptians, perhaps understandably, exaggerated their accomplishments, since they came easily, and since Egyptians were unaware of the contributions from the deep past. Conditions were otherwise in Sumeria, where the Tigris and Euphrates thwarted human endeavor—drought and flood seemed to oscillate capriciously, crops withering into dust one year, overwhelmed by mud and water the next. The Mesopotamians, in comparison to the Egyptians, were relatively modest in assessing the significance of human action. But like the Paleolithic mind, the Neolithic mind was intensely conscious of humankind's close relation to nature, indeed, of living within nature. On close inspection we see that certain elements of the mythic structure of the era of the Great Hunt were preserved, even while the vestiges of a hunting-gathering economy and social organization were disappearing. Both Sumerian and Egyptian civilizations identified with natural patterns and cycles; nature was seen as alive, animistic, its forces conceptualized as gods (often with human forms).

By the fourth millennium B.C.E. Egyptian culture was stratified into religious-political elites and a rural peasantry, and power was concentrated in the hands of a priestly class. Animal idolatry was stabilized by the priests into a bull-god of fertility, called Apis. This god was thought to incarnate himself in the form of an earthly bull. During the lifetime of this Apis-incarnate the animal was tended and nurtured by priests, fed a special diet, bathed and massaged, and generally treated as a god. Apis played important roles in a variety of fertility ceremonies—among them, rituals associated with the yearly flood, when Apis was bred to cows, and the annual celebration of the king's ascension, when Apis accompanied the king in a trek around state boundaries, thereby ensuring fruitful fields in the coming season. On his death Apis was mummified, with the same great ceremonial dignity and elaborate ritual accorded a pharaoh, so that his spirit could return to the next world, and his body entombed with bull statues of solid gold at Saqqara (city of the dead).

Apis was not the only sacred animal of Egypt, though perhaps the most important because of his antiquity and association with the founding dynasty.[20] Among other animals were the black-and-white ibis (then abundant) that, with its long, graceful bill, probed the muddy fields of the Nile Delta. This behavior was believed to mark the unending search for truth; thus, the sacred ibis was associated with Thoth, god of wisdom or truth. The crocodile was interpreted as a source of both evil and good, being not only Sobek (an associate of Seth, god of evil) but the Lord-of-the-Island-in-the-River (the god who brought land back to the earth). The falcon was interpreted as the god of the sun (Horus), and associated, like Apis, with the pharaoh. By the sixth century B.C.E., Egyptians believed that mummification of any animal brought favor from the patron spirit incarnate; the catacombs of Saqqara contain untold embalmed animal remains, each encased in a clay sarcophagus. Estimates are that 4 million ibis and 800,000 falcons were offered to Thoth and Horus.

Sumeria, located between the Tigris and Euphrates rivers in the area known as the Fertile Crescent, some five hundred miles northeast of Egypt, presents an equally fascinating picture of ancient agriculturists coming to conceptual grips with an ecological transition. The Sumerians can claim many firsts, including the distinction of forming the first nation-state. Writing is the most famous and perhaps most important creation (c. 3300 B.C.E.) of these people. The essential genius of their insight was in moving beyond the pictographic images of hieroglyphics to words constructed of letters used to make syllables. This new form of writing, called cuneiform (Latin *cuneus* means wedge, as in the stylus used to mark clay tablets), was a powerful tool that supported not only sophisticated commerce but the creation of literature and stable codes of law. The *Epic of Gilgamesh,* which dates from at least the second millennium B.C.E., is perhaps the first written rationalization of human existence, and the laws of Ur-Nammu of Ur (c. 2100 B.C.E.) and the more famous Code of Hammurabi (c. 1750 B.C.E.) are the earliest known legal codes. Other Mesopotamian inventions include a plow with an attachment to sow seeds and a potter's wheel (the first machine with continuous rotary motion).[21]

In many ways Sumerian and Egyptian history run on parallel courses. Sumeria was fashioned (c. 3000 B.C.E.) out of a host of city-states, each with its own divinity, by a strong man who became the first king, Etana of Kish. And like Egypt, ancient Sumeria was a hydraulic culture; but here the Egyptians enjoyed an enormous advantage, for the Nile's annual flood during the cool months created conditions ideal for cultivation. (The pyramids were constructed at least in part by farmers who had nothing else to do during the annual inundation.) Circumstances were otherwise in Mesopotamia, where historically unprecedented modification of nature was required to irrigate croplands. By building canals from the Euphrates, the largest river in western Asia, to the Tigris, approximately ten thousand square miles of land could be cultivated (compared with some thirteen thousand square miles along the Nile); water flowed downhill from the Euphrates toward the Tigris and was channeled into the fields as required. But the seeds of environmental ruin were being planted, for the annual inundation was unfortunately timed. Summertime evaporation gradually increased the salinity of the soil. Further, the lower, marshier areas between the junction of the Tigris-Euphrates and the Persian Gulf were subject to a constant battle between crop-sustaining flows of freshwater and saltwater infiltrating from the sea. Forest clearing exacerbated environmental problems; the *Epic of Gilgamesh* reveals that the Sumerians realized this. Book II recounts Gilgamesh's awe on first entering the forest (with his friend, Enkidu).

> They stood in awe at the foot
> Of the green mountain. Pleasure
> Seemed to grow from fear for Gilgamesh.
> As when one comes upon a path in woods
> Unvisited by men, one is drawn near
> The lost and undiscovered in himself;
> He was revitalized by danger.[22]

Gilgamesh's wonder was soon lost in the battle with Humbaba, the mighty forest god. Gilgamesh slew Humbaba, symbolically representing the relentless Sumerian encroachment on the ancient forests and the triumph of civilization over the wilderness. And perhaps the death of Humbaba symbolically parallels the recognition by the Paleolithic mind of apostasy: human existence seems to entail an awareness that transgressions against nature are inevitable.

Predictably, most Sumerian divinities were identified with natural forces, the four principal gods being sky (An), earth (Ki), air (Enlil), and water (Enki). Tiamat was the mother of all gods, and she was associated with saltwater (perhaps symbolizing the water associated with the womb).

The gods were believed to control the processes of nature; the dry season was a consequence of the death of Dumuzi (god of vegetation) and his return to the underworld, there to await the appearance of his wife, Inanna (goddess of the evening star). In time, Inanna rescued Dumuzi from the underworld, the rains returned, and the fertile earth again flowered. The rescue of Dumuzi was celebrated in a ritual ceremony on New Year's Day by the Sumerian king and a priestess. They acted out a marriage rite between Dumuzi and Inanna to ensure fertility for the coming season of growth and to legitimate the monarch's authority as "the beloved of Inanna, fit for her holy lap."[23] To the modernist, such rites and beliefs appear mundane and superstitious, peculiar manifestations of mythically inspired behavior.[24] Such a view is fallacious, rooted in the modern mind's secularism: time was sacred for Homo religiosus, and sacred rituals reunited the agricultural mind with the basic creative forces of nature. As Eliade states, the notion of reenacting sacred time makes it possible for Homo religiosus "to experience the cosmos as it was *in principio,* that is, at the mythical moment of Creation."[25]

Theology provided the intellectual base for Egyptian and Sumerian society. Priests served the essential function of giving existence meaning—creating, maintaining, and repairing the sacred mythology.[26] Ra (the sun god), greatest of the later Egyptian pantheon, was the creator of all things, and the pharaohs claimed descent from him; the pharaoh was a god incarnate who theologically justified Egyptian culture. His presence symbolized a bond between Egyptians and the eternal cycles and mysteries of creation. Sumerians believed in transcendent gods, but the differences are inconsequential—Sumerians also celebrated rituals that reunited them with cosmic forces and perpetuated life. Sumerian temples were sacred places through which the culture proclaimed to the universe its legitimacy, its privileged place in the cosmos. The pyramids similarly celebrated the glory of the gods (symbolizing in fact the very presence of Ra). Politically and economically, the temples, pyramids, and priestly class thus provided cohesion for the spread-out populace.[27] Yet here, too, Egyptian and Sumerian culture differed in important ways. The purpose of human existence for the Sumerians was stated in the *Epic of Creation:* "Let him [man] be burdened with the toil of the gods that they may freely breathe."[28] The Egyptians had a rather more concrete idea of god: god was pharaoh.

In spite of continuities (for example, a belief that nature was fundamentally feminine), the gulf between the hunter-gatherers and the agriculturists, insofar as this involves conceptualization of humankind and its relation to nature, widened steadily. Hunting-foraging was for Paleolithic people the basis of existence; the civilized peoples of the ancient Mediterranean lands still hunted, but only for sport—the game was no longer sacred. (Sometimes the hunt was merely utilitarian, as in clearing the Nile of hippopotamus and crocodiles.) The agriculturists of Sumeria and Egypt were increasingly alienated from nature as they bent the earth to human purpose—even if in the name of the gods. In this the fertility cults were important, since the theological rationalization and economic transformation of culture went hand in hand. The ancient myths of Sumeria and Egypt recognize a twofold difference—between humankind and nature on the one hand and humankind and the divine on the other. From the beginning of civilization, it seems, people have understood themselves as singular, different from other things in nature and from the divine, yet interacting with and orienting their lives toward both. Human beings see themselves as having power over nature, control exhibited through the ever-increasing *technē* of hands and mind. Yet again and again we realize that the world is not ours to master, that some forces operate outside our control.[29]

The discovery that humankind is an agent of geographical change came gradually. A sense of history—that is, the passage of time where changes fundamentally alter the natural landscape—is required before such an idea can be grasped.[30] To the Neolithic peoples who settled in the floodplains of the Nile and the Tigris-Euphrates, humans were simply living as their ancestors had since the dawn of time. The Sumerians and Egyptians later theologically rationalized the agricultural civilizations they had built. Almost certainly they thought of nature as a sometimes capricious but essentially orderly, even designed process. Such ideas were anthropomorphic, modeled especially on the orderly design of cities and roads, canals and fields, homes and gardens. Further, as Egyptian and Sumerian culture developed, some notion that humans fundamentally affected nature must have developed, though a clear conception of this idea—Plato's and Aristotle's notions of the artisan—was an achievement of Greek thought.

The Tribes of Yahweh and Old Testament Outlooks on the Wilderness

Scholarship has reached a remarkable level of sophistication and insight into ancient Mediterranean culture. Barely a century ago no one had the slightest inkling that Sumerian civilization had ever existed; today it is common knowledge. Similarly, our understanding of the so-called tribes of Yahweh, those disparate peoples who became a nation under David (the kingdom of Israel, c. 1000 B.C.E.), has increased dramatically.

Our knowledge of these people was formerly limited almost exclusively to literary sources, primarily the Bible; today a wealth of archaeological, sociological, ethnological, and ecological knowledge animates our understanding. Of course, problems remain in understanding Yahwism generally, and its relation to the idea of wilderness more specifically, not the least of which is the nature of scholarship. Norman Gottwald's admonition goes to the heart of the matter. "There are few who take responsibility for synthesizing the discoveries of specialists." In consequence, "fragmented lines of inquiry are reinforced by scholarly vanity and the encrusted traditions of learning. Students of the Bible are socialized to believe that it is 'scholarly' to limit sharply the scope of what is researched."[31] The demands of this study require a synoptic view. Since the argument proceeds briskly, the following outline may be useful.

I contend (1) that the conventional critiques of Judeo-Christianity made by environmentalists of various hues and stripes are not particularly helpful, in part because they view the Bible and Judeo-Christianity through the lens of history rather than studying Yahwism, and then early Christianity, as religions fundamentally related to the problems of living in a determinate sociomaterial context. (2) The rise of Yahwism itself (c. 1400–1050 B.C.E.) is best understood as a further evolution in the ecological transition from hunting-gathering to farming-herding. (3) This evolution is confirmed by the Yahwist ambivalence about culture and nature. The Old Testament in particular can be read as rejecting the high culture of the ancient Near East, as well as affirming a conception of life as taking place outside nature. The Hebrews reject not only nature gods and mythology but also natural place as having any basic importance. God (Yahweh), the supremely important concept for the tribes of Yahweh, is entirely outside nature.[32] (4) In Yahwism, however, we detect lingering reverberations of the Paleolithic mind, especially as revealed in the symbolic significance of shepherd and wilderness for the Hebrews. Even Yahweh is equated with a shepherd. (5) Yahwism nevertheless sounds the death knell of mythic consciousness and the rise of historic consciousness as the dominating sensibility in the West. The Hebrews do not seek to restore an eternal mythical present but look upon time (history) as filled with novel events of singular significance (for example, the Exodus as a testing of resolve and faith). (6) All these developments, finally, are consistent with the basic pattern of ancient Mediterranean outlooks on nature. Although the Hebrews cannot be seen as agricultural innovators, they were the first people to conceive of themselves as living a life whose meaning was defined apart from nature. And Yahwism is clearly the most abstract of ancient belief systems, for

Yahweh was not a nature god but a god above nature who had designed the world expressly for his chosen people.

CONTEMPORARY HISTORIANS and wilderness philosophers, even while they recognize the role of modern science and technology in environmental crisis, often place more blame on Judeo-Christianity.[33] The biblical notion that God gave *man* dominion over the earth, with injunctions to be fruitful and multiply does appear to foster an aggressive, exploitative orientation toward nature. Lynn White's article "The Historical Roots of Our Ecologic Crisis" is perhaps the most famous scholarly essay to advance such a thesis, and he minces no words, arguing that "we shall continue to have a worsening ecologic crisis until we reject the Christian axiom that nature has no reason for existence save to serve man." White holds "Judaism" culpable in that "Christianity inherited from Judaism not only a concept of time as nonrepetitive and linear but also a striking story of creation." This story, he contends, was deeply anthropocentric; by asserting that humankind was made in God's image, Judeo-Christianity created a radical split between humankind and the rest of God's creation. And "by destroying pagan animism, Christianity made it possible to exploit nature in a mood of indifference to the feelings of natural objects."[34] Roderick Nash similarly interprets the influence of Judeo-Christianity, arguing that the Europeans who came to America brought with them an anthropocentric wilderness heritage inspired by Judeo-Christianity. Even so insightful a thinker as Aldo Leopold believes that an "Abrahamic concept of land" lies at the root of abuse and mistreatment of the land (see chapter 7).

Judeo-Christianity is better understood, however, as bound with a long, complicated process of cultural evolution, not the least part of which is the agricultural revolution. But the lens of history makes our appropriation and interpretation of Judeo-Christianity problematic. For if religion reflects in some ways the conditions of human existence, then our changed environment—the modern world—affects our understanding of religion. So understood, Judeo-Christianity is no one thing that serves as a primal explanatory substance but is bound up with the mutable human world—*both influencing and influenced*. As contemporary students of Judeo-Christianity we are involved in a hermeneutic circle, for "when we exegete the Bible we are also exegeting ourselves in our own socio-literary worlds."[35] In short, no definitive or Archimedean point exists from which any scholar can judge Judeo-Christianity. We cannot escape our Judeo-Christian cultural tradition; we can only reinterpret it. Any scholar who ignores this is questing for an Olympian objectivity that simply does not exist. But this is to say that we, too, are caught up in the human predicament—history and philosophy books begin and end, but the ongoing sociomaterial process does not.

Again, as in understanding the Paleolithic mind, we should try not to impose our own categories on the tribes of Yahweh. Yahwism must be understood first as the ideological manifestation of a social community that existed for several centuries in the ancient Near East. So viewed, the Yahwistic religion represents both a social and a religious evolution. Socially, the tribes of Yahweh slowly forged a corporate identity, broke from the elitism and statism of the more ancient hieratic societies that dominated the Near East, and became (for a while) a nation that flourished amid more powerful nations. Religiously, Yahwism represented the symbolification of sacred truths that legitimated the Israelites as a people. As Gottwald explains, "The covenant charter of early Israel mirrored and legitimated commitment in struggle toward the intentional 'destratification' of the human world, to the elevation of all Israelites to the status of free producers—both of their physical lives and their religiocultural identities." As modernists we turn this religiocultural actuality into a theological puzzle: Yahweh, and his choice or divine election of the Israelites, becomes a mystery, since we no longer live the form of life that produced Yahwism. "Our changed socioeconomic and intellectual-cultural conditions have severed our bondage to the ancient gods, and to Yahweh as well, for Yahweh too fell victim to the process of objectifying and falsifying collective human experience." [36]

From the perspective of a posthistoric primitivist the Hebrew experience is in most ways a further elaboration of sociomaterial processes already some millennia old, rather than a radical new point of departure. Such a perspective does not absolve it from any responsibility for environmental crisis; rather, it emphasizes that any attempt to seize on one historical variable to explain the Western world's relentless humanizing of the wilderness is intrinsically narrow. Yahwism ultimately became *the* legitimating rationale for agriculture. As a result, the two factors (religion and agriculture) in combination provide keener insight into history (changing ideas of wilderness and contemporary environmental crisis specifically) than either alone. Indeed, only in the context of the agricultural revolution, and the later Protestant Reformation, and industrial, scientific, and democratic revolutions, can any sense be made of the claim that environmental malaise is rooted in Judeo-Christianity. Paradoxically, such an exegesis undercuts the cogency of that very hypothesis. More fundamentally, Judeo-Christianity marks the emergence of a distinctively historical, and therefore modern, consciousness—a moment in history that culminates the Neolithic revolution.

For our purposes the Pentateuch (the first five books of the Hebrew Bible, or Old Testament) is of particular interest. These books are not the work of a single author who expresses a unitary view of life but the result of communal insights often preserved in oral traditions amalgamated with authorship that accumulated over several hundred years.[37] The Pentateuch contains inconsistent ideas of the wilderness. There is compelling evidence of a *wilderness religion* that resonates with vestiges of the Paleolithic mind. Yet the Hebrew Bible represents the ultimate rationalization of sedentary agriculture. In short, the Old Testament is multidimensional, shot through with inner tensions. It is, however, consistent in one thing: its unremitting attack on the high cultures (the powerful nation-states of the ancient Mediterranean) and their nature myths and religions. The Hebrews desacralized nature and viewed it as the creation of a transcendent God who had given them an exclusive claim to the land. Genesis 12.1–3 states clearly the Hebrew belief that there is but *one God* who has entered into a sacred *covenant* with the Israelites, his chosen people. There is nothing unique about this kind of belief: mythology has always served such a legitimating role. More interesting is the ideological (and psychological) effect, for the Hebrews—of all the world's ancient peoples—are the most intensely conscious of history.

THE SPREAD OF AGRICULTURE was pervasive throughout the eastern Mediterranean basin. Settlement at Çatal-Hüyük dates from 8400 B.C.E., and farming had been practiced in Palestine for nearly ten thousand years. Another famous site of the early Neolithic is Ras-Shamra, also known as Ugarit (*ugar* means field). The oldest stratum there (7000 B.C.E.) contains clay figurines (Venuses) and other artifacts indicating that its inhabitants believed in a primitive fertility religion. This Ugaritic culture, situated roughly at the intersection of the later Egyptian and Hittite empires, flourished until 1200 B.C.E. The most important finds from the upper strata are cuneiform texts (c. 1400 B.C.E.) that illuminate the Old Testament, confirming among other things that the gods of Canaan included El (El or Elohim is *the* God of Abraham), as well as Baal, Asherah, and Anat. These texts establish continuities between early agriculturists and those who came later. Baal (Hebrew *baal* means lord, husband), perhaps the most important god of fertility, also controlled the rains and weather and figured prominently in the Ugaritic religion; the remains of a grand temple built to celebrate his glory have been found. The relative importance of Baal and El in Canaan remains conjectural, but Abraham (likely an eponymous name), who led his people into the wilderness, clearly believed Elohim to be the only god. Thus, the Hebrews, from their beginnings as an identifiable people, apparently opposed the worship of Baal.[38]

The Hebrew Bible, in sociomaterial context, can be read virtually as a coming to historical consciousness, as the story of a slow but inexorable ecological transformation of the ancient world. As we have seen, farming-herding grew up alongside hunting-gathering; the band society character-istic of the Paleolithic gradually changed to the tribal organization char-acteristic of the Neolithic; finally, (c. 4000 B.C.E.) the great cultures of the Near East emerged. These historical developments frame the saga of the Old Testament. The tribes of Yahweh were almost certainly agriculturists, practicing a form of *rain agriculture* (as distinct from the irrigation agri-culture of Egypt and Sumeria), using iron implements to clear and cultivate the land, and holding water through the dry season in watertight cisterns of slaked lime plaster. John Passmore observes that "by the time the Gene-sis stories were composed—in Mesopotamia—man had already embarked on the task of transforming nature. In the Genesis stories man *justifies* his actions. He did not set about mastering the world—any more than he set about multiplying—because Genesis told him to. Rather, Genesis salved his conscience."[39]

Passmore is correct, but the story is even more complicated.[40] The Old Testament must be read not only as the rationalization of agriculture but more fundamentally as the tale of a cultural dialectic between rural Yah-wist tribalists and urban statists. Recent scholarship reveals that the tribes of Yahweh were agriculturists who longed to live free from the oppres-sion of the hieratic nation-states. The Exodus likely reflects diverse bands of people fleeing from tyranny, rather than any one group with an estab-lished identity making a planned escape—or wholesale migration to a new land. Premonarchic Israel was probably tribal in character; over several centuries these diverse peoples forged the "interconnective tissues of cross-cutting group identities and activities" as they struggled for an identity as a community distinct from the great nation-states *and* for a legitimate claim to the land.[41] The word *Hebrew* means *Hab/piru, 'apiru*, which connotes outlaws, rebels, fugitives—that is, an identity based on socio-political rather than genetic or economic traits.[42] The tribes of Yahweh became Hebrews through their actions; in the beginning no one was born a Hebrew.

The Pentateuch (J source) is not blind to the history of the continual battles over land. (Apparently, invaders had once taken the Egyptians by surprise, attacking them by crossing the land of Canaan; by c. 1450 B.C.E. the pharaohs had subjugated the Canaanites.) Throughout the ancient Mediterranean every "state explained its origins and justified its existence and its practices by recourse to the declared will of divine beings. Everywhere religion served as an ideology to legitimate the existing social and political order."[43] As Herbert Schneidau observes, "We must remember the situation of Israel among its neighbors: the ones, bearers or satellites of high and mighty cultures whose deep-rooted traditions went back beyond the Stone Age, and the other, a puny band of shepherds and farmers identified more as a tribe than a nation, who for a brief time developed a second-rate empire when the greater powers were in decline." At issue was the rightful claim to Canaan, a right the Hebrews vindicated through Yahweh. From their perspective, the nature religions of their neighbors had become corrupt, no longer rooted in authentic experience—in the sociomaterial conditions of upper Paleolithic and early Neolithic life—but empty rites and superficial shells, sustained primarily by the self-interest of elites. These were "cold cultures," frozen in place by a "slavish awe of mighty cities, temples, and tombs."[44] The great cities of the high civilizations were perceived as places of abomination, where the few prospered at the expense of the many. The Yahwists rejected everything fundamentally associated with Egyptian and Babylonian civilization: the worship of nature, the cities, the megalithic architecture. We might expect the tribes of Yahweh, as Frankfort puts it, "to have assimilated alien modes of thought, since these were supported by such vast prestige. . . . But assimilation was not characteristic for Hebrew thought. On the contrary, it held out with a peculiar stubbornness and insolence against the wisdom of [their] . . . neighbours." So viewed, Hebrew identity was forged in two primary ways. First, by rejecting the nature religions of their rivals. And second, by affirming Yahweh as the one true God who had chosen them as his people. "When we read in Psalm xix that 'the heavens declare the glory of God; and the firmament sheweth his handiwork,' we hear a voice which mocks the beliefs of the Egyptians and Babylonians."[45]

Although farming is a dominant theme throughout the Bible (both Old and New Testaments, from Genesis 1, especially 1.26–31, through Revelations 22.2), there is also another tradition—the heritage of the seminomadic wanderer.[46] And though these two ways of life share many features, such as monotheism and rejection of idolatry, antipathy exists between them. The story of Cain and Abel (Genesis 4), for example, symbolizes cultural conflict between shepherds and farmers. The Hebrew Bible is conventionally viewed as revealing a sociomaterial transition from a seminomadic to a settled, agrarian way of life that fundamentally changed "the" Hebraic outlook on nature.[47] Interpreted thus, it reveals the story of an ideological struggle between an ancient seminomadic people, at home and practicing religion in the wilderness, and a later agrarian people, who abhorred the wilderness and institutionalized religion (by building temples and creating a priestly class to administer them).[48] But another reading is possible; though somewhat more complicated, it is perhaps more illuminating. This viewpoint refuses to see the tension between shepherds and farmers either as one of dialectical consequence, where thesis inevitably leads to antithesis, or as an ecological consequence, where a more complicated mode of existence (agriculture) emerges from simpler beginnings (herding). Instead, the relation between the Hebraic seminomads and agriculturists is seen as one of symbiosis, where the shepherds are a later economic subspecialization that came about (at least in part) from the fissiparous tendency characteristic of cultural evolution. Shepherds serve a larger community—with which they are associated by crosslinkings— by herding domesticated livestock onto forage beyond regions adjacent to permanent settlement.[49] Yet, as the conflict between Cain and Abel demonstrates, tension (if not overt hostility) clearly existed between seminomads and farmers throughout the Near East; the Hebrews were probably no exception. We must separate these two elements within one cultural tradition, especially insofar as they differ in their concept of the wilderness and humankind's relation to it. But in doing this we must, so far as possible, not overlook similarities in their outlooks.

Herbert Schneidau's analysis is unexcelled for this purpose; he identifies a "shepherd-farmer mythology" that maintains an identity with difference. The shepherd-farmer mythology gave the Hebrews a corporate identity as a culture while preserving skepticism about the value of culture or even civilization. "The shepherd-farmer mythology . . . then can be seen as a symbolic node likely to have preoccupied those who wanted to remember or invent traditions that placed them in opposition to cultured neighbors; for these the shepherd could become a potent signifier of independence, austerity, loyalty, and content."[50] In other words, much like the guerrillas of Vietnam, who defied the mighty United States, the Yahwist seminomads—by refusing to stay put—resisted the enslaving demands of the predatory nation-states all around. But more important, the shepherd-farmer mythology "bespeaks a deeper psychic conflict" than any simple antipathy between herders and farmers. It represents a persistent opposition to civilization. In this mythology the wilderness assumes a deep symbolic meaning, representing both (in Genesis) the shepherd's departure from the detested city (itself symbolic of the high cultures) and the exodus from slavery into the desert to face Yahweh's challenge. The importance of the shepherd-farmer mythology is underscored by the characterization of Yahweh as a shepherd, as in Psalm 23. "The LORD is my shepherd, I shall not want; he makes me lie down in green pastures. He leads me beside still waters; he restores my soul."[51] And David, the first king of Israel, is prepared for kingship by assuming his pastoral duties (2 Samuel 7.8).

Abraham (literally, father of the multitude; *Abram* means exalted father) is perhaps the pivotal figure in understanding the wilderness religion tradition of the Hebrew Bible.[52] Abraham sees himself as a shepherd, as do all the patriarchs. He lived (Genesis 11.27–30) near Ur, a city on the edge of the Fertile Crescent. His people were probably refugees who inhabited marginal lands on the edges of the surrounding high cultures, where armies could not easily go. The primary purpose of Genesis, and the Hebrew Bible generally, is to narrate God's dealings with human beings and especially "to interpret Israel's special role in his historical plan. Thus the call of Abraham ([Gen.] 12.1–3) is the great turning point."[53] This point is critical, for it is the death knell of the mythic consciousness.[54] Clearly, Genesis 12 can be viewed as the basis of a shared outlook with later Hebrew agriculturists that testifies to a common faith in the reality of Yahweh's covenant. And, since the covenant is part of God's plan, it serves to explain the intense consciousness of history, and therefore the significance of linear time, so characteristic of Judeo-Christianity. In the context of later events (see chapter 3) this abiding awareness of history encouraged the humanizing of nature, for such came to be understood as *the plan.* In Genesis also lie the roots of a difference in outlook on the wilderness between the E and J traditions.[55]

Abraham's people are called *from civilization,* that is, a way of life near or within a settled and increasingly specialized agricultural community, *into the wilderness.* Abraham was a "dropout," to use a modern term. Perhaps he felt the discontents of civilization, perhaps he saw his people falling from the paths of their fathers as they gained urban sophistication, or perhaps environmental exigency prompted a migration. Such details are lost in time, and in any case the "symbolic memorialization of the conflict becomes more important in retrospect than its presumable origins."[56] Whatever the reason, Abraham received a message from God to found a nation, and he led his people into the wilderness to do so. Wild nature is not here, as for agriculturists, an implacable foe to be conquered but a spiritual oasis where God can be known directly, where humankind in some sense returns to Eden (before the Fall, the agricultural turn), however obscure that idea might be. The shepherd goes into the wilderness, a symbolic journey away from the tyranny of civilization. Such a belief can be understood in part as a primitive survival of the Paleolithic mind, as well as a precursor to later Romantic and philosophic ideas of wilderness (see chapter 4).

The E source contains suggestive parallels to various Paleolithic beliefs, in particular the idea that the natural world manifests the presence of divinity. The lingering beliefs that God might reveal himself in nature and that the natural world (for example, groves of trees) might harbor divine spirits, are consistent with earlier Paleolithic and Neolithic belief systems. And even in passages where the agenda of the J or P sources controls the narrative, elements of the Elohistic vision of nature survive, as in Genesis 9.13: "My [rain]bow I set in the cloud, sign of the covenant between myself and earth." (See also Genesis 9.16–17.) For the tribes of Yahweh, God's covenant is *not* only with humankind. Elohim has a divine relation with all creatures, great and small, and the earth itself. The rainbow is a natural symbol—though not totemic—of God. As a rainbow God metaphorically parallels the Magna Mater—virtually a palpable presence revealing himself to those who will see.[57] Similarly, Moses' encounter with the burning bush is a natural theophany, a revelation of God's existence. Such theophanies separate Yahweh from the rigid pantheons of the high cultures, associated with the temples, fields, and cities. The desert, Schneidau argues, is a fitting place for Moses' revelation, since "the unearthly landscape of the desert is not God's 'home' but a scene appropriate to him, for he too is unearthly."[58] But Yahweh is not a desert God per se, not literally in the desert: he is a god above nature.

Natural symbols occur elsewhere as well, as for example in Exodus 19.9: "The LORD said to Moses, 'I am now coming to you in a thick cloud, so that I may speak to you in the hearing of the people, and their faith in you may never fail.'" And Exodus 24.15–16: "So Moses went up the mountain and a cloud covered it. The glory of the LORD rested upon Mount Sinai, and the cloud covered the mountain for six days; on the seventh day he called to Moses out of the cloud."[59] Furthermore, the Hebraic wilderness religion contains survivals of the Paleolithic idea that the divine presence will provide sustenance.

> While Aaron was speaking to the community of the Israelites, they looked towards the wilderness, and there was the glory of the LORD appearing in the cloud. The LORD spoke to Moses and said, "I have

heard the complaints of the Israelites. Say to them, 'Between dusk and dark you will have flesh to eat [the quail] and in the morning bread [probably the honeydew from the tamarisk] in plenty. You shall know that I the LORD am your God.' " [Exodus 16.10–15]

The E and J sources contain other similarities to long-established Mediterranean beliefs concerning relations between humankind and nature. In Genesis 4, Cain—the paradigmatic farmer—offers sacrifice of the fruit of the ground, while Abel—the paradigmatic seminomad—offers the "firstlings of his flock."[60] Such sacrificial practices are characteristic of ancient fertility religions and represent a continuity of tradition. Parts of Genesis 1–11 reflect a widely shared belief system concerning the origin of earth, life, and humankind (the original pair). Some ancient myths are preserved, even when these add nothing to the narrative, as for example Genesis 6.1–4, which recounts how gods copulated with mortal women, thereby producing a race of giants *(nephilim)*. (This detail undercuts any narrow interpretation of the Fall as due to sexual misconduct.) The ideas that the world rested on and had been created from a watery chaos and that the sea (personified as a great dragon) had fathered the serpents of the deep were also widespread. But the J source makes it clear that God created the sea and everything else (Genesis 2.5–6). And even though the earth is viewed as resting on the sea (Psalms 24.1–2), the P source explicitly rejects polytheistic nature religion, as in Genesis 1.20: "God said, 'Let the waters teem with countless living creatures, and let birds fly above the earth across the vault of heaven.' "[61] To worship either plants or animals (such as the bull) was thus senseless, since the effect or appearance of divinity rather than the power itself was paid homage.[62] Although Genesis 1–11 gives no evidence of direct theological reflection, the idea that God is transcendent to his creation is clear. Nature and the animal and vegetable world are no longer sacred. "Yahweh," as Gottwald explains, "is a 'high god,' not to be confused with nature spirits, but an overarching root metaphor of a living reality to be pictured necessarily in human imagery."[63] Alternatively, as Schneidau puts it, "the most striking fact about Hebrew ideology in its context is that it claims nothing from nature: all origins, if they come into question, are from Yahweh, who is beyond nature."[64]

After the earth had been made, Yahweh saw that there was no "man [Hebrew *'ādām*] to till the earth," so "God formed man from the dust of the ground [Hebrew *'adāmāh*]." Genesis 2.15 (J source) observes that "the LORD God took the man and put him in the garden of Eden to till it and care for it." Man of the *'adāmāh* means literally "man of the ground," or farmer, as in the story of Noah, "a man of the soil" (Genesis 9.20). Thus Adam—the paradigmatic human being—is the cultivator, the tiller of the soil. *'Adāmāh* can also mean the inhabited land and especially arable land as distinct from wilderness (Hebrew *midbar*), and the land given by Yahweh to the Hebrews (see Genesis 28.13–15). However, Genesis 1.26–31 (P source) is perhaps the supreme manifestation of an agriculturist viewpoint:

> Then God said, 'Let us make man in our image and likeness to rule
> the fish in the sea, the birds of heaven, the cattle, all wild animals
> on earth, and all reptiles that crawl upon the earth.' So God created
> man in his own image; in the image of God he created him; male and
> female he created them. God blessed them and said to them, 'Be fruit-
> ful and increase, fill the earth and subdue it, rule over the fish in the
> sea, the birds of heaven, and every living thing that moves upon the
> earth.' God also said, 'I give you all plants that bear seed everywhere
> on earth, and every tree bearing fruit which yields seed: they shall be
> yours for food. All green plants I give for food to the wild animals,
> to all the birds of heaven, and to all reptiles on earth, every living
> creature.' So it was; and God saw all that he had made, and it was
> very good.

This language is most revealing, for here lie the roots of an intense anthropocentrism. *Man,* of all the animals, is alone made in Yahweh's image, and the remainder of creation—the wild animals—is given by God to his *son* to rule over. Furthermore *man* is "to subdue" the earth, liter- ally to be free from nature's tyranny *and* idolatry of things in nature, and to be fruitful and multiply (a foregone conclusion once agrarian culture is established).[65] The settled Hebrews perhaps saw the farming life, whatever its insufficiencies, as a relief from the misery of the desert in which Abra- ham's people had wandered; the midbar was a place of hunger, drought, and danger. This urban and agriculturalist worldview explained for the Hebrews the existence of the world, Israel, and themselves.[66]

In Yahwism begins much that is fundamental to our actions and con- sciousness; as Harold Bloom suggests, that primal writer J has had an influence in the West that, for whatever reasons, overdetermines us all.[67] Although the Hebrew Bible primarily offers a justification for agriculture and perceives the wilderness as antithetical to that enterprise, its meaning goes beyond any simple interpretation. As Schneidau argues,

> The pastoral motifs that have such force in the Bible derive their sig-
> nificance from the emergence of what we call civilization, but what

they portray is the contingent nature of it. . . . Though the pastoral symbolism does not recognize nature as an antidote to culture, it does emphasize the sense in which urban culture took a turn away from the older way of things, in which culture had been integrated with nature, and which before 10,000 B.C. had served man for over a million years. Man as hunter-collector and forager-fisher was all the world knew of him for the vast majority of human time. Then a set of circumstances fell together, and he began to do quite different things and live in different ways: some of these carrying the seeds of specialization out beyond the tribal 'division of labor,' so that the possibilities of withdrawal and conflict appear. When fissiparous specialization begins the integrated culture is called in question, and pastoral symbolism arises to oppose those who substitute regimentation for integration.

Of course, Yahwism has influenced Western culture primarily through its fusion with Christianity; our account of ancient Mediterranean ideas of wilderness thus remains incomplete. Standing between the Yahwists and the early Christians are the Greeks, and without Greek rationalism any merger of Yahwism with the early Christian community is difficult to imagine. Nonetheless, although Plato may be the thinker who defined our Western idea of objective knowledge—that is, as drawing a separation between knower and known—the Hebraic prophets preceded him by several hundred years. They were the first to dissociate themselves from the restrictive confines of culture and associate truth with the supernatural. As Schneidau succinctly summarizes it, "The Bible, read objectively, tells us why we read objectively." [68]

The Rise of Reason and Classic Culture

During classical antiquity human effort was effectively redirected from the physical and economic world to the intellectual and spiritual. The repeated invasions by marauding armies and concomitant decline of culture in the Near East (c. 1200 B.C.E.) indirectly contributed to the rise of Greco-Roman civilization, for the people who settled the Aegean islands and adjacent coasts were refugees fleeing "barbarians." Although agriculturists had settled in Attica as early as in the Fertile Crescent and Egypt, civilization came later. The Greeks, as these people came to be known, borrowed heavily from those who had preceded them. Aristotle himself observed, "For it is owing to their wonder that men both now begin and at first began to philosophize" (*Metaphysics* I.2.982b). By the sixth century B.C.E. the great coastal cities of Greek civilization were engaged in almost continual commercial and intellectual intercourse with the leading civilizations of the Western world. Yet whatever they borrowed from either the ancients or their contemporaries they transformed through their commitment to reason.

No serious student of Western civilization underestimates the importance of the rise of Greek rationalism on our own lives, for *Reason* lurks always beneath its surface (even surviving today as a noble if perhaps unattainable ideal). Greek rationalism is often presented "as a unique vantage point from which to view the evolution of the European mind towards civilization. The historical documents that survive show clearly a breaking away from primitive attitudes into progress and elementary science, from myths into disciplined acquisition of knowledge about the universe." [69] But one is wise to question the "received wisdom" that interprets the past for us through the lens of history. From such a perspective the Greeks present an unqualified success story, the triumph of logic and method over intuition and emotion, science and philosophy over myth and religion.[70] Viewed from the stance of a posthistoric primitivism (or viewed hermeneutically, for that matter), things are more complicated. No doubt the discovery of deductive reason and the method of proof is a monumental cognitive achievement: our world would clearly have a radically different cast without the Greek influence. Yet even today mathematicians turn upon the Euclid myth, arguing that the Greek ideal of certain knowledge is not only unattainable but potentially dangerous in encouraging foolish action.[71] If we look closely, we find among the Greeks themselves the primitive survivals of the past, as manifest in the strain between the Dionysian and Apollonian elements in Greek culture; mythic consciousness even penetrated the discourse of those paragons of reason, Socrates, Plato, and Aristotle. Our purpose, however, as we trace the web of belief in the ancient Mediterranean, is not to deconstruct but ultimately to reconstruct the legacy of Greek rationalism to modern culture and our own idea of wilderness.[72] For what unites distinctively Western culture across its moments is its relentless demythologizing.

PHILOSOPHY BAKES NO BREAD, but once the supply of bread is sure, then that speculative enterprise begins. Agriculture gives rise not only to the hieratic nation-states, writing, and law but also to philosophy: the attempt to understand the world on the basis of *Reason*. The Pre-Socratics were essentially the first physicists, interested in questions concerning the nature of the physical world and motion. Thales (c. 600 B.C.E.) stands first in line. Often called the father of Western philosophy, he believed that water was the fundamental principle in terms of which everything else could be explained. On its surface this notion seems ignorant, uninformed, simplistic beyond belief. And yet, as Frankfort observes, "This change in viewpoint is breath-taking. It transfers the problems of man in nature from the realm of faith and poetic intuition to the intellectual sphere. A critical appraisal of each theory, and hence a continuous inquiry into the nature of reality, became possible."[73]

Thales' turn to reason is remarkable in two ways: first, he did not appeal to a water god or spirit lying behind the visible, and second, his philosophy was literally an argument, based on sensible evidence and logic. Life, he contended, perhaps observing the desiccation of corpses or the fluids associated with the womb, is impossible without water. He also maintained that the earth itself is supported in space by water (here mirroring a widespread ancient belief: compare Genesis 1), a conjecture that perhaps rests on observing floating ships. Thales may be commended for attempting to develop a conceptually elegant and simple theory to explain what a later philosopher called "the blooming, buzzing confusion" of the world, but other Pre-Socratics achieved more lasting success. Leucippus and Democritus believed that the world was made of fundamentally homogeneous atoms, an insight partially vindicated in today's atomic theory. Nature's diversity was a manifestation of different arrangements of these atoms. Anaximander, in another remarkable foreshadowing of later scientific theory, argued that the world was actually in process—that is, evolving. The two giants of the Pre-Socratic world, however, are Heraclitus (c. 535–c. 475 B.C.E.) and Parmenides (born c. 515 B.C.E.), intellects of such creative insight that they may be interpreted as laying down the channels in which later Western thought about nature characteristically flows.

Both fixed on the so-called problem of natural change: the passing of the seasons; the cycles of birth, growth, decline, and death; the tremendous diversity of plants and animals. "Life," according to Heraclitus, "is a moving river into which we cannot step twice." Here he grasped the problem that defines the locus of scientific knowledge: the perceptual flux or sensorial manifold (to use Kantian terms). Even the Paleolithic mind, though prescientific, manifests the human attempt to grapple with the kaleidoscopic face of nature. "All is one," counters Parmenides, "Motion is an illusion." This doctrine is the conceptual antithesis, indeed, the eternal foe of the Heraclitean spirit: permanence is the form of objective truth. Viewed individually, the philosophies of Heraclitus and Parmenides are diametrically opposed, and yet together they draw the blueprints for constructing Athenian epistemology. They have thus had a fateful effect on Western history.

An interesting parallel exists between Heraclitus's outlook and our reconstruction of the Paleolithic mind: he conceives the good life essentially as the maintenance of natural order. Although Heraclitus's idea of nature is philosophical and logical, and thus distinct from the mythological and intuitional character of Paleolithic thought, continuities exist. Like Xenophanes, Heraclitus ridiculed the conventional religious sensibility of his day: Homeric mythology, and polytheistic and anthropomorphic idolatry. Unlike Xenophanes, he did not deny that a sacred force pervaded nature.

> 227 The wise is one thing, to be acquainted with true judgement, how all things are steered through all.
> 228 One thing, the only truly wise, does not and does consent to be called by the name of Zeus.[74]

This claim, however obliquely stated, is "the real moral of Heraclitus' philosophy, in which ethics is for the first time formally interwoven with physics."[75] Alternatively stated, Heraclitus's claim was that only by understanding the natural order of the world, and accommodating their own actions to it (the Logos), could human beings achieve a good, ordered, and balanced life. As Frankfort puts it, "Heraclitus asserted that the universe was intelligible because it was ruled by 'thought' or 'judgment,' and that the same principle, therefore, governed both existence and knowledge."[76] This is a profound insight—crucial to any postmodern idea of wilderness—for unless science and ethics, or fact and values, can find a reconstructive integration, then there is some question as to the future (see chapter 10). Heraclitus's vision also mirrors that ancient dawning of human self-consciousness: human existence is contingent, in at least some ways, on nature-in-its-order-of-operation.

In spite of the achievements of Heraclitus and Parmenides, the glory of Italy and the eastern shore of the Aegean was short-lived, and the center of philosophical thinking moved to Athens.[77] Here arose one of the essential thinkers of Western civilization, a philosopher whose very life is used as a point of intellectual demarcation: all before are Pre-Socratics.[78] In distinction from the Pre-Socratics, Socrates was a philosopher not of nature but of humankind, and in this way he gave all later Western thought a homocentric cast. "For man," he argued eloquently in perhaps the most famous speech from *The Apology*, "the unexamined life is not worth living." In this alone there is nothing radical or unprecedented. What is revolutionary is the Socratic conception of the good life as essentially a reflective attending to and nurturing of the soul *(psyche)*. The effect is to turn attention inward, from nature as a connected order of being with which humankind is intrinsically bound toward human beingness as distinct from the non-human other—a turning from myth to self-conscious reason.[79] As with the Hebrews, so with the Greeks: old ways were ridiculed, demythologized, and abandoned in favor of new legitimating rationales. There is no problem with an appeal to reason per se, since the very survival of Homo sapiens gives value to intelligent behavior. At issue is the limited idea of reason that the Greeks had: they appealed to a universe of timeless knowledge that was fully accessible only in a dimension beyond space and time.

Socrates thus continued in the Parmenidean tradition. Although human life was lived amid an ever-changing panoply of immediate experience, he identified this play of the world as the problem to be overcome. Images, smells, sounds, and feelings were for Socrates mere appearances, obscuring eternal forms implicit within those images. Knowledge, or a rational understanding of a wise course of action in the world, depended on the forms behind (above, outside of) nature. In *Phaedo* (and elsewhere, such as *Meno*) Socrates argued that "the invisible"—that is, the transcendent realm of universal definitions, *eidos,* the forms themselves—"always remains the same, whereas the visible"—that is, the spatio-temporal realm of evanescent particulars—"does not." In this attitude lurks the germ of a pervasive dualism and logocentrism, sometimes called Eurocentrism, that since the Greeks has infected virtually all Western philosophy, science, and religion.[80] Its effects on Western civilization have been far-reaching and long-lasting. Knowledge (conceptualized as *epistemē*) and the essence of the psyche have been associated with a transcendent and immaterial domain beyond space and time. Further, this invisible, supernatural realm (Parmenides' One) has been associated with the sacred—divine because knowable through unchanging universals, the knowledge that gods alone have. The palpable world of experience—the natural world of the Paleolithic mind—becomes profane, a manifestation only of mere particulars, pallid reflections of transcendent, universal forms.

Plato raised the Socratic theory of forms to maturity in *The Republic*. Scholars point out that Plato's theory of forms offers an epistemological solution to the problem of change first identified by the Pre-Socratics. By viewing all forms as connected in hierarchical fashion with the ultimate form—the Beautiful or the Good—Plato met "the Parmenidean requirement for unity, which, taken together with the permanence and indestructibility of the forms, saved knowledge, thought, and language from Parmenides' [skeptical] arguments."[81] Crucially, Plato also redirected philosophical attention to the idea of nature, especially in *Timaeus,* advancing beyond the relatively thin account of creation given in Genesis.[82]

An analogy can be drawn between Plato's concept of the Divine Artificer, imposing divine mind upon matter to make the world, and everyday artificers or skilled workers who impose their plans upon matter (as with the potter, the woodworker, and even the farmer). Glacken argues that the "Greeks' respect for the artisan and for the beauty and order produced by intelligence and manual skill lies deep in their history. . . . The respect for artisanship could lead to two general ideas: (1) the creator as artisan, and (2) man as a being who can create order and beauty out of brute material, or more broadly, who can control natural phenomena with a combination of intelligence and skill."[83] In the Greek scheme, just as undisciplined matter (or matter *simpliciter*) is mutable, and thus inferior to the unchanging realm of the Platonic universals, so wild nature is inferior to the agriculturist's results, or those of any other skilled worker who imposes form on the naturally given. Plato's Divine Artificer is an intensification of Socratic homocentrism: God is a perfected and magnified version of the human soul, an all-powerful soul free of the encumbering body.

Plato's social and political philosophy reflects the maturation of agriculture; as Mediterranean culture unfolded, the sociopolitical world became harder to comprehend. Cities and nations, tyrants and kings, rose and fell. Perhaps war is inevitable once people abandon hunting-foraging, settle permanently, and acquire property, since the quickest path to wealth is to take from those who have it. So, too, the rise of socioeconomic classes confirms the advance of agriculture; as the simple world of the hunter-foragers is left behind, tribal forms of organization are abandoned and society becomes stratified along lines of wealth and power. The problems of peace and human settlement, and questions of the ideal form of governance and society, were thus much on the minds of the Greek philosophers. *The Republic* is the definitive expression of Plato's ideal society. He envisions a hierarchical society, a community where individuals fill their allotted roles according to a so-called natural division of labor. Such a society, Plato concludes, is inherently just, since every person performs the task for which he or she is naturally suited. But Plato's appeal to a natural order is illicit, since no appeal to history (as a genuine temporal process) is consistent with a Platonic epistemology. Plato lacks awareness of the deep past. His idea of a natural order reveals that his society was agrarian, and therefore hierarchial. Although the republic Plato envisions might be ideal for agriculture, it is an incomprehensible form of social organization for Paleolithic culture. Paul Shepard suggests that a model such as Plato's comes from the pasture and the field. "The model of the caste [Plato's natural arrangements] is the farmer's pure strain of livestock or plants, rather than the food chain [the Paleolithic model]. It emphasizes discontinuity between castes instead of connectedness. This diversity within the society impairs its outward relationships to other groups of people as well as to other species. All others become remote and alien." [84]

Aristotle culminates the rich tradition of Athenian philosophy. He offers a metaphysical solution to the problem of change in nature by arguing that the forms are not above nature, as Plato thought, but in nature. Every natural kind possesses its own form as a potential that, if not thwarted by circumstance, will actualize itself through time. This development is of some significance, for Aristotle's idea of nature both resembles and dramatically differs from that of the Paleolithic. As Ernst Mayr suggests, "No one prior to Darwin has made a greater contribution to our [rational or scientific] understanding of the living world than Aristotle." [85] The *Biology* shows the keenness of Aristotle's eye and the fascination nature—in its infinite detail—held for him. In this sense he represents a survival of the savage mind's interest in nature. For Aristotle, nature is itself animate, and each natural entity contains its own vital principle. Change in nature is a consequence of the essence of natural objects themselves: nature-in-its-order-of-operation. " 'By nature,' " Aristotle writes, "the animals and their parts exist, and the plants and the simple bodies (earth, fire, air, water)— for we say that these and the like exist 'by nature.' " Further, "All the things mentioned present a feature in which they differ from things which are *not* constituted by nature. Each of them has *within itself* a principle of motion and of stationariness (in respect of place, or of growth and decrease, or by way of alteration)" (*Physics* II.192b). Change in the world—in the biological world of plants and animals—is thus in the first analysis a result of animate nature. So Aristotle might be viewed as baptizing in the fount of reason an ancient, even prehistoric, idea of nature as alive.

But lurking within Aristotelian biology is a subtle yet unmistakable difference between any prephilosophical outlook on nature and Aristotle's own. The point is that Aristotle wanted to gain rational knowledge and thereby control over nature, rather than to maintain harmony with it. Totemism, its associated taxonomy, and the mythology of the Great Hunt were for Paleolithic people effective although unconscious (mythic) modes of consciousness for relating culture and nature. In distinction, the Greek mind—arising in the context of agriculture—views culture as an achievement that separates the human enterprise from the rest of nature. Accordingly, although Aristotle's outlook on nature is in part savage, since he is a cataloger extraordinaire of natural plants and animals, his idea of nature is also quite different. The rich classificatory schemes of prehistoric people, transmitted by oral tradition and rooted in the concrete world of plants and animals, are thrown over, replaced by the syllogism and Aristotle's notion of cause. In making nature a focus for strictly philosophical thought, Aristotle (and the Greeks generally) desacralizes the wilderness. Nature is no longer the Magna Mater but a challenge to rational (scientific and philosophic) understanding. The Aristotelian taxonomy and logic represent a continuation of the Pre-Socratic quest for knowledge of nature, not a renewal of a primal bond between humankind and Eden. Aristotelian knowledge of biological categories is achieved through observation rather than intuition and stabilized not into mythology but into an explicit theory that explains change through causal syllogism.[86]

The Greeks, it is fair to say, were intensely anthropocentric and conceived of nature as analogous to the human mind. For them, as R. G. Collingwood notes, "the life and intelligence of creatures inhabiting the earth's surface and the regions adjacent to it . . . represent a specialized local organization of this all-pervading vitality and rationality." Thereafter, critical inquiry and reasoned argument became the distinctive human approach to nature. Our modern idea of nature originates with the Pre-Socratics, who bracket any archaic sense of wonder in the presence of nature by initiating the quest for rational understanding of and thereby control over nature. Of course, the Greeks believed that natural entities are alive—self-moving, animate centers of activity seeking their own ends. From this perspective a plant or animal participates "psychically in the life-process of the world's 'soul' and intellectually in the activity of the world's 'mind,' no less than it participates materially in the physical organization of the world's 'body.'"[87] In this animistic view we recognize a vestige of the Paleolithic mind. But unlike archaic peoples, who attempted only to live in harmony with nature, the Greeks—as agriculturists—sought to impose their order on the world. This notion was rooted in the Greeks' experience of themselves as artisans, as practicing *techne* by which the naturally given might be transformed into utilitarian goods.[88] And just as humans imposed order on natural elements, as in metalworking, sculpting, or farming, so the Divine Artisan had created the world.

Greek Rationalism and the Leavening of Christianity

In chapter 1 I advanced the premise that the agricultural revolution cannot be viewed simply as the glorious Rise of Civilization. Those human beings who preceded it made enormous contributions, including the development of language. We have introduced the theme of the Fall as a dangerous but perhaps workable metaphor for recovering the deep past so that a Paleolithic idea of wilderness might inform our own. The memory of the Fall (regardless of the religious conventions that encrust it) reflects the self-conscious recognition by sedentary agriculturists that the *green world* from which the human species had come was irretrievably lost. In this chapter we have explored the theme of the Fall, gathering the pieces of a puzzle yet to be assembled: the consummation of ancient Mediterranean ideas of humankind and nature in Judeo-Christianity.

As we look to the past we see no abrupt breaks, only gradual and sometimes shadowy transitions. The Greeks and early Christians follow on the heels of the Egyptians, Sumerians, and Hebrews, who in an almost unbroken chain saw the earth as an abode designed for humankind. The consciousness of humankind as distinct from and superior to the rest of the natural world slowly became more firmly established. Judeo-Christianity climaxes the Neolithic revolution, a restructuring that began when humans took up the hoe and staff and abandoned the mythology of the Great Hunt. Judeo-Christianity negates the ideas that humans are simply one among the many children of the Magna Mater and that the natural order is sacred, and affirms the ideas that *man* is the son of God, and therefore a privileged creation superior to wild nature, created by God to dominate creation. Clarence Glacken argues that the Hebrew-Christian conceptions "of God and of the order of nature were often combined by the early Church Fathers with both the classical argument of design and the idea of an artisan-deity or demiurge, creating a conception of the habitable world of such force, persuasiveness, and resiliency that it could endure as an acceptable interpretation of life, nature, and the earth to the vast majority of the peoples of the Western world until the sixth decade of the nineteenth century."[89]

The Hebrew Bible, as we have seen, is no one thing; even within its most ancient sacred document competing ideas of wilderness are presented. What remains to be explored is that peculiar historical reality whereby elements of Greek rationalism were fused with Hebrew and early Christian thought. In that combination lies the genesis of the idea of wilderness that has ruled Western civilization for these past two millennia. So understood, Christianity culminates earlier Mediterranean ideas of the earth as designed for humankind and is therefore the conceptual apotheosis of the Neolithic revolution. This assertion underscores the idea that the roots of environmental crisis are buried far deeper than we usually think. Indeed, we are compelled to recognize that Christianity is no one thing but a combination of historical determinants, including human nature and the agricultural revolution, which together introduced a historically unprecedented direction to human relations with wild nature: the natural world came to be conceived as valueless until humanized.[90]

THE CONCEPT OF THE SOUL as the seat of human personality has become so much a part of our worldview, so accepted a notion, that its existence seems self-evident, requiring neither philosophical explanation nor historical justification. This familiarity is almost unquestionably due to the role of Judeo-Christianity in the past two thousand years. But Christianity did not originate the idea of the soul, for when it "came to the Greco-Roman world it found the general conception of the soul which it needed already prepared for it by philosophy."[91] The Greeks conceived of the soul as eternal, capable of existing independently of the body in a realm beyond space and time. They also recognized the soul (psyche) as the distinguishing characteristic of humans, and thus as the seat of intellect and personality. That this came from the Greeks is almost certain, since it is unlike any other ancient Mediterranean ideas of the soul. More important, the Pentateuch is devoid of any such conception. The Hebrews did not believe in the duality of body and soul, either that the soul was the seat of personality or that the soul was a perdurable, eternal substance.[92]

Neither does the Old Testament articulate—as does the New Testament—a philosophical theory of time or theology of history. Elohim or Yahweh is portrayed through simple narrative, and time is a passage of events ad seriatim from today to tomorrow. History is simply the arena of God's activity, and what is most important about history (or the cumulative record of time's passing) are the events that lead to the revelation of God's name, the Exodus, and the giving of the covenant on Mount Sinai. In the New Testament a significant change occurs: the Greek concept of the soul is fused with the God of the Hebrew Bible. In the Christian scheme of things God reveals himself through Jesus Christ. Crucially, Christ's death and resurrection confirms for Christians the reality of eternal salvation—proof of a kingdom beyond the earthly pale and thus beyond time. The claim that Christian theology revolves around the soul and the problem of its salvation is no exaggeration. And the abiding Christian concern with the nature of life after death establishes continuities with the deep past, beginning with the burials of *Homo neanderthalensis.*

Again, we see a primitive survival in the evolution of consciousness, for through its coming to self-consciousness the Paleolithic mind almost surely grasped the temporal tragedy of existence. If such a working through of

these fundamental questions of human existence is inevitable, then historical Christianity necessarily confronted the problem of the soul's existence
in a temporal dimension during life, and then its later existence in some
eternal afterlife. The problem of time, or the meaning and significance of
temporal existence itself, thus became acute for early Christianity, and it
was Paul who attempted to provide an answer.[93]

There is also another, critical dimension to the Christian conceptualization of time—namely, the idea of time as a second coming when God
would *return to and redeem the world* from its fallen condition. Jesus
speaks of this future time, when the faithful might gain divine forgive-
ness and fellowship, warning his audience that "whoever speaks against
the Holy Spirit will not be forgiven, either in this age or in the age to
come" (Matthew 12.32). Time, in this apocalyptic sense as an age or eon,
is of such a scope that even the lives of several generations of people do
not encompass its beginning or end. (Time in its fundamental sense as an
eon is meaningless to the Greeks.)[94] Within the Judeo-Christian tradition,
Charles Sherover argues, time was never merely

a neutral container of events, but somehow intrinsic to their essential
nature. Time [even in the Old Testament] was to be an important guide
to men concerning the propriety or appropriateness of possible alternative actions which, whatever else be true of them, had an integral
temporal component. . . .

The New Testament, although composed in a later Hellenistic
world, carried this theme forward; time was portrayed as linear, as
history, as the vehicle for fulfillment, as the carrier of meaning.[95]

The claim that both the Hebrews and the early Christians were intensely
conscious of time is perhaps an understatement, for Judeo-Christianity is
singularly bound up with the idea of meaningful and singular events (for
example, God's covenant with the children of Israel, the resurrection of
Jesus) that have occurred over a long period of history. The Old Testament
prophet Jeremiah predicted a second and more perfect covenant between
God and the children of Israel five hundred years before the birth of Christ.
To the faithful, the New Testament, or New Covenant, is perhaps more
than anything else the revelation of that second covenant. From a Christian perspective the Old Testament itself recounts *the Fall of humankind
into time*—into a world of suffering and an awareness of death—as a consequence of its evil nature, and prepares humanity for the coming of Christ
and the possibility of redemption in heaven. The Messiah comes not only
to save the chosen few but to offer salvation to all. "The Incarnation was

not only the end of the old dispensation; it was, much more importantly, *the beginning of a new order of things.* The problem of time and history arose once more, within the new context of Christianity."[96]

The second covenant is no less than a redirection of human attention from mundane affairs toward a world beyond—a time that is not yet but will be, a time where the soul exists forevermore.[97] For Christianity is oriented "towards the future. Its purpose and value can only be judged in relation to eternity: 'We have here no abiding city, but we seek that which is to come' " (Hebrews 13.14).[98] From the Hebrew tradition came the idea that time has a beginning and a sense that God is an active presence in the unfolding of history. For Christians time acquires a new dimension: a linear succession of moments through which history moves as the Divine Plan unfolds. "The plan may not always be clear to us; it may suffer, to our way of thinking, serious setbacks or modifications. Nevertheless, the movement towards its fulfillment does give a direction and purpose to the time series; it makes sense in a way in which it would not if, for instance, we thought of it as unfolding in the reverse order."[99]

Paul, it has often been said, baptizes Greek philosophy, despite the protestations of Colossians 2.8, where he warns believers to "see to it that no one makes a prey of you by philosophy and empty deceit, according to human tradition, according to the elemental spirits of the universe, and not according to Christ." The techniques of dialectical argument and the lessons of the Platonic dialogues clearly help Paul rationalize the seeming contradictions inherent in the resurrection of Jesus, and in a faith in the Kingdom of Heaven and eternal salvation. Employing the resources of Greek rationalism, he articulates a lucid distinction between two aspects of existence: the mortal and natural (the fall into time due to original sin), and the immortal and supernatural (the escape from death into the eternal and nontemporal).[100] The New Testament also testifies to Paul's persuasive powers, for he constantly uses agrarian metaphors in appealing to what remained largely an unsophisticated audience of Mediterranean agriculturists. Although the New Testament is ideologically innovative, when viewed from the perspective of posthistoric primitivism we see that it continues in the agriculturist tradition of the Old Testament.[101] In addressing those whose faith wavered or who doubted, Paul returns again and again to the central paradox of the soul. The question was, and remains, how can anything survive death? And Paul answers that "the truth is, Christ was raised to life—the firstfruits of the harvest of the dead" (1 Corinthians 15.20). Just as the firstfruits of the harvest symbolize the whole harvest, so Jesus' resurrection (the firstfruit) symbolizes the rebirth of all believers. The analogy could not have been missed.

For Paul and the early Christians the second covenant was superior not only to the first but also to Greek rationalism and its conception of the good life.[102] The better world of the beyond (Plato's heaven) was to be reached not through symbolic allusion (like shadows on the walls of Plato's cave: see *Republic* 514a–517c) but rather through faith in the reality of the Incarnation and Resurrection. The Kingdom of God—the eschatology of the future—although not yet present in this life was manifested by both the presence and the salvation of Jesus. This was the power of the "word of the cross" (1 Corinthians 1.18), and the new covenant that Jeremiah prophesied (Jeremiah 31.31–34), surpassing the first covenant because of the confirming reality of Christ and the universality of the message. Salvation was possible for all human beings, not just the Israelites. This universalizing of salvation is a significant evolution in thought, for it overcomes the intrinsic narrowness of the Hebrew outlook. Paul not only attempted to break down the barrier between humankind and God, through the twin notions of the Incarnation and the Atonement, but also extended the good news to all who could hear and see the Light. Such an evolution of consciousness, Collingwood argues, "represents the high-water mark of religious development, and it is difficult to see that religion in its essential form can ever achieve anything higher and more ultimately or absolutely satisfying than the twin conceptions of the Incarnation and the Atonement. In these conceptions the task of religion is accomplished and its problem solved. Man is by them redeemed in very truth from his sins, that is to say from the alienation between him and God."[103] Accordingly, Christianity represents a solution—however tenuous—to that ancient fall when humankind crossed from the Paleolithic into the Neolithic.

With the Socratic-Platonic doctrine of soul incorporated into Christian theology, Western civilization was set inexorably on an anthropocentric course. The human soul now lay at the center of all things, and Western culture was intellectually alienated from the Great Mother of the Paleolithic mind. For the archaic mind humankind has no task higher than to live in an eternal mythical present, maintaining through ritual the sacrality and timeless harmonies of natural existence.[104] The Judeo-Christian mind claims nothing from nature. God alone is of importance, and human attention shifts irreversibly from any idea of an eternal mythical present to the hopeful awaiting of the future. For the Christian, time has two poles: the beginning (as depicted in Genesis 1) and the end (the Day of Judgment,

Table 2. Outlines of an Early Christian Idea of Wilderness

EARLY CHRISTIANS (C. 100 C.E.) probably believed that
- God created the world and all things in it
- nature is a *fallen* and profane world, and Heaven is home
- God is transcendent and above the fallen world; *He* alone is divine and sacred
- *man*kind is made in *His* image and is therefore distinct from the rest of creation
- *man*kind is to rule over God's earthly creation
- time is diachronic and headed somewhere
- God has a plan, however inscrutable

when the dead shall rise). This conception leads to a revolutionary rethinking of the relation between humankind and nature as momentous as that first arrival at self-consciousness in the era of the Great Hunt. Ortega's insight into this revolutionary shift of perspective is unsurpassed, for

what had seemed real—nature and ourselves as part of it—now turns out to be unreal, pure phantasmagoria; and that which had seemed unreal—our concern with the absolute or God—that is the true reality.

This paradox, this complete inversion of perspective, is the basis of Christianity. The problems of natural man have no solution: to live, to be in the world, is perdition, constitutional and unchangeable. Man must be saved by the supernatural.[105]

This dichotomization—of the supernatural from the natural, the sacred from the profane, the transcendent and eternal from the corporeal and evanescent—is the heart of the Greek legacy to Christianity. And thereby metaphysical boundaries were drawn between culture and nature, borders that did not exist for the savage mind. As later events in Western civilization confirm, human attention was riveted on Heaven and salvation (see table 2). Christianity "gives this world a definition which is more serious and more profound than all the definitions of Greek philosophy, a simple geographic definition, when it tells us that this world is 'a vale of tears.' "[106]

Later theologians, throughout the medieval period, amplified these themes. Thomas Aquinas, for example, argued (here perhaps still hearing psychic reverberations of the Earth Mother) that humankind lives as it does because of original sin. The Fall had led to a confrontation between humankind and the natural order. Nature, therefore, must be subdued through work, through pain and suffering. "For what was brought on him as a punishment of sin would not have existed in paradise in the state of innocence. But the cultivation of the soil was a punishment of sin" (Genesis 3.17).[107] Indeed, Aquinas and other medievalists believed that only through the grace of God was salvation possible. The human animal—the natural man or woman—was to medieval Christianity intrinsically flawed; only God's grace led to redemption. Of course, this notion of the natural world as fallen was clearly, if dimly, foreshadowed by Paul (see Romans 8.19–23; 1 Corinthians 15.24–28; Ephesians 1.9–12, 22–23), since he almost certainly "regarded the whole of nature as being in some way involved in the fall and redemption of man. He spoke of nature as 'groaning and travailing' (Rom. 8.22)—striving blindly towards the same goal of union with Christ to which the Church is tending, until finally it is re-established in that harmony with man and God which was disrupted by the Fall."[108] As we shall see in chapter 3, this outlook influenced later conceptualizations of the use of science; technology was viewed as the means to subdue nature and create a New Jerusalem.

CHAPTER THREE

creation / transformation

The Alchemy of Modernism
The Transmutation of Wilderness into Nature

> *What unites Western culture in all its phases, tying in with the ambivalence that produces the continuity of change, is a series of demythologizings and consequent "losses of faith"—some gradual, some traumatic. Nothing is so characteristic of our traditions, with the result that we can say more truly of Western culture than of almost anything else,* plus ça change, plus c'est la même chose. *The Western world, in short, uses up myth at a tremendous rate, and often has to borrow frantically from other cultures, or to allow the cultural changes and oscillations that "time and chance" will bring but which mythological societies will manage to dampen effectively.*
> —Herbert Schneidau, *The Sacred Discontent*

THROUGHOUT THE MIDDLE AGES human beings dreamed of transmuting common metal into precious gold through alchemy. Although this aspiration led to a handsome living for many an alchemist, employed by those who desired the proverbial something for nothing, the hope was never realized. *Modernism*—understood as a historical movement that begins with the Renaissance and extends to the present—is in this sense analogous to alchemy, for through science, technology, and liberal democracy modern people hoped to transform a base and worthless wilderness into industrialized, democratic civilization. Modernism, like the classicism of antiquity, thus continued the humanization of wild nature initiated by the early agriculturists; and, like alchemy, it was never completely successful. But Modernism was unquestionably the ideological cutting edge that, reinforcing the Judeo-Christian perspective on nature and time, led to the wholesale conversion of first the European, and then the American, wilderness into civilization.[1]

To understand the alchemy of Modernism the principal elements of historical change must be examined as they affected older ideas of wilderness. Modernism consists of several component historical processes, which intertwine and interrelate in typically messy fashion. Among these currents of change are the Renaissance, the Reformation, the Enlightenment, and the democratic, industrial, and scientific revolutions. Modernism cannot be reduced to these components, since the whole is effectively greater than the sum of the parts. The various aspects of the modernist movement tend to reinforce each other, as for example the Reformation and the scientific revolution, or industrial technology and the growth of capitalism. Obviously the term *Modernism* represents a simplification of a tangle of historical events, ideas, and periods; yet it is meaningful in the same way as are the terms *classicism, feudalism,* or *capitalism.*

The forces of history together challenged the hegemony of the Church, elevated "natural reason" over faith, and legitimated the pursuit of worldly success. A tidal wave of rising material demands inundated wild nature. The Industrial Revolution, reinforced in its later phases by scientific technology, provided a means to satisfy the economic aspirations of liberal-democratic people. Modernism also effected an ideological conversion of the wilderness into material nature, both as an object of scientific inquiry and as the means to fuel economic progress.[2] Modernism thus underlies the emergence of a profound homocentrism, still dominant in the world, which may be characterized as *the ideology of man infinite* or the rise of *Lord Man,* that is, a radical change in humankind's sense of relative proportions. Unlike Paleolithic and Neolithic people, and unlike even the Greeks and early Christians, modern human beings think of themselves as existing without natural limits.[3] And nature, a mythless nature conceived of as nothing more than matter-in-motion, is thought to be infinitely plastic. "The hierarchy of substances is abolished: a single one replaces them all: the whole world *can* be plasticized, and even life itself since, we are told, they are beginning to make plastic aortas."[4]

Medieval Christendom

We have a tendency to expect Christianity to present one view of the environment, be it positive or negative. This is not historically realistic. Judaism and Christianity are complex social phenomena, extending over many centuries and moving through numerous urban and rural cultures.

—Susan Bratton, "The Original Desert Solitaire:
Early Christian Monasteries and Wilderness"

The Middle Ages stretch roughly from the demise of the Roman Empire to the beginnings of the Renaissance (c. 1350).[5] The *middle* Middle Ages have sometimes been called the Dark Ages, a characterization now in disrepute; and yet, relative to the idea of wilderness, the Middle Ages epitomize a calm before the storm. Sweeping generalization is always subject to exception, but the medieval mind conceived of nature as an earthly abode over which humankind had been given dominion by a beneficent God. Salvation of the soul was the ultimate goal, and thus life on earth was merely transitory. While ensconced in this vale of tears the human lot was to toil in order to bring forth the fruits of the earth. From the governing medieval Christian perspective, wild nature had to be tamed, and thereby civilized or brought into harmony with the Divine Order. Clarence Glacken's summary of the medieval outlook on nature is apt: "If a dominant idea existed, it was that man, blessed with the faculty of work, assisted God and himself in the improvement of an earthly home even if the earth were, in Christian theology, only a sojourners' way station."[6] To the medieval mind, as epitomized by the monk, nature was no more than a symbolic schematism celebrating the glory of God (the red rose symbolized Christ's blood; the white snow, the Virgin's purity).[7] By understanding nature the medieval mind believed itself witness to the glory of God. Knowledge revealed God's presence and divine wisdom in creating the splendors of the universe and served as an instrument of human dominion over nature so that his will might be realized.

Acting out their beliefs, medieval people altered the environment. Permanent human settlement goes hand in hand with agriculture, and so it came later to the northern European landmass than to the Near East.[8] Population increases led steadily to the elimination of the vast European deciduous forest for pasture and food.[9] Wood, the principal source of fuel, was also used in many other ways, as in building houses and making household goods. The British Isles, a Roman outpost located at the edge of European civilization, was covered with timber at the beginning of the Middle Ages. All who came to the British Isles unrelentingly pressured the woodlands—through unrestricted grazing by pigs and cattle, unrestrained logging for charcoal (used to smelt iron) and for building timber, and widespread clearing and burning of forestland to create pasture. By the end of the Middle Ages, Great Britain had been largely stripped of its native forests, except for patrician hunting preserves.[10] More than one historian has argued that the seeds of the Industrial Revolution lie in deforestation. Disruption of wood-fueled energy supplies literally forced conversion to coal and steam power, harbingers of the industrial age.

Although theological disputes and heresies were prevalent throughout the Middle Ages, this was an age of intellectual tranquillity and surety. The medieval mind had a unity quite foreign to our own: art, religion, politics, economics, and philosophy interpenetrated and revolved about a common focal point—God.[11] The Bible was the ultimate authority on all matters and, of course, a source of constant argument as conflict almost inevitably arose as to the true meaning of biblical passages.[12] Philosophy preoccupied itself with religious issues, primary among which was the friction between faith and reason. Art celebrated the glory of God and the celestial kingdom; medieval stained glass today seldom fails to impress even a religious skeptic with its stunning beauty and implicit divine presence. Medieval culture was hierarchical, as the first agrarian societies had been, and society was understood as a manifestation of the divine plan, each element in its ordained place. The monarch, charged with upholding natural law— God's law—as well as the civil law, ruled by divine right. Church and aristocracy formed a mutually reinforcing power structure. Papal authority, though theoretically superior to secular rule, usually acted in concert with worldly authority. Eternal damnation was promised for the miserable serf who dared upset the divine plan by challenging the entrenched order. A small social elite of clerics and nobles was thus supported largely by the masses who worked the feudal estates. However, a small body of skilled tradespeople, aligned into guilds, and a merchant-trader class burgeoned near the end of the Middle Ages. They were instrumental in laying the economic foundations of the Renaissance.[13]

The economy of the Middle Ages differed little from that of the classic age: land and agriculture remained the foundation of material life. From a modern economic viewpoint this was the age of the feudal economy— which some characterize, not altogether facetiously, as the futile economy. There was neither a market nor an idea of a market, in the modern sense, which combined the elements of production (land, capital, and labor) and consumption; neither did any concept of economic society or *Homo oeconomicus* exist. Rather, custom, tradition, and the teachings of the Church ruled economic affairs. The monk, with his vow of poverty and renunciation of material possessions, was the ideal upon which Christians were to model their behavior. Labor in the fields was simply part of the divine plan for salvation. The serf's role was to work contentedly for lord and master, believing that poverty was a blessing and that the dutiful would be rewarded in Heaven. The role of the noble was to manage the estate, distributing the means for life to the underclass and passing the excess of nature's largess on through charity to the Church and monastic orders. The accumulation of wealth and worldly possessions was, in theological terms, a sure path to ruination. In practical terms, the Church maintained vast holdings and possessed wealth generally exceeding that of the aristocrats.

Cloistered societies were possibly the *single* largest agent of environmental change during the Middle Ages.[14] The scope of this influence resulted from several factors. Monasteries were typically located in relatively remote, wild places. These uncivilized locales, often thickly forested, presented a challenge to the medieval mind—the conquest of *horridae quondam solitudines ferarum* (the formerly horrid desert of wild beasts).[15] Paganism, furthermore, remained as an enemy of medieval Christianity. A constant theme of medieval theology is the insistence that nature, though proof of God's existence (the argument from design), was not divine. The sacred groves worshiped by pagans, and reputedly the denizen of witches, shamans, and Lucifer himself, had to be eliminated from the face of the earth.[16] Woodlands were ravaged by ax-wielding monks who, in the attempt to extirpate "heathen" belief in spirits, attacked sacred groves or other sites of nature worship. To revere wild nature was to the medieval mind a blatant heresy. By taming the wilderness the holy brothers fulfilled God's plan, simultaneously exercising human dominion over nature and exterminating paganism.[17] Their work also meshed practically with the needs of a demographically expanding society.

The views of Albert the Great (1193–1280), a dominant intellectual figure and prolific writer, epitomize the medieval outlook on wild nature: God created nature to serve human needs.[18] The medieval mind had no misgivings about Genesis 1, for humankind was intended to have dominion over all creation. Mirroring his age, one in which human settlement was rapidly encroaching on wilderness, much of Albert's work deals with the practicalities of farming. He argued that just as the plow improves the soil, allowing cultivation and the distribution of its energies to seeds sown by human hand, so domestication improves wild plants and animals (for example, vegetables become larger and milder, and cattle smaller and meeker). By bending nature to cultivation, humans were doing God's bidding.

Albert's coeval, Francis of Assisi (1182–1226), differs from the dominant medieval view, yet he is not sui generis. Susan Bratton points out that Francis was not "an aberration, but the product of a thousand-year tradition beginning with Antony in the inner desert and kept alive by the great monastic libraries of Europe that harbored numerous tales of wildlife and wilderness loving saints."[19] Often categorized as a pantheist, Francis is better understood as a panpsychist, believing that God's spirit animates all creation and that humankind is merely one life-form among many. He advocated the cultivation of humility and the joyful affirmation of the the Creator's presence as revealed through the natural world. Viewed from a contemporary standpoint, Francis abandoned the abiding Judeo-Christian presupposition of human superiority and replaced the anthropocentric outlook of the Bible with what is analogous in part to a biocentric perspective. Panpsychism does not, as does biocentrism, affirm the existence of a web of life, where species are effectively bound with land and sun into a living tapestry. But Francis refused to see the natural world as organized around and serving human interests only. God smiled on all creatures equally.

To assert that the Middle Ages were static—culturally, ideologically, technologically—is an exaggeration, since many changes did occur. The agricultural revolution necessarily transformed the natural environment, and Judeo-Christianity culminated the rationalization of the ecological transition from hunting-gathering to *agri*-culture. Humankind had lived in the wilderness as foragers for 200,000 years or more, but in fewer than 10,000 years all that had been swept away before the advancing front of agriculture. In context, the Middle Ages is perhaps best understood more as a continuation of previous ideas and techniques than as a sociomaterial revolution. The process of humanizing the landscape, developing new strains of plant and animal stocks, clearing more acreage for production, and refining the techniques of field and barnyard steadily proceeded. By the end of the Middle Ages (c. 1400) subsistence forager economies had—with few exceptions, such as the Laplanders and others living in "hostile" environs—been displaced from the European landmass. The era of the Great Hunt had ended. Similarly, the philosophical mind felt no great stirrings; the Greek conception of the soul suffused Judeo-Christianity, and Plato and especially Aristotle ruled the intellectual pale. Yet with Albert and his ilk the end of the Middle Ages was at hand: a maelstrom of change lay in the offing.

The Renaissance and the Reformation

The Renaissance began in Italy with a renewal of interest in art, science, and philosophy. Although historians write tomes simply on the general events of the Renaissance, we are concerned with the effect of the great reawakening on the idea of wilderness. The nuances of economic, political, and religious transformations in time and place are similarly beyond our scope. And yet the idea of wilderness exists only within a larger cultural context: politics, economics, technics, and other variables resulted in subtle but significant shifts in the conception of wild nature.

Renaissance political philosophy shattered the theological justification of feudal society in favor of secularized, democratic principles.[20] Marsilius of Padua (1270–1342) marks a dividing line between the Middle Ages and the Renaissance. He argued that the general assembly of the people constituted the legislator for society and that the executive authority was a servant of the legislator; in sum, the people were sovereign. This notion of society as organized around the will of the people themselves, rather than according to God's plan, subtly but unmistakably undermined papal authority, and not only in the secular or temporal realm. Marsilius also adopted an Aristotelian, teleological view of the state: the end of the state was to achieve the good life for the people.[21] Later and better known philosophers, such as Niccolò Machiavelli (1469–1527), Jean Bodin (1530–96), and Thomas Hobbes (1588–1679), provided enormously amplified theories of the secular state. Machiavelli's argument that power was the essence of the state, and that those who sought power were justified in using any means to achieve it, is incommensurable with medieval views. Bodin argued for an absolute separation of church and state, and Hobbes outlined a contractual theory of the state (itself modeled on the emerging paradigm of natural science).

In spite of a gradual lessening of papal authority and a relative rise in the power of secular authority during Marsilius's own time, actualization of democratic principles was yet some time away. The temporal relation between ideas *(theorie)* and practice *(praxis)* has always been inexact, since established institutions and patterns of behavior usually resist rapid change. Simply by raising questions that went beyond a naive faith in the existing order, Marsilius heralded the possibility of cultural revolution. By broaching the issue of the relation of the Church to the secular state, he set off a historical movement (culminating in the French and American revolutions) that led to radically increased demands for "the good life"— that is, material success. So long as the Church remained at the center of society, any notion that "the good life" was to be achieved during earthly tenure was incomprehensible. With the rise of the secular state, the emergence of an entrepreneurial class, and the revolutionary ideology that the state's end was to promote the citizenry's well-being, the claims made on the physical and biological capacities of wild nature escalated dramatically. Inevitably, the idea of wilderness itself was to change.[22]

An unprecedented growth of commercial and mercantile activity, and a reinvigoration of urban life, took place during the Renaissance. The first phase of economic expansion (c. 1300–1400) was basically a quickening of economic currents already present in medieval society. The Church resisted the growth of commerce and industry, primarily because the pursuit of wealth, as well as the lending of money at interest, was viewed as detrimental to the soul and its prospects for salvation. But the rise of the commercial class—merchants who fostered the growth of towns, and traders who traveled the world over, simultaneously making money and establishing lines of communication and transportation—was instrumental to the Renaissance. With the revitalization of urban life, municipal government grew as a challenge to ecclesiastical authority. Through most of the Middle Ages towns had been little more than regional centers for religious power, and town markets existed simply for bartering and trading produce and necessities. But with the strengthening of urban settlement a more worldly minded artistic and intellectual class appeared. To this day the belles lettres appear to flourish best where a community of participants possess the economic means adequate to sustain creativity.

The Reformation (c. 1517–55) marks a second phase of changes in economic life.[23] If the rise of the merchant class was the first economic blow to the Church, the Reformation sounded its death knell. The seeds of Marsilius began to flower: the gradual secularization of authority left the mercantile class free to expand, and the Reformation invested worldly activity with social dignity and psychic significance. By proclaiming the central place of the individual in the realization of grace, rather than sacramental ritual administered by the priesthood, Protestantism affected all elements (political, economical, intellectual) of the medieval world, however unclear the exact lines of influence.[24] And worldly success, rather than being prohibited by holy sanction, was now religiously reinforced. The Protestant believer saw no surer indication that one was chosen (predestined for salvation) than the accumulation of wealth: economic success was a sign of God's favor. Today, of course, the economic sphere is largely separated from religion; but the spiritual justification for the pursuit of wealth was perhaps an initial necessity.

The Reformation did not change the idea of wilderness per se. What had changed, however subtly, was perspective: humankind increasingly looked at the world through economic rather than religious spectacles. Wealth was viewed as virtue, not vice. Wholesale exploitation of the naturally given ensued, for the Protestant goal was to capitalize on nature as rapidly and prosperously as possible. The consumer society lay just around the corner; all that was needed was democratic revolution, techniques of mass production, and the idea of a market society. But even after the Reformation, modern economic society had not yet arrived; the affairs of material life were still governed largely by tradition. "The Middle Ages, the Renaissance, the Reformation—indeed the whole world until the sixteenth or seventeenth century—could not envisage the market system for the thoroughly sound reason that Land, Labor, and Capital—the basic agents of production which the market system allocates—did not yet exist [that is, as theoretical ideas]."[25] The Western world awaited the Enlightenment, the industrial and democratic revolutions, and the galvanizing influence of Adam Smith, whose *Inquiry into the Nature and Causes of the Wealth of Nations* (1776) revolutionized economic life.

The Scientific Revolution

Perhaps no aspect of Modernism has had a greater effect on the idea of wilderness than science. Thomas Aquinas, an unrepentant Aristotelian, helped to clear the way for scientific revolution, ironically, by distinguishing between faith and reason. Once recognized as autonomous, if subservient, natural reason—that peculiar combination of logic and observation—was to run roughshod over mystical faith in things illogical and unseen: that is, the entire mythology of Judeo-Christianity. Of course, such progressive demythologizations are, as Herbert Schneidau maintains, characteristically Western. The rest is history. To challenge theological orthodoxy, as the seventeenth century began, was to risk one's life; but heliocentrism, however cautiously advanced, was the first loose thread in the unraveling of the prevailing medieval scientific paradigm. Giordano Bruno (1548–1600), the most famous philosopher of the Italian Renaissance, was burned at the stake in the square of Rome in 1600 for advocating heliocentrism.[26] Nicholas Copernicus's (1473–1543) monumental work on heliocentrism, *De Revolutionibus,* was published posthumously because of the repressive intellectual and political atmosphere of the time. Galileo Galilei (1564–1642), brought before the Inquisition for the heretical implications of *The Starry Messenger,* shown the instruments of torture, and reminded of Bruno's fate, capitulated and recanted—knowing full well that his assertions were logically consistent and corroborated by physical evidence.[27]

To single out any three or four figures as essential to the scientific revolution is a simplification and partial falsification. However, Galileo's new science, Bacon's new logic, Descartes's mechanistic reductionism, and Newton's physics are central to our study. Collectively they represent a *paradigm shift* so radical that the very meaning of the word *nature* was changed. This conceptual change is reflected in such twentieth-century usages as "wild nature" as distinct from "nature" *simpliciter*. Nature is now believed to be the object of scientific study, and nothing remains in it of anything that is identifiably wilderness.[28] The nature of the ancient world—of colors, sights, and sounds, of touch and smell—has been replaced by a world devoid of secondary qualities—that is, characteristics associated with the primary sensory modalities. Similarly, the idea of nature as animate and living, where species seek to realize their natural ends, has been displaced by the idea of a cold and lifeless mechanical nature. In explanatory terms, the Aristotelian syllogism has been replaced by causal explanation; thus, natural motion is understood no longer as the consequence of biological entelechy but rather as the consequence of external forces acting upon a body.[29] As Newton argued, summarizing the modernist view of motion, every action is the consequence of some other distant action. The modern mind has come to view nature as nothing more than matter-in-motion, whether planets, projectiles, or even animals.

The essential differences between the classical idea of nature as an organism and the modern idea of nature as a mechanism are apparent. But to think that such a transformation in outlook was based on purely theoretical considerations is misleading. The idea of nature as a machine was deeply rooted in the experience of the Industrial Revolution and the pervasive influence of machines on life.[30] Johannes Kepler (1571–1630) wrote, "I am much occupied with the investigation of physical causes. My aim is to show that the celestial machine is to be likened not to a divine organism but rather to a clockwork."[31] These assertions do not imply that Greek rationalism and Modernism are absolutely distinct, since the modernist project is Parmenidean in its cognitive quest for certain knowledge. The mechanical metaphor, however, offered a strategy whereby science could proceed unimpeded by the Church, for God was the cosmic clockmaker, and the divine plan was revealed through the knowable natural order that he had created. Science merely disclosed the underlying regularities of the mechanism.[32]

THE REVOLUTIONARY SHIFT from an organismic to a mechanistic paradigm might be understood as beginning with Galileo—so often called the father of modern science. This is not to say that Galileo lacked predecessors but rather to observe that "with Galileo the modern science of nature reaches maturity."[33] Widely known for his encounters with ecclesiastical authority, Galileo is often acclaimed as a champion of the critical spirit and the freedom of inquiry. Clearly his so-called new science represents a radical departure—a scientific revolution, in Kuhnian terminology—from Aristotelian physics and Ptolemaic astronomy, and this for several reasons.

Galileo led the way into the scientific age in part through his use of the telescope, here understood as the prototypical scientific instrument. Although he did not invent the telescope, he was the first to employ it in scientific inquiry. In retrospect, it is but a short step from the telescope to the cyclotron, mass spectrometer, electron microscope, and computer. A radically positivistic wing of the philosophy of science has argued that science consists only of readings made by instruments.[34] This is doubtless an overgeneralization, but instrumentation is essential to research and the acquisition of knowledge.[35] By using the telescope, Galileo's eyes gathered additional light, and the telescopic image itself was magnified, thus extending his normal vision. But scientific instruments, or more accurately the data that they convey about the world, represent both an amplification and a reduction of sensation. Through the telescope Galileo confirmed the Copernican hypothesis. What he lost was the sweeping field of view of naked eye astronomy, the relation of the Milky Way to the starry sky, and the movement of the wandering stars across the ecliptic plane. And perhaps, in his intense concentration, he lost also the sounds and smells of the night and the awareness of himself as a conscious man beholding a grand and mysterious stellar spectacle. Galileo was standing no longer within nature, but outside it. He became a scientific observer apart from nature, for it had been replaced with a theoretical object of inquiry.[36]

The physical world conceptualized by Galileo is quite unlike the natural world that humankind had experienced immediately through the longueurs of space and time. His world of nature is explicitly not a world of concrete experience: the objects he observed were tasteless, colorless, odorless, soundless.[37] For Galileo the size and shape of a physical body were *real* or *objective*—that is, attributes of a physical world presumed to exist independently of human cognition. Such notions as heaviness, redness, sweetness, roughness, natural places, and natural ends play no role in his physics, however real they seem to the scientifically naive.[38] (Under the spell of Galileo, secondary and tertiary qualities still seem insignificant to today's Galileans, the scientific scholastics of the modern university, for their radical faith is that only the scientific worldview has cognitive significance.[39] Characteristics capable of mensuration and quantification, and thus arithmetical manipulation, are primary and thus real qualities; felt qualitative experiences are secondary and subjective.[40] Scientism, an ideological offshoot of Modernism, views nature as an objective, mechanical process and denies validity to either nonreductionistic or intuitive modes of consciousness as legitimate avenues of knowledge and understanding. And yet it cannot be denied that implicit in the scientific quest is a profound two-sided amplification-reduction: something is gained, something lost.)[41]

Galileo also proposed a revolutionary logic for the new science. Induction and deduction, observation and mathematics, were essentially wedded, and the natural kinds *and* syllogistic inferences of Aristotle relegated to oblivion.[42] "Philosophy [natural philosophy]," wrote Galileo, "is written in that vast book which stands ever open before our eyes, I mean the universe; but it cannot be read until we have learnt the language and become familiar with the characters in which it is written. It is written in mathematical language, and the letters are triangles, circles and other geometrical figures, without which means it is humanly impossible to comprehend a single word."[43] For Galileo mathematical analysis provided the essential rigor of scientific inquiry; syllogistic reasoning was an empty and sterile exercise revealing nothing.[44] Lacking the calculus, an almost simultaneous development of Newton and Leibniz, Galileo's algorithms lack the predictive accuracy of Newton's. Yet Galileo was but one small step removed from the theoretical elegance and predictive utility of Newton's equations.

The new science was also revolutionary in arguing that motion was *not natural* but inertial. Even from our contemporary vantage point the paradoxical nature of this hypothesis is apparent: the sun, moon, planets, and indeed all the constellations appear to circle the earth *naturally*. If, for example, the earth orbits the sun, why is there no evidence of a wind (as felt when sailing in a ship or riding a horse)? And what keeps people from falling off the moving earth? Galileo had no rejoinder to such commonsense refutations. His contention that the earth moved inertially through space thus testifies to the influence of systematic observation on his thinking. His painstakingly gathered evidence supported the conclusion that Jupiter, like the Earth, had moons that circled it; inertial motion seemed to explain that phenomenon (celestial physics). Likewise, he tested his theory of inertial motion on earth (terrestrial physics) with an ingenious experiment—rolling two iron balls of differing weights down an inclined plane, confirming for himself that Aristotelian "heaviness" was a mere secondary quality. Inertial motion was the true explanation of the movement of the balls. The picture of the natural world, accordingly, was radically changed for Galileo. The theory of inertia explained the motion of both the heavens and the earth, and there was therefore only one true science (physics).[45]

Galileo, however, divorced final cause not from the modern world-view but only from the scientific picture of the world. Nature as a system of matter-in-motion was to be understood through knowledge of efficient cause and inertial motion, not final cause; but the traditional Judeo-Christian view of nature as an earthly abode designed by God in Heaven for humankind was left intact. Glacken notes that "the Copernican theory had not called the creation into question; the cosmic system was a product of divine design and order. Galileo deftly said that to prohibit the teaching of Copernican astronomy 'would be but to censure a hundred passages of holy Scripture which teach us that the glory and greatness of Almighty God are marvelously discerned in all his works and divinely read in the open book of heaven.' "[46] Regardless, Galileo earned the enmity of the Church. What was to prevent Galileo's challenge to ecclesiastical authority from spreading beyond the domain of "facts" to "values"?[47] He had no answer.

IF GALILEO WAS THE prototypical scientist, his coeval Francis Bacon (1561–1626) was the epitome of the new Renaissance person. He had an answer to the respective roles of biblically inspired faith and scientifically grounded reason: science was to restore what sin had put asunder. Bacon figuratively wore three hats—scientist, philosopher, and politician—and was thus uniquely positioned to see the human parade. And he lived in an age of optimism; the English Renaissance was in full swing. Humankind was increasingly full of itself, the smell of the Enlightenment belief in progress was in the air, and an awareness of the possibility and actuality of controlling nature was growing rapidly.[48] The idea that knowledge is power was rooted partly in the practical successes of agriculture and industry in bending the environment to human purpose and partly in the theoretical promise of the scientific revolution. William Leiss argues that Bacon's work was so conclusive, so overwhelming, "that the history of all subsequent stages in the career of [the idea of the domination of nature] . . . down to the present can be arranged as a set of variations on a Baconian theme."[49]

Bacon shared with Galileo the same paradigmatic view of nature and method of experimental inquiry, and he, too, made original contributions to scientific method. His theory of induction was not surpassed, even by the great nineteenth-century logician, J. S. Mill, until the twentieth century. Of crucial importance was his conceptualization of scientific inquiry as involving a logic of question (hypothesis) and answer (data). He viewed the scientist as a detective (to use a modern idiom) and realized that to understand nature *she* must be put to the test. True to his principles, he put nature to the test himself, reputedly contracting a fatal case of pneumonia as a consequence of experimenting with the retardation of "spoiling" by cold. These tests were closely tied to his kinetic theory of heat, which some believe to be his greatest substantive contribution to science.

Yet the best measure of Bacon's significance lies neither in his contributions to scientific method nor in his experimental findings. As Galileo irrevocably changed the fundamental conception of science, and thereby divorced the scientific idea of nature from the idea of wild nature, so Bacon envisioned a second world, or *mundus alter*, that humankind might create through science. In one philosophical stroke he revolutionized the idea of humankind's relation to the natural or first world, abandoning the prevailing ideology with its intrinsically conservative orientation and affirming Modernism with its inherent dynamism. Neither the prehistoric ideal of life in harmony with nature nor the classical ideal of nature as a bountiful world that sustained humankind was acceptable: Bacon's ideal was no less than a complete mastery of nature. He achieved a radically modern viewpoint, surrendering the classical and medieval notion that humankind was acting out a role upon an externally fixed cosmic stage and asserting that everything in the world could be fashioned to human purpose through science.[50] "For while men are occupied in admiring and applauding the false powers of the mind [the idols], they pass by and throw away those true powers, which, if it be supplied with the proper aids and can itself be content to wait upon nature instead of vainly affecting to overrule her, are within its reach."[51]

Bacon championed a radically anthropocentric perspective on creation in professing that human beings were potentially master of all things, including their destiny. He viewed prescientific people as barbarians who lived in a godforsaken wilderness without the benefits of civilization. "Let a man only consider what a difference there is between the life of men in the most civilized province of Europe, and in the wildest and most barbarous districts of New India; he will feel it be great enough to justify the saying that 'man is a god to man,' not only in regard of aid and benefit, but also by a comparison of condition. And this difference comes not from soil, not from climate, not from race, but from the arts."[52] Bacon clearly shared and suffered from the same unrestrained ethnocentrism as his fellow philosopher Thomas Hobbes, who also saw humans-in-the-state-of-nature as savage and barbaric. Civilized humans-in-the-modern-age would employ the power of science to remake the wilderness, the world with which humans-in-the-archaic-age had empathetically identified themselves. The *modern* project Bacon envisioned was to convert wild nature as rapidly as possible into the New Atlantis. Standing near the end of the twentieth century there can be no reservation that succeeding generations took Bacon to heart, for he irrevocably drew the boundaries between civilization and wild nature. He thus symbolizes much of what is at issue in contemporary intellectual life.

The genius of Bacon, and his pivotal role in the historical stream as "the man who saw through time" (Loren Eiseley's felicitous appellation), is confirmed by his texts—not only their substance, but their use of language. His style reveals a deep understanding of human psychology, for he wrote of a radically new human future in traditional Elizabethan language strongly colored with biblical precepts, allegories, and metaphors. Language speaks, as Heidegger says, serving not only as a tool of communication but as the veritable wellspring of the traditions by and through which we exist. "Reality," Hans-Georg Gadamer points out, "does not happen 'behind the back' of language, it happens rather behind the backs of those who live in the subjective opinion that they have understood 'the world' (or can no longer understand it); that is, reality happens precisely *within* language."[53] Necessarily, then, Bacon wrote in a familiar genre, for he wanted to see the power of science implemented in his own time. Bacon, Eiseley writes, "was attempting to project for the masses a new definition of culture and inventiveness extending into the remote future. Semantically it involved as difficult a task as Darwin was later to encounter in his attempts to explain natural selection."[54]

Here, however, we must go slowly and carefully, for problems of interpretation are concealed in the Baconian corpus. Although Bacon wrote to advance the cause of science, he also wrote, John Passmore observes, from "within the Judeo-Christian tradition. He thought of his projects for the advancement of science as restoring man to his prelapsarian dominion over the animals, that dominion which was ceremonially symbolised when God called upon Adam to give them names."[55] Yet to state that Bacon wrote from within this tradition is to observe no more than he was part of Western civilization. We must recall that even now the primal author J yet powerfully influences our lives—regardless of our religious dispensation. Bacon was interpolating between the old and the new, between the age of faith gone by and the dawning age of reason—*the modern age.* That he would couch his arguments, then, in biblical terms was essential. Bacon's

New Atlantis was the *New Jerusalem,* the Kingdom of Heaven on earth—
the rescue of human beings from their fallen condition.

The Great Instauration begins with an affirmation that through scientific knowledge humankind might restore the earth to its "perfect and
original condition," for ignorance caused the Fall from Eden. "For it
was not that pure and uncorrupted natural knowledge," Bacon wrote,
"whereby Adam gave names to the creatures according to their propriety,
which gave occasion to the fall. It was the ambitious and proud desire of
moral knowledge to judge of good and evil, to the end that man may revolt
from God and give laws to himself, which was the form and manner of the
temptation." Again Bacon acts in concert with the Judeo-Christian worldview. People had long existed through ignorance in a fallen condition—a
result of the revolt against God's law. Through science, however, humankind could escape; a way had been "opened for the human understanding
entirely different from any hitherto known," a way to "exercise over the
nature of things the authority which properly belongs to it."[56] Thus, as
Passmore concludes in his insightful reading of Bacon, what "sin had shattered, science could in large part repair: man could become not only the
titular but the actual lord of nature. This was by no means the orthodox
Christian teaching; it amounted to saying that *man,* as distinct from God,
could bring the world into the ideal state which Isaiah had prophesied."[57]
Bacon's vision, though radical, has proven to be both accurate and problematic. The insight that knowledge is power, that science gives humankind an unprecedented ability to intervene in the naturally given, is irrefragable. But Bacon's dream of the mundus alter, a second world where
poverty and sickness is vanquished and where humankind enjoys dominion over nature, has not come to pass. This failure of the modern project
reflects in part a pervasive ambiguity inherent in the very idea that knowledge is power; students of Bacon's thought have reached fundamentally
different interpretations of his texts. It is disputed whether Bacon's position is that technological modification of the naturally given is intrinsically
beneficial—that is, good without qualification—or that ends had to be
considered before the means of technology might be employed.

One interpretation of Bacon's philosophy is that virtually any technological transformation of the wilderness is an improvement, an almost
automatic enhancement of civilized life. Glacken argues that "there is no
hint [in Bacon] that environmental change by man might ever be undesirable." Quoting Bacon from *New Atlantis,* Glacken continues: "The end of
our foundation is the knowledge of causes, and secret motions of things;

and the enlarging of the bounds of human empire, to the effecting of all things possible."[58] John Passmore shares the interpretation that Bacon believed the use of science to be unqualifiedly good.

> As early as 1597, indeed, Bacon had proclaimed that "knowledge itself is power." Eight years later, he was to argue once more that "learning should be referred to use and action." He now added that this is true not only in the case of such obviously "practical knowledge" as navigation, but also in the case of what Bacon called "philosophy and universality" and we should call scientific theory. "The empire of man over things," as he elsewhere puts it, "depends wholly on the arts and sciences." Man does not, on this view, "rape nature." Rather, to continue the metaphor, he seeks to gain intellectual knowledge of her, overcoming her resistance not by force but by his intimate knowledge of her secrets, by seduction.[59]

If so, Bacon clearly lies at the germinal core of the intense anthropocentric orientation characteristic of our modern age, a perspective that seems to have almost inevitably led to the unrestrained exploitation of nature. But a different reading of Bacon advances a contradictory thesis. In his interpretation of *The Advancement of Learning*, Loren Eiseley finds what he thinks a pivotal qualification by Bacon of the power of technology. "Bacon makes clear his concern, not only with knowledge, but its application for human benefit and freedom. He knew that man himself, unless well studied and informed, was part of the darker aspect of that unknown country which, as he said, 'awaited its birth in time.' 'Mere power and mere knowledge exalt human nature but do not bless it,' he insisted. 'We must gather from the whole store of things such as make most for the uses of life.' "[60] On this reading Bacon appears to be aware of the difficulties inherent in harnessing science with human agency, since knowledge is power but does not in its own right exalt human nature. "I would address one general admonition to all," Bacon observed in *The Great Instauration*, "that they [those who sought power through science] consider what are the true ends of knowledge, and that they seek it not either for pleasure of the mind, or for contention, or for superiority to others, or for profit, or fame, or power, or any of these inferior things, but for the benefit and use of life, and that they perfect and govern it in charity."[61]

The question immediately arises, however, as to how humankind was to find the path of exaltation, to know those ends "for the benefit and use of life." Bacon, having theoretically sundered himself from the wisdom of the ages (that is, the traditions of religion and philosophy), had no ready answer. How was such knowledge to be gained? Through science? Or faith? Scientific method proceeds inductively—that is, on the basis of experience—and the lessons of the near past revealed more a picture of human woe and struggle than inspiring insight into the true ends of the human estate. And the role of faith for Bacon was narrowly circumscribed. Faith's domain was the Kingdom of Heaven, not this vale of tears. In *The Advancement of Learning* Bacon attempted to answer this conundrum by appealing to natural reason in its function as *radius reflexus* "whereby man beholdeth and contemplateth himself."[62] Yet his conception of reflective reason was untenable. The ends he envisioned essentially reflected the conventional wisdom of the emerging Protestant bourgeoisie: the power of science was to be used to develop and exploit the economic resources of nature while humankind built the New Jerusalem. By sundering fact and value—a dichotomy from which the modern age yet suffers—Bacon begged a fundamental question. As Leiss puts it, "Why is the recovery of the divine bequest not the result of moral progress rather than scientific progress? This will not seem to be such an empty question [for the modern mind] if we recall the legend of the early saints in the wilderness . . . : it was their exemplary moral life, not their superior scientific knowledge, which was believed to be the basis of their restoration of that dominion over the animals possessed by Adam."[63] Bacon simply ignored earlier models, such as the wilderness sage tradition, where the saints reestablished a mastery of nature by living an exemplary life in the wilderness.

BACONIAN OPTIMISM ENDURED through the nineteenth century. Yet concealed by the Baconian outlook are perplexing questions about technology and our relation to nature: most fundamentally, the issues regarding the ends to which the power of science is a means. And twentieth-century events have shattered the Baconian dream. True, humans now fly almost like birds and swim in the ocean deeps almost like fish. We light up the night, make crooked legs straight, and cause the deserts to bloom. Surely such accomplishments are the stuff of dreams. And yet there also appear—in the specter of nuclear war or global ecocrisis—nightmares, as an apparently autonomous technology leads humankind not toward a New Jerusalem but toward Sheol.[64] What has gone wrong? This question is difficult to answer, but part of the problem concerns the idea of nature itself.

Here the work of René Descartes (1596–1650) is important, for he proposed the metaphysical schematism—that is, the absolute presuppositions that mind *(res cogitans)* and matter *(res extensa)* are distinct, and that the natural world is a machine—that undergirds the modernist idea of nature. Though such metaphysical presuppositions were implicit in Bacon's philosophy, he did not explicitly draw them.[65] Like Bacon, Descartes was iconoclastic, believing in the power of natural reason (or the "new science") to transform the world. He, too, looked to the future rather than the past. And like Bacon he was a visionary and propagandist, seeing the radical potentiality of a new world implicit in science. Bertrand Russell notes that Descartes wrote "not as a teacher, but as a discoverer and explorer, anxious to communicate what he has found" to the modern world.[66] Leiss agrees, arguing that Bacon and Descartes were "the twin prophets of a new age for mankind." They argued that through scientific method humankind could achieve domination over nature.

> This formula encompassed two distinct thoughts: (1) the new method would permit an explanation of natural phenomena far superior to what obtained in their day with respect to such criteria as generality, consistency, and conceptual rigor; (2) the fruits of the method also would consist in social *benefits*—notably an increased supply of goods and a general liberation of the intellect from superstition and irrationality—that would enable men to control their desires and to pursue their mutual concerns most justly and humanely.[67]

Reflecting the repressive intellectual tenor of the times, and the still real danger of the Inquisition, Descartes observed (Part VI, *Discourse on Method*) that he could find nothing in the disavowed physical theory of Galileo "prejudicial either to Religion or the State." Here Descartes shows an almost Baconian circumspection and caution: science must neither be perceived as a rival to the Church nor challenge ecclesiastical authority over the heavenly realm. Nonetheless, he was convinced that his thoughts about the new science must be published, since he had learned through experience "how much they differ from the principles of which we have made use up to the present time"—Aristotelian physics, scripture, and the philosophy of the Schoolmen.

> I believed that I could not keep them concealed without greatly sinning against the law which obliges us to procure, as much as in us lies, the general good of all mankind. For they [the general notions of the new science] caused me to see that it is possible to attain knowledge which is very useful in life, and that, instead of that speculative philosophy which is taught in the Schools, we may find a practical philosophy by means of which, knowing the force and the action of fire,

water, air, the stars, heavens and all other bodies that environ us, as distinctly as we know the different crafts of our artisans, we can in the same way employ them in all those uses to which they are adapted, *and thus render ourselves the masters and possessors of nature.*[68]

In this regard, then, Descartes is a virtual clone of Bacon, extolling the power of science to modify nature while avoiding confrontation with the Church.

Interestingly, Descartes's *Rules for the Direction of the Mind,* a logical masterpiece in the Euclidian tradition, reflected both a rich philosophical heritage and—ironically, since he was a Catholic—the spread of Protestantism. Lutheranism and Calvinism had attacked authority in all guises, whether in the domain of science, ethics, politics, or religion; for the Protestant an individual knowledge of God and grace was primary, rather than a sacramental relation to God grounded in faith. Considered in context, Descartes simply extended this idea of the primacy of the individual consciousness over faith and sacramental tradition in religion to epistemology. Only what the mind could clearly and distinctly confirm was, according to Descartes, knowledge. "In the subjects we propose to investigate, our inquires should be directed, not to what others have thought [*doxa*], nor to what we ourselves conjecture [*doxa,* again, since undemonstrable], but to what we can clearly and perspicuously behold and with certainty deduce [*episteme*]; for knowledge is not won in any other way." [69] Employing his famous method of doubt, he reached the conclusion *cogito ergo sum.* This insight was the ground of his philosophy, yet it also reflected philosophical tradition. Socrates himself manifested a radical skepticism vis-à-vis all conventional claims to knowledge. More pointedly, Augustine had advanced an argument much like Descartes's. But Descartes's use of these insights was boldly original, for the inquiring mind became the very locus of truth about the natural world.[70] Paradoxically, Descartes's *res cogitans* was a disembodied mind, standing outside nature.

Yet, above all else, Descartes's most important effect on the idea of wilderness was the view that animals were no more than machines.[71] In the *Discourse* Descartes undertook an elaborate analysis of the circulatory system to show that God was the divine artisan who had fashioned a marvelously complicated organic world as mechanical in its action as a clock. Animals "have no reason at all, and . . . it is nature which acts in them according to the disposition of their organs, just as a clock which is only composed of wheels and weights is able to tell the hours and measure the time more correctly than we can do with all our wisdom." [72] This view is founded on the premises that an absolute understanding of nature is possible and that the physical, chemical, and biological worlds can be completely reduced to mechanical principles and laws. From this perspective even the so-called higher animals are nothing more than matter-in-motion. The devastating implications of this analogy, though initially hidden from view, are nonetheless real. Since animals are mere machines, they are incapable of such feelings as pain. And, like machines, animals have use value only. This view represents the triumph of the Parmenidean spirit and the death of an archaic awareness of the natural world as filled with living and therefore kindred organisms.[73]

Cartesian dualism is also problematic; once mind and matter are separated, how can a disembodied mind affect the natural world?[74] For dualists like Descartes all human relations to nature are mere epiphenomena. To say that his idea of human beings as disembodied thinking substances (that is, archetypal physicist-mathematicians) is problematic is an understatement; and to say that his answer to the question of how the knowing mind might affect action in the material world is ingenuous is to gloss over the fact that he advanced notions that are far from clear and distinct. As Bertrand Russell points out, a fundamental contradiction lies at the foundation of Cartesianism, since by assuming "that all physical action is of the nature of impact, dynamical laws suffice to determine the motions of matter, and there is no room for any influence of mind."[75] Even more fundamentally, Descartes unknowingly entrenched the distinction between wild nature, as immediately known through primary experience, and nature, as a second-order theoretical object. The consequence, according to Max Scheler, was a "fantastic exaggeration of the unique position of man now completely torn loose from the maternal arms of nature. . . . For Descartes, the world consists only of thinking 'points' and of a gigantic mechanism to be explored mathematically."[76]

Descartes's aggressive outlook on the natural world mirrors the dynamism of Bacon's perspective. Both foresaw a new world—the *mundus alter*—coming through human effort. This vision, Passmore suggests, was the philosophical "charter of the Industrial Revolution." The Baconian-Cartesian view of nature and humankind's relation to it has since dominated in our culture,

> at first merely as an aspiration, eventually as an achievement. Its emphasis was not on the diversity of forms but on the uniformity of laws. The qualities which make nature so attractive, notably colour, it denied nature to possess; it looked, for control over nature, to the

structure of particles rather than to roles in a wider system. It saw in man's operations on nature not destruction—for what man transformed had, in its eyes, no intrinsic value—but simply the reshaping of matter and energy to a form more suitable for human use. So the only obstacles, in its eyes, to man's dominion over nature were set by the limits of his knowledge and skill, and these limits were never more than temporary.[77]

The Baconian-Cartesian dream, thus, was that humankind might transcend the Fall, rise up from its sinful condition, and create a heaven on earth. Through science human beings might realize the covenant of the Old Testament and become the master of nature. Even more, science promised a New Jerusalem and held out the hope that the second covenant might be fulfilled. Only a lack of imagination might limit human accomplishment. Here, then, lie the ideological roots of Lord Man.

ALTHOUGH THE CORRELATION is a mere contingency, Isaac Newton (1642–1727) was born the year that Galileo died. Newton's life might be understood as marking a clear transition in Western civilization from the Middle Ages to modernity, for he brought that great wave of intellectual ferment now known as the scientific revolution to theoretical culmination.[78] Although he borrowed heavily from those who preceded him, he undoubtedly remains one of the world's great creative geniuses. *Principia* was almost instantly acclaimed across the Western world, and not only firmed up the physicalist model of nature but laid the foundations for a dramatically new view of economic society.[79] Newton was quite aware, much like Galileo before him, of the sweep of his new perspective. He observed in his "Preface" of 1686 that "since the ancients . . . esteemed the science of mechanics of greatest importance in the investigation of natural things, and the moderns, rejecting substantial forms and occult qualities, have endeavored to subject the phenomena of nature to the laws of mathematics, I have in this treatise cultivated mathematics as far as it relates to [natural] philosophy." However, Newton cautioned, his project involved more than mere geometry and mathematics; it also involved mechanics:

In the third book I give an example of this in the explication of the System of the World; for by the propositions mathematically demonstrated in the former books in the third I derive from the celestial phenomena the forces of gravity with which bodies tend to the sun

and the several planets. . . . I wish we could derive the rest of the phenomena of Nature by the same kind of reasoning from mechanical
principles, for I am induced by many reasons to suspect that they may
all depend upon certain forces by which the particles of bodies, by
some causes hitherto unknown, are either mutually impelled towards
one another, and cohere in regular figures, or are repelled and recede
from one another.[80]

Newton's idea of the *System of the World* completes the methodological revolution that began in ancient Greece with the Pre-Socratics. The
new physics realized humankind's desire for a logical and ostensibly absolute understanding of the natural world—a desire rooted, we have suggested in chapter 2, in the Fall. Newton is thus a figurative reincarnation
of Parmenides; yet the Newtonian world of matter-in-motion is superior
to the Parmenidean one in that natural change is not reduced to an illusory status. Rather, change is understood as the mechanical repetition of
a predictable and determinate sequence of phenomena. Through mathematics Newtonian mechanics elucidates the phenomenal world, rendering
it intelligible in a theretofore unprecedented way. In this sense Newton
can be understood as taking a Pythagorean route to resolve the impasse
between Parmenides and Heraclitus. But whatever the effect on physical
science, *the Newtonian paradigm had an impact on far more than physics.*
As Ortega argues, "the development of physics is the most important event
in human history," since through physics came the "possibility of infinite
technique." With infinite technique came the potential to remake the world
in harmony with the human imagination, so that every desire might be
fulfilled. Physics promised to be "the *instrument*" of human happiness.[81]

The Western world was awe stricken when the great comet appeared in
1758, exactly as Edmund Halley, using Newtonian physics, had predicted.
A new faith in science arose; Newtonian science, in this sense, essentially
ushers in the modern age that Bacon and Descartes had foreseen. "Men
and women everywhere saw a promise that all of human knowledge and
the regulation of human affairs would yield to a similar rational system of
deduction and mathematical inference coupled with experiment and critical observation. The eighteenth century became 'preeminently the age of
faith in science' . . . ; Newton was the symbol of successful science, the
ideal for all thought—in philosophy, psychology, government, and the science of society."[82] The world of Adam Smith now loomed on the horizon.

The Enlightenment and the Industrial Revolution

The Enlightenment (c. 1700–1800), initiated and sustained by a remarkable succession of scientific and philosophic thinkers, combined a number of diverse intellectual elements and historical moments into a powerful, virtually overwhelming cultural paradigm—one centered around the Industrial Revolution. This paradigm, termed Modernism, still rules the world. More than one historian has argued that only the Neolithic revolution has had as profound an influence on human existence as the Industrial Revolution.[83] In classic understatement Heilbroner notes that "it was a complex concatenation of events which finally brought about that eruption we call the Industrial Revolution."[84] Indeed, the Industrial Revolution involves a coalescing of so many variables that it appears almost a coincidence: but for the Renaissance there would not have been the growth of trade; but for the growth of trade there would not have been the wealth of the British Empire (extracted from colonial nations through imperialism); but for wealth there would not have been capital; but for industrial technology there would not have been the machines to engender mass production; but for the Reformation there would not have been the religious justification for pursuing worldly success; but for the market there would not have been the division of labor; but for mass production there would not have been mass product; and so on.

Of all Enlightenment thinkers, Adam Smith (1723–90) most successfully recognized and blended the diverse elements of Modernism into a comprehensive cultural paradigm, epitomized by his monumental work, *The Wealth of Nations*. Consistent with the rise of natural science, this book can be regarded as an observation of changes that had occurred during the grinding shift from feudalism to mercantilism and then capitalism. Smith saw the economic potential of industrial technology, the specialization of labor, the factory system, and the entrepreneur. He realized that self-interest can be a powerful motivation and that wealth cannot be adequately conceived in terms of gold bullion. His conception of wealth and well-being as economic throughput (the production-consumption cycle that converts the naturally given into the goods desired by society) has *in fact* been realized. Remarkably, Smith recognized how different cultural, technological, and social components interrelate to produce (in contemporary terminology) beneficial systems-level effects. In essence, he bore descriptive witness to the demise of feudalism, the errors of mercantilism, and the material promise of industrial technology.

The Wealth of Nations purports to be a scientific treatise whereby the actions of atoms (individual human beings) are described as behaving according to natural laws (specifically, the Law of Accumulation and the Law of Population) and moving in a predictable upward spiral. Little wonder that Smith is known as the father of the science of economics, since the isomorphisms between Smith and Newton are pervasive: both were essentially mechanistic reductionists. The only *deus ex machina* in Smith's model of the economic world was the invisible hand—perhaps the most famous theoretical construct in social science—which orchestrated the actions of selfish individual actors (economic atoms) into harmonious outcomes at the societal level (the level of nature). The invisible hand itself, however, mirrored the Enlightenment belief that Progress was a law of nature.

A normative dimension is also present in *The Wealth of Nations*—namely, a vision of how things should be. Smith presupposed that consumption was fundamental to human well-being; the happy person, therefore, was necessarily a wealthy one. In short, Smith could not conceive of any limit to the desire for pleasure-producing consumption. Like Bacon he envisioned a mundus alter, a world where the engine of economic growth drove society relentlessly forward in a ceaseless expansion of the production-consumption cycle. Poverty—and the dreadful horrors, as he imagined them, that accompany a subsistence economy—were to be overcome by the Laws of Accumulation and Population. These, like Newton's laws of motion in relation to nature, would govern the human system. Unlimited growth—both material and demographic—was the ethical justification for capitalism, and the reason why Smith believed it preferable to all other forms of human economy. Adam Smith almost singlehandedly built, to use Sahlins's terminology, that modern "shrine to the Unattainable: *Infinite Needs.*"[85]

LACKING KNOWLEDGE OF the subsistence economies of archaic society, Smith greatly exaggerated the importance of economic throughput. From his perspective hunter-foragers lived, just as Hobbes said, lives that were nasty, brutish, and short.

Among the savage nations [sic] of hunters and fishers, every individual who is able to work, is more or less employed in useful labour, and endeavours to provide, as well as he can, the necessaries and conveniences of life, for himself, or such of his family or tribe as are either too old, or too young, or too infirm to go a hunting and fishing. Such nations [sic], however, are so miserably poor that, from mere want, they are frequently reduced, or, at least, think themselves reduced, to the necessity sometimes of directly destroying, and sometimes of abandoning their infants, their old people, and those afflicted with lingering diseases, to perish with hunger, or to be devoured by wild beasts.[86]

Smith's presupposition that the Industrial Revolution was the salvation of humankind provided at best an emotive rationale for accepting the persuasive argument to follow; today we know better. Poverty, he claimed, was the cause of the savages' fallen estate, and thus wealth must be the guarantee that humankind will live in a civil fashion. Here the influence of Protestantism is clearly manifest, as is the Baconian dream of the New Jerusalem. Leaving aside the patent falsehoods of Smith's characterizations of hunting-gathering culture (among other things, cynegetic peoples were not organized into nations, Smith had no evidence of infanticide among archaic peoples, and he was unaware of the dubious semantics inherent in using such relative terms as *poverty* cross-culturally), we nonetheless see clearly the general Enlightenment orientation toward wild nature. The wilderness condition was something repugnant in which human beings lived mean and savage lives.[87] Smith, the apotheosis of a civilized European, associated human beingness completely with culture—nature played no part.

On the Continent, others like Jean-Jacques Rousseau (see chapter 4) were extolling the virtues of the noble savage. But the Englishman would have none of it. He believed that human happiness laid not in some return to a golden age or Garden where human beings lived in harmony with the natural world but in taking a new path.

Among civilised and thriving nations, on the contrary, though a great number of people do not labour at all, many of whom consume the produce of ten times, frequently of a hundred times more labour than the greater part of those who work; yet the produce of the whole labour of the society is so great that all are often abundantly supplied, and a workman, even of the lowest and poorest order, if he is frugal and industrious, may enjoy a greater share of the necessaries and conveniences of life than it is possible for any savage to acquire.[88]

The assertion that Adam Smith invented the concept of an engine of economic growth—a theoretical explanation of how that great ideal of the Enlightenment, progress, was to be initiated and sustained—is unassailable. Through economic alchemy, wild nature—the streams and forests, the plants and animals, the land itself—was transformed into material *resource*—matter-in-motion, a means to some other end. The *Wealth of Nations* represents the realization of Merlin's dream: the base and value-less could now, with the facility of natural science and industrial tech-nology, be transformed into a Heaven on earth.[89] Consumption, and its never-ending growth, is the summum bonum of the *Wealth of Nations,* an ideal yet living today in the relentless pursuit of economic develop-ment. Through legerdemain, Smith transformed the first world from which humankind came into a standing reserve—a nature of significance only within a human matrix of judgment, devoid of intrinsic value.

We now understand how this was done, for we see nature only through the eyes of Homo oeconomicus. As Eliade reminds us, modern people live in a world that is absolutely profane, and we think of ourselves as living en-tirely outside nature. Yet as Georgescu-Roegen suggests, "we should note that it would be utterly absurd to think that the economic process exists only for producing waste [that is, endlessly increasing economic through-put and thereby accelerating the production of entropy]. The irrefutable conclusion is that the true product of that process is an immaterial flux, the enjoyment of life."[90] Nevertheless, economic alchemy in no way sur-prises us, for it mirrors the separation of primary and secondary qualities in physics. For Smith, and for Homo oeconomicus more generally, those qualities of nature experienced through empathetic awareness were now insignificant. Primary attributes of nature alone remained—those capable of quantification through monetary value. Even to entertain such a ques-tion as "How much is wild nature worth?" implies a radical reorientation of perspective. For Smith, and all industrialized democracies since, this question has been answered through the market *mechanism,* sometimes supplemented by cost-benefit analysis (an enormously questionable and politically oriented practice itself rooted in Modernism).[91] With the publi-cation of Smith's *Wealth of Nations,* the line between civilization and the wilderness was clearly drawn.[92]

Conclusion

Perhaps, had only physical theory been at stake, the Church would not have reacted with such hostility to heliocentrism and Galileo's new science. But physics fundamentally influences the world beyond matter-in-motion.[93] Bacon was likely the first to grasp the cultural implications of the scientific revolution. "While Bacon himself had no intimation as to where his goals might ultimately lead," Carolyn Merchant observes, "nor was he [entirely] responsible for modern attitudes, he was very sensitive to the trends and directions of his own time and voiced them eloquently. The expansive tendencies of his period have continued, and the possibility of their reversal is highly problematical."[94] Science has played a major role in revolutionizing our Western worldview, if for no other reason than to challenge the cognitive hegemony of the Church. And applied science (technology) has drastically altered the relations, in force since the agricultural revolution, between culture and nature.

As the eighteenth century gave way to the nineteenth, the forces of history—the scientific, democratic, and industrial revolutions, the Reformation, and the Enlightenment—amalgamated themselves into a cultural paradigm so powerful and pervasive that it yet rules the West. Modernism, dressed in myriad guises, has framed the principal categories that define our existence. Not surprisingly, therefore, Modernism has transformed the idea of wilderness. The Great Mother of Paleolithic culture is a lingering memory. Nature now, so far as she retains feminine qualities, has "become a mindless, submissive body. Not only did this new image function as a sanction, but the new conceptual framework of the Scientific Revolution—mechanism—carried with it norms quite different from the norms of organicism."[95] The vestiges of humankind's tie to nature, still manifest throughout the Middle Ages in the day-to-day texture of economic life, were erased by the alchemy of Modernism. Adam Smith, and thus capitalism, bears particular responsibility for this, for he "undermined all the social foundations upon which naturalistic modes of behavior were based. . . . The notion of a complete equality among all individuals, together with the idea of the opposition between nature and society, are the cornerstones of the social-contract theory, which was itself the great intellectual weapon used against the defenders of the old society."[96]

The separation of humankind from nature's embrace began long ago with the Neolithic turn and the advent of civilization in Sumeria and Egypt. The Pre-Socratics intensified the separation by making nature an object of intellectual study; the paragons of Athens reanimated the natural world, conceiving of nature as organic and self-moving, yet they divorced the essence of our humanity *(psyche)* from nature. Judeo-Christianity both desacralized nature—since only God was divine—and raised humans above it, thinking the world God's gift to his most favored creation: *man*. The scientific and industrial revolutions were the ultimate realization of the alchemist's dream: through science the biological and physical world was conceptualized as a machine that could be understood simply as so many atoms of matter-in-motion. Merchant argues that "the metaphor of the earth as a nurturing mother was gradually to vanish as a dominant image as the Scientific Revolution proceeded to mechanize and to rationalize the world view."[97] Capitalism and democracy coalesced with machine technology to effect the conversion of nature into a standing reserve possessing market value only. Modernism thus completes the intellectual divorce of humankind from nature.

And yet, even as the Enlightenment was in full swing, countervailing tendencies appeared. The Church, of course, resisted the intellectual advances of science. Yet faith was not the only source of opposition; in intellectual terms, it was perhaps the least important. Challenges to the cognitive hegemony of Modernism came from within scientific, philosophic, and literary communities. Scientists, such as the physico-theologists, denied the universality of efficient cause and affirmed final cause as lying within the purview of the scientific world picture. Philosophers, such as the primitivists, objected to the idea that civilized Europeans were the ideal for humanity. And litterateurs, such as the Lake Poets, insisted on the reality of qualities intuitively known and immediately experienced. Modernism, though it ruled the world, did not suppress a minority report.

CHAPTER FOUR

Wild Nature
Critical Responses to Modernism

Remembering the poetic rendering of our concrete experience, we
see at once that the element of value, of being valuable, of having
value, of being an end in itself, of being something which is for its
own sake, must not be omitted in any account of an event as the
most concrete actual something. "Value" is the word . . . for the
intrinsic reality of an event. Value is an element which permeates
through and through the poetic view of nature.
  —Alfred North Whitehead, *Science and the Modern World*

S INCE THE PUBLICATION of Descartes's *Discourse on Method*
(1637) and *Meditations* (1641) and Newton's *Principia Mathe-*
matica (1687), the mechanistic model has dominated natural science. The
Cartesian-Newtonian paradigm enjoys cognitive hegemony in the modern
world, displacing any aesthetic, religious, or philosophical claim to insight
or knowledge. And long before the social sciences emerged, such thinkers
as Thomas Hobbes and Adam Smith were modeling their treatises on the
structure of political and economic society on the mechanistic paradigm,
attempting to capture in human affairs what was being achieved in natural
science: theoretical elegance and precision leading to predictive knowledge
and causal control. The root metaphor, borrowed from science by both
Hobbes and Smith, was the machine. These normative ideologies combined with the idea of progress, itself deeply rooted in Judeo-Christianity,
to power an unprecedented era of economic and demographic growth.
Modernism, that combination of the power of science and technology with
political and economic ideologies modeled on the machine metaphor, rules
the world. Practically everyone, save a few ecologists and kindred spirits,
thinks of wild nature as scientific nature, and the wilderness itself has become a mere landscape.[1] Modernism draws, perhaps unconsciously but

absolutely, a boundary between an objective or scientific and a poetic or aesthetic view of nature.[2]

Even though Modernism has intellectually ruled "reason" in the Western world for some four hundred years, challenges to its cognitive adequacy have been numerous. Of course, there was not historically nor is there now any one alternative paradigm to Modernism. This is one reason Modernism prevails, providing a normative standard under which any number of disparate kinds of inquiry find common ground. At least three identifiable streams of criticism flourished from 1650 to 1900, however: one literary, one philosophical, and one scientific. Clearly, these critical reactions have many important differences. The Romantic writers, for example, valued an immediate, personal, and affective relationship to nature, while the philosophical mind was more concerned with the conceptual underpinnings of science and its alternatives. Even within a genre, say Romantic poetry, there are pronounced differences. Wordsworth, for example, despised scientific method ("we murder to dissect") and knowledge, while Shelley admired it. And yet there are also important isomorphisms among the many critics of Modernism. The concept of a baseline is appropriate, since any one rejoinder to mechanistic materialism or Modernism is more a variation on a theme than a novel response. Collectively considered, the critics of Modernism engendered an opposition between two rival ideas of nature: *the idea of nature-as-a-machine* as against that of *nature-as-an-organism*.[3]

The scientific counteraction to Modernism was grounded in an attempt to recast traditional axiological and teleological beliefs in a manner consistent with the advancing front of positive knowledge. Blind faith in ecclesiastical pronouncements and biblical authority was no longer acceptable, but the waters of Judeo-Christianity ran deep. Most seminal scientific thinkers, among them Galileo and Newton, retained belief in final cause. Although efficient cause supplanted final cause within the scientific paradigm, these men thought that final causes operated in the cosmological sweep of events. Within the scientific community there was also a minority tradition, the "lesser lights" (practitioners of normal science) who retained grave doubts about mechanistic materialism. Such scientists believed that factual evidence about the world (geology) and the creatures in the world (biology) supported the idea of a divine plan.[4] These *arcadian ecologists* and *physico-theologists* set out on a road that led to Charles Darwin in the nineteenth century. (In the twentieth century this critical tradition— which refuses to accept a mechanical model of nature that denies organicity and self-initiated motion—culminates in ecology, general systems theory, and nonequilibrium thermodynamics.)

Romanticism epitomizes the literary (and artistic) response to Modernism. Like the physico-theologists, the nineteenth-century English Romantic poets were defenders of the faith. To the Romantics nature was not a lifeless machine, mere matter-in-motion, but a living organism created by divine providence; they believed that God's presence was revealed through an aesthetic awareness of nature's beauty. To the Romantics the scientific idea of nature-as-matter-in-motion was sterile, objective, and stultifying. The poetic view of nature gravitated toward its wild and mysterious aspects, the felt qualitative rather than measured quantitative dimensions of experience, known through immediate contact rather than through experimentation. Feeling instead of thinking, and concrete emotion rather than abstract conception, were the essence of the Romantic awareness of nature. Romanticism also spilled over into social criticism: modern society, the Romantics believed, threatened human freedom and individuality, and poets like Lord Byron and Percy Bysshe Shelley proclaimed the justice of revolution against tyranny. They also rejected the Hobbesian-Smithian idea that society was nothing more than a mechanism orchestrating the actions of human atoms—individuals blindly pursuing self-interest. And, like the wilderness prophets of old, the Romantics reacted adversely to the city, finding it oppressive.

Beyond scientific and literary attempts to salvage religious beliefs, there was a critical philosophical reaction to Modernism that centered on its basic assumptions—namely, the beliefs that mind and matter are metaphysically distinct substances, that the whole of nature equals the simple sum of its parts, that all relations are external, and that efficient causation entirely explains natural motion. Mechanists held these presuppositions as articles of faith. The first wave of philosophical resistance to the metaphysics of Modernism was dominated by Benedict Spinoza (1632–77), who found mechanistic materialism and Cartesian dualism conceptually untenable and attempted to create a system where humankind was part of rather than apart from the natural world. Following in this tradition, even as he attempted to vindicate classical science as a rational project, Immanuel Kant (1724–1804) confronted the yawning gap between the nature-as-a-machine he knew as a scientist and the nature-as-an-organism he knew as a living man. Georg Wilhelm Hegel (1770–1831) attempted to reconcile the demands of Judeo-Christian faith with scientific inquiry through his system of absolute idealism. The Hegelian Absolute is virtually the reincarnation of the historic God of Judeo-Christianity within the context of a burgeoning scientific revolution that produces knowledge incommensurable with traditional biblical claims. Hegel viewed European society and the scientific revolution as the inevitable dialectical outcome of the biblically promised millennium. Nineteenth-century philosophers like Arthur Schopenhauer (1788–1860) and Friedrich Nietzsche (1844–1900) continued the tradition of criticism. The philosophical critics of Modernism continually questioned the idea that the scientific paradigm provided an accurate model for comprehending humanity either individually or culturally.[5] Throughout this period of philosophical criticism, however, no one dominant countervailing paradigm to Modernism emerged—waves of opposition rose and fell, swirling around a variety of issues.

Scientific Responses to Modernism: Physico-Theology, Arcadian Ecology, and the Organic View of Nature

The scientific revolution prompted a veritable explosion of knowledge; never had such a tool for production of knowledge, such a method of inquiry, been loosed upon the world.[6] Science, by giving nature over to efficient causation, threatened the traditional Judeo-Christian account of the cosmos. Even as scientific discoveries proliferated—in astronomy, geology, and biology—however, so too did astro- and physico-theology. The physico-theologist interpreted scientific knowledge as evidence in favor of the argument from design. The astro-theologist could not look at the celestial firmament and its regular motions without finding confirmation of God's handiwork. Even on the cutting edge of the scientific revolution there were those who appealed to the doctrine of final cause. God for both Kepler and Newton was the cosmic guarantor of scientific certitude, a creator who had produced a rational, comprehensible universe.[7] Yet positive science was moving in another direction: the phenomenal world had been given over to efficient cause, and nature was conceived on the model of the machine. Accordingly, even as experimental science advanced, there was an uneasy truce between secular understanding and biblical traditions. Mechanistic science and theology were often wed, as in physico-theology, but the marriage was largely one of convenience.

The physico-theologist movement (also known as natural theology) is epitomized by John Ray (also Wray, 1627–1705) and his book, *The Wisdom of God Manifested in the Works of the Creation* (1691). Widely recognized as a prominent figure in the history of biology, he contributed enormously—and ironically, since natural theology was based on creationism—to the emergence of both evolutionary theory and ecology.[8] Ray argued that nature could not be understood simply as inert matter-in-motion, believing that the biological and geological evidence overwhelmingly indicated that nature was more than a mere collection of its parts. Mechanistic materialism, in short, failed to account for nature as actually observed. Regardless of the evident success that physical science had achieved in explaining the motion of strictly material objects, Ray argued that there was no conflict between faith and reason when it came to the world of animate-matter-in-motion. The marvelous and intricate adaptation of living plants and animals to one another in specific geographic context, and the sheer diversity of life on earth, could not be mechanistically explained. Newton's laws clearly could not cope with the observed complexities and interrelations of life on earth. Accordingly, Ray argued, nature was incomprehensible without a supreme creator who had designed the earth. Ray thus attacked the Cartesian-Newtonian scientific program and developed a positive account of nature as a living entity created by God.

Ray had been influenced in his own thinking by the Cambridge Platonist Henry More (1614–87), the most insistent anticartesian of his age.[9] More believed that mechanism was a sure route to atheism, and he dedicated his life to the critique of mechanistic materialism. He denied the tenability of dualism, arguing that both mind and matter are extended and that space is but a reflection of the mind of God. And he argued that efficient cause cannot explain the existence of either material or biological entities, since something must bind atoms in place even within material objects, and since living organisms exhibit behavior that cannot be accounted for mechanistically. This something else beyond efficient cause, he maintained, was spirit. More was echoing ancient animist notions that the natural world was alive and capable of self-initiated as well as efficiently caused behavior. In More we see the reemergence, in a Judeo-Christian framework, of Greek nature philosophy: spirit, rather than matter, was the primordial explanation of being. This position entails, if only tacitly, belief in the continuity of nature and does not suffer from the most obvious defect of Cartesian dualism, which assumes an absolute break between matter and mind. Unlike a mechanistic materialist such as Descartes, an animist such as More can maintain distinctions between humankind and everything else simply by recognizing spirit as existing at levels below the rational and sensitive.

Enter John Ray who, Donald Worster suggests, dressed More's animism "in acceptable garb." In the intellectual atmosphere of the seventeenth century, no animist, and especially one rooted in Aristotelian learning, could gain a hearing.[10] Like More, Ray was convinced that mechanistic materialism undermined faith, for God was reduced at best to cosmic spectator, observing the results of his creation—matter-in-mechanical-motion—from the sidelines. Yet as a natural historian with an enormous reach of information that seemed consistent with the machine metaphor, he did not want to overthrow the new science. So Ray struck a compromise: he could not find sufficient reason through efficient cause to explain the harmonious interrelations among the diverse elements of the natural world, for these testified to the existence of a divine creator. Therefore, God did exist, and he made the world (the argument from design), which largely worked as a mechanism. Living creatures themselves, though part of the grand design, retained a sensitive spirit, itself subordinate to divine spirit. Ray's solution to the impasse of faith and reason was ingenious. Natural theology seemed to sustain all the cognitive advantages of mechanistic materialism (the knowability of natural order) while preserving the possibility of self-initiated behavior, since deviations from the presumed regular order of nature resulted from organismic freedom—what Ray termed the "plastick" power. Here was an obvious analogy to the sinful nature of human beings, for just as Adam and Eve had been expelled from the Garden for exercising their will, so might other natural species deviate from God's perfect plan.

The historical God of Judeo-Christianity was no mere abstract Supreme Being for Ray. Like the ancient nature religion of the Old Testament, he believed that God's existence was manifest through his myriad works on planet earth. The *Wisdom of God* begins with the twenty-fourth verse of Psalm 104. "O lord, how manifold are thy works! In wisdom hast thou made them all: the earth is full of thy riches." Although Psalm 104 might be read as an expression of the wilderness sage tradition of the Hebrew Bible, Ray was equipped with an array of observed facts, unknown to the Hebraic psalmist, that he used to buttress the argument from design. Thus, in the *Wisdom of God* Ray affirmed his faith in God while maintaining his credentials as a scientist. He was struck by the diversity of plant and animal life, the distribution of species in accordance with variations of terrain and climate, the organic interdependencies of the creatures, and the harmony of these associations. These patterns were proof of the existence of some supremely wise and powerful being, since neither human agency nor Newtonian science could account for them. Just as the watch implies the watchmaker, so Ray argued that the marvelous complexity and harmony of the natural world, far exceeding any human achievement, necessarily implied a cosmic designer. All nature was testimony to the existence of God. Ray's *Wisdom of God* is in some ways as grand a seventeenth-century synthesis of what had theretofore been a mélange of observation and description as Darwin's nineteenth-century integration, the *Origin of Species*. Ray, of course, was not an evolutionist, believing in one act of creation only. But he fused natural history into a comprehensive theory that demonstrated, to his satisfaction, *the unity of nature,* thus planting the seeds of modern ecology.

Predictably, Ray's work remained enframed by the anthropocentrism of Judeo-Christianity. He thought that the Bible prescribed acceptable practices for human exploitation of creation. God put the bounty of the earth at human disposal; the uses that humans find are "little less than a Demonstration, that they were created intentionally, I do not say only, for these Uses."[11] As Glacken concludes, Ray's view of humankind in its "relation to the earth is a gracious, almost idyllic one: a friendly abode for man has been created by Ray's beneficent Creator, who is full of hints and advice (often gratuitous) about its use, and grateful man, endowed with reason and inventiveness, uses the beautiful earth, and in using it changes it, even if it was not designed specifically for him."[12] Ray advocated a kind of comfortable *Christian stewardship*—a view that still finds currency in the twentieth century—based on the Bible (see chapter 10). The events of the nineteenth century, however, first Darwin and then Marsh, destroyed the notions of the designed earth and the ethic of Christian stewardship.

AS THE SEVENTEENTH century gave way to the eighteenth two rival streams of ecology emerged. Donald Worster aptly terms these *pastoral* or *arcadian ecology* and *imperial ecology*. Pastoral ecology "advocated a simple, humble life for man with the aim of restoring him to a peaceful coexistence with other organisms," and imperial ecology aimed "to establish, through the exercise of reason [materialistic mechanism] and by hard work, man's dominion over nature."[13] These streams emerged, however, from the same source: Francis Bacon. He dreamed of restoring a prelapsarian harmony to the world through science; what the Fall had created, the power of science might restore. Yet Bacon's solution to the human predicament was more complicated than it appeared, for science was no one thing. In spite of More and Ray, the larger scientific community was moving in the direction of abstract physical and chemical theories that interpreted the natural world as mere matter-in-motion and sought above all else knowledge of efficient cause. Such theories left room for neither theology nor final cause. Carolus Linnaeus (Carl von Linné, 1707–78) epitomized this tendency in natural history. Yet earlier ideas of nature did not perish under the scientific onslaught. A minority community of researchers—arcadian ecologists—sought not knowledge of efficient cause but the understanding of how the many parts of the natural world meshed as a whole. Arcadian ecology was personified by Gilbert White (1720–93), who moved not toward increasing scientific rigor and causal knowledge but toward an empathetic view of wild nature.

White was the parson of the village of Selborne, England, and was thus given to an intellectual orthodoxy rooted in the precepts of Judeo-Christianity. He had no doubt that divine providence had played an active role in creating the wonderfully diverse yet carefully integrated natural world in which he trekked and with which he communed. Like Ray, White was a virtual encyclopedia of nature lore. He filled the pages of his journal (published as *The Natural History of Selborne*, 1789) with accurate observations and hypotheses, as for example his discoveries that swallows not only eat on the wing but also drink, copulate, and bathe in the air, and that cattle, standing in cooling pools to escape afternoon heat, fueled a rich and varied aquatic life with their droppings. Through years of close study he came to understand that each organism, no matter how insignificant to human eyes or in the human economy, had a role to play in nature's economy.[14]

White's idea of nature had a philosophic dimension beyond that of Ray and the physico-theologists, who saw nature, despite or perhaps because of its divine origin, through utilitarian spectacles. But White, along with such contemporaries as poets William Cowper (1731–1800) and Thomas Gray (1716–71), believed that human beings could reestablish an arcadian harmony with the natural world. White had read the pagan literature of Greece and Rome and had been especially influenced by Virgil's *Georgics* (30 B.C.E.) and *Eclogues* (37 B.C.E.).[15] Worster observes that "the overwhelming impression in this arcadian writing . . . is of a man eager to accept all nature into his parish sympathies. That desire is what the rediscovery of pagan literature in the eighteenth century was primarily about: a longing to reestablish an inner sense of harmony between man and nature through an outer physical reconciliation."[16] Ecology for White was thus a means not to the Cartesian end of power over nature but rather to recreate or rediscover and maintain a primal bond with the natural world.

Arcadian ecology, however, was rivaled in the eighteenth century by imperial ecology, a tradition that sought the mastery of nature White eschewed. Imperial ecology found its champion in Linnaeus, whose *Systema Naturae* (1758) proposed a remarkable system for classifying the plant world and whose essay "The Oeconomy of Nature" (1749) provided a foundation for the domination of wild nature.

> All these treasures of nature, so artfully contrived, so wonderfully propagated, so providentially supported throughout her three kingdoms [animal, mineral, vegetable], seem intended by the Creator for the sake of man. Every thing may be made subservient to his use; if not immediately, yet mediately, not so to that of other animals. By the help of reason man tames the fiercest animals, pursues and catches the swiftest, nay he is able to reach even those, which lye hidden in the bottom of the sea.[17]

Like Ray and White, Linnaeus had a static view of the natural world in which every entity performed its established role in maintaining the harmony of nature. Unlike White, Linnaeus was both Cartesian, attempting to classify clearly and distinctly all the natural world, and Baconian, believing that the end of such knowledge was the control of nature. Linnaean ecology does not recognize that humankind is part of nature. Clearly, Linnaeus's root metaphor was the machine, a mechanism designed by a beneficent creator that could be exploited through ecological knowledge. Worster argues that

> the climate of opinion in the Age of Reason was unblushingly utilitarian, and the Linnaean naturalists did no more than follow the attitude toward nature that dominated in Anglo-American culture. Almost everyone was sure that God intended for all His creation, and for man above all, to be happy on earth; and happiness, in this period, meant material comfort if it meant anything. While scientists busied themselves in collecting and classifying the facts of nature and in aligning their piety with their science, they also managed to create an ecological model that accurately mirrored the popular bourgeois mood. Its fundamental assumption was that the "economy" of nature is designed by Providence to maximize production and efficiency.[18]

Accordingly, all parts of nature were—like a machine—interchangeable and expendable. And the natural world was analogous to a factory to manufacture an unending stream of products for human consumption, and thus the landscape had only instrumental and not intrinsic value. God and humankind, his most favored and privileged creation (made in his image, and endowed with an eternal soul), stood above the rest of creation.

THE PUBLICATION OF two books—Charles Darwin's *Origin of Species* in 1859 and George Marsh's *Man and Nature; or, Physical Geography as Modified by Human Action* in 1863—knocked the props out from under the idea of a pre-established harmony between humankind and the natural world that Ray, White, and Linnaeus presupposed.[19] And the tension between science and theology, and the strain between the facts determined by research and traditional beliefs established by faith, soon rendered the argument from design untenable. Much as More had feared in the seventeenth century, divine providence was on the verge of becoming otiose within the framework of efficient causation. Darwin's *Origin of Species* destroyed the uneasy truce between science and theology. After Darwin, supernatural explanations of the origin of life on earth were scientifically verboten—a credible argument from design simply could not be made by an appeal to facts. Indeed, the facts were embarrassing, since an overwhelming array of paleontological and geological evidence suggested that even if God had created the earth and all the species in one divine act, he had not been of certain mind, for the geological record showed constant upheaval and change in the earth's crust and the fossil record showed literally thousands of terminated experiments.[20] Darwin himself had grown up with orthodox beliefs and had been greatly influenced by the natural theology of William Paley. Yet his own research revealed the untenability of the argument from design. The facts of nature could be explained by natural selection: God was superfluous.[21]

The Darwinian revolution, while part of the scientific revolution, presented irresolvable difficulties for classical theology.[22] Whereas classical physics and astronomy were inconvenient for the ecclesiastical authorities, *the new physics* could be and often was justified against a theological backdrop. Galileo, Bacon, Descartes, and Newton were not disbelievers, arguing that science was a more perfect account of God's glory since he was the architect of the natural world. Physics was therefore not a heresy but a more accurate narration of God's creation. Darwin's revolution was a different matter, for the philosophical implications of *the new biology* were less easily reconciled with Judeo-Christian orthodoxy. On one hand, the evolutionary hypothesis was merely another chapter in the scientific revolution; on the other, the new biology represented an unprecedented challenge to faith, for what was at stake was no less than the origin of the human species. Special creation was the prevailing dogma: the human animal was a privileged creation of an almighty and provident God, who had created not only humankind but the rest of nature.

Evolutionary science ran counter to the thesis of special creation, for the evidence showed that humankind was bound with nature, itself no more than a mutable world of biological and geological forms with no final configuration. Darwin minced no words in stating his conclusion in his *Descent of Man*, published in 1871, some twelve years after the *Origin of Species*. "The main conclusion here arrived at, and now held by many naturalists who are well competent to form a sound judgment is that man is descended from some less highly organised form. . . . He who is not content to look, like a savage, at the phenomena of nature as disconnected, cannot any longer believe that man is the work of a separate act of creation. . . . [The facts] all point in the plainest manner to the conclusion that man is the co-descendant with other mammals of a common progenitor."[23] The human species, in short, was more deeply involved with the unity of nature than either the physico-theologists or the arcadian and imperial ecologists had realized. The Darwinian revolution forced two questions on the nineteenth-century mind. First, was the human species truly the favored creation of a supernatural creator, itself endowed with a supernatural spirit, and set upon earth to rule creation? And second, given the untenability of the modernist idea of nature-as-resource-only, an ecomachine to be exploited through science and technology, what was the relation of the human species to the natural world?[24] Ironically, in destroying the orthodoxy central to Gilbert White's arcadian view of our relation to nature, evolutionary science led to new understandings of our environmental role. Here, too, the work is unfinished: humankind has barely begun to think ecologically. But the evolutionary paradigm is now established, unquestionably the paradigmatic underpinning of postmodern science.[25]

Darwin's bombshell was only the first blow to the prevailing worldview. Four years later came George Perkins Marsh's *Man and Nature*. Contemporary environmental studies—regardless of methodology and sophistication of analysis—trail in its wake. A careful reading of *Man and Nature* leaves one incredulous, since Marsh marshaled almost irrefragable evidence, spanning an enormous array of activities, that humankind was on balance a destabilizing environmental force whose impacts portended an uncertain future. As he explained, his purpose was

to indicate the character and, approximately, the extent of the changes produced by human action in the physical conditions of the globe we inhabit; to point out the dangers of imprudence and the necessity of caution in all operations which, on a large scale, interfere with the spontaneous arrangements of the organic and inorganic world; to suggest the possibility and the importance of the restoration of disturbed harmonies and the material improvement of waste and exhausted regions; and, incidentally, to illustrate the doctrine that man is, in both kind and degree, a power of a higher order than any of the other forms of animated life, which, like him, are nourished at the table of bounteous nature.[26]

Marsh's vantage point reflected his place and time, escaping neither supernaturalism nor utilitarianism, which is to say that his idea of nature was clearly anthropocentric. His view of a proper balance between the human species and nature was modeled on the ideal of Christian stewardship. He thus indicted humankind for wantonly slaughtering animals and for practices that wasted or destroyed nature's largesse, but he was certain of humankind's superiority over the remainder of creation. Yet Marsh's study was so comprehensive in its account of environmental despoliation that no unbiased reader could ignore its message: humankind was entering terra incognita in its relentless humanization of the earth. His book concludes with an observation remarkably modern in the depth of its ecological insight:

> It is a legal maxim that "the law concerneth not itself with trifles," *de minimis non curat lex;* but in the vocabulary of nature, little and great are terms of comparison only; she knows no trifles, and her laws are as inflexible in dealing with an atom as with a continent or a planet. The human operations mentioned [above] . . . , therefore, do not act in the ways ascribed to them, though our limited faculties are at present, perhaps forever, incapable of weighing their immediate, still more their ultimate consequences. But our inability to assign definite values to these causes of the disturbance of natural arrangements is not a reason for ignoring the existence of such causes in any general view of the relations between man and nature, and we are never justified in assuming a force to be insignificant because its measure is unknown, or even because no physical effect can now be traced to it as its origin.[27]

Whatever the shortcomings of Marsh and Darwin, they reduced to tatters the Baconian-Cartesian belief that science enabled creation of the New Jerusalem.[28] The cumulative effect of the inherent contradiction between faith and reason, and the ongoing course of the scientific and industrial revolutions, engendered the downfall of an ideology. "By the 1850s," Worster suggests, "the synthesis of piety and science represented by Linnaeus, Ray, and White had been reduced to a cracked and dried-out shell; little of its inner vitality remained."[29] Humankind was not only not God's special creation, but the idea that humankind could exploit wild nature without consequence (since God's grace ensured that human stewardship was ultimately benevolent) was philosophically untenable; environmental malaise demonstrated the inadequacy of scriptural guides to developing the earth's resources. And Thomas Malthus had planted the festering seeds of doubt that events might be beyond the power of human control. Malthusian specters of famine caused misgivings about the sagacity of the biblical admonition (Genesis 1.28) to "be fruitful and multiply, and fill the earth and subdue it; and have dominion over the fish of the sea and over the birds of the air and over every living thing that moves upon the earth."[30]

Although the theoretical program of physico-theology failed (the breakdown of the doctrines of special creation and preestablished harmony, and the collapse of the argument from design), the movement played a positive role. Not only was physico-theology the first scientific challenge to the cognitive hegemony of mechanistic materialism but, as Glacken claims, "it had already—before 'Darwin's web of life'—prepared men for the study of ecology."[31] Though both physico-theology and arcadian ecology came to naught as positive sciences, from their ruins emerged modern biological science. By advancing the hypothesis of the unity of nature, the physico-theologists and arcadian ecologists contributed to the intellectual future.[32] Of course, the idea of nature as a unitary living whole had existed since the Paleolithic. Yet never before had such an array of empirical evidence been combined into a meaningful gestalt. Although contemporary ecology is devoid of theological dress, the underlying notion that every element in an ecosystem has a role to play is historically grounded in natural theology.

The question of the unity of nature remains a live issue, since neither classical science nor natural theology have provided a comprehensible account of that order. In fact, neither God (final cause) nor mechanism (efficient cause) can account for the orderly world or the unity of natural process. As we shall discuss in chapter 10, telos exists from the vantage point of contemporary ecology, but the ends are purposeless purposes: self-creating order out of chaos has replaced God or the cosmic machine or both. Ernst Mayr's idea of evolutionary process as *teleonomic* at least partially captures this idea of purposeless purpose. He insists that telic language is legitimate in evolutionary studies, although we cannot legitimately describe these "processes or trends as goal-directed (teleological).

Selection rewards past phenomena (mutation, recombination, etc.), but does not plan for the future, at least not in any specific way."[33] Ilya Prigogine's study of thermodynamics amplifies the idea of purposeless purpose, since "irreversibility is the source of order at all levels." Classical science arose in part in "opposition to the biological model of a spontaneous and autonomous organization of natural beings. But it was confronted with another fundamental alternative. Is nature intrinsically random? Is ordered behavior merely the transient result of the chance collisions of atoms and of their unstable associations?"[34] The evolutionary paradigm (alternatively: organicism and not mechanism) will likely rule the postmodern world. Yet at this moment humankind still treads a Baconian-Cartesian path, still views nature as matter-in-motion, which through technology is converted into the accoutrements of advanced industrial civilization. And the imperial ecologist reigns supreme, wielding the band-aids and tourniquets, the palliatives of Modernism, that so desperately try to forestall ecocrisis.

The Romantic Reaction to Modernism

Roderick Nash believes that the Romantic idea of wilderness began, paradoxically, in the cities, where artists and gentlemen experienced nostalgic remembrances of other times and places when human life was bonded more closely to nature.[35] Tales of the New World, now being colonized by Europeans, accentuated the desire for the wild, the primitive. The scientific and industrial revolutions, and Enlightenment philosophy more generally, had transformed European life. Nash offers a useful summary of the Romantic idea of wilderness, arguing that "in regard to nature Romantics preferred the wild. Rejecting the meticulously ordered gardens at Versailles, so attractive to the Enlightenment mind, they turned to the unkempt forest. Wilderness appealed to those bored or disgusted with man and his works. It not only offered an escape from society but also was an ideal stage for the Romantic individual to exercise the cult that he frequently made of his own soul. The solitude and total freedom of the wilderness created a perfect setting for either melancholy or exultation."[36]

Yet the Romantic wilderness was more than this; the idea had social implications as well. Jean-Jacques Rousseau's (1712–78) concept of the natural man *(l'homme naturelle)* was grounded in his observation of the social conditions in which most of humanity lived. The masses, though freed from the tyranny of the manor, now obeyed a new lord: the secular state, which protected, above all else, the rights of property.[37] Human beings are born free, yet everywhere they are in chains, echo his famous words. Rousseau believed that the state, science, and other elements of culture, including property and law, had corrupted the human estate; the true path to happiness and well-being lay in finding the way back to a natural existence. This notion is often associated with that complex of ideas known as *primitivism*, essentially the thesis that culture and happiness are inversely related; thus the concept of the noble savage was engendered. In almost absolute contrast with Hobbes, Bacon, and Smith, Rousseau saw the savage life as a virtuous one. Wild nature was idealized as an oasis free of the ills of civilization, a retreat to which the harried and battered, the suppressed or oppressed, might turn for relief. The original sin, as Rousseau saw it, was the turn to agriculture, and its inevitable accompaniment: private property. But the human animal was naturally good, and civilization was the distorting element that turned humans against one another. The good life, accordingly, was the primitive life.

Rousseau also fueled the aesthetic turn in nineteenth-century Romanticism with his *Julie, ou La Nouvelle Héloïse* (1761). The Romantic attitude, whatever else, was characteristically one of intense personal involvement with and aesthetic response to nature. The eighteenth-century Romantic cultivated *la sensibilité*—the affective relation to and bonding with the natural world (rather than an objective relation based on reason and logic). Rousseau's praise of the sublimity of the Alps and their effect on the soul stimulated a generation of artists and poets. He had been influenced in his thinking by natural theologians, who had attempted to account for the mountains, deserts, dark forests, and other seemingly godforsaken areas devoid of civilization. Such geographical features had long been a theological problem, for they embodied an imperfection of the earth. How could the Supreme Being, possessing omnipotent power, allow such randomness and irregularity? The physico-theologists answered this question by distinguishing the beautiful and the sublime.

The beautiful elements of nature expressed God's care and benevolence, while the wild (sublime) elements, such as mountains and hurricanes, represented his power and capacity for wrath. So viewed, the wilderness was a consequence of humankind's sins, punishment by a wrathful God for transgressions from his way. Thomas Burnet, one of Ray's contemporaries, argued in *The Sacred Theory of the Earth* (1681–89) that original sin had motivated God to expel Adam and Eve from Eden, which was an uncorrupted paradise. The great flood and the resulting cataclysms led to the present "ruined" state of the world. Yet in just these aspects (mountains, chasms, deserts) Burnet found proof of God's existence and of his omnipotent, wrathful, and just essence.

> There is something august and stately in the Air of these things, that inspires the mind with great thoughts and passions. We do naturally, upon such occasions, think of God and his greatness: and whatsoever hath but the shadow and appearance of infinite, as all things have that are too big for our comprehension, they fill and over-bear the mind with their Excess, and cast it into a pleasing kind of stupor and admiration.
>
> And yet these Mountains . . . are nothing but great ruins; but such as show a certain Magnificence in Nature.[38]

Thus were the seeds of the Romantics' aesthetic response to the wilderness sown, for the feelings of the sublime were, in the tradition of physico-theology, contemporary evocations of the same feelings humankind experienced in the prelapsarian condition when God manifested himself directly.

In part, the Romantics were defending the traditions of Judeo-Christianity. Blind faith would no longer do; Modernism, both theoretically and existentially, necessitated adjustment of religious sensibility. Mechanistic rationalism threatened to overturn the grounding of Western culture in the traditions of Judeo-Christianity.[39] Were human beings just matter-in-motion obeying the blind dictates of natural law? Where in fact was God and Heaven if no empirical evidence (scientific observation) could be found to verify their existence? How could faith in things unseen, and in the values of truth, justice, and charity be maintained in the face of science? And could faith be reconciled with the dramatically changed view of the cosmos? Viewed thus, as Morris Abrams explains, "the Romantic enterprise was an attempt to sustain the inherited cultural order against what to many writers seemed the imminence of chaos; and the resolve to give up what one was convinced one had to give up of the dogmatic understructure of Christianity, yet to save what one could save of its experiential relevance and values, may surely be viewed by the disinterested historian as a display of integrity and of courage."[40]

Romanticism may also be understood as an aesthetic reaction to a specific intellectual framework—mechanistic materialism, nature understood as matter-in-motion.[41] "The literature of the nineteenth century, especially its English poetic literature," Whitehead argues, "is a witness to the discord between the aesthetic intuitions of mankind and the mechanism of science."[42] The Romantic poets addressed themselves to the concept of nature-as-an-organism, an idea clearly opposed to nineteenth-century scientific cant. Neil Evernden suggests that "the Romantics were not so much nature poets as reality-experimenters working in the environment least hostile to their project."[43] The new science stripped the world of those attributes of which individuals were—as part of the natural world—most immediately aware. *Scientific nature* was devoid of taste, sight, sound, and feeling; it was known only through mass, velocity, position, and repetition of invariant patterns. *Poetic nature*, in contrast, was alive, subjective, capricious, a riot of colors and sounds, and a source of aesthetic delight and philosophical inspiration. Romantics like Shelley and Wordsworth simply could not reconcile what presented itself immediately to their conscious awareness with scientific representation, and they thus developed a deep distrust of mechanistic rationalism. Maurice Mandelbaum observes that the Romantics were deeply suspicious of the scientific perspective because it merely "*represents* an object, without *re*-presenting it" and was thus a mere abstraction (or convention) that simply "stands for, or symbolizes, that which we seek to know."[44]

The Romantic movement can thus be understood as a project that self-consciously took an aesthetic turn.[45] Unlike the strictly philosophical reaction to Modernism, where such thinkers as Spinoza and Schopenhauer systematically worked through conceptual (epistemological, metaphysical, and ethical) issues, the Romantics were concerned with affective immediacy: they followed a direct intuitive path to a realization of the unity of nature. No invidious comparison of the aesthetic turn taken by the Romantics to the philosophical temper is here intended, however. As the work of Alfred North Whitehead illustrates, the influence of the Romantics on philosophical thought is consequential.[46] In fact, there is reason to think that the Romantic poets went through a philosophical door that Kant opened in his *Critique of Judgment*. So viewed, the Romantic poets are not tender-hearted nature lovers but address issues of fundamental philosophical import—concerns central to the nineteenth-century idea of nature and humankind's relation to it. Here we must go slowly, beginning with Kant.

The Kant of the *Critique of Pure Reason* (1781) gave the world over to mechanistic materialism: this was the Cartesian-Newtonian world of scientific surety, which he believed had realized the ancient Parmenidean ideal. Humankind, Kant was confident, had achieved through physics a certain knowledge of the phenomenal world that would be good for all people in all places and times. The first critique, a brilliant synthesis of British empiricism with Continental rationalism, is an explanation of how

scientific knowledge of the natural world is possible. Kant sailed—to use
Norwood Russell Hanson's metaphor—between the Scylla of formalism
(Continental rationalism) and the Charybdis of sensationalism (British
empiricism). Concepts without percepts are empty, Kant argued, thus exposing the empirical vacuity of Cartesian rationalism; but, he continued,
percepts without concepts are blind, thus overcoming the naive realism of
Lockean empiricism. The rational mind necessarily understood the world
from the standpoint of Newtonian space-time (as a priori intuitions) and
the categories of physics (for example, causality).

Here arose a dilemma, for if the phenomenal world was given over to
the dictates of natural law, how then to explain choice? ethics? human
freedom? Could individuals be held accountable for their actions if simply
acting out natural imperatives? And what was God's place in the universe?
How could he be known, since there seemed no place for him in the scientific purview? Science could not answer these questions. The second critique (1788) dealt with these issues by drawing an ontological distinction
between the phenomenal realm, the world known through science, the experience of nature-as-matter, and the noumenal realm, the world known
through ethics and religion, the experience of nature-as-value. Here Kant
extended the Parmenidean project, believing that he had found a categorical imperative for the practical sphere. Rational human beings necessarily
accepted the categorical imperative, and thus acted as if the maxim of their
actions were to become through their wills a universal law.[47] Yet this solution extracted a philosophical price, for the world was now split into phenomenal and noumenal realms. There seemed no escape from Cartesian
dualism.

Kant recognized the limits of his apparent reconciliation of nature-as-
matter and nature-as-value. The introduction to the conclusion of his *Critique of Practical Reason* is an open admission of the reality of the poetic
view of nature by the man whose philosophy epitomizes the scientific
worldview, a confession to the validity of intuition:

> Two things fill the mind with ever new and increasing admiration and
> awe, the oftener and the more steadily we reflect on them: *the starry
> heavens above and the moral law within*. I have not to search for them
> and conjecture them as though they were veiled in darkness or were
> in the transcendent region beyond my horizon; I see them before me
> and connect them directly with the consciousness of my existence.
> The former begins from the place I occupy in the external world of
> sense, and enlarges my connection therein to an unbounded extent

with worlds upon worlds and systems of systems, and moreover into limitless times of their periodic motion, its beginning and continuance. The second begins from my invisible self, my personality, and exhibits me in a world which has true infinity, but which is traceable only by the understanding, and with which I discern that I am not in a merely contingent but in a universal and necessary connection, as I am also thereby with all those visible words.[48]

Thus Kant suspends the Parmenidean project (he wrote ex cathedra) by recognizing the reality of immediate vision. "I have not to search" for the starry heavens above or the moral law within, since they are encountered in lived experience. Here is the recognition that all human beings are rooted in a natural world that is not merely matter-in-motion, a prelinguistic, precultural, primal world of *human experience*. Alternatively, Kant recognized a natural subjectivity or experience of a lived body (to use Merleau Ponty's term) that existentially existed before the transcendental subject. In effect the introduction to the conclusion of the *Critique of Practical Reason* is the report of a philosophical anthropologist who has uncovered a primal consciousness still reverberating in his mind.

But what was this mode of apprehension, of sensibility? The *Critique of Judgment* (1790) is Kant's attempt to deal with this question.[49] Allan Megill argues in his insightful *Prophets of Extremity* that the third critique "is important because it unequivocally maintains the autonomy of aesthetic judgment. In so doing, it appears to suggest that there exists an independent realm of the aesthetic, a realm quite distinct from the other realms of morality and of nature."[50] In short, the third critique is a Kantian legitimation of poetic nature, just as the first critique is a justification of scientific nature. (There is yet another reading consistent with the idea that the third critique points to the possibility that scientific, ethical, and aesthetic judgment are not independent but related.)[51] Accordingly, the third critique opens the door to Romanticism generally, and Coleridge, Wordsworth, and Shelley in particular. Yet Kant's position is problematic at the least, and we cannot here unravel the many intricacies of his aesthetic. Is Kant asserting that humans might find a moral path by coming to know nature's beauty? That wilderness sojourns are good for the sensitive soul? That the good life is somehow intrinsically bound with aesthetic appreciation of the starry sky above? Clearly Kant believed (§57) in a "transcendental rational concept of the supersensible," itself the basis of "sensible intuition" and "therefore, incapable of being further determined theoretically." The *Critique of Judgment* thus suggests at least the possibility of understanding why Kant or any other human being is affected by the starry heavens above or the moral law within: such sentience is a direct manifestation of an unmediated (prelinguistic, precultural) mode of awareness. It might also be explained as a faint but lingering reflection of the Paleolithic mind.[52]

THE CLAIM THAT Samuel Coleridge (1772–1834) brought Kant to England is not too far from the truth (as is the contention that Emerson brought Coleridge, and thus the Romantic outlook, to America). No defensible argument can be made that Coleridge advanced Kantian philosophy; rather, he found in Kant an armory of ideas to be employed in his struggles with British empiricism and utilitarianism.[53] To Coleridge the greatest threat of mechanistic materialism was its displacement of God from the center of existence: from the scientific purview, God was irrelevant. Echoing More, Coleridge saw in Cartesian dualism an opening through which he might press an attack on mechanism, and so defend his faith; yet in defending his faith his most important philosophical accomplishment was in further working through the relation between mind and nature. He believed that Friedrich Schelling's (1775–1854) *Naturphilosophie* (a Continental response to Modernism) went too far in asserting the intuitive primacy of the external world, whereas the Cartesians had sundered mind entirely from nature.

Coleridge took a Kantian via media, finding in aesthetic intuition a middle ground between reason and understanding.[54] By cultivating aesthetic sensibility Coleridge believed that he escaped either horn of the dualistic dilemma, which posited mind and nature (matter) as autonomous substances. We find for example in his "Frost at Midnight" an empathetic Coleridge who imaginatively recognizes in a "low-burnt fire" lying on his grate almost a kindred animate spirit.

> Only that film [flickering embers], which fluttered on the grate,
> Still flutters there, the sole unquiet thing.
> Methinks its motion in this hush of nature
> Gives it dim sympathies with me who live,
> Making it a companionable form,
> Whose puny flaps and freaks the idling Spirit
> By its own moods interprets, everywhere
> Echo or mirror seeking of itself,
> And makes a toy of Thought.[55]

The natural world, even a fire, was for Coleridge alive and conscious, having "dim sympathies with me who live." The poem transcended any absolute mind-matter distinction by drawing a discrimination not of type or substance but of degrees of consciousness. Clearly, this natural world (independent of human consciousness) was unconscious of itself, and therefore lacked freedom, an important and distinguishing human characteristic. But nature was not alien but rather kindred to human spirit.

Even more important, God was for Coleridge the first cause of all, including mind and nature; in this sense God was the identity of mind and nature. In effect, reality was a continuum of being that had been erroneously distorted by the operations of the rational (scientific) intellect. Coleridge believed that God could be known immediately and directly through perception of simple phenomena, as in "the secret ministry of frost" in building "silent icicles,/Quietly shining to the quiet Moon." Here there was no longer any scientific abstraction from the phenomena of nature but an immediate presenting of reality. As the fire reflected in his mind and made "a toy of Thought," Coleridge believed himself led to even deeper insight: the recognition that God was one with both nature (fire) and humankind (Coleridge). Through *sensibilité* the Romantic consciousness thus achieved the unity of mind with nature through God.

From our vantage point Coleridge's resolution of the mind-matter impasse is not entirely satisfactory, for he overcame that dualism only by reaffirming an absolute distinction between God (a supernatural and transcending creator) and creation, including both nature and humankind. Even while employing a Kantian aesthetic, Coleridge succumbed to the orthodoxies of faith that Kant had managed to escape. Kant's first critique had mounted a scathing attack on the conventional arguments for God's existence; in the second critique he adopted an essentially deist position, emphasizing that the value of natural religion was its moral instruction (and not its supernaturalism). The third critique, as we have seen, enabled the aesthetic turn taken by Coleridge and the other Romantic poets. As Kant envisioned it, however, the aesthetic imagination was not merely a vehicle of consciousness to return human beings to faith in things unseen (supernaturalism). Judeo-Christianity was a purely moral religion, and its most fundamental precepts were entirely in accord with the categorical imperative. By forgetting the lessons of Kant, Coleridge's critique of Modernism is a legitimate protest but only a partial success. As Michael Moran suggests, for thinkers like Coleridge, "philosophy inevitably becomes a form of theosophy. Religion is the highest exercise of the human spirit, and philosophy is a kind of rational prolegomenon that prepares the way for man's fuller appreciation of his relationship with God."[56]

WILLIAM WORDSWORTH, a close friend of Coleridge's, was a more forceful critic of Modernism, and Whitehead even insinuates that in conceptualizing humankind's relation to nature Coleridge "is only important by his influence on Wordsworth."[57] Wordsworth shared the Romantic's commitment to discovery of the hidden depths of the self by encounters with the natural world, but unlike Coleridge he was not a theosophist. Wordsworth's poetry is not that of a mystic, describing mysterious revelations of God, but of a person deeply immersed in the wonder and beauty of nature. He ultimately found God through and in nature, but his affirmation of divine presence was more a genuine discovery of a deity through wilderness experience than confirmation of an article of faith.[58] A passionate Romantic, Wordsworth unabashedly wore his heart on his sleeve, making clear the depth of his involvement with wild nature. His *Excursion,* a promised study "On Man, on Nature, and on Human Life,/Musing in solitude . . . ," and surely one of the most remarkable literary texts of our culture, begins with the line " 'Twas summer, and the sun had mounted high."[59] It is not Humankind, and not Human Life with which Wordsworth began, but with Nature itself, and not scientific Nature but the Romantic wilderness, encountered individually, immediately, and spontaneously. Wordsworth's lifelong odyssey was a communion with nature: he sought enlightenment, not power.

> My heart leaps up when I behold
> A rainbow in the sky:
> So was it when life began;
> So is it now I am a man;
> So be it when I shall grow old,
> Or let me die![60]

"Wordsworth in his whole being," Whitehead observes, "expresses a conscious reaction against the mentality of the eighteenth century. This mentality means nothing else than the acceptance of the scientific ideas at their full face value."[61] In short, Wordsworth believed his contemporaries to be living the unexamined life, blind to the hold of scientific methods and categories on thought, and oblivious to the hidden presuppositions (mechanism, dualism, and the theory of external relations) of Modernism. What the Newtonian-Cartesian paradigm lacked was any comprehensible account of the relations between mind and matter, and humans and nature, those relations most important to the Romantics in their critical reaction to Modernism. Wordsworth marveled at these relationships and often described them in his poetry, as in the Preface to *The Excursion*.

How exquisitely the individual Mind
(And the progressive powers perhaps no less
Of the whole species) to the external World
Is fitted:—and how exquisitely, too—
Theme this but little heard of among men—
The external World is fitted to the Mind;
And the creation (by no lower name
Can it be called) which they with blended might
Accomplish:—this is our high argument.[62]

In short, Wordsworth had come face to face with the dilemma that both Bacon and Kant had recognized. Science enabled an enormous expansion of humankind's power to effect change in the natural world, yet its underlying mechanism and materialism rendered it bereft of moral significance. To what end, Wordsworth wondered, was this cultural project to come? Modernism provided no answer save material progress: from a Smithian perspective society was nothing more than a mechanism following economic laws. Civilization's only goal was material progress (to satisfy the supposed infinite needs of Homo oeconomicus), enabled by the exploitation of nature. Such a society would presumably grow ever richer, and thus able to satisfy better the insatiable demands of human consumers. Although Wordsworth never resolved the economic problem per se, he did recognize the essential sterility of the prevailing view. And he envisioned the possibility of some other relationship, recognizing in his poetry that the World, nature itself, and the Mind, the individual psyche, might be blended in some new creation.

Of course, Wordsworth's high argument was visionary, fundamentally discordant with the predominating Cartesian-Newtonian perspective. He knew too well the imperfections of the modern mind, and he realized that the world was imperfect in other ways: loved ones died, roses faded, and humans exploited their fellows. But Wordsworth feared neither the mutability of nature nor human cruelty. His lifelong odyssey with wild nature allowed him to accept life's transitoriness in what is arguably a Heraclitean way, for he recognized that there was a Logos beneath the flux, a natural way that might inform the philosophic mind.

> Though nothing can bring back the hour
> Of splendor in the grass, of glory in the flower;
>   We will grieve not, rather find
>   Strength in what remains behind;
>   In the primal sympathy
>   Which having been must ever be;
>   In the soothing thoughts that spring
>   Out of human suffering;
>   In the faith that looks through death,
> In years that bring the philosophic mind.[63]

WE COME TO SHELLEY, who in his embrace of science provides an interesting counterpoint to Wordsworth and Coleridge. Whitehead suggests that Shelley loved science "and is never tired of expressing in poetry the thoughts which it suggests. It symbolizes to him joy, and peace, and illumination. What the hills were to the youth of Wordsworth, a chemical laboratory was to Shelley."[64] Thus the insights of geometry, physics, chemistry, geology, and biology animated his poetry, not just as illustrations but informing his perspective. For example, the Earth says in *Prometheus Unbound* that

> The joy, the triumph, the delight, the madness!
> The boundless, overflowing, bursting gladness,
> The vaporous exultation not to be confined!
>   Ha! Ha! the animation of delight
>   Which wraps me, like an atmosphere of light,
> And bears me as a cloud is borne by its own wind.[65]

Here is a poetic application of Robert Boyle's experiments and laws ("The boundless, overflowing, bursting gladness"), so crucial to Newton's thinking. Yet Shelley reanimated the lifeless world of matter-in-motion, bringing the gases joyfully alive as they caressed the earth. Similarly, he employed the geometric perspective of Galileo and Copernicus through personification of the Earth.

> I spin beneath my pyramid of night,
>   Which points into the heavens dreaming delight,
> Murmuring victorious joy in my enchanted sleep;
>   As a youth lulled in love-dreams faintly sighing,
>   Under the shadow of his beauty lying,
> Which round his rest a watch of light and warmth doth keep.[66]

Whitehead argues that this passage "could only have been written by someone with a definite geometrical diagram before his inward eye."[67] More specifically, only a person with a Copernican model of the solar system in mind, and a Newtonian understanding of the phenomenon of light, could write such poetry. Neither the ancients nor the medievals could have understood a spinning globe and its relation to the diurnal cycle (for the earth does not seem to move), nor could they have understood the metaphor of the "pyramid of the night" (for the earth, not the sun, was the center of their cosmos, and the earth was presumed flat). Yet in spite of the role of science in his poetry, Shelley's idea of wilderness was not nature-as-matter-in-motion but nature-as-alive, full of animate entities revealing themselves to humankind through a rich panoply of secondary qualities. "The bright blue sky of Rome," he wrote in the Preface to *Prometheus Unbound,* "and the effect of the vigorous awakening spring in that divinest climate, and the new life with which it drenches the spirits even to intoxication, were the inspiration of this drama."[68]

Shelley, like other Romantic poets, drew inspiration from an immediate aesthetic encounter with the natural world. Coleridge, Wordsworth, and Shelley sought to enter into a personal relation with a living world. They did not aim to know nature through symbolic quantification and scientific law, nor to use such knowledge to manipulate nature. Their goal was to experience beauty, for through beauty one might know divine presence. And through such experience the individual might gain knowledge of self as part of the world—immersed in and bound with wild nature. The Romantic project, in this sense, is post-Kantian, an attempt to transcend aesthetically the bifurcation of knowing subject and known object, the theoretical and the practical, even the phenomenal and the noumenal. In Romantic poetry, Abrams explains, "an individual confronts a natural scene and makes it abide his question, and the interchange between his mind and nature constitutes the entire poem, which usually poses and resolves a spiritual crisis."[69] The denouement is realization of the unity of mind and nature.

Philosophical Reactions to Modernism

The view of nature-as-a-machine, as nothing more than matter moving according to natural law, encountered almost immediate philosophical opposition. The foremost philosophical critic of Modernism was Benedict Spinoza. From the Cartesian-Newtonian perspective *knowledge was power,* the ability to dominate the natural world. For Spinoza *knowledge was enlightenment,* an understanding of the true relations between human beings and nature.[70] Spinoza argued that since humankind was bound with the order of nature, human happiness depended on recognizing this relation.[71] Classical science denied the possibility of such a reflexive understanding of the human place in nature, for the cognizing subject had been excluded from scientific purview (except insofar as humankind was comprehensible as mere matter-in-motion). Spinoza recognized that nature-as-matter-in-motion was a comprehensible object of inquiry, but nowhere in scientific nature was there an account of the relation between humans as agents in the world and nature itself. Spinoza's view, in this regard, was like Bacon's. (Descartes was oblivious to any such question of ethics, and simply counseled humankind to use science to master the world.) His subsequent aim was to ground humankind ethically—before scientific knowledge was put to technological use. In effect, what classical science had put asunder—that is, a relation between humans as ethical agents and nature as the environment in which they acted—Spinoza sought to restore. Spinozism can thus be understood as a part of and consistent with the perennial quest, initiated by the Paleolithic mind, to understand our relation to the natural world in which we are immersed and through which we live our lives.

In metaphysical terms, Spinozism is a kind of neutral monism predicated on the presupposition of the *unity of nature.* Unlike the physico-theologists (Ray and Burnet were contemporaries), Spinoza separated neither divine substance nor the cognizing mind from nature. Both were interpretations of the One substance, or Reality. This reality could be regarded either as Nature by the scientist or as God by the religionist, but either path viewed philosophically led to an *infinita idea Dei* (infinite idea of God). The universe was for Spinoza one connected system, as expressed in the doctrine *Deus sive natura:* God or Nature. God and Nature were names not for two independent substances but one and the same substance. An enlightened individual who understood the principle of Deus sive natura necessarily recognized the inquiring consciousness as *being a part of* rather than *apart from* the natural world. Viewed ethically, in light of Spinoza's metaphysics, the summum bonum was knowledge of the mind and body as a part of the system of nature. Such knowledge produced felicity, the knowledge of necessity.

Nature, Spinoza argued, shows us two faces: *natura naturans*—nature as initiative center of activity—and *natura naturata*—nature as passive product. The idea of natura naturans recognized spirit or God as the creative and self-sustaining center of nature: God was the immanent cause of nature and was not apart from that creation. Viewed passively, from the standpoint of science per se, nature is natura naturata, a created product understood as a rational system of natural law and efficient cause. Science was, however, a retrograde form of knowledge for Spinoza, being only a partial grasp of the nature of reality, just as orthodox faith was an inferior mode of rational conviction. Although the Bible might satisfy the masses, and Newtonian physics the scientist, neither faith nor scientific reason were intellectually adequate to comprehending the fundamental nature of reality. *Scientia intuitiva*, or intuitive knowledge (rather than scientific generalization) was the highest form of knowledge, by which mind apprehended the necessity of all that exists and thus became identical with the infinite idea of God. From this standpoint Spinoza believed that humans could escape narrow, selfish grasping and be moved by a full awareness of their place in the universe—not as some vast mechanism to be dominated by human beings but as an interrelated hierarchical system that was ultimately an infinite idea of God.[72]

At philosophical base Spinozism is a rigorous pantheism, going far beyond any panentheistic leanings of the physico-theologists.[73] Even Gilbert White's "paganism," an attempt to commune with nature as if it were filled with living spirits, stops far short of pantheism. Both theism and panentheism retain a supreme being independent of the natural world; panentheism differs from theism basically in that God is allowed *both* a separate and an immanent existence. Thus, panentheism is understood as a difference in degree, but not kind, from theism, since God remains separate and primary. Nature is merely secondary, a temporal and finite manifestation of an underlying eternal and infinite supreme being.[74] Pantheism (*pan* means all, and *theos* means god, thus all is god) allows no separation between God and creation. Divinity is both *causa sui* and *causa omnium*. Spinoza argued that God is immanent in the world and that ultimately everything that is is a manifestation of this divine principle. "By God," Spinoza wrote, "I understand Being absolutely infinite, that is to say, substance consisting of infinite attributes, each one of which express eternal and infinite essence."[75] For him the highest of all virtues, the summum bonum, was the unabashed pursuit of knowledge of this divine substance that led to the realization of the unity of nature. Spinoza was not, of course, the first pantheist, but his system remained until the twentieth century the most powerful challenge to orthodox theism and panentheism.[76] Much of later European thought, including that of Hegel and Johann Goethe (1749–1832), received its impetus from Spinoza. (Hegel tended toward pantheism in that the Absolute had no existence apart from the actuality of spatio-temporal process understood as either history or nature. Goethe's pantheism aimed at combining pagan orientations toward wild nature with what he understood as the redeeming values of Judeo-Christianity.)

Spinoza also attacked mechanism and the theory of external relations, although this was for him a secondary philosophical mission. Since Spinoza explained the world in its myriad guises through the reality of one pervading divine substance, the machine metaphor was therefore otiose. Animals were not, as Descartes believed, functional machines but finite "modes," self-determining parts of the larger order of nature. For Spinoza life was a process of intercommunication and adjustment among the elements that constitute nature. Natural things are what they are only in relation to the whole; there is no separate existence.[77] Given this interpretation, Spinoza verged on a profoundly postmodern science where location is not tied to any position in absolute space or time, and existence is not a state of being but a process. Alternatively (and simplistically) stated, a thing is what it is (identity) in relation to a surrounding environment, and it has being (existence) only through its interrelationships.

Yet, for a number of reasons, Spinoza did not develop his implicit philosophy of organicism. First, his primary mission was to ground rationally—consistent with classical science—his belief in God: above all else justification of the infinita idea Dei animates Spinozism. Second, although Spinoza in part transcended the Heraclitean-Parmenidean impasse, his solution is ultimately unsatisfactory. His principle of Deus sive natura reflects more the ancient Parmenidean ideal of complete and necessary knowledge than the Heraclitean ideal of becoming. Though Spinoza was clearly a pantheist, he was not an animist: wild nature was not fully alive for him, since spontaneity would undercut permanent knowledge. Spinoza's God was a creative will that, paradoxically yet necessarily, engaged only in a single creation, rather than in an ongoing evolutionary process. George Sessions and others believe that Spinozism escapes this limitation, arguing that Spinoza has a process metaphysics; yet this reading is difficult to sustain.[78] As we have argued, and as Bertrand Russell claims, the "metaphysical system of Spinoza is of the type inaugurated by Parmenides," and thus overwhelming emphasis is placed on the knowability of one unchanging substance.[79]

Like Newton, Spinoza was cognitively entangled in Modernism's Parmenidean project: he sought certain, universal knowledge. Spinoza followed Descartes in denying the Aristotelian ontology that divides nature into kinds, thus making the notion of a unitary physics possible; but, as Stuart Hampshire observes, he went beyond Descartes and "took an equally large step towards the project of a single system of organized knowledge when he challenged the last remaining division of reality into two irreducibly separate compartments, somehow causally related—the mental and the physical."[80] He thus avoided the perils of metaphysical dualism, since there is no intrinsically unbridgeable gulf between mind and matter in Spinoza's system: the cognizing mind was part of the natural world. But the relation of mind to nature was at base arithmomorphic (deductive); consistent Spinozans would proceed deductively, and therefore boldly and aggressively, in the natural world, confident that they had knowledge of the necessary arrangements of nature. "Everything [for Spinoza]," Russell observes, ". . . is ruled by an absolute logical necessity. . . . Everything that happens is a manifestation of God's inscrutable nature, and it is logically impossible that events should be other than they are."[81] Thus, though he eschewed mechanism and the rule of efficient cause, Spinoza gave the natural world over to necessity: evolution is not possible in a Spinozan world.

WE COME NOW TO Arthur Schopenhauer, a neglected but important critic of Modernism. *The World as Will and Idea*, Schopenhauer's masterpiece, is essentially a critique of the metaphysics of Modernism. Like Spinoza, Schopenhauer rejected the concept of scientific nature as either an adequate or a self-sufficient account of reality. Unlike Spinoza, who presented an alternative but rational system, he had grave reservations about the role of reason and the possibility of objective knowledge. This position represents a radical break with Western rationalism, and in this regard Schopenhauer is the antithesis of Parmenides. Schopenhauer believed that nature could not be reduced to either an infinita idea Dei or to Kantian-Newtonian categories. Alternatively, Schopenhauer recognized that *the idea* of nature-as-a-machine was precisely that—a human construction arbitrarily imposed on an independent or autonomous other. Schopenhauer labored to make his point by attacking Kant, ironically the philosopher he most admired and respected. He surmised that theoretical science revolved around the causal category—at base an attempt to stabilize the Heraclitean flux through the permanence of causal law. Echoing Hume, and anticipating the futility of J. S. Mill's efforts to guarantee causal law, Schopenhauer argued that the "causal connection merely gives us the rule and the relative order of their [perceptions] appearance in space and time, but affords us no further knowledge of that which so appears. Moreover, the law of causality itself has only validity for ideas, for objects of a definite class, and it has meaning only in so far as it presupposes them. . . . We wish to know the significance of these ideas; we ask whether this world is merely idea; . . . or whether it is also something else, something more than idea, and if so, what." [82] The what, Schopenhauer continued, was the will itself: the vital but irrational force that moved the world.

Schopenhauer had realized that the scientific picture of the world— or causal explanation of matter-in-motion, of change—did not explain reality but was itself a fact to be explained. Only from *within* nature, Schopenhauer argued (here paralleling Spinoza), could the scientific idea of nature be made comprehensible. Science itself was a mere manifestation of humankind becoming self-conscious of its situatedness in the natural world. [83] The natural world was not just our idea of nature; it was alive and organic, subjective and striving, manifesting itself through a mysterious power Schopenhauer called the *qualitas occulta.* This enigmatic power— which the individual could know directly and immediately—explained the animate qualities of nature. Scientific inquiry itself could never reveal the reality of the will (of the qualitas occulta) to the inquiring thinker, since "we can never arrive at the real nature of things from without. . . . In fact, the meaning for which we seek . . . would never be found if the investigator himself were nothing more than the pure knowing subject. . . . But he is himself rooted in that world; he finds himself in it as an *individual,* that is to say, his knowledge, which is the necessary supporter of the whole world as idea, is yet always given through the medium of a body, whose affections are . . . the starting-point for the understanding in the perception of that world." [84] Schopenhauer thus glimpsed—even before the advent of evolutionary theory—the inescapable fact that humankind can know nature because it is within nature, not a disembodied Cartesian-Newtonian ego apart from nature but a sentient part of it.

In effect, Schopenhauer revivified the Paleolithic consciousness of nature as living entity with which human beings were bound in order to ground scientific knowledge. Such an insight is truly justification for viewing Schopenhauer as the arch-Romantic, for *The World as Will and Idea* posits an Archimedean point for understanding the compelling attraction for human beings of wilderness experiences. In rejecting the Kantian thing-in-itself—a noumenal realm underlying the phenomenal realm—standing behind the world of human sensation and perception, Schopenhauer affirmed the immediate reality of meadows with green grass and grazing elk, blue skies with soaring eagles, and mountainsides with gurgling streams and jumping trout: in sum, nature was a reality irreducible to mere matter-in-motion known through causal law. Thus Schopenhauer opened the door to the reanimation of the natural world and to an idea of wild nature that was truly alive and evolutionary.

IN ADDITION TO Spinoza and Schopenhauer, others raised voices of philosophical protest against Modernism and the idea that nature was nothing but a machine. Leibniz, following on Spinoza's heels, argued for a view of nature-as-an-organism, virtually a living continuum of consciousness ranging from material monads through the human soul to the supreme monad (God).[85] Hegel proposed a system of absolute idealism, a view of reality as an all-pervading spirit wending its way toward the absolute. This system ostensibly transcended Cartesian dualism and the conflict between Judeo-Christian faith and objective reason. Yet neither Leibniz nor Hegel could make a convincing case for panpsychism. Schopenhauer, though an unrecognized genius, was more successful in his attack on scientific nature. But his critique of the modern idea of nature was imperfect, since the will, though animate—and therefore capable in principle of explaining natural motion and the assumed regularity lying behind causal law—was empirically empty.

In spite of philosophical criticism, optimism about the human prospect pervaded the nineteenth century: the spirit of Modernism ruled the world. In France, August Comte (1798–1857) argued for a new kind of philosophy, known as positivism, that was virtually a religion of humanity, and that promised—mirroring Bacon and Descartes—virtually infinite progress in human affairs. He claimed that science represented true knowledge and that through scientific method would come the power to ensure unlimited social progress. Hegelianism implied a similar hope, since science and technology, as well as the Industrial Revolution, indicated to Hegel that society was inevitably progressive, each new generation destined to overcome the failures and limitations of the previous. And in England such thinkers as Jeremy Bentham and J. S. Mill extended the basic premises of mechanistic materialism to psychology and society. Bentham's psychological hedonism was perfectly suited to a society bent on nothing more than an unlimited expansion of consumption. More pleasure could always be had, and gratification as such was always good; consistent with Modernism, Bentham actually believed that a calculus of pleasure, a quantitative assessment, was possible (thus laying philosophical groundwork for welfare economics). And Mill's utilitarianism virtually defined the ethical underpinning of the new industrial state: the good state provided satisfactions (pleasure) for the largest number of people.

Amid this optimism, however, the doors of Modernism were coming off their hinges, a fact both reflected in and aided by Schopenhauer's insights. The later course of nineteenth-century science vindicated Schopenhauer in some ways. Darwin advanced the hypothesis that *no* understanding of human beings—be this biological or epistemological—could be credible unless it reflected natural evolution. Rudolf Clausius (1822–88) discovered the second law of thermodynamics, enabling later twentieth-century accounts (Whitehead, Prigogine) of *will* as a metaphor for the reality of self-creating order out of chaos (thereby giving Schopenhauer's qualitas occulta empirical content). And Karl Marx exposed the irrational antitheses of the most sacrosanct of categories, including property itself; after Marx no informed intellectual could believe that socioeconomic progress was necessary (even if they denied the cogency of Marx's thesis that class war was inevitable). Schopenhauer's legacy was to bear its greatest return in the thought of Nietzsche, who perhaps culminates the nineteenth-century Romantic challenge to Modernism. Following Schopenhauer, Nietzsche rejected the prevailing rationalism (in effect, the nineteenth-century worldview), making clear his repudiation of the Apollonian and support for Dionysian aspects of Western culture.[86]

The Autonomy of Wild Nature

Modernism is no one thing but a collective process greater than the sum of its parts: the scientific and industrial revolutions, the Reformation and the Renaissance, and many other movements have played roles in the Western cultural drama. Opposition to the prevailing cultural currents arose almost immediately, but no one stream of resistance dominated. Viewed retrospectively, the critical responses to Modernism illuminate many difficulties with the prevailing belief system. Viewed prospectively, as Western culture wends its way toward an unpredictable future—perhaps toward a postmodern idea of wilderness—these divergent currents still show life. Ernst Mayr contends that the consequences of the dominance of Modernism, specifically the mechanical model, are a "tragedy," since the "prevailing framework of our social and political ideals developed and was adopted when the thinking of [the Western world] . . . was largely dominated by the ideas of the scientific revolution, that is, by a set of ideas based on the principles of the physical sciences."[87] Ilya Prigogine concurs in this judgment, arguing that the paradigm of classical science has led to a "tragic, metaphysical choice" between an idea of nature as alive and with which we enjoy "a fundamental corelatedness," and an idea of nature-as-a-machine and "fidelity to a rationality that iso-

Table 3. Mechanistic and Organismic Models Compared

Nature as a Machine	Nature as an Organism
– reductionistic atomism	– synoptic holism
– external relations	– internal relations
– invariant repetition	– emergent novelty

lates [us] . . . in a silent world."[88] And part of the tragedy, he continues, is that we seem to have had to choose between the mechanistic paradigm of classical science, and the extraordinary successes it has achieved, and the "qualitatively different way of understanding nature, as, for example, is attempted by Whitehead."[89] The problem in choosing, as Whitehead notes, is that if we pick something other than the idea of nature-as-a-machine, then we presumably lose connection with science. Yet, he continues, "if science is not to degenerate into a medley of *ad hoc* hypotheses, it must become philosophical and must enter upon a thorough criticism of its own foundations."[90]

Perhaps such a questioning begins with a study of the immediate counteractions to Modernism, and especially with the contemporaneous implications of these historic responses. Generalization is always subject to exception, and yet virtually all of the scientific, Romantic, and philosophic critics of Modernism appear to have *collectively* pointed toward an idea of nature-as-an-organism as an alternative to the idea of nature-as-a-machine (see table 3).[91] The idea of nature-as-an-organism lets us view ourselves as part of an evolving cosmos, "manifestations of a complex universe; we are not apart, but are moments in the open-ended, novelty-producing process of cosmic evolution." The idea of nature-as-a-machine lets us view ourselves as standing apart from the environment and as exercising control over it. The cosmos is understood, Michael Zimmerman suggests, as "a gigantic clockwork whose character and destiny are prefigured according to strict, unchanging causal laws."[92] The differences between these two worldviews—*mechanism* and *organicism*—are important.

Simply put, the mechanist employs a machine, such as a clock, and the organicist a living entity, such as an animal, as the root metaphor of reality. The mechanist—assuming the Cartesian premise that knowledge is to be gained only through relentless reduction until an unanalyzable atom is reached—believes that the world can be reduced to a set of basic elements, such as atoms or even subatomic particles such as quarks, just as a clock might be disassembled to expose its works. Opposed to this is the organismic idea of synoptic holism, or the notion that a whole is greater than the sum of its parts, having characteristics that are neither predictable nor deducible from knowledge of constituent parts.

The mechanist presupposes that the basic components that make up the world machine are related only externally. Each basic entity is what it is independent of all others. As David Bohm explains, though the fundamental elements may mechanically affect each other, they "do not grow organically as parts of a whole, but are rather more like parts of a machine whose forms are determined externally to the structure of the machine in which they are working. By contrast, organic parts, the parts of an organism, all grow together with the organism."[93] A useful distinction between external and internal theories of relation is that the external theory presumes that discriminated entities (such as atoms) are fundamentally real and unchangeable, whereas the internal theory assumes that even atoms are sometimes changed through association (as in a star). In other words, a theory of external relations implies that any organism or natural system is merely a collection of its parts and that any collectivity can be resolved into its previous elements. A theory of internal relations, in contrast, implies that irreversibility, not reversibility, is the fundamental nature of reality.

Finally, the idea of nature-as-a-machine presupposes that basic constituents are not fundamentally changed through association, since they "only interact mechanically by sort of pushing each other around." So viewed, interactions among natural things (atoms, molecules, organisms) "do not affect their inner natures."[94] In contrast, when nature is viewed organically, emergent novelty represents a genuine evolution rather than a consequence of human ignorance or lack of predictive knowledge, literally a qualitative infinity of nature. "In this process there is no limit to the new kinds of things that can come into being, and no limit to the number of kinds of transformations, both qualitative and quantitative, that can occur. This process, in which exist infinitely varied types of laws, is just the process of *becoming*, first described by Heraclitus several thousand years ago (although, of course, by now we have a much more precise and accurate idea of the nature of this process than the ancient Greeks could have had)."[95]

Unquestionably there presently exists an intense suspicion of organicism and the evolutionary paradigm generally. Much of this misgiving has centered on the theory of internal relations, which has often been interpreted as a *metaphysical principle* that proves, among other things, that time is not real and that everything in existence is merely a reflection of the One—usually God. In its most overstated form, such as in the absolute idealism of an F. H. Bradley or John McTaggart, the theory of internal relations has been interpreted to mean that any one thing implies everything else, or that everything is related to everything else.[96] Such a viewpoint may have psychic benefits, as for example the Romantic belief that not a leaf falls to earth without God's knowledge, but the theory lacks predictive utility. Considered as a metaphysical absolute, rather than as grounding principle of inquiry, a theory of internal relations seems to lead to a Parmenidean outcome, as in McTaggart's arguments against the reality of time. But empirically considered, a metaphysical theory of internal relations is sterile (even Hegel recognized that pure being is nothing).

The organismic idea of nature does not entail an absolute idealism, however. The question is basically one of theoretical and empirical viability at the subatomic, atomic, molecular, organismic, and systemic levels. Any theoretically adequate answer to the many questions that surround organicism is beyond the limits of our study.[97] A single example must suffice: the science of ecology. Ecology presupposes a principle of internal relations, but this principle is relative rather than absolute since the value of the organic metaphor is paradigmatic rather than metaphysical. That is, such an assumption has heuristic value: knowledge of internal relations is gained only through research. The work of such chemists as Prigogine and such ecologists as Eugene Odum has been instrumental in empirically confirming the value of the presupposition that internal relations are real. Prigogine's work is here nearly definitive, since the irreversibility of time (which poses an infinite entropy barrier) confirms that pervasive interconnections between elements constitute the fabric of life. These relations emerge spontaneously, transforming both the context in which interaction occurs and the nature of the component parts. As we have painfully discovered in the twentieth century, nature is not simply a causal mechanism that technological society can control as an engineer does a train. There are environmental complexities and ecological interrelations that are incapable of being known through external relations and the mechanistic model.[98]

Interest in the earlier critical responses to Modernism has today reawakened. Not only have environmental despoliation (Chernobyl, Three Mile Island, Los Angeles smog, the Amazon rain forest), burgeoning masses of impoverished and hungry human beings, and dwindling supplies of nonrenewable natural resources caused consternation, but the pervasiveness of crime, drug addiction, and such atrocities as Auschwitz and My Lai, have prompted much twentieth-century soul-searching. Questions long since thought of as settled, specifically those pertaining to the origin and nature of the natural world, and those concerning humankind's relations to nature, have again come to the fore. Chapters 5, 6, and 7 examine a trio of wilderness thinkers, beginning with Henry David Thoreau, whose way was collectively prepared by the previous two centuries of intellectual ferment. As a group, these thinkers—Thoreau, John Muir, and Aldo Leopold—questioned the divide between civilization and wilderness established by Modernism. These developments begin with Thoreau, for he clearly had a significant influence on those who came after. Thoreau is best understood as a wilderness philosopher whose subject was the continuities and discontinuities between culture and nature. Almost universally misunderstood as a transcendentalist in the Emersonian tradition, Thoreau explicitly rejected the mechanistic rationalism that enslaved Emerson's view of nature. So understood, Thoreau is a thinker whose kindred spirits were simultaneously arcadian, Romantic, and philosophical; more important, he extended the critique of Modernism in a fashion that remains relevant. Thoreau thus bridges between all that went before and that which is yet to come in the age of ecology.

CHAPTER FIVE

Henry David Thoreau
Philosopher of the Wilderness

Though there is a general progress in his overall development, there is no single Thoreauvian stance vis-à-vis nature . . . . The movements of his imaginative life show a continual series of struggles (most of them met with delight) because he was aware of nature's infinite variability and he wanted to face every fluctuation with the mode which it required of him. Each voice that he heard from nature demanded a slight shift in his own voice.
    —Frederick Garber, *Thoreau's Redemptive Imagination*

HENRY DAVID THOREAU cuts a most unusual figure in the fabric of American life, for he died largely unknown and unrecognized by his peers, perceived as a satellite orbiting an Emersonian center of gravity.[1] Today Thoreau's reputation has largely eclipsed Emerson's. The older transcendentalist is viewed more as a popularizer of European ideas than as a progenitor of a unique philosophy. Although Emersonian transcendentalism is moribund, Thoreau's ideas yet animate reflection on the human condition and are recognized as crucial to the birth of a distinctively American idea of wilderness. He was in the vanguard of the nineteenth-century criticism of Modernism, in some ways an American analogue to Schopenhauer, Marx, and Nietzsche.[2] More important, Thoreau had the brilliance to recognize, before Darwin published his theory of evolution, an organic connection between Homo sapiens and nature—a natural world from which the species had come and to which it was bound. This evolutionary insight puts Thoreau on the leading edge of a postmodern view of the relation between humankind and nature.

There is little doubt why Thoreau has been reappraised: his life and writings exemplify an attempt to grapple with the pivotal questions of human existence: Who or what is humankind? nature? and how are they related? What is the good life? the good economy? the good government? the good society? And, finally, what are knowledge, beauty, justice, and truth? Central to Thoreau's thought is his idea of wilderness and the natural life. The most recent readings of Thoreau, such as Jerome and Diane Rothenberg's and Frederick Turner's, find him to be a thinker who discovers the essential and creative affinity between wild nature and Homo sapiens, questions the presumed ontological dichotomy between the primitive and civilized, and affirms the grounding of the social in the presocial.[3] As Neil Evernden argues, human beings are culture-dwelling animals, and we cannot avoid creating categories "any more than we can avoid the social construction of reality. The inclination to tell the story of 'how the world is' seems basic to being human. . . . We can only hope that when the story turns out to be too far removed from actual experience to be reliable, we still have the skill to return to the world beneath the categories and re-establish connection with it."[4] Such a skill is the essence of Thoreau's great genius. Virtually no article of faith, ideology, or institution—be this sacred or profane, this worldly or otherworldly—escapes his scrutiny.

Transcendental Inclinations

Those determined to interpret Thoreau from a transcendental perspective often begin with Ralph Waldo Emerson's essay "Nature," pointing out parallels between this work and Thoreau's.[5] Undeniably, Thoreau read the essay during his collegiate days at Harvard, and he responded enthusiastically to its message. "Nature" espouses maxims for action that Thoreau actualized. Clearly he, among all the Concord circle, was the most actively engaged in encountering nature firsthand. Setting out from his transcendental inclinations, Thoreau developed through ceaseless reflective effort a remarkable philosophical position revolving around the ideas of self, society, and wilderness and the interrelations among them. Thus, although he followed Emerson's practical maxim in "Nature," he did not reach the same conclusions. His mentor's key contribution was helping Thoreau to establish a belief that nature can be known through the immediate activity of inquiring consciousness (or, alternatively, an absolute separation between consciousness and nature does not exist). This transcendental axiom, or first principle, was the heart of the Emersonian philosophical legacy. But comparison of Emerson's "Nature" and other relevant writings, such as "The Over-soul," with Thoreau's mature work underscores the differences in their use of the imagination. Unlike Emerson, Thoreau uses transcendentalism as a departure point, that is, as justifying the intuitive apprehension and active questioning of nature.

For Emerson consciousness is nothing more than a vehicle to carry him toward a pre-existing conclusion. "Nature" is not a philosophical inquiry but a literary exercise designed to rest a pre-established belief in God on rational, rather than scriptural, footing. The conceptual focal point is the human soul and God, not nature or the wilderness. For Emerson a wilderness odyssey is an occasion for the individual mind first to discover a reflection of itself (nature as a system of laws, concepts, and commodities) and then to confirm God's existence. So viewed, Emerson's "Nature" merely goes over the ground covered by the physico-theologists, like them discovering purpose and final cause in nature, the difference being that his argument is leavened by transcendental philosophy rather than proto-ecology. He discovers the design of nature not through its inner unity and order but rather through the workings of the transcendental consciousness. The organic world, full of sights and sounds and smells, was through his philosophical spectacles mere appearance, a visible promontory obscuring something more real than the phenomenal face of nature—namely, mind itself, and ultimately God, who unifies all seeming diversity into the One. Emerson believes that human beings can recapture a prelapsarian condition, transcending the dichotomies that separate them from nature and God. "We do not understand the notes of birds. The fox and the deer run away from us; the bear and tiger rend us." Yet through personal encounter with nature a human being might rediscover the truth of the Bible.

> *Know then, that the world exists for you.* For you is the phenomenon perfect. . . . As fast as you conform your life to the pure idea in your mind, that will unfold its great proportions. A correspondent revolution in things will attend the influx of the spirit. So fast will disagreeable appearances, swine, spiders, snakes, pests, mad-houses, prisons, enemies, vanish; they are temporary and shall be no more seen. . . . *The kingdom of man over nature,* which cometh not with observation,—a dominion such as now is beyond his dream of God,—he shall enter without more wonder than the blind man feels who is gradually restored to perfect sight.[6]

This passage, the conclusion of "Nature," unmistakably reveals Emerson's orientation toward the natural world. The position is conventionally anthropocentric and androcentric, enframed by a Baconian-Cartesian perspective: nature is mere putty in human hands, bestowed by God upon his most favored creation, *man.* Sentient Man is master of all that lies before him, the phenomenon perfect for whom the world was made. How comforting such an "argument" must have been to the Boston Brahmins and to Emerson, with a supreme being restored to the cosmological throne through "Transcendental Reason," rescued from the clutches of blind faith resting on Scripture and the revealed word—a God reached not through the Bible but through recitation of a transcendental litany. Although "Nature" does not commit the *petitio principii,* a fallacy inherent in all biblically based arguments for God's existence, the argument is tortured, to say the least, and inconsistent with Kant and the German idealism from which New England transcendentalism sprang.[7]

Emerson and the other transcendentalists unquestionably left their mark on Thoreau, but transcendentalism is a poor framework for understanding Thoreau's idea of wilderness. As with all first-rate minds, his cannot be reduced to the ideas of his progenitors. Thoreau asks questions and finds interrelations between the human species and nature about which Emerson never dreamed. If Thoreau's idea of wilderness can be understood from a transcendental perspective, then he is a mere Emersonian epigone, and "Nature" rather than *Walden* contains the seminal American idea of wilderness. But if Thoreau's idea of wilderness goes beyond transcendentalism, then any view of his work that reduces it to transcendentalism commits the genetic fallacy. Clearly, Thoreau had transcendental inclinations; yet Emerson and the other transcendentalists did not realize the revolutionary potential of European idealism. Thoreau, not Emerson, is the American heir to Kant's critical philosophy. Unlike Kant, who reduces wild nature to Cartesian-Newtonian nature in the first critique, however, Thoreau encounters wild nature without an established repertoire of categories, attitudes, and responses. In the final analysis, the Thoreauvian idea of wilderness has more in common with the Kant of the third than the first critique (see above, chapter 4), and with Schopenhauer's idea of the world as will, for the Kantian aesthetic opened the door to a genuinely original relation to the wilderness.

Thoreau's Wilderness Explorations: The Evolution of an Idea

Thoreau's idea of wilderness is rooted in a lifetime of primary experiences or firsthand meetings with nature. Not only did he live in the wilderness alongside Walden Pond for more than two years, but he ranged widely and frequently over New England and journeyed on occasion to Canada and Minnesota. Thoreau climbed mountains, explored the vast, densely forested regions of Maine, and floated rivers. And he walked—day-hiked, in the popular idiom—almost every day of his life. These journeys were the existential substratum for his intellectual investigations, the folding back of consciousness on his immediate experiences. Thoreau was no rhapsodic Romantic or Lake Poet singing hymns of praise to nature's beauty. His excursions, as he called them, were not mere physical journeys but contemplative odysseys through which he gradually overcame the alienation of the person, both as living body and as sentient being rooted in culture, from nature. *Walden* is customarily viewed as Thoreau's masterpiece; yet a new perspective on the Thoreauvian corpus is that the *Journal*, traditionally viewed as a daily record and ultimately a source book for Thoreau's more formal works, takes precedence over all his other work.[8] However, if we are to have any chance of understanding the radical, even revolutionary implications of his idea of wilderness, and in reconciling the multitudinous "definitive" scholarly studies, then we must retrace the route he took. No reader of the Thoreauvian corpus can fail to notice the evolution of his thought, even perhaps in a single work, given his penchant for folding time into his writings.

The height of early Thoreau is a "Natural History of Massachusetts" (1842), "A Walk to Wachusett" (1843), and "A Winter Walk" (1843).[9] Of the three, "A Walk to Wachusett" is the most conventionally transcendental. As with Emerson's "Nature," where an encounter with nature is only a means to ground a pre-existent conclusion, "Wachusett" seems to be less about Thoreau's philosophical explorations (search for meaning) while climbing the mountain of that name than an imposition of a conventional interpretation on the experience. The first sentence sets the tone for the piece and shows the mark of Emerson's belief that universals always underlie contemporaneous experience. From a transcendental perspective, the classic and therefore timeless insights of a Virgil or a Homer are the true meaning of wilderness encounters. "Summer and winter our eyes had rested on the dim outline of the mountains on our horizon, to which distance and indistinctness lent a grandeur not their own, so that they served equally to interpret all the allusions of poets and travelers; whether with Homer, on a spring morning, we sat down on the many-peaked Olympus, or with Virgil and his compeers roamed the Etrurian and Thessalian hills, or with Humboldt measured the more modern Andes and Teneriffe."[10]

This less than flowing beginning is followed by a long and stiff poem.[11] Unlike the later nature writing, the reader here continues only as a labor of love. Thoreau struggles to suffuse "Wachusett" with classical sensibilities. The essay lacks spontaneity and intensity; the prose is stilted as he strains

derived from heaven

to achieve an empyrean view connecting the immediacy of the present moment with universal truth. Rather than using intuition and reflection to uncover meaning organically rooted in the encounter with nature, Thoreau tries to discover the significance of this present mountain excursion by subsuming it under classical and therefore timeless categories. Only after his engagement with Mount Katahdin (the highest peak in Maine) could he reconcile the natural and cultural in a complementary fashion. On the summit of Wachusett, Thoreau is incapable of finding meaning except through classical categories that frame the significance of his experience.

Near the end of the essay, reflecting an almost letter-perfect rendition of Emerson's "Nature," Thoreau reaches the conclusion of an orthodox transcendentalist, echoing the traditions of physico-theology and the argument from design, by finding evidence of divine plan in the mountainscape. "We could at length realize the place mountains occupy on the land, and how they come into *the general scheme of the universe*. When first we climb their summits and observe their lesser irregularities, we do not give credit to *the comprehensive intelligence* which shaped them; but when afterward we behold their outlines in the horizon, we confess that *the hand* which moulded their opposite slopes, making one to balance the other, worked round a deep centre, and was privy to *the plan of the universe*." [12] Here, then, is Emerson's idea of nature, capital "N" Nature over which humankind ruled, strutting its stuff for the transcendental consciousness.

THE "Natural History of Massachusetts" and "A Winter Walk" are more felicitous pieces, in some ways almost vintage Thoreau. Some critics believe "Natural History" to be the first piece in the Thoreauvian nature writing genre. Both essays show the modern reader a Thoreau reveling in the presence of wild things, plants and animals, as well as his emerging talent for close observation of particulars—minutiae that an orthodox transcendentalist would recognize only as exemplifying universals. Thoreau had not yet accumulated that wealth of nature lore that he later drew on, and "Natural History" relies heavily on information from books—an observation confirmed by the uneven discussions of the various plant and animal species, some long and detailed, others no more than a few sentences. In this essay, however, Thoreau diverges from a narrow path, espousing ideas that were heresies to mainline New England transcendentalists. "In society you will not find health," he writes, "but in nature. . . . Society is always diseased, and the best is the most so." He also indicates that no merely conventional appreciation of nature is adequate; the parlors and polite conversation of Concord are wearing thin.

"We fancy that this din of religion, literature, and philosophy, which is heard in pulpits, lyceums, and parlors, vibrates through the universe, and is as catholic a sound as the creaking of the earth's axle; but if a man sleep soundly, he will forget it all between sunset and dawn."[13] Expressing such ideas publicly would not in any social circle, and particularly one as geographically centralized as that of the New England transcendentalists, win friends and influence people.[14]

"Natural History" confirms Thoreau's critical bent, for conventional wisdom of any kind is suspect, mere opinion to be tested by immediate experience and later reflection.[15] Emerson's teaching, for example the belief that a person might find in Nature proof positive of God's existence and the underlying order of things, is questioned. Thoreau's iconoclasm even leads him to criticize the scientific method, a platform that to Emerson and other transcendentalists reveals the eternal laws of nature, helping to confirm the existence of an Over-soul. Thoreau knew intuitively that if one gives a boy a new hammer, he will want to hammer everything he sees. The Cartesian-Newtonian paradigm epitomizes such an instrument, and in "Natural History" Thoreau rejects it.

> The true man of science will know nature better by his finer organization; he will smell, taste, see, hear, feel, better than other men. His will be a deeper and finer experience. We do not learn by inference and deduction and the application of mathematics to philosophy, but by direct intercourse and sympathy. It is with science as with ethics, *—we cannot know truth by contrivance and method; the Baconian is as false as any other,* and with all the helps of machinery and the arts, the most scientific will still be the healthiest and friendliest man, and possess a more perfect Indian wisdom.[16]

Thoreau is not advocating scientific book burning but is seeking a kind of cognitive balance, an "Indian wisdom" that restores organic qualities to a world of scientific quantities and reintegrates human consciousness with the cognizable world. The seeker of Indian wisdom is clearly not a classicist imposing timeless Virgilian and Homeric categories on nature. Rather the search is for presocial meaning through primary experience in the wilderness, through encounter with a nonhuman other outside the domain of conventional wisdom. Thoreau here clearly questions the boundaries between wilderness and civilization that are absolutes to Emerson and his fellow transcendentalists. Thoreau's goal—however imprecisely formulated in "Natural History"—is to rekindle a primitive (savage, Paleolithic, archaic, or Indian) awareness of the Magna Mater. "Natural History" makes clear the Thoreauvian notion that meaning can be found through an immediate (nonmediated) encounter with wild nature. This is the legacy of idealism and Romanticism unrealized in Emerson's "Nature."

The Thoreauvian exploration of the natural history of Massachusetts cannot be defined, then, in terms of either scientific or transcendental category. To escape the parlor's din he recommends a natural antidote: sleep, unconsciousness, a letting go of the categorically focused concentration on Nature. And in the morning, a fresh beginning, a walk into wild nature sans the categories of culture. Nature is alive with the sights and sounds that science excludes, and these secondary qualities Thoreau finds central to understanding nature-as-an-organism with which he is bound as distinct from nature-as-matter-in-mechanical-motion over which he stands as thinking subject. "Natural History" also sharpens our understanding of Thoreau's perspectives on nature as modified by human action. Massachusetts had been colonized two hundred years earlier, and those colonists confronted a true wilderness that they were determined to civilize. A long history of bloody encounters with the "Indians" and the depredations of hunters and trappers finally led to the "taming" of both wild people and the animals. "Natural History"—published six months before "Wachusett"— reveals a different perspective than that of literary pastoralism. Clearly, even at the beginning of his career when he was most influenced by Emerson, Thoreau was aware of humankind's adverse impact on nature. "The bear, wolf, lynx, wildcat, deer, beaver, and marten have disappeared; the otter is rarely if ever seen here at present; and the mink is less common than formerly."[17]

"A Winter Walk" begins with sentimental descriptions of waking and rising on a winter morning. Thoreau wishes to emphasize natural rhythms, the slow pace increasing as waking gives way to walking. Within a few pages Thoreau strikes a pace—close to the quality of description reached in *Walden*—that shows him as the very "true man of science" addressed in "Natural History." Sauntering through the winter landscape, free of the parlor's din, he establishes an intuitive bond with nature. Many of the ideas present in "Natural History" are again examined, rooted now in the winter wilds. "Meanwhile we step hastily along through the powdery snow, warmed by an inward heat, enjoying an Indian summer still, in the increased glow of thought and feeling. Probably if our lives were more conformed to nature, we should not need to defend ourselves against her heats and colds, but find her our constant nurse and friend, as do plants and quadrupeds." Yet Thoreau still attaches Emersonian interpretations to this insight, observing that "what stays out [in winter] must be part of the original frame of the universe, and of such valor as God himself." [18]

"A Winter Walk," while echoing "Natural History," foreshadows themes developed in both *Walden* and "Walking," Thoreau's greatest essay on the idea of wilderness. He observes that "a healthy man, indeed, is the complement of the seasons, and in winter, summer is in his heart"—a structural theme in *Walden*. He also discovers in an abandoned woodsman's hut a model for his cabin at Walden Pond. And he finds in wilderness ramblings the inspiration so central to the message of "Walking." "The chickadee and nuthatch are more inspiring society than statesmen and philosophers . . . . In this lonely glen, with its brook draining the slopes, its creased ice and crystals of all hues, where the spruces and hemlocks stand up on either side, and the rush and sere wild oats in the rivulet itself, our lives are more serene and worthy to contemplate." Rather than marching unconsciously to the dictates of society, a person-in-the-wilderness is more natural, in tune with organic fundamentals, and thus not a philosopher or scientist but a person of Indian wisdom. Similarly, the fisher "does not make the scenery less wild, more than the jays and muskrats, but stands there as a part of it . . . . He belongs to the natural family of man, and is planted deeper in nature and has more root than the inhabitants of towns." [19]

"Natural History" and "A Winter Walk" reveal a Thoreau in process, exploring the wilderness for meaning, and slowly progressing toward mastery of his medium of expression. An abstract quality, although muted, remains in these essays, which sometimes fall back on transcendental universals rather than develop original conclusions drawn from intuition. But we see Thoreau's imagination beginning to stretch the categories—both transcendental and classical—of experience, as he explores new methods of knowing. The Thoreauvian art form is yet imperfect, but the use of natural metaphors (for example, a healthy man has summer in his heart; the fisher has roots in nature) has ensued. Thoreau has not yet reconciled the natural and the cultural, but he has set out on a singular path. [20]

A Week on the Concord and Merrimack Rivers was written during Thoreau's sojourn at Walden Pond, and his intent to draft the book may have influenced his decision to make such a retreat. [21] *A Week* exemplifies his lifelong habits of working and reworking his literary efforts and of incorporating materials accumulated over years into a single work. The book includes fragments from his journal of 1837 (his elliptical record of the voyage), a poem he wrote in 1839, pieces of essays he published in *The Dial* in the early 1840s, and the essay "Friendship," written in 1848. *A Week,* as might be anticipated for a first book, lacks the craftsmanship of *Walden* (Joseph Wood Krutch calls the work "scattered and unfocused") and again shows the lingering influence of Emersonian transcendentalism. As in "Wachusett," abstruse passages interrupt the narrative flow.[22] Nevertheless, the book reveals advances in Thoreau's idea of wilderness: he set out on the river in search of something like the eternal mythical present or point of origin (original face) of the Paleolithic mind.

> I had often stood on the banks of the Concord, watching the lapse of the current, an emblem of all progress, following the same law with the system, with time, and all that is made; the weeds at the bottom gently bending down the stream, shaken by the watery wind, still planted where their seeds had sunk, but ere long to die and go down likewise; the shining pebbles, not yet anxious to better their condition, the chips and weeds, and occasional logs and stems of trees, that floated past, fulfilling their fate, were objects of singular interest to me, and at last I resolved to launch myself on its bosom, and float whither it would bear me.[23]

A Week begins with a passage that provides a vantage point on Thoreau's sorting out of the interrelations between the cultural and natural and on his increasingly adept use of language to uncover these meanings. In fact, *A Week* returns again and again to fundamental questions of language and expression, of contrasts between "white man's poetry" and Indian muses.

> The Musketaquid, or Grass-ground River, though probably as old as the Nile or Euphrates, did not begin to have a place in civilized history, until the fame of its grassy meadows and its fish attracted settlers out of England in 1635, when it received the other but kindred name of CONCORD from the first plantation on its banks, which appears to have been commenced in a spirit of peace and harmony. It will be Grass-ground River as long as grass grows and water runs here; it will be Concord River only while men lead peaceable lives on its banks. To an extinct race it was grass-ground, where they hunted and fished, and it is still perennial grass-ground to Concord farmers, who own the Great Meadows and get the hay from year to year.[24]

This passage manifests a deepening appreciation of the philosophical complexities inherent in language and sound. Thoreau views "Musketaquid" as the true name of the river, as a name rooted in a natural and therefore primary rather than merely cultural and thus contingent history. Something in the Indian name captures his imagination as it flows from the tongue. "If we could listen but for an instant to the chaunt of the Indian muse, we should understand why he will not exchange his savageness for civilization."[25] "Concord," although kindred, is a merely conventional name, an imposition of a recent social order upon natural fact. By emphasizing the name of the grass-ground river as "Musketaquid," Thoreau attempts to disclose a presence concealed by conventional designation, a presocial, primal, and therefore genuine meaning.[26] Further, as grass-ground river the river endures beyond the reign of civilization. Thoreau here achieves a hermeneutical insight into the linguisticality and historicity of the human predicament. *Language speaks,* as Heidegger says, language is the house of Being.[27] (Thoreau is intuitively aware of this encompassing linguistic reality; what eludes his attention is the further realization that all language, as a human phenomenon, takes on conventional meaning and that the passage of time ultimately carries away any and all phenomena, including the grass-ground river and its Indian name.)

Throughout *A Week* Thoreau weaves archaic languages—as in selections from Virgil—through quotation into the text. Unlike "Wachusett," where the citations seem mere ornamentations, the material is integrated into the philosophical exploration, essential to the realization of nature's priority over culture. Ancient and dead languages now held a fascination for Thoreau, particularly when they recognized living nature; that element bonded him with archaic sensibilities and thus with a time before the enfolding of meaning within the merely present. "These are such sentences as were written while grass grew and water ran." Thoreau seeks to write sentences like those written when the grass first grew and the water ran fresh, unsullied by humankind. Though unusual, these are perfectly healthy sentences that "are, perhaps, not the nicest, but the surest and roundest."[28]

A Week, then, reveals the germs of Thoreau's quest for mastery of his medium, his goal to communicate through the written word the very pulse of human encounter—naked experience, without transcendental universals or other armament—with wild nature. A true seeker of wisdom must, Ortega y Gasset observes, lay down the merely traditional and orthodox and seek the wild beast of truth in the jungle where it lives.[29] Geoffrey O'Brien suggests that "Thoreau dreaded the sterility of purely denotative language." As a result he struggled to maintain contact with the natural world that remained vital, outside the printed page. "The 'perfectly healthy sentence' that he wants to write is not a dissection of reality but a spontaneous manifestation of it, a human utterance equivalent to 'the crowing of cocks, the baying of dogs, and the hum of insects at noon, . . . evidence of nature's health or *sound* state.' "[30] The structuring of *A Week* around two natural metaphors—the days and the river—is part of Thoreau's endeavor to ground consciousness in nature. A day is a natural cycle beginning with a dawn that finally gives way to night, as Sirius and the constellations replace Sol. Similarly, the river is a natural metaphor for a sentient life, a never-ending flow through time, freed from the confines of convention.

Thoreau digresses in *A Week* to recount his exploration of Mount Greylock in July 1844. Approaching the mountain along a "romantic and retired valley," he crosses a stream whose "constant murmuring would quiet the passions of mankind forever."[31] Here he encounters a last outpost of civilization, a man named Rice—crude and gruff, an aboriginal man unsuited to Concord yet at home in the mountains. "He was, indeed, as rude as a fabled satyr. But I suffered him to pass for what he was, for why should I quarrel with nature? and was even pleased at the discovery of such a singular natural phenomenon. I dealt with him as if to me all manners were indifferent, and he had a sweet wild way with him. I would not question nature, and I would rather have him as he was, than as I would have him. For I had come up here not for sympathy, or kindness, or society, but for novelty and adventure, and to see what nature had produced here."[32] The contrast between a man like Rice and the members of the Concord circle must have been overwhelming. Rice is not a gentle-man but a natural-man, living in close consort with nature, as Thoreau would soon do at Walden Pond. Obviously, there is a rationale for including this incident in *A Week* on more than one score. While living at Walden Pond, Thoreau likely drafted the episode because Rice, too, rejected social convention for a wild life.

Thoreau's idea of wilderness and his unique way of seeing is not complete in *A Week*, nor is his quest to write "perfectly healthy sentences" fulfilled. When pressed for conclusions, he often falls back into comfortable cubbyholes of thought. Yet his close observation of Rice and attention to Indian words reveal an increasing awareness of organic, presocial layers of meaning: he is abandoning the methods of transcendentalism for those of philosophical anthropology.[33] As readers like Jerome Rothenberg and Fred Turner suggest, Thoreau was ideally placed in time, since during the nineteenth century the idea that archaic societies might serve as models for European society came into currency. *A Week* reveals in part an anthropological inquiry just underway, an idea of wilderness in process. Thoreau has abandoned the Emersonian position outlined in "Nature," which assumes as givens the categories (economic, religious, political, scientific) of Modernism and searches for alternatives. So viewed, the Walden experiment represents Thoreau's self-conscious step across the boundary between wilderness and civilization. He is trying to recreate "the economic condition of the savage, in search of the place where we took our false turning .... [At Walden] Thoreau is being historically, as well as personally, reflexive; just as he is seeking the foundations of his own experience, he is seeking the foundations of the experience of his culture." [34]

AT THIS JUNCTURE our path becomes less defined, as contemporaneously and posthumously published works, and material from the *Journal,* begin to intertwine. Even determining a strict chronology is difficult, given Thoreau's penchant for continual revision. Yet there is justification for considering the posthumously published *Maine Woods* (1864), edited by his sister Sophia and his lifelong friend Ellery Channing, as the next step in the unfolding of Thoreau's idea of wilderness. The book is an amalgamation of three essays based on three trips to Maine (1846, 1853, 1857). Yet *Maine Woods* is essential because of the excursion to Ktaadn.[35] "Ktaadn" is an Indian word meaning highest land, substituted by Thoreau for the Anglicized "Katahdin." The journey to Ktaadn's summit was an existential encounter that dealt a death blow to the Emersonian notion that the world existed for humankind. Thoreau began his trip to Ktaadn—which is, at precisely one mile above sea level, the highest and most precipitous mountain in Maine—on August 31, 1846 (thus interrupting his stay at Walden), but he had had the plan in mind for some time.[36] There is no reason to think that he even remotely conceived of what awaited him, for he left Walden a somewhat unorthodox transcendentalist with romantic tendencies. He returned with an understanding of the fundamental untenability of the Emersonian stance toward wild nature, having learned that there was no easy equation between consciousness *(psyche)* and nature, between the cultural and natural, between humankind and the wilderness. To this point in life, including his experiences at Walden Pond, Thoreau's intercourse with wild nature had been pleasant, if occasionally uncomfortable, but never threatening. The Ktaadn excursion tested him, physically and psychically, in a new and radical way.

Maine Woods reveals a Thoreau in high spirits as the journey begins, but as his party works deeper into the wilderness his outlook subtly shifts. He begins to sense evil within nature—a position in some ways not unlike a conventional Judeo-Christian orientation. Thoreau, seeker of Indian wisdom, a man who had admired Rice for his rough and uncivilized ways, is suddenly taken aback by the true wilderness. The contrast is obvious. Walden Pond, though once removed from Concord, is on the edge of civilization, where even in his criticism of conventional wisdom Thoreau remains within a safe world with known boundaries. The Maine woods, once removed from Walden, is terra incognita with life-endangering circumstances—a true psychological and physical divide.

The text brilliantly shows his awareness of the crossing, as he becomes increasingly attentive to the evidences of civilization, seeking to maintain a psychic balance between the civil and the natural. He comments favorably on the signs of human existence: the scarring of the forest by loggers, a ring-bolt drilled into rock, even a brick someone had left behind. He characterizes trout caught for supper as "the fairest flowers, the product of primitive rivers," "these bright fluviatile flowers, seen of Indians only, made beautiful, the Lord only knows why, to swim there!" thus reassuring himself that nature is not evil. That night Thoreau dreams of the beautiful trout, but the doubts—the psychic foreboding—emerge again. Questioning the dream's veracity, Thoreau rises before dawn to "test its truth": "There stood Ktaadn with distinct and cloudless outline in the moonlight; and the rippling of the rapids was the only sound to break the stillness. Standing on the shore, I once more cast my line into the stream, and found the dream to be real and the fable true. The speckled trout and silvery roach, like flying-fish, sped swiftly through the moonlight air, describing bright arcs on the dark side of Ktaadn, until moonlight, now fading into daylight, brought satiety to my mind, and the minds of my companions who had joined me."[37] To all appearances, Thoreau is striving to maintain an Emersonian view of the wilderness even on the verge of his climb.

The ascent soon disabused him of any vestiges of a romantic view of nature. Breaking camp, Thoreau moved to head the party, being the "oldest mountain climber." Reaching a south-running ridge extending from the main peak (the proposed route of ascent), he was rewarded with his best view yet, one unlike any he had seen before. "Ktaadn presented a different aspect from any mountain I have seen, there being a greater proportion of naked rock, rising abruptly from the forest; and we looked up at this blue barrier as if it were some fragment of a wall which anciently bounded the earth in that direction." From this point the party almost immediately lost sight of the peak, being "buried in the woods."[38] By four o'clock the group had not reached the summit, and all except Thoreau returned to camp. He continued alone, climbing alongside a precipitous waterfall into the clouds, until he came to a raging river, approximately thirty feet wide, where he paused to survey the country below.

The wildness of the country was again affecting his perception. "I began to work my way, scarcely less arduous than Satan's anciently through Chaos, up the nearest, though not the highest peak," through the "most treacherous and porous country I ever traveled," where "rocks, gray, silent rocks, were the flocks and herds that pastured, chewing a rocky cud at sunset. They looked at me with hard gray eyes, without a bleat or a low." Nature was losing its human countenance, turning from familiar friend to potentially hostile stranger: this was no Emersonian excursion. Thoreau returned to camp, perhaps glad to be back in human company. After a fitful night's sleep, with the wind whipping embers from the fire around the camp, and the party unsettled by the howl of the wind and flapping tent fabric, Thoreau awoke and again contemplated the mountain. The experiences of the previous afternoon were beginning to crystallize into more definite impressions.

> The mountain seemed a vast aggregation of loose rocks, as if some time it had rained rocks, and they lay as they fell on the mountain sides, nowhere fairly at rest, but leaning on each other, all rocking-stones, with cavities between, but scarcely any soil or smoother shelf. They were the raw materials of a planet dropped from an unseen quarry, which the vast chemistry of nature would anon work up, or work down, into the smiling and verdant plains and valleys of earth. This was an undone extremity of the globe; as in lignite, we see coal in the process of formation.[39]

The wilderness was becoming before his eyes a world of evolving matter-in-motion upon which the impersonal chemistry of nature worked. Beautiful trout were no longer inscribing bright arcs on the side of Ktaadn: the mountain was but raw materials of a planet dropped from some unseen quarry. As an Emersonian transcendentalist armed with conventional categories and comfortable conclusions, Thoreau had died on Ktaadn's ridge, and he verged on achieving a primordial, if threatening, relation to the universe.

Impatient to begin the climb, and perhaps eager to test his courage, Thoreau left camp alone. As he climbed he was engulfed by "the hostile ranks of clouds . . . . It was, in fact, a cloud-factory,—these were the cloud-works, and the wind turned them off done from the cool, bare rocks." All the Homeric odes and poetry of Virgil, the transcendental principles of Emerson, and even the romanticizing of nature's beauty were suddenly meaningless. Thoreau was disoriented, struggling not only against the mountainside and the clouds to find his way but also for understanding.

> Æschylus had no doubt visited such scenery as this. It was vast, Titanic, and such as man never inhabits. Some part of the beholder, even some vital part, seems to escape through the loose grating of his ribs as he ascends. He is more lone than you can imagine. There is less of substantial thought and fair understanding in him than in the plains [or the parlors of Concord, or even Walden Pond] where men inhabit. His reason is dispersed and shadowy, more thin and subtile, like the air. Vast, Titanic, inhuman Nature has got him at disadvantage, caught him alone, and pilfers him of some of his divine faculty.[40]

Thoreau's education atop Ktaadn was not yet finished, but the principles of Emerson's "Nature" had already been bracketed. As the clouds thickened, he abandoned the ascent and returned to camp. The significance of the journey now struck home with sudden impact.

> Perhaps I most fully realized that this was primeval, untamed and forever untameable *Nature,* or whatever else men call it, while coming down . . . . And yet we have not seen pure Nature, unless we have seen her thus vast and drear and inhuman . . . . Nature was here something savage and awful, though beautiful. I looked with awe at the ground I trod on, to see what the Powers had made there, the form and fashion and material of their work. This was that Earth of which we have heard, made out of Chaos and Old Nights. Here was no man's garden, but the unhandseled globe. It was not lawn, nor pasture, nor mead, nor woodland, nor lea, nor arable, nor waste-land [that is, eludes all conventional categorization]. It was the fresh and natural surface of the planet Earth, as it was made forever and ever,—to be the dwelling of man, we say, [a notion Thoreau is clearly questioning]—so Nature made it, and many may use if he can. Man was not to be associated with it. It was Matter, vast, terrific,—not his Mother Earth that we have heard of, not for him to tread on, or be buried in,—no, it were being too familiar even to let his bones lie there,—the home, this, of Necessity and Fate. There was clearly felt the presence of a force not bound to be kind to man. It was a place for heathenism and superstitious rites,—to be inhabited by men nearer of kin to the rocks and to wild animals than we. . . . Perchance where *our* wild pines stand, and leaves lie on their forest floor, in Concord, there were once reap-

ers, and husbandmen planted grain; but here not even the surface had been scarred by man, but it was a specimen of what God saw fit to make this world. What is it to be admitted to a museum, to see a myriad of particular things, compared with being shown some star's surface, some hard matter in its home! I stand in awe of my body, this matter to which I am bound has become so strange to me. I fear not spirits, ghosts, of which I am one,—*that* my body might,—but I fear bodies, I tremble to meet them. What is this Titan that has possession of me? Talk of mysteries! Think of our life in nature,—daily to be shown matter, to come in contact with it,—rocks, trees, wind on our cheeks! the *solid* earth! the *actual* world! the *common sense! Contact! Contact! Who* are we? *where* are we?[41]

This is surely one of the two most remarkable pages of prose ever penned by Thoreau.[42] If we believe that his constant quest is to elucidate the relations between human consciousness and nature, then Ktaadn defines one endpoint: brute facticity, the material world, even his own material body within which his consciousness existed, could be alien. Ktaadn rekindles for Thoreau a primal or Paleolithic coming-to-consciousness of humankind's naked rootedness in and absolute dependence upon nature. If *Walden* and "Walking" later refine his definitions of the positive side of the wilderness, then Ktaadn deals with its negative promontory. Yet Ktaadn represents more: the encounter was crucial to the evolution of Thoreau's idea of wilderness. Positively viewed, (1) the position developed in "Ktaadn" is antithetical to Emerson's philosophy, the final step in Thoreau's development from transcendentalism to a genuine relation to the universe. His writings hereafter carry the mark of his singular experiences, of his unique vantage point on the wilderness, and of his genius. More important, (2) the encounter with Ktaadn sharpens Thoreau's understanding of interrelations between humankind and nature. "Talk of mysteries! . . . Think of our life in nature. . . *Contact! Contact! Who* are we? *where* are we?" Thoreau's allusion to being shown a star's surface is closer to cosmological truth than he knew (see below, chapter 10). By the time he returned to Walden Pond he was enroute to developing—independently of Darwin and Wallace specifically, and the paleontological and geological advances in Europe more generally—a profound evolutionary perspective on nature. By the time *Walden* was published Thoreau had worked this problem through.

Thoreau returned to the Maine woods twice more. Although the Ktaadn excursion liberated him from transcendentalism, both "Chesuncook" and

"The Allegash and East Branch" (included as part of *Maine Woods*) clarify the distinctions between Emerson and Thoreau. Foreshadowing John Muir's observations, and clearly deviating from the Emersonian commodities view of nature, Thoreau begins "Ktaadn" by observing how even the vast Maine forest had been scarred by logging. So much timber had been harvested and floated downstream to the sea that ships were sometimes becalmed, hemmed in by vast rafts of floating logs. Thoreau notes that there is something nearly tragic in cutting a living tree, for it becomes "lumber merely." "Think how stood the white-pine tree on the shore of the Chesuncook, its branches soughing with the four winds, and every individual needle trembling in the sunlight,—think how it stands with it now,—sold, perchance to the New England Friction-Match Company! . . . The mission of men there seems to be, like so many busy demons, to drive the forest all out of the country, from every solitary beaver-swamp, and mountain-side, as soon as possible."[43] Thoreau is asserting, as he argues more systematically in both *Walden* and "Life without Principle," that economic categories blind human beings, destroying not only living entities, which are reduced to use value only, but also the human soul. There can be no easy equation between Thoreauvian and Emersonian views of natural entities. For Thoreau they exist in and for themselves, whereas for Emerson they are ultimately commodities, provided by a benevolent God for his most perfect creation.[44]

Thoreau extends his critique of the economic appropriation of the forest (and wild nature generally) in the later essays. In "Chesuncook," the second part of the book, we see his increasing hermeneutical sophistication. In a passage that reverberates with echoes of the Paleolithic mind, Thoreau recognizes the wilderness as composed of natural entities living self-sufficiently and contrasts this view with the masses of people who are oblivious because of the imprisoning effects of customary categories. He writes that "the pine is no more lumber [despite our human designation of it as 'lumber'] than man is, and to be made into boards and houses is no more its true and highest use than the truest use of a man is to be cut down and made into manure. . . . Every creature is better alive than dead, men and moose and pine-trees, and he who understands it aright will rather preserve its life than destroy it."[45]

Neither a clearer nor an earlier statement of the preservationist's credo can be found. Thoreau denies the unquestioned validity of conventional categories, which ostensibly define the forest, animals, and all wild nature. The true meaning of the wilderness, he insists, is rooted in the spirit of living nature and in the relation of human consciousness to that world,

not in human categorization or use or both. Further, he recognizes that
if humans are to understand the wildness that lies across the divide, then
conventional wisdom (Modernism) must be bracketed. By expressing his
intuitions, Thoreau is revealing a presence concealed by language, simultaneously exegeting himself and his relations to wild nature. This is the
hermeneutical circle. Thoreau's writing here threatens a quantum leap into
a new wilderness mythology beyond the realm of convention—exposing
through his art form a world that all might see.

AFTER KTAADN, THOREAU returned to Walden Pond and finished drafting *A Week on the Concord and Merrimack Rivers.*[46] September 6, 1847, marked his final departure from Walden Pond—the classic
experiment in the woods lasted two days beyond twenty-six months. Soon
after, he began to draft the Walden manuscript, a process that extended
over several years through seven major drafts. Although *Walden* was originally intended for publication in 1849, the dismal sale of *A Week* set
Thoreau's plans back, undoubtedly to the benefit of posterity.[47] The book
was finally published in 1854. *Walden* gives the *appearance* of orthodox
transcendentalism, but the book itself belies that interpretation. Thoreau
clearly rises above Emersonian transcendentalism and reintegrates human
consciousness with wild nature by erasing the fence that conventionally
separates wilderness and civilization. *Walden* also transcends the paradox of Ktaadn, where the material world stood opposed to human consciousness. For Thoreau, Ktaadn reveals the excesses of transcendentalism; Walden (the working in the bean field, the palpable reality of the
seasons, the melting of the sandbank, and the reflection upon these experiences) allows him to advance from that encounter to a unique wilderness
philosophy. *Walden* reveals the human ego as nature grown self-conscious,
a theme Thoreau developed further in "Walking."[48] It also unequivocally
expresses a grasp of the essential triadic integration of matter, life, and
consciousness.

The book begins with "Economy," almost three times longer than "The
Ponds" and perhaps five times longer than any other section. "Economy"
subtly offers a critical analysis of the economic forces that rule human
lives, and a reflective justification of why Thoreau came to the pond. Explaining that he embraces wild nature to free himself from civilization's
grip, he confesses his ultimate goal: to discover life's essentials. The argument flows gently along, and yet the Thoreauvian dialectic cuts a deep
channel, questioning both the presuppositions of Adam Smith's *Wealth
of Nations* and the very idea of knowledge. "Economy" begins by strip-

ping bare the social illusions—the force of custom, of opinion—that govern most human lives. The most famous and often quoted line of *Walden* comes to the point. "The mass of men lead lives of quiet desperation." Underlying these ruined lives is Modernism: the liberal-democratic industrial state that promises so much and delivers so little. "Most men, even in this comparatively free country, through mere ignorance and mistake, are so occupied with the factitious cares and superfluously coarse labors of life that its finer fruits cannot be plucked by them. . . . [The laboring man] has no time to be any thing but a machine. How can he remember well his ignorance—which his growth requires—who has so often to use his knowledge? . . . The finest qualities of our nature, like the bloom on fruits, can be preserved only by the most delicate handling." [49]

Here Thoreau only hints at the positive function of ignorance—an Indian wisdom achieved through spontaneous encounter with nature—an idea he develops in "Walking." He does, however, explore the trap that the claim to knowledge, or the belief that something is known absolutely, represents, again validating the distinction between opinion that enslaves the mind and the wisdom that is the goal of inquiry. "The greater part of what my neighbors call good," Thoreau writes, "I believe in my soul to be bad, and if I repent of any thing, it is very likely to be my good behavior." His point is that knowledge of truth, justice, and virtue have little or nothing to do with tradition, custom, or popularity even if conventional wisdom rules the world. "The millions are awake enough for physical labor," he writes, "but only one in a million is awake enough for effective intellectual exertion." In these insights Thoreau shows a remarkable sense of ideas later developed by twentieth-century sociologists, philosophical anthropologists, and social psychologists. [50]

Having recognized humankind's social predicament, and the resultant force of mere opinion on thought, he turns to societal institutions and traditions; these, too, he finds wanting. "It would be some advantage to live a primitive and frontier life, though in the midst of an outward civilization, if only to learn what are the gross necessaries of life . . . . For the improvements of ages have had but little influence on the essential laws of man's existence; as our skeletons, probably, are not to be distinguished from those of our ancestors." Thoreau's immediate concern is with the effect of economic society on the individual, since he believes that mainstream New England culture represents an untenable answer to an essentially simple problem—living a good life. A necessary though not sufficient condition for such a life, he argues, is simply to maintain one's "vital heat," requiring only food and shelter—those essential laws of human existence.

But, anticipating the consumer culture and conspicuous consumption of the twentieth century, Thoreau observes that "most of the luxuries, and many of the so called comforts of life, are not only not indispensable, but positive hindrances to the elevation of mankind. With respect to luxuries and comforts, the wisest have ever lived a more simple and meagre life than the poor." And later, again with penetrating sociological insight, he writes that "it is the luxurious and dissipated who set the fashions which the herd so diligently follow." [51] Thoreau thus rejects one of the cardinal presuppositions of Adam Smith—namely, that human well-being can be equated with the consumption of material goods. Although Modernism still rules the world and society has not yet understood Thoreau, his essential insight is irrefragable: beyond the minimum necessary for sustenance, material consumption becomes a parody of itself.

As "Economy" ends, Thoreau hints at the thesis developed in detail in the following section: "to maintain one's self on this earth is not a hardship but a pastime, if we will live simply and wisely." The Walden experiment thus straddles the physical and the intellectual: Thoreau seeks to simplify the business of maintaining vital heat and, once free of social illusions, to uncover the good life. "Economy" prepares the way for the conclusion offered in "Where I Lived, and What I Lived For."

I went to the woods because I wished to live deliberately, to front only the essential facts of life, and see if I could not learn what it had to teach, and not, when I came to die, discover that I had not lived. I did not wish to live what was not life, living is so dear, nor did I wish to practise resignation, unless it was quite necessary. I wanted to live deep and suck out all the marrow of life, to live so sturdily and Spartan-like as to put to rout all that was not life, to cut a broad swath and shave close, to drive life into a corner, and reduce it to its lowest terms, and, if it proved to be mean, why then to get the whole and genuine meanness of it, and publish its meanness to the world; or if it were sublime, to know it by experience, and be able to give a true account of it in my next excursion. For most men, it appears to me, are in a strange uncertainty about it, whether it is of the devil or of God, and have *somewhat hastily* concluded that it is the chief end of man here to "glorify God and enjoy him forever." [52]

This paragraph is pivotal. Thoreau went to Walden to discover primal ways of living. By experiencing an organic life he hoped to find an alternative to "the lives of quiet desperation." So viewed, the Walden project is an anthropological inquiry: an attempt to uncover the outlines of archaic culture, to recapture a Paleolithic consciousness, and to become a man of Indian wisdom. Thoreau intends to "suck out all the marrow of life," a carefully chosen metaphor that underscores the unconventionality of the experiment. There is also a post-Ktaadn flavor to this account, for he suggests at least a possibility that life in the wilderness might be mean. Yet he enters his wilderness laboratory without either classical categories or transcendental principles, specifically rejecting a conventional intellectual's life, as epitomized by Emerson and the other members of the Concord circle. "There are nowadays professors of philosophy, but not philosophers. . . . They make shift to live merely by conformity, practically as their fathers did, and are in no sense the progenitors of a nobler race of men. . . . The [true] philosopher is in advance of his age even in the outward form of his life. He is not fed, sheltered, clothed, warmed, like his contemporaries. How can a man be a philosopher and not maintain his vital heat by better methods than other men?" [53]

Neither transcendental philosophers nor ordinary laborers pass the Thoreauvian test for living the good life. Philosophers are prisoners of abstract systems of ideas, workers the captives of the factory system. [54] The good life, Thoreau is confident, involves living in harmony with nature and the essential laws of human existence, and knowledge of these essentials can be found only in the wilderness, away from the entangling vines of civilization. Thoreau vividly contrasts adults, locked in the world of convention, with children, who spontaneously approach the world, open to its teachings. "By closing the eyes and slumbering, and consenting to be deceived by shows, men establish and confirm their daily life of routine and habit every where, which still is built on purely illusory foundations. Children, who play life, discern its true law and relations more clearly than men, who fail to live it worthily, but who think that they are wiser by experience, that is, by failure." [55] Children at play do not impose adult schemes upon the world but interact imaginatively with their environment through games. A child might look at a forest as a refuge for hide-and-seek, or a place of mystery and adventure, begging for exploration, whereas an adult might look at the same forest in terms of its value as lumber or as an obstacle to pasturing cattle. More crucially, in the adult world time is money, an attitude rooted in the Protestant ethic. In the child's world time is an infinite sequence of moments, each to be appreciated fully in and of itself.

Thoreau concludes that "time is but the stream I go a-fishing in." This statement implicitly contradicts both the conventional idea of scientific time (Newton's absolute time, part of the structure of the universe, and fundamental to the modern worldview that sure and certain knowledge is possible) and religious time (Christian time, a secular vale of tears to be endured before salvation). Thoreauvian time is organic, a temporal flow to be enjoyed immediately, then savored through later reflection. It is also cyclical, as with the change of the seasons. Given this organic stream of time, Thoreau continues, he wants to do nothing more than

> drink at it; but while I drink I see the sandy bottom and detect how shallow it is. Its thin current slides away, but eternity remains. I would drink deeper; fish in the sky, whose bottom is pebbly with stars. I cannot count one. I know not the first letter of the alphabet. I have always been regretting that I was not as wise as the day I was born. The intellect is a cleaver; it discerns and rifts its way into the secret of things. I do not wish to be any more busy with my hands than is necessary. My head is hands and feet. I feel all my best faculties concentrated in it. My instinct tells me that my head is an organ for burrowing, as some creatures use their snout and forepaws, and with it I would mine and burrow my way through these hills. I think that the richest vein is somewhere hereabouts; so by the divining rod and thin rising vapors I judge; and here I will begin to mine.[56]

The epistemological implications of this passage are complicated yet elementary. The path to knowledge is to engage time—the flow of life—like a child. Perhaps Thoreau should have spelled out his theory of knowledge with more precision; and yet, read in context, the passage summarizes his previous observations concerning knowledge and lays a foundation for later chapters. Like a child, he spends his time fishing, playing in a stream whose current (portending evolutionary process) reveals eternity—nature's way as manifested in an eternal mythical present. The idea of time as a stream, pebbled with stars on the bottom and fish in the sky, is a richly imaginative and powerful metaphor, childish in a way that surely nettled Emerson, yet more profound than anything he had written. Yet, paradox on paradox, Thoreau cannot count even one star and claims not to know the alphabet. Why? Because the path to Indian wisdom is not through mensuration, quantification, differentiation. Thoreau is in the wilderness to fish for the essential laws of existence, for some sense of the cosmic whole. School learning has made him less wise than the day he was born. But Walden presents the opportunity, away from society, to practice contemplative fishing. Common sense, Thoreau realizes, is a cleaver that names, categorizes, and discriminates in a conventional pattern. "My head," Thoreau claims, "is my hands and feet" (yet another trope). So he keeps his hands free from workaday demands, since his best faculties for knowing are concentrated in his head—that is, his hands and feet. He will therefore engage himself with walking, and he will burrow, because he intuits a "rich vein" of knowledge nearby. The hoeing in the bean field is about to commence.

Having told us Thoreau's purpose, *Walden* settles into a comfortable pace, recounting his life alongside Walden Pond. He relates that he sometimes read, but not newspapers, rather Homer and Æschylus, the classics—something with roots deeper than the immediate moment, deeper than prevailing opinion. He laments that "most men have learned to read to serve a paltry convenience, as they have learned to cipher in order to keep accounts and not be cheated in trade; but of reading as a noble intellectual exercise they know little or nothing." Yet even the classics contain a trap, however important the messages or insights therein. Thoreau is no longer the classicist who wrote "Wachusett," straining to impose Virgil and others upon contemporary experience, for "while we are confined to books, though the most select and classic, and read only particular written languages, which are themselves but dialects and provincial, *we are in danger of forgetting the language which all things and events speak without metaphor,* which alone is copious and standard. . . . What is a course of history, or philosophy, or poetry, no matter how well selected, or the best society, or the most admirable routine of life, compared with the discipline of looking always at what is to be seen [and heard]."[57]

The differences between this Thoreau, mature in thought and master of his medium, and the early Thoreau are evident: the empyrean quest has been abandoned. Once free of society, wilderness sights, sounds, and events might intuitively register on consciousness, much like a leaf landing on the surface of a pond, gently supported by surface tension of the water, registering its presence in spreading ripples. Sights, sounds, smells, textures—these are the unmediated language of reality, and they, unlike the abstract generalities of Emerson's "Nature," become the substance of his prose. Clearly Thoreau has reached an explicit awareness of language as an organic medium of expression, in part a mirror of nature that therefore reflects truths about the human condition. Meaning is to be found in wild nature, and it can be best expressed through natural metaphor and trope. Thoreau's use of these is part of his genius, and a reason for working in the bean field, since "some must work in fields if only for the sake of tropes and expression, to serve a parable-maker one day."[58]

Remarkably, Thoreau achieved insight into the imprisoning subtleties and liberating potentialities of language from a mid-nineteenth-century vantage point—there was no rich tradition of hermeneutics to draw upon

—realizing through his own persistent efforts that *humankind is language* and that conventional language enframes the human project.[59] The consequences of this enframing, left unrecognized, are stifling. Thus Thoreau aims to break free, not through a romantic retreat to some prelapsarian age of innocence but through recovery of words that speak granitic truth. Thoreau's goal is to ground his language in nature and thereby (to paraphrase Paul Ricoeur) empty language of its conventional meaning while filling it anew—in short, his project is no less than the "hope of a re-creation of language."[60] Thoreau's earlier use of ancient languages and Indian words gives way in *Walden* to his own imaginative re-creation of the elemental, the primordial or presocial dimension of human experience that grounds all language.

Thoreau's journal gives evidence of his "hermeneutical" reflections, and the entry for May 10, 1853, combines his hermeneutical insights with his critique of conventional science and his quest to become a person of Indian wisdom—the true science.

> He is the richest who has most use for nature as raw material of tropes and symbols with which to describe his life. If these gates of golden willows affect me, they correspond to the beauty and promise of some experience on which I am entering. If I am overflowing with life, am rich in experience for which I lack expression, then nature will be my language full of poetry,—all nature will *fable,* and every natural phenomenon be a myth. The man of science, who is not seeking for expression but for a fact to be expressed merely, studies nature as a dead language. I pray for such inward experience as will make nature significant.[61]

These are remarkable statements. "I pray for such inward experience as will make nature significant." Such visions would animate a new natural mythology, recapturing a sense of meaning (presence) that scientific language and philosophical abstraction stripped from the world.[62] By going into the wilderness, Thoreau empties his mind of conventional wisdom and prepares to receive life through primary experience: epiphanies which reveal an eternal mythical present, dimensions of being hidden from ordinary consciousness. And "all nature will *fable,* and every natural phenomenon will be a myth." If we view *Walden* through this lens, then it represents a new wilderness mythology, an alternative to all that "Nature" and the Cartesian-Newtonian concept of nature represent, a world beyond nineteenth-century conventionality. Wild nature will fable (from *fabulari,* to talk), that is, speak through a person if that person will but let natural phenomena have voice, and such a speaking will be as if literally true, alive, and organic. The facts of science, imprisoned within conventional language (including mathematics), are inert human inventions, at best useful fictions. So, too, is Emersonian transcendentalism, and the idea that nature has been created by a transcendent God for *man*.

"Solitude" complements this line of analysis, for freed from convention, including the classics, Thoreau becomes a sensitive register of what surrounds and sustains him. "This is a delicious evening, when the whole body is one sense, and imbibes delight through every pore. I go and come with a strange liberty in Nature, a part of herself." Through life in solitude by the pond, Thoreau achieves an organic yet conscious unity with wild nature. "What do we want most to dwell near to? Not to many men surely, the depot, the post-office, the bar-room, the meeting-house, the school-house, the grocery, Beacon Hill, or the Five Points, where men most congregate, but to *the perennial source of our life,* whence in all our experience we have found that to issue, as the willow stands near the water and sends out its roots in that direction." Thoreau has transcended Judeo-Christian presuppositions about time, the scientific idea of nature, Cartesian dualism, and the Baconian dream: wilderness is neither an alien enemy to be conquered nor a resource to be exploited but "the perennial source of life." Here Thoreau verges on a Paleolithic awareness of living life within nature: all nature is alive, filled with kindred spirits, and he is at home in it (see above, chapter 1). "Every little pine needle expanded and swelled with sympathy and befriended me. I was so distinctly made aware of the presence of something kindred to me, even in scenes which we are accustomed to call wild and dreary, and also that the nearest of blood to me and the humanest was not a person nor a villager, that I thought no place could ever be strange to me again." Thoreau's attitude or outlook is, anthropologically considered, archaic. "While I enjoy the friendship of the seasons I trust that nothing can make life a burden to me." "Solitude" also foreshadows the evolutionary insights developed near the conclusion of *Walden*. "Shall I not have intelligence with the earth? Am I not partly leaves and vegetable mould myself?"[63]

"The Bean-Field" is a crucial experiment for Thoreau and a virtuoso demonstration of reflective thought and anthropological insight expressed through natural metaphor. In philosophical terms, the chapter is a dialectical movement as the actual experience of working in the field shapes and reshapes understanding. Thoreau marries human intentionality to wild nature through his hands and feet. He finds an intrinsic pleasure in selfless work, where hoe and hand, muscle and soil, seed and sun become one. The beans "attached me to the earth." Any gardener can understand Thoreau's pleasure. Beyond the virtue of work itself, Thoreau discovers affinities between his self and the organic materials with which he worked, rising above a commonsense categorization of weeds and critters. His initial understanding is conventional. "My enemies are worms, cool days, and most of all woodchucks." By the end of his labors Thoreau discovers that from a mythic viewpoint—one that escapes human centeredness and includes larger, natural cycles of existence—the "beans have results which are not harvested by me. Do they not grow for woodchucks partly? . . . How, then, can our harvest fail? Shall I not rejoice also at the abundance of the weeds whose seeds are the granary of the birds?" Rain is part of a larger cycle that lies outside the ordinary purview of human experience, even that of a farmer. "If it should continue so long as to cause the seeds to rot in the ground and destroy the potatoes in the low lands, it would still be good for the grass on the uplands, and, being good for the grass, it would be good for me."[64]

While hoeing in the bean field, Thoreau stumbles on a metaphor for rooting culture in wild nature—an idea developed fully in "Walking." "When my hoe tinkled against the stones, that music echoed to the woods and the sky, and was an accompaniment to my labor which yielded an instant and immeasurable crop. It was no longer beans that I hoed, nor I that hoed beans." The insights gained in the bean field are methodologically distinct from the results of either scientist or transcendental philosopher. Thoreau is a seeker of Indian wisdom, a proto-anthropologist digging for organic truth. The arrowheads in the soil he tills become a metaphor for the interpenetration of the natural with the cultural and sentient—all woven into a moment of time. Thoreau extends the analogy a few lines later, as hawks circle overhead, "alternately soaring and descending, approaching and leaving one another, as if they were the imbodiment of my own thoughts." He brings the metaphor full circle by comparing the seeds he plants in the bean field to "sincerity, truth, simplicity"—human virtues, which themselves can become "wormeaten" or lose vitality.[65] Just as with beans, virtues must be planted from seeds and cultivated, and only vital stock yields an abundant harvest. Most human beings neglect the lessons of the bean field and are therefore oblivious to life's essentials: virtue, like beans, must be seeded from good strains and nurtured.

Reverberations from "Economy" now come stage center in the "Beanfield," for not only are human beings more concerned about their crops than virtue, their motivation is mercantile. The prototypical modern person is Homo oeconomicus, and the sole value of farming the land is profit.

Such activities do not bring the human spirit closer to the soil and larger organic process but render nature of use value only—a boundary (common to Adam Smith and Karl Marx) Thoreau is determined to transgress, or at least question.

> Ancient poetry and mythology suggest, at least, that husbandry was once a sacred art; but it is pursued with irreverent haste and heedlessness by us, our object being to have large farms and large crops merely. We have no festival, nor procession, nor ceremony, not excepting our Cattle-shows and so called Thanksgiving, by which the farmer expresses a sense of the sacredness of his calling, or is reminded of its sacred origin. . . . By avarice and selfishness, and a grovelling habit, from which none of us is free, of regarding the soil as property, or the means of acquiring property chiefly, the landscape is deformed, husbandry is degraded with us, and the farmer leads the meanest of lives. He knows Nature but as a robber.[66]

By tilling in the bean field Thoreau hears the faintly lingering melodies of the Earth Mother, realizing that the worship of Mammon and Judeo-Christianity together desacralizes nature. Accordingly, he seeks to reinvest wild nature with sacrality: to create a new wilderness mythology through an organic language that combines words of granitic truth in perfectly natural sentences. He underscores his notion of wild nature's sacredness in a later chapter, wryly extending his critique of Christianity with favorable allusions to pagans and polytheists. "Sometimes I rambled to pine groves, standing like temples, or like fleets at sea, full-rigged, with wavy boughs, and rippling with light, so soft and green and shady that the Druids would have forsaken their oaks to worship in them; or to the cedar wood beyond Flints' Pond, where the trees, covered with hoary blue berries, spiring higher and higher, are fit to stand before Valhalla."[67]

We come now to "Higher Laws," the title perhaps a thrust at the abstract sterility of transcendentalism. The chapter begins with a compelling passage that, ringing with reverberations of the encounter on Ktaadn, reveals a consciousness now capable of embracing nature through recognition of its visible promontory *within* human nature itself.

> As I came home through the woods with my string of fish, trailing my pole, it being now quite dark, I caught a glimpse of a woodchuck stealing across my path, and felt a strange thrill of savage delight, and was strongly tempted to seize and devour him raw; not that I was hungry, then, except for the wildness which he represented. Once or

twice, however, while I lived at the pond, I found myself ranging the woods like a half-starved hound, with a strange abandonment, seeking some kind of venison which I might devour, and no morsel could have been too savage for me. . . . I found in myself, and still find, an instinct toward a higher, or, as it is named, spiritual life, as do most men, and another toward a primitive rank and savage one, and I reverence them both. I love the wild not less than the good. . . . I like sometimes to take rank hold on life and spend my day more as the animals do.[68]

To eat a woodchuck raw is to behave as a savage, even perhaps as an animal living unconsciously and spontaneously, and instinctively following primordial patterns. In the woods there is no polite conversation over glasses of wine and veal served on fine china in a Concord dining room, no discussion of nature as a system of laws or manifestation of God, but a Schopenhauerian realization of the vital center—nature as will—of organic life. Thoreau immediately moderates his position by claiming to love the good as well as the wild. Yet most human beings, he correctly observes, love only the good and are oblivious to the wild: the line between the primitive and civilized is drawn absolutely. Yet he loves the wilderness and wants to experience its wildness completely. The problem, as he had learned on Ktaadn, is to embrace its existence *within* himself without threatening his identity as a distinctively human being: Thoreau is the most civilized of men, and he knew it. Although he stops short of adopting the woodchuck as a totemic symbol, he again verges on recovery of the Paleolithic mind.

"Spring" is the crux of Thoreau's idea of wilderness. No doubt archaic people first associated spring with nature's rejuvenation after winter's austerity. In any case, Thoreau's choice of spring as the season for summing up his philosophy was deliberate. He uses a melting sandbank as a natural metaphor to illustrate "the principle of all the operations of Nature." The sandbank fascinated him as it melted and, freed from winter's grip, began slowly to shift. As the sand flowed, Thoreau recognized in its metamorphosis the very process of cosmic creation.

When the frost comes out in the spring, and even in a thawing day in the winter, the sand begins to flow down the slopes like lava, sometimes bursting out through the snow and overflowing it where no sand was to be seen before. Innumerable little streams overlap and interlace one with another, exhibiting a sort of hybrid product, which obeys half way the law of currents, and half way that of vegetation. As it flows it takes the forms of sappy leaves or vines, making heaps of pulpy sprays a foot or more in depth, and resembling, as you look down on them, the lacinated lobed and imbricated thalluses of some lichens; or you are reminded of coral, of leopards' paws or birds' feet, of brains or lungs or bowels, and excrements of all kinds.[69]

These observations are richly imaginative; Charles Darwin almost simultaneously was making his epic cruise to South America and, ultimately, the Galapagos. But Darwin's imaginative leap, given the abundance of organic forms with which he worked, is perhaps not so great as Thoreau's, for Thoreau derives his principle of the mutability of natural form from inorganic material.[70] And, going far beyond Darwin, he extends his description of evolutionary process from elemental matter through life to cosmological principle.

[When I see the flowing sand] I am affected as if in a peculiar sense I stood in the laboratory of the Artist who made the world and me,— had come to where he was still at work, sporting on this bank, and with excess of energy strewing his fresh designs about. I feel as if I were nearer to the vitals of the globe, for this sandy overflow is something such a foliaceous mass as the vitals of the animal body. You find thus in the very sands an anticipation of the vegetable leaf. No wonder that the earth expresses itself outwardly in leaves, it so labors with the idea inwardly. The atoms have already learned this law, and are pregnant by it.[71]

As with Darwin, Thoreau does not describe the actual workings of genetics. Yet clearly he has grasped the principle of evolution of complex from simple forms—in this case living vegetative matter from inorganic materials. Earlier anticipations of evolutionary process, as on Ktaadn's ridge, are now brought to completion. The cosmos is alive and in flux, virtually a living continuum in which the higher is an elaborated or articulated arrangement of the lower. This is a bold step toward resolving the paradox of Ktaadn, and Thoreau accomplishes it in part by metaphorically extending the melting sandbank to the human body.

When the sun withdraws the sand ceases to flow, but in the morning the streams will start once more and branch and branch again into a myriad of others. You here see perchance how blood vessels are formed. . . . In the silicious matter which the water deposits is perhaps the bony system, and in the still finer soil and organic matter the fleshy fibre or cellular tissue. *What is a man but a mass of thawing clay?* The ball of the human finger is but a drop congealed. The fingers and toes flow to their extent from the thawing mass of the body. . . . Is not the hand a spreading *palm* leaf with its lobes and veins? . . . The nose is a manifest congealed drop or stalactite. The chin is still a larger drop, the confluent dripping of the face.[72]

The fundamental weakness of metaphor and analogy, of course, is dis-analogy. "This" can never be exactly like "that" in all regards without undercutting the essentially inductive logic of analogy. If an *x* is identical in all regards with a *y*, then logically they are both *x*, an empty identity rather than analogy. A Thoreauvian dissertation on fetal development, for example, is sure to fail, since he seeks meaningful comparisons grounded in immediate experience rather than scientific explanations based on theory. Thoreau knew this, clearly acknowledging the fanciful nature—viewed from a physiological perspective—of his fable. Indeed, he is playing with words, as the many puns reveal; there is no literal assertion that any particular person is a mass of thawing clay. Thoreau's point is that evolution is pervasive, and not only within the inorganic realm. The organic evolves from the inorganic, and evolution continues within the organic realm, a process including the human animal, however unclear the sequencing.

What Champollion will decipher this hieroglyphic for us [Darwin's *Origin of Species* was published in 1859, some five years after *Walden*], that we may turn over a new leaf at last? This phenomenon is more exhilarating to me than the luxuriance and fertility of vineyards. True, it is somewhat excrementious in its character, and there is no end to heaps of liver lights and bowels, as if the globe were turned wrong side outward; this suggests at least that Nature has some bowels [a Thoreauvian arrow aimed at the heart of Emerson's "Nature"], and there again is mother of humanity. . . . [The melting sandbank] convinces me that Earth is still in her swaddling clothes, and stretches forth baby fingers on every side. Fresh curls spring from the baldest brow. There is nothing inorganic. These foliaceous heaps lie along the bank like the slag of a furnace, showing that Nature is "in full blast" within. The earth is not a mere fragment of dead history, . . . but living poetry like the leaves of a tree, which precede flowers and fruit,—not a fossil earth, but a living earth; compared with whose great central life all animal and vegetable life is merely parasitic. . . . You may melt your metals and cast them into the most beautiful moulds you can; they will never excite me like the forms which this molten earth flows out into. *And not only it, but the institutions upon it, are plastic like clay in the hands of the potter.*[73]

The implications are profound. Thoreau's discovery of fundamental evolutionary principles is the mark of genius. Not until the later nineteenth century, with Charles Sanders Peirce and William James, was America to produce thinkers who so clearly understood Heraclitean metaphysics and cosmology. And Peirce and James, of course, are post-Darwinian figures: Thoreau is on the cutting edge of evolutionary thought.[74]

Walden did not offer Thoreau opportunity to pursue his evolutionary insights, and thus we come to "Walking," his great evolutionary essay, best read as applying and extending the insights gained at Walden Pond to culture and knowledge. Some consider "Walking," along with "Life without Principle," the best overview of Thoreau's philosophy. "Walking" is undoubtedly the finest short statement of his idea of wilderness. "I wish to speak a word for Nature," Thoreau begins, "for absolute freedom and wildness, as contrasted with a freedom and culture merely civil,— to regard man as an inhabitant, or a part and parcel of Nature, rather than a member of society." This is necessary, he believes, because most human beings are alienated from nature. "Here is this vast, savage, howling mother of ours, Nature, lying all around, with such beauty, and such affection for her children, as the leopard; and yet we are so early weaned from her breast to society, to that culture which is exclusively an interaction of man on man,—a sort of breeding in and in, which produces at most a merely English nobility, a civilization destined to have a speedy limit."[75] Therein lies the role of walking. By removing the individual from the social cocoon such excursions enable immediate and potentially liberating encounters with wild nature.

Walking is no mere exercise, Thoreau cautions, "nothing in it akin to taking exercise . . . but is itself the enterprise and adventure of the day. If you would get exercise, go in search of the springs of life." Further, walkers must prepare themselves for the adventure, essentially by clearing the mind, forgetting the conventional wisdom, the din of parlors, thoughts of work. "What business have I in the woods, if I am thinking of something out of the woods?" So prepared, the walker need merely follow nature's "subtle magnetism . . . which, if we unconsciously yield to it, will direct us aright." Humans beings are like the needle of a compass, and nature would direct them westward. "It is hard for me to believe that I shall find fair landscapes or sufficient wildness and freedom behind the eastern horizon." Thoreau's metaphor is easily misunderstood; wilderness, for example, lies east of Los Angeles and north of San Francisco. But the West for Thoreau is the wild, as contrasted to the settlements along the eastern seaboard, Boston and New York, which he had known as either student or erstwhile

American scholar. The East symbolizes tradition, a cultural shell encasing and restraining life, and the West represents creativity and freedom, the palpable essence of life. "We go eastward to realize history and study the works of art and literature, retracing the steps of the race; we go westward as into the future, with a spirit of enterprise and adventure."[76]

Beyond freedom for the individual, and its increase through walking, the essay extends Thoreau's evolutionary insights to culture itself. "The West of which I speak is but another name for the Wild; and what I have been preparing to say is, that *in Wildness is the preservation of the World*."[77] *Walden* focuses on the evolution of the organic from the inorganic; "Walking" applies the same evolutionary principle to culture. Society, being a collectivity of individuals, is endangered when wilderness is destroyed, thereby stultifying its potential to revivify culture. Thoreau believes that the essence of freedom resides not in culture but in nature, and the closer human beings live to nature, the more likely they are to realize their freedom. Moreover, and crucially, society more often hinders than aids the actualization of freedom—the ephemeral and contingent (a monetary economy), the artificial (conventional morality), and the trivial (money), supplanting the permanent and necessary (nature's economy), the natural (joy), and the essential (higher laws).

Walking is a path to freedom, an organic activity that redirects humankind's attention to the natural, organic, and essential. Thoreau's insight is astute, however imperfect the idea of "wildness" might be in conveying the essential notion that *cultural forms,* just as inorganic and organic ones, *must evolve in response to changing circumstance.* His essential insight is that the same evolutionary process that underpins life also nourishes the individual and that the creative (novel) individual is in turn necessary to sustain cultural evolution.

> My spirits infallibly rise in proportion to outward dreariness. Give me the ocean, the desert, or the wilderness! . . . When I would recreate myself, I seek the darkest wood, the thickest and most interminable and, to the citizen, most dismal swamp. I enter a swamp as a sacred place, a *sanctum sanctorum.* There is the strength, the marrow, of Nature. The wildwood covers the virgin mould, and the same soil is good for men and for trees. . . . In such a soil grew Homer and Confucius and the rest, and out of such a wilderness comes the Reformer eating locusts and wild honey.

Here is Emerson's American Scholar, transformed from a ministerial or professorial role into a seeker of Indian wisdom. Evolution moves the cosmos, and when its renewing potentials are thwarted, both the individual and culture are endangered. "The civilized nations—Greece, Rome, England—have been sustained by the primitive forests which anciently rotted where they stand. They survive as long as the soil is not exhausted. Alas for human culture! little is to be expected of a nation, when the vegetable mould is exhausted, and it is compelled to make manure of the bones of its fathers."[78]

"Walking" also advances Thoreau's project of developing an evolutionary epistemology, or naturalistic theory of knowledge true to the precepts of a seeker of Indian wisdom rather than those of a scientist or philosopher. He reinforces the idea that the value of wilderness experience is its unconventionality, since the meaning of a wilderness excursion can neither be defined in conventional terms nor have its meaning appropriated by the market. Furthermore, insight into the essentials of existence is irreducible to any kind of Emersonian transcendentalism or scientific law. Every walker can achieve an authentic, inherently creative relationship, with nature. "Beautiful knowledge," surely a deliberate juxtaposition of terms, is the outcome. "We have heard of a Society for the Diffusion of Useful Knowledge. It is said that knowledge is power, and the like. Methinks there is equal need of a Society for the Diffusion of Useful Ignorance, what we will call Beautiful Knowledge, a knowledge useful in a higher sense: for what is most of our boasted so-called knowledge but a conceit that we know something, which robs us of the advantage of our actual ignorance? What we call knowledge is often our positive ignorance; ignorance our negative knowledge."[79]

How such notions must have rankled the hardworking Yankees of Concord and confirmed their opinion of Thoreau as a slacker, more interested in bird-watching and dreaming than in contributing to the cultural enterprise. These ideas were also stinging barbs directed at the heart of transcendentalism. Little wonder that Emerson ultimately dismissed him as little more than Captain of a Huckleberry Party, for Thoreau challenges all that customarily passes for knowledge.[80] And with brilliant insight "Walking" proposes what is in effect a bracketing of both scientific and philosophic method—an *epoche* as relentless, if not as incisive, as that of twentieth-century phenomenology.

My desire for knowledge is intermittent, but my desire to bathe my head in atmospheres unknown to my feet is perennial and constant. *The highest we can attain to is not Knowledge, but Sympathy with*

Intelligence. I do not know that this higher knowledge amounts to anything more definite than a novel and grand surprise on a sudden revelation of the insufficiency of all that we called Knowledge before,—a discovery that there are more things in heaven and earth than are dreamed of in our philosophy. It is the light up of the mist by the sun. Man cannot *know* in any higher sense than this.[81]

Nonsense, thought the good citizens of Concord, and Emerson as well. The typical New Englander could understand the practical people who came to gather ice from Walden during winter or to catch fish during summer; but to sit contemplating the water as if it were the eye of the earth was something else again. "Sympathy with Intelligence"? The utility of theoretical science, let alone such a philosophical flight of fantasy, was difficult enough for most to grasp. Yet the almost automatic tendency to reject this idea as mere romanticism rather than intuitive insight must be questioned. Thoreau brilliantly weds the implications of evolution with epistemology itself: *knowledge itself evolves, and intuition is fundamental to the process.*[82] Again, we must emphasize that Thoreau is a thinker far ahead of his time in realizing that humankind is enframed by language and history. Walking—that is, wilderness excursions taken without preconception—was one way to rediscover the mythic point of origin.

The nineteenth century is rightly called Darwin's century. But Thoreau's anticipations of things to come are remarkable. "Walking" forcefully advances the premise that no culture achieves perfect form, being only one variation in a never-ending sequence. A culture cannot, Thoreau knew, simply live in the fashion of the past, since the world is dynamic, and the very definition of life is the ability to respond to a changing environment. "Life consists with wildness. The most alive is the wildest."[83] Emerson never understood that the societal road into the future is tied to the organic realm and that the path of advance must be in harmony with nature. For Emerson the categories of the Enlightenment and Judeo-Christianity, buttressed by transcendental argument, were adequate for cultural reformation. Progress was to his mind a law of nature. Tied to the city (his pulpit, lectern, or desk), Emerson never experienced a fundamental kinship with the organic realm, its seasons, its landscapes, and its myriad plants and animals. In contrast, by reflecting upon his wealth of experience, by seeking an original relation with the universe, Thoreau confirmed that species Homo sapiens is part of the evolutionary flux—material and biological. From our modern vantage point, his notion that in "wildness lies salvation of the world" is perhaps an imperfect reflection of the evolutionary nature of life. Nonetheless, his insight is essentially accurate: culture evolves or dies.

Walden and "Walking" form the heart of Thoreau's wilderness philosophy, outlining both the critical—his pervasive critique of Modernism and conventional wisdom, be this common sense or New England transcendentalism—and the positive—his evolutionary insight and recognition of the pervasive continuities between the human and the natural—sides of his thought. But we would be remiss not to discuss briefly at least three additional works: "Life without Principle," *Cape Cod*, and the *Journal*.

"Life without Principle" is, in the opinion of Krutch, Thoreau's "most important and the most influential" shorter essay, an "unqualified statement of his defiant individualism and his plea for the individual's right to march to the sound of his own drum." [84] For all its brilliance, "Life without Principle" does not add much to the idea of wilderness found in other works. The essay contains little of the striking nature writing found elsewhere and is as abstract as anything Thoreau ever wrote. And its themes are not originations but continuations, with many parallels to and isomorphisms with *Walden* and "Walking." The essay is perhaps best understood as a synopsis or gloss of the critique of Modernism found in *Walden*, especially the chapter "Economy," now organized into a format suitable for a listening rather than a reading audience. His point is the familiar one that when humankind rediscovers its primordial grounding in the natural world, then life might be set aright. "Life without Principle" also contains at least a hint of pessimism, recognizing that the opinions that wealth was the highest value and that working for a living was the most important human activity dominated the world. Thoreau writes, "There are those who style themselves statesmen and philosophers who are so blind as to think that progress and civilization depend on precisely this kind of [economic] interchange and activity—the activity of flies about a molasses-hogshead." [85]

Cape Cod was published posthumously in 1864 (edited by Thoreau's sister Sophia and his best friend, Ellery Channing). The book, a collection of ten essays covering his three trips to the cape, lacks the profundity and craftsmanship of *Walden* and the incisive evolutionary insights of "Walking" but deserves more attention than it is accorded. Of the critics, only Paul Theroux has been lavish in praise. Walter Harding calls it Thoreau's sunniest but least profound book. [86] Yet only *Maine Woods* gives one as clear a sense of Thoreau's ability to grasp a place, the nuances of life and vegetation, and the interactions between humankind and the environment. *Cape Cod* captures the effect of ocean and beach, wind and tides, on the people who lived there. And, like *Walden,* the encounters with nature, such as observing the rotting bodies of shipwrecked animals washed up on shore, provide grist for contemplation. While beachcombing Thoreau would ponder the waves and tides, and the vast expanse of water, fading off yet ultimately washing onto distant shores, and observe the diverse flora and fauna that comprise the Cape Cod community. "There is naked Nature, inhumanly sincere, wasting no thought on man, nibbling at the cliffy shore where gulls wheel amid the spray." Thoreau was fascinated by the depths and floor of the ocean, hidden beneath the surface, and characteristically drew parallels between this aspect of the sea and the human mind. And, crucially, he came to see the ocean as the wildest of all wildernesses.

> I think that [the sea] . . . was never more wild than now. We do not associate the idea of antiquity with the ocean, nor wonder how it looked a thousand years ago, as we do of the land, for it was equally wild and unfathomable always. . . . The ocean is a wilderness reaching round the globe, wilder than a Bengal jungle, and fuller of monsters, washing the very wharves of our cities and the gardens of our sea-side residences. . . . Ladies who never walk in the woods, sail over the sea. To go to sea! Why, it is to have the experience of Noah,—to realize the deluge. Every vessel is an ark.[87]

No reading of Thoreau's texts could be complete without some mention of the *Journal.* It offers an unequaled record of thought and intuition, of human encounter with wilderness. Not published until 1906, the *Journal* has long been popular with serious amateur and professional natural historians. Thoreau's eye for detail in nature is rivaled only by his eye for humanity; anthropologists find the *Journal* a treasure of information about nineteenth-century ways of life. Meteorologists turn to them to glean a picture of nineteenth-century weather. And botanists recognize Thoreau as the American equivalent of Gilbert White of Selborne; in the later years the *Journal* presents increasingly detailed descriptions of plant and animal species, the seasons and cycles of nature, and the interrelations between them. John Dolan suggests that "the connection between Thoreau's absorption in the rich world of living plants, in particular, the plants of Concord, and his creative growth as an artist and thinker is quite intimate."[88] Thoreau himself notes, anticipating a biocentric perspective, that "I am interested in each contemporary plant in my vicinity, and have attained to a certain acquaintance with the larger ones. They are *cohabitants with me of this part of the planet,* and they bear familiar names. Yet how essentially wild they are! as wild, really, as those strange fossil plants whose impressions I see on my coal." [89] The *Journal* also contains an explicit statement of the ideal of creating national parks. The wilderness traveler

> merely has the privilege of crossing somebody's farm by a particular narrow and maybe unpleasant path. The individual [property owner] retains all other rights,—as to trees and fruit, and wash of the road, etc. On the other hand, these should belong to mankind inalienably. The road should be of ample width and adorned with tress expressly for the use of the traveller. There should be broad recesses in it, especially at springs and watering-places, where he can turn out and rest, or camp if he will. I feel commonly as if I were condemned to drive through somebody's cowyard or huckleberry pasture by a narrow lane, and if I make a fire by the roadside to boil my hasty pudding, the farmer comes running over to see if I am not burning up his stuff. You are barked along through the country, from door to door. [90]

Thoreau in Cultural Context

Although Thoreau is widely recognized as the greatest American nature writer and one of the world's best, his works are not mere belles lettres of the nature genre. At his best—as in *Walden*—he achieves that rarest kind of writing, the fusion of form and content. *Walden* perhaps rivals Plato's Dialogues in embodying philosophy as an art form. The contrast between Thoreau and Emerson underscores the point. When we compare Emerson's "Nature" and Thoreau's *Walden* the titles themselves speak, "Nature" abstract and general, *Walden* specific and concrete. In "Nature" Emerson writes as a disembodied transcendental spectator who brings with him abstract principles to impose on nature. In *Walden* Thoreau directly engages his subject, becoming its living manifestation. *Walden* exemplifies both the life he lived and the philosophical principles he discovered. He becomes a man of Indian wisdom, a person-in-contact with wild nature, with the Great Mother. His genius is not that he turned his back on civilization—Thoreau is no hermit, no misanthrope—but that he affirms the reality of organic process and the vital importance of understanding that humankind, too, is part of this larger, enframing realm—life within nature. Thoreau is a natural classicist who argues that humankind is wild nature grown self-conscious and that creativity—that is, evolutionary response to changing cultural circumstances—depends essentially on systematically acting upon this insight: in wildness lies the preservation of the world.

Given Thoreau's now evident genius, the case might be made that he, not Emerson, is the culmination of the mid-nineteenth-century American Renaissance. Thoreau formulates a rich philosophy that scarcely resembles the abstract, sterile theorizing of Emerson. He senses both the insufficiencies of his age and the path beyond; he is acutely conscious of the limitations of the scientific worldview; and his insights into nineteenth-century Yankee society are as penetrating as Marx's on European capitalism and more relevant to American culture. His intuitive grasp of the evolutionary character of the cosmos, and the intertwining of matter, life, and consciousness in the human animal, has been vindicated, first by Darwin and later by ethology, human ecology, cultural anthropology, and cultural geography. Thoreau in many ways anticipates the two great American philosophers of the later nineteenth century, Charles Sanders Peirce and William James. All share a common pragmatic interest in knowledge, an evolutionary viewpoint, and a belief that creativity is essential to survival.

Thoreau's idea of wilderness remains as vital today as when he wrote. In 1861, near the end of his life, Thoreau wrote that most people "do not care for Nature and would sell their share in all her beauty, as long as they may live, for a stated sum—many for a glass of rum. Thank God, men cannot as yet fly, and lay waste the sky as well as the earth! We are safe on that side for the present. It is for the very reason that some do not care for those things that we need to continue to protect all from the vandalism of a few."[91] Thoreau's ideas and example clearly influenced such essential wilderness thinkers as John Muir and Aldo Leopold. Indeed, the Thoreauvian spirit animates the cutting edge of contemporary critiques of Modernism, be it critical economics, ecocentric philosophy, or boldly visionary views of alternative human futures. This fact puts us in a position to understand the reflexive implications of Thoreau's work better than his coevals. The conventional wisdom that Thoreau is of little more than literary interest, and that his philosophy is little more than an application of Emersonian transcendentalism, must be reconsidered. It is no exaggeration to say that today all thought of the wilderness flows in *Walden*'s wake.

CHAPTER SIX

John Muir
Wilderness Sage

If there is such a thing as an awakening, Muir's eyes were opened by the mountains in the early seventies. His journals and letters from Yosemite are filled with references to baptism in light and water. . . . He was living in a sacred world, and as he partook of its reality and being he became a part of a world which was not a chaos, but a cosmos. . . . Like Thoreau, he recognized his sacred spiritual state as opposite to the profane. He was cleansed by being converted from conventional or traditional man back into natural man. This was what it meant to be awakened. This is what he meant when he wrote to his brother that he had been baptized three times in one day and had "got religion."   —Michael P. Cohen, *The Pathless Way*

POSTERITY HAS TREATED John Muir well, for the richness of his intellectual and institutional legacy continues to grow. In two decades, and especially in the ten years since the Muir archives were opened, the traditional view that he merely reiterated the tired truths of transcendentalism has been abandoned. A case can be made that he stands intellectually with Henry David Thoreau and Aldo Leopold as a thinker whose work yet exerts major influence on contemporary American ideas of wilderness. In instrumental terms, Muir is the father of the American conservation (now preservation) movement; his influence is most visibly manifest in the activities of the Sierra Club, direct contributions to the creation of no fewer than six of America's premier national parks, and the radical amateur tradition in conservation. He is best understood as one of that rare breed whose life unifies *theorie* and *praxis:* an American scholar who not only speculated about but also changed the world.

Inevitably, reinterpretations of men like John Muir (1838–1914) must occur, and in his case the past decade has been an unusually fruitful period of reassessment.[1] Yet, in spite of his evident achievements, the intellectual and cultural significance of his life and thought is difficult to categorize and comprehend. The established view is that Muir is simply a lesser transcendentalist, dimly mirroring the insights and following the methods of Emerson and Thoreau. He has also been interpreted as a Romantic, as a primitivist, and as one whose primary contribution to American culture was the popularization of wilderness philosophy. In short, Muir is often seen as *merely* bringing the idea of wilderness to public attention rather than contributing to its evolution. Justification for interpreting him as a "publicizer" rests in the popularity and influence of his writings, which converted countless Americans to the conservation cause. But to think of him as a nineteenth-century public relations person for conservation is to miss the philosophical meaning of his idea of wilderness.[2] Muir's journal and published works from 1867 on confirm his dismantlement of a Judeo-Christian–based anthropocentrism and an unmistakably clear grasp of a biocentric perspective on wild nature. His writings separate his wilderness philosophy from New England transcendentalism and include dimensions even Thoreau's idea of wilderness did not attain.[3] Furthermore, his wilderness theology—a profoundly insightful evolutionary pantheism— is a complementary development that revivifies an archaic sense of the sacrality of all being.

At least three problems deny ready passage to understanding Muir's idea of wilderness, however. One is that he wrote voluminously, more as a naturalistic essayist in the tradition of Gilbert White than as a systematic philosopher. Although there are passages of philosophical prose in his writings, he is not one to push an argument. One of his contemporary biographers candidly states that his forte is not "philosophical argument; he tends to make discrete statements, a series of insights and apercus, that pile up but don't really build a case. I often find myself wishing he would go into some point more deeply, instead of skipping past it."[4] As a result, Muir's insights must be sifted out line by line, since nowhere is there a complete gathering of his philosophical writing. Even then, any assertion of a systematic bent or conceptual center in the collection faces a formidable challenge.[5] To claim that Muir advances a biocentric idea of wilderness is thus to take on the burden of proof. Yet throughout his work we find a relentless questioning of the anthropocentric viewpoint on nature— the stance of the modernist, designated by Muir as Lord Man—and a continual affirmation of a biocentric perspective, where the human being has become an empathetic part of rather than scientific observer apart from nature.

As Richard Rorty explains, the aim of edifying philosophers "is always the same—to perform the social function which Dewey called 'breaking the crust of convention.' " In his wilderness philosophy, as his recent biographers unanimously agree, Muir challenges the prevailing sociocultural paradigm: Modernism, the paradigm that reduces nature to matter-in-mechanical-motion and sees in the wilderness only a challenge to the imposition of human values. So viewed, Muir's idea of wilderness presents an alternative view of humankind's relation to nonhuman others. Edifying philosophy is a protest, a reaction "against attempts to close off conversation by proposals for universal commensuration through hypostatization of some privileged set of descriptions."[6] Muir breaks with the Cartesian-Newtonian paradigm and advances a rival idea of nature-as-an-organism that in many ways resembles earlier ideas of nature that rose in critical response to Modernism. In striving to achieve an empathetic relation with nature, and in viewing it as alive, Muir's idea of wilderness has a clear affinity with the Paleolithic mind. In other words, Muir's idea of wilderness is incommensurable with the idea of nature-as-a-machine.

A second problem is that Muir's nature vocabulary appears to be more theological than philosophical. Some passages in his texts give the appearance of being a popularized but orthodox version of physico-theology, where proof of God's eternal and transcendent existence is found in the beauty and design of nature. One early biographer observes that his "love of nature was so largely a part of his religion that he naturally chose Biblical phraseology when he sought a vehicle for his feelings. No prophet of old could have taken his call more seriously, or have entered upon his mission more fervently."[7] Yet Muir's use of biblical phraseology illuminates his deepest thoughts, for the substrate of his psyche was grounded in the rigorous biblical instruction he received as a child. As Northrop Frye suggests, such socialization, apart from any religious value per se, provides, an "imaginative survey of the human situation which is so broad and comprehensive that everything else finds its place inside it."[8] Recent biographies confirm that Muir's idea of wilderness would likely be cast in a religious rather than a philosophical or scientific vocabulary. Although his writings abound with scriptural allusions and metaphors, his seemingly orthodox religious vocabulary does not carry traditional Judeo-Christian presuppositions with it.[9] In his late twenties, Muir underwent a religious conversion in the wilderness, a hierophany that suffused nature with sacrality and underlay the conceptualization of his mission. Animated by this epiphany, he achieves a level of cosmological sophistication that few have noticed, mistaking his biblical metaphors as an expression of either conventional religious sentiment or transcendentalism. Michael Cohen, however, catches the essence of Muir's religious language, observing that his "was a wild and true voice which revealed the most radical, that is to say the most essential and deeply rooted Muir, pantheistic, ecstatic, and possessed by the cosmic vision."[10]

Finally, Muir's original ideas are sometimes overlooked because he wore so many hats. Known well as a wilderness trekker, scientific observer, prolific and popular writer, and passionate conservationist, he is not often considered from a philosophical perspective. Yet that Muir attempts to comprehend the cosmic context—the entirety of the world, the things in the world, and the relations among them—creates a third problem in understanding his wilderness philosophy. While we live in an age of specialization, his intellectual reach was immense. Accordingly, philosophical interpretation presents a trying task since he knew not only science but politics, not only the wilderness but human ways. One mark of intuitive geniuses is that, in climbing to the top of the mountain, they can share that vantage point with ordinary men and women. John Muir not only climbed mountains, but he was able to communicate at least part of the importance of what he contemplated to the public; his writing achieved almost immediate popular acclaim. Educated Americans of the later nineteenth century were ready to read about the wilderness, mountain vistas, and giant sequoias, perhaps motivated by some lingering sense of what had been lost within the course of their own lifetimes. So, in spite of his lack of recognition as a fundamental thinker, we find in his work the very "underpinning of granitic truth," to use Thoreau's phrase, for a comprehensive wilderness philosophy.

Roots of a Wilderness Sage

The seeds of Muir's passionate lifelong attachment to the wilderness were planted in his childhood. Nature in any guise was a vital source of solace throughout his life, and especially during his youth. Escaping the routines of the farm, John would revel in the wild plants, animals, and vistas of the Wisconsin countryside. Flocks of migrating waterfowl set his mind wandering; bugs and tadpoles, trees and plants, virtually any life-form, were of equal interest to him. By retreating alone into wild nature the harsh, even perverse treatment experienced in human company literally vanished. The contrast of the peace and beauty experienced in nature with the conflict and abuse imposed by his father—in the name of God— cannot have failed to have had a deep, albeit unmeasurable, influence on the adult Muir. Frederick Turner argues that Muir's "experiences with the natural world of his Scots childhood had given him a kind of psychic and spiritual base, and in his early years at Fountain Lake he had drawn sustenance from this during the apparently endless days of his servitude until the kinship he felt for nature had deepened into a genuine need." [11]

In his twenties, after leaving the University of Wisconsin, he lived for a time in Canada, exploring the Canadian shores of Lakes Huron and Ontario. Here the countryside presented opportunities for extended sojourns into areas devoid of humankind. On one such trek Muir experienced an epiphany, collapsing into tears over the sight of an exquisite flower *(Calypso borealis)*. "So unexpected was it," Turner writes, "and so surpassing its beauty here in the monochromatic swamp that Muir sat down beside it and wept. In the very center of his loneliness, here was this joyful beauty, fully at home." A skeptic might interpret such an episode as a result of fatigue or anxiety or as a meaningless outbreak of emotion. Yet this experience might also be seen as hierophany, as a religious experience occurring during a solitary wilderness encounter.[12] This flower-engendered epiphany was not the only time wild nature provided a psychological catalyst for Muir, confirming for him the unity of self with cosmos. In letters to his sisters and to Jeanne Carr he observes that he took "more intense delight from reading the power and *goodness* of God from 'the things which are made' than from the Bible. The two books, however, harmonize beautifully, and contain enough of divine truth for the study of all eternity." [13] Increasingly, Muir turned to nature rather than the Bible; but as Cohen points out, he thought of nature as a book, the Book of Nature, and he "read it largely as an early nineteenth-century scientist might, with the assurance that it was a sacred book." [14]

In the eyes of his father and all religious fundamentalists young Muir was on the path to spiritual ruin, since to them the wilderness was an abhorrent and evil place. From our vantage point he was verging on recognition of the sacrality of all existence. So viewed, Muir's Canadian epiphany was important in determining, both practically and intellectually, the course of his life. His breakdown on seeing the solitary *Calypso borealis* was not an index of fatigue or neurosis but a religious experience, a sign of psychic development, of self *imaginatively* becoming one with cosmos. Only many years later was this process completed, springing forth into a full-blown wilderness theology—a remarkable post-Darwinian pantheism. But through his epiphany in the Canadian wilderness, divinity and its pervading sacrality—now free of the strictures of society—were manifest for him in nature. Muir now recognized nature as a reality that enframed and transcended all being, including himself.[15]

At this time it cannot be fairly said that Muir was a pantheist. Though the customary Judeo-Christian view of wild nature, and of God's relation to creation, was becoming increasingly untenable, the God that he conceptualized was still transcendent and apart from creation. Arguably, he was now passing from an orthodox theism through a panentheistic zone of transition toward pantheism. Muir's new idea of God as manifest in nature helped him reconcile his developing sense of self with the streams of past influence: his religious indoctrination in supernaturalism and his love of the wilderness. By equating God with nature, Muir served the motive for metaphor—that is, the human desire to identify with the world of which we are a part—and reconciled these divergent streams of influence: supernatural and natural. Perhaps he had also intuitively realized John Dewey's explicit objection to supernaturalism as standing "in the way of an effective realization of the sweep and depth of the implications of natural human relations."[16]

Interestingly, and perhaps crucially, Muir never became an atheist, never explicitly rejected the Calvinistic theology of his youth. He simply outgrew the constrictions of conventional faith and developed a theology of the wilderness. By 1868, at age thirty, he had undergone what is best described as a religious conversion experience, and this transformed his view of nature and virtually everything else. After his conversion Muir's life was marked by a sense of mission. He became a "mountaineer," part sauntering scientist (geologist and botanist) and part wilderness theologian. Muir ultimately found God and celebrated the divine presence in the wilderness; the churches in town were part of civilization and all its torments. He abandoned the anthropocentric theology of Calvinism, replacing it with a biocentric wilderness theology rooted in a consciousness of the sacrality of wild nature. In his life "he was led from mystery to mystery with a deepening, widening religious awe, one that went far beyond the confines of conventional Christian practice. There would always be a certain amount of orthodox baggage that he carried within him . . . . But it would become lighter and lighter over the years so that in his late years some would call him a mystic or pantheist."[17] Nature became his temple. He wrote, "The clearest way into the Universe is through a forest wilderness."[18] And as with Thoreau, intuition was his principal avenue of access to the truths of wild nature; his idea of wilderness grew through later reflection on these immediate encounters.[19]

Muir was atavistic, a specimen as exotic as an aborigine walking the streets of New York City, a throwback to the Paleolithic mind. The visible details of his life tend to obscure the remarkable character of the man and his experiences—a life in which so many variables interrelated in such an unpredictable way that, in retrospect, he appears almost as a hero in a Thomas Hardy novel. In the final analysis one must say that John Muir lived to experience the wilderness, to seek that Thoreauvian "Sympathy with Intelligence" that is the greatest end to which some people aspire. If anyone lived and thought according to the credo of Thoreau's masterful essay "Walking," John Muir did.[20] For Muir "home," in the most fundamental sense of the word, became the wilderness. Civilization, rather than defining the locus of human beingness, was something to be tolerated, not celebrated. He wrote that "going to the woods is going home; for I suppose we came from the woods originally."[21] Crucially, Muir recognized that whatever humankind might be, one's essential human beingness could be known only in relation to the nonhuman other. Thus Muir's mature idea of wilderness eradicated the ontological boundaries drawn between wilderness and civilization. The flowing whole of nature was the ultimate reality, the process in which life and death (and all other human conceptualizations) were merely part of everything else.

> Contemplating the lace-like fabric of streams outspread over the mountains, we are reminded that everything is flowing—going somewhere, animals and so-called lifeless rocks as well as water. . . . Rocks flow from volcanoes like water from springs, and animals flock together and flow in currents modified by stepping, leaping, gliding, flying, swimming, etc. While the stars go streaming through space pulsed on and on forever like blood globules in Nature's warm heart.[22]

John Muir and Emersonian Transcendentalism

The longstanding scholarly view of Muir as transcendentalist is rooted in the assumption—not grounded in Muir's writings—that his idea of wilderness mirrors an Emersonian perspective. Transcendental philosophy did influence Muir. As Muir read the writings of Emerson and Thoreau at the University of Wisconsin, the theocratic paradigm of his father faced an intellectual challenge beyond the felt insufficiencies of childhood. Although his university experiences helped prompt the kind of intellectual reevaluations that many students experience on leaving home and parents, by no stretch of the imagination can even the Muir of his university years be thought of as above all a transcendentalist. The fabric of his early intellectual life was woven of many threads; among these sources might be included the Bible, Milton, Shakespeare, and the Romantics more generally, as well as the thinking of various members of the scientific community who were moving toward an evolutionary view of not only the earth but the cosmos. Muir's thinking, his worldview, was already in process before he encountered New England transcendentalism.

Emerson's ideas provided psychological support for a young man who, like Thoreau before him, was out of step with materialism and everyday American culture. But there was no Copernican revolution, no sudden conversion to Emersonian transcendentalism. Muir's idea of wilderness is closer to Thoreau than to Emerson. As Michael Cohen argues, although a transcendental tradition "flowed from Emerson to Thoreau and Muir, neither of the younger men were strict followers of Emerson. If the self they began to discover was suggested in Emerson's essays, both men found in practice that they had to entrust themselves to Nature far more than Emerson did. The old sage had argued that Nature was the first influence upon the mind of Man, but for Muir Nature became the alpha and omega of life. And so he parted with his teacher when he realized that he would be more faithful to the primary influences on his life."[23] Others have argued that Muir's wilderness philosophy differs in several ways even from that of Thoreau. George Sessions contends that Muir "overcame the subjectivism of Transcendentalism to a much greater extent than did Thoreau."[24] However this may be, the basic issue is whether Muir is to be understood as either an epigone of Emerson and the school of New England transcendentalism or as a fundamental, independent contributor to the idea of wilderness. If the former, then students of the idea of wilderness need read Muir merely to find concrete illustrations of the philosophical principles set forth in Emerson's essay "Nature." So viewed, Muir's writing is reduced to a mere exemplification, through concrete description, of the universal forms described by Emerson. In fact, the record shows that although Muir admired "Nature," he disagreed with much that Emerson claimed, and in any case went fundamentally beyond the shallow idealism of Emerson vis-à-vis wild nature.[25]

In chapter 5 I attempted to show through textual example that Emerson's nature philosophy, though he insisted on the importance of immediate, individual encounter, is rooted in an abstract idealism where wild nature is reduced to a mirror of the human mind, thereby facilitating the discovery of Absolute Spirit or God. "Nature" is Emerson's working out of this part philosophical, part theological position. A more representative title for "Nature" would have been "The Discovery of God through the Human Use of Nature," since Emerson interprets nature against a traditional religious and anthropocentric backdrop of human purpose and meaning. George Santayana suggests the difference between the genteel tradition and a thinker such as Muir in the following paragraph.

> A Californian whom I had recently the pleasure of meeting observed that if the philosophers had lived among your mountains, their systems would have been different from what they are. Certainly very different from what those systems are which the European genteel tradition has handed down since Socrates; for these systems are egotistical; directly or indirectly they are anthropocentric, and inspired by the conceited notion that man, or human reason, or the human distinction between good and evil, is the center and pivot of the universe. That is what the mountains and the woods should make you at last ashamed to assert.[26]

In contrast to Emerson, the mature Muir does not approach nature with an established belief in a transcendent God and then find in nature's beautiful panoply confirmation of that belief. Rather, he actually finds divinity in wild nature. Understandably, since his writings are suffused with passages that attribute nature's beauty to God's glorious handiwork, and even confirm God's existence through encounter with wild nature, he may appear merely to be reiterating Emersonian notions.[27] But this is not the case; Muir achieves an original relation to the universe to which "Nature" alludes. In effect, Muir becomes Homo religiosus, whereas Emerson simply substitutes transcendentalism for a conventional religious orientation based on Scripture.[28] For Emerson the ultimate outcome of encounter with nature—confirmation of God's existence—is virtually the same as biblically based faith, except that it is intellectually more justifiable since the conclusion appears as consequence of philosophical argument rather than religious conditioning, and is psychologically more convincing since faith rests on transcendental reason rather than the Bible. But nature has been reduced to epiphenomenon, mere phenomenal surrogate for God, confirming the glory of the human soul that can comprehend such a marvelous truth.

A second fundamental difference between Emerson and Muir is that the New Englander always remains a theist. In contrast, through his original relation to the universe Muir experienced a religious conversion that led him to realize the sacrality of wild nature. The traditional anthropocentric God of Judeo-Christianity—the God of Daniel Muir and Ralph Waldo Emerson, who privileges humans above all other elements of creation—is metaphysically transformed from an eternal and transcendent creator (theism) into a temporal, immanent, and continuing process of divine creation (pantheism). This God incarnate suffuses the natural world, a world still in process; wild nature is ensouled, and no aspect of creation is privileged over any other, for all is sacred. Muir, of course, did not arrive at his wilderness theology all at once; but a close reading of his journal and published works confirms the progression of his thought toward an evolutionary pantheism.

Unquestionably, Muir revered Emerson and benefited by reading his work. He apparently believed that Emerson had a better way of explaining God's relation to creation. Not satisfied with his own exposition of this relation, Muir greatly anticipated Emerson's visit to the Sierras in 1871. "I had read his essays, and felt sure that of all men he would best interpret the sayings of these noble mountains and trees. Nor was my faith weakened when I met him in Yosemite. He seemed as serene as a sequoia, his head in the empyrean." This is strong praise, but Muir was to be disappointed; Emerson was not allowed to accompany him on an extended backwoods excursion. "His party, full of indoor philosophy, failed to see the natural beauty and fullness of promise of my wild plan, and laughed at it in good-natured ignorance, as if it were necessarily amusing to imagine that Boston people might be led to accept Sierra manifestations of God at the price of rough camping." The Bostonian attitude gave Muir second thoughts about the transcendental school that surrounded Emerson. "And to think of this being a Boston choice! Sad commentary on culture and the glorious transcendentalism." But he remained loyal to Emerson the man, still thinking of him as a friend even though he was disappointed in the visit and with the "glorious transcendentalism": "I quickly took heart again,—the trees had not gone to Boston, nor the birds; and as I sat by the fire, Emerson was still with me in spirit, though I never again saw him in the flesh." [29]

The question of method is also instructive. Muir approaches nature from the standpoint of a radical and intuitive empiricism rather than an abstract idealism. By *directly seeing* God in nature, Muir cuts through the cake of social convention and achieves an immediate felt unity with the web of life. [30] To Muir books are essentially sterile, "at best signal smokes to call attention." His manner of approach was direct encounter without scientific category, religious presupposition, or philosophical method. "One day's exposure to mountains is better than cartloads of books. See how willingly Nature poses herself upon photographer's plates. No earthly chemicals are so sensitive as those of the human soul. All that is required is exposure, and purity of material. 'The pure in heart shall see God!' " [31] The methods of transcendentalism are to Muir just so much encumbering baggage. The qualitative dimensions of experience, which for the modernist are ephemeral, contingent, and merely subjective, are for Muir real and objective characteristics immediately known. The learned treatises of scientist, philosopher, or religionist—which assume the truth and validity of socially defined categories—were themselves subjective. Muir's books, all that he needs, are found in nature. "Reading these grand mountain manuscripts displayed through every vicissitude of heat and cold, calm and storm, upheaving volcanoes and down-grinding glaciers, we see that everything in Nature called destruction must be creation—a change from beauty to beauty."[32] Of course, only the truly awake, the intuitively aware, the "sensitive soul," can read these messages; if there is to be any method then we must silence the mind and thereby bracket *doxa*. "Only by going alone in silence, without baggage, can one truly get into the heart of the wilderness. All other travel is mere dust and hotels and baggage and chatter."[33] Thoreau, not Emerson, is Muir's true kindred spirit.[34]

The Fundamentals of Muir's Wilderness Theology

In marked contrast with Emerson, the mature Muir equates nature with divinity. He is not a transcendentalist but a pantheist who, over the course of a lifetime of intuitive encounter with and subsequent reflection on the wilderness, develops an authentic wilderness theology. The entire world becomes a living and sacred community in which all creatures have purpose in their own right and no species enjoys special privilege. This totality is still in process, a living and glorious manifestation of God incarnate. Muir also abandons any conventional scientific view of nature (mechanistic materialism) and sees in the plants and animals, even the water and rocks, a world of living creatures and spirits that are more than mere matter-in-motion. Therein lie the outlines of his wilderness philosophy and a formidable challenge of exegesis. The development of Muir's idea of wilderness is marked by three moments, beginning with his realization that all of nature is animate, passing through a panentheistic zone of transition, and culminating in a biocentric-pantheistic wilderness paradigm.[35]

Muir's idea of wilderness perhaps pivots on his one-thousand-mile journey to the Gulf of Mexico (1867). He left Indianapolis with fairly orthodox religious beliefs. Embarked on an odyssey of discovery, he was able to resolve intellectually what he must have realized, if only intuitively, as a contradiction from his earliest days in Wisconsin. Muir's Calvinist father had forced him to bend nature to agricultural purpose. How it must have pained Muir to clear and burn the trees and brush, turn the soil, and reduce nature to a mere servant of human purpose. What had provided a home for myriad creatures was reduced to smoke and ash, a diverse biotic community transformed into a biological monoculture that soon depleted the soil.

Set in the context of our study (see above, chapters 1 and 2), the apostasy that Muir struggled to overcome was perhaps grounded in the Neolithic revolution: the age when humankind left Eden. Of course, we run the risk of overstating the importance of the agricultural revolution in determining the course of Western history. Yet surely that change initiated a process of sociocultural transformation that (for many reasons) created an ostensibly absolute divide between civilization and wilderness, between the primitive forager and the sophisticated agriculturist. Christianity can be seen as culminating the rationalization of agriculture, and Daniel Muir personified the Christian outlook on the natural world. No sooner had the first family farm been "won" from nature than Daniel Muir acquired a new property, nearly a half-section of timbered land, and set young John to clearing the forest. The harvest from the first farm had declined through the elder Muir's failure to maintain soil fertility. Yet Daniel Muir was simply living out the practical implications of his theology. Nature to him was primarily a commodity, and he was enervated theologically from feeling anything for wild nature; at stake were his soul and worldly success.[36] Wealth was a clear sign that one was among the elect, predestined for a Heaven above this godforsaken wilderness.

John Muir was nearly thirty when he began to walk from Indianapolis toward the gulf. "My plan," he observed in a fashion reminiscent of Thoreau, "was simply to push on in a general southward direction by the wildest, leafiest, and least trodden way I could find, promising the greatest extent of virgin forest."[37] Like Thoreau's retreat to Walden, Muir left society behind, in search of something vital to life. As he trekked into the wilderness, he dropped traditional interpretations of wild nature by the wayside. He found not only the wilderness, the Cumberland Mountains, myriad plant and animal life-forms, but something else as well: the beginnings of a new way of experiencing wilderness, of perceiving and thinking. He was becoming a radical empiricist, opening his mind to speculative thought and the truths of intuition. Turner explains that Muir's jottings, recorded in the journal of 1867, take on an "aboriginal tone . . . in which the distinctions prevalent in Western civilization between men, plants, and animals begin to be broken down and are replaced with a kind of mystical reverence for all forms of life."[38] This assertion is correct, and yet

Muir's dawning awareness of the animate nature of all creation, and his so-called mystical reverence for life, are two distinct though complementary developments.

The phrase "mystical reverence for life" carries pejorative connotations, implying that the veneration of organic being is independent of reason, grounded only in some intrinsically private feeling that objective thinkers do not experience.[39] Yet paradoxically, respect for the web of life is consistent with present-day biological and ecological knowledge. All organic being is intertwined into a living whole apart from which the existence of any single organism or species is not possible.[40] Muir's appreciation of these facts was revolutionary, far in advance of the conventional wisdom, but speculative rather than mystical is a more accurate appellation. Through *speculative thought* Muir realized that an animistic or organismic viewpoint possessed far greater explanatory possibilities than mechanism. Immediate experience revealed to him that mechanistic materialism —that is, nature viewed from a Cartesian-Newtonian perspective—was an enormous simplification of and abstraction from the reality of the natural world. The animate vitality of nature pervaded the cosmos. And since all of creation was alive rather than inert, it followed that a human being might feel kinship with the natural world: Muir here verged on recovery of the Paleolithic mind. Yet he did not reach this idea in one speculative insight. It was the outcome of a three-stage process (chronology) that was simultaneously psychological and intellectual.

His *A Thousand-Mile Walk to the Gulf*, drawn from his journal of 1867, exemplifies the beginnings of this process. The book does not present a rigorous, ad seriatim account of philosophical analysis but rather reveals a psyche in transition. Throughout his childhood, much like cynegetic or archaic people, Muir had felt wild plants and animals to be kindred spirits, sources of solace, of wonder and adventure. Farming, as Turner suggests, threatened his sense of an affinity with the wilderness. "Placed in an adversarial, exploitative relationship, an unremitting hand-to-hand combat with the land, he began in his adolescent years to imagine some way of being and thinking that would allow him to continue to love that with which he struggled."[41] So framed, the walk was the beginning of Muir's search for meaning, for a path with a heart.[42]

Near the end of his trip he contracted malaria and was bedridden; this protracted period of inactivity permitted him to reflect on his experiences of the previous months, and during his recovery Muir broke through to a clearly defined animistic perspective. On the journey this pattern had been obscured by the vivid details if his adventures. So pervasive was the transformation that he perceived even plants and inorganic matter—in what surely must be seen as an evolutionary insight far in advance of its time—as endowed with spirit. "Plants," he wrote, "are credited with but dim and uncertain sensation, and minerals with positively none at all. But why may not even a mineral arrangement of matter be endowed with sensation of a kind that we in our blind exclusive perfection can have no manner of communication with?"[43]

Virtually all of Muir's later works (beginning in 1868, during his first summer in the Sierras) manifest this animistic vision.[44] After viewing Vernal and Nevada falls in Yosemite he was struck by the impression that "water does not seem to be under the dominion of ordinary [Newton's] laws, but rather as if it were a living creature, full of the strength of the mountains and their huge wild joy."[45] Even glaciers (frozen water) seemed alive and to have a mind of their own. Cohen captures this speculative bent to Muir's thinking; Muir witnessed (at Tuolumne Divide) that "a glacier had flowed *uphill* and over a ridge into Tenaya Canyon. This was a lesson about life. The tops of the mountains flowed into the bottom of heaven, the finite merged with the infinite. The message of an old Zen saying was clear: 'When you get to the top of the mountain, keep on climbing.'"[46] On his trip to Alaska in 1879, after a glorious day's ascent to Glenora peak that concluded a two-hundred-mile trek, Muir felt the spirit of life pervading all creation. "The plant people seemed glad, as if rejoicing with me, the little ones as well as the trees, while every feature of the peak and its traveled boulders seemed to know what I had been about and the depth of my joy, as if they could read faces."[47] And in *Our National Parks,* perhaps his most widely read book, he clearly expressed his animistic vision. "When I entered this sublime wilderness the day was nearly done, the trees with rosy, glowing countenances seemed to be hushed and thoughtful, as if waiting in conscious religious dependence on the sun, and one naturally walked softly and awe-stricken among them. I wandered on, meeting nobler trees where all are noble, subdued in the general calm, as if in some vast hall pervaded by the deepest sanctities and solemnities that sway human souls."[48]

Although the notion of natural entities as animate pervades Muir's 1867 journal, his pantheism and biocentrism developed more slowly. The first apparent movement away from a Judeo-Christian–inspired anthropocentrism began on his walk to the Gulf of Mexico. "The world, we are told, was made especially for man—a presumption not supported by all the facts. A numerous class of men are painfully astonished whenever they find anything, living or dead, in all God's universe, which they cannot eat or render in some way what they call useful to themselves. They have precise dogmatic insight of the intentions of the Creator."[49] This was a radical departure from the conventional wisdom and a logical extension from an animistic perspective. If all of creation was animate, then no absolute distinction of human life from the remainder could be metaphysically legitimate. (Compare this to Emerson's comfortable and traditional viewpoint that distinguishes the human soul from the rest of creation.) Almost simultaneously Muir extended the logic of the position and *began* to develop a biocentric perspective.

> How narrow we selfish, conceited creatures are in our sympathies! how blind to the *rights of all the rest of creation!* With what dismal irreverence we speak of our fellow mortals! Though alligators, snakes, etc., naturally repel us, they are not mysterious evils. They dwell happily in these flowery wilds, are part of God's family, unfallen, undepraved, and cared for with the same species of tenderness and love as is bestowed on angels in heaven or saints on earth.[50]

Yet Muir's wilderness philosophy remained incomplete. He had rejected orthodox Christian theology and its accompanying anthropocentrism but had not yet experienced the religious conversion that allowed him to see wild nature as itself divine.[51] The Muir of *A Thousand-Mile Walk* is best understood as a *panentheist* rather than *pantheist,* for he yet held God's essence apart from wild nature. Charles Hartshorne explains that "if 'pantheism' is a historically and etymologically appropriate term for the view that deity is the all of relative or interdependent items, with nothing wholly independent or in any clear sense nonrelative, than 'panentheism' is an appropriate term for the view that deity is in some real aspect distinguishable from and independent of any and all relative items, and yet, taken as an actual whole, includes all relative items."[52] This distinction helps us understand the evolution of Muir's wilderness theology. The philosophically pivotal section of *A Thousand-Mile Walk* occurs at the end of Muir's recovery from malaria. A lengthy entry for October 15—"a great wild day" he spent wandering among the palmetto—confirms the thoroughgoing nature of his animistic vision, and his conviction that orthodox Christianity was both selfish and narrow-minded. He knew that the conventional wisdom was "that plants are perishable, soulless creatures, that only man is immortal, etc.; but this, I think, is something that we know very nearly nothing about. Anyhow, this palm was indescribably impressive and told me grander things than I ever got from human priest." Muir now explicitly recognized that all creatures were as alive as he and that they spoke a language more truthful than the priest, for the cleric in any guise viewed the world of nature in an orthodox way. All nature will fable, Thoreau reminds us, if we but let it. Muir did.

I am now in the hot gardens of the sun, where the palm meets the pine, *longed and prayed for and often visited in dreams,* and, though lonely to-night amid this multitude of strangers, strange plants, strange winds blowing gently, *whispering, cooing, in a language I never learned,* and strange birds also, everything solid or spiritual full of influences that *I never before felt,* yet I thank the Lord with all my heart for his goodness in granting me admission to this magnificent realm.[53]

But Muir remains at this juncture a panentheist, for he thought of God's essence as apart from creation and prayed to this God for revelation. In this regard his view paralleled Emerson's, for nature confirmed that which could not be otherwise known. And yet he was breaking though the barriers of Modernism to a depth of sensibility both paralleling and transcending that of the Paleolithic mind.

After completing his walk to the gulf, Muir left by boat for Cuba, and while there (thwarted in his plans to journey on to South America) learned of an economical passage to California. He later looked back on the still-born plans for an epic trek through South America as fortunate, for in California he finally found his path with a heart. There he discovered Twenty Hill Hollow, a beautiful valley near Yosemite. This section of *A Thousand-Mile Walk to the Gulf* is reminiscent of Thoreau's "Natural History of Massachusetts," replete with detailed geological descriptions and observations of all manner of plants and animals. Most important, Muir experienced another epiphany. "Never," as he put it, "shall I forget my *baptism* in this font. It happened in January, a *resurrection day* for many a plant and for me." The sun washed down in what Muir described as a golden flood, illuminating the flowers. The parallel here to the blinding light that Paul experienced on the road to Damascus is obvious, for that light ultimately lead to revelation. So, too, would this California light, the "sunshine for a whole summer . . . condensed into the chambers of that one glowing day," be the key to Muir's own revelation.

Every trace of dimness had been washed from the sky; the mountains were dusted and wiped clean with clouds—Pacheco Peak and Mount Diablo, and the waved blue wall between; the grand Sierra [Range] stood along the plain, colored in four horizontal bands:—the lowest, rose purple; the next higher, dark purple; the next, blue; and, above all, the white row of summits pointing to the heavens.

It may be asked, What have mountains fifty or a hundred miles away to do with Twenty Hill Hollow? To lovers of the wild, these mountains are not a hundred miles away. Their spiritual power and the goodness of the sky make them near, as a circle of friends. They rise as a portion of the hilled walls of the Hollow. You cannot feel yourself out of doors; plain sky, and mountains ray beauty which you feel. You bathe in these spirit-beams, turning round and round, as if warming at a camp-fire. *Presently you lose consciousness of your own separate existence: you blend with the landscape, and become part and parcel of nature.*[54]

Mensuration, and therefore a Cartesian-Newtonian perspective, was but a puny tool that disguised rather than revealed truth. The Sierras, of course, were one hundred miles away. But to the lover of wild nature those mountains were immediately present, a palpable reality indicative of nature's ever-present and enframing backdrop. Muir no longer confronted a nature reduced to mere matter-in-motion, known only by quantification of objective characteristics frozen in timeless mathematical truth, but was embraced by a living nature of which he was a part. Through his thousand-mile walk to the gulf, a path which ultimately led him to the mountains of California (1868), Muir had found his place in the cosmos, becoming part of a living world of kindred spirits.

A second conversion experience, one that moved him beyond the pan-entheistic remnant of his Calvinistic past, occurred during his first summer (1869) in the high Sierras. He left society, in Thoreauvian fashion, so that "I might learn to live like the wild animals, gleaning nourishment here and there from seeds, berries, etc., sauntering and climbing in joyful independence of money or baggage." In the mountains the revelation of the previous summer was reaffirmed in a new vision.

We are now in the mountains and they are in us, kindling enthusiasm, making every nerve quiver, filling every pore and cell of us. Our flesh-and-bone tabernacle seems transparent as glass to the beauty about us, as if truly an inseparable part of it, thrilling with the air and trees, streams and rocks, in the waves of the sun,—a part of all nature, neither old nor young, sick nor well, but immortal. Just now I can hardly conceive of any bodily condition dependent on food or breath any more than the ground or the sky. How glorious a conversion, so complete and wholesome it is, scarce memory enough of old bondage days left as a standpoint to view it from![55]

Muir's cognitive revolution was nearly complete: the conversion experiences cleared the way for a radical new wilderness paradigm. He now saw earth as one community of life everlastingly in process and virtually unlimited (infinite in its manifestations), and he had transcended the egotism that set humankind apart. Furthermore, he had abandoned the religious cant that salvation lay in eternal life after death. Such dogma was now revealed as a sterile human conceptualization reinforced by social convention and practice. Life and death were now understood as aspects of a larger cosmic scheme—the natural, wild process was the reality, the immortality, the glory, and the beauty. "Life seems neither long nor short, and we take no more heed to save time or make haste than do the trees and stars. This is true freedom, a good practical sort of immortality."[56] Muir was not concerned with the salvation of one individual's insignificant and selfish soul, for he had left that orthodoxy behind. Near the end of the summer (September 2) he reached what can only be understood as an abiding understanding of the Heraclitean reality of the natural world— an insight that was to strip the stings of mutable existence, and the notion of death, of their pain.

> One is constantly reminded of the infinite lavishness and fertility of Nature—inexhaustible abundance amid what seems enormous waste. And yet when we look into any of her operations that lie within reach of our minds, we learn that no particle of her material is wasted or worn out. It is eternally flowing from use to use, beauty to yet higher beauty; and we soon cease to lament waste and death, and rather rejoice and exult in the imperishable, unspendable wealth of the universe, and faithfully watch and wait the reappearance of everything that melts and fades and dies about us, feeling sure that its next appearance will be better and more beautiful than the last.[57]

This insight remained constant throughout his life. In August 1872 he observed that "there need be no lasting sorrow for the death of any of Nature's creations, because for every death there is always born a corresponding life."[58] And near the end of his life he wrote, in *Our National Parks,* that

> to an observer upon this adamantine old monument in the midst of such scenery, getting glimpses of the thoughts of God, the day seems endless, the sun stands still. Much faithless fuss is made over the passage in the Bible telling of the standing still of the sun for Joshua. Here you may learn that the miracle occurs for every devout mountaineer,

for everybody doing anything worth doing, seeing anything worth seeing. One day is as a thousand years, a thousand years as one day, and while yet in the flesh you enjoy immortality.[59]

Yet there remained a missing piece in Muir's wilderness theology—God incarnate. Although the idea that everything that exists is unified in a single process pervades his journal as early as 1867–68, he had not yet reached the conception that this all-inclusive unity was itself divine. In *A Thousand-Mile Walk* he prayed to God for a revelation, and in *My First Summer* he spoke of angels, implying that he still maintained supernaturalistic convictions. But by 1873 Muir's belief in such a transcendental realm apart from the evolutionary process appears to have been abandoned. At the least he had reached a middle ground, that is, a panentheism that allowed for both the divinity of creation and a separate existence for a divine cosmic presence.[60] He had long studied the wonder of creation, the myriad species, and the interrelations among animate entities and the land, and he now saw nature itself as divine, for "all of the individual 'things' or 'beings' into which the world is wrought are sparks of the Divine Soul variously clothed upon with flesh, leaves, or that harder tissue called rock, water, etc." A few months later Muir observed that the "rocks and sublime canyons, and waters and winds, and all life structures—animals and ouzels, meadows and groves, and all the silver stars—are words of God, and they flow smooth and ripe from his lips." Although the journal for 1873 allows no definitive interpretation, it reveals a pantheistic perspective in that nature is conceived as a temporal manifestation of a divine soul. Read in context (that is, his conversion experiences and the evolutionary framework underlying his research), there is some reason to think that he was verging on denial of any absolute distinction between Divine Soul or God—as eternal and infinite—and creation itself—as temporal and finite. "What is 'higher,' what is 'lower' in Nature?" was the question he posed to himself. And he answered that "all of these varied forms, high and low, are simply portions of God radiated from Him as a sun, and made terrestrial by the clothes they wear, and by the modifications of a corresponding kind in the God essence itself."[61] Such a position—that the *essence of God is changed*—cannot be reconciled with any variant of pantheism that conceptualizes nature as a divine *but merely temporal* manifestation of a divine *and eternal* cosmic spirit.

By 1879 Muir had reached a conception of God as entirely incarnate. Ten years in the mountains, free of religious convention while living in the immediacy of ongoing evolution, had revealed that *God was nature*, a sacred living temporal presence in *everlasting* process. This was a speculative insight of sweeping proportion, for it restored wholeness and meaning to a world rent asunder by Modernism. Muir now understood Genesis as religious metaphor, for through actual encounter with wild nature he knew that "the world, though made, is yet being made; that this is still the morning of creation."[62] As Joe Barnhart explains, "Pantheism has not known what to do with the idea of God as experiencing succession. Pantheism [typically] cannot recognize time as a part of God's own being."[63] Muir appeared to have accepted the reality of time and its implications, for he no longer believed in a transcendent God remaining apart from nature. In the mountains of California he realized that he was witnessing an unending process of creation. He felt that "in very foundational truth we had been in one of God's own temples and had seen Him and heard Him working and preaching like a man."[64] This analogy must not be taken lightly, for it is incongruent with conventional Judeo-Christian theology (theism). Muir's God was like a human—temporally bound with a natural world. The heresy here is overwhelming, for the human being was not made in God's image, but God was fashioned by analogy in the same fashion as humankind, and thus was grounded in process: birth, life, and death. Muir had committed the same apostasy as Giordano Bruno: by making divinity incarnate, providence was denied, since there could be no supernatural spectator apart from the world with a divine plan in mind. And humankind could no longer be *the* chosen species awaiting eternal salvation while witnessing an essentially meaningless because preordained passage of time. Time for Muir had become real and irreversible, and the human being—both body and soul—bound totally with time.

Muir, in other words, had realized that humankind enjoyed no special dispensation, and therefore he abandoned the doctrine of special creation and any supernaturalistic account of the human soul. In a passage (written in 1873) that parallels Thoreau's description of the sandbank in *Walden,* he posited the terrestrial origin of the human species. "Such a being is man, who has flowed down through other forms of being and absorbed and assimilated portions of them into himself, thus becoming a microcosm most richly Divine because most richly terrestrial, just as a river becomes rich by flowing on and on through varied climes and rocks, through many mountains and vales, constantly appropriating portions to itself, rising higher in the scale of rivers as it grows rich in the absorption of the soils and smaller streams."[65] Muir thus overturned that dramatic inversion of Western culture by which the palpable reality of nature had been denied as mere appearance and the phantasmagorical, that is, the transcenden-

tal—God and Heaven—claimed as reality. This rejection of supernaturalism was fundamental to the evolution of Muir's biocentric outlook on the
natural world.

Muir believed in God throughout his life, but his God was neither
the Cosmic Hitler of Daniel Muir nor the Transcendental Oversoul of
Emerson, but a God incarnate and in process. Muir's completed wilderness paradigm thus represents a theological antithesis of orthodox Judeo-
Christianity. His panentheism was perhaps an understandable zone of
transition; but given his adolescent conditioning, the years of intimate,
emotionally charged intercourse with wild nature, and his sense of the
cosmos's unity, pantheism seems an inevitable outcome. Muir's outlook
is clearly more a wilderness theology than metaphysics. A thoroughgoing
evolutionary metaphysics did not appear until the process-relational philosophers of the twentieth century (Samuel Alexander and Whitehead).
Indeed, Muir was not versed in the technical language of metaphysics.
He was more interested in working through theological questions about
creation and the origin of the human species than scholarly philosophical
issues. Yet, as Alasdair MacIntyre argues, "Pantheism as a theology has a
source, independent of its metaphysics, in a widespread capacity for awe
and wonder in the face both of natural phenomena and of the apparent
totality of things. It is at least in part because pantheist metaphysics provides a vocabulary which appears more adequate than any other for the
expression of these emotions that pantheism has shown such historical
capacity for survival."[66]

Some, of course, would point to Muir's wilderness theology as generally
muddled thinking, an unlikely combination of faith and reason. Environmental malaise is one thing, so they might argue, but there is nothing to
be gained in our endeavors to clean up the earth and conserve the wilderness by bringing in "god-talk."[67] Yet Muir's god-talk provides an alternative vocabulary to that of Modernism. His pantheism was a reflective
outgrowth from his childhood religious indoctrination, his adult religious
experiences in the mountains, and his evolutionary perspective on nature.
Pantheism allowed him to see the world steadily, and whole, and was thus
complementary with both his psychic needs and his intellectual commitments. Indeed, all these were woven into a seamless fabric. And, crucially,
there is no inconsistency in such a pantheistic reconciliation of faith and
science. True, Charles Hartshorne explains,

the Bible . . . nowhere says in so many words that God is the whole
of things, but no more does it say that he is not the whole. The "pan-

theistic" issue had not arisen, and so the wrong solution could not yet be given. (We so easily forget that our sophistication is a danger as well as an opportunity.) Of course "no graven image" of God was permitted, but what sculptor knows how to image the whole of things? What is there in the Bible to show that the word "God" refers to less than, or even other than, the all-inclusive reality—except a few passages which would discomfort traditional theists as much as they would any pantheist, e.g., "God walked in the garden." And Paul says that we live, move, and have our being "in" God. Precisely.[68]

John Muir, Evolution, and Biocentrism

John Muir was squarely in the center of the first generation of human beings who began to struggle with the lessons of evolution, and he attempted to do so geologically, biologically, and ultimately philosophically. Muir grew up with Genesis 1.26: "Then God said, 'Let us make man in our image, after our likeness; and let them have dominion over the fish of the sea, and over the birds of the air, and over the cattle, and over all the earth, and over every creeping thing that creeps upon the earth.'" Genesis, as many commentators observe, emphasizes humankind's "supreme place at the climax of God's creative work."[69] Once set upon his life's work, Muir came almost immediately into opposition with creationism, achieving an evolutionary and proto-biocentric point of view in *A Thousand-Mile Walk*. "This star, our own good earth, made many a successful journey around the heavens ere man was made, and whole kingdoms of creatures enjoyed existence and returned to dust ere man appeared to claim them. After human beings have also played their part in Creation's plan, they too may disappear without any general burning or extraordinary commotion whatever."[70] Within a few years Muir also came to reject the catastrophist theory of geology, seeing with his own eyes that Yosemite Valley had been created by glaciers. The notion that Yosemite was primarily a consequence of a cataclysmic subsidence, and only secondarily or tertiarily the result of glaciation, harmonized with religiously inspired *doxa* but not with the speculative mind of a radical empiricist. Yet Muir went far beyond geology in his evolutionary outlook, ultimately bracketing the prevailing nineteenth-century ideology of Lord Man. He came to believe that humankind was merely one among many natural kinds existing within an interrelated community of life on earth and that through a combination of religiously inspired arrogance, economic greed, and sheer ignorance Lord Man was blindly destroying that web of life.

The idea that human rights were not privileged above all others further extend the dimensions of Muir's apostasy beyond pantheism. So farseeing was this idea, so out of step with mainstream culture, that it remains to this day a subject of philosophical, legal, and economic debate. The Endangered Species Act, designed to protect flora and fauna from eradication at human hands, has been criticized as blocking economic progress and human interests. The argument, advanced by C. D. Stone, that trees and other natural entities, such as rivers and perhaps even ecosystems, should have legal standing has been assailed as nonsense, since (according to Stone's critics) nothing has value independent of cultural context.[71] And Aldo Leopold's land ethic—which advances from Muir's premise that all creation has rights—has been denied cognitive validity by a generation of analytic philosophers. The wilderness philosopher Holmes Rolston suggests that the nub is simply put: "Can there be an environmental ethic in a primary, naturalistic sense, one where natural things are morally considerable in their own right?" Further, *ought* nature in some sense be followed? "Can it be a tutor of human conduct?"[72] Muir answered these questions affirmatively.

Once freed of his father's immediate influence and creationism's shackles, Muir began to realize that all things on earth, indeed, in the cosmos, are interrelated. His evolutionary studies at the university were merely a first step. By the time he spent his first summer in the Sierras his viewpoint had surpassed that of his mentors at Wisconsin, and he was beginning to suspect that his idea that nature could be read like a sacred book was not entirely accurate. "When we try to pick out anything by itself, we find it hitched to everything else in the universe. One fancies a heart like our own must be beating in every crystal and cell, and we feel like stopping to speak to the plants and animals as friendly fellow mountaineers. Nature as a poet, an enthusiastic workingman, becomes more and more visible the farther and higher we go; for the mountains are fountains— beginning places, however related to sources beyond mortal ken."[73] Muir was here thinking ecologically, although he did not characterize himself as an ecologist; he thought of himself as a mountaineer. Nevertheless, his position is consistent with the idea of nature-as-an-organism and an ecological worldview.

The question is to define as precisely as possible the term *ecology*.[74] By suggesting that Muir was thinking ecologically we mean that he not only began with the insight that all things are interrelated but heeded the methodological implications of that premise. The idea that the life world is exactly that—a seamless living whole—is, as Neil Evernden argues, "something conventional ecology begins with but quickly forgets. For the very notion of interrelatedness contradicts the Cartesian premises which biology, in seeking to be scientific, readily accepts. Hence, there is a substitution or re-interpretation effected whereby 'interrelated' is taken to mean 'causally connected.' The two terms may sound similar, but they reflect different beliefs about the nature of relationship."[75] In adopting an ecological perspective Muir cast off the methodological constraints of Modernism, and therefore a traditional perspective on the human species, nature, and civilization. The knowledge Muir sought was not to the end of a Baconian-Cartesian power over nature but insight into (among other questions) humankind's place in nature: not as Lord Man but as a biotic citizen.

George Sessions characterizes Muir as a mystical ecologist; evidence of an almost prehistoric empathy or Thoreauvian sympathy with the plant and animal world pervades Muir's work. Muir observed that "most people are *on* the world, not in it—have no conscious sympathy or relationship to anything about them—undiffused, separate, and rigidly alone like marbles of polished stone, touching but separate." But perhaps *proto-ecologist* is a better term than mystical ecologist, for he was far more a radical empiricist than mystic. "There are," Muir argued, "no square-edged inflexible lines in Nature. We seek to establish a narrow line between ourselves and the feathery zeros we dare to call angels, but ask a partition barrier of infinite width to show the rest of creation its proper place." His affinity with nature was (in methodological terms) grounded in an openness to relations that are as arguably real as the notion that nature can be understood through a machine metaphor and efficient causation. Muir knew through his observations that the Cartesian-Newtonian worldview was merely a perspective, not the definitive scientific viewpoint. And he was intuitively aware of organic wholeness. "Most civilized folks cry morbidness, lunacy upon all that will not weigh on Fairbanks's scales or measure to that seconds rod of English brass. But we know that much that is most real will not counterpoise cast-iron, or dent our human flesh."[76] Here Muir was bearding the lion in its den, for the modernist believes that only primary qualities capable of mensuration are real and that wholes are simply collections of parts. But for a radical empiricist, much that is real eludes the cognitive grasp of Modernism, including comprehension of Homo sapiens as a part of nature.

Roderick Nash argues correctly that Muir anticipated the ecological insights of Aldo Leopold, for Muir never systematically developed his thinking on ecology per se.[77] Yet this is entirely understandable, for ecology did not yet exist as a discipline. And neither did an explicitly holistic and organismic paradigm. There were neither such process-relational philosophers as Alfred North Whitehead nor such systems theorists as Ludwig von Bertalanffy for Muir to consider. His incipient holism and organicism came from the Romantics and Thoreau, and the traditions of natural theology, rather than from any paradigmatic reformation. Ernst von Haeckel (1834–1919), usually recognized as the founder of ecology, was Muir's coeval, and though the smell of ecology was in the air, even Haeckel did not fully realize its theoretical (inferential) dimensions.[78] He thought of *Oekologie* as a descriptive term, and it remained for others to comprehend the dynamic principles inherent in the ecological paradigm. In consequence, ecology as an evolutionary science did not flourish until well into the twentieth century. Interestingly, Haeckel was—like Muir—a pantheist. Anna Bramwell insightfully argues that "the extraordinary influence of Haeckel and his successors can be attributed, in part, to the quasi-religious appeal, the incipient pantheism of his picture. But there is a deeper appeal; the return to a god-impregnated nature, which had been banished from the North [and Western culture more generally] by Christianity. This void . . . could now be filled, and filled by a convincing science-oriented ethic, that did not depend on received myths."[79] Clearly, Haeckel and Muir were in many ways responding to the same cultural circumstances, most pointedly the collapse of the argument from design and the realization that faith in God's providence was untenable. So viewed, both Haeckel and Muir were confronting the scientific question of *how* the human species was related to the rest of nature and the ethical question of *what*—if anything—did life mean?[80] Classical science, as epitomized by the Baconian-Cartesian perspective, provided no answers and therefore no ethical guidance, for humankind was conceived as nothing more than the master and possessor of nature.

Even during his first summer (1868) in the Sierras Muir was struck again and again by human blindness to the community of life. Reflecting on poison ivy he observed that "it is somewhat troublesome to most travelers, inflaming the skin and eyes, but blends harmoniously with its companion plants, and many a charming flower leans confidingly upon it for protection and shade. . . . Like most other things not apparently useful to man, it has few friends, and the blind question, 'Why was it made?' goes on and on with never a guess that first of all it might have been made for itself." Viewing nature ecologically, Muir recognized that in the wilderness all plants and animals, including poison ivy and rattlesnakes, were parts of an organic whole. Only from a narrow anthropocentric and eco-logically false human perspective were these things pernicious. Similarly, Muir observed that " 'sheep men' call azalea 'sheep-poison,' and wonder what the Creator was thinking about when he made it—so desperately does sheep business blind and degrade." [81] Yet azalea had more right to exist on mountain slopes than sheep. Muir even questioned an anthropo-centric view of climatological variation. "When an animal from a tropical climate is taken to high latitudes, it may perish of cold, and we say that such an animal was never intended for so severe a climate. But when man betakes himself to sickly parts of the tropics and perishes, he cannot see that he was never intended for such deadly climates." [82]

In retrospect, Muir appears more a proto-ecologist, or even deep ecolo-gist, than a nature mystic. Through observation he repeatedly confirmed that all things were in process, and that Homo sapiens—like it or not—was part of the web of life. From his ecological vantage point Muir antici-pated the shape of our own so-called environmental crisis, for he recog-nized that Lord Man lived in oblivion to the fact that all living things are interconnected. Farmers and ranchers provided almost perfect examples of what Muir now understood to be the environmental consequences of human short-sightedness and narrowness. His own experiences in Wis-consin were sufficient grounds to indict the farmer, and he had seen in California that ranchers would graze hordes of "hoofed locusts" on moun-tain meadows with often ruinous results—destruction of rare species or even an entire alpine ecosystem. "The glory of these forest meadows," Muir wrote, "is a lily *(L. parvum).* . . . And to think that . . . sheep should be allowed in these lily meadows! after how many centuries of Nature's care planting and watering them . . . . And so the beauty of lilies falls on angels and men, bears and squirrels, wolves and sheep, birds and bees, but as far as I have seen, man alone, and the animals he tames, destroy these gardens." [83]

Muir was perhaps most sensitive to the assault on North American forests set in motion by unrestrained deforestation. Logging dramati-cally affected watersheds. Rainfall, formerly slowed naturally by the forest canopy and root system, and allowed to percolate into the ground, now rapidly ran off denuded mountain slopes, eroding and carrying off the life-sustaining soils (themselves accumulated over eons), and causing siltation and flooding problems at lower elevations in the watershed. Muir equated the unrestrained cutting of virgin forest with "robbery and ruin," and argued "that a change . . . to a permanent rational policy is urgently needed nobody with the slightest knowledge of American forests will deny."[84] Muir had realized that human avarice, particularly the economic greed engendered by capitalism, was virtually unchecked.

Foresters would fell titans hundreds, even thousands of years old, take out only the heartwood and abandon the rest, failing even to replant the forest, raped and pillaged in a matter of years. "Any fool," Muir argued, "can destroy trees. They cannot run away; and if they could, they would still be destroyed,—chased and hunted down as long as fun or a dollar could be got of their bark hides, branching horns, or magnificent bole backbones." He wondered why humans would cut a tree thousands of years old for no more reason than to use a cross-section to build a dance floor, since from his empathetic and ecologic perspective the tree was a living patriarch to be revered. "Great trees and groves used to be venerated as sacred monuments and halls of council and worship. But soon after the discovery of the Calaveras Grove one of the grandest trees was cut down for the sake of a stump! The laborious vandals had seen 'the biggest tree in the world,' then, forsooth, they must try to see the biggest stump and dance on it."[85] Perhaps it is fair to say that John Muir, in recapturing an almost Paleolithic awareness of the relations between humankind and nature, began *thinking like a forest:* the trees were kindred spirits, and going into the woods was going home. A green world with its forests intact was a far richer and more interesting world, and a better world than one where humankind exploited nature for the ephemeral, merely economic purposes of Lord Man. Almost beyond question Muir had rejected the notions that humankind could be adequately understood as Homo oeconomicus and that human beings stood in merely economic relations to nature. He had become Homo religiosus, and through the wilderness a window onto the universe had been opened, for in the wilderness he stood reunited with an eternal mythical present—the point of origin.

Crucially, Muir advanced from his ecological vantage point on the community of life to the then radical notion that infrahuman species had rights. Given the intellectual context of the nineteenth century, any premise that the land, plants, and animals had rights bordered on lunacy.[86] Even such luminaries as George Marsh, whose *Man and Nature* revealed the adverse consequences of human modification of the natural landscape, stayed within the encompassing frame of Modernism. Marsh was primarily concerned with using resources efficiently and maximizing social utility. And the U.S. Supreme Court, ostensibly a citadel of enlightened mid-nineteenth-century opinion, viewed Negro slaves as property and thus denied them recognition as human beings. The Northern victory in the

Civil War, of course, ended the practice of slavery and extended basic rights to all human beings. But Muir's idea that natural entities had rights just as human beings started no war. Although legions of idealists were prepared to battle for the rights of slaves, few were prepared to uphold the rights of flora and fauna to free existence.

Muir realized early in life that Judeo-Christian attitudes, reinforced by the Protestant ethic and industrial technology, underlay the economic exploitation of wild nature. As his thinking developed, questions of both guiding ends and appropriate controls on human actions became increasingly important. Although such concerns had probably nagged him as he pressed nature into service on the farm in Wisconsin, once he saw the larger world they grew even more urgent. Muir could not think that Homo sapiens was the ultimate climax of God's work or that human purposes were more important than any other. Sheep were more than "food and clothing," whales more than "storehouses of oil," plants more than other useful items "for us." Yet he realized that the conventionally pious could not see that humankind was deeply entwined in the community of life. He began to notice the inner contradictions in the modern view that humans were born to reign over nature, arguing that those who proclaimed that God made nature for Lord Man, those "profound expositors of God's intentions," had glossed over the other side of nature, such as human-eating animals and crop-eating insects. "Doubtless man was intended for food and drink for all these?," he asked wryly. "Oh, no! Not at all!," replied his Euthyphro, his Everyman. "These are unresolvable difficulties connected with Eden's apple and the Devil." Muir could no longer accept the doctrine of original sin any more than special creation, nor the explanation that evil was the Devil's work.

> Now, it never seems to occur to these farseeing teachers that Nature's object in making animals and plants might possibly be first of all the happiness of each one of them, not the creation of all for the happiness of one. Why should man value himself as more than a small part of the one great unit of creation? And what creature of all that the Lord has taken the pains to make is not essential to the completeness of that unit—the cosmos? The universe would be incomplete without man; but it would also be incomplete without the smallest transmicroscopic creature that dwells beyond our conceitful eyes and knowledge.[87]

Muir also came to question human arrogance and pride in dominating nature, believing that nature's ways were superior to prevailing cultural practices and that human beings who lived in harmony with nature's economy lived a better life. One example was his outlook on the relative merits and demerits of wild and domesticated animals. Compared to human methods that produced such animals as domestic sheep, "nature's method of breeding and teaching seems to lead to excellence of every sort."[88] In a famous essay entitled "Wild Wool," Muir argued that the wool of wild sheep was superior to that of the domestic breeds and that both human beings and sheep would be improved by an infusion of wildness. "A little pure wildness is the one great present want, both of men and sheep."[89] Reveling in the beauty of butterflies, he observed that even if we regard them "only as mechanical inventions, how wonderful they are. Compared with these, Godlike man's greatest machines are as nothing." Observing the cleanliness and orderliness of natural plants and animals, he noted how "strange that mankind alone is dirty."[90]

John Muir in Cultural Context

Regrettably, Muir's seminal work has generally been ignored by the intellectual community.[91] Contemporary environmental philosophy and history too often disregard the past. Since, as Morton White suggests, we live in an age of analysis, then perhaps we can understand why the past is neglected. Time, and therefore history, is not real to the children of Descartes. Furthermore, Muir never organized the elements of his biocentric philosophy into a comprehensive treatise. Clearly, his work was more than anticipatory; he was on the cutting edge of nineteenth-century evolutionary thought and the associated attempt to understand its ethical implications. Donald Worster argues that the Darwinian paradigm and theory of evolution returned to Western "thought an awareness of natural kinship that appears to be universal among pagan cultures, including the so-called primitive peoples of the world."[92] Insofar as our contentions that the Paleolithic mind was rekindled in Muir and that he saw the world evolutionarily and therefore ecologically are correct, then any systematic study of his writings must recognize that he advanced many of the principles that define contemporary biocentrism. Simply stated, John Muir had realized that humankind was merely one species among many; that the human species was bound with the community of life through interdependent relationships; that all members of the community of life had their own (teleonomic) ends, the actualization of which was necessary to their well-being and survival; and that Homo sapiens had neither intrinsic right nor religious justification to thwart those purposes. Consequently, it was incumbent upon the human species to rethink its ethical relation to the rest of creation.

Like the conservation movement itself, determination of the consequence of Muir's wilderness philosophy is in process. Steven Fox argues that Muir was the philosophical inspiration for the radical amateur tradition in conservation, especially as this movement was and remains distinct from the professional, utilitarian tradition epitomized by Gifford Pinchot and the conservation establishment. (See below, chapter 9, for further discussion.) According to Fox, the radical amateur tradition revolves around the philosophical center established by Muir and is at base profoundly antimodern. "Drawn from an incongruous range of intellectual and political backgrounds, antimodernist thinkers converge on a single point: modern progress—implying cities, technology, and human arrogance—as ambiguous at best, probably nothing more than a harmful illusion that exchanged sanity and wholeness for less important physical improvements." [93] Fox attempts to establish his case (that Muir's thought is antimodernist) by distinguishing antimodernism from another stream of critical thought which he calls the *radical tradition*. He contends that this radical tradition—flowing out of Marx—has found a home in America through the "progressive-New Deal lineage in government." Among its identifying characteristics are its materialism, skepticism of religion, urban orientation, and, crucially, its "liberal [here read Judeo-Christian and Marxian] view of history as progress." According to Fox, the *antimodernist* tradition, in distinction from the *radical* tradition, views the history of civilization as "decline and regression." Further, it is "quirkily religious," "oriented toward rural and wilderness areas," and "esthetic and spiritual in values." Interestingly, Fox believes that antimodernism has been "overcome by the general course of events," even though "antimodernist thinkers comprise an impressive roster of the most powerful and original minds [Thorstein Veblen, Henry Thoreau, Henry George, T. S. Eliot, Lewis Mumford] in American history." [94]

If Fox is correct that antimodernism is pragmatically moribund, then the answer to the question as to whether wild nature has a future is academic. For in terms of his own argument the institutions of Western liberal democracies will inexorably grind on, grounded in the beliefs that progress is a law of nature and that humankind is superior to and apart from the rest of creation, in a last fey surge of economic growth and environmental imperialism. [95] Fox's view is much like the opinion expressed by Roderick Nash near the end of *Wilderness and the American Mind:* neither sees the wilderness as having any realistic future, and both agree that the professional conservation movement—which dominates both governmental policy-making and implementation, as well as educational policy in the nation's colleges and universities—is merely part of the modern project. As Robert Paehlke observes, "Too often agencies established to protect and conserve end up indistinguishable in outlook from the interests they are established to regulate."[96]

What Fox proposes in his study is in effect a revisionist reading of the American conservation movement, pivoting in part on the thought of Muir and more generally upon antimodernism. His point, as a historian of the conservation movement, is that the official view of conservation has neglected the antimodern strain, and that in consequence much of the reforming potential of conservation has been thwarted.[97] Even more pointedly, "the Muir tradition of the radical amateur in conservation has barely been acknowledged, much less interpreted."[98] The ecologist David Ehrenfeld advances a similar and supporting thesis in his book, *Conserving Life on Earth,* distinguishing between resource and holistic schools of conservation, and explicitly associating Muir with this latter view. *Resource conservation* (Fox's professional tradition) uses the bandages and palliatives of mainstream ecology to ensure that advanced industrial societies extract the last measure of value from the natural world, and accordingly does not question the underlying ethical assumptions of that culture. *Holistic conservation* (Fox's radical amateur tradition) actually attempts to reconcile "the needs of men with the requirements for stability of the natural world."[99] Neil Evernden's remarkable study, *The Natural Alien,* goes beyond Ehrenfeld's analysis toward Fox's point—humankind's efforts to conserve life on earth paradoxically conceal from view the underlying presuppositions of Modernism itself.

Muir might also be understood as a postmodernist instead of an antimodernist. Insofar as antimodernism ideologically converges on a rejection of the idea of progress, then it is an oversimplification of a complicated historical movement, and an interpretation of Muir as a postmodernist is preferable. Modernism is a complicated concatenation of ideological presuppositions, including ideas that progress is inevitable, that the power of science and technology is unlimited, that humankind represents the apex of creation, and that the natural and cultural worlds can be understood on the basis of a machine metaphor. Truly, Muir's wilderness paradigm *is* radically disconcordant with these assumptions. Accordingly, Fox is correct in arguing that Muir's wilderness philosophy possesses all the identifying characteristics of antimodernist thought, although we demur from thinking of Muir's pantheism as "quirkily religious," since theism, for example, appears profoundly peculiar from the perspective of philosophical naturalism.

But to think of Muir and kindred spirits like Thoreau as antimodernists is to enable the continued dominance of the environmental movement by resourcism or resource conservation.[100] The world-in-force, as all the lessons of anthropology and sociology confirm, is resistant to fundamental change. If Muir's thought, and that of the radical amateur tradition in conservation, is itself defined only through opposition to the status quo (Modernism), then it is at best a final, futile effort of protest against nearly overwhelming forces of history. Yet if we understand Muir as representing the leading edges of postmodern thought, then our assessment of the contemporary relevance of his life and thought changes dramatically. Setting Muir in a postmodern context is based in part in understanding him as a proto-ecologist—that is, as a thinker who in the late nineteenth century started to come to grips with the lessons of evolution and the failures of modern culture. John B. Cobb argues that postmodern thought generally is identified by an ecological or holistic perspective, which, among other attributes, eliminates mind-matter and subject-object dualism. A postmodernist is one "for whom the vision of the interconnectedness of all things has become the inclusive context within which" virtually all things and relations—both theoretical and practical—are seen.[101] In short, to think as a postmodernist is to presuppose, as Muir did, that the world is an interdependent and unified whole in which the whole is greater than the sum of its parts; in other words, the many parts that constitute the world system are internally related.

Viewed thus, Muir's work bears all the marks of constructive postmodernism rather than deconstructive antimodernism. Muir's idea of wilderness is not so much antimodern as positively visionary; he presents an alternative set of presuppositions, concepts, and/or vocabulary for understanding reality. Constructive postmodernism, David Griffin argues, "involves a new unity of scientific, ethical, aesthetic, and religious intuitions. It rejects not science as such but only that scientism in which the data of the [classical] . . . natural sciences are alone allowed to contribute to the construction of our worldview." As we have seen, Muir's wilderness paradigm affirmatively incorporates all of these elements (the scientific, ethical, aesthetic, and religious). Furthermore, constructive postmodernism "opens itself to the recovery of truths and values from various forms of premodern thought and practice that had been dogmatically rejected by modernity," but does not seek to return to some golden age in the past.[102] Muir seeks to revivify an ancient idea of a living, organic nature that can be known immediately and qualitatively. The final chapter has yet to be written; but insofar as Rorty is right in asserting that "we are well on the way to seeing *conversation* as the ultimate context within which knowledge is to be understood," then Muir's role in the history of the West shall continue to grow.[103] His is a bold and alternative vision, yet consistent with fundamentals of the human project: for he believes that human beings can know God, truth, and beauty.

CHAPTER SEVEN

Aldo Leopold and the Age of Ecology

Ecology was, and is, a science which does not fit readily into the familiar mold of science erected on the model of classical physics, and it deals with phenomena which frequently touch very close to the quick of human sensibilities, including aesthetics, morality, ethics, and, even worse in some minds, economics.
—Robert P. McIntosh, *The Background of Ecology*

ALDO LEOPOLD, THE third giant of wilderness philosophy, is a thinker whose ideas outline the living context of the idea of wilderness. Like Thoreau, he helped to define an intellectual framework within which to formulate questions involving the concept of wild nature. And like Muir, he was instrumental in founding an organization dedicated to wilderness preservation; the Wilderness Society remains a potent legacy, forming with Muir's Sierra Club an effective advocacy for wildlife protection. But unlike Thoreau or Muir, Leopold could find a "path with a heart" that legitimated his life's work. He became what is today termed a wilderness ecologist, beginning his career as a "forest assistant" and ending as a wildlife researcher and professor at the University of Wisconsin. Judged against the standards of Thoreau and Muir, he was not a prolific writer, publishing just four books, though he penned many essays, scientific articles, newspaper columns, and handbooks. His *Game Management* (1933), recognized as a classic in the field, presents concepts of wildlife ecology and management still used today. His philosophical masterpiece, *A Sand County Almanac and Sketches Here and There*, was published posthumously in 1949 and in fewer than forty years has achieved a popularity in wilderness philosophy second only to Thoreau's *Walden*.[1]

Sand County Almanac advances *the land ethic*, unquestionably Leopold's greatest contribution to contemporary wilderness philosophy. Broadly considered, the land ethic is a remarkable statement of what is termed a "biocentric perspective," an idea grounded in Leopold's notion of ecology as a normative science. The term *normative science* is an oxymoron if classical physics is granted status as *the* final vocabulary.[2] The land ethic is clearly a revolutionary departure from the stance of modern science, which permits the scientist to describe but never prescribe. Yet Leopold was convinced that ecological knowledge must be brought to bear upon prescriptive questions concerning the interrelations between Homo sapiens and the larger biotic community. The justification of this belief and the explanation of how science might inform ethical choice are complicated issues that lie at the philosophical heart of the land ethic, and the crux of this chapter.

Classical science denies cognitive status to the ethical activities of human beings, as reflected in the Cartesian commitments to mind-matter and fact-value dualism. Erwin Schrödinger and many others argue that science modeled on physics as an exemplar excludes human beings as ethical agents from the cognizable world picture. In other words, humankind nowhere appears within the classical picture of nature, unless reduced to matter-in-motion. Leopold, however, came to understand that the human species, when viewed from an ecological (and temporal) perspective, is a part of nature. Therein lies the cognitive power of the land ethic, which is inherently synoptic and organismic rather than reductionistic and mechanistic, and which includes human beings as initiative centers of activity within a community of life. Leopoldian ecology, or *foundational or arcadian ecology* as distinct from a more narrow and traditional *imperial or utilitarian ecology*, recognizes that human beings are sentient elements in the evolutionary process and thus obligated to evaluate their action from a reflexive standpoint.[3] The land ethic, which states that humans ought to act to preserve the integrity, stability, and beauty of natural systems, gives Leopoldian ecology an explicitly normative dimension. Such a recognition of telos is forbidden within the framework of classical science, which understands nature only as a machine moved by efficient cause: from that perspective humankind is related to nature only through external causes, acting at a distance upon indifferent matter-in-motion. In Leopold's normative ecology the human species is viewed as a part of rather than apart from nature. Subsequently, the membership of sentient beings in the community of life entails obligations to preserve the land.

Leopold knew that there was no methodologically defined path by which ethics and ecology might be synthesized, and he candidly and concisely stated the point in the 1948 foreword to *Sand County Almanac*.

That land is a community is the basic concept of ecology, but that land
is to be loved and respected is an extension of ethics. That land yields
a cultural harvest is a fact long known, but latterly often forgotten.

These essays attempt to weld these three concepts.

In the foreword Leopold also states the reason he thought this effort incumbent upon himself. America had become "so obsessed with its own
economic health as to have the lost the capacity to remain healthy. . . .
Nothing could be more salutary at this stage than a little healthy contempt
for a plethora of material blessings." He never denied, although some of
his critics fail to recognize this point, the necessity of human efforts to use
the land economically. What concerned him was an apparent overemphasis
on economic criteria of judgment that seemed to lead to the destruction of
not only things natural but things cultural—a harvest that included everything from freedom and privacy to art and philosophy. Of course he was
not overly sanguine about the prospects for any Copernican revolution in
human values. He concluded the foreword in a one-sentence paragraph,
ringing with Thoreauvian harmonics, that in wildness lay the preservation
of the world. "Perhaps such a shift of values can be achieved by reapprais-
ing things unnatural, tame, and confined in terms of things natural, wild,
and free."[4]

Unquestionably, even in Leopold's judgment, the land ethic is an attempt to synthesize three rival and often conflicting perspectives on the
land: the ecological, ethical, and aesthetic. That Leopold writes that *Sand
County Almanac* is an "attempt to weld" these concepts underscores the
provisional nature and methodological uncertainty of the work: the intellectual means to his philosophical ends were not altogether clear even to
him. This perplexity is easily understood—he was enframed by the fissure
between theory and practice, between knowledge of means and ends, that
has dominated Western culture since Bacon, Descartes, and Kant. Leopold
struggled throughout his career with an implicit opposition between the
atemporal, mechanistic, and reductionistic slant of classical science and
the temporal, organismic, and holistic cast of the natural history tradition
and its successor, evolutionary science. (The struggle between these contending "paradigmatic forces" within ecology remains alive and shows no
sign of resolution; McIntosh notes that the urge for a holistic view continues among ecologists yet is "deplored by some ecologists, or critics of
ecology, as obscuring the understanding and predictability demanded of
a 'hard' science.")[5] Interestingly, the land ethic retreats from an earlier

period of Leopold's thinking, when he was relatively sanguine about the possibilities of almost deductively passing from ecology to a conservation ethic. *Sand County Almanac* is a paradigmatic proposal for an ecological science that goes beyond mere description of lawful regularities to prescription of ethical obligations; but Leopold carefully avoided the methodological issues thereby raised.[6]

So viewed, the land ethic is more a posing of questions central to a clear conceptualization of relations between ecology and ethics than a final answer. Yet in raising these issues—and here lies the essence of Leopold's genius—he abandoned a traditional, human-centered ecology, itself the child of modern science, for a brave new ecology. Donald Worster's distinction between arcadian and imperial ecology bears meaningfully on understanding Leopold. So, too, does the contrast drawn by the Norwegian philosopher Arne Naess between *shallow ecology*, essentially a resource-management approach predicated on the values of efficiency and utility, and *deep ecology*, which transcends conservation in favor of preservation and biocentric values. In cultural context Leopold is best understood not only as author of the land ethic but also as progenitor of a new, critical ecology that epitomizes what Paul Shepard and Daniel McKinley call the "subversive science."[7] This second element—the potential of ecology to reorder the cultural paradigm—of Leopold's work is often overlooked, yet it is perhaps his most important contribution to contemporary thought. Worster argues in *Nature's Economy* that just as economics has ruled the twentieth century, so ecology promises to rule in the twenty-first century: the only question is just what kind of ecology this will be. As McIntosh puts it, "The question for ecologists is: Are there any ergodic properties in ecological phenomena?"[8] Late twentieth-century ecology clearly remains in a preparadigmatic condition: the real ecology has not yet stood up.[9] Leopold was clearly a harbinger: ecology has been thrust by environmental exigency into an increasingly visible and important—if sometimes controversial—sociocultural role.[10] Worster's thoughtful metaphor—the Age of Ecology—speaks to the point; his book, *Nature's Economy*, whatever else it might imply, is a relentless argument that ecology is essential if humankind is to save itself from destroying the biological underpinnings of civilization. Anna Bramwell, by contrast, believes that ecology (as a political movement and as a subversive science) "is advocating a return to primitivism . . . . Consciously or otherwise, this is a death-wish. . . . The father of the movement is an utter rejection of all that is, and for at least three millennia all that was."[11]

The Evolution of Leopold's Land Ethic

In 1893 Frederick Jackson Turner published his monumental work *The Frontier in American History*. Turner argued that American culture had in less than a century transformed itself from a country of pioneers looking for economic opportunity on the advancing edge of civilization to a country of settled farmers and merchants.[12] He believed that this transformation was reflected in the disappearance of wild lands to be "conquered" and the subsequent diminution of opportunity for people to be tested in the crucible of experience where Indians, wild animals, and the "hostile" elements were daily challenges to survival. Further, the problem that had dominated public policy since the American Revolution—namely, the expeditious mobilization of natural resources for the productive enterprise, whatever the cost in waste and environmental despoliation—was now seen with different eyes.

By the turn of the century the economy had turned a corner, the nation's gross national product evenly divided between agriculture and industry. The Jeffersonian ideal now seemed an anachronism, and no one needed George Marsh to see the adverse environmental consequences of agriculture and industry. Americans were beginning to wonder if perhaps the time to preserve wilderness had not come. Responding in part to the growing perception of the changing face of America's land and economy, President Teddy Roosevelt and Gifford Pinchot made efficiency rather than expediency the watchword for resource use. Conservation became a governmental policy initiative, soon followed by the creation of agencies mandated to promote husbandry of natural resources for the public good. Yet the so-called *progressive conservation movement* was philosophically grounded in Modernism. Wild nature was conceived as little more than a stockpile of raw materials of no intrinsic value; only through the productive enterprise—the humanizing of the wilderness—did nature gain value. And even though efficiency replaced expediency as the guiding value, utility was still the grand arbiter of judgment (as measured by the dollar). The greatest good for the greatest number was increasingly construed in narrow economic terms.

Leopold's life (1887–1948) coincides with these changes, for society now sanctioned such professions as forestry that were dedicated to the scientific study and management of wilderness, as well as, ostensibly, the more efficient use of resources.[13] Ecology, history, and Aldo Leopold were running on convergent courses. Out of the Darwinian revolution came the ecological revolution; out of American history—the disappearance of the frontier and a growing public consciousness of waste and abuse—grew a need for conservation; and out of these circumstances and others, such as his love for nature, young Leopold found a direction for his life. Aldo Leopold mirrors his time almost as perfectly as any person can.[14]

For these reasons, Leopold is best understood in historical context. Yet just as we cannot comprehend either Thoreau's or Muir's wilderness philosophy by imposing some explanatory rubric like transcendentalism on them, so Leopold's idea of wilderness is neither second-hand merchandise nor old wine in new bottles. The land ethic is the culmination of a lifetime of experience and reflective thought, and thus a "natural history" of Leopold's thought is instructive. Susan Flader argues that his "intellectual development mirrors the history of ecological and evolutionary thought, while his professional career spanned the first half century of the movement for conservation and resource management in America. His enduring achievement was to integrate the two strands—the scientific basis and the conservation imperative—in a compelling ethic for our time."[15]

Leopold graduated from Yale in 1909 with a degree in forestry; the silviculture he was schooled in rested on a Baconian-Cartesian premise that knowledge is power. Accordingly, forest management presupposed knowledge of efficient causes that facilitated control of timber resources, and aimed to manage wild nature guided solely by considerations of economic efficiency and social utility. Although this approach, rooted in the tradition of imperial ecology and now often termed *resourcism* or *shallow ecology*, still rules the contemporary world, Leopold became aware of the limitations of that paradigm and then attempted to transcend them. In maturity he advocated integrity, stability, and beauty as the governing values of ecology; efficiency and utility were secondary though still important considerations.[16] The evolution of Leopold's thinking reflects the changing circumstances of the first half of the twentieth century: the dust bowl of the 1930s underscored humankind's effects on nature, and ecology promised both theoretical understanding of environmental malfunction and practical guidance toward at least reducing if not preventing destructive human behavior. However, ecology lacked an established paradigm and systematic procedures for research, as well as degree programs for training the necessary personnel.[17] But society generally, and government specifically, wanted immediate solutions for environmental havoc.

Looking at ecology historically, Leopold's niche seems relatively clear. Most creative in his thought is his synoptic approach to a new idea of wilderness through a philosophically leavened science: the *ethical ecology* implicit within *Sand County Almanac* represents an evolution, if not a quantum leap, from modern (classical) science.[18] The Darwinian revolution had set the science of ecology in motion. And subtly but crucially evolutionary science was irreconcilable with Modernism in almost all regards, including mechanistic materialism and laissez-faire economics. Darwin himself attempted to articulate a new ethic for humankind based on the evolutionary paradigm.[19] Leopold thus had a rich heritage on which to base the land ethic; "the two great cultural advances of the past century," he wrote, "were the Darwinian theory and the development of geology. The one explained how, and the other where, we live. Compared with such ideas, the whole gamut of mechanical and chemical invention pales into a mere matter of current ways and means."[20] The upshot of Darwin's century, Leopold realized, was that any scientifically credible twentieth-century understanding of human nature and culture itself had to reflect some variant of post-Darwinian naturalism.

Post-Darwinians, however, hold a range of opinions, both epistemological and ethical. Some are (paradoxically, since the basic message of evolution is that things change, if slowly) by all appearances mechanistic-reductionists. "Only when the machinery can be torn down on paper at the level of the cell and put together again will the properties of emotion and ethical judgment come clear," writes E. O. Wilson.[21] Others, for example, Leiss, however, might see Wilson's so-called modern synthesis as symptomatic of the disease of Modernism rather than as a cure. And those such as Ilya Prigogine might deny that Wilson's description of evolution and its implications is anything more than one alternative among many. Finally, some biologists would flatly disagree with Wilson's reading of the ethical implications of evolution. As Mayr puts it, "*Genuine* human ethics *emerged* from the inclusive fitness altruism of our primate ancestors," but we do not learn how to judge what is ethically good by understanding cell biology.[22] The land ethic is framed by such a historical problematic. But we have gotten ahead of our narrative.

FRESH FROM COLLEGE, Leopold began his career with the National Forest Service in the forests of New Mexico and Arizona. The first adaptation in his thought occurred near the end of his Southwestern experience (1909–24) when he realized that the real world did not always mesh with scientific theory and Forest Service policies. This discovery was prompted by his field research into erosion. He knew that the indigenous peoples of the Southwest had over several millennia evolved cultural systems that minimally altered nature. In the past century and a half, however, humans had dramatically affected the Southwestern landscape, and erosion was one of the clearest indications of this. Over eons Southwestern ecosystems had evolved into stable forms, resistant to natural climatological fluctuations.[23] Yet prevailing agricultural practices, driven primarily by the profit motive, upset this stability. The established methods of farming and ranching were ecological disasters waiting to happen. But agriculture was not the sole cause of erosion. Uncontrolled logging of mountain forests damaged watersheds, and even Forest Service policies (for example, encouraging grazing in forest land to reduce fire hazards) also upset the natural equilibrium.

Such policies were a mélange of progressive and ecologically uninformed ideology grounded in the guiding concepts of utility and efficiency, and reinforced by a presupposition that nature was a virtually infinite stockpile of resources. Progressive conservation ideology arose partly in response to environmental abuse, attempting to control the wasteful and inefficient actions of entrepreneurs. During his years in the Southwest Leopold started to realize that utility and efficiency, though better than the profit motive alone, were inadequate guides to action. Further, forestry alone was incapable of dealing with the range of issues involved in erosion; geology, plant ecology, history, economics, and other disciplines were all relevant. And even if all the scientific data were available, Leopold knew that knowledge would not eliminate erosion: human attitudes—that is, the prevailing views of wilderness—were crucial, for these ideas determined how power was brought to bear on the environment. Yet here lay a complex problem, since Leopold lacked a conceptual and methodological paradigm equipped to deal with the transdisciplinary issues he had raised.

He drafted an article in 1923—"Some Fundamentals of Conservation in the Southwest"—in which he began to lay out the issues, showing a remarkable awareness of the importance of value questions in conservation. Quoting Muir (near the end of the essay), Leopold suggested that environmental malaise was grounded in either a religion that assumes humankind is the end of creation or a mechanistic science dedicated to dominating nature. In either case the result was the same. "Erosion eats into our hills like a contagion, and floods bring down the loosened soil upon our valleys like a scourge. Water, soil, animals, and plants—the very fabric of prosperity—react to destroy each other and us. Science can and must unravel those reactions, and government must enforce the findings of science. This is the economic bearing of conservation on the future of the Southwest." The problem went beyond economic issues to fundamentally moral questions, since "one cannot round out a real understanding of the situation in the Southwest without likewise considering its moral aspects."[24] The leap from ecology and economics to ethics may have been intuitive, but it seemed legitimate. The problem was how to ground his view, since by itself the scientific insight he had earlier extolled provided no guidance. He was familiar with the work of leading turn-of-the-century ecologists, such as F. E. Clements and H. C. Cowles, but their work remained descriptive although holistic and organismic: there was no call to conservation as a moral issue.[25] Leopold attempted to bridge this impasse between science and ethics through intuition, the path followed by many who had influenced him, such as John Muir and Walt Whitman.

> Possibly, in our intuitive perceptions, which may be truer than our science and less impeded by words than our philosophies, we realize the indivisibility of the earth—its soil, mountains, rivers, forests, climate, plants, and animals, and respect it collectively not only as a useful servant but as a living being, vastly less alive than ourselves in degree, but vastly greater than ourselves in time and space—a being that was old when the morning stars sang together, and, when the last of us had been gathered unto his fathers, will still be young.[26]

Leopold's words reflect the strain between his training as a scientific observer and his intuitions of wild nature. While recognizing that not everyone discerned the "indivisibility of the earth," Leopold believed that in principle such a vision was open to everyone, and he used the word "possibly" to emphasize the point. Particularly influential on his thinking at this time was P. D. Ouspensky's book *Tertium Organum,* which advanced the thesis that things which appeared outwardly to be merely material were actually living, conscious beings. For a modernist, such a doctrine was heresy. Leopold knew that any appeal to vitalism was fraught with scientific peril and that he should not be understood as a vitalist. Callicott and Flader argue that "Fundamentals of Conservation" actually advocates organicism. Leopold's "scientific predecessors Clements, Cowles, and S. A. Forbes had pioneered organicism, conceiving ecology as an extension of physiology—the 'physiology' of plant and animal associations. . . . He may not have cited any American ecologist [and leaned on Ouspensky] because none had explicitly expanded the organismic model of plant and animal associations to comprehend the whole earth."[27] "Fundamentals of Conservation" was not published during Leopold's lifetime, perhaps because of his own uncertainty.[28]

In his approach to erosion he was on descriptively firm ground, able to bring a variety of scientific insights to bear on the problems of amelioration and prevention. But Leopold was dissatisfied because the question ineluctably involved an ethical dimension. He knew that humans were not simply doing what comes naturally, since the species had existed as hunter-foragers for all but a few thousand years of very recent history. Yet he could find no rationale to mandate any modification of prevailing attitudes. Ouspensky at least offered the prospect of grounds for change: the entire world could be seen as a living, conscious organism. But as a scientist Leopold had been trained to cross all the *t*'s and dot the *i*'s (more than once he emphasized that science was above all an objective method). Two unresolved philosophical issues lurked in the background as he finished "Fundamentals of Conservation." Could the case be made that matter was conscious?[29] And, even granting Ouspensky's thesis, no prescriptions necessarily followed, since nature was red in tooth and claw. This was the infamous problem of natural evil, the seemingly endless chain of life itself requiring death in order to be sustained.[30] Clearly, "Fundamentals of Conservation" did not solve the question of natural evil. It did, to Leopold's enormous credit, recognize that the earth did not exist simply to serve the needs of Homo sapiens. After completing this essay Leopold pulled in his philosophical wings and stuck for some time thereafter to fieldwork, objective analysis, and technical writing.[31]

As he neared the end of his stay in the Southwest, Leopold was treading a tightrope between two rival traditions in ecology. *Arcadian* ecologists, like White, Thoreau, and Muir, resonated with the wilderness, with the birds and animals, the grass and the sky, feeling themselves to be a part of the larger and enveloping whole, even while recognizing that their culture exploited nature, thereby creating estrangement. Leopold undoubtedly had affinities with arcadian ecology, intuiting his bonds with nature, its palpable presence and influence on him, and believing that wild nature had some ethical claim on human behavior ontically prior to economy and technology. Yet as a forester Leopold was an *imperial* ecologist, seeking to dominate and manage wild nature. These two poles almost certainly created cognitive dissonance; his "imperial self" was likely uncomfortable with his "arcadian self," viewing such as nostalgic and subjective and therefore lacking either logical or empirical justification, and vice versa.[32] The Leopold of the Forest Service used the tools of an imperial ecologist—he proceeded methodologically as a scientist, pursuing knowledge of cause and effects—but had the feelings and perceptions of an arcadian ecologist—that is, he affectively bonded with wild nature, a relation that produced intense aesthetic and ethical responses. Such a creative tension can only be understood as beneficial; Leopold struggled throughout his life to resolve this psychic split, and the land ethic may be understood at least in part as the upshot.

Leopold's long years of field experience in the Southwest started to yield dividends just as he was preparing to leave for a new position. Suddenly he recognized that venality was not the only factor underlying environmental devastation: inappropriate governmental policies also bore responsibility. His *Watershed Handbook* criticized the federal policy that encouraged grazing to reduce the risk of fire. With extensive fieldwork in the Tonto and Prescott national forests to support his conclusions, he argued that the policy was both misguided and environmentally unsound. Extensive grazing of cattle, though it cut down the grass and browse conducive to forest fires, was ruinous to the watershed. And fire was not an enemy but a natural part of the forest cycle (the Ponderosa pine, for example, requires fire for germination of its seeds and as a mature specimen is virtually impervious to fire).

He also delivered an address in late 1923 entitled "A Criticism of the Booster Spirit" in which he extended his critique of the almighty dollar. Sinclair Lewis's *Main Street* (1920) and *Babbitt* (1922) likely figured in his thinking, since these books satirized the worship of Mammon and the almost irresistible pressures to conformity characteristic of small-town America. Leopold lashed out against the "Babbittian" mentality of those who wanted to build a monument to the War Mothers of America and to preserve Pueblo Indian communes not through any "unselfish and lofty motives" but through simple avarice: the war monument and pueblos would attract tourists and line the pockets of local business people. He looked, perhaps nostalgically, at the past. "Growing away from the soil has spiritual as well as economic consequences which sometimes lead one to doubt whether the booster's hundred percent Americanism attaches itself to the country, or only to the living which we by hook or crook extract from it." These insights parallel Thoreau's in "Life without Principle," for Leopold saw that unrestrained materialistic impulses were as pernicious to the spirit of Southwesterners in Albuquerque as they were to Yankees in Concord. "Is it too much to hope," he concluded, "that this force [boosterism], harnessed to a finer ideal, may some day accomplish good as well as big things? That our future standard of civic values may even exclude quantity, obtained at the expense of quality, as not worthwhile?"[33]

Leopold left the Southwest in 1924, bound for a new position in the Forest Products Laboratory in Madison, Wisconsin. The move likely fanned the tension between his arcadian and imperial selves; Flader suggests that we can "imagine that he felt constrained in an institution whose primary concern was with utilization of the tree after it was cut, when everything about him made him interested in the forest as a living community."[34] In any case, the move was to prove eventful far beyond expectation. Hereafter his writings reveal an increasing sophistication, an ability to see the world ecologically. He could now examine a piece of land, its vegetation and inhabitants, read its natural history, and begin to correlate what he saw in one area with what he had learned in others. His new assignment allowed him more time for writing, and a veritable torrent of essays and reports flowed from his desk during the late 1920s and early 1930s. Many of the ideas were embryonic, but they became persistent themes of inquiry, evolving fully in later works. He wrote, among more than forty essays and handbooks, "The Game Survey and Its Work," "Game Management in the National Forests," "Game Restoration by Cooperation on Wisconsin Farms," "A History of Ideas in Game Management," and "Management of Upland Game Birds in Iowa: A Handbook for Farmers, Sportsmen, Conservationists and Game Wardens." Leopold was blazing a trail toward the science of game management. Although the Europeans had a game management tradition (the term *science* is not descriptive of their practices) some three centuries old, nothing comparable existed in America. The science of game management simply did not exist anywhere in the world. Leopold's writings were instrumental in forging a new discipline.

During this period Leopold came to understand, more clearly than ever, the interconnections between the cultural and natural worlds. Although he still did not think of himself as an ecologist, his research involved a close study of human ideas and attitudes since they were crucial in determining environmental outcomes. In a paper entitled "Game and Wild Life Conservation" (1932), Leopold confirmed the explanatory power of his emerging ecological perspective—a wildlife science oblivious to its cultural context was a sterile exercise, just as were the arguments of "preservationists" who believed that game management was an exploitation of helpless animals and birds. Ostensibly, the essay was a defense of his view of conservation and game management. Its cutting edge, however, was the critique of "the national game of economic expansion."

> I realize that every time I turn on an electric light, or ride on a Pullman, or pocket the unearned increment on a stock, or a bond, or a piece of real estate, I am 'selling out' to the enemies of conservation. When I submit these thoughts to a printing press, I am helping cut

down the woods. When I pour cream in my coffee, I am helping to drain a marsh for cows to graze, and to exterminate the birds of Brazil. When I go birding or hunting in my Ford, I am devastating an oil field, and re-electing an imperialist to get me rubber. Nay more: when I father more than two children I am creating an insatiable need for more printing presses, more cows, more coffee, more oil, and more rubber, to supply which more birds, more trees, and more flowers will either be killed, or what is just as destructive, evicted from their several environments.

What to do? I see only two courses open to the likes of us. One is to go live on locusts in the wilderness, if there is any wilderness left. The other is surreptitiously to set up within the economic juggernaut certain new cogs and wheels whereby the residual love of nature, inherent even in 'Rotarians,' may be made to recreate at least a fraction of those values which their love of 'progress' is destroying. A briefer way to put it is: if we want Mr. Babbitt to rebuild outdoor America, we must let him use the same tools wherewith he destroyed it. He knows no other.[35]

Some might criticize Leopold here for being utopian, since the "new cogs and wheels" within the economic process to preserve wild nature still do not exist. Neither have human attitudes changed. The dollar remains for Mr. Babbitt the highest of all values and economic progress the dominating end of American life. Others might critique Leopold for a narrowness of vision: for demanding changes in some abstract economic process, when changes of the hearts and minds of Americans are first required, and for worrying about wildlife and lands while the needs of poor people go unmet. Yet Leopold's thinking transcends such criticism. First, he was criticizing his critics for being utopian and defending his plan as a realistic means to achieve a difficult end. Although Leopold's language was popular (by design), his words reflect a keen ecological insight—namely, that humankind was related to nature not externally but internally. What people did, regardless of their motives, had effects that rippled throughout culture and nature, destroying both the environment and blighting human lives. A narrowness of economic vision (itself predicated on Modernism) lay at the root of both evils. Yet there was a potential solution, for humans possessed a "residual love of nature" that might spark a refashioning of liberal-democratic life. Leopold was here abandoning the Baconian-Cartesian dream of dominating nature and Adam Smith's political economy. The human economy was not one of action at a distance, where mere matter-in-motion was transformed into the goods to sustain a consumers culture, but action that immediately affected the living world, and thus human beings: nature's economy and the human economy were intrinsically, intimately linked.

In 1933 Leopold published two pivotal works: *Game Management* and "The Conservation Ethic." *Game Management,* along with Herbert Stoddard's *The Bobwhite Quail,* virtually created a profession, giving game management a shape and texture that remain today. One writer cites *Game Management,* along with the National Environmental Policy Act (1969) and the Endangered Species Act (1973), as "milestones in the evolution of America's conservation history."[36] *Game Management* outlined a core conception of ecological science that endured for Leopold's professional life, anticipating the transdisciplinary position he later advanced in *Sand County Almanac,* and it touched now and again on fundamental questions of human nature and ethical behavior. "The Conservation Ethic" was more philosophical than *Game Management* and marked a significant evolution in Leopold's thinking from his earlier unpublished paper "Conservation in the Southwest." It was also one of three foundational articles, along with "A Biotic View of the Land" (1939) and "The Ecological Conscience" (1947), that Leopold synthesized in writing the essay "The Land Ethic." Leopold wrote the concluding section of *Game Management* and "The Conservation Ethic" almost concurrently, and together they give us an accurate picture of his thinking in 1933.[37]

The concept of game management implies the associated activities of hunting and killing game animals for human recreation. Animal rights advocates and preservationists who believe that wildlife and lands should be absolutely free from human encroachment are thus unlikely to find *Game Management* appealing, since the book appears to be a practical scientific treatise that serves only the values of efficiency and utility. But the case is not as simple as critics like to think. First, the text reveals some of the breadth inherent in Leopold's idea of wilderness, such as his concern with the preservation and management of non-game species, his recognition that all species of wildlife, not just game species, were adversely affected by unrestrained humanization of the land, and his realization that human life was enriched by preserving wildlife and land.

> The objective of a conservation program for non-game wild life should be . . . to retain for the average citizen the opportunity to see, admire and enjoy, and the challenge to understand, the varied forms of birds and mammals indigenous to his state. It implies not only that

these forms be kept in existence, *but that the greatest possible variety of them exist in each community.*

In times past both of these categories of opportunity [to hunt game and to observe non-game] existed automatically, and hence were lightly valued. Both are now, by reason of their growing scarcity, perceived to be immensely valuable. Conservation is nothing more or less than a purposeful effort to perpetuate and extend them as one of our standards of living.[38]

Clearly, the rationale for game management assumes human use of the managed species and thus appears narrowly anthropocentric; but implicit in Leopold's argument is a deeper rationale, neglected by his antihunting critics, lying in human nature itself. He asserted at the beginning of the text that "the practice of some degree of game management dates back to the beginnings of human history." Always cautious when advancing from facts to conclusion, he may have been somewhat ahead of his data in making this claim. He cited a dubious source that suggested that "tribal taboos" regulated hunting even among primitive people. The truth not of the specific anthropological details but of the ecological insight per se is crucial here: humankind has interacted with natural species since prehistory, and ideology has been fundamental in determining the character of that association. By predicating discussion of the origin of tribal taboos and game laws on ecology (the study of dynamic interrelations between the human species and game), Leopold was opening the door to the study of the biology of human behavior—a persistent theme that, once loosed, he pursued tenaciously. Only a few other twentieth-century thinkers have probed so thoroughly in such directions.

Leopold was keenly aware of antihunting sentiment, but he effectively met such critiques by raising difficult issues that go to the nub of human nature. So complex are these considerations, involving questions of genetic structure, psyche, and brain, that they have yet to be answered. But the evidence is unmistakable: as early as 1933 Leopold was probing into the biological bases of human behavior, beginning to question boundaries drawn too readily, and too easily, between civilization and wild nature.

Hunting for sport is an improvement over hunting for food, in that there has been added to the test of skill an ethical code, which the hunter formulates for himself, and must live up to without the moral support of bystanders. That the code of one hunter is more advanced than that of another is merely proof that the process of sublimation, in this as in other atavisms, is still advancing.

The hope is sometimes expressed that all these instincts will be "outgrown." This attitude seems to overlook the fact that the resulting vacuum will fill up with something, and not necessarily with something better. *It somehow overlooks the biological basis of human nature,—the difference between historical and evolutionary time-scales.* We can redefine our manner of exercising the hunting instinct, but we shall do well to persist as a species at the end of the time it would take to outgrow it.[39]

Leopold's insights into human nature parallel Thoreau's, as when Thoreau wrote in *Walden* that "I love the wild not less the good" and that he "felt a strange thrill of savage delight" as he contemplated seizing a woodchuck and devouring it raw. *Game Management* also rings with reverberations of Thoreau's insights into lives of quiet desperation, for modern people were—by implication—living lives out of synchronization with nature. Throughout the Paleolithic era the human species had existed in an ecologically balanced relation with the land. Leopold saw that civilization was a cultural overlay on a long natural history and that its "Abrahamic concept of the land" was upsetting the integrity and stability of natural ecosystems. *Game Management* simultaneously advocated the preservation of wild species while recognizing that hunting—within even the context of advanced industrial society—was not only a natural human activity but often essential to the well-being of game species and even eco-systems.[40] Leopold never forgot the lessons of the mismanagement of the whitetail deer in the Kaibab forest. More important, he was beginning to see civilization for what it was and is: a veneer overlaid on a human nature fashioned in the geological and biological longueurs of time. Although we may quarrel with Leopold's hypothesis of a "hunting instinct," there can be no argument with the underlying rationale: humankind has a nature, a genetic structure that is essentially fixed when viewed against a cultural time line, and this nature has—regardless of any illusions that deny our grounding in nature—profound implications for human behavior.

Although *Game Management* lacks the philosophical sophistication of *Sand County Almanac*, focusing primarily on destructive human encroachments on wild game habitat and on strategies for ameliorating these adverse impacts, it is clearly the precursor: an ecological perspective animates both books.[41] By the time *Sand County Almanac* was published Leopold viewed wilderness as a necessity for the human animal: as an ontic foundation underlying culture and a backdrop essential to any measure of the human estate that sought to escape the merely transitory and contingent categories of culture. Meine suggests that in 1917 Leopold saw the wilderness as "a place to hunt, fish, and camp." By 1947 the wilderness was an idea or "cerebral entity, an alternative to which civilization could turn to assess not only its ecological health, but even its social and psychological well-being." [42] *Game Management* led the way to this vision, for Leopold predicated this book upon recognition of the dynamic interrelation of the human species and nature. *Game Management* revealed a concern for wild nature, later amplified in the land ethic, that went beyond mere efficiency and utility.

> We of the industrial age boast of our control over nature. Plant or animal, star or atom, wind or river—there is no force in earth or sky which we will not shortly harness to build "the good life" for ourselves.
>
> But what is the good life? Is all this glut of power to be used for only bread-and-butter ends? Man cannot live by bread, or Fords, alone. Are we too poor in purse or spirit to apply some of it to keep the land pleasant to see, and good to live in? [43]

Thus Leopold reached the very question that Bacon had raised at the beginning of the Modern Age: science is a power that does not in its own right exalt nature. To what ends that power? Leopold would ask that question, again and again, for the rest of his life.

"The Conservation Ethic" (1933) is animated by this question and systematically explores the limits of efficiency and utility as the guiding ends of conservation. In this essay Leopold refines the idea that ethics can be understood both historically, as a strictly cultural phenomenon, and biologically, as reflecting human nature. Economic criteria alone, he argued, do not provide adequate guides to land usage. He believed that ethical criteria were also necessary and that ethics reflected a genetically based tendency for humans to evolve modes of cooperative behavior. Evolution, as manifest in rapidly changing technologies and changing patterns of land use, engendered a concomitant need for further ethical development. [44]

> There is as yet no ethic dealing with man's relationship to land and to the non-human animals and plants which grow upon it. Land, like Odysseus' slave-girls, is still property. The land-relation is still strictly economic, entailing privileges but not obligations.
>
> The extension of ethics to this third element in human environment is, if we read evolution correctly, an ecological possibility. . . . Individual thinkers since the days of Ezekiel and Isaiah have asserted that

the despoliation of land is not only inexpedient but wrong. Society, however, has not yet affirmed their belief. I regard the present conservation movement as the embryo of such an affirmation.

In short, Leopold was contending that however successful humankind had been in developing cooperative modes of behavior, the dynamic nature of the relations between Homo sapiens and the environment now compelled further change. "A harmonious relation to land is more intricate, and of more consequence to civilization, than the historians of its progress seem to realize. Civilization is not, as they often assume, the enslavement of a stable and constant earth. It is a state of *mutual and interdependent cooperation* between human animals, other animals, plants, and soils, which may be disrupted at any moment by the failure of any of them."[45]

Here, albeit embryonically, were ideas that *Sand County Almanac* crystallized into a land ethic. Leopold's emerging ecological perspective was now far more than environmental engineering. It had become subversive—that is, socioculturally critical and reflective. Indeed, he found no grounds for faith in any of the present modes of cultural governance: the Cartesian dream of mastering nature was an illusion. Lord Man could not stand above the kingdom of nature, for the human project was grounded in and inextricably bound with that green world. The cultural recipes that ostensibly led to or presumed the triumph of Homo sapiens over nature were ecologically bankrupt. Leopold argued that, so far as he could see,

all the new isms—Socialism, Communism, Fascism, and especially the late but not lamented Technocracy—outdo even Capitalism itself in their preoccupation with one thing: The distribution of more machine-made commodities to more people. They all proceed on the theory that if we can all keep warm and full, and all own a Ford and a radio, the good life will follow. Their programs differ only in ways to mobilize machines to this end. Though they despise each other, they are all, in this respect of this objective, as identically alike as peas in a pod. They are competitive apostles of a single creed: *salvation by machinery.*[46]

Though the critical edge in Leopold's thought was advancing rapidly, he was still groping for a positive conception of a land ethic, for some effective way of articulating a "vital proposal for adjusting men and machines to land." Clearly, he had progressed from "Fundamentals of Conservation" (1923)—now he did not even tacitly appeal to either a superorganic or supernaturalistic ground for ethical behavior. And he had realized that the values he subscribed to as a conservationist were intrinsically connected with an ecological perspective. The issue was simply how to bring these two foci—ends and means, values and facts—together.[47] Leopold's inability to marry science with ethics and then bring this knowledge to bear on environmental malaise was at base a reflection of the rupture between humankind and nature created by Modernism. Yet he thought that he was making progress. He had read Ortega y Gasset's *Revolt of the Masses* and believed that the book accurately raised the issue of "whether the mass-mind *wants* to extend its powers of comprehending the world in which it lives."[48] Progress, Leopold recognized, was not inevitable, not a law of nature: humankind and Western culture remained unfinished projects. Leopold had also learned of the new ecology of Charles Elton (as distinct from the more descriptive, holistic tradition of natural history) and believed that it might provide the intellectual means to the end he envisioned.

Leopold had met Elton, a brilliant theoretical ecologist at Cambridge University, two years before he wrote "The Conservation Ethic."[49] Elton had published *Animal Ecology* in 1927, when he was only twenty-six. Intensely theoretical, the book delineates a functional approach to ecology that undoubtedly influenced Leopold; the key issue is how. Callicott maintains that "Elton's community paradigm (later modified . . . by Arthur Tansley's ecosystem idea) is the principal and morally fertile ecological concept of 'The Land Ethic.'"[50] So understood, the community concept allowed Leopold to abandon the organismic metaphor (thinking of the land as an organism) and the machine metaphor (thinking of land as a mechanism) in favor of a more readily comprehensible social metaphor: thinking of land as a community. Worster largely agrees with Callicott: "In Elton's account of the natural community as a simplified economy, twentieth-century ecology found its single most important paradigm."[51] Meine argues that "Elton shot a lasting dose of intellectual vitality back into the veins of . . . [the natural history] tradition. *Animal Ecology* outlined many of the concepts—trophic layers, food chains, food webs, the 'pyramid of numbers,' population dynamics, and so forth—that underlay the new science [ecology], and that would usher in a revolution in conservation philosophy."[52] Perhaps, as McIntosh implies, Elton's community model appealed to Leopold because it offered a "coherent verbal model linking several concepts of a functional animal community and its component populations."[53] Such a verbal model was precisely what Leopold needed to help harness scientific fact with ethical judgment. His paper "A Biotic View of the Land" (1939) realized an Eltonian-inspired, functional understanding of "the land" consistent with his growing interest in the ethical issues raised by conservation; and his paper "Conservation: In Whole or in Part?" (1944) was structured around the community metaphor.[54]

Yet the new ecology of Elton was not realized in the profession at large: mainstream ecology soon took a radical turn toward physics as its exemplar—perhaps an understandable turn, given the enormous prestige and financial support accorded physics in the modern world.[55] At Oxford University A. G. Tansley bared the mechanistic cast of the new ecology, introducing the term *ecosystem* into the language of theoretical ecology as an alternative to the term *community*. The title of his paper "The Use and Abuse of Vegetational Concepts and Terms" (1935) is revealing. From Tansley's perspective, ecosystem, set in the immediate context of the new ecology, was quite unlike community, set historically in the context of natural history. For one reason, an ecosystem was ostensibly quantifiable in all regards. Thus Tansley thought that the new ecology led to a denial of the organismic doctrine (originating with Clements, a plant ecologist) that the whole—a living ecological community—was greater than the sum of its parts.[56] Wholes were no more than the aggregate of components, an unquestionably Cartesian position. "And although Tansley himself did not emphasize energy dynamics in his seminal paper, his suggestion that ecology draw upon physics for a conceptual model invited quantification of Elton's qualitative 'trophic pyramid'—in which plant 'producers' are eaten by animal 'consumers'—as solar energy measurable at each point of capture, coursing through food chains."[57]

In denying organismic doctrine, however, Tansley made a tacit metaphysical appeal to the verification criterion of meaning, and consequently his arguments are themselves unsustained by the "hard facts" as he imagined them. The timing of Tansley's mechanistic attack on the "old" ecology coincides with the flourishing of realism at Oxford, as epitomized in the philosophy of Cook Wilson. Worster argues that Tansley

> wanted to strike the word "community" from his science's vocabulary because of connotations that he considered misleading and anthropomorphic; some, he feared, might conclude from such language that human associations and those in nature were parallel. Plants and animals in a locale cannot constitute a genuine community, he argued, for no psychic bond can exist between them, and thus they can have no true social order. In short, Tansley hoped to purge from ecology all that was not subject to quantification and analysis, all those ob-

scurities that had been a part of its baggage at least since the Romantic period. He would rescue it from the status of a vaguely mysterious, moralizing "point of view" and make of it instead a hard-edged,
mechanistic, nothing-but discipline, marching in close ranks with the
other sciences.[58]

So viewed, the so-called new ecology inspired by Tansley was yet another variation on Descartes's dream, a power directed to ends that themselves remained unexamined. Leopold's vision of ecology must thus be
seen as diverging from the mainstream, becoming increasingly critical,
qualitative, and historical—edging toward the normative ecology of the
land ethic. At base his dawning idea of ecology (1935) and that of the modern tradition stretching from Linnaeus to Tansley (and beyond) were irreconcilable.[59] Leopold knew from three decades of research that the human
species was capable of impairing any "objective order" or ecological equilibrium that might be discovered through quantitative research. And he
had abandoned faith in Modernism's doctrine of "salvation by machinery," even as Tansley was revitalizing Descartes's dream. The overriding
goal of ecological inquiry for Leopold was not knowledge whereby Homo
sapiens might be "the master and possessor of nature." He was looking
for a scientific perspective adequate to understand humankind and nature
as dynamically interrelated and to undergird changes in the categories
through which human relations to nature were conceptualized. Leopold
was truly deviating from the path of Modernism: the land ethic was to be
the final outcome.[60]

A PRESENTATION TO the University of Wisconsin chapter of
Sigma Xi (a science honor society) entitled "Land Pathology" (1935) sharp-
ened Leopold's grasp of the issues on several advancing fronts. His talk
was understandably alarmist—these were the dust bowl years—in suggesting that humankind's impact on the environment had reached pathological proportions. Leopold did not shirk from either diagnosing the
nature of the infirmity or showing that what Tansley had dismissed as
"communitarian cobwebs," that is, the idea of a web of life, remained
viable.

Equipped with this excess of tools, society had developed an unstable
adjustment to its environment, from which both must eventually suffer damage or even ruin. *Regarding society and land collectively as
an organism, that organism has developed pathological symptoms,*

i.e., self-accelerating rather than self-compensating departures from normal functioning. The tools cannot be dropped, hence the brains which created them, and which are now mostly dedicated to creating still more, must be at least in part diverted to controlling those already in hand.[61]

Leopold's solution was in part Baconian, for the brains that had created the tools of environmental exploitation bore responsibility for directing their use. If anything, science and technology had functioned historically to exacerbate land pathology. In clear distinction from the modernist main-stream, Leopold here restated his arcadian view that society and the land are collectively an organism, and therefore that society could employ the power of science to manipulate nature only at potential risk.

Leopold was becoming dissatisfied with any approach that studied either society or the land atomistically, as if nature were one thing and society something else entirely. By ignoring the land and dwelling on soci-ety, philosophers had vitiated their analyses, and in studying nature but ignoring society, scientists, too, had failed. Both camps overlooked the dynamic interactions between society and the land. Leopold called on his fellow scientists to lead the way in reshaping the governing ideology.

> Philosophers have long since claimed that society is an organism, but with few exceptions they have failed to understand that the organ-ism includes the land which is its medium . . . . We may never put society and its land into a test tube, but some of their interactions are discernible by ordinary observation. . . . Conservation is a protest against destructive land use. It seeks to preserve both the utility and the beauty of the landscape. It now involves the aid of science as means to this end. Science has never before been asked to write a pre-scription for an esthetic ailment of the body politic. The effort may benefit scientists as well as laymen and land.[62]

Most interesting, however, is Leopold's continued oscillation between verbal models in this paper: he employed both organismic and mechanis-tic metaphors. Using a machine analogy, he argued that "America presents the first instance of a society, heavily equipped with machines, invading a terrain set on a hair-trigger. The accelerating velocity of destructive inter-actions is unmistakable and probably unprecedented. Recuperative mecha-nisms either do not exist, or have not had time to get underway."[63] What could be done to halt the ruin of the land? Three things.

One is the formulation of mechanisms for protecting the public interest in private land. The other is the revival of land esthetics in rural culture.

The further refinement of remedial practices is equally important, but need not here be emphasized because it already has some momentum.

Out of these three *forces* may eventually emerge *a land ethic* more potent than the sum of the three, but the breeding of ethics is as yet beyond our powers. All science can do is to safeguard the environment in which *ethical mutations* might take place.[64]

Meine suggests that Leopold's top priority, even above consistency, was making the case. On one hand, he used terms consistent with classical physics, such as *mechanism* and *forces*, as well as terms like *breeding* and *ethical mutations* that metaphorically adapted biology to history. On the other, the talk marked the first use of the term *land ethic*. Obviously, Leopold's thought was in process as he attempted to wed science and ethics. Explicitly he appears to be a mechanist, believing that some new mechanism could be fashioned to govern nature. Implicitly the paper manifests an organismic perspective, as in its assertion that a land ethic would be more potent than the sum of the forces that created it. A more comprehensive discussion of a theory of organicism and internal relations was in order. Although Leopold never escaped entirely from thinking of ecological facts as "out there," he knew that the objective order of nature was a useful fiction.[65] His research had repeatedly confirmed that Homo sapiens and nature were internally related. "Granted that science can invent more and more tools, which might be capable of squeezing a living even out of a ruined countryside," Leopold concluded, "yet who wants to be a cell in that kind of a body politic? I for one do not."[66]

Science generally, and the ecologist specifically, had an ethical function to serve—a position that assumed a theory of internal relations and transcended the fact-value distinction implicit within Modernism. Modernism, by granting the theory of external relations the status of a cognitive absolute, entrenched the fact-value distinction. The problem with that distinction, as Rorty points out, "is that it is contrived precisely to blur the fact that alternative descriptions are possible in addition to those offered by the results of normal inquiries."[67] Yet the so-called new ecology was predicated on the distinction between fact and value: the ecologist could study the assumed objective order of the world but not the underlying ideology and assumptions. For the imperial ecologist, economic efficiency and social utility would remain the guides to action. The only question was how to ascertain "the ecological facts" the better to serve these sacrosanct values. Leopold, in contrast, wanted to explore questions pertaining to the good life. What ends was the power of science to serve?

In 1937 Leopold also wrote "Marshland Elegy," an essay that, though more natural history than technical treatise or professional paper, is consistent with his emerging ecological perspective. He took the long view of a marsh, recounting its evolutionary history and the myriad species it had supported. The first few lines call the reader to an almost palpable awareness of a living presence. "A dawn wind stirs on the great marsh. With almost imperceptible slowness it rolls a bank of fog across the wide morass. Like the white ghost of a glacier the mists advance, riding over phalanxes of tamarack, sliding across bogmeadows heavy with dew. A single silence hangs from horizon to horizon." In the next paragraph Leopold flew (with his words) a flock of cranes—whose marsh this was, by right of their presence through the unrecorded ages—across the morning sky. The crane became "the symbol of our untameable past, of that incredible sweep of millennia which underlies and conditions the daily affairs of birds and men." Yet the human animal, in its greed, drained and ditched the marsh, endangering the continued existence of this species and other life-forms of the marsh. For the cranes "the song of the power shovel came near being an elegy. The high priests of progress knew nothing of cranes, and cared less. What is a species more or less among engineers? What good is an undrained marsh anyhow?" This was a familiar theme: economic spectacles, Leopold had long realized, rendered humankind blind to the land. But the implied notions, that *natural species possessed intrinsic rights* to existence and that these sometimes took precedence over human rights, were new. Leopold also began to reconsider the very idea of conservation. "The ultimate value in these marshes is wildness," he wrote, "and the crane is wildness incarnate. But all conservation of wildness is self-defeating, for to cherish we must see and fondle, and when enough have seen and fondled, there is no wilderness left to cherish."[68]

"Marshland Elegy" helps us recognize that Leopold's thinking was being restructured; he was moving toward *a biotic view of land*. Significantly, he had abandoned the notion that one could identify some objective ecological equilibrium that might restore what humankind had rent asunder. The question was increasingly one of the ethical responsibilities of humankind vis-à-vis wild nature and decreasingly one of means. Leopold now believed that conservation, so long as it was grounded in progressive ideology, was incapable of preserving what was most fundamental: the land, the grand, wild march of evolution with which the human species—a newcomer—was bound. In "Marshland Elegy" Leopold crossed the Kantian divide between the objective and theoretical sphere of science, and the subjective and practical spheres of ethics and aesthetics.

Three encounters with the land helped to formulate his questions about the philosophical foundation of conservation. In 1935 Leopold had traveled to Germany—a landscape almost totally humanized—discovering that an "engineering mentality" had produced catastrophic mistakes in forest management. In 1936 and again in 1937 he journeyed to the Rio Gavilan region of Mexico, a true wilderness. The juxtaposition of the landscapes led him to realize that his conservation work had always been "a post-mortem cure." In the Chihuahua Mountains of the Rio Gavilan Leopold found "the cream of creation," "a picture of ecological health." Diversity of plant and animal species, and stability of the ecosystem, appeared to be the rule, and the beauty was overwhelming. In the German forests the consequences of human-centered management (for wood and game) had promoted turbulent changes in species diversity as well as environmental instability. The contrast was catalytic, and Leopold started to think through the implications for conservation. For one thing "the Sierra Madre offers us the chance to describe, and define, in actual ecological measurements, the lineaments and physiology of an unspoiled mountain landscape." He was now more convinced than ever that governmental programs that relied on intensive scientific management were more part of the problem—the domination of nature—than solution. "I point no moral except that we seem ultimately always thrown back on individual ethics as the basis of conservation policy. It is hard to make a man, by pressure of law or money, do a thing which does not spring naturally from his own personal sense of right and wrong." [69]

In 1938 Leopold presented a paper—with a conclusion about the limits of management similar to his "Conservationist in Mexico"—entitled "Engineering and Conservation," to the faculty of the College of Engineering at Wisconsin. In it he critiqued those who confused mechanical knowledge with ecological wisdom, confirming his grasp of the Baconian insight that knowledge is a power that in its own right does not exalt nature. He also observed that times were changing. Granted, "engineering is clearly the dominant idea of the industrial age." But, he continued, "what I have here called ecology is perhaps one of the contenders for a new order. In any case our problem boils down to increasing the overlap of awareness between the two." Leopold's ideas about the grounds of conservation were clearly changing. "We end . . . at what might be called the standard paradox of the twentieth century: our tools are better than we are, and grow better faster than we do. They suffice to crack the atom, to command the tides. But they do not suffice for the oldest task in human history: to live on a piece of land without spoiling it." [70]

Shortly thereafter he delivered an address entitled "Natural History, the Forgotten Science," in Missouri. Leopold again noted that the methods of Modernism unquestionably yielded a knowledge of the separate parts of the environment. But he was looking for a wider purview to see things steadily, and whole, particularly as this related to viewing the human species and nature as dynamically interrelated, and recognizing that society and land constitute a community of ongoing life—bound into one natural history. "Here is a farmstead. Look at the trees in the yard and the soil in the field and tell us whether the original settler carved his farm out of prairie or woods. Did he eat prairie chickens or wild turkey for his Thanksgiving? What plants grew here originally which do not grow here now? Why did they disappear? What did the prairie plants have to do with creating the corn-yielding capacity of this soil? Why does this soil erode now but not then?" [71]

Leopold presented yet another important paper—one of the three folded into "The Land Ethic"—entitled "A Biotic View of the Land" in 1939. [72] In this essay he attempts to analyze the relation between ecology (as *theorie*) and conservation (as *praxis*) and thereby reveals his continuing struggle with two rival paradigms: organicism and mechanism. Crucially, Leopold now recognized that "ecology is a new fusion point for all the natural sciences." Mirroring Eltonian ecology, the paper first discusses the biotic pyramid, addressing questions of food chains, trophic layers, energy flows, and circuits (a strategy designed in part to offer an alternative to the older notion of the balance of nature—accepted "only with reservations" by ecologists). [73] More important, Leopold now looked at the biotic pyramid from the perspective of a natural historian, grounding it in *time,* since creation of the pyramidal structure of life could not be explained on the basis of a pre-existent objective order and must therefore have been created through (irreversible) evolutionary change. [74] Evolution, he argued, is "a long series of self-induced changes, the net result of which has been probably to accelerate the flow [of energy], certainly, to lengthen the circuit [of flora and fauna, that is, biological diversity]." In the normal geological and biological course of events such changes were slow and local. But the misuse of human tools, specifically modern technology, was producing changes in the biotic pyramid "of unprecedented violence, rapidity, and

scope." Humankind was a remarkable agent of change in the biotic pyramid, exceeded in consequence only by such cataclysms as volcanic erup-
tions or ice ages. "The process of altering the pyramid for human occupa-
tion releases stored energy, and this often gives rise, during the pioneering
period, to a deceptive exuberance of plant and animal life, both wild and
tame. These releases of biotic capital tend to becloud or delay the penal-
ties of violence."[75] Implicitly, in spite of the objective language, Leopold
was making his strongest ethical statement to date. As Meine notes, and
as Worster and Bramwell would surely agree, "a 'biotic view' of nature,
however objective it tried to be, could not help but imply a deep criticism
of trends in human history."[76] Leopold was struggling mightily with the
negative environmental consequences of the alchemy of Modernism and
the theoretical consequences of the two-culture split. Mirroring "Marshland Elegy," "A Biotic View of the Land" implied that nature possessed
intrinsic value.

The creative tension between Leopold's arcadian and imperial selves
continued to animate his intellect into the 1940s. He explored functional
approaches to ecology in a variety of technical papers, and he started to
write more papers in the tradition of natural history. Even in his technical
writings, such as "Biotic Land Use" and "Biotic Theories and Conservation," Leopold pressed beyond the limits of imperial ecology and began to
entertain the crucial questions of ends rather than means only. What were
the aims of conservation? He now believed that conservation could not
"be accomplished by any mere mustering of technologies. Conservation
calls for something which the technologies, individually or collectively,
now lack." Further, neither economic nor recreational criteria were adequate to guide conservation technology. Reflecting on his earlier observations in Germany and the Rio Gavilan, Leopold argued that conservation's
purpose was to stabilize the land and maintain species diversity. Simultaneously he recognized that such a notion went beyond the province of
positive science. "It seems improbable that science can ever analyze stability and write an exact formula for it. The best we can do, at least at
present, is to recognize and cultivate the general conditions which seem
to be conducive to it. Stability and diversity are associated. Both are the
end-result of evolution to date. To what extent are they interdependent?
Can we retain stability in used land without retaining diversity also?"[77]
This was then as now a supremely important and difficult question. Leopold discussed the issue with Elton, Wehrwein, and others. As McIntosh
suggests, though this matter remains unresolved, Leopold was one of the
first to grasp its import.[78]

By 1944 Leopold had been transformed from an imperial ecologist, whose goal was to understand the mechanical workings of nature and through resource management impose society's unexamined values on nature, to a foundational ecologist, whose aim was to understand the natural and cultural worlds as a community of life and through such knowledge serve society's needs consistent with conserving its ecological underpinnings. Following Susan Flader, Donald Worster argues that this conversion occurred about 1935, when Leopold was engaged with others in founding the Wilderness Society. That was the year of Leopold's trip to Germany, where he had found that German methods of managing nature were far from ideal. "And during that watershed year, too, he found an old, abandoned shack near Baraboo, Wisconsin, where until his death he would at odd moments live the life of a Gilbert White or Henry Thoreau—a rural naturalist living apart from a technological culture, seeking to intensify his attachment to the earth and its processes."[79]

Meine, in contrast to Worster, argues that the change in Leopold's orientation—away from a progressive, Pinchotlike management philosophy toward a radical, Muirlike preservationist philosophy—was more gradual. In either case, the result was the same. Leopold now believed that the progressive ideology and managerial ethos that had controlled conservation ran roughshod over any rights wild nature might possess and ignored questions of human duties to the land. His thinking became more philosophical, more concrete and qualitative, and less abstract and quantitative. Of course, Leopold was still deeply involved, both at the university and through his role in professional organizations, in attempts to guide the rise of a new professional elite: the wilderness manager. His writings, however, confirm a shift away from technical concerns toward a more personal relation to the land community. Leopold was embarked on a quest, much like that of Thoreau, to become a person of Indigen wisdom seeking a sympathy with intelligence.

The natural history essays of this period (collected in *Sand County Almanac*) are remarkable statements—Thoreauvian in their literary quality and much of their underlying philosophy. "Thinking Like a Mountain" (1944) is representative of the changes in Leopold's outlook: a confession (in some ways almost Augustinian) that through his own short sightedness and human centeredness he had sinned against nature.[80] As in "Marshland Elegy," nature was animated through Leopold's unique prose. "A deep chesty bawl echoes from rimrock to rimrock, rolls down the mountain, and fades into the far blackness of the night. It is an outburst of wild defiant sorrow, and of contempt for all the adversities of the world." Leopold's intuition was grounded in a personal relation to the mountain itself (rather than any philosophical commitment to vitalism), a mountain which recognized in the cry of a wolf a "deeper meaning, known only to the mountain itself. Only the mountain has lived long enough to listen objectively to the howl of a wolf." [81] This statement metaphorically endows the mountain with sentience—the basis of an interconnectedness between the massif and the timber and animals that inhabit its slopes. What in imperial ecology would be a mechanical equilibrium of the ecosystem had been animated and metaphorically personified, but not anthropomorphized. [82] Crucially, the mountain has lived through the longueurs of geological and biological time: long enough to be free of the prejudice that taints human perception of the wolf.

Some humans listened only with the ears of ranchers, who believed the wolf a threat to their livelihood, or the bounty hunters, who saw pelts as income. But others heard the howl differently, though "unable to decipher the hidden meaning [they] know nevertheless that it [a deeper meaning] is there, for it is felt in all wolf country, and distinguishes that country from all other land." Leopold here verged on recapturing a Paleolithic consciousness of *nature in its order of operation*—escaping the prison of conventional categories and finding his way back to the green world from which his kind had come, becoming one with the mountain. But, mea culpa, in younger days and full of trigger-itch, he too thought not like a mountain but a human, a manager who "thought that fewer wolves meant more deer, that no wolves would mean hunters' paradise." Even then (1918) "after seeing the green fire die, I sensed that neither the wolf nor the mountain agreed with such a view." Leopold now drove his point home: people must learn to think like a mountain and allow wild nature to take its course, not only on the mountain, but throughout the world. Human intervention—whether for recreation, as with the hunter, or commerce, as with the rancher—too often promoted instability and reduced diversity. Killing predators was thinking like a human, not a mountain.

We all strive for safety, prosperity, comfort, long life, and dullness. The deer strives with his supple legs, the cowman with trap and poison, the statesman with pen, the most of us with machines, votes, and dollars, but it all comes to the same thing: peace in our time. A measure of success in this is all well enough, and perhaps is a requisite to objective thinking, but too much safety seems to yield only danger in the long run. Perhaps this is behind Thoreau's dictum: In wildness is the salvation of the world. Perhaps this is the hidden meaning in the howl of the wolf, long known among mountains, but seldom perceived among men.[83]

During the war years Leopold completed thirteen of these nature essays, works that seemed to relax the tension between his arcadian and imperial selves. He was uncharacteristically pessimistic, however, on the prospects for preservation of the land community. The war had likely taken its toll. A written response to his friend Bill Vogt, who was organizing a conference on the South American environment, illuminates *Sand County Almanac* and the land ethic. The culturally prevailing paradigm and Leopold's idea of wilderness were now clearly incommensurable.

> The only thing you have left out is whether the philosophy of industrial culture [Modernism] is not, in its ultimate development, irreconcilable with ecological conservation. *I think it is.*
>
> I hasten to add, however, that the term industrialism cannot be used as an absolute. Like "temperature" and "velocity" it is a question of degree. Throughout ecology, all truth is relative: a thing becomes good at one degree and ceases to be so at another.
>
> Industrialism might theoretically be conservative if there were an ethic limiting its application to what does not impair (a) permanence and stability of the land [and] (b) beauty of the land. *But there is no such ethic, nor likely to be.*[84]

In 1923 Leopold had posed the question whether the forces destroying the land were inherent in a "mechanistic conception of the earth."[85] Two decades of reflection had led him to conclude that they were; but he was now on the verge of his most important work, about to venture forth a statement of the missing ethic.

IN *Nature's Economy* Donald Worster asserts that we live in the Age of Ecology—a time when ecology as a discipline has achieved a position of influence only slightly behind physics and economics. And *Sand County Almanac* has been assessed as "one of the central documents—some would say, *the* central document—of the modern conservation movement."[86] Yet the dominant ecology of science, academe, and management is rooted in an ethos that Leopold himself embraced and then abandoned. Today's ecology is a house divided between the resource (imperial) ecologist who, armed with environmental impact statements, cost-benefit analyses, differential equations, and energy transfer models, champions the values of utility and efficiency and the normative (foundational) ecologist who values wild nature's beauty, stability, and integrity in addition to and sometimes more than efficiency and utility. This bifurcation mirrors the split between Leopold's own arcadian and imperial characteristics. An anthropocentrically biased ecology of management is entirely consistent with the prevailing cultural paradigm. Perhaps Leopold's *Game Management* epitomizes this side of his thought. But *Sand County Almanac* is of a different order, no longer predicated on the assumption of human needs as absolute but grounded in an awareness that those needs are conditional. The land ethic advances a biocentric perspective, where foundational knowledge and aesthetic judgment have supervened merely scientific, economic and technical judgment—that is, an anthropocentric perspective. Although the land ethic perhaps raises more questions than it answers, it is clearly a dramatic reconceptualization of the relations between Homo sapiens and nature.

The land ethic itself, articulated most persuasively within *Sand County Almanac*, culminates Aldo Leopold's lifetime of action and contemplation. The book is an extraordinary statement—stretching the categories of Western experience beyond conventional meaning—of a near postmodern idea of wilderness. In final analysis it was the wilderness, wild nature in all its beauty and evolutionary complexity, that became (as with Thoreau and Muir) the focal point of Leopold's thought. As he stated in the foreword,

> There are some who can live without wild things, and some who cannot. These essays are the delights and dilemmas of one who cannot.
>
> Like winds and sunsets, wild things were taken for granted until progress began to do away with them. Now we face the question whether a still higher "standard of living" is worth its cost in things natural, wild, and free. For us of the minority, the opportunity to see geese is more important than television, and the chance to find a pasque-flower is a right as inalienable as free speech.
>
> These wild things, I admit, had little human value until mechanization assured us of a good breakfast, and until science disclosed the drama of where they come from and how they live. The whole conflict thus boils down to a question of degree. We of the minority see a law of diminishing returns in progress; our opponents do not.[87]

Sand County Almanac might be viewed as having two poles: one negative and critical, which prepares the way for the land ethic, and the other positive and affirmative—the statement of the land ethic. Leopold criticized virtually all secular absolutes: government, Judeo-Christianity, economics, even science. Paralleling Muir, he argued that Judeo-Christianity was in part culpable for environmental ruin. "Conservation is getting nowhere because it is incompatible with our Abrahamic concept of land." He also put aside economic criteria as the yardstick by which all other things might be measured. Outright worship of the almighty dollar by the business community had disastrous ecological consequences, and the progressive conservation movement was but a small improvement, since "a system of conservation based solely on economic self-interest is hopelessly lopsided. It tends to ignore, and thus eventually to eliminate, many elements in the land community that lack commercial value. . . . It assumes, falsely, I think, that the economic parts of the biotic clock will function without the uneconomic parts." Furthermore, governmental action in the name of conservation was piecemeal and therefore inadequate. "The practices we now call conservation are, to a large extent, local alleviations of biotic pain. They are necessary, but they must not be confused with cures." Leopold also saw that the mainstream of the scientific community had been coopted. With devastating sociological insight and logic he argued that scientific method "means doubting everything except facts; it means hewing to the facts, let the chips fall where they may. One of the facts hewn to by science is that every river needs more people, and all people need more inventions, and hence more science; the good life depends on the indefinite extension of this chain of logic."[88] Science, then, was no secular absolute, but was itself bound up with the cultural matrix. Reform was needed, and here Leopold placed his faith in perhaps humankind's most important genetic endowment: the possibility of individuation.[89] Having critiqued the cultural infrastructure, the institutions of science, government, and economy, he had no other alternative. So throughout *Sand County Almanac* he struggled to promote the possibility of perception of the land; individual awareness was a starting point toward ecological sanity.

His *wilderness* or *land aesthetic* crossed the modernist divide between subject and object, and achieved a Thoreauvian unity of knowing subject (the individual) and known object (nature). As for Kant, the role of imagination was fundamental for Leopold, for it is a knowing subject who sees and hears and smells the wilderness. Leopold's land aesthetic, as J. Baird Callicott argues, "involves a subtle interplay between conceptual schemata and sensuous experience. . . . The 'world,' as we drink it in through our senses, is first filtered, structured, and arranged by the conceptual framework or cognitive set we bring to it, prior, not necessarily to all experience, but to any *articulate* experience."[90] Leopold's aesthetic, in distinction from

Kant's, is that of an ecologist rather than physicist: this is an important difference. To follow Callicott's lead, "the ontological primacy of objects and the ontological subordination of relationships, characteristic of classical Western science [Modernism], is, in fact, reversed in ecology."[91] Such ontological subordination had been based in a theory of external relations (as well as subject-object and fact-value dichotomies), and existentially manifested in humankind's unrelenting endeavor to humanize wild nature and view it only as a standing reserve. By promoting perception of the beauty of things, Leopold opened up perceiving subjects to an awareness of their relatedness to the land. A wilderness aesthetic, Leopold wrote, "entails no consumption and no dilution of any resource" but engenders awareness "of the natural processes by which the land and the living things upon it have achieved their characteristic forms (evolution) and by which they maintain their existence (ecology). That thing called 'nature study,' despite the shiver it brings to the spines of the elect, constitutes the first embryonic groping of the mass-mind toward perception."[92] Such nature study for the individual need not necessarily be carried to Thoreauvian extremes, but ecological literacy begins with a categorical openness to and perceptual awareness of nature as a community of life possessing integrity, stability, and beauty.

The land aesthetic, then, complements the land ethic. Together, Callicott concludes, "they represent a coherent environmental axiology."[93] Indeed, philosophically considered, one is not possible without the other, for a wilderness aesthetic opens the possibility of recognition that we as sentient subjects are bound with all of creation, including the starry sky above and the moral law within. Although Kant restricted scientific imagination to nature, no philosophical requirement in principle limits perception to matter-in-mechanical-motion; Leopold's ecological imagination opens a vantage point (closed by Modernism) onto an entirely different domain of experience (and is in this sense part of a continuing scientific revolution, now informed by Darwin and Clausius). The land aesthetic is in effect Leopold's transcendental aesthetic, reflecting the culmination of his career as a wilderness ecologist, much as Kant's aesthetic reflected his experience as a physicist. Such an aesthetic is presupposed by Leopold's notion of an *ecological conscience,* which in turn was the foundation for the land ethic. A land ethic, Leopold argued, "reflects the existence of an ecological conscience, and this in turn reflects a conviction of individual responsibility for the health of the land."[94] The appeal here to an ecological conscience is grounded not in a "faculty" psychology but in a Kantian recognition that unless reason can universalize itself—that is, take the vantage point of *the other*—no ethic beyond utilitarianism is possible. But no such movement in thought is in principle possible unless the land or wild nature, as distinct from nature, exists as a perceptual entity.

Leopold stated the land ethic as succinctly as possible. "A thing is right when it tends to preserve the integrity, stability, and beauty of the biotic community. It is wrong when it tends otherwise." From the Leopoldian vantage point any line drawn between the cultural and the natural or between humans and brutes was tenuous. The human animal was no longer absolute ruler above the web of life but a biotic citizen who recognized that the very endeavor to perpetuate material progress—that shrine built to the unattainable assumption of infinite needs—was an illusory and self-defeating goal. He wrote that "the combined evidence of history and ecology seems to support one general deduction: the less violent the man-made changes, the greater the probability of successful readjustment in the [biotic] pyramid." And then he offered a conclusion.

> Ability to see the cultural value of wilderness boils down, in the last analysis, to a question of intellectual humility. The shallow-minded modern who has lost his rootage in the land assumes that he has already discovered what is important; it is such who prate of empires, political or economic, that will last a thousand years. It is only the scholar who appreciates that all history consists of successive excursions from a single starting-point, to which man returns again and again to organize yet another search for a durable scale of values. It is only the scholar who understands why the raw wilderness gives definition and meaning to the human enterprise.[95]

Reflections on the Land Ethic

A survey of the critical reaction to and assessment of Leopold's place in American life and culture reveals a diversity of opinion. Some, such as the deep ecologist George Sessions and the wilderness philosopher Holmes Rolston III, find in the land ethic the leading edge of a new paradigm for thought and action. Others, such as L. W. Sumner, characterize the land ethic as dangerous nonsense, and Paul Taylor uses the land ethic to exemplify the is-ought fallacy. David Ehrenfeld, surely sympathetic to Leopold's philosophy, nonetheless finds reason to believe that it remains at base anthropocentric. In a reading opposite to Ehrenfeld's, John Passmore finds the land ethic to be so biocentrically centered as to lack meaning. And these are only a few of many judgments made of Leopold, a mélange of inconsistent, often contradictory interpretations. Can Leopold's ideas be so hopelessly ambiguous and vague as to defy consistent interpretation or so poetic as to permit any interpretation?[96]

Although inconsistent with our dominating cultural tradition, which insists on truth as single and permanent, diversity of opinion is not necessarily bad and may have positive benefits by promoting discussion of the land ethic. Indeed, part of Leopold's genius is that he invites us as sentient subjects to reconsider our relations to the land. And therein arises the possibility of the many alternative interpretations of his writings, since they mesh with the tides of Western culture: the land ethic is a twentieth-century manifestation of perennial questions about humankind's relation to wild nature, questions to which—given the inescapable reality of evolutionary process—no final answers may be given. As Leopold realized, even attempting to resolve such questions requires an exacting synthesis of theoretical knowledge, practical experience, and creative vision. Here our purpose is not to survey the many interpretations of Leopold's thought, but to develop a reflective perspective on his idea of wilderness: that is, to set the land ethic in the continuum of thought developed throughout this book. In other words, the significance of Leopold's idea of wilderness can be seen most clearly against the backdrop of history—those transitions of thought from Paleolithic through and including Modern ideas of wilderness.

A fact sometimes ignored by his admirers and critics is that Leopold's wilderness philosophy is deeply entwined with the historical stream.[97] His ecology builds upon the thought of those who preceded, and must thus be seen as part of a continuing intellectual and cultural revolution that began in the nineteenth-century with Darwin and Clausius. Leopold's synthesizing tendencies resemble in some ways those manifest in Hegel's idea of history or Darwin's theory of evolution.[98] If we view Leopold as theoretically and existentially immersed within a cultural matrix that transcended merely disciplinary issues, then the land ethic can be understood as part of an ongoing twentieth-century struggle to link the descriptive world of classical science and the prescriptive world of ethics. In learning how "to think like a mountain," Leopold necessarily reconceptualized science in general, and ecology in particular, since he recognized that science is inextricably entangled with the culture that sustains it. Only a few intellects of our century have grasped this crucial fact: Einstein was one and Leopold another.

Leopold's premise—that science and ethics intertwine and that at base they are streams that diverge from one source—coincides with the advance

of postmodern reason. To view Leopold from the standpoint of modernistic interpretative schema is to miss the underlying tension, the period of
revolutionary science, that animated his life's work. While often viewed
as definitive, the land ethic is perhaps best understood as the product of a
transitional ecology, part of an unfinished intellectual process that began
with the Darwinian revolution and has yet to work its way through. As
our century begins to give way to the next, an incomplete sociocultural
agenda awaits. As Leopold said, "Ecology is an infant just learning to talk,
and, like other infants, is engrossed with its own coinage of big words. Its
working days lie in the future." [99] Wallace Stegner echoes Leopold's assertion, observing that the "land ethic is not a fact but a task. Like old age, it
is nothing to be overly optimistic about. But consider the alternative." [100]
However procedurally perilous the path on which he embarked, Leopold
has been vindicated, for the issues central to his thought are fundamentally
entwined with contemporary events: questions about the limits of economic growth, water and air quality standards, designation of wilderness
areas within the national forests, and protection of endangered species all
reflect the land ethic.

Of those who have examined Leopold's philosophy, perhaps Peter A.
Fritzell best sets him in the historical stream. Fritzell finds *Sand County
Almanac* a quintessential "American book" because it reveals so clearly
the competing allegiances of the American mind.

> In so doing, the book proves the continuing vitality of that paradoxi-
> cal American determination, on the one hand, *to reform or redeem
> history*—in the process, restoring or reclaiming an original harmony
> between human and nonhuman nature—and, on the other hand, *to
> escape history entirely,* by turning (or returning) to nature, as we say,
> by letting nature take its course, by leaving nature to its own devices,
> or by simply appreciating nature and its workings in all their deep evo-
> lutionary power and ecological complexity, wherever they may lead.[101]

This interpretation seems cogent. Yet the American mind manifests a
variety of purposes and motives. Some Americans, and by all indications
they remain a majority, think of nature as only a stockpile of resources,
no more than a materially necessary substratum for cultural and personal
achievement. Thus, the land ethic is more radical than Fritzell suggests, for
Sand County Almanac brackets the categories of Modernism (economic,
scientific, ethical) in terms of which the interface between the human
species and nature has been habitually and unreflectively conceptualized.
The beauty of Fritzell's interpretation is that he views Leopold's normative

ecology in the context of a larger historical process: humankind's ever-changing yet somehow constant idea of wilderness. Such a positioning is sound, for adequate judgment cannot be made by imposing ahistorical criteria on Leopold's thought. As Fritzell intimates, Leopold was a part of a wilderness tradition that sought through contact with wild nature some primal sense of being, or even an *Ur* experience—an awareness of the green world from which the human species had come. He was simultaneously part of an emerging science of ecology, itself the child of the scientific and Darwinian revolutions, that aimed at remaking culture and ameliorating environmental damage.

If we so view Leopold, then the land ethic seems susceptible to the same bifurcation that Fritzell observes in the American character. Leopold's ecological reading of history at least tacitly recognizes the one-way movement of evolutionary process. But if he envisions "thinking like a mountain," then he seeks to go home again. However, as Fritzell argues,

> if man *is* a plain member and citizen of the land community, one of thousands of accretions to the pyramid of life, then he *cannot* be a nonmember or conqueror of it; and his actions (like the actions of other organisms) *cannot* but express and affect his position within the pyramid of life. . . . Conversely, if man's technology *has* enabled man to make unprecedented changes in the circuit of life, then evolution is *not* simply a long series of self-induced changes in that circuit. . . . If man *is* simplifying the flow mechanisms and shortening the circuits of the biotic pyramid, then the trend of evolution is *not* to elaborate and diversify the biota, at least not so long as man is a functioning member of it. If man is an exploiter and conqueror of the land community, then he is not a plain member and citizen of it, or least he is a citizen only part of the time.[102]

Leopold was too much of a realist to believe that industrial-democratic people could go home again, even if we "think like a mountain." His point was that we might learn to follow in culture those ways of nature which promote integrity, stability, and beauty. Humankind, Leopold saw clearly, is part of a grand evolutionary process, and our species cannot only recognize but preserve and promote beauty, thus reforming or redeeming history; similarly, those activities that destabilize ecosystems or threaten environmental integrity can be redirected.

Near the beginning of this chapter we observed that American history, ecology, and Aldo Leopold were running on convergent courses. His land ethic perhaps confirms that assertion, for his philosophy comes as close as any other to resolving the many paradoxes of modernity. As we have pursued the Cartesian dream of becoming the masters of nature we have painfully rediscovered the essential wisdom of Bacon's insight: the illusion that we are master of all things obscures the truth that we are not even masters of ourselves. Thus, it is plausible to read Leopold's ecology as a subversive science, a foundational or deep ecology that promises not only paradigmatic (*theorie*) but cultural revolution (*praxis*) as well. Leopold saw as a whole—essentially the natural history of species *Homo sapiens*—what most only see as disparate pieces and parts. He is perhaps the harbinger of Worster's Age of Ecology. Gregory Bateson observes that "the major problems in the world are the result of the difference between the way nature works and the way man thinks."[103] Leopold seized on such a problematic, and came close to resolving it, for thinking ecologically means that the way (Modernism) that Western people characteristically think has been found wanting in some regards, and therefore we must at least consider the possibility of beginning to think in terms of the way nature works. "It is only the scholar," Leopold argued, "who appreciates that all history consists of successive excursions from a single starting-point, to which man returns again and again to organize yet another search for a durable scale of values."[104]

CHAPTER EIGHT

The Idea of Wilderness in the Poetry of Robinson Jeffers and Gary Snyder

Is there in the end any fundamental difference between the thinking poet and the poetic thinker? The poet need not think; the thinker need not create poetry; but to be a poet of first rank there is a thinking that the poet must accomplish, and it is the same kind of thinking, in essence, that the thinker of first rank must accomplish, a thinking which has all the purity and thickness and solidity of poetry, and whose saying is poetry.

—Albert Hofstadter, "Introduction" to
Martin Heidegger, *Poetry, Language, Thought*

THIS CHAPTER FOCUSES on the idea of wilderness in the poetry of Robinson Jeffers and Gary Snyder, consequently ignoring other writers and poets whose work also reflects that concept. The selection of Jeffers and Snyder delimits an otherwise impossibly large field, and there is some reason to think that the choice is sound since "ecological consciousness seems most vibrant in the poetic mode. The poetic voices of Jeffers and Snyder, so rare in modern poetry but frequently found in primal people's oral tradition, are a virtual cascade of celebration of Nature/God and being." [1] We have already argued that Modernism—or, more precisely, its language, its philosophic and scientific literature—obscures wild nature. Humankind has seemingly left the green world behind and today embraces only the world of culture. It follows, according to Joseph Meeker, that if literature is a defining characteristic of the history of civilization, then "it should be examined carefully and honestly to discover its influence upon human behavior and the natural environment—to determine what role, if any, it plays in the welfare and survival of mankind and what insight it offers into human relationships with other species and with the world around us."[2]

Immediately the so-called literary ecologist discovers the overwhelming reality that as civilization develops its literature dwells increasingly on humankind and its problems, on Lord Man—reified *Man* that humanizes nature for *His* purposes—and less and less on nonhuman others and our relations with them.[3] Our dreams and sacred myths are not of a mother goddess incarnate but of a divinity beyond who rules over an earthly vale of tears. Nevertheless, there remain among us a few thinking poets whose creative work incorporates the wilderness into its heart.[4] Such artists are grappling with "the nature of the human predicament: how nature is to be reentered; how man, the relatively unthinking and proud creator of the second world—the world of culture—may revivify and restore the first world which cherished and brought him into being."[5] The wilderness poet calls forth ancient connections of the wild and human worlds that Modernism has obscured. In ontogenetic terms, the poetry of Jeffers and Snyder allows the reader to reestablish roots in that fertile soil which nurtures all life. They question the belief that humankind is unproblematically separate from and superior to wild nature and poetically affirm an awareness of primordial being. They reveal in their language that we are—although the proud creators of a second world towering over nature—still bound with the larger course of evolution. Even our contemporary problems intrinsically involve nature.

Robinson Jeffers (1887–1962) and Gary Snyder (1930–) are not unique in reflecting on the human condition, in exploring the wilderness, and in plumbing the depths of our relations with creation. In their basic commitment to the natural and wild they appear to mirror the Romantic poets. Although the Romantics initiated a poetic reaction to Modernism, especially to mechanistic materialism and dualism, they remained partially enframed within its conceptual outlines, essentially taking a linear view of history (itself rooted in Christian eschatology) and believing that progress toward perfection of the human estate was inevitable.[6] Jeffers and Snyder abandon such a viewpoint. Jeffers believes that humankind is doomed inevitably first to rise and then to fall, perpetuating a cosmic cycle of suffering that is neither good nor evil but simply the way things are.[7] Snyder also abandons any idea that the present time culminates historical process in favor of a tranquil and cyclical, and therefore organic and presumably satisfying, mode of human beingness.[8] And although the Romantics eschewed logic in favor of *sensibilité*, Jeffers and Snyder have little faith in either intuition or reason. Both are skeptical that humans can know ultimate truth, since the human enterprise is eternally in flux. Jeffers believes that enlightenment necessitates pain and that even then any vision defies conventional categorization: the seer must seek truth alone. Snyder replaces faith in reason with a poetry that discloses an ancient wisdom: an *Ursprung* that can be accessed by dwelling poetically. So viewed, Jeffers and Snyder are post-Romantics who have made more a quantum leap than a linear progression from their predecessors. Jeffers believes that only from the ashes of Judeo-Christian culture and the categories of the Enlightenment might rise a grounded human beingness that loves the "beauty of things" and God more than itself. Snyder, too, departs from the modern mainstream, finding in ancient myth a premodern wisdom that underlies a psychologically satisfying, intellectually liberating, and ecologically feasible mode of postmodern existence, where humankind is again bound with the land, the plants, and animals.

Robinson Jeffers's Poetic Vision: Inhumanism and the Beauty of Things

The idea that Robinson Jeffers is a neglected genius of American poetry persists, but the notion is poorly defined. His poetic vision is incongruous with the world-in-force, and thus appears aberrant and irrational to any modernist critic. Little wonder that Jeffers has been called a poet without critics. George Sterling wrote (1925) that *Tamar* was the "strongest and most dreadful poem that I have ever read or heard of" and recommended that people "who shrink from the hidden horrors of life" should avoid reading it.[9] Even today "interest in Jeffers remains negligible. No longer considered prominent enough to attack by critics, he is now ignored."[10] Jeffers is not considered by most academic critics to be in the first rank of twentieth-century poets with, for example, T. S. Eliot, Wallace Stevens, or Ezra Pound.

Outside the "poetic establishment" Jeffers has a thriving group of readers. His poems are well known to lovers and defenders of wild nature, particularly those interested in the idea of wilderness and in exploring relationships between nature, God, and humankind. His poetry also finds ready reception abroad, both in English and in translation, most recently Japanese and German.[11] And even within the larger community of critics a minority views him as one of the preeminent twentieth-century American poets.[12] A few scholars and graduate students are writing books and dissertations on Jeffers, and new collections of his poetry abound.[13] Robert Brophy writes that "after decades of neglect during which he appeared only sporadically in anthologies, his poetry is once again being appreciated by critic and reading public alike. There are those . . . who think he will be one of the few great poets of our century."[14]

Time has helped heal the wounds Jeffers's poetry inflicted on the public psyche. The poet Dana Gioia argues that "now—sixty years after he began his radical redefinition of human values—his answers still seem disturbingly fresh and cogent" and that his poems "constitute an American realist and regionalist alternative to the mandarin aestheticism of international modernism."[15] Gioia's insight is doubly perceptive, for in recognizing that Jeffers offers a regionalist alternative to the culturally prevailing conception of poetry, he also affirms the postmodern character of the poetry. Regionalist poets are by definition tied to the land and necessarily develop a sense of their place in the natural scheme.[16] So understood, they are not preoccupied, as is modern literature, with human life; rather their subject is more often humankind's relations to nature. Yet another contemporary critic, Robert Ian Scott, sees Jeffers similarly, finding in his work a viable and connected poetic vision that forms an affirmative alternative to the pessimistic and disconnected visions of Eliot and Pound. Scott concludes, "If I had to sum up the characteristic choice of subject and point of view of the two leading American poets of this century by quoting them, I'd choose: 'I can connect nothing with nothing' for Eliot; his confusions were his subject. For Jeffers, I'd chose: 'The enormous beauty of things.' His subject is not himself but the universe as the beautifully visible God he loved."[17]

Inhumanism is the term most often used to characterize the philosophical vision that animates Jeffers's poetry, and the poet portrays himself as an inhumanist.[18] And yet the term begs clarification since it implies that Jeffers is a misanthrope and oversimplifies his philosophical outlook. The term is accurate in that the poetry redirects attention from the human toward the inhuman and "the beauty of things," but only a thorough study, such as Brophy's, begins to capture the complexity and richness of the inhumanist perspective.[19] The best short statement of Jeffers's inhumanist philosophy is his own, found in the *published* preface to his last major book, *The Double Axe*. He explains that the burden of the poems

> is to present a certain philosophical attitude, which might be called
> Inhumanism, a shifting of emphasis and significance from man to not-
> man; the rejection of human solipsism and recognition of the trans-

human magnificence. It seems time that our race began to think as an adult does, rather than like an egocentric baby or insane person. This manner of thought and feeling is neither misanthropic nor pessimist, though two or three people have said so and may again. It involves no falsehoods, and is a means of maintaining sanity in slippery times; it has objective truth and human value. It offers a reasonable detachment as rule of conduct, instead of love, hate and envy. It neutralizes fanaticism and wild hopes; but it provides magnificence for the religious instinct, and satisfies our need to admire greatness and rejoice in beauty.[20]

The original preface, not published in the 1948 Random House edition but included in the 1977 Liveright edition of *The Double Axe*, amplifies. Jeffers suggests that section 45 of Part II, entitled "The Inhumanist," briefly expresses "the intentions implicit in these poems and previous ones. I take the trouble of this note, not for the sake of the verses, but because it seems to me that the attitude they suggest—the devaluation of human-centered illusions, the turning outward from man to what is boundlessly greater—is a next step in human development; and an essential condition of freedom, and of spiritual (i.e., moral and vital) sanity."[21] Undoubtedly, Jeffers saw inhumanism as a paradigmatic alternative to and incommensurable with the modern worldview. In the original preface he also states that the poems explicitly capture "a new attitude, a new manner of thought and feeling" which first came to him through his disillusionment with World War I. This novel outlook is "based on a recognition of the astonishing beauty of things, and on a rational acceptance of the fact that mankind is neither central nor important in the universe; our vices and abilities are insignificant as our happiness. We know this, of course, but it does not appear that any previous one of the ten thousand religions and philosophies has realized it."[22] This declaration is as extreme as Thoreau's in *Walden* that "only one in a million is awake enough for effective intellectual exertion, only one in a hundred millions to a poetic or divine life."[23] As Thoreau realized, only by making such emphatic statements can the poetic thinker or thinking poet be heard over the din of civilization. Jeffers knew that he had kindred spirits. He also knew that those who spoke for the inhuman were an endangered species, and he realistically assessed inhumanism's public prospects, observing that it "is particularly unacceptable at the present, being opposed not only by tradition, but by all the currents of the time."[24]

Inhumanism, then, can be understood as the philosophical crux of Jeffers's poetry. In other words, Jeffers's poems articulate his inhumanism: a postmodern perspective grappling with the fundamental ontological question—What is being? As the Inhumanist, an old man with a double-bit ax (Jeffers's persona) says (§45, Part II),

> "O future children:
> Cruelty is dirt and ignorance, a muddy peasant
> Beating his horse. Ambition and power-lust
> Are for adolescents and defective persons. Moderate kindness
> Is oil on a crying wheel: use it. Mutual help
> Is necessary: use it when necessary.
> And as to love: make love when need drives.
> And as to love: love God. He is rock, earth and water, and
>   the beast and stars; and the night that contains them.
> And as to love: whoever loves or hates man is fooled in a
>   mirror." He grinned and said:
> "From experience I speak. But truly, if you love man,
> swallow him in wine: love man in God.
> Man and nothing but man is a sorry mouthful."

Such a dramatic statement elliptically outlines the essence of his idea of wilderness: *outside of the cosmic process there is no being whatsoever, be this human or divine.*[25] Viewed in toto, his poetry embraces three principles. First, (1) the inhumanist brackets the intense and unreflective anthropocentric bias of Modernism by recognizing "transhuman magnificence." But (2) in acknowledging transhuman magnificence the inhumanist is neither antihuman nor inhumane but celebrates the possibility of a sane human beingness that has cured "the fever of self-involvement, and contemplate[s] the living God."[26] Accordingly, inhumanism represents an alternative worldview that rejects the profane twentieth-century world while affirming the sacrality of existence. Finally, (3) in comprehending the beauty of things, the inhumanist discovers the transitory nature of all things, including humankind and its works: the cosmic process is the reality, and the human species is inextricably bound with that process.

The inhumanist's bracketing of the categories of Modernism and the turning away from the merely human and socially defined reality toward the transhuman magnificence of things (1 above) is remarkably similar to the phenomenological *epoche,* an opening up of human consciousness to the transhuman truths of lived experience.[27] Jeffers calls the quest for such truth the return: a return to the source of existence. "It is time for us to kiss the earth again, / It is time to let the leaves rain from the skies, / Let the rich life run to the roots again." Jeffers's sensibility is premodern, for he taps into an primeval materialism—a *prima materia* or connectedness with the very substance of life—with which modern materialism, in its second-order abstraction, has lost contact. "I will touch things and things and no more thoughts, / That breed like mouthless May-flies darkening the sky."[28] Robert Bringhurst argues that the models for Jeffers's poems were geophysical rather than literary, that his inspiration was not in ideas but came instead from natural things and processes. His intent was to get "away from the human surfaces of language and into its rhythmic and narrative depths. Poetry must have rhythm, he insisted, not to tell us its human contents but because rhythm is a test of external reality." "Continent's End" epitomizes Jeffers's poetics. "Mother, though my song's measure is like your surf-beat's ancient rhythm I never learned it of you. / Before there was any water there were tides of fire, both our tones flow from the older fountain."[29] Bringhurst notes that "students of prosody are often taught that the word 'verse' comes from versus, the furrow and turn of the plow, and by implication that verse, if not poetry, is an achievement of agricultural societies. Jeffers knew that it is older than the neolithic, that its roots are the roots of the world."[30]

The inhumanist perspective also (2 above) leads to a rediscovery of the living-God in the world. Brophy writes that Jeffers "has 'fallen in love outward,' swept away by the beauty of the universe which he sees as divine. This is one side of his poetics, a psalmist for this pantheistic god; the other side is critic of this time, a relentless voice, pronouncing doom to men's egocentric hopes, a prophet like Isaiah, demanding holiness and wholeness and renunciation of false gods." This characterization—which underscores the persistent religiosity of Jeffers's poetry—hints at the intricacy of inhumanism, a perspective Brophy describes as "a consistent, thoroughgoing world-view based on his scientific insights, paced by astronomic perspective, and inspirited by a mystic sense of immanent divinity. For him, the world became the ongoing self-discovery of God who unfolds in the secrets of atoms and galaxies all the possibilities of being."[31] Jeffers's religious vision reflects, of course, the inhumanist bracketing of conventional wisdom and turning away from the merely human. The poetry recognizes that the modern person—the humanist of modern culture—has become Homo oeconomicus, and the world in which life plays out its course merely profane. The inhumanist, however, is a specimen of Homo religiosus, and celebrates an eternal mythical present: a living-God in the world.

Finally (3 above), the inhumanist perspective leads to the realization that process alone is reality, that life is a temporal flux in some ways beyond comprehension. Jeffers, however, is not an anti-intellectual, since he contends that inhumanism has both "objective truth and human value." His poetry is informed by the second scientific revolution—the evolutionary paradigm, in contrast to the static paradigm of modern science—and brings the truths of Darwin and Clausius to bear on the perdurable questions of human nature and humankind's relation to nature. For Jeffers science is not simply a tool by which humankind stands above nature, since it also functions reflexively, revealing that the human experiment is grounded in and subject to nature's way.

JEFFERS WAS THE SON of an Old Testament theology professor, cutting his intellectual teeth on the Bible and the categories of the Enlightenment. The complexity of his poetry is rooted in this erudition, since he knew not only the Bible but Hebrew, Greek, and Latin, and not only the classics but Nietzsche, Wordsworth, and Spengler. Jeffers's poetry is aptly understood as an abiding inquiry into the nature of religious experience (as distinct from religion). Although often characterized as godless, Jeffers is not an atheist, believing that some experience of an ego-transcending and culture-enframing context is essential to any distinctive sense of human beingness. Many of his poems explore the traditional answers of the world's religions and philosophies, although he invariably finds them inadequate to answer the questions of God's existence.[32] "To His Father" addresses the break between his father's Judeo-Christian perspective and his own inhumanism. Jeffers's father, a dour Presbyterian, was as remote from the family as the God he sought. In one critic's view Jeffers's poetry is, "almost from first to last, a testimony to his sense of abandonment and to his quest for a father who had hidden himself as the God of his own fathers had been gradually hidden from him."[33] Jeffers could neither lie to his father nor hide what he took to be the inherent flaws of Judeo-Christianity: the reification of humankind into Lord Man and the isolation of both Lord Man and God from the cosmic process which sustains all being. Yet to follow alternate paths was painful: they led to the acceptance of human finitude and death.

They also led to authentic religious experience. The necessity of suffering and the pain of existence, truths Jeffers learned from Buddhism and the harsh realities of life, were essential to ultimate insight—hierophany or the vision of God's living-presence. His tortured god, at the end of the long poem "At the Birth of An Age," expresses this idea clearly.

> If I were quiet and emptied myself
> of pain
>   breaking these bonds,

Healing these wounds: without strain there is nothing. Without
     pressure, without conditions, without pain,
Is peace; that's nothing, not-being; the pure night, the perfect
     freedom, the black crystal. I have chosen
Being; therefore wounds, bonds, limits and pain; the crowded
     mind and the anguished nerves, experience and ecstasy.
Whatever electron or atom or flesh or star or universe cries
     to me,
Or endures in shut silence: it is my cry, my silence; I am the
     nerve, I am the agony,
I am the endurance. I torture myself
To discover myself; trying with a little or extreme experiment
     each nerve and fibril, all forms
Of being, of life, of cold substance; all motions and netted com-
     plications of event,
All poisons of desire, love, hatred, joy, partial peace, partial
     vision. Discovery is deep and endless,
Each moment of being is new: therefore I still refrain my burn-
     ing thirst from the crystal-black
Water of an end.[34]

The poem implies that once recognized and accepted, pain can lead to some glimmer of the cosmic godhead. For Jeffers, grace comes only through experiencing anguish and identifying with the process of suffering.

Jeffers had no quarrel with the great religious seers per se, such as the Buddha, Lao Tzu, Mohammed, or Jesus Christ. Each had struggled to the top of the mountain following his own path, and there had encountered divinity. His poetry affirms such questing as inevitable for all human beings, as an inescapable consequence of self-consciousness. "Theory of Truth" identifies three fundamental questions that underlie the religious quest: "First, is there a God and of what nature? Second, whether there's anything after we die but worm's meat? / Third, how should men live?"[35] The failure of orthodox religion lies primarily in its inevitable reification of the intuitive insights of the prophets into dogma, into Religious Truth.[36] Jeffers is also skeptical of saviors per se (as in Isaiah 43.3). All ideologies, religious or secular, are potentially enslaving, since they are irretrievably human.

Jeffers was uncomfortable with his own potential role as savior, believing that the highest truths and beauty can only be known individually. In a passage that is Thoreauvian in its suspicions of collective authority he writes that

> There is no valid authority
> In church nor state, custom, scripture nor creed,
> But only in one's own conscience and the beauty of things.
> Doggedly I think again: One's conscience is a trick oracle,
> Worked by parents and nurse-maids, the pressure of the people,
> And the delusions of dead prophets: trust it not.
> Wash it clean to receive the transhuman beauty: then trust it.[37]

Obviously, Jeffers does not totally avoid affirmations, but his answers are always carefully qualified. "Then what is the answer?—Not to be deluded by dreams." Delusion by dreams. The fevered imaginings of the human brain. The passions of the human heart. These are perhaps the reasons Jeffers believed that religious seers (as exemplified by Arthur Barclay in "The Women at Point Sur") become, in the end, insane. "Theory of Truth" reveals that the religious experiences of Jesus, Lao Tzu, and the Buddha were authentic but that each seer lost the way through madness.

> Why does insanity always twist the great answers?
>   Because only
>   tormented persons want truth.
> Man is an animal like other animals, wants food and
>   success and women, not truth. Only if the mind
> Tortured by some interior tension has despaired of happiness:
>   then it hates its life-cage and seeks further,
> And finds, if it is powerful enough. But instantly the private
>   agony that made the search
> Muddles the finding.[38]

The poem closes with yet another question.

> Then search for truth is foredoomed and frustrate?
> Only stained fragments?
>
>   Until the mind has turned its love from itself and
> man, from parts to the whole.[39]

The turning from parts to the whole is central to Jeffers's inhumanist perspective, for in that direction lies connectedness to God, the holy order of the universe. This is as far as Jeffers cared to go in his affirmation of a path: turn love outward from humankind to the transhuman magnificence of the beauty of things, the cosmic whole that enframes the human odyssey and, indeed, is itself divine. In articulating such a religious perspective—an *eco-*

logical vision of divinity—Jeffers ran far ahead of conventional wisdom.[40] Only a few poetic thinkers, such as Alfred North Whitehead and Charles Hartshorne, achieve a similar depth of insight.[41] As Whitehead suggests, "Between them the Hebrews and the Greeks provided a program for discontent," a radical discontent lying in the denial of our human nature, our rootedness in a natural world.[42] The combined effect of Greek and early Christian thought on our culture led to the belief that to exist in the natural world is to live in perdition. Only the supernatural could save us. Jeffers stands this orthodoxy on its head: the inhumanist accepts pain and death, for all is part of the holy, transhuman magnificence of things. The psychic allure of Jeffers's ecological vision is that nature and God, rent asunder by the modern mind, are reunited.[43]

From the inhumanist vantage point all things are connected—life and death, humankind and nature, heaven and earth. "The Answer" casts aside the dreams of the Western world for "universal justice and happiness" and offers in their place an objective realism suffused with the natural values of integrity and beauty.

> A severed hand
> Is an ugly thing, and man dissevered from the earth
>   and stars and his history
>   . . . for contemplation or in fact . . .
> Often appears atrociously ugly. Integrity is wholeness,
>   the greatest beauty is
> Organic wholeness, the wholeness of life and things,
>   the divine beauty of the universe.
>   Love that, not man
> Apart from that, or else you will share man's
>   pitiful confusions,
>   or drown in despair when his days darken.[44]

The lessons of ecology were not always ironic. Jeffers sometimes sets the human animal in a natural context, as for example in "Boats in a Fog." Fishing boats with "throbbing engines" move out of the Monterey harbor in a heavy fog, "trailing each other / Following the cliff for guidance, / Holding a difficult path between the peril of the sea-fog / And the foam on the shore granite." And then they return.

> Back to the buoys in Monterey harbor. A flight of pelicans
>   Is nothing lovelier to look at;
>   The flight of the planets is nothing nobler; all the arts lose
>   virtue

> Against the essential reality
> Of creatures going about their business among the equally
> Earnest elements of nature.[45]

The unstated conclusion is that humankind might endure if it would follow nature's way.

In his longer works, Jeffers's dramatis personae are often set in a natural context where outcomes are a consequence of instinctive forces rather than human rationality. Nietzsche and Schopenhauer unquestionably influenced this poetic vision. Jeffers endows his characters with foreknowledge and mystical insight; they experience powerful dreams, act out deep-seated impulses, and are often caught in conflict between societally approved channels of behavior and their own subconscious inclinations. Rape, murder, jealously, psychosis—these are familiar if painful themes in the poems. Jeffers was not afraid to tackle such issues, believing that only a considered look at the human predicament held any prospect for salvation—that is, saving us from ourselves.

In "Tamar" the sexual desires that awaken in Tamar and her brother are amplified through biblical allusion and metaphor, and we see the influence of Nietzsche's theory of eternal return on the poem. The principals are caught in a cosmic cycle that both grounds and transcends. "The ancient water, the everlasting repetition of the dawn. You shipwrecked horseman / So many and still so many and now for you the last." Tamar reflects the wildness of the coast and the ocean where she lives—the impulse to commit incest with her brother dominates her mind.

> Was it the wild rock coast
> Of her breeding, and the reckless wind
> In the beaten trees and the gaunt booming crashes
> Of breakers under the rocks, or rather the amplitude
> And wing-subduing immense earth-ending water
> That moves all the west taught her this freedom?[46]

Such reflections on the human condition are bitter draughts, hard to swallow when we cannot even accept the relatively objective lessons of ecology. Although Jeffers's analysis of human nature is not irrefragable, his insistence that sentient beings must probe into the implications of evolution for human nature is correct.

Science, or more accurately philosophical insight leavened by objective fact, is essential to Jeffers's quest for understanding. His studies in medicine "impressed him with a romance-deflating outlook on human aspirations, a clinical assessment of glands and nerve fibrils. It also put him in touch with pain, death, and corruption of the flesh."[47] Jeffers's investigations in anthropology and comparative religion helped break him free from hand-me-down Christianity. He uses one of the earliest insights of modern science—the heliocentric theory of Nicholas Copernicus—to restrain human egotism in "The Double Axe." The Inhumanist builds a cairn of stones to surround an iron boundary marker, and while contemplating the result, the old man finds it aesthetically pleasing and decides to dedicate the work.

> "To whom this monument: Jesus or Caesar or Mother
>   Eve?
> No," he said, "to Copernicus: Nicky Kupernick: who first
>   pushed man
> Out of his insane self-importance and the world's navel,
>   and taught him his place."
>
>   "And the next one to Darwin."[48]

Other poems draw on twentieth-century science, including the concept of the expanding universe ("We have counted the stars and half understood them, / we have watched the farther galaxies fleeing away from us, wild herds / Of panic horses—or a trick of distance deceives the prism") and thermodynamics ("The heroic stars spending themselves, / Coining their very flesh into bullets for the lost battle, / They must burn out at length like used candles").[49] Science, Brophy contends, gave him "the ultimate metaphor, the oscillating universe in which the big bang yielded to imploding galaxies—the rhythm of successive cosmoses which he called the heartbeat of God."[50] Jeffers plumbs the depths of science for its reflexive implications, understanding that the relatively objective truth of twentieth-century science is helpful in overcoming humankind's inevitable tendency to anthropocentrize. The two great nineteenth-century insights into the reality of becoming—the discovery of evolution and the second law of thermodynamics—provide a scientific backdrop against which the profile of the inhumanist can be seen most clearly.[51]

What are the implications of Darwin's theory for self-understanding? Jeffers understood that this question goes far beyond squabbles with creationists. He looks steely-eyed at what the Romantics and others glorify, debunking any idealization of the soul and human nature. "Original Sin" openly poses the question whether humankind might be an evolutionary mistake, especially since the species is capable of unprecedented acts of natural evil. The poem dramatically juxtaposes "man-brained and man-handed apes," who have captured a mammoth in a pit and, unable to slay the beast with their spears, have lit a fire and are literally roasting it to death, with the beauty, the nobility, of natural process.

Still, science is neither a cognitive nor an ontological absolute for Jeffers, since it, too, is intrinsically human-centered. "Science" (1925), a poem thoroughly Baconian in perspective, expresses reservations about human-kind's use of science. "A little knowledge, a pebble from the shingle, / A drop from the oceans: who would have dreamed this infinitely little too much?"[52] Science alone cannot solve any of the problems that afflict humankind. After the horrors of World War II, and the reality of Hiroshima and Nagasaki nuclear Armageddon, Jeffers's concerns intensified. One of the giants in "The Inquisitors" splits open a human skull and, squinting at the contents, remarks

> "A drop of marrow. How could that spoil the earth?"
> "Nevertheless," he answered,
> "They have that bomb. The blasts and the fires are nothing:
> freckles on the earth: the emanations
> Might set the whole planet into a tricky fever
> And destroy much." "Themselves," he answered. "Let
> them. Why not?" "No," he answered, "life."[53]

"Curb Science? " one of the infamous poems deleted by the Random House editors from the 1948 edition of *The Double Axe,* observes that

> Science, that gives man hope to live without lies
> Or blast himself off the earth:—curb science
> Until morality catches up?—But look: morality
> At present running rapidly retrograde,
> You'd have to turn science too, back to the witch-doctors
> And myth-drunkards. Besides that morality
> Is not an end in itself: truth is an end.

One wonders at the editorial judgment that suppressed such a penetrating perspective. Then again, it is comprehensible; the editors were caught in the grip of the modern age. Jeffers was ahead of his time in understanding the issues posed by the power of science. Alternatively, he recognized the two-culture split before C. P. Snow gave his famous Rede lecture. Jeffers's inhumanism attempts to bridge the fissure of fact and value. "Diagram" bears witness to the demise of the metaphysical and cognitive hegemony of Judeo-Christianity and the rise of a new age "that began at Kittyhawk."

The failures of Judeo-Christianity are reflected in the Frankensteinlike character of a modern technology run amok. "Truly the time is marked by insane splendors and agonies. / But watch when the two curves cross: you children / Not far away down the hawk's-nightmare future: you will see monsters." [54]

Jeffers's sense of the importance of time, however, goes beyond mere history. He had read Heraclitus, and time is central to the inhumanist perspective. His poems frequently set the human parade within a transitory cosmic process. "Shine Perishing Republic" (1925) reminds the reader that "the flower fades to make fruit, the fruit rots to make earth. / Out of the mother; and through the spring exultances, ripeness and decadence; and home to the mother." America, too, shall have its moment in the sun, and then will inevitably decline. Jeffers renders no value judgment here. The point is to realize the evanescence of cultural forms and to identify whatever abiding pattern, if any, that exists in the flux of experience. "You making haste haste on decay: not blameworthy; life is good, be it stubbornly long or suddenly / A mortal splendor: meteors are not needed less than mountains: shine, perishing republic." Jeffers's scorn is reserved for those who try to reify categories in a futile attempt to deny the reality of the flux. "And boys, be in nothing so moderate as in love of man, a clever servant, insufferable master. / There is the trap that catches noblest spirits, that caught—they say—God, when he walked on earth." [55]

Jeffers's poetry belies the outlook that behind this world lies an all-pervading, timeless reality: change is the central reality. Yet he also looks to establish culture in some deeper, perdurable surrounding context of being—something beyond the dollar, progress, democracy, and all the measures that the modern mind assumes are a part of the basic furniture of the universe. For Jeffers *the one abiding pattern* is the beauty of things.[56]

> When the imbecility, betrayals and disappointments become
>   apparent—what will you have, but to have
> Admired the beauty? I believe that the beauty and nothing
>   else is what things are formed for. Certainly
>   the world
> Was not constructed for happiness nor love nor wisdom.
>   No, nor for pain, hatred and folly. All these
> Have their seasons; and in the long year they balance
>   each other, they cancel out. But the beauty stands.[57]

"To the Stone Cutters" (1924) further discloses his Heraclitean perspective on both human endeavor—"stone-cutters fighting time with marble, you foredefeated / Challengers of oblivion"—and stone, which inexorably if slowly disintegrates, crumbling into oblivion. Not only are such material things as statuary impermanent, but the human mind's products are anchored only in the shifting sands of time—the poet "builds his monument mockingly." Entropy, ultimately, will have its way with all that exists or can be conceived. "For man will be blotted out, the blithe earth die, the brave sun / Die blind and blacken to the heart."[58] Some may choose to see this poem as pessimistic; more likely it is realistic, since we are what we are, evanescent creatures bound in time, beset by finitude. Jeffers finds a nobility in our foredefeated challenges to oblivion, for stone, though impermanent, holds the sculptor's form if only for a time, and old poems yet find ways to bring "the honey of peace" to the human heart. Thus, even while he affirms change as the central reality, he recognizes the possibility of a limited knowledge of permanencies within the process, such as the beauty of things—a view remarkably similar to Whitehead's. And insofar as there are similarities between Whitehead's and Jeffers's ideas of time, then we can better understand the pervasive religiosity of Jeffers's poetry. As Whitehead argues, "The most general formulation of the religious problem is the question whether the process of the temporal world passes into the formation of other actualities, bound together in an order in which novelty does not mean loss."[59]

These many strands of the inhumanist perspective—the necessity of pain, the beauty of things, the pervasiveness of the flux, and the reality of God—come together in some of Jeffers's longer poems, especially in "At the Birth of an Age." Jeffers writes that this poem had a "calculated origin. I was considering the main sources of our civilization, and listed them roughly as Hebrew-Christian, Roman, Greek, Teutonic." As the poem grew he suddenly realized that he was treading familiar ground, since the Teutonic element began "to warp and groan under the tension of Christian influence. The symbol of the self-tortured God, that closes the poem, had appeared to me long before in *Apology for Bad Dreams* and in *The Women at Point Sur*—Heautontimoroumenos, the self-tormentor— but it stands most clearly in the self-hanged Odin of Norse mythology."[60] Brophy's perceptive analysis of this poem precisely captures Jeffers's synthesis.

> Whatever one fantasizes about other modes of being theoretically possible, the mode which man experiences has a simple formula: Being is a dynamism, a building-up and a breaking-down of forms. This means violence, no form yielding itself without resistance, which in turn im-

plies pain for sentient beings. For Jeffers this violence makes beauty—an effulgence and radiation of being in its straining, excruciating course—and this beauty is so deeply itself and so totally permeating as to be transcendental—to be God.

BEING = DYNAMISM = VIOLENCE = PAIN = BEAUTY = GOD

The mark of the hanged god, that is, this process of painful self-discovery, is on everyone.[61]

Brophy's insight goes to the core of Jeffers's inhumanism, for by turning from the love of humankind to the world, God can again be experienced as immediately present. Living astride the wild Pacific shore, following that same path in the wilderness that countless others had followed before, Jeffers became Homo religiosus.[62]

> There is one God, and the earth is his prophet.
> The beauty of things is the face of God: worship it;
> Give your hearts to it; labor to be like it.[63]

The depth of Jeffers's insight into the central reality of evolutionary process and its implications for humankind are easily overlooked, for what he proposes is no less than an open window through nature on to the possibility of hierophany. The inhumanist perspective effectively weds humankind, God, and nature by first (1) bracketing the prevailing Judeo-Christian notion of a linear, progressive time (itself retained within classical science, the Enlightenment, and Romanticism). For the modern mind, God is necessarily outside of time and nature, and the reality of suffering is only a manifestation of sin. The inhumanist (2) grasps that time does not run on a human schedule and that humankind is no more than a way station on a cosmic journey. Such a realization, as the Inhumanist says,

> "is more than comfort: it is deep peace
> and final joy
> To know that the great world lives, whether man dies or
> not. The beauty of things is not harnessed to
> human
> Eyes and the little active minds: it is absolute.
> It is not for human titillation, though it serves that. It is
> the life of things,
> And the nature of God."[64]

Of course, (3) suffering for sentient beings is inevitable in the grinding away of the Heraclitean flux, most poignantly in death and human finitude; but through acceptance of this reality the gate to theophany is opened, for the process is divine, "transcending" (better, enframing or grounding) the evanescent. Thus, as Jeffers maintains, inhumanism has both objective truth, being consistent with the known facts, and human value, serving as a guide to human action. The morale is to eschew the merely contingent and affirm the relatively permanent—the beauty of things. From such a vantage point humankind might cure "the fever of self-involvement" and contemplate the "living-god." Only in solitude, however, can such a god be encountered.

Jeffers is intensely conscious not only of cultural evanescence but of individual mortality as well. "What a wretched fisherman is death, / That lets his catch lie kicking in the nets of delusion like living men."[65] Death assumes a cosmic importance in Jeffers's inhumanism, since from the ashes of ruin rises new life. He lived some ten years after the death of his wife, Una, and during this decade his thoughts often turned to his own encapsulation in time. "The Deer Lay Down Their Bones," written shortly after Una's death, is Jeffers's reconciliation to that fact; in spite of the loss of his great love ("We have been given life and have used it—not a great gift perhaps—but in honesty / Should use it all. Mine's empty since my love died"), the poem testifies to his will to carry on. "I am bound by my own thirty-year-old decision: who drinks the wine / Should take the dregs; even in the bitter lees and sediment / New discovery may lie. The deer in that beautiful place lay down their bones: I must wear mine." His "Vulture" (1963, published posthumously) revolves around the vulture who on "great sails" mistakes a reclined and resting Jeffers for a meal. As Jeffers heard the wind whistling in the bird's wings he was again struck by the transhuman beauty of things.

> But how beautiful he looked, gliding down
> On those great sails; how beautiful he looked, veering
>   away in the sea-light over the precipice. I tell you
>   solemnly
> That I was sorry to have disappointed him. To be eaten
>   by that beak and become part of him, to share those
>   wings and those eyes—
> What a sublime end of one's body, what an enskyment;
>   What a life after death.[66]

Thus we see, ultimately, that the great cosmic cycle—the stars wheeling in their heavenly course, the endless cycle of birth, growth, decline, and death, and the divine beauty of things—enframes the human condition and that any man or woman oblivious to this central reality is, in Jeffers's estimate, lost in a sea of illusions.

Gary Snyder: Poet Laureate of Deep Ecology

If we think of Robinson Jeffers as standing astride wilderness poetry during the first half of this century, then Gary Snyder's poetry straddles the second. In contrast to Jeffers, Snyder has been lionized in his own time, receiving among other honors a Pulitzer Prize in 1975 for *Turtle Island*. Unlike *The Double Axe*, published in the psychic glow of victory in war and thus fated to destroy Jeffers's reputation, *Turtle Island* was published almost simultaneously with the peaking of public consciousness of environmental crisis, the burgeoning of the counterculture, and the Vietnam War protest movements. Here an inexact but useful analogy seems appropriate: just as few if any of Thoreau's coevals were prepared to understand his idea of wilderness, so Robinson Jeffers; and just as a large segment of society was ready to receive John Muir's message, so with Gary Snyder. If Jeffers is a poet of protest against human vanity and myopia, then Snyder is more a poet of a *quiet revolution* that might transform the way in which the earth's peoples interact with the land and among themselves. This is not to say that Snyder's poetry lacks a critical edge but rather to affirm that his poetry—more than Jeffers's—addresses the issue of healing the rift between humankind and wild nature. Particularly among deep ecologists, Snyder has been recognized as both a critic of Modernism—the mainstream scientific-technocratic-industrialized culture of both socialism and capitalism—and a visionary whose poetry calls forth an alternative grounded in the oral traditions of primal peoples and contemporary ecological insight.[67]

What is sui generis about Snyder is not that he is a utopian, for visionaries abound, but rather that he achieves a singular philosophy combining East (religion, philosophy, psychology) and West (ecology, anthropology) with ancient wisdom (especially Amerindigen mythology) into what Sessions and Devall characterize as a "spiritual ecology."[68] The conventional connotation of the term *ecology* implies that to look at things ecologically is to see them as connected, as constituting a whole that is greater than the sum of its parts. That definition, however, suits either a functional (shallow) or a foundational (deep) ecologist, and so there must something more involved if Snyder is to be characterized as the poet laureate of deep ecology *and* a spiritual ecologist to boot. Paradoxically, a modernist perspective is particularly suited to helping us understand Snyder as a spiritual ecologist. Although Anna Bramwell, for example, does not include him in her study, surely she would read him as advocating primitivism, since he advances a premise that by exploring the "primitive" we can identify primary human potentials thwarted by modern society and that by actualizing these potentials we not only will cease burdening the earth's living systems but will become more fully human. As we shall see, nothing in Snyder's spiritual ecology suggests a return to primitivism. His poetic vision distinctly reveals the marks of a postmodern consciousness: he is a *thinking poet* whose poetry calls into being an ancient wisdom that resonates with contemporary ecology and whose saying transcends the dichotomies of Modernism.

Another way of gaining perspective on Snyder's spiritual ecology is by attending to his "Eastern connection"—his abiding interest in Oriental philosophy, psychology, religion, and poetry. During his Japan years (Snyder lived in Japan from 1956 to 1968) he discovered Miyazawa Kenji (1896–1933) and translated eighteen of his poems. Kenji, Snyder notes, was "born and lived his life among the farmers: school-teacher (Chemistry, Natural Sciences, Agriculture) and a Buddhist. His poems have many Buddhist allusions, as well as scientific vocabulary."[69] The description fits Snyder, for his poetry is difficult to understand without familiarity with both ecology and Eastern philosophy, religion, and poetry, as well as knowledge of paleoanthropology, mythology, and Amerindigen lore.

Snyder's spiritual ecology was forged at least in part in the crucible of his Japanese experiences, and he remains a Zen Buddhist.[70] The Eastern tradition (foreign to the linear, logical Western mind-set) is crucial to his exploration and appreciation of nonlinguistic, nonegocentric, nonethnocentric modes of consciousness.[71] In other words, the spiritual dimensions of Snyder's poetry flow forth from premodern sensibilities; Zen is a way of liberation for him, and there is more than a little affinity between Japanese poetry (especially haiku) and his own. If Snyder is influenced by an Eastern tradition, then the importance of silence looms prominently. If we are to hear the Earth Mother, welling up through the poet's song that sings of ancient animist sensibilities, then we must first listen. As Lao Tzu reminds, the name that can be named is not the Tao, the Mother of the ten thousand things.[72] Snyder's poems invite us to listen, to look, to feel the Mother Earth that we have either forgotten in our busyness or obscured with words and categories, the entangling vines of civilization. As Master Dōgen suggests,

> Even if you see mountains as grass, trees, earth, rocks, or walls, do not take this seriously or worry about it; it is not complete realiza-

tion. Even if there is a moment when you view mountains as the seven treasures shining, this is not returning to the source. Even if you understand mountains as the realm where all buddhas practice, this understanding is not something to be attached to. Even if you have the highest understanding of mountains as all buddhas' inconceivable qualities, the truth is not only this. These are conditioned views. This is not the understanding of buddha ancestors, but just looking through a bamboo tube at a corner of the sky.[73]

AS WITH JEFFERS, some understanding of Snyder's life illuminates his poetry. Born in 1930 in San Francisco, Snyder and his family settled on a dairy farm outside Seattle. His childhood was punctuated with forays into the wild Pacific Northwest. "Back-country skiing and snow-peak mountaineering" were early interests, and he became a self-conscious representative of the wilderness before he was twenty; Snyder's first poems dealt with these wilderness themes.[74] He explains that as a youth he "had an immediate, intuitive, deep sympathy with the natural world which was not taught me by anyone. In that sense, nature is my 'guru' and life is my sadhana. That sense of authenticity, completeness, and reality of the natural world itself made me aware even as a child of the contradictions that I could see going on around me in the state of Washington, in the way of exploitation, logging, development, pollution."[75] Early influences were not only natural, however: cultural events also played their role. The Great Depression at a minimum encouraged a healthy skepticism of the rhetorical excesses that can accompany economic theory. World War II also affected him; the world had gone mad just as he was coming of age. Western civilization was coming apart at the seams: Germany—which had cradled and nourished Bach and Goethe, Kant and Einstein—became a nation of homicidal barbarians, and his own country incinerated hundreds of thousands of civilians in Japan.

After the war Snyder worked as a merchant seaman, logger, and forest lookout, among other things; he was apparently fired from this last job because his interest in Marxism made him a "security risk."[76] He also undertook an ambitious program of study at Reed College, where he became friends with Lew Welch and Philip Whalen (who were later influential in the West Coast "beat" movement). His interdisciplinary studies at Reed culminated in a senior thesis that gave (as we shall see) an early if preliminary definition to the course of his work. Snyder moved to San Francisco in 1953, pursuing graduate studies in Oriental languages at the University of California. During his Berkeley years he got to know "Kenneth Rexroth,

Robert Duncan, Jack Spicer, Allen Ginsberg, Jack Kerouac, William Everson, and many others who were instrumental in the great flowering of west coast poetry that started in the fifties." The beat philosophy was a powerful antidote to the materialistic poisons that swept post–World War II America, and this influence is still reflected in Snyder's poetry. In 1956 he received a scholarship for study in Japan, and he spent the next two years there immersed in the study of Oriental philosophy and religion. The trip marked the inception of what Snyder calls "the Japan years," although he frequently left. Living in Kyoto, he "took up residence in the Zen temple of Shokoku-ji" and "worked part time as a researcher and translator of Zen Buddhist texts at the First Zen Institute of America's Kyoto facility, directed by Rush Sasaki, and then became a full time student of Rinzai Zen Buddhism at the Daitoku-ji monastery under Oda Sesso, Roshi." [77]

Since 1970 Snyder has lived in the northern reaches of the Sierra Nevadas "on the edge of the Tahoe National Forest, developing a mountain farmstead and working with the old and new settlers of the region." Zen remains a focus in his life, and he "is the founder of the Ring of Bone Zendo, a north Sierra association of creative lay Zen Buddhists." A functional although inexact analogy is that just as Christianity to Milton and *Paradise Lost,* so Zen to Snyder and his poetry; the spirituality that animates his poetry and life flows from Zen. Snyder writes that "along with many of his neighbors he lives by a combination of 19th and 21st century technologies: wood stoves for heat and cooking, photo-voltaic cells for electricity." [78] Much of his work over the past twenty years might be construed as an attempt to reestablish connections with the earth in a way that is beneficial to humankind without harming the community of life. In other words, this phase of his life can be understood as a twentieth-century Thoreauvian experiment, though he has sustained it for nearly two decades rather than twenty-six months. Snyder writes that his attempt to return to the land is "not some nostalgic replay of the nineteenth century. Here is a generation of white people finally ready to learn from the Elders. How to live on the continent as though our children, and on down, for many ages, will still be here (not on the moon). Loving and protecting this soil, these trees, these wolves. Natives of Turtle Island." [79]

During all these years Snyder has produced a steady stream of poetry (nine books) and prose (five books).[80] Viewed chronologically, the prose and poetry seems to go through changes in perspective. Work completed during and immediately after his Japanese sojourn, such as *The Back Country,* seems intensely Oriental, while later work, such as *Turtle Island,* seems more ecological and mythological than Eastern. *Axe Handles* (1983), his first collection of new poems after *Turtle Island,* seems to have muted the Eastern influence, instead exploring in Thoreauvian fashion the intimate bonding between a man and place, man and life. Snyder seems to be ever exploring new perspectives, creating an appearance of fitfulness, even uncertainty. Yet viewed retrospectively (from last to first), what is most important about the many streams of influence are not their differences but their convergence on a spiritual or sacred ecology. Snyder's work might be interpreted as a kind of poetic bricolage, a pastiche somewhat like William Blake's piecing of disparate parts into a remarkable whole of poetic vision. Yet his poetry is not just a collage but rather a fusion of myth-fact-vision-religious experience. *Turtle Island* is perhaps the best example of this fusion—a new vision of old ways in both prose and poetry that points toward an alternative path for modern people.[81]

Snyder's prose mirrors the poetry and vice versa, both expressing an ever changing conception of poetics that remains steadfast in its orbit about an ancient and natural center of gravity. His essay "The Politics of Ethnopoetics" (1975) lays out the grand design for *Turtle Island,* and is the most complete and mature statement of his poetics.[82] Other essays, both earlier, such as "Poetry and the Primitive" (1967), and later, such as "Poetry, Community, and Climax" (1979), also bear materially on any interpretation of Snyder's work. And the core of Snyder's poetics is rudimentarily present in *He Who Hunted Birds in His Father's Village* (1951), his senior thesis at Reed. Although Snyder has since called that work flawed, *He Who Hunted Birds* anticipates his mature poetry in its use of oral tradition, myth, and sense of community. The foreword to the 1978 edition recognizes the importance of *He Who Hunted Birds,* even though, when Snyder wrote it, he was a "green would-be scholar" who employed methods that can be seen as either internally contradictory or "downright wrong," and even though he would revise a second edition.

> What I'd emphasize now, even more than I did when I wrote it, is the *primacy of performance:* in the dark room, around the fire, children and old people, hearing and joying together in the words, the acting and the images. It's there that the shiver of awe and delight occurs, not in any dry analysis of archetypes or motifs—or the abstractions of the structuralist.
>
> I went on to other modes of study and writing, but never forgot what I learned from this work. Folklorists and anthropologists have done bins of research and writing since then, but somehow nobody has yet followed through with a multidimensional approach. So I pub-

lish it finally, with its many flaws, . . . hoping it will . . . [help to] push
others more trained than I, to do the work that will show how deeply
important the world heritage of story is to all of us, now and always.
And, to again point out that all peoples in all places share in a rich
prehistoric international lore—no group is "culturally deprived" until
oppressed by an invader or exploiter. The *indigenas* are bearers of the
deepest insights into human nature, and have the best actual way to
live . . . . May this be realized before they are destroyed.[83]

In *He Who Hunted Birds* Snyder grasps, however imperfectly, the ontogenetic function of oral literature and takes the first step on a long poetic
odyssey that celebrates the primal mythos. Turtle Island, so understood,
is a wellspring for postmodern existence, a series of poems that call forth
an "old-new" way of being. (The juxtaposition of "old" and "new" is an
unusual but apt characterization of Snyder's cultural vision, and he has
often so characterized it himself.)

Snyder refined this kernel of thought and sensibility—that is, the importance of recapturing the primitive and giving it voice—in a later essay,
"Poetry and the Primitive: Notes on Poetry as an Ecological Survival Technique," published in *Earth House Hold* in 1967. "Poetry must sing or
speak from authentic experience. Of all the streams of civilized tradition
with roots in the paleolithic, poetry is one of the few that can realistically
claim an unchanged function and a relevance which will outlast most of
the activities that surround us today. Poets, as few others, must live close
to the world that primitive [people] . . . are in: the world, in its nakedness, which is fundamental for all of us—birth, love, death; the sheer fact
of being alive."[84] Here the term *primitive* is not used pejoratively, since
Snyder's work avoids the modernistic fallacy that unreflectively assumes
the categories that rule the world to be ontic and epistemic absolutes. Instead, he is in some sense an archaeologist who digs not for bones and material relics but for premodern oral tradition. In recovering the primitive
the poet finds not the outmoded and contingent, the savage and barbaric,
but the perdurable roots of life and human beingness.

By 1975, after the publication of *Turtle Island,* Snyder reached what
might be considered as the presently governing characterization of his
poetry: *ethnopoetics.*[85] In "The Politics of Ethnopoetics" he writes that
"looking at our poetry of North America—Turtle Island—in the light of
the past, of other traditions, and this old new sense of the Earth, it seems
to me that we are just beginning."

We're just starting, in the last ten years here, to begin to make songs that will speak for plants, mountains, animals and children. When you see your first deer of the day you sing your salute to the deer, or your first red-wing blackbird—I saw one this morning! Such poetries will be created by us as we reinhabit this land with people who know they belong to it; for whom "primitive" is not a word that means past, but *primary*, and *future*. They will be created as we learn to see, region by region, how we live specifically (plant life!) in each place. The poems will leap out past the automobiles and TV sets of today into the vastness of the Milky Way (visible only when the electricity is turned down), to richen and humanize the scientific cosmologies. These poesies to come will help us learn to be people of knowledge in this universe in community with other people—non-human included—brothers and sisters.[86]

It is a misinterpretation of Snyder to see him as a nineteenth-century Romantic manqué advocating a failed theory of the noble savage. In fact his idealization of the primitive is empirically grounded in ecology and paleo- and Amerindigen anthropology. Snyder's poetry questions the sacred articles of our Enlightenment faith, such as the idea of progress, and corrects some of the excesses of Romantic poetry, such as its idealization of the noble savage. Augmented by the rich stream of twentieth-century anthropological studies, he argues that Rousseau's insights were profound. "One of the most remarkable intuitions in Western thought was Rousseau's Noble Savage: the idea that perhaps civilization has something to learn from the primitive." Yet Snyder's vision of the archaic is not nostalgic.

We all know what primitive cultures don't have. What they *do* have is this knowledge of connection and responsibility which amounts to a spiritual ascesis for the whole community. Monks of Christianity or Buddhism, "leaving the world" (which means the games of society) are trying, in a decadent way, to achieve what whole primitive communities—men, women, and children—live by daily; and with more wholeness. The Shaman-poet is simply the man whose mind reaches easily out into all manners of shapes and other lives, and gives song to dreams. Poets have carried this function forward all through civilized times: poets don't sing about society, they sing about nature . . . . Class-structured civilized society is a kind of mass ego. To transcend the ego is to go beyond society as well. "Beyond" there lies, inwardly, the unconscious. Outwardly, the equivalent of the unconscious is the wilderness: both of these terms meet, one step even farther on, as one.[87]

SNYDER BELIEVES THAT poems must celebrate the world and reestablish human bonds with wild nature. Poetry becomes a bridge to primal forms of consciousness and ways of being-in-the world: oral literature in performance is ontogenetic, world-making or evoking. Snyder's poetry, especially *Turtle Island,* rings true with this message. The book begins with a remarkable sequence of poems, "Anasazi," "The Way West, Underground," and "Without." The central myth—a panhuman myth of ancient peoples—is Turtle Island, where the landmass that supports life is understood as the back of a (cosmic) turtle sticking above the water. "Anasazi," the first poem, celebrates the Amerindigen culture of the American Southwest and grounds the poems that follow. "The Way West, Underground" extends the Turtle Island myth both geographically and temporally—from America to Japan, Tibet, and Finland through a pancultural prehistoric wisdom to, ultimately, the cave paintings of Paleolithic culture:

> Bears and Bison,
> Red Hands with missing fingers,
> Red mushroom labyrinths;
> lightning-bolt mazes,
> Painted in caves,
>
> Underground.

Finally, "Without," the third poem of the sequence, fuses the ancient wisdom of East and West:

> the silence
> of nature
> within.
>
> the power within.
> the power
>
> without.
>
> the path is whatever passes—no
> end in itself.
>
> the end is,
> grace—ease—

healing, not saving.

singing
the proof

the proof of the power within.[88]

Here in outline we see the postmodern cast to Snyder's vision, for his poetry achieves a fusion of the natural and human, the within and without—*a spiritual ecology* that calls into vision an old-new way of being.

The first poem of this sequence begins with a rhythmical "Anasazi,/ Anasazi," that sets a mood for not only the lines following but all *Turtle Island*. The poem discloses that the ancient ones were rooted in the earth in ways that elude modern people; steel and concrete have replaced sandstone, supermarkets and fast food have supplanted fields of corn and beans. And the Anasazi were in touch with the divine, "sinking deeper and deeper in earth/up to your hips in Gods." Their cosmos was ordered: the kiva—the holy lodge or sacred space, an axis mundi—central to existence. The feathers of the eagle, itself an instantiation of divinity, adorned the heads of the shaman, who ritualistically (using pollen to trace intricate designs that symbolized the structure of the cosmos) maintained the cosmic order. Snyder gives the poem a concrete, almost tactile, quality through the odor of the guano, and the flavor of sandstone in the breads made from the maize, further binding these premodern people with the Magna Mater.[89] Nature related to them in a feminine and nurturing (rather than masculine and domineering) way, and the people were bound with the land in an organic cycle, as in "women/birthing/at the foot of ladders in the dark."[90] Reverberations of the Paleolithic cave rituals are also heard in the poem, for life is sustained within a dark opening in the earth (womb), suggesting the eternal mystery of life and death. And so a new generation of wide-eyed red babies was born and held to earth, under the lips of rock, nourished by life-giving streams in the semiarid desert.

"The Way West, Underground" amplifies these themes and gives them a panhuman significance, for hunting-gathering people across the earth lived in similar fashion and had analogous ideas of Turtle Island. We encounter archaic peoples living through fishing ("split-cedar/smoked salmon/cloudy days of Oregon"), hunting and gathering ("tracking bears and mushrooms,/eating berries all the way"), and united via an archaic wisdom, as symbolized by the many names of the bear: "*Karhu—Bjorn —Braun—Bear.*"[91] These primal peoples are not degraded "primitives" living nasty, brutish, and short lives but healthy people rooted in the land, embracing all plants and animals. Snyder stretches the boundaries of human time beyond our culturally relative definitions by drawing attention to the cave art of Paleolithic peoples: they, too, were human, not simply barbaric savages, and they had a wisdom that modern people have lost. The introduction of the cult of the Bear, the predominating mythology of the era of the Great Hunt, into the poem is rife with possibilities of interpretation along totemic lines.

These introductory poems are followed, in the "Manzanita" section, by a number of poems paired on facing pages. These poem-pairs develop the themes of spiritual ecology, presenting first yin and then yang, together a centered vision of a larger whole. "Front Lines" and "Control Burn," for example, mirror each other in recognizing that life necessarily involves ecological transaction but juxtapose modern and ancient ways of human relations with wild nature. "Front Lines" reveals a modern technology that is disruptive and destructive. Civilization is characterized as a spreading cancer, which Snyder diagnoses as caused by the virus of money. Developers see the land only as potential profit, thus exploiting and raping the Mother.

> Sunday the 4-wheel jeep of the
> Realty Company brings in
> Landseekers, lookers, they say
> To the land,
> Spread your legs.

Snyder extends the sickness metaphor to cardiac disease. "Every pulse of the rot at the heart / In the sick fat veins of Amerika / Pushes the edge up closer—."[92] In contrast, "Control Burn" articulates a vision of a healthy relation between humankind and the land. The fires which the Amerindigens set burned out the brush,

> keeping the oak and the pine stands
> tall and clear
> with grasses
> and kitkitdizze under them,
> never enough fuel there
> that a fire could crown.

By contrast, modern Americans view fire as pernicious and invite disaster by letting brush accumulate.[93] Snyder then envisions—clearly a reconstructive act of postmodern consciousness—using this ancient and natural tool, fire, much like the Indigens before, to help the land upon which he now lives. "And then / it would be more / like, / when it belonged to the Indians // Before." [94]

Other poems in the "Manzanita" section harmonize with the melody established by the first three, helping us to hear the poet's song. "Prayer for the Great Family" is fashioned after a Mohawk prayer and reanimates through its saying some ancient sensibility of the Magna Mater. Each part begins with an expression of reverence to one aspect of the Great Mother: the first three lines ("Gratitude to Mother Earth, sailing through night and day— / and to her soil: rich, rare, and sweet / *in our minds so be it*") deal with the feminine and nurturing aspects of life; the last stanza ("Gratitude to the Great Sky / who holds billions of star—and goes yet beyond that— / beyond all powers, and thoughts / and yet is within us— / Grandfather Space. / The Mind is his Wife. // *so be it*"), directs consciousness toward a higher level of abstraction (the cosmic dimensions of human experience) that itself confirms identity in difference. Between these first and last stanzas the poem-prayer pays spiritual homage to the plants, air, wild creatures, water, and the sun, each stanza ending with the refrain "*in our minds so be it*." [95] For the Paleolithic mind all natural things are suffused with sacrality, and through prayer (oral ritual) the Magna Mater's presence is celebrated. Such poem-song-prayers of the aboriginal mind are viewed by Snyder as manifestations of the reality of primary experience, springing up from nature into aboriginal consciousness as "seed syllables." [96]

"The Bath," another powerful poem in the "Manzanita" section, confirms Snyder's Zen practice. A simple act of daily life—bathing his son, Kai—becomes a meditation on cosmic process and the nature of being. Again, the dominant metaphor is that of the female.

> The body of my lady, the winding valley spine,
>> the space between the thighs I reach through,
>> cup her curving vulva arch and hold it from behind,
>> a soapy tickle   a hand of grail
> The gates of Awe
> That open back a turning double-mirror world of
>> wombs in wombs, in rings,
>> that start in music,
>>> *is this our body?* [97]

Here the female principle symbolizes the life force: his wife becomes a manifestation of the female *sub specie aeternitas*, both an opening into the mysterious recesses of the cosmic process and an explanation of the poetic voice. Snyder writes in "Poetry and the Primitive" that the voice giving rise to poetry

> is anything other that touches you and moves you. . . . Man in his
> sexual nature has found the clearest mirror to be his human lover.
> As the West moved into increasing complexities and hierarchies with
> civilization, Woman as nature, beauty, and The Other came to be an
> all-dominating symbol, secretly striving through the last three mil-
> lennia with the Jehovah or Imperator God-figure, a projection of
> the gathering power of anti-nature social forces. Thus in the West-
> ern tradition the Muse and Romantic Love became part of the same
> energy, and woman as nature the field for experiencing the universe
> as sacramental. The lovers' bed was the sole place to enact the dances
> and ritual dramas that link primitive people to their geology and the
> Milky Way.[98]

The second and third sections of *Turtle Island*—"Magpie's Song" and "For the Children"—contain what is sometimes called the "healing poetry" where the "stored energy" from the primal layers below wells up to heal, to transform. Through rediscovery of ancient ways and wisdom Snyder hopes to transform Modernism, to escape the entangling vines of civilization, to reestablish contact with the Tao. "Mother Earth: Her Whales" pierces to the heart of the malaise that afflicts the modern age, revealing that even the Japanese, who nurtured Zen in its infancy, torment Mother Earth, having lost touch with their roots.

> And Japan quibbles for words on
>   what kinds of whales they can kill?
> A once-great Buddhist nation
>   dribbles methyl mercury
>   like gonorrhea
>   in the sea.

And the Chinese, too, have become exploiters of the Mother Earth.

> Père David's Deer, the Elaphure,
> Lived in the tule marshes of the Yellow River
> Two thousand years ago—and lost its home to rice—
> The forests of Lo-yang were logged and all the silt &
> Sand flowed down, and gone, by 1200 AD—[99]

Not only "Amerika," then, afflicts the Earth; all humankind has turned against Her.

Snyder also rejects any hope of salvation through technology, one of the shibboleths of our time.[100] "L M F B R" reveals that the liquid metal fast-breeder reactor portends destruction and death rather than salvation. "Death himself, / (Liquid Metal Fast Breeder Reactor) / stands grinning, beckoning." Other poems in the second section, such as "Affluence" and "Ethnobotany," employ the same technique of Eastern opposition (ying and yang) used in the first section. "Affluence" shows how the virus of money has infected the loggers who hastily exploit the forest, leaving their residue ("they didn't pile the slash and burn then") to litter the ground, posing an unnatural fire hazard. "Ethnobotany" describes a natural process of life and death in the forest; two oaks, rendered vulnerable by rot in their roots, have fallen. One has been converted (presumably by Snyder himself) into firewood, and the other (symbolically) left for the deer and the mushrooms, fungus, bacteria, and other lives that thrive in forest detritus. With Indigen wisdom, Snyder tastes the growth. "Taste all, and hand the knowledge down." [101]

The second section also manifests an almost palpable sense of the Magna Mater and her life processes. Snyder writes in *The Old Ways* that "the original poetry is the sound of running water and the wind in the trees." [102] "By Frazier Creek Falls" epitomizes that idea.

> Standing up on lifted, folded rock,
> looking out and down—
>
> The creek falls to a far valley,
> hills beyond that
> facing, half-forested, dry
> —clear sky
> strong wind in the
> stiff glittering needle clusters
> of the pine—their brown
> round trunk bodies
> straight, still;
> rustling trembling limbs and twigs
>
> listen.
>
> This living flowing land
> is all there is, forever
>
> We *are* it
> it sings through us—

> We could live on this Earth
> without clothes or tools![103]

Listen! the poet tells us. This is the Eastern axis of Snyder's spiritual
ecology: by listening one quiets the mind, calms the senses, and reestab-
lishes contact with the earth. The mind forgets intellectual conventions—
nature as lifeless matter-in-mechanical-motion—and the mores of culture.
Go into the wilderness; stand on the rock of granitic truth. Hear the Ur syllables, the seed syllables, of mother earth: *the wind! the moving water! the*
sighing boughs! We are her children, she is our mother, we are it, the flowing land: here then is the ecological axis of *Turtle Island.* "We could live
on this Earth / without clothes or tools!" Hyperbole? Or a poetic disclos-
ing of a divine presence concealed from us by Modernism? A postmodern
hierophany? A shaman's vision?

"Tomorrow's Song" underscores the dual role of shaman-poet that
Snyder plays as spiritual ecologist, for the poem is a vision that is sung.
Reverberating with the overtones of Jeffers's "Shine Perishing Republic"
("While this America settles in the mould of its vulgarity"), Snyder assesses
the present. He suggests that America lost its mandate in the twentieth
century. Yet even "myths die" and "continents are impermanent." But, the
poet sings, "we look to the future with pleasure / we need no fossil fuel /
get power within / grow strong on less," for rising phoenixlike from the
ruins of Amerika reemerges Turtle Island. Humankind can then be "At
work and in our place: // *in the service / of the wilderness / of life / of death /*
of the Mother's breasts!"[104]

The poet's song revivifies the Magna Mater of the Paleolithic mind: one
can hear the chants, "Anasazi, Anasazi, Anasazi," see Paleolithic people
celebrating the miracle of life as they paint the walls of Lascaux, hear the
call of the marshland crane. This vision is immediately enframed by the
following poem, "What Happened Here Before." Snyder obliterates the
importance of human time through geological time, beginning 300 million years ago—when there was no Turtle Island, but only a sea. Through
time, soils were formed and the topographical and biological features of
the earth shaped and reshaped, again and again in a ceaseless kaleidoscope of change. And then, forty thousand years ago, came humankind—
first the Indigens, who lived in peace with the land, and then "the white
man." But

> *now*
> we sit here near the diggings
> in the forest, by our fire, and watch
> the moon and planets and the shooting stars—

my sons ask, who are we?
drying apples picked from homestead trees
drying berries, curing meat,
shooting arrows at a bale of straw.

military jets head northeast, roaring, every dawn.
my sons ask, who are they?

> WE SHALL SEE
>
> WHO KNOWS
>
> HOW TO BE
Bluejay screeches from a pine.[105]

The prose section ("Plain Talk") of *Turtle Island* makes clear that Snyder is neither a nihilist nor pessimist but a realist who looks to a future that begins from where we are now yet has regrounded itself in a premodern past. "There are many things in Western culture that are admirable. But a culture that alienates itself from the very ground of its own being—from the wilderness outside (that is to say, wild nature, the wild, self-contained, self-informing ecosystems) and from that other wilderness, the wilderness within—is doomed to a very destructive behavior, ultimately perhaps self-destructive behavior."[106] The rediscovery of the wilderness is thus central to Snyder's spiritual ecology. Snyder's primary accomplishment, argues L. Folsom, "is a rediscovery and reaffirmation of wilderness, a clear rejection of Turner's (and America's) closure of the frontier. Snyder announces the opening of the frontier again and attempts to push it eastward, to reverse America's historical process, to urge the wilderness to grow back into civilization, to release the stored energy from layers below us."[107]

Contact with the wild leads to transformation through categorical change, as in "a new definition of humanism and a new definition of democracy that would include the nonhuman, that would have representation from those spheres." Snyder mentions the Amerindigens as having categories large enough to admit *the other*. "In Pueblo societies a kind of ultimate democracy is practiced. Plants and animals are also people, and, through certain rituals and dances, are given a place and a voice in the political discussions of the humans." Reaffirmation and discovery of the wilderness also widens human horizons through ecological understanding. "You cannot communicate with the forces of nature in the laboratory." If we set aside conventional wisdom, we can recognize that "there is more information of a higher order of sophistication and complexity stored in a few square yards of forest than there is in all the libraries of mankind. Obviously, that is a different order of information. It is the information of the universe we live in." As with Thoreau and Muir, Snyder encourages us to become seekers of Indigen wisdom, to pursue knowledge not to dominate nature but to find our proper place in the web of life. Finally, through contact with the elemental and wild, modern man and woman might be whole again. "Our own heads: Is where it starts. Knowing that we are the first human beings in history to have so much of man's culture and previous experience available to our study, and being free enough of the weight of traditional cultures to seek out a larger identity; the first members of a civilized society since the Neolithic to wish to look clearly into the eyes of the wild and see our self-hood, our family, there." [108]

The prose of *Turtle Island* also underscores Snyder's commitment to a process of personal and social transformation called *bioregionalism*. [109] A modernist would offer an explicit economic and political program for reform and palliatives for the psychic travails of modern life. In contrast, Snyder envisions an old-new way of being where land use "is sensitive to the properties of each region." Such a culture is rooted in the land rather than some a priori ideology, the grounds for which have been long forgotten, thus obviating much of what has become an increasingly burdensome bureaucratic state. "Stewardship means, for most of us, find your place on the planet, dig in, and take responsibility from there—the tiresome but tangible work of school boards, county supervisors, local foresters—local politics." [110] In an interview ("Tracking Down the Natural Man") given in 1979 Snyder observes that "some of the solidity in *Turtle Island* is because of my sense of place, living here in Nevada County." So understood, *Turtle Island* redirects the reader's attention from the evanescent facade of culture to its organic foundation. Thinking ecologically is, he admits, difficult. "We're so impressed by our civilization and what it's done, with our machines, that we have a difficult time recognizing that the biological world is infinitely more complex." [111] But if modern people, bound up in the second world, can rediscover that sense of place in the green world, that awareness of being grounded in nature that was characteristic of ancient people, then the second world might be transformed.

In "The Bioregional Ethic" (another 1979 interview) Snyder points out that "no political movement in the United States that came out of left field with so little beginning public support has had as much effect on the whole American political and economic system in such a short time as the environmental movement." [112] He recognizes that not everyone will have an ecological awareness, in part because "they have worked all their lives part of the industrial machinery." But "real people," as he puts it, have an "interest in not ruining the place." He gives an example grounded in the Sierra Nevadas—long a treasure house of metal ores exploited by humans.

If your mining is controlled by Saint Joe Minerals, which has operations going in Rhodesia, South Africa, and California all at the same time, you know not only that all the money is going to be taken away from your area, to banks in Switzerland, or whatever, but also that the owners have no concern for the viability of where you live, later on down the line. They don't care if the area becomes a wasteland. So the ecological benefit of rootedness is that people take care of a place because they realize that they're going to live there for a thousand years or more.[113]

More recently he writes (in an essay to be included in his next book) that "being solid with the place, the people turn up at hearings and in front of trucks and bulldozers to defend the land. Showing solidarity with a region! What an odd idea at first. Biogregionalism is the entry of place into the dialectic of history—we are not limiting our analysis of *difference* to class. And there are 'classes' that Marx overlooked—the animals, rivers, and grasses—that are now entering history."[114]

Ecological awareness is only one side of Snyder's poetics: the complementary side is that of spiritual vision. Through rediscovery of place flow spiritual benefits because "by being in place, we get the largest sense of community. We learn that community is of spiritual benefit and of health for everyone, that ongoing working relationships and shared concerns, music, poetry, and stories all evolve into the shared practice of a set of values, visions, and quests. That's what the spiritual path really is." To his credit, Snyder is not overly sanguine about the prospects for such change, arguing that the evolution of consciousness moves slowly.

In our present over-speeded and somewhat abnormal historical situation, the long stability of traditional peasant cultures or primitive hunting and gathering cultures seems maybe dull. . . . But from the spiritual standpoint, the evolution of consciousness goes at a different pace. . . . When we steer toward living harmoniously and righteously on the earth, we're also steering toward a condition of long-term stability in which the excitement, the glamour will not be in technology and changing fads. But it will be in a steady enactment and reenactment over and over again of basic psychological inner spiritual dramas, until we learn to find our way through to the next step.[115]

Modern people, however, are not bereft of resources, as the first two poems in *Turtle Island* demonstrate. First, "the objective eye of science, striving to see Nature plain, must finally look at 'subject' and 'object' and the very Eye that looks. We discover that all of us carry within us caves;

with animals and gods on the walls; a place of ritual and magic." [116] And second, the poet's role is to aid and abet the process of spiritual growth, particularly through healing songs.

> I like to think that the concern with the planet, with the integrity of the biosphere, is a long and deeply-rooted concern of the poet for this reason: the role of the singer was to sing the voice of corn, the voice of the Pleiades, the voice of bison, the voice of antelope. To contact in a very special way an "other" that was not within the human sphere; something that could not be learned by continually consulting other human teachers, but could only be learned by venturing outside the borders and going into your own mind-wilderness, unconscious wilderness. [117]

Snyder's poetic vision is that of a spiritual ecologist. Caught up in the flow of our times, the modern mind thinks of wild nature as standing reserve, as an alien "other." Through ethnopoetry, however, Snyder believes that the modern mind might learn to see itself as living in a relationship of complementarity with rather than superiority to nature. "Thus nature leads into nature—the wilderness—and the reciprocities and balances by which man lives on earth." [118]

Conclusion: Dwelling Poetically

What is the role of the wilderness poet in society? What is society? What is poetry? Is there ultimately any difference between the thinking poet and the poetic thinker? These are difficult questions which threaten to take us afield from our study of the idea of wilderness in poetry. Further, there are neither ready-made answers nor a framework within which to seek answers. Both poetic thinkers and thinking poets, unlike scientists, who may rely upon the genius of method, must confront their quandary sans methods and instruments. Our questions about wilderness poets force thought outside modern channels into an uncharted wilderness. As Heidegger sees so clearly, the very expression "dwelling poetically" affronts the modernist sensibility, that world-in-force which holds the modern mind in an iron grip. We know absolutely, do we not, that poetry is either "a frivolous mooning and vaporing into the unknown, and a flight into dreamland, or is counted as a part of literature" and is therefore worthy of no one's attention save academics and the literary intelligentsia. To assert, as does Heidegger, that poetry is ontogenetic is to the modernist the worst kind of nonsense; such a judgment confirms for Heidegger the insufficiencies of the modernist worldview. "Man acts as though *he* were the shaper and master of language, while in fact *language* remains the master of man. Perhaps it is before all else man's subversion of *this* relation of dominance that drives his nature into alienation."[119] Language, in short, is the house of being.

Language, as Heidegger says, speaks. *Language speaks.* Language is ontogenetic, world making, whether this be the language of the scientist, the religious seer, or the poet. Yet such insight is hidden behind the conventional wisdom that believes language to be solely representational and expressive, an activity of an already thinking and speaking humankind. The interpretation of poetry is typically so infected. Such criticism remains, Heidegger tells us, "confined by the notion of language that has prevailed for thousands of years. According to this idea language is the expression, produced by men, of their feelings and the world view that guides them. Can the spell this idea has cast over language be broken? Why should it be broken? In its essence, language is neither expression nor an activity of man. Language speaks. We are now seeking the speaking of language in the poem."[120] Upon realizing that language speaks, we also understand that the poet does not aspire to use descriptive language, as do those who function within the confines of conventional speech. The thinking poet reaches toward a presence obscured by the obvious, toward what is absent because of its concealment behind language, behind opinion, behind ideology: *the wilderness poet calls forth being.* Gadamer writes that poetry, and literature more generally, "can be understood only from the ontology of the work of art, and not from the aesthetic experiences that occur in the course of the reading." Books appear to be lifeless relics. But, Gadamer contends, "literature is not the dead continuance of an estranged being made available to the experience of a later period. Literature is a function of intellectual preservation and tradition, and therefore brings its hidden history into every age."[121]

What must be recognized absolutely, if the idea of wilderness implicit in the poetry of Jeffers and Snyder is to be understood as something other than a nostalgic longing for noble savages and forested mountainsides, clear waters, and blue skies, is that language speaks. Their poetry resonates with Paleolithic and archaic myth and through its saying reveals a world in which humankind might again be an integral part, a world in which mortals and immortals, the sacred and profane, God and humans might again be whole. Jeffers's "beauty of things" and Snyder's "Turtle Island" are neither scientific description nor emotive expression; they are, rather, the unconcealment of presences obscured behind the visible promontory of the world-in-force. Both Jeffers and Snyder, as thinking poets, create a poetry that is informed by the basic physical-chemical-biological-ecological facts of existence; and both write a poetry that energizes latent human sensibilities. Yet the focus of the thinking poet is not on the world as that which is culturally given but rather on that dimension of being concealed behind that presence. The thinking poet necessarily abandons conventional categories to explore the hidden meanings of terms with primal (autochthonous) connotations. Through such speaking, the old categories—GNP, Man, Nation, Progress, Economic Growth, Standard of Living—are abandoned and primordial being revealed. Such poetry is ontogenetic—world making. As Joseph Campbell observes, such has always been the function "of the great seers (known to India as 'rishis,' in biblical terms as 'prophets,' to primitive folk as 'shamans,' and in our own day as 'poets' and 'artists') . . . by recognizing through the veil of nature, as viewed in the science of their times, the radiance, terrible yet gentle, of the dark, unspeakable light beyond, and through their words and images to reveal the sense of the vast silence that is the ground of us all and of all beings." [122]

Jeffers's poetic vision—his theophany—calls us back to a sense of the elemental and divine beauty of things. The inhumanist philosophy is not the outlook of a lunatic but a deeply informed bracketing of the orthodox view that holds Lord Man apart from wild nature. The antipode to his inhumanism is the implicit "humanism" of his work, a human beingness enframed by the beauty of things and entwined with a process of cosmic proportions. Jeffers returned to nature in search of a durable scale of values, a sense of belonging founded in re-cognition of nature's integrity, stability, and beauty.

Snyder's poetic vision is rooted in earth consciousness, a rediscovery of the wisdom of the ages, known to primal peoples across the face of earth during the Paleolithic era and even thereafter among archaic hunteringgathering societies. His is a poetry more healing than Jeffers's poetry of protest. Snyder sees not doom but a world in which computer technicians might walk in autumn with migrating elk. Snyder's poetry rings with the clarity of rams butting heads, and thus captures our attention, but flows with the sounds of mountain streams and thereby allows nature to speak. Snyder, like Thoreau, seeks the Red Face of Humankind—for a kind of Indigen wisdom that eludes description and logic. Like Muir, Snyder resonates with the plant people and wild California mountains through a primal bonding rather than scientific understanding. As with Leopold, Snyder's poetry cannot help but promote perception of the land.

CHAPTER NINE

Contemporary Wilderness Philosophy
From Resourcism to Deep Ecology

Men increase; country suffers. Though I sign up with organizations that oppose the process, I sign without great hope. . . . Islands of wildlife and native flora may be saved, as they should be, but the big, sloppy, rich, teeming spraddle will go on. It always has.
—John Graves, *Goodbye to a River*

There is no built-in mechanism restraining the human proclivity to use, and expand the use, of natural substances—this has to be consciously developed under special circumstances. In all other cases, the historical record is one of progressive expansion of resource conversion and growing impact on Nature.
—John W. Bennett, *The Ecological Transition*

CONTEMPORARY IDEAS OF WILDERNESS are implicit within activities as diverse as the legislative and judicial decision-making processes, policy implementation, and philosophical speculation. Ideally, some distinct idea might cut across this array of subjects and unite them along a continuum, much as the principles of liberal democracy unite diverse elements of the body politic. As Samuel Hays observes, environmentally oriented inquiry has not led "to a single system of thought such as social theorists might prefer, and it would be difficult to reduce its varied strands to a single pattern."[1] Typically, however, those concerned with the idea of wilderness offer either a stipulative definition that suits their purposes or, more characteristically among scholars, a potpourri of positions. This second approach, though it sometimes achieves a near exhaustive listing, suffers from a lack of rigor and clarity. The idea of wilderness is whatever anyone or group cares to think.

Although a definitive idea of wilderness does not exist, a reflective synthesis emerging from a diversity of inconsistent positions might be possible. At a minimum, such a synthesis would transcend the impasse between the resource management or conservationist approach to wild nature and the preservationist school of thought and practice. Of course, the possibility as well as the methodology of such a philosophical reconciliation is at issue. Aldo Leopold's struggle to develop a land ethic belies the dream of an easy passage from resourcism to preservationism and beyond. Even more complicated are the issues involved in articulating a wilderness philosophy that brings the principles of foundational ecology into an affirmative and pragmatic relationship with the ongoing cultural stream. Can such revolutionary paradigms for thought and action be effectively related to present-day intellectual, political, and economic process?[2]

The mainstream of wilderness philosophy is in some respects a house divided along the same lines as John Muir and Gifford Pinchot. The battle between contending forces, generally but imprecisely characterized as "conservationists" and "preservationists," yet rages, perhaps reflecting the uncertainty of the past century and a half of American history.[3] By attending briefly to the historical grounds that underlie contemporaneous wilderness philosophies, then at least the lines of battle among competing ideas can be drawn. The obvious place to begin is with Thomas Robert Malthus, who shocked the world in the early nineteenth century by arguing that population would increase geometrically and the means of production only arithmetically.[4] Although Europeans were concerned, his predictions seemed not to apply to the United States, since the American economy rapidly converted wilderness into means for the good life. Two bombshells followed Malthus, however. Darwin's *Origin of Species* showed that humankind did not stand above the natural world but was part of the web of life. Soon afterward George Marsh's *Earth as Modified by Human Action* warned of the "dangers of imprudence and the necessity of caution in all operations which, on a large scale, interfere with the spontaneous arrangements of the organic or the inorganic world."[5] Suddenly an awareness dawned that human activity, however long established and well intentioned, could destroy environmental equilibrium.

As the nineteenth century ended many Americans, including members of the socioeconomic elite, became conscious of these discoveries, realizing that the supply of natural resources was finite. These ideas took hold in the corridors of power. In 1907 President Theodore Roosevelt organized the Governors' Conference, an event sometimes cited as dating the emergence of conservation as a public philosophy influential at the highest levels. In a letter to the governors, Roosevelt wrote that "it is evident the abundant natural resources on which the welfare of this nation rests are becoming depleted, and in not a few cases, are already exhausted."[6] The conference participants convened with a sense of Malthusian urgency, although the question before them was practical, not philosophical. How could America more efficiently manage its natural resources? They concluded that fundamental changes were needed in the American political economy since laissez-faire economics promised environmental and, ultimately, economic ruin.

Many dramatic changes in the way our nation conceptualizes and approaches nature have followed in the wake of the Governors' Conference. Propelled by the ideology of resource conservation, the federal government has assumed an ever larger role in managing nature. World War I hastened the move toward the rationalization and scientific management of natural resources.[7] New inventions and technologies—especially the automobile—also had a dramatic impact. The automobile had a spreading economic effect: cars required roads and fuel, steel and rubber, and businesses to sell, repair, finance, and insure them.[8] Wave after wave of consumer products—from appliances and cars to televisions and washing machines—helped propel America, in spite of temporary recessions and wartime disruptions, on an upward spiral of socioeconomic growth. Continued increases in population also contributed to increases in demand, intensifying the effort to manage nature. And the economic boom after World War II led to an enormous escalation in demand for wilderness resources (land and game) to provide recreational outlets for increasingly well-to-do middle and upper classes. Growing numbers of people with discretionary income and leisure time turned to the outdoors for alpine and cross-country skiing, white-water rafting, rock climbing, backpacking, motorized touring and camping, hunting, and fishing. The federal government responded with far-reaching public works, managing the nation's parks and forests, building alpine highways and trails, providing water and electric hookups for campsites, restaurants, bathrooms, and even so-called wilderness exhibits.[9] Yet, given the evolving system, the fundamental challenge of the twentieth century has been to provide natural resources to fuel socioeconomic growth.

In this century the resource management approach has dominated the conceptualization and management of nature. The Governors' Conference perhaps marked the formal emergence of *resourcism* as governmental policy; two world wars, rapid socioeconomic growth, and deterioration of environmental quality further legitimated federal action and reinforced the conservationist philosophy.[10] Resource conservation has grown beyond concern for a mere husbanding and efficient use of non-renewable resources to include both environmental quality and renewable resources.[11] Immense federal bureaucracies (the National Forest Service, U.S. Army Corps of Engineers, Department of Energy, Environmental Protection Agency, Bureau of Land Management, National Park Service) support this rationale; private sector contractors have carried out the plans of these bureaucracies; and university programs that provide the technicians to administer public policy and manage wild nature have flourished. In short, there has grown and developed in America a resource management elite consisting of academic theoreticians, politician-administrators, and technicians who attempt to impose cultural purpose on and thereby control nature. The tools of the resource conservationist vary, ranging from the concrete and instrumental, such as bulldozers and dynamite used to build dams, to the abstract and theoretical, as in cost-benefit analysis used to account for such expenditures of public funds.[12] Cost-benefit analysis is a theoretical bulldozer, clearing the way through thickets of ethical and legal questions, ostensibly by justifying resource conservation in terms of the public interest and economic efficiency.[13]

Resourcism, though it enjoys cognitive hegemony, has not gone unchallenged. Critics have been abundant, and many resource conservation projects proposed in the name of the public's interest have been vigorously opposed, both through direct political action and acts of civil disobedience. However beleaguered, the record shows that the American wilderness would probably be worse off today had the conservation movement not appeared. Given the inherent economic and technological dynamism of American society, and a basically unfettered ambit of opportunity for the entrepreneur, what is remarkable is that we have such things as air and water quality standards and that any significant wilderness areas yet remain. Whatever the theoretical insufficiencies of resourcism, it has afforded wild nature some protection. Earl Finbar Murphy's perceptive study, *Governing Nature,* provides a useful vantage point on the issues before us: the facts of human metabolism and culture must be confronted.[14] Life for any species is possible only in relation to an environment on which its continued existence depends. All species, except one, live in a naturally determined relationship with their environment, subject to change only through the workings of evolutionary process. The human animal, in distinction from all others, interposes culture between itself and environment, which is to say that Homo sapiens is a culture-dwelling animal. Given the cultural status quo—the multitudes that must be fed, clothed, and sheltered—and a commitment to maintenance of the present liberal-democratic value system, then nature must be managed: there is no apparent alternative. By all indications the question is not whether advanced industrial society can choose to govern nature but how to do so.

Ironically, Marsh himself criticized the rationale underlying resource management. He wrote that "the equation of animal and vegetable life is too complicated a problem for human intelligence to solve, and we can never know how wide a circle of disturbance we produce in the harmonies of nature when we throw the smallest pebble into the ocean of organic life." [15] Contemporary ecological studies appear to support Marsh's judgment, for not only are things environmental complicated, they are more complicated than they seem; and yet manage we must. Whatever an individual's idea of wilderness, mere stockpile of natural resources or Mother Earth, the mass of humanity so fundamentally alters nature that no laissez-faire position is rational. Neither is a romantic retreat to some contemporary Walden Pond, like Alaska or Montana, anything more than a temporary escape from the looming reality of advanced industrial society. [16] Rather the conservation question arises at a more fundamental level: the issue involves the *theorie* upon which *praxis* will rest—the idea of wilderness itself. Whatever this idea, the conceptual difference will be reflected in practice.

To the modern mind such a contention seems a priori nonsensical. Any talk of wilderness, of unpolluted blue sky and noble savages living in harmony with nature, seems mere nostalgia for a way of life gone forever, a romantic belief that threatens the advance of modern civilization. In other words, the idea of wilderness represents primitivism. Yet the postmodern mind believes—or at least the posthistoric primitivist believes—that wildness is not just the preservation of the world, it is the world—self-organizing order out of chaos. Accordingly, our study has reached a critical juncture, confronted with a choice between two paradigms: Modernism and Postmodernism. These alternatives are themselves entangled in that natural and cultural stream which is history.

Here we shall hold in abeyance any assumption about the ultimate meaning of historical process. We refuse the ideas that history is either sound and fury signifying nothing, a position grounded in scientism and mechanistic materialism, or headed toward some Absolute or Omega, a position rooted in that peculiar Western fusion of Attica and Jerusalem. We accept the postmodernist position that we stand within a hermeneutic circle and that by examining the idea of wilderness we are also coming to understand the course of natural and cultural history that enframes human life. Such a study necessarily begins with resourcism—the conservationist ideology that is supported by and therefore entirely consistent with Modernism; follows the rise of preservationism and other competing ideas of wilderness that, though inconsistent in some ways with Modernism, do not escape its grasp; and concludes (in chapter 10) with a conjectural articulation of a postmodern idea of wilderness. What the challenges to resourcism reveal most clearly are the many anomalies of Modernism. These puzzles warrant the conjecture that we are probably entering a revolutionary period of theorie and praxis. Here Glacken's penetrating study again bears on ours, for his *Traces on the Rhodian Shore* concludes just as the second scientific revolution—engendered by Darwin and Clausius—began. As Anna Bramwell notes, he "decided to end his study at 1800, because after that date a qualitative change began in man's view of his place in the world. . . . 'What follows is of an entirely different order, influenced by the theory of evolution, specialization in the attainment of knowledge, acceleration in the transformation of nature.'"[17]

Resourcism

The resource conservation idea of wilderness has a familiar appearance, since its roots lie in the Neolithic revolution. Unquestionably the dominant idea of wilderness, resourcism is the child of Western history, reflecting the intense homocentrism of Judeo-Christianity and the alchemy of Modernism. Neil Evernden contends that "resourcism is a kind of modern religion which casts all of creation into categories of utility." From another vantage point, resourcism represents the transformation of modern people from Homo religiosus to Homo oeconomicus. Since resource conservation is the visible facade of a largely unquestioned and therefore absolute worldview, it short-circuits the potentially subversive power of foundational ecology. Evernden points out that ecology has in this century become little more than "a branch of classical physics, in spirit if not in exact content. The results of ecological research are therefore predetermined in some measure. Starting with mechanistic assumptions, it can only discover machines. Consequently it will always seem reasonable to assume that we can manipulate the ecomachine."[18] Here we have reached the same impasse that Aldo Leopold reached in his life and thought: the modern mind is confronted with a choice, whether that choice is recognized, between foundational and functional ecology (see table 4).

From a resource conservation perspective the wilderness in whatever guise is effectively reduced to an environment, a stockpile of matter-energy to be transformed through technology, itself guided by the market and

Table 4. Defining Characteristics of Resourcism

RESOURCE CONSERVATIONISTS believe that
- natural systems are no more than collections of parts
- Homo sapiens is related externally to the ecomachine
- the ecomachine can be engineered to produce desired outcomes and prevent undesired consequences
- the market objectively determines the worth and value of all things, cultural and natural
- the national and per capita income accounts are the ideal measure of societal well-being
- progress can be determined according to the utilitarian formula of the greatest good for the greatest number

theoretical economics, into the wants and needs of the consumer culture. The new industrial state would not be possible without science, for such knowledge of nature makes causal control possible. Humankind can produce desired effects, as in a technologically based agriculture that increases crop yield by hybridizing plant stocks and fertilization, and prevent undesired events, by using pesticides and herbicides to eliminate "pests" and "weeds." Utilitarianism is the sacrosanct ethical justification for the industrial democratic state, since the good society is believed to be that which produces the greatest good for the greatest number.[19] The "good" is itself reduced to a Benthamite calculus of pleasure, consumption is equated with pleasure, and high rates of economic throughput are thus equated with the good life.[20] Mutatis mutandis, the better able each individual to achieve similar pleasure, the better off society. Therein, as we have seen, lies the great genius of *The Wealth of Nations,* for an "invisible hand" orchestrates the actions of all these selfish, pleasure-seeking consumers into the "good society."

Although resourcism is a secular ideology, in some ways it mirrors Judeo-Christian traditions, especially in its anthropocentric outlook. Nature and natural entities are not sacred, have no end or justification in and of themselves, and exist solely as means in terms of which human ends might be fulfilled. Resourcism is bereft of any archaic sense of wilderness as the Mother Earth, of any Romantic sense of the connection of human purpose with nature, and of any Leopoldian sense of value in the wilderness. Human life takes place outside nature, and the boundaries between wilderness and civilization are definite. The value of wild nature is construed strictly in economic terms, either directly through operation of the market according to "laws" of supply and demand, or indirectly through cost-benefit analysis.[21] The market makes a mountain meadow worth more as a ski development and resort, complete with condominiums and shopping centers, than as a wilderness preserve; a forest preserve worth more as timber than as a home for wildlife; a mountain worth more as oil extracted from its shale than as a noble rock promontory thrusting into the sky. Cost-benefit analysis, a function of a resource conservation elite, reinforces the market. To take one example, a species of fish was destroyed by construction of the Tellico Reservoir. By a cost-benefit calculus of value, the economic benefits of the water provided for human consumption and the enjoyment of water-skiers and fishers was worth more than the existence of the snail darter. Little matter that such thoughtless acts are, as Holmes Rolston argues, "like tearing pages out of an unread book, written in a language humans hardly know how to read, about the place where they live."[22] The so-called renewable resource concept further exemplifies the homocentric rationalism implicit in resourcism. The idea of forests as renewable resources, much publicized by Weyerhauser and other leviathans of the timber industry, exemplifies the model of nature as ecomachine—a virtual factory system pouring out an unending stream of commodities.

Within the context of American history the conservationist idea of wilderness can be seen as inevitable—the outcome of some ten thousand years of history. The exploitation of wilderness areas has continued without ideological limit or restraint: nature has been conceived as a limitless supply of convertible matter-energy, and production-consumption has been guided almost solely by the political and economic imperatives of the industrial state. Accordingly, modern society appears to evade not only the laws of ecology but the second law of thermodynamics. Of course, the laissez-faire approach of the nineteenth and early twentieth centuries has been replaced by a more rationalized system of management: resource conservation. To the conservationist nature remains an adversary to be conquered by technology, and thereby brought into productive and sustaining relationship with human wants and purposes. Ecology becomes a tool by which this idea of wilderness is sustained. In other words, theoretical ecology provides the means through which industrial-democratic culture pursues its unquestioned goal. Namely, as Evernden states so clearly, "the maximum utilization of the earth as raw material in the support of one species." Functional ecology becomes a self-fulfilling prophecy, since both dwindling supplies of natural resources and pollution confirm that nature is an adversary: an unruly force that can be harnessed to human purpose only through science and technology. Further, control of nature-as-adversary necessitates an academic, political, and technical elite who create and wield the instruments of domination. Yet the question never asked, Evernden argues, is "the question of ends—why are we doing all this in the first place?"[23]

Preservationism

Although resourcism dominates contemporary thought and action, its triumph has not been complete. Preservationist ideas of wilderness, although clearly minority reports, have often manifested themselves in public policy debate (see table 5). The professional resource conservationist has largely controlled public policy administration, but a radical amateur tradition in preservation has persisted. A fundamental distinction between conservationist and preservationist ideas of wilderness revolves around the concept of a holistic as distinct from an atomistic view of nature. Preservationists, in contrast to resource conservationists, think of nature as an ecosystem, where the whole is greater than the sum of its parts, rather than as a stockpile of essentially interchangeable parts.[24] The influence of holism (theorie) on the world (praxis) has not been inconsequential. Carolyn Merchant argues that holism underlies such laws as the Endangered Species Act (1973) and that ecology is "the most important example of holism today," since it has led toward preservationism by "pointing up the essential role of every part of an ecosystem . . . . Each part contributes equal value to the healthy functioning of the whole. All living things, as integral parts of a viable ecosystem, thus have rights." Consequently there arose "the necessity of protecting the ecosystem from

Table 5. Distinguishing Characteristics of Preservationism

PRESERVATIONISTS believe that natural systems are
- self-creating, evolutionary wholes with synergetic characteristics that preclude complete reduction and analysis
- coordinating interfaces in natural hierarchies where all elements are internally related
- Homo sapiens is related internally to the environment
- human actions can impair the ability of natural systems to maintain themselves or to evolve further
- human values go beyond those measured by the national income accounts to include the preservation of wild lands and life

collapse due to the extinction of vital members," as in endangered species legislation.[25] Donald Worster makes the same point somewhat more dramatically when he observes that we are now living in an age of ecology.

For the modernist, who assumes the Cartesian-Newtonian paradigm as an absolute, the concept of a whole or an ecosystem is a lapse into what is derisively called "mystical ecology."[26] The idea that natural systems are wholes with irreducible properties represents an alternative to the atomistic-reductionistic foundations of conservationist philosophy. To the preservationist, synergetic phenomena are irreducibly real outcomes of the interaction of component elements of natural process. Accordingly, there is no surprise when DDT devastates the reproductive cycle of fish-eating birds or acid rain pours down on the northeastern United States and southeastern Canada. Such phenomena are a consequence of the ecological reality that natural systems are functioning wholes greater than the sum of their parts. Barry Commoner eloquently expresses this principle by arguing that the first law of ecology is that "everything is connected to everything else."[27] Consequently, synergetic phenomena cannot be explained satisfactorily in terms of either mechanical and reversible relations or external causation. By implication we can begin to understand the contemporary revolution in the physical sciences, where a dramatic reconceptualization of nature's basic processes is underway. As Prigogine puts it, the sciences "are moving from deterministic, reversible processes to stochastic [random] and irreversible ones."[28]

Whitehead characterizes change in natural systems as the creative advance of nature into novelty; Prigogine terms such self-creation as the emergence of order out of chaos. The hypothesis of self-creation does not necessitate the assumption of extrasystemic purpose, such as Teilhard de Chardin's Omega point, but only the continuation with modification of already established patterns. Purpose exists but is revealed only through the irreversible movement of a natural system through space and time.[29] Natural systems thus manifest "purposeless" purpose, which can be defined as a telic direction created by evolutionary process: the parts of a natural system find their reason-to-be within temporal context. The appearance of life was an inventive step into novelty from an already established order, as was the evolution of the genetic structure, and neither requires either extrasystemic purpose or agency for explanation. Natural history supports the judgment that evolution over time replaces the simple with the more complex. Stated somewhat differently, evolutionary process alone can account for the existence of life on earth.

From a preservationist perspective time is real and irreversible. Nature is not simply an ecomachine moving regularly and mechanically but an intrinsically organic phenomenon that can be irreversibly damaged by human actions. Natural systems—consistent with the second law of thermodynamics—husband high-energy, low-entropy matter-energy, thus maintaining themselves in uniform configurations. The most stable natural systems are such physical phenomena as atoms and stars. Our sun fuels life on earth and concurrently balances the entropic account books, since the evolution of self-creating and self-maintaining biological systems on earth has occurred simultaneously with the increase of solar disorder (entropy). *Gaia* may be characterized as an *open system* operating within the constraints of the second law.[30] Environmental changes (volcanism, ice ages, sunspots) can significantly influence evolution, as witness the disappearance of dinosaurs some 63 million years ago; yet ecosystems generally become increasingly resistant to change as their size and complexity increase.[31] Strictly natural systems, relative to cultural systems, achieve a near steady state. Cultural systems are to natural ecosystems what daylilies are to *Sequoia sempervirens:* a moment of splendor followed by a rapid wilting. Preservationists argue that natural systems, left to their own ends and free of catastrophic disruption, maintain themselves in a changing environment. Alpine and desert ecosystems are marvelous examples of nature's way of maintaining order in the face of challenging circumstances. Leopold's observations and comparison of the Rio Gavilan's integrity and stability with the precarious state of managed ecosystems in Germany illustrate the point.

Preservationists also argue that natural systems are coordinating interfaces in natural hierarchies. Through time, order increasingly prevails over chaos, without foreclosing further creative advance into novelty, by building on or developing from some existing structure. Such a principle almost defines an ecosystem: through functional coordination the constituent elements comprising the whole achieve integrity and stability. Preservationists think ecosystemically rather than atomistically, and so they view nature as an organic system of internally related parts rather than as an ecomachine made of externally related parts. Their idea of wilderness thus diverges in fundamental ways from resourcism, and therefore from the impress of Modernism. Ecosystems generally, and life in particular, are understood as fundamentally irreducible to, although consistent with, the laws of classical science. More important, preservationism paradigmatically reflects the second law of thermodynamics—here understood as a law of irreversible process that, when transgressed, results in the collapse of a natural system to a more primitive level of organization.

In spite of its evident dissimilarities with resourcism, preservationism has sometimes been equated with shallow ecology, little more than an instrument to sustain the economic development of Western civilization while forestalling such environmental disasters as the greenhouse effect. Deep ecologists argue that the preservationist agenda remains committed to the domination of nature through an ostensibly "value-free" science and technology. So viewed, ecology is simply a sophisticated tool that, in conjunction with such other Modernist techniques as cost-benefit analysis, will ensure that a full measure of value is gained from wild nature. Preservationists are also charged with being Modernist manqués, "green bigots" who place the interests of wildlife and lands over the legitimate needs of impoverished masses of humanity. Accordingly, preservationists are easily stereotyped as people who have made their fortune and become more interested in protecting birds and wildflowers, guaranteeing their access to unspoiled wilderness and cleaning the air and water rather than ameliorating the plight (health care, housing, education, and income) of the underprivileged.[32] Finally, preservationism is sometimes seen as too little, too late by biocentric thinkers, and thus an inherently flawed idea of wilderness.

Biocentrism and Ecocentrism

Notwithstanding its virtues, the preservationist idea of wilderness *simpliciter* remains anthropocentric. By abandoning the view that nature is no more than an ecomachine or a stockpile of resources to fuel the human project, preservationists tend not to be bulls in an ecological china shop. They typically reject a strictly economic approach to valuing wilderness, and entertain other considerations such as rarity, species diversity, and even beauty. And by adopting a holistic view, preservationists are attentive to the pervasive linkages and interactions essential to any concept of a wilderness ecosystem. Yet from an ecocentric or biocentric perspective, preservationism remains anthropocentric, since human interests are the ultimate arbiters of value. In other words, biocentrism and ecocentrism go beyond strict preservationism by questioning speciesism: the idea that humankind is somehow superior to and therefore entitled to impose its values on nature.

Workable distinctions among the terms *anthropocentrism, biocentrism,* and *ecocentrism* are difficult and take us into the perilous waters of value theory and environmental ethics.[33] In a preliminary way, we can understand anthropocentrism as commencing with the rise of agriculture, bio-centrism as beginning in the nineteenth century with Charles Darwin, and ecocentrism as originating recently, after World War II. Aldo Leopold's land ethic is a representative (if not definitive) example of an ecocentric outlook. Anthropocentrists see the human species as the most significant fact of existence, and accordingly evaluate all else from a human stand-point. Biocentrists take life rather than the human species as the central verity and thus assign value to all other things relative to life; protection of a single organism (as distinct from a species) is therefore important to a biocentrist. Ecocentrists take natural systems as the dominant reality, such that even life itself must be set in a larger evolutionary frame of reference that contains inorganic components; protection of a species (rather than an individual) *and* its supporting context is therefore critical to an ecocen-trist. Ecocentrism, biocentrism, and anthropocentrism can be understood as in some ways connotatively and therefore denotatively overlapping. For example, the concept of life and the individual organisms presupposed by biocentrists are an abstraction (increasing connotation, decreasing denota-tion) from a larger ecosystemic reality that includes both biotic and abiotic parts organized into a synergetic whole. Similarly, the concept of human life presupposed by anthropocentrists is an abstraction from the web of life on the basis of some distinguishing characteristic (as for example the child of God or the rational animal).

Biocentrism and ecocentrism are clearly contradictory with resourc-ism. For the resource conservationist nature has use-value only. Beyond resourcism, however, biocentrism and ecocentrism are inconsistent even with preservationism, since it rests essentially on instrumental values. Preservationism expands evaluative criteria beyond those of resourcism, but strict preservationists continue to justify their prescriptive statements by an appeal to human utility, as in claiming that a wilderness area ought to be preserved because future generations will enjoy it. To biocentrists and ecocentrists this is a self-defeating prescription, since if wildlife and land are to be protected, then human interests must sometimes give way to bio-centric and ecocentric interests. Strict biocentrists claim that wilderness areas ought to be preserved for reasons, such as the intrinsic value of life, that are independent of any instrumental value. Obviously, the idea of in-strumental as distinct from intrinsic values is complicated, but it is funda-mental to comprehending differences between preservationism and either biocentrism or ecocentrism (see table 6). Hereafter *ecocentrism* is assumed to include *biocentrism* on the presupposition that life cannot exist outside

Table 6. Distinguishing Characteristics of Ecocentrism

ECOCENTRISTS believe that
- natural systems are the basis of all organic existence, and therefore possess intrinsic value
- humankind is an element within rather than the reason to be of natural systems, and is hence dependent upon intrinsic value
- ethical human actions (actions which promote the good life for humankind) necessarily promote all life on earth (preserves such intrinsic values as diversity, stability, and beauty)

---

an ecosystemic context; thus a biocentric argument that contradicts ecosystem values is self-defeating. Further, ecocentric arguments remain open to both human and biological values but also include ecosystemic values.

The first principle advances from the preservationist understanding of nature as a living system of interrelated parts to the idea that natural ecosystems possess value in their own right, independent of human value judgments. The ecocentrist recognizes a level of organization and integration within wild nature that is independent of human purpose, whereas the strict preservationist, while recognizing that natural systems are organized wholes, understands and values nature strictly in the context of utility. Accordingly, ecocentrists recognize that human values do not exhaust the set of all possible values. But, even granted the premise that wild nature possesses intrinsic value, a number of complicated philosophical questions immediately arise. How is the idea of intrinsic value to be defined? How are such values manifested in nature? And how could such intrinsic values conceivably be related to instrumental values?

The nineteenth-century evolutionary insights of Thoreau again find contemporary relevance. What, he asked, is the human species but a mass of thawing clay? This question led him to the conclusion that "at least Nature has some bowels, and there again is mother of humanity." In short, sentient creatures such as himself had descended from the inorganic through a grand yet mysterious evolutionary process. The idea that nature is the mother of humanity is irreconcilable with mainstream Western culture and yet another idea flying in the face of Emersonian transcendentalism and Modernism more generally: for nature has a radical and absolutely autonomous value independent of humankind and the Oversoul. As Thoreau understood, the naked ape is dependent upon a primordial fount of value, and not vice-versa. Some twentieth-century evolutionists, such as Teilhard de Chardin, have gone too far in claiming that "man, the centre of perspective, is at the same time the centre of construction of the universe." [34] Jan Smuts observes more accurately that the realization that humankind is part of cosmic process also "impresses on us the necessity of that great lesson of humility which is the ethical message of Evolution." More specifically, evolution obliges humankind to recognize that "the Great Society of the universe leaves a place for the most humble inanimate inorganic structure no less than for the . . . soul. To conceive the universe otherwise is to indulge in anthropomorphism, which may be pleasing to our vanity, but in reality detracts from the richness and variety of the universe." [35]

From an ecocentric perspective, Homo sapiens no longer lies at the center of all things (anthropocentrism) or culminates evolution (speciesism). An ecocentrist understands the human species as part of a natural community, a society that includes (as radical empiricists like John Muir saw clearly) poison ivy and azalea, rattlesnakes and scorpions, hurricanes and tornadoes. [36] Ecocentrism weds the preservationist idea that nature is a living process with the idea that natural systems possess intrinsic values that undergird and are independent of human values. Such a position, though consistent with ecology and nonequilibrium thermodynamics, is cognitively meaningless to the modernist for two reasons. First, the modern mind assumes an absolute separation between mind and nature, fact and value; second, nature therefore cannot in its own right be a locus of value, for humankind (mind) assigns all value. In contrast, to the evolutionist an ecocentric perspective is required since the idea of Human Infinite—as the absolute locus of value—is empirically empty and logically inconsistent. Alternatively, Lord Man is extinct, since humankind (Human Finite) cannot live without even such elementary phenomena as sunlight and photosynthesis. In short, the human species is thermodynamically and biologically, and therefore inescapably, bound with natural process.

The third distinguishing characteristic of ecocentrism extends the logic of the first two principles to the conclusion that human values must be brought into harmony with intrinsic natural values. In other words, Homo sapiens must do certain things because of its membership in a natural community (just as a member of the civil community is obligated to do certain things). Ecocentrism moves beyond preservationism, for the idea of promoting all life entails a radical claim that human values which destroy intrinsic value must therefore be either modified or abandoned. Holmes Rolston argues that "the key idea [underlying an ecocentric perspective] is of nature as source of values, including our own. Nature is a generative process to which we want to relate ourselves and by this to find relationships to other creatures. Values include far more than a simplistic human-interest satisfaction. Value is a multifaceted idea with structures that root in natural sources."[37] Advancing from this premise, Rolston specifies several ecocentric maxims, including those of reversibility and scarcity, predicated on a holistic understanding of nature. The reversibility maxim assumes the vantage point of nonequilibrium thermodynamics and states that humankind ought to avoid introducing irreversible changes in natural process. Humankind can destroy beyond repair delicate ecosystemic processes that have required literally millions of years to create.[38] The scarcity maxim assumes the vantage point of foundational ecology and states that humankind ought to take special measures to protect rare ecosystems (such as alpine tundra and old-growth forests) and endangered species. Crucially, in transcending the barriers of Modernism that have divorced humankind from nature, Rolston does not erect new barriers. As he points out, there is no necessary antagonism between human and natural values, since natural values face both inward and outward. Inward-facing natural values are values independent of humankind, as for example the snail darter or photosynthesis, and outward-facing values are values in a specifically human context, as for example the value of native genetic plasm to agronomists attempting to perfect hybrid plant stocks. Further, Rolston contends that nature itself—the evolutionary process—was enriched by species Homo sapiens: for in that experiment nature became self-conscious.

However appealing an ecocentric perspective is to defenders of the wilderness, it engenders several difficulties. John Passmore argues that apart from human experience there is no idea of wilderness, and therefore ecocentrism is an inherently flawed and nonsensical position since humankind cannot in principle view the environment from other than a human perspective.[39] And Rolston observes that any argument that the human species is obligated to promote intrinsic natural values seems paradoxical, since nature "runs automatically and, within her more active creatures, instinctively; but persons do things by design, which is different, and we for the most part have no trouble distinguishing the two kinds of events." Yet according to this argument "no human has ever acted deliberately except to interfere in the spontaneous course of nature. All human actions are in this sense unnatural because they are artifactual, and the advice to follow nature is impossible. We could not do so if we tried, for in deliberately trying to do so we act unnaturally."[40] The issue, simply stated, is this: If humankind is part of nature, then human actions cannot be construed as anything other than natural even if detrimental to the larger natural community. By contrast, if Homo sapiens is distinguished by its cultural being from other natural kinds, then no consistent argument that humankind must follow nature's way seems possible. Stated somewhat differently, natural or evolutionary process led to human nature, and human nature to culture; but culture has paradoxically enabled behavior that impairs the integrity of nature. Thus no return to nature seems possible without contravening human nature and the reality of the past ten thousand years of history.

Passmore's observation that all ideas are linguistically and culturally enframed is neither unique nor a refutation of ecocentrism. Just as he maintains, Homo sapiens cannot escape having a human perspective on the wilderness, whether this be resourcism, preservationism, or ecocentrism. But in his critique of ecocentrism, Passmore assumes a modernistic and therefore anthropocentric perspective as the rule to measure all others. Such criticism is external, underscoring rather than resolving the inconsistencies and contradictions between anthropocentric and ecocentric vocabularies. The issue is not choosing between a human and a nonhuman viewpoint but discussing the relative adequacies and inadequacies of anthropocentric and ecocentric perspectives. As Duerr observes, "Not *all* facts become apparent in *every* language, certainly not in the castrated variety customarily employed in academe. Not *all* wheels turn *everywhere*."[41] More fundamentally, the question is the relation of thinking to reality. Passmore assumes that there is a necessary or logical rather than a culturally determined and therefore contingent correspondence between reality and an anthropocentric idea of wilderness, as if it were the only possible vocabulary for description and evaluation. Yet, as William James argues, " '*Reality' is in general what truths have to take account of.*" But reality cannot in principle equal whatever human beings merely think it is, for that is a self-defeating position. Consequently, James continues, "what we say about reality thus depends on the perspective into which we throw it. The *that* of it is its own; but the *what* depends on the which; and the *which* depends on *us.*"[42] So understood, ecocentrism is a human but nonanthropocentric perspective on nature.

Here, however, a naive ecocentrist might object, and complain that through philosophical analysis we have fallen back into the subjectivism of the resource conservationist, where human beings have again become the measure of all things. The beauty of wild nature is often cited as an example of values in nature independent of humankind, that is, objectively real features of the environment. To assert that there is "beauty in nature" is clearly different than to say that "beauty is in the eye of the beholder." The same mountain meadow, for example, might be beautiful to one person in and of itself, a beauty independent of human action. From this perspective people bear witness to or celebrate the beauty of wild nature, but they in no way create that state of affairs. To the ecocentrist, intrinsic beauty needs unconditional protection from human encroachment, since to intervene is to destroy the condition that makes beauty possible. Furthermore, the naive ecocentrist might contend, if judgment of beauty is made relative to human standards, then the beauty of the mountain meadow might conceivably be enhanced by a ski resort and the pleasures and profits it might bring. Indeed, virtually anything might be justified under aesthetic criteria. Here, then, is a seemingly absolute distinction between anthropocentric and ecocentric aesthetics.

The problem with asserting that "beauty is in nature" simpliciter—independent of sentience—is that the idea rapidly leads to mysticism. To speak of values in nature, such as beauty, as if these were utterly objective qualities of the environment is to commit what Whitehead defines as the fallacy of misplaced concreteness. Thus naive ecocentrism is ironically both mystical and modernist: mystical because the experience of beauty is private, and modernist because dualistic. The question is whether natural beauty is beautiful simpliciter or relationally, that is, independently of or conjointly with human understanding and appreciation of the marvels creation presents to sentience. To choose "the beautiful" simpliciter is, paradoxically, to reaffirm the very modernistic perspective against which the ecocentrist protests, for sentient humans have again been absolutely alienated from nature.

Ecocentric arguments encounter a second fundamental difficulty in the is-ought fallacy.[43] Ecocentrists argue that wild nature has ends independent of human intentionality, that these are privileged, and that human agency ought to recognize these ends. Aldo Leopold's land ethic is a paradigmatic case, for he asserts that humankind must "quit thinking about decent land-use as solely an economic problem. Examine each question in terms of what is ethically and aesthetically right, as well as what is economically expedient. A thing is right when it tends to preserve the integrity, stability, and beauty of the biotic community. It is wrong when it tends otherwise."[44] The land ethic, however, has been used to exemplify the is-ought fallacy by analytic philosophers, the philosophical heirs to Modernism. They argue that no ethical prescription (an ought statement) can be validly deduced from any scientific description (an is statement), be it physics, chemistry, or ecology. Given this premise, the land ethic does commit the is-ought fallacy, for Leopold moves from statements of fact, the observed integrity and stability of natural systems, to the claim that humankind ought to promote integrity and stability.[45]

In *Respect for Nature* P. W. Taylor argues that the land ethic "is not sound from a logical point of view. It confuses fact and value, 'is' and 'ought.'"[46] But this judgment is itself rooted in a paradigmatic framework assumed as an absolute. The land ethic is not, as Taylor claims, unsound from a logical point of view but rather incommensurable with his self-imposed final vocabulary and its logic. Only if the modernist paradigm is assumed as definitive (as an ultimate vocabulary unproblematically used to evaluate all other vocabularies) can Taylor's criticism be sustained. Yet Modernism, as we have seen, (1) is a cultural project lacking any isomorphic relation with an independent empirical reality to sustain its truth claims; even worse, (2) Modernism is bereft of an internally consistent theoretical demonstration of its cogency.[47] We have no quarrel with the idea that any claim to knowledge of either truth or virtue must be justified: the issue is precisely that of the paradigmatic standards by which the justification itself is made—Taylor's? or Leopold's?

Here again lurk difficulties grounded in the modern age. If humankind is the measure of all things, and nature no more than matter-in-motion, then the Cartesian dream of absolute control over nature might appear to be realized. So viewed, science is merely a means to human ends, one of which is to dominate nature. Leopold attempted to face the paradoxical fact that the insights of science, and therefore knowledge of what is, have been divorced from ethical considerations, that is, knowledge of what ought to be. Granted, there can no immediate deduction (in a strictly logical sense) of legitimate normative statements from a collection of descriptive statements. Social Darwinism, for example, reveals the problematic side of basing prescriptive norms on any loose assemblage of scientific fact. Indeed, Social Darwinism reflected more than anything else the hidden value assumptions of a laissez-faire political economy. Yet it is equally clear, as Aristotle argued nearly 2,500 years ago, and John Dewey more recently, that factual information is crucial to making informed ethical decisions. Leopold lacked a philosophically adequate paradigm to transcend fact-value, means-end dualism, and thus the land ethic, from the unreflective vantage point of the modern mind (external criticism), appears to commit the is-ought fallacy. But the land ethic can be defended from a postmodern philosophical viewpoint that accepts the reality of time as irreversible process and the inevitability of interpretation.[48]

Finally, once past the is-ought fallacy and the phenomenalistic predicament, ecocentric ideas of wilderness face a host of problems in application. Do the needs of burgeoning masses of Third World peasants and the privileged elites of the developed world take precedence over the values of natural systems? And how can Western society argue to the Third World that the global ecosystem no longer permits "underdeveloped" nations to exploit their natural resources? Further, by what methods and strategies might reconciliation between culture and nature be achieved? And what is the value of the anopheles mosquito? poison ivy? and the smallpox virus? since these natural kinds seem to lack intrinsic value. And who represents nature's interests, for the plants and beasts are mute?[49]

Resourcism does not confront such problems, since from its perspective wild nature has only instrumental value. Neither does preservationism confront these issues, since its primary claim is that human values (economic, scientific, and aesthetic) beyond those of efficiency and utility are thwarted by resourcism. But the ecocentrist has, in effect, no hiding place: there is neither any appeal to a human yardstick by which natural things might be instrumentally evaluated nor any petition to an inherent superiority possessed by species Homo sapiens that privileges human judgment, be this scientific, economic, or philosophic. Further, a consistent ecocentric position implies that wild nature actually teaches or reveals knowledge and values. Holmes Rolston advises us to respect an ecosystem as a proven, efficient economy. "When we step in, we need to be careful with our massive, irreversible, simplifying innovations, because the chances are that our disturbance will have some unintended bad consequences."[50] The ecologist Barry Commoner catches this dimension of ecocentric thought in his prescription that *nature knows best,* which he calls the third law of ecology. But what is nature's way? Does a natural mode of existence imply that humankind must go back to a hunting-gathering way of life? Or is it enough that we heed lessons of ecology (everything goes somewhere), steady state economics (minimize throughput, maximize the quality of life), and thermodynamics (haste makes waste, pollution, and entropy)? Crucially, recognition that the human species is merely an element within the web of life, and that nature's way offers alternatives, brings to the fore not the practical questions of economics and politics but the philosophical questions posed by Leopold, Evernden, and many others. Namely, why does Lord Man do what he does in the first place? Why has the human species assumed that nature's role is to serve only as the means to the good life of humankind? By raising such questions—even if unable to answer entirely the formidable philosophical problems raised by its prescriptive claims—ecocentrism directly confronts resourcism and goes beyond the cognitive bounds of preservationism.

Deep or Foundational Ecology

Deep or foundational ecology (also called radical environmentalism) presents an idea of wilderness contradictory to resourcism and inconsistent with preservationism since it moves beyond any appeal to instrumental values as a ground for guiding human action.[51] And deep ecology, while theoretically consistent with ecocentrism, goes beyond it by developing a pervasive critique of advanced industrial culture. In other words, foundational ecology advances from the idea that humankind is an element within natural systems, and therefore obligated to promote life on earth, to an ecocentric critique of Modernism. Deep ecologists also offer a variety of paradigmatic alternatives to the Cartesian-Newtonian paradigm. Warwick Fox argues that deep ecology hinges on the idea that there is no ontological divide between human and nonhuman, implying that the perception of any absolute bifurcation between these elements of evolutionary process is grounded in a priori assumptions rather than any a posteriori appeal to facts. When "we perceive boundaries, we fall short of deep ecological consciousness."[52] George Sessions catches the critical side of radical environmentalism when he argues that "urban-industrial society is a dinosaur causing immense destruction in its death throes. New intellectual-social paradigms for postindustrial society are emerging. The paradigm which embodies contemporary ecological consciousness is called the 'deep ecology movement.' "[53]

These arguments are problematic, as Sessions is well aware; deep ecology is more a collection of diverse ideas than a well-defined paradigm (in contrast, for example, to resourcism). In the language of T. S. Kuhn, the many anomalies of the modern mind are apparent, and thus we find ourselves amid an intellectual revolution. Yet a new paradigm—which will enable normal science—has yet to appear. So the deep ecologist lives in a pre-paradigmatic age that abounds in "pretenders" to the cognitive throne long occupied by Modernism. Sessions lists Jeffers's inhumanism, the eco-poetry of Snyder, the philosophy of Lao Tzu and Spinoza, the counterculture of Rozak, the steady state economics of Daly, and so on ad infinitum as all being part of or relevant to the deep ecology movement. Many of the pivotal figures in this study, such as Thoreau, Muir, and Leopold, are also mentioned as seminal deep ecologists. This diversity perhaps indicates that radical environmentalism is presently more of a conjectural umbrella, under which a family of critical responses to Modernism gathers, than a paradigm. Clearly the movement is edging toward a new and comprehensive vision of the relation between humankind and the natural world. Just as clearly the basic framework for a new paradigm that enables normal science is not yet in place.[54]

Deep ecology is presently in a preparadigmatic period and thus partly defined in opposition to the status quo. Radical environmentalism is cognitively revolutionary apropos of *shallow ecology* in at least two respects. First, deep ecology does not accept the modernistic premise that science is value free but draws on the many resources of both philosophic and scientific critics of Modernism. Part of the research program of deep ecology, itself not a single discipline, is to explore alternative social ideals and values. In this regard deep ecology is part of a postmodern reformation of science. Second, deep ecology is committed to an explicitly ecocentric orientation where humankind is understood as a part of rather than apart from wild nature. Shallow ecology is the ecology of the resource conservation movement, and hence of the modern university and research institute; the shallow ecologist believes that "reforming human relations towards nature can be done within the existing structure of society."[55] Deep ecology, in contrast, is interested in the question of what is good for the natural system itself of which humankind is only a part. Unlike shallow ecology, which considers only questions of the means to achieve the established ends of advanced industrial societies, deep ecology questions ends; in other words, foundational ecology moves beyond purely functional inquiry to entertain explicitly ethical questions. However, Sessions cautions that deep ecology is misunderstood or misinterpreted when people assume "that its goal is to produce an ecological ethic in the sense of modern Western ethics," since modern ethical theory has been based on the assumptions that the human species stands apart from and is superior to the rest of creation.[56]

The Norwegian ecophilosopher Arne Naess, viewed by many as the preeminent deep ecologist, has attempted to give the movement a defined profile through his many articles and books. In his recent work he argues that deep ecology might also be called *ecosophy*, in part to distinguish the movement from the science of ecology and in part to gather from the Greek root *sophia* the connotation of eco- (or ecological) wisdom.[57] Ecosophy encompasses three research foci: wild nature, society, and the interrelations of society and nature. This set of distinctions discloses why so many seemingly different kinds of inquiry are categorized as "deep ecology," since

Table 7. Fundamentals of Deep Ecology

DEEP ECOLOGISTS believe that
- all life on earth has intrinsic value
- the richness and diversity of life itself has value
- human life is privileged only to the extent of satisfying vital needs
- maintainance of the richness and diversity of life mandates a decrease in human population
- humankind's relations to the natural world presently endanger the richness and diversity of life
- changes (consistent with cultural diversity) affecting basic economic, technologic, and ideological cultural components are therefore necessary
- "Green societies" value the quality of life (e.g., beauty) more than the quantity of life (e.g., GNP)
- individuals subscribing to these fundamentals of deep ecology are obligated to promote sociocultural change

---

each opens a different door for research. Thus a wilderness ecologist might study wildlife and land, a social ecologist might examine society, and an energy ecologist might explore relations between market economics and the production-distribution-consumption of energy. Yet this diversity of approaches, while creating a wealth of information, generates an embarrassment of riches: for there is apparently no theory which ensures that the perspectives ultimately converge on a common center.

Naess has attempted to delineate the principles that cut across the deep ecology movement (see table 7). Clearly, many deep ecologists focus on questions of value rather than method and paradigmatic structure.[58] The need for a personal relation to wild nature is often mentioned as prior to any environmentally oriented action or the ecological reform of society. Still, deep ecology entails an implicit methodological commitment perhaps best described as a radical bracketing of the categories of modern existence, although no allegiance is given any one method. Such a methodological freedom is simultaneously a strength and a weakness. Because deep ecology is methodologically underdetermined, its project is open to input from multiple sources, including wilderness ecology, social ecology, ethnopoetry, history, philosophy, anthropology, and sociology. Thus, Heidegger, Spinoza, Leopold, Muir, Jeffers, and Snyder all have contributions of one kind or another to make to radical environmentalism. Yet this very wealth is also an embarrassment, for there seems to be no sense of the relative value of any idea. Because of its theoretical freedom deep ecology invites criticism that it is (1) more a secular religion than a legitimate philosophy, and (2) more a mystical than a scientific discipline. And because of their ecocentric commitments deep ecologists invite the charges that (3) they are green bigots who ignore the legitimate needs of underprivileged human beings and that (4) their program for social reform borders on hopeless utopianism. Yet these criticisms are not entirely accurate, and in fact are better interpreted as pointing toward areas that need further consideration and development—before a deep ecology paradigm might legitimately be said to be in place—rather than fatal weaknesses.

The claim that deep ecology is more a secular religion or social phenomenon (like the counterculture) than a legitimate science or philosophical discipline results from its methodological openness. If, for example, both a Heidegger and a Leopold are members of the deep ecology research community, then by what criteria are they included? And by what criteria might anyone be excluded? Any one who attempts to reconcile Heidegger's with Leopold's contributions to deep ecology finds the going rugged. Granted, once terminological differences are settled, points of similarity, even isomorphisms, can be identified. Both argue that nature has been exploited through technology in the name of social progress and that fundamental changes in human behavior and ideology are needed. Heidegger calls for humankind to dwell in the fourfold and to let Being be; Leopold calls for the evolution of the land ethic and an ecological conscience. And yet their differences are enormous, both in method and in subject. Heidegger is a hermeneutical phenomenologist (a workable, if not entirely accurate categorization) who dwells on the reality of humankind's historicity and linguisticality. His writing is intensely abstract, as in *Being and Time*. Further, the question of reflexivity is central to his project.[59] Consequently, the pragmatic implications of Heideggerian deep ecology are obscure to all except the most determined students of his thought. Leopold is a wilderness ecologist whose writing is often practical, as in *Game Management*. In *Sand County Almanac* Leopold flirts with the theoretical boundaries of science and philosophy, yet even here the implications for practice remain relatively clear. The land ethic, whatever its insufficiencies, is firmly tied to ecological observation. But if both Heidegger and Leopold are part of the deep ecology movement, then the implications are devastating, for it must account for itself as both a philosophical discipline and an ecological science.

Although such an account may be possible in principle, radical environmentalism presently lacks any explicitly defined and widely accepted paradigmatic platform. Naess and Sessions, in an effort to provide such a base, appeal to Spinozism. They argue that Spinoza's ideas of nature as a hierarchical system with which humans as knowing subjects are intrinsically bound, and his demonstration of the reliability of direct intuitive knowledge of God-Nature, are particularly suited to deep ecology's research program: that is, knowledge of both ends and means. Sessions also argues that Whiteheadian-inspired process-relational approaches merely reinforce existing anthropocentric ideas of nature and that Spinozism enables a true ecocentric perspective.[60] True, Spinozism counters the atomistic-reductionistic tendencies of Modernism; but it is irreconcilable with evolutionary science and cosmology. And the ecocentric idea of intrinsic value in nature, surely a principle central to deep ecology, can be defended without appealing to Spinozism. Further, there is no uniformity of belief in Spinozism among deep ecologists, and no deep ecologist has shown any necessary connection between Spinoza and, for example, Heideggerian or Leopoldian deep ecology.

While the foregoing analysis is philosophically incomplete, at least one implication is clear. Deep ecology is in part guilty as charged—more an intellectual movement in process than a paradigm. So viewed, radical environmentalism adds nothing methodologically to the work of Leopold and Heidegger—indeed, to anyone who has found shelter under its research "umbrella." But collectively considered, not only Leopold and Heidegger but all those termed *deep ecologists* point toward a common problematic—that is, Modernism itself and the idea of nature as an ecomachine. What is more, the deep ecology movement not only can but perhaps should be understood, whatever else it might be, as part of a postmodern movement. Of course, Postmodernism itself is poorly defined, referring more "to a diffuse sentiment rather than to any common set of doctrines—the sentiment that humanity can and must go beyond the modern."[61] Some argue that all constructive postmodernists share, as a minimum, a commitment to an ecological and organismic perspective on evolutionary process. Yet even accepting this stipulation does not resolve the question of understanding just what deep ecology represents, for some avowed postmodernists explicitly distinguish the deep ecology worldview, on the basis of its explicitly ecocentric value orientation, from a second ecological worldview that is consistent with the traditions of personalism and humanism.[62]

Even beyond questions raised by its diversity of methods, deep ecology is vulnerable to charges that it is an exercise in mysticism and irrationalism. Here the critic can admit to the reality of ecological dysfunction but can claim that, given radical environmentalism's lack of methodological rigor, society cannot trust the deep ecologist's ecstatic vision any more than that of the religious or political seer. Why should we believe that all life on earth has value? or that a decrease in human population is obligatory? or that fundamental sociocultural changes are necessary? Critics of the European, deep ecology–based "green movement" charge that its policy proposals are nothing more than "scare based legislation" that in final analysis are "anti-people." Deep ecologists "give no credit at all to the achievements of human civilization, achievements which have often involved the conquest of nature's cruelty. The Earth is not really a separate living entity with rights of its own."[63] This position is perhaps too extreme a criticism to be taken seriously. More judicious critics might admit that individuals like John Muir have had Ur experiences, that such visions have psychically bonded those who have them with nature, and that such epiphanies might change the lives of all who have them. Then they lower the boom, pointing out that intuitions of any and all kinds have proven to be notoriously unreliable (just what are they, how are they to be interpreted, and what do they mean) and are often fraught with peril.

But the deep ecologist has an immediate rejoinder to this kind of criticism, drawing a clear distinction between "mystical ecology," which depends on achieving states of mind that are by definition private and incapable of communication, and the public and communicable cutting edge of deep ecology—that is, arguments resting on logic and evidence even if methodologically diverse.[64] Further, once fundamental principles are questioned, then the "facts" are subject to change. For example, the resource conservationist assumes that the gross national product is an accurate index of the good life; to the deep ecologist, who frames human beings within the terms of a radical anthropology such as that of a Paul Shepard, a Stanley Diamond, or a Marshall Sahlins, the virtues of conspicuous consumption, and the quest for an ever greater quantity of life, appear illusory, self-defeating. Still, to so reduce contemporary experience appears mystical to those who do not so frame experience. Yet this is perhaps the greatest value of the deep ecologist's program: dialogue about and inquiry into fundamental questions of human beingness is opened, sustained, and encouraged with the aim of developing new insights and meaningful alternatives. If, as Aristotle and Hartshorne argue, wisdom lies in moderation, then deep ecology sometimes goes too far; for example, some deep ecologists imply that if modern people would live like archaic people, then the problems of urban-industrial society would be overcome. Such an apparently immoderate contention opens radical environmentalism to attack from a number of directions, and yet moderation can only be defined relative to the end points that mark a continuum. Deep ecology, however mystical and ineffable it appears to the conservationist or shallow ecologist, nevertheless challenges the conventional wisdom. By so "stirring up the blood" deep ecology is inherently healthy: hardening of the categories is an insidious disease of culture, and by deconstructing the modernist categories of existence the radical environmentalist helps society begin to grapple with its problems. Although we cannot go back in time, we can—as deep ecologists contend—learn something from premodern culture.

The charge that deep ecologists are "green bigots" has been leveled by an offshoot from the main trunk of radical environmentalism: namely, the social ecologists who follow the lead of Murray Bookchin. Bookchin has made important contributions to environmental philosophy, not the least of which is his ecological critique of Marxist ideology.[65] But recently Bookchin has become highly critical of the deep ecology movement (a problematic endeavor at best, since deep ecology is an elusive target). He charges that "deep ecology is becoming one of the most pernicious ideologies to invade the ecology movement in the United States," largely because it identifies the wrong source of environmental malaise (which for Bookchin appears to be the traditional leftist scapegoat, that is, the exploitative capitalist bourgeoisie), denies the fundamental human rights of exploited masses of human beings, and mystically confuses wilderness with the real world. Social ecology, Bookchin continues, in contrast to deep ecology, "advances the view that the conflict between society and nature stems overwhelmingly from the conflict between human and human, notably within hierarchies and classes, and generally within a system of widespread oppression and economic exploitation. . . . Deep ecology . . . only deflects ecologically concerned people from the all-important need for radical social change."[66]

Individuals such as Kirkpatrick Sale and George Sessions have defended deep ecology against Bookchin's criticism, and Robyn Eckersley has published a critique of Bookchin's own ecological ethics.[67] Sessions argues that Bookchin's social ecology is actually a radical reinterpretation of the word *ecology*, indeed, that social-ecology is "a pre-ecological anthropocentric Enlightenment view of human technological progress, human domination over nature, a Lockean view of land as useless until developed, and a refusal to admit that there is a human overpopulation problem."[68] Eckersley—who recognizes the merits of portions of Bookchin's work—believes that it contains a self-contradiction. She argues that his claim—that social ecology can best deliver freedom for all life-forms to express their unique nature—is undercut by his privileging of "second nature over first nature and from his presumptuous conclusions concerning the state of human understanding of ecological and evolutionary processes." [69] Although we cannot dwell here on the ongoing debate, a few observations are in order. In-house battles within the larger framework of ecologically conscious Postmodernism are self-defeating; moderation remains a virtue, even among intellectuals. Clearly, different groups have different agendas for action in the world; just as clearly, mutual self-criticism—which points to errors of logic and fact, and openly discusses paradigmatic fundamentals —is beneficial to finite intellects. As C. S. Peirce observes in "Fallibilism," those interested in bringing about existential change must not—above all else—block the way of inquiry; doctrinal purity serves only dogmatists.[70] Deep ecology is clearly no panacea; neither is social ecology. And insofar as Bookchin insists that class opposition is the cause of ecological malaise, he blinds himself to a wealth of relevant data. Granted, as social ecology claims, ameliorating a global ecocrisis entails social reorganization, not only among individuals and classes within nations but between nations.[71] But just as deep ecology claims, reorganization of relationships between human and nonhuman others is also required.

Another criticism of the deep ecology movement, usually made by proponents of either resourcism or preservationism, is that it is hopelessly utopian—or ecotopian, as deep ecologists themselves claim.[72] Utopias by definition are visionary, radically imaginative, and opposed to the cultural mainstream; in addition, the checkered history of utopian communes illustrates that the best of intentions often fail to bring about lasting change in human ways. Conservationists and preservationists argue that the greater good for the greater number will come about through small but incrementally cumulative changes, rather than any attempt to create, for example, Paul Shepard's techno-cynegetic society or Baker Brownell's ecological society. Even the arguments for bioregionalism—the idea of a politically and economically decentralized culture where human beings attempt to live in accord with nature's way—seem radically discordant with the modernist outlook.

Sessions and Devall partially meet this kind of criticism by observing that "nothing can be done, everything is possible."[73] In being methodologically open and culturally utopian the deep ecologist aims to do what the resource conservationist does not: that is, achieve a theoretical posture adequate to the rapidly changing picture of life on earth by grappling with the very categories that define the modern mind and then transcending the anomalies of that worldview. Radical environmentalism is therefore weakest precisely where resource conservation at least partially succeeds: we cannot be idle while we engage in a Chineselike critical purging of the spirit. And deep ecology is strongest where resource conservation and shallow ecology are weakest; the cure proposed by resource conservationists betrays the fundamentally impoverished nature of Modernism. Humankind is left out of the picture; economics, politics, ethics, and philosophy are not seriously reconsidered. Thus, deep ecology recognizes the inherently dynamic potential of our species to modify the naturally given and then envisions this being done in a "sophisticated" and "unobtrusive" way in the context of an environment "left natural."

Ecofeminism

Ecofeminism is a relatively new way of thinking about the relations between the human species and the earth, so contemporary that Roderick Nash does not discuss it in *Wilderness and the American Mind* (1967). Yet viewed from the perspective of posthistoric primitivism, ecofeminism is in part a rediscovery of an ancient and premodern way of thinking about the natural world as intrinsically feminine that has grown out of the intersection of the women's consciousness and environmental movements since World War II. As we have seen, the environmental movement is no one thing, and neither is the feminist movement, since feminist thought encompasses at least four distinct schools (liberal, traditional Marxist, radical, and socialist). We shall examine ecofeminism only insofar as it is related to other contemporary ideas of wilderness, attempting thereby to avoid entanglement in the nuances and "in-house" arguments of feminist thought.

Rosemary Ruether's *New Woman, New Earth* (1975), Dolores LaChapelle's *Earth Wisdom* (1978), and Carolyn Merchant's *Death of Nature* (1980) could be used to mark the beginnings of what is now a burgeoning ecofeminist literature.[74] Each of these women, however, is a distinguished scholar whose work transcends feminism: Ruether is a prominent theologian, LaChapelle a consequential deep ecologist (who denies association with ecofeminism), and Merchant a widely recognized historian of science. Four characteristics generally define ecofeminist thought (see table 8). Here we confront the standard paradox of definition: we can make clean lines of separation only by preparing a procrustean bed. Given the criteria in table 8, ecofeminism overlaps ecocentrism and deep ecology at least in part.[75]

One characteristic of ecofeminist thought is the deceptively obvious idea that the earth is fundamentally feminine rather than masculine. Merchant observes that "women and nature have an age-old association—an affilia-

Table 8. Defining Characteristics of Ecofeminism

ECOFEMINISTS believe that
  – Mother Earth is a nurturing home for all life and should be revered and loved as in premodern (Paleolithic and archaic) societies
  – ecosystemic malaise and abuse is rooted in androcentric concepts, values, and institutions
  – relations of complementarity rather than superiority between culture and nature, the human and nonhuman, and male and female are desirable
  – the many problems of human relations, and relations between the human and nonhuman worlds, will not be resolved until androcentric institutions, values, and ideology are eradicated

---

tion that has persisted throughout culture, language, and history." [76] Thus ecofeminists almost uniformly are engaged in a project to disclose a way of thinking about wild nature that has been hidden behind the androcentric face of Modernism. We have seen that the concept of the Magna Mater is nearly as old as self-consciousness itself. The idea that nature is feminine persists among archaic peoples today, as for example the Sioux's belief in the Maká Iná. Similarly, Thoreau believed that nature is feminine and that "we are so early weaned from her breast to society, to that culture which is exclusively an interaction of man on man . . . [that in consequence we are] a civilization destined to have a speedy limit." [77] Gary Snyder's spiritual ecology also brings the female principle to the foreground, as an animating principle not only of nature but of cosmos. Thus ecofeminism—in reawakening ancient sensibilities of the Mother Earth—is not sui generis. Merchant believes that interest in this ancient wisdom was dramatically reawakened "by the simultaneity of two recent social movements—women's liberation, symbolized in its controversial infancy by Betty Friedan's *Feminine Mystique* (1963), and the ecology movement, which built up during the 1960s and finally captured national attention on Earth Day, 1970." [78]

Dolores LaChapelle uncovers a connection between the female principle and mountainous landscape forms venerated by archaic peoples in her book *Earth Wisdom*. She insightfully traces the symbolic and psychological connections between veneration of Mother Goddess mountains and the feminine principle, particularly as represented in the voluptuous feminine statuary characteristic of Paleolithic peoples. These statues were

"carved as the child knows the mother, all breasts, hips, and *mons veneris*, full and round." Notice the word *mons*. Latin for mountain in this anatomical word for the female genital region. The combination of gently rounded *mons veneris* and the two breasts is the same combination as the conical hill between the cleft mountain or ridge, the "cross valley." Possibly, the power of this combination of landscape forms has something to do with the actual birth of the baby. Recent discoveries by Leboyer and others have proved that the newborn baby . . . can see her [mother's] face and recognize it later. This may indicate that the first combination of shapes the baby sees after birth is the gently rounded *mons veneris* between the two breasts.[79]

In revering a mountain landscape displaying the V cleft, the archaic mind celebrates the mysteries of all creation, since the miracle of life is intrinsically bound with the female. To the modern—and therefore, according to ecofeminists, androcentric—mind, such beliefs in Mother Goddess mountains are mere superstitions; from a reflective standpoint, such worship is an enormous leap in consciousness from the immediate reality of birth, and thus life, to the explicitly self-conscious realm of the symbolic. Mother Goddess mountains re-present at a distance the same form present to a child as it comes to life, and the psychological association of mountains with birth experience thus symbolizes the intrinsically feminine character of life. From the modernist vantage point such a belief is clearly nonsensical. Just as clearly, the modernist can render such judgment only by holding personal beliefs as absolute standards used to measure all others.

For the ecofeminist the feminine principle is relevant to resolving the ecocrisis, since "the Earth's house and the human house are habitats to be cherished."[80] Metaphorically, Lord Man has behaved toward the earth as if he were in a whore's rather than his mother's house: the relation has been one of physical exploitation rather than spiritual veneration.[81] For the modernist an idea that nature is intrinsically feminine is incomprehensible, for the earth is nothing but inert matter subject to usurpation according to human plan: that is, phallo-technic society, as Mary Daly calls it, or the prevailing androcentric culture. Daly argues in *Gyn/Ecology* that "phallic myth and language generate, legitimate, and mask the material pollution that threatens to terminate all sentient life on this planet."[82] The ecosystemic consequences of the attitude of Lord Man are all too evident (although the extent to which life itself is threatened is unknown); but here important questions arise as to just how nourishing and cherishing relationships between Mother Earth and her wayward sons and daughters might be reawakened.

LaChapelle argues that modern people might—indeed, must—recover these ancient sensibilities through ritual, breaking away from our homocentric and rationalistic schemes of thought. Nature is not just an occasionally unruly "other," a standing reserve to be harnessed through technology to the wants of the consumer culture, but an avenue of discovery leading toward concealed foundations of existence. Yet these realities remain hidden, and nature mute, because "we have idolized ideals, rationality and a limited kind of 'practicality,' and have regarded the conscious rituals of . . . other cultures as at best frivolous curiosities. The results are all too evident. We've only been here a few hundred years and already we have done irreparable damage to vast areas of this country now called . . . [the United States of America]." Through earth rituals and ceremonies LaChapelle believes that we might escape the imprisoning effect of the linear-logical side of our brain and thousands of years of cultural conditioning.[83] In making her case, and we cannot begin to do justice to her arguments here, she draws on a rich variety of psychology, anthropology, ethology, and philosophy. "Ritual provides us with a tool for learning to think logically, analogically and ecologically as we move toward a sustainable culture. Most important of all, perhaps, during rituals we have the experience, unique in our culture, of neither *opposing* nature nor *trying* to be in communion with nature . . . but of *finding* ourselves within nature, and that is the key to sustainable culture."[84]

A second characteristic of ecofeminist thought is the hypothesis that present-day environmental malaise results from gender conversion—a shift from thinking of nature as a nurturing mother to the masculine idea of nature as a foe to be conquered. According to Merchant,

> The metaphor of the earth as a nurturing mother was gradually to vanish as a dominant image as the Scientific Revolution proceeded to mechanize and rationalize the world view. The second image [of nature as female], nature as disorder, called forth an important modern idea, that of power over nature. Two new ideas, those of mechanism and of the domination and mastery of nature, became core concepts of the modern world. An organically oriented mentality in which female principles played an important role was undermined and replaced by a mechanically oriented mentality that *either eliminated or used female principles in an exploitative manner*. As Western culture became increasingly mechanized in the 1600s, the female earth and virgin earth spirit were subdued by the machine.[85]

A difficulty, not necessarily a fatal flaw, with this thesis is that machines in and of themselves are neither masculine nor feminine; some people view machines, such as ships and cars, as feminine. More fundamentally, gender conversion, a shift from thinking of the natural world as revered female to thinking of it as a hostile foe or inhuman "other," occurred much earlier than the scientific revolution—perhaps in the transition from Paleolithic to Neolithic culture. Through the domestication of animals and the cultivation of grains nature slowly lost its feminine mystery and became a masculine foe requiring domination; the feminine principle retained currency only through association with fecundity or as a source of chaos and through assimiliation into patriarchal ideology and institutions.[86]

The work of Rosemary Ruether is particularly relevant to understanding how the feminine came to be conceptualized as a source of disorder, thwarting human purpose. She argues that Judeo-Christianity has been and remains androcentric, and correlates "femaleness with the lower part of human nature in a hierarchical scheme of mind over body, reason over passions. Since this lower part of the self is seen as the source of sin—the falling away of the body from its original unity with the mind and hence into sin and death—femaleness also becomes linked with the sin-prone part of the self." Male monotheism subsequently reinforced this metaphysical distinction between male and female, spirit and matter, becoming "the vehicle of a psychocultural revolution of the male ruling class in its relationship to surrounding reality." From Ruether's perspective the Western world's relentless humanizing of wild nature is implicit in abandoning the matriarchal nature worship of our archaic ancestors and embracing Yahweh as the one, absolute God.

> Whereas ancient myth had seen the Gods and Goddesses as within the matrix of one physical-spiritual reality, male monotheism begins to split reality into a dualism of transcendent Spirit (mind, ego) and inferior and dependent physical nature. . . .
>
> Both the Hebrew Genesis story and the Platonic creation story of *Timaeus* retain reminiscences of the idea of primal matter as something already existing that is ordered or shaped by the Creator God. But this now becomes the lower pole in the hierarchy of being. Thus the hierarchy of God-male-female does not merely make woman secondary in relation to God, it also gives her a negative identity in relation to the divine.[87]

Ruether's analysis both theoretically and practically reinforces the work of others in the ecofeminist movement, especially the idea that humankind's unrelenting exploitation of the earth is a consequence of androcentric ideas and values. Contemporary feminist theology may very well, as Ruether claims, help expose "the Big Lie" (Modernism) as an illusion, and disclose "the Divine Wisdom" as an alternative way of thinking about ourselves and our relations to the natural world. The big lie is, in part, that "man must drive the devils and witches from the world, restore order, put himself in charge, reduce nature to his control. With numbers and formulas he can search out her innermost secrets, learn all the laws of her ways; become her lord and master. The cosmos is reduced to elements, molecules, atoms, positive and negative charges, infinitely manipulatable, having no nature of her own, given to him to do with what he will."[88] But mere criticism is in the end incomplete, and Ruether thus necessarily addresses the positive pole of ecofeminist theology: the Divine Wisdom.

> Through the fissures of the system we glimpse the forgotten world of our homeland. We learn to walk again; to watch sunsets; to examine leaves; to plant seeds in soil. Turn off the TV; talk to each other to ease the frenetic pace; get in touch with our circulatory system, with the rhythms of our menstrual cycle that link us to the pull of the moon and tides of the sea.
>
> The scales begin to fall from our eyes, and all around us we see miracles. Babies grow in wombs without help from computers. The sun rises every day. Con Ed sends no bill for sunshine. The harmony is still there, persisting, supporting, forgiving, preserving us in spite of ourselves. Divine Grace keeps faith with us when we have broken faith with her.[89]

Again, from a modernist perspective this claim is nonsense. What do women know of pollution and its causes, or the economics of cleaning up acid rain? Then again, as Gary Snyder writes, we shall see who knows how to be.

A third characteristic of ecofeminist thought is its egalitarianism. Ecofeminists almost uniformly advocate reconsideration of male-female roles —both in the family and society—and relations between human and infra-human species, and thus oppose long-established patterns of human behavior. By articulating a need for reexamination of gender-based roles, ecofeminism draws from its roots in the women's movement. And whatever the theoretical strengths and weaknesses of ecofeminism, its agenda for action underscores the idea that we live in an age of ecology. An ecological paradigm, with its emphasis on holism and internal relations, forces us to reconsider questions of human nature and culture that have usually been thought of as closed. Such reexaminations are difficult, in part because the age-old nature-nurture controversy immediately thwarts us, and in part because we are the subject of inquiry. Further, the data become increasingly murky as we peer into the dim recesses of the Paleolithic and even dimmer as we look back to the protohumanoids. Archaeologists heatedly dispute the role of women in the Paleolithic age. Was our human beingness fundamentally shaped more by "woman the gatherer" than "man the hunter"? Did the erect posture of protohumanoids lead to premature birthing and thus cause females to seek out males for protection during the now extended period of caring for children? We cannot resolve these issues here, but have again encountered the fundamental questions of human beingness that so many wilderness philosophers and poets raise.

Once the assumptions of the intrinsic superiority of the human species over nature and of man over woman are held in abeyance, then alternative views of these relations—the human to the nonhuman, and male to female—become possible. Michael Zimmerman observes that "it is plausible to suggest that . . . women are in a better position than most men to help reconstruct the humanity-nature relation in light of their ongoing sensitivity toward and involvement with their own bodies and the rest of nature. We must be careful, however, not to fall prey to the sex-based stereotyping that has been so crucial to maintaining patriarchy." Obviously ecofeminism contradicts resourcism, and just as clearly ecofeminism seems difficult to reconcile with preservationism, which does not presume to challenge such idées fixes as the respective roles of male and female. And some ecofeminists have argued against biocentrism, believing that at base it remains androcentric by extending male rights to the nonhuman other. If so, then biocentrism "fails to include moral categories that arise from a feminine experience of self and world. The experience of relatedness reported by many women gives rise to a morality of caring for the concrete needs of those with whom one is related." Yet viewed ecologically either male or female simpliciter is an abstraction from a natural kind (the human species) and biological process (evolutionary history) and thus risks becoming a metaphysical entity independent of human experience. To believe that hormones and sexual organs are destiny is to denigrate the full potentiality of our human beingness. Zimmerman argues that "if patriarchy is an interpretive framework, is feminism itself not another such framework? Does feminism pretend to provide a nondistorted, impartial way of interpreting experience? Are feminists raised under patriarchy motivated by their own version of the power drive that is essential to patriarchy?" Male and female do not exist apart from a natural and cultural continuum, and in any case "authentic [nonsexist] human existence would inevitably transform the current exploitative treatment of nature."[90]

This assertion finds parallels in the ecofeminist literature. Merchant, for example, believes that once we begin to view the world of human experience ecosystemically, rather than either homocentrically or androcentrically, we realize that "nature cannot continue to provide free goods and services for profit-hungry humans, because the ultimate costs are too great." But transforming the relations between the human species and nature inevitably involves transforming male-female relations, since

> the dualism of separate public and private spheres should be severed and male and female roles in both the household and the workplace merged. Cooperation between men and women in each specific context—childrearing, day-care centers, household work, productive work, sexual relations, etc.—rather than separate gender roles could create emotional rewards. Men and women would engage together in the production of use-values and would work together to scale down the production of commodities that are costly to nature. Technologies appropriate to the task, technologies having a low impact on the environment, would be chosen whenever possible.[91]

The Idea of Wilderness and the Hermeneutic Circle

Our inquiry into contemporary ideas of wilderness seems to have reached an impasse, where articles of faith preclude further discussion. Opposition among the contending forces appears irreconcilable. RESOURCISM rules the modern world, and this is no surprise. Humankind must live, and the conservationist idea of wilderness is entirely consistent with that cultural plan for existence called *Modernism*. The resource conservationist and shallow ecologist view wild nature as a means only to human ends. Accordingly, humankind is understood not as a part of but apart from the green world. Nature is presumed to be merely inert matter-energy devoid of value until the humanizing force of civilization is forced upon it. PRESERVATIONISM abandons the modernist faith that nature is only a collection of parts that obey the mechanical laws of nature, embraces the idea that nature is a living whole in evolutionary process, and affirms the importance of aesthetic and scientific values. But preservationism at paradigmatic base remains anthropocentric since all values rest on the assumption that human beings are the apex of creation and the measure of all worth. ECOCENTRISM attempts to escape this bias by inverting the relation between our species and the natural world. So understood, ecocentrism embraces holism and overcomes speciesism. Yet culture refutes any thesis that the human project is strictly natural or that the good life can be equated with a natural life: to be human is to be enframed by language and history. DEEP ECOLOGY is the leading and therefore ragged edge of a postmodern idea of wilderness—consistent with preservationism (holism) and ecocentrism (rejection of speciesism) even while going beyond these ideas of wilderness by embracing a mélange of additional ideas: bioregionalism, ecofeminism, and green politics. Yet deep ecology suffers from limitations of both theorie and praxis. Pragmatically considered, green politics is likely too little too late, too radical to have more than a minimal influence on the cultural mainstream.[92] More fundamentally, although deep ecology has exposed many of the anomalies of Modernism, it provides no philosophically adequate undergirding (ontological, cosmological, epistemological) for a postmodern project. Foundational ecology is now more multifaceted process than finished paradigm. And last, but not least, is ECOFEMINISM, engendered by the same historical circumstances that have created preservationism, ecocentrism, and deep ecology. Yet ecofeminism is more identification of a complicated problematic involving sex-based ideology than a solution, for the modern world obliviously, and therefore androcentrically, marches on. Although the feminist critique offers insightful, often original perspectives on the anomalies of Modernism, it appears at its radical edges to be paradigmatically incapable of transcending them without falling into "feminarchy."

Perhaps there is a way beyond, since the idea of wilderness conceivably entails larger questions that might transcend the conceptual quandary now confronting us. My conjecture, however preposterous this might seem to the modern mind, is that the theoretical spectrum before us—from resourcism through deep ecology and ecofeminism—remains entangled with that cultural project that is the West. Modernism yet rules the world, even if surreptitiously, and thus only by going beyond its bounds to Postmodernism can our dilemma be overcome. In this presumption I claim neither privileged dispensation nor insight, only to be carried along in a natural and cultural stream set in motion long, long ago. I admit to the inadequacy of the arguments to follow, for the matters of which I speak are those of possibility, not probability. And yet a new synthesis— *a postmodern idea of wilderness that is a profoundly ecological and evolutionary point of view*—is possible.[93] This idea of wilderness presumes to cover the evolution of human consciousness from its first glimmerings of self-consciousness in the Paleolithic mind to the entirely reflexive consciousness of the postmodern mind, and to see the human project as taking place within rather than outside nature.

In hypothesizing that a transformation from Modernism to Postmodernism is underway I invite criticism from those of Cartesian-Newtonian persuasion: that is, the majority of Western intellectuals. Yet, maybe, as many have suggested in different ways, we might emerge from the repressiveness that is the history of Western rationalism.[94] Just as evolution was to any intellectual of the nineteenth century—that is, a stubborn factum that could not be denied without rendering any consequent argument irrelevant and fallacious—so Postmodernism.[95] Clearly we cannot deny that the method of tenacity, as Peirce so aptly termed it, still rules the world and that the final vocabulary of the modernist worldview will abide as a privileged and putatively absolute perspective.[96] Any pretense, however, to intellectual viability forces consideration of the questions of postmodernity. Here my critics might justifiably remark that I have lapsed into prophesy: but either history is sound and fury signifying nothing, or, as I have argued for nine chapters, this brief interlude of cosmic history—the history of humankind—does mean something. The question is what?

Let us proceed cautiously from what Neil Evernden has recognized as the common core of contemporary ideas of wilderness: environmentalism.

> Environmentalism, like Romanticism, constitutes a defence of value. I am now asserting an even more fundamental role, the defence of meaning. We call people environmentalists because what they are finally moved to defend is what we call environment. But, at bottom, their action is a defence of cosmos, not scenery. Ironically, the very entity they defend—environment—*is itself an offspring of the nihilistic behemoth they challenge.* It is a manifestation of the way we view [and speak of] the world.[97]

Thereby Evernden invites us to abandon the modernist worldview that is either explicitly or tacitly assumed by existing ideas of wilderness and to think like postmodern men and women. Yet paradox of paradoxes, we are people who conceive of the world in terms of the learned categorical scheme of Modernism. It seems impossible to understand any alternative, for that would entail abandoning the cultural project on which we have been so long embarked: the modern mind is inescapably enframed by language and history. Still, there is the possibility of understanding something beyond for those who are willing to stand within the hermeneutic circle, and to listen to the words of the edifying philosophers. "Where is the literature," Thoreau asks, "which gives expression to Nature?"

> He would be a poet who could impress the winds and streams into his service, to speak for him; who nailed words to their primitive

senses, as farmers drive down stakes in the spring, which the frost has heaved; who derived his words as often as he used them,—transplanted them to his page with earth adhering to their roots; whose words were so true and fresh and natural that they would appear to expand like the buds at the approach of spring, though they lay half smothered between two musty leaves in a library,—aye, to bloom and bear fruit there, after their kind, annually, for the faithful reader, in sympathy with surrounding Nature.[98]

And so we wend our way toward a postmodern idea of wilderness, one that is necessarily fragmentary. I have no illusions of solving the many problems of theory and practice that have confronted us throughout this study. Chapter 10 is grounded in the work of Martin Heidegger, who reveals so insightfully that humankind is language, and suffers from the illusion that it masters and possesses language; Paul Ricoeur, whose hermeneutic phenomenology turns attention toward the essential bidirectionality of language, and thereby helps reestablish contact with the bios, the Ursprung, the elemental and primitive that underlies the logos; and Marjorie Grene, among the first to see that the way back to the green world, or the path to healing the rift between wilderness and civilization, lies in taking a hermeneutical step back. But the most immediate linkage to the hermeneutic community is with Richard Rorty, who argues in *Philosophy and the Mirror of Nature* that we—and by we he means anybody who ever looked beyond the end of his or her culture-bound nose— "are well on the way to seeing conversation as the ultimate context within which knowledge is to be understood."[99] More recently, Rorty argues for solidarity, an idea that can be extended to include nonhuman others: the land, the plants, and the animals.[100] The dramatic implication of all this is that wilderness philosophy and literature is the cutting edge by which nature's experiment in humanity is transforming itself from the modern to the postmodern era. In chapter 10 I attempt in part to confirm and exemplify the validity of the hermeneutical thesis—that conversation is the ultimate context within which knowledge is to be understood—by looking generally at the wilderness philosophy and literature genre during the past 150 years. In doing this we shall again gaze upon the work of the poetic thinkers and the thinking poets we have previously encountered.

CHAPTER TEN

Cosmos and Wilderness
A Postmodern Wilderness Philosophy

The truly apocalyptic view of the world is that things do not repeat
themselves. It isn't absurd, e.g., to believe that the age of science and
technology is the beginning of the end for humanity; that the idea of
great progress is a delusion, along with the idea that the truth will
ultimately be known; that there is nothing good or desirable about
scientific knowledge and that mankind, in seeking it, is falling into a
trap. It is by no means obvious that this is not how things are.
—Ludwig Wittgenstein, *Culture and Value*

THE ANOMALIES OF MODERNISM, that paradigm for thought
and action upon which the contemporary world rests, are
reflected throughout the conceptual spectrum of chapter 9. Yet paradigmatic revolution—a profound change in consciousness, however foolish
that idea seems—is in the wind, and humankind may be on the brink of a
postmodern age. Of course such qualifiers as anti- or post- tend to obscure
the central issue: Modernism.[1] Crucially, the idea of wilderness appears
to undergird a new paradigm for understanding humankind as embodying
natural process grown self-conscious. The wilderness paradigm might be
viewed as only an outgrowth of the environmental movement of the past
few decades, spilling over into a related yet different concern, for if environmentalism could always be and often was justified homocentrically,
our concern for the wilderness, the preservation and protection not only
of endangered species but of entire ecosystems, seems rooted in ecocentrism. But the emerging postmodern wilderness philosophy is more than
environmentalism in new guise. It represents a convergence of scientific research and reflective thought on the premise that the human and cultural—
including the ethical, theological, and philosophical—are linked with the
material and organic. In other words, there are no grounds to draw radical

distinctions in kind between ends and means, or facts and values, for what is known to exist is known only in relation to something else, and that is most fundamentally an evolutionary continuum. Just as the modern idea of nature as nothing more than matter-in-motion is best understood as rooted in mechanistic materialism, so the postmodern conception might be understood in terms of *cosmic synergism*. More important, the idea of wilderness in postmodern context is, as Neil Evernden and others imply, a search for meaning—for a new creation story or mythology—that is leading humankind out of a homocentric prison into the cosmic wilderness. And if that new creation story is to ring true in a postmodern age, then it must have both scientific plausibility and religious distinctiveness.[2]

Enter Postmodernism

The second scientific revolution of Darwin and Clausius is just now, in its cosmological implications, reaching critical mass. Who am I? echoes a questioning voice from the nineteenth century. What are we? Where are we going? Only when we are lost, Thoreau reminds, can we begin to find ourselves. Once we abandon the signposts, the directions that define the conventional world, we see wild nature, and there, in wildness, lies preservation of the world. In the wilderness the phenomenological epoche is no longer conscious strategy, no longer method, but reality: nature becomes an immediate and palpable presence no longer obscured by the cake of custom.[3] Yet Thoreau's insights are perhaps more opaque to the modern mind than to his coevals, who understood him not at all, for the twentieth century is more deeply ensnared by Modernism than the nineteenth. So fundamentally entwined with culture, and thus life, is the modernist paradigm that even alternatives are typically envisioned through its hidden and uncriticized presuppositional framework. Governmental policy, economic theory, business decision-making, higher education—virtually the entire panoply of contemporaneous human experience—are conceptualized in modernist terms. Even contemporary ideas of wilderness are enframed by Modernism, for in trying to address ecological malaise we have not thought beyond nature as environment—that is, as standing apart from and inferior to us, serving only as a resource to fuel the human project.

Paradigmatic changes are inevitably messy, creating havoc within the world-in-force as connotative shifts in the categories of experience occur. As Modernism has slowly revealed its theoretical insufficiencies, that monumental achievement of the human intellect—science—has been discomfited enormously, and yet it remains central to all that lies ahead. "The ethic of knowledge that created the modern world is the only ethic," proclaims Nobel Laureate Jacques Monod, "compatible with it, the only one capable, once understood and accepted, of guiding its evolution."[4] Modernism, however, precludes inference from descriptive to prescriptive statements. Yet science, Einstein tells us, is unable to warrant its own existence, "so little capable of acting as a guide that it cannot prove even the justification and the value of the aspiration toward that very knowledge of truth. Here we face, therefore, the limits of the purely rational conception of our existence."[5] Modern science offers no remedy. Schrödinger suggests that the assumption that makes pursuit of scientific truth possible is the exclusion of the observing scientist or the "subject of cognizance from the domain of nature that we endeavour to understand."[6] Similarly, C. F. von Weizsäcker writes that "if empirical scientific theory is itself science, then it must establish its concept of empirical science empirically, meaning historically and descriptively."[7] An adequate account *necessarily* includes science in its cultural context since "scientific findings, even those which at the moment appear the most advanced and esoteric and difficult to grasp, are meaningless outside their cultural context."[8] These insights bear pivotally on this chapter, for the idea of wilderness pulls contemporary scientific findings into human context, even while acknowledging with Whitehead that "almost all really new ideas have a certain aspect of foolishness when they are first produced."[9]

As this century turns to the next a new evolutionary paradigm is emerging, set in motion almost simultaneously with the *rediscovery of time.*[10] The continuing scientific revolution impels reconsideration of time, since the prevailing Judeo-Christian and Newtonian-Cartesian conceptions have been intellectually discredited, though not socioculturally overthrown. The bifurcation of the temporal and eternal, and the natural and supernatural, reflects the influence of Greek rationalism on Judeo-Christianity: a peculiar combination of Attica and Jerusalem that has fatefully influenced history. Western culture, almost from the onset, has thought of nature as designed for the human species, a physical world conceptualized as a mere working out of a Divine Plan with an established beginning and end. Between this origin and terminus humankind would fulfill God's plan by humanizing the earth. The later Cartesian-Newtonian universe, at base a Parmenidean vision of an eternal One, was itself bound with its Judeo-Christian roots, presupposing that God had made a rational and intelligible nature that was therefore open to systematic inquiry. Nature was a fallen world, since it was material; yet behind its apparent changing facade lay a world of permanent form, that is, the laws of nature. Space and time were conceived as essentially empty, sterile containers through which matter moved in uniform fashion.

The mutable face of the phenomenal world was thus understood as nothing more than an appearance that obscured the unchanging reality of an underlying nature. Classical science permits creative activity only for the initial act of Deity, for if new forms eventuate through the passage of time, then the presumed power of that Deity is contradicted.[11] Accordingly, classical physics adopts a machine metaphor for nature; God is the master engineer who designed the world mechanism. Natural motion is reduced to mechanical and lawful, and thereby uniform, predictable, and reversible motion. The moon, for example, could move just as well in the other direction as does a pendulum, for in either direction the same laws and mechanical forces underlie motion. To recognize the possibility of genuine novelty in either material (an unpredicted movement) or biological nature (a novel kind) upsets perfect knowability. Consequently, beyond the sociopolitical necessity of accommodation between scientific and ecclesiastic authority, the demand of science for complete knowledge cannot be reconciled with evolution. Under the impress of classical physics the question of change in nature was reduced in toto to the question of trajectories—the descriptions of classical dynamics.[12]

Newtonian dynamics culminates a long movement in Western thought, a battle that commenced with those giants of antiquity, Parmenides and Heraclitus. Mechanistic materialism represents a virtual triumph for the children of Parmenides, following Galileo in articulating *one* consistent scheme to explain motion in both celestial and terrestrial spheres, and Descartes in its mathematization of motion or change. But the nineteenth-century revolutions of Darwin and Clausius belie the Newtonian separation of space-time from matter. Darwin attempted to remain a good Newtonian, searching for *the mechanism* of evolution so that the course of change in biological form might be predicted. Today that quest is recognized as impossible in principle. "Evolution," Loren Eiseley remarks at the conclusion of *Darwin's Century*, "if it has taught us anything, has taught us that life is infinitely creative. Whether one accepts Henri Bergson's view of the process or not, one of the profoundest remarks he ever made was the statement that 'the role of life is to insert some *indetermination* into matter.'"[13]

For Modernism this idea is heretical. Similarly, the implication of the second law—that time moves in one direction only—is unwelcome, and late nineteenth- and early twentieth-century science struggled to deny the reality of irreversibility. Ludwig Boltzmann's project to extend classical dynamics (through a theory of probability) to cover the situation described by thermodynamics failed. Yet, as Prigogine argues, modern cosmology, indeed Modernism itself, marched on in oblivion to a dramatically new understanding of the reality of time and therefore nature.[14] As a result, the confirmation of time as an irreversibly real process awaited the rise of quantum mechanics and Werner Heisenberg. The culmination of the "golden age" of physics (1925–27) was Heisenberg's discovery that the unquestioned *realism* of classical physics was untenable, since all measurement necessitates human choice of a measuring device (itself a construction), and thus any description of reality is contingent upon the result of that selection. Thus, Prigogine argues, "no single theoretical language articulating the variables to which a well-defined value can be attributed can exhaust the physical content of a system. Various possible languages and points of view about the system may be complementary. They all deal with the same reality, but it is impossible to reduce them to one single description."[15]

Ilya Prigogine may be seen as leading the advance of postmodern science in response to the anomalies of Modernism. In such works as *Being and Becoming* and *Order Out of Chaos* (with Isabelle Stengers) he exposes the inadequacies of Modernism and advances the case for a postmodern worldview. "We now understand," he writes, "that we live in a pluralistic world." The problem is that much of this world is excluded from the descriptions of classical science, and perhaps most crucially, there is no place in its theoretical frame for "the vast areas of relationship between" the human species and nature. Prigogine points out that modern science leaves unanswered certain fundamental questions. For example, "How can we recognize ourselves in the random world of atoms? Must science be defined in terms of rupture between man and nature?" Significantly, the near simultaneous revolutions of Darwin and Clausius have begun to revolutionize the scientific worldview. The consequences are profound; the linear view of truth is being abandoned, and the hold of Parmenidean logic, Cartesian dualism, and Newtonian mechanism are being broken. We now know, Prigogine argues, that "time and reality are closely related. For humans, reality is embedded in the flow of time."[16]

Most important, through discovery of the reality of time there is a chance to weld the fissure between Homo sapiens and the earth, since the belief that time is not real has contributed to the alienation of humankind from nature and hence the ecological crisis.[17] Simply stated, we can credibly believe neither that the earth is a designed abode for the human species nor that the earth maintains itself eternally in some pre-established harmony. The consequences of human actions in the present, like those of the past, have real ecological consequences in the future. Thus the upshot of the second scientific revolution has been to break the cognitive hegemony of classical physics and objectivism: *process is reality, and the order of cosmological process is irreversible.* "Who would have believed, fifty years ago," Prigogine wryly observes, "that most and perhaps all elementary particles are unstable? Or that we would speak about the evolution of the universe as a whole? Or that, far from equilibrium, molecules may communicate?"[18] The inescapable reality of time has also made clear the impossibility of a divine or Parmenidean vantage point from which to describe reality. The second scientific revolution emphasizes "the wealth of reality, which overflows any single language, any single logical structure. Each language can express only part of reality."[19] In short, with the discovery that humankind is embedded in an evolving universe, the Parmenidean foundations of Modernism crumble; the description of a Parmenidean One or a static universe is conceivable only to the extent that one set of descriptions is granted unquestioned status as a cognitive absolute. Heraclitean descriptions, which depict human beings as part of an evolutionary flux, have assumed a new cogency insofar as the good life is contingent upon understanding the shifting panoply of experience. The implications for praxis, once the historicity and linguisticality of science are recognized, are profound, and such thinkers as Kuhn, Feyerabend, and Rorty have masterfully explored these dimensions of the scientific enterprise.[20] Truth is not out there, in a world independent of a community of scientific researchers, but is enabled by the linguistically articulated assumptions and human practices (including scientific instrumentation) that enable inquiry.

The crucial question, faintly but unmistakably present on the horizon of our inquiry, is to determine how culture—that is, the continuing process of choice called the West—presently influences science. Yet with recognition of this question the reflexive paradox appears with a cognitive vengeance, for language is caught within its own circle. Historically considered, "certainty has been found in God [religion], in phenomenological experience [phenomenology], in empirical observation [natural and social science], and in the beliefs of common sense. But today, because of the irreducibly textual character of our beliefs, all arenas of certainty are in question."[21] In other words, recognition that language plays a central role in all knowledge and thought, indeed, in culture and therefore life, has also called into question claims to absolute certitude. Yet this is a frightening specter. Truth was for the Greeks and remains for the modern mind the hallmark of knowledge. Today, wherever we might look, relativity *seems* to rule, for the Parmenidean One has been shattered into a million pieces. Even mathematics, long the sole holdout against relativity, has suffered from an insufficiency of basic principles, and mathematicians have taken the lead in warning of the dangers of Parmenides' dream. Philip Davis and Reuben Hersh argue that although "the social and physical worlds are being mathematized at an increasing rate," we would do well to question this process, "*because too much of it may not be good for us.*" They also point out that alternative mathematizations of reality are possible and that all are equally fraught with peril for the human species since none ask the "why" of reality, just the "how." "In days gone by the ideas of intent, purpose, harmonies, imposed a reality on science that was derived from human values. Now, in the reverse direction, [modern] science, in its abstract mathematical formulations, has imposed its own reality on human values and behavior." [22] More precisely, modern science has forgotten its past, its own origination in a grounding set of human values.

Of course, the admission that certitude is beyond the reach of human inquiry and any subsequent conclusion that therefore all claims to knowledge are equally valued are two things entirely. The difference between the second conclusion and the acknowledgment of intellectual finitude is that of (1) a vicious and complete cognitive relativism as over and against (2) an evolutionary theory of knowledge or contextualism. Precisely at this epistemological juncture lies the possibility of recognizing (affirming the potential) and creating (actualizing the potential) an old-new way of being. If the modern predicament is in part reflexive crisis, it is also capable of resolution, for with recognition that Homo sapiens is enframed by language and history comes the possibility of a new era of being. Marjorie Grene observes that human beings have "the image of a human world shorn of any roots in nature and a natural world devoid of places for humanity to show itself." [23] From our vantage point within the hermeneutic circle we now know that this is a false dichotomy. Once we accept language as ontogenetic, and the necessity of oral performance, then we can show that fact and value or nature and history are not rivals but intrinsically conjoined.

The Idea of Wilderness in Cosmological Context:
An Evolutionary Drama

ACT 1: Irreversible Process and Cosmic Synergy

As randomness, complexity, and irreversibility enter into physics as
objects of positive knowledge, we are moving away from [the] rather
naive assumption of a direct connection between our description
of the world and the world itself. Objectivity in theoretical physics
takes on a more subtle meaning.

—Ilya Prigogine and Isabelle Stengers,
Order Out of Chaos

Twentieth-century humankind is a study in paradox. Approximately one-third of the earth's people live in unprecedented health and material well-being; another third live in so-called developing nations; and the remainder live in abject poverty. The biosphere, upon which all life on earth depends, is doubly assailed by the sheer mass of humanity and its level of demand. The twentieth-century humanizing of the planet's surface has accelerated, and depredations by agricultural-industrial culture upon archaic peoples continues unabated. Humankind's assault on wild lands and life has been an almost unlimited attack on all fronts, from the biological, such as the clearing of the Amazon rain forest and extinction of plant and animal species, to the physical, such as insatiable consumption of nonrenewable natural resources and rending of the ozone layer. Near the end of *Wilderness and the American Mind*, Roderick Nash suggests that the idea of wilderness is likely romantic baggage from a bygone age and proposes that humanity might best spend its energy adapting to a total civilizing of the earth's surface. Unfortunately, for his study is a fine one, Nash has posed the wrong issue: the question is not whether wilderness has a tomorrow but whether Homo sapiens has a future without wild nature. The twentieth century is in some features the *mundus alter* that Francis Bacon envisaged as he stood on the doorstep to the modern age. Humankind, *apparent* master of all things, except itself. We have ventured into the macrocosmic universe—with space shuttles and vehicles that have left the solar system—and probed the microcosmic universe—with knowledge of the atom and our genetic structure. We have achieved new levels of understanding about the origins of cosmos and the evolutionary process, although the technical details of contemporary cosmology are in this context less important than the narrational gestalt. Ethology, anthropology, ecology, and other disciplines also contribute to a remarkable new picture of the human place in cosmic process; such a postmodernist perspective is just now coming into focus. To this evolutionary drama our account of the idea of wilderness must now turn. Here the sociology of science, and social epistemology generally, bears on the question of the legitimacy of our narrative, for the "one-eyed scientists and theologians" of modernity have not concerned themselves with the cosmic creation story.[24]

AS OUR PLANET hurtles through space and time we are enveloped by cosmic history. What informed stargazer has not meditated on the significance of time as photons from the Andromeda Galaxy, some two million years in transit, register faintly on retinal tissues that see meaning in such sensation. These intergalactic travelers trigger a consciousness not yet in existence when they began their journey. Even one hundred years ago they fell on blind eyes, for in the past century no one had the slightest idea of the realm of the nebulae. More staggering is the realization that those photons from M31 are only yesterday's news on a cosmic time scale, for astronomers now study quasars that stretch time beyond twelve billion years. And with our ears we hear almost the beginning of the process that is reality, for Earth is bathed in the cosmic reverberations of the Big Bang.[25]

In the first instants after the Big Bang, consistent with the cosmological constants, hydrogen atoms came into existence. Perhaps it is too poetic to assert that time preceded existence, but a finite interval of time preceded the evolution of atomic structure. As cosmic evolution continued, clouds of undifferentiated hydrogen were condensed by gravity, and within these vast clouds, protogalaxies began to emerge (ultimately reshaped into clusters of galaxies), commonly in the spiral configuration of our Milky Way and its sister, M31. Galaxies are evolutionary species within the cosmic zoo.[26] The "force" of gravity inexorably collapses a protogalaxy (hydrogen cloud) into smaller and smaller knots or increasingly dense masses which themselves yield emergent novelty: stars are born and begin to emit light. Each star is essentially a nuclear furnace that generates awesome energy; Einstein's equation $E = mc^2$ here applies. A star does more than emit photons (light), however, for through fusion the elements—the building blocks of our earth and life itself—are created. This process is both fascinating (for example, it takes a photon about a million years to move to Sol's surface) and complex. In simple terms, through developmental process the elements of the periodic table, beginning with lighter ones like helium and lithium and terminating in heavy elements like gold and lead, are produced.

But the course of stellar evolution over eons was studied long before fusion theory and the origin of the Big Bang hypothesis. In 1910 two scientists began to plot stellar luminosity against spectral type; the results are known as a Hertzsprung-Russell or H-R diagram. One's first impression of such a diagram can be overwhelming, for it graphically depicts the course of stellar, and thus a significant portion of cosmic, evolution.[27] After formation, a star moves onto what is known as the main sequence, the longest, hydrogen-burning phase of its life. Almost paradoxically, the more glorious a star—if bigger and brighter constitute glory—the shorter its lifespan. The process can be *simply* explained as follows: gravity and fusion are locked in a stellar tug of war. As a star ages, gravity inevitably loses out to fusion, and the star cataclysmically falls apart, that is, explodes. With giant stars the event is known as a supernova; the incredible brilliance of supernovas within our galaxy have long captivated human attention yet have only been recently understood as evolutionary phenomena. Smaller stars, such as Sol, become rather ordinary novas and fade away with mere cosmic whispers.

This brings us to the local vicinity of space and time, the solar system and spaceship earth. The Earth, as well as Mercury, Mars, and Venus, is a byproduct of evolution, composed of the denser elements flung spasmodically into space by the death throes of stellar giants. Yet, just as detritus on a forest floor is a basis for new life and growth, so the passing of the first generation solar titans of the Milky Way galaxy nourished second growth. Almost five billion years ago, in an obscure location in the Perseus arm of that howling, cosmic wilderness which is the Milky Way, a small stellar-planetary nursery came into being, pulled none too gently into determinate form through gravity. By all evidence our sun is an ordinary, second generation star—a fortuitous accident essential to life on earth, since Sol's energy animates the solar system. Carbon-based life-forms exist only within a narrow range of conditions; ambient temperature is one such decisive variable, and thus the size of a planetary body and its distance from any local stellar mass is critical in determining its potential to support life. Our sun will remain on the main sequence for about 10 billion years; this long period of stellar homeostasis provides enough time for life to evolve. Sol is literally a magnificent nuclear engine driving life on earth, delivering its energy through space via photons captured by green plants. These photosynthetic organisms are of such gravity as to humble those industrial plants rooted in the soil of modern culture.

Since the solar system is about 5 billion years old, and the fossil record of life on earth ensues at 3.2 billion years, roughly 2 billion years were required for biological process to ensue from the merely physical and chemical. That this chronology necessitates an evolutionary hypothesis is beyond question: life was impossible 5 billion years ago. Not only did Earth lack a life-supporting atmosphere, but by all available evidence the planet was an inhospitable molten mass. Over space and time—how many passages around the gravitational center of our galaxy?—the planet cooled and the conditions became right for life to spring forth.[28] Consistent with the idea of evolutionary process, these primordial conditions no longer exist; yet scientific investigation confirms that life began as a synergetic phenomenon. Consider also that the appearance of life must be considered as a "historical incident in the evolution of the planet—i.e., as an event limited in place and time by prevailing physical and chemical conditions," but not strictly reducible to these conditions.[29]

With the appearance of life there is a tendency to rush by the longueurs of space and time to what, in biological terms, happened an instant ago: the appearance of our species. Such anthropocentric intoxication make human consciousness drunk with itself and forgetful of the bits and pieces that makes Homo sapiens possible, like flowering plants, grains, soil, and microorganisms—that is, the ongoing activity of Creation. But a few thoughtful men and women have caught some sense of the deeper meaning of this immense journey and have realized that our lives are inconceivable except on the supposition of cosmological process. Thoreau apprehended the pulse of life through a lifetime of encounter with wild nature: the melting sandbank in *Walden* is a cosmological tour de force that connects the inorganic, organic, and human. Similarly, Loren Eiseley's insightful prose exemplifies evolutionary sensibilities.

> Through how many dimensions and how many media will life have to pass? Down how many roads among the stars must man propel himself in search of the final secret? The journey is difficult, immense, at times impossible, yet that will not deter some of us from attempting it. We cannot know all that has happened in the past, or the reason for all of these events, any more than we can with surety discern what lies ahead. We have joined the caravan, you might say, at a certain point; we will travel as far as we can, but we cannot in one lifetime see all that we would like to see or learn all that we hunger to know.[30]

ACT 2: Mythopoeic Interlude

"In the beginning was the Word," and God said "Let there be Light."[31] Is it the case that the universe is language, thought, and finally the Word? In the beginning was the Word. Can this statement have meaning in the Modern Age? Some believe in a convergence between ancient mythopoetry, such as the Bible and the Vedas, and postmodern evolutionary cosmology.[32] Robert Jastrow argues that since the origin of the universe remains couched in mystery, and scientific certitude is not possible, the dream of modern science for a rational account of the cosmos "ends like a bad dream. [The scientist] has scaled the mountains of ignorance; he is about to conquer the highest peak; as he pulls himself over the final rock, he is greeted by a band of theologians who have been sitting there for centuries."[33] In contrast, Paul Davies argues that such a leap of faith to supernatural explanation is not logically required, however psychologically comforting. He concludes that although contemporary cosmology does *not* deny the existence of God, it militates against the idea of a transcendent God-the-creator. Still, evolutionary cosmology "does not rule out a universal mind existing as part of that unique physical universe: a natural, as opposed to supernatural God. Of course 'part of' in this context does not mean 'located somewhere in space' any more than our own minds can be located in space. . . . [T]he entire physical universe would be the medium of expression of the mind of a natural God. In this context, God is the supreme holistic concept, perhaps many levels of description above that of the human mind."[34] The process-relational theologian Schubert Ogden argues for a similar creation story, where absolute distinctions among humankind and nonhuman others, nature, and God are replaced by an evolutionary and thus historical view. The problem, according to Ogden, is that the modern mind has lost sight of the primitive worldview where "nature was seen as one grand symbiotic system of which man is integrally a part." Nature has become lifeless-matter-in-motion, "at best the alien arena of our historical strivings, and at worst the object of our domination and ruthless exploitation."[35]

Perhaps we are on the edge of articulating *a new mythology,* a fresh and profound creation story within which humankind can again be at home in a cosmos that, though infinite and ever changing, is the ground of all that is eternal and sacred. At this juncture the modern mind encounters obstacles, for the postmodern mind seems to go too far, assume too much, move too fast. Better that we live with the insufficiencies of Modernism, the modern mind proclaims, than go beyond the demonstrably true. The modernist might in a weak moment admit that there are things that exceed us, such as the starry sky at night and the purple mountain's majesty, even that the human species is little more than a nonentity compared with the infinity of nature. But the modernist soon sobers, for rationality precludes such a blurring of ontological lines between the real and factual, that world known and revealed to experimental science, and the imaginary and fantastical, that world of the postmodern creation story. Even more tellingly, the modern mind no longer thinks of the world as a creation of a Personal God but as a consequence of blind and impersonal Natural Laws. Thus Homo sapiens no longer exemplifies the fundamental nature of the cosmos, for the world is mere matter-in-motion that moves in oblivion to such categories as truth, justice, and beauty; such things as those are not part of reality and the nexus of efficient causation but mere ideals of Homo sapiens. For the modern mind only one thing is of ultimate consequence: to master and possess nature through causal control. The modernist creation story has cast humanity adrift into a material cosmos moving forever in mechanical motion. We have become *natural aliens* living on an ecomachine where human consciousness is thought at best to be an epiphenomenon—a paradoxical and confusing manifestation of our bodies in motion.

"But wait!" cries the voice of a postmodern herald. Is the postmodern cosmic creation story of no consequence? Or does that story provide the backdrop for all other stories, scientific or religious, political or economical, that a culture tells? Is it not the case that through evolutionary process spaceship earth has acquired consciousness? and that this mind has slowly become aware of its place in the cosmos? and that through dramatic narrative finds itself at home in a cosmos charged with meaning? Has not our kind—including Homo neanderthalensis—since time beyond recall sought purpose by grounding the human project in some enfolding and thus transcending milieu? In the beginning was the word, argues J. T. Fraser, and communication through language, however elementary, "tied the fate of the individual to that of the community, the coherence of the community to the effectiveness of its language."[36] Through the art of language, including painting, humankind was able to give cognitive structure to a world of which it had suddenly and painfully become aware.

In a passage of apparent doggerel from the *Book of Bolkonon*, Kurt Vonnegut writes that "Tiger got to hunt,/Bird got to fly;/Man got to sit and wonder 'Why, why, why?'/Tiger got to sleep,/Bird got to land;/Man got to tell himself he understand."[37] Vonnegut here sees deeper into the human predicament than most critics realize, for Homo sapiens has had to tell itself that it fathoms the nature of existence. In crossing a Paleolithic threshold of self-consciousness humankind encountered finitude— most fundamentally, the reality of death. Paleolithic burial sites are more than facts to be cataloged and more than superstitious rituals of an extinct race (Homo neanderthalensis) that lacked the good sense to worship a proper God in Heaven who would tend their souls forevermore.[38] These relics reveal the deepest truths of human nature, unmistakable evidence of the loss of the innocence of Eden—*our first mind, that of animal innocence*—and the rise of our so-called second mind, our self-conscious knowledge and fear of death.[39]

Quickly following on the self-conscious awareness of personal oblivion came that dawning realization of the reality of time. As Vonnegut implies, the human niche is time, for only the human animal wonders Why? Why? Why? In our culture—in our language, our institutions, our literature, our altars raised to unseen gods—we find confirmation of our species's intimate relations to time: we are truly *time binders*. But becoming aware of time was a doubled-edged sword, for with it came the Fall. "The story of Eden is a greater allegory than man has ever guessed," Loren Eiseley writes. For what was lost was the blissful ignorance of the natural animal that walks "memoryless through bars of sunlight and shade in the morning of the world." Since that coming to self-consciousness, as wondering hands crossed heavy foreheads, "time and darkness, knowledge of good and evil," have been constant companions.[40] The awareness of time, Fraser explains, "conferred upon the members of our species their peculiar restlessness, rooted in chronic [temporal] insecurity. From then on, people very seldom, if ever, could maintain the inner peace that a satisfied animal seems to have." The consequence was a foregone conclusion. "Our ancestors, therefore, began to bargain with passing, in the hope of avoiding the inevitable. That bargaining, which is still going on, created the great cultural continuities: the religions, the philosophies, the arts and letters, and the sciences."[41]

These cultural continuities and the lingering reverberations of the human revolution are reflected in the transition from Paleolithic to modern ideas of wilderness. In the beginning was the Word—the mythopoetry of archaic peoples—and the seed syllables that bound them with the running water, the flowers in the meadow, the animals with whom their lives intermingled, and the starry sky above. Today we are thousands of years away from the Paleolithic mind, the modern ego swollen with pride in our cultural achievements. We cannot see the heavens wheeling overhead in their cosmic course—our city lights and smog have rendered them indistinct. And from inside our human-made habitats we cannot feel the winds and rain, smell the flowers and animal herds, or hear the running water and singing birds. Yet we remain, in spite of the myths of modernity that blind us to primordial insights into the mystery of existence, the human animal, bound with the cosmic flux.

ACT 3: Recovery of Value

The serpent said, "Of course you will not die. God knows that as soon as you eat it, your eyes will be opened and you will be like gods knowing both good and evil." When the woman saw that the fruit of the tree was good to eat, and that it was pleasing to the eye and tempting to contemplate, she took some and ate it. She also gave her husband some and he ate it. Then the eyes of both of them were opened and they discovered that they were naked; so they stitched fig-leaves together and made themselves loincloths. —Genesis 3.4–7

Through space and time speaks the voice of that nineteenth-century genius Henry David Thoreau: *In wildness lies the preservation of the world.* Only when we are lost—and isn't the testimony of the twentieth century evidence that humankind is lost amid the very splendor and potential of the civilization it has created?—can we begin to find ourselves. Once we lay down our conventional system of directions, then we see that we are cosmic orphans. Who is our Mother? Our Father? Where are we going? Where is our Home? Amid the swirling clouds on Ktaadn's ridge, just at the point where his idea of wilderness might have collapsed into New England transcendentalism, Thoreau firmly seized the idea of cosmic process. His words ring true for the postmodern mind, for amid these rocks he discovered granitic truth and realized the ongoing nature of Creation. "The highest that we can attain to is not Knowledge, but Sympathy with Intelligence. . . . [T]here are more things in heaven and earth than are dreamed of in our philosophy." Cosmos, he intuited, is Heraclitean, and capital "K" knowledge, be this scientific or humanistic, philosophical or theological, is a Parmenidean deception, since the human animal is bound with creative process.

Rather than supposing that some Supreme and Almighty Transcendent Creator who serves as the Cosmic Guarantor of Certitude and Value exists, let us assume the reality of time and therefore evolution: that is, let us imagine that Act 1 of our cosmic drama has been staged. Does this not lend at least some credibility to the weak anthropic cosmological principle? In short, *cogito ergo mundus talis est* (I think therefore the world is such as it is).[42] Homo sapiens is the consequence of a natural history of the universe that is precisely the one which it is. If we change the fundamental variables (the cosmological constants), then the course of evolution as revealed to us from our present vantage point becomes inconceivable.[43] Again, we are latecomers to the evolutionary process, and we do not know all that we might care to know. What we do know is that we are bearing sentient witness to Creative Evolution: we are bound with time, that is, with the historic character of *Kosmos*.[44] Perhaps the weak anthropic principle serves adequately as a background—however seemingly inconsistent with the traditional epistemological and axiological underpinnings of our culture—against which the recovery of value might take place. We must recall that black on black is nothing, an identity without a difference that disappears, for there is no ground against which such a figure might appear. Just as black cannot be seen save against white, so there can be neither vision nor understanding of human value except in relation to a background. Value, in other words, cannot be grounded in humankind, for to do so is to catch ourselves in an infinite regress: human value exists only in context.

The Paleolithic mind perhaps intuited human finitude, the miracle and utter gratuity of existence, yet by all indications the modern mind is devoid of any similar sensibility. We have relentlessly pursued the vision of ourselves as Lord Man. Yet even in our midst there have been a few, the Thoreaus, Muirs, and Snyders, open to religious experience, to some sense of an absolute presence in nature. Among our contemporaries Henry Nelson Wieman has seen deeply into the grounding of human value in an encompassing and therefore sacred context. "The thin layer of structure characterizing events knowable to the human mind by way of linguistic specification is very thin compared to that massive, infinitely complex structure of events, rich with quality, discriminated by the noncognitive feeling-reactions of associated organisms human and nonhuman." The cosmos is a vast society of interacting organisms whose history stretches far back into the dimmest recesses of space-time, and thus beyond the grasp of the human intellect to articulate in scientific terms. We cannot go back in time, for that would violate the second law of thermodynamics, yet our existence as conscious beings presupposes evolutionary process. Those structures knowable to the human mind, which we have articulated and codified into science, philosophy, and religion, retain their qualitative richness only "if they continue conjunct and integral with this deep complex structure of quality built up through countless ages before even the human mind appeared and now accessible to the feeling-reactions of the human organism. But when the human mind in its pride tries to rear its knowable structures as supreme goals of human endeavor, impoverishment, destruction, conflict, and frustration begin because these structures are then cut off from the rich matrix of quality found in organic, nonintellectual reactions."[45]

Here, however, we must guard against our apparently inevitable tendency to anthropomorphize. We can neither justify the belief that Creative Evolution exists for us nor think that we are its goal and purpose. By realizing that we are part of Cosmic Process we confirm that we are finite beings bound in the reality of Becoming. There are fixities beyond human control, and perhaps foremost among these is the second law of thermodynamics. The second law is the law of the historic character of nature and it confirms the *one-way* process of Creative Evolution.[46] Today, stretching back into time with our instruments of technology, we reawaken the profound longing in all human beings for the ground of being. Ironically, with these instruments we discover not being but the reality of Becoming. We now hear the Cosmic Hiss, the Beginning of Time, and we intuit, as profoundly modern humans, the finitude of our being. We understand that only in this universe could carbon-based finitude such as us come into existence. We are not the privileged children fashioned in the image of God but coordinate interfaces of the historical process of nature. We do not impose value on a valueless cosmos; rather, we are sensitive registers of values created through the unfolding of time.

ACT 4: Postmodern Hierophany

Countless are the things thou hast made, O Lord.
Thou hast made all by thy wisdom;
and the earth is full of thy creatures,
beasts great and small.   —Psalm 104

Our vaunted power is part of a cultural web, spun from the language of politics and economics, religion and theology, physics and philosophy. Yet humankind is encompassed by a reality independent of which existence is impossible and compared to which our significance is minuscule. We are no more than reflections of cosmic process, an ephemeral phenomenon like ripples spawned by a falling leaf on an alpine pool. *And, simultaneously, we are no less.* Here, however shaky beneath our feet, is the ground of postmodern hierophany, of rediscovery of the sacrality of Creation—the theme that animates Psalm 104. We now stand in position to reawaken a primordial consciousness of the Great Mother who sustains us all. And yet we cannot walk the same path of those who have gone before, for we are farther along that road.

In 1689 John Ray published the *Wisdom of God*, one of the most remarkable integrations of science and theology that the Western world has seen. Yet the argument from design has been shattered by our own thoughtless blunders and the advance of reason. On one hand, it is ironic that any belief in a cosmic teleology has been rendered meaningless by the acts of the animal to whom it meant so much: we cleave the flesh of the world, rending its surface, polluting its air and water, killing its inhabitants. The principle of plenitude—the belief that a beneficent God created the earth for humankind—has been overturned by unrestrained human appetite. And on the other hand, the advance of evolutionary science worked against the notions of cosmic finalism and pre-established harmony. "The more the studies of the naturalists progressed," Ernst Mayr argues, "the more phenomena were found which contradicted the excellence of design."[47] Malthus irrevocably undressed the belief that a burgeoning human population was a sign of God's favor, for the human animal is constrained by limits to growth. However dismal his message, Malthus understood that poverty, hunger, and even war were the consequence not of the devil's work but of too many human beings with demands that exceeded the means available for satisfaction. Charles Darwin concluded *The Descent of Man* by observing that the geological, archaeological, and biological facts militated against special creation and that thereafter such a belief would lie outside the province of reason. The argument of design in nature that had seemed so conclusive "fails," he wrote in his *Autobiography*, "now that the law of natural selection has been discovered. We can no longer argue that, for instance, the beautiful hinge of a bivalve shell must have been made by an intelligent being, like the hinge of a door by man. There seems to be no more design in the variability of organic beings and in the action of natural selection, than in the course which the wind blows."[48] George P. Marsh dealt a final blow to the argument from design by documenting the adverse environmental consequences of the modification of the earth; the notion of any primal consonance simply could not be reconciled with the facts.

Mircea Eliade argues that modern humanity lives in an irreverent culture from which any sense of the sacred has been meticulously removed. Accordingly, the Modern Age represents a "new existential situation" where we regard ourselves "solely as the subject and agent of history, and . . . [we refuse] all appeal to transcendence. In other words . . . [we accept] no model for humanity outside the human condition as it can be seen in the various historical situations."[49] In short, we have become Modernists: species Homo religiosus is extinct. If Eliade is correct, then there is little prospect for dealing with ecological crisis. On his terms, the modern mind cannot escape seeing Creative Evolution—that is, the natural history of cosmos—as anything more than environment. Here is that nihilistic behemoth to which Evernden refers in *The Natural Alien:* environment is what nature has become in the Modern Age, and we stand in relation to nature only as Homo oeconomicus. In other words, the arguments of either the religionist or the humanist provide no compelling grounds for modern people to reconsider who and what they are, or why they do what they do. In consequence, the earth—the veritable source of life—is conceptualized as no more than a re-source to serve human purpose. We are precluded by our idea of nature from recognizing its own being, its history and elaboration. The modern mind has lost any sense of human dependence on an enveloping and therefore transcending *source of value.* Crucially, and paradoxically, the argument that the ecological status quo—the historically established relations between Western humanity and the earth—cannot be meaningfully changed within the framework of Modernism cannot be refuted by either the theist or atheist.

If we grant the traditional theistic presupposition that God exists, then humankind has been created in that image to stand supreme atop the designed universe.[50] Of course, theism per se does not entail total indifference to the ecological realities of existence. Indeed, supernaturalists proclaim that human beings must exercise God's stewardship and save his creation from continued abuse. But Christians are *called* to redeem the earth, not from an awareness of impending disaster for the ecosystem, but out of a faith in "our being in Christ, who is the life of the world."[51] The prophet Isaiah is often cited by those who advance the argument of Christian stewardship, finding in Isaiah 2.7–9 an indictment of materialism (and by implication the relentless pursuit of economic growth by advanced industrial societies), as well as parallels between the words of the prophet that God will humble humankind and the present-day environmental malaise. Homilies then follow to the effect that "guided by the Word of God—Incarnate and in Scripture—we must arm ourselves to the task of being new Isaiahs, witnessing to God's judgment and mercy in our times—and above all, to his ability to redeem and transform the values and strictures of the world. And our armor consists no longer of sackcloth and ashes, but of a redeemed wonder at, knowledge of, and *power over God's creation.*"[52] Yes, onward Christian soldiers, marching off to war, in oblivion to the biological and cultural complexities that have led to the earth's present precarious state.

Yet, if we grant the atheistic presupposition that there is no god, then any action is permissible, and humankind is the measure of all things. For humanists there is neither shame nor a sense of defeat in such an admission, for they believe absolutely that the human species makes itself and its way in a godless and forsaken cosmos. Yet humanists—and all humanists are at base modernists—are not oblivious to ecological malaise, and, here echoing the religionists, humanists exclaim that we must behave ethically in relation to the environment. The conservationist idea of wilderness is one such attempt to deal with ecological malaise through ethical arguments based on the appeal to efficiency (waste not, want not) and utility (the greatest good for the greatest number). Yet *resourcism* clearly can neither transcend nor change the cultural matrix that has created environmental crisis. In other words, the resource conservationist idea of wilderness is not a cure for but a manifestation of the underlying etiology of the abuse of nature.

Other humanistic arguments are more sophisticated than those of the resource conservationist (in that they do not assume mechanistic materialism as a starting point), but they, too, are enframed by modernistic presuppositions. Consider, for example, the ecohumanist argument (also called Kantian holism) for an environmental ethic. Since "we *are* our environment, to harm the environment is to harm ourselves, and rationally autonomous persons cannot consistently will to harm themselves. To harm the environment is to undermine one's own rationality and identity."[53] Yet Kantian holism is refuted by its own historically established premise that humankind is a rational species that makes itself. In other words, the ecohumanist mind is merely a subspecies of the modern mind. Kantian holism thus inevitably reduces the natural world to environment—a rational object of scientific and philosophical inquiry. Ecohumanists, however good their motives to save a suffering world, remain Cartesian thinking things apart from wild nature. Furthermore, if humankind were a rational species, then nature would be treated ethically. Nature is not treated ethically. Therefore humankind is not an entirely rational animal. It follows that any appeal to positive reason alone as a ground for environmental ethics must fail.

Since neither religionist nor humanist can cogently ground an environmental ethic, we must wonder if any environmental ethic is feasible without some abiding sense of the sacrality of the cosmic wilderness? without some grounding of the human estate in natural process? without a postmodern hierophany?[54] In other words, if we are to deal realistically with the environmental question, then we must confront those questions of who and what we are and where we are going. And in dealing with those issues we necessarily encounter something beyond positive reason and secular religion, some ineffable presence, some sense of the *source*. But our insistence upon the necessity of raising cosmological questions neither precludes nor replaces other kinds of inquiry. Paehlke makes abundantly clear, for example, that meaningful action in the context of Western liberal democracies entails political action *within* existing institutional frameworks. He also emphasizes that the environmental movement involves the kinds of questions raised in this chapter. As he puts it, "The environmental movement must remain conscious of its roots in a value-laden appreciation of the human condition. Technical administration (and science itself), when left without moral and political guidance, is at the root of many of the problems discussed throughout this book."[55]

We argued in chapter 9 that environmentalism is more than just protecting endangered species, cleaning up the air and water, and leaving blue skies unmarred by pollution and free-running streams unobstructed by water resource projects. We must wonder if either Christian or secular environmental ethics are not more symptomatic of the disease than part of the cure. So long as the modern mind, religious or secular, believes that nature is simply a stage on which humans act, then—ironically—we are mere puppets mindlessly reenacting assigned roles in the drama that is the history of Western civilization (from the Neolithic revolution through the alchemy of Modernism). However, as Evernden's *Natural Alien* explains, our attempts to defend the wilderness confirm our search for meaning; they represent a defense of absolute value, a defense of cosmos, that is, something beyond human measure, and not scenery. Since environmental crisis has grown out of the presently governing system of ideas and institutions, redress of ecological malaise can be realized only through a postmodern sociocultural paradigm.[56]

George Sessions is one of a few environmental philosophers to realize that Modernism contains no cures for the malaise of Western culture. The horrors of two world wars, the burgeoning population, and the looming reality of ecological apocalypse in the twenty-first century provide him a springboard. But what is the solution? Sessions argues that we are

> clearly in need of a "perennial philosophy" with which to pick up the pieces of the shattered dream, the wreckage of both Nature and our own psyches, and begin the process of healing and integration. But this perennial philosophy, this new way of thinking about Being and beings, needs to be both scientifically and philosophically sophisticated at its base. It must accommodate itself to the new Presocratic

non-anthropomorphic and non-anthropocentric . . . science which has progressively developed since the sixteenth and seventeenth centuries, and it must avoid the ontological and epistemological dualisms and metaphysical claims against which Heidegger . . . argued. It must avoid absolute subjectivism. And it must provide us with an adequate and true representation of God/Man/Nature in which each "component" is placed in proper perspective and given due weight.[57]

Sessions argues that Spinozism undergirds a perennial philosophy—a moot conclusion. But he accurately describes the shaky cultural ground upon which we stand—which Prigogine calls the consequence of a "tragic metaphysical choice"—for the modern mind has sundered itself from the sacred nature of the world. The Creation has become either an empty formula divorced from facts by religious orthodoxy or a value-free scientific explanation equally stifling because devoid of any sense of transcending (beyond human power to change) and absolute (all human value is contingent upon it) value.

We cannot here probe into the many possibilities for theology and religion, or for mythology and mythopoetry, in the postmodern era. Indeed, recapturing some sense of deity and the sacrality of creation transcends any one account, religious or poetic. But our study of the idea of wilderness requires some consideration, however brief, of the possibility of a postmodern hierophany. Such a revelation of deity is, for the postmodern mind, rooted in our awareness, however tenuous, of the reality of creative evolution on a cosmic scale, and therefore is also a revelation necessarily devoid of finalism—be this personalistic or theistic. Alternatively, whatever is revealed to us of deity must be consistent with the reality of becoming. But the second scientific revolution encourages the possibility of religious experience: that is, the reality of creative evolution is fully consistent with the possibility of reawakening a primordial sense of the fundamental mystery and gratuitousness of human existence, some sense of the infinite and transcendent beyond merely human purpose and life. Unquestionably, even discussion of the possibility of a postmodern hierophany promotes uneasiness in the modern mind, and all the more because of the rise of New Age mysticism, esoteric cults of enlightenment, and the almost inevitable naïveté of the people who act in good faith. Erazim Kohák maintains that any affirmation of

the incoercible presence of God may at first appear marginal in the context of the conceptualization of nature. Nature appears dead to us in great part because we have grown accustomed to thinking of God as "super-natural," absent from nature and not to be found therein. That, though, is itself a measure of how far our quest for theory has deviated from the reality of lived experience, not ours alone, but that of humankind throughout history. For, in lived experience, in the radical brackets of the embers and the stars, the presence of God is so utterly basic, the one theme never absent from all the many configurations of life's rhythm.[58]

Some light can be shed on our predicament—that is, the seemingly ludicrous idea that deity is revealed in nature—by examining the past. Both Spinoza and Leibniz, although unknowing of the second scientific revolution that was to come, discovered elements of a postmodern position from their seventeenth-century vantage points. Living in an age when the advance of science seemed almost certain to destroy faith in God's existence, they were determined to reconcile faith and reason: the positive reason of Descartes and Newton with the faith of their fathers in a supreme and transcendent Creator. Leibniz coined the term *philosophia perennis* to describe that age-old human quest, apparently precluded by the rise of natural science, for knowledge of the divine ground of all existence. Clearly there are attractive features to Spinoza's and Leibniz's arguments that point toward the possibility of hierophany, and thus some sense of the unity of humankind with God and all creation. Sessions argues that Spinozism is singularly suited to understanding reality as an interconnected unity, and is thus a philosophical precursor to our contemporaneous ecological worldview. Walter O'Briant makes similar claims apropos of Leibnizianism (while arguing that Spinozism is infected with a fatal dualism that precludes Sessions's claim). Yet although ecological or holistic inclinations are present in both Spinoza and Leibniz, neither can ground a postmodern hierophany since they remain enframed within a static and substantialistic, and therefore modernistic, view of the universe.[59] The fundamental difficulty, however, is not in the concept of God or deity per se; more to the point is the issue Henri Bergson raises. "It must not be forgotten that the force which is evolving throughout the organized world is a limited force, which is always seeking to transcend itself and always remains inadequate to the work it would fain produce. The errors and puerilities of radical finalism are due to the misapprehension of this point. It has represented the whole of the living world as a construction, and a construction analogous to a human work."[60] No Spinozistic or Leibnizian philosopher can meet this objection without self-contradiction.

The thought of Samuel Alexander stands in distinction from those Parmenidean and eternalistic visions of Spinoza and Leibniz. Our account, as we wind our way toward a conclusion, is necessarily restricted to the question of the conceivability of postmodern hierophany. Alexander's *Space, Time, and Deity* affirms that possibility in a manner consistent with creative evolution, and therefore does not assume the existence of a universal teleology. Understood from the postmodern vantage point of process-relational cosmology, which accepts the reality of natural selection and the second law, God is part of the evolutionary process.[61] For Alexander, deity *exists in and through time and space*, where *the body of God* is the cosmos of the present, and where deity per se is the nisus or inherent restlessness of time that leads to emergent novelty. Space-time is the fundamental reality which through evolution engenders matter, life, mind, and ultimately deity; each moment of evolutionary process can be understood as an element in an evolutionary scale of forms. Life presupposes but is irreducible to matter, possessing a genuinely qualitative distinction. And similarly, so mind (sentience) to life, and ultimately deity to mind. Deity, Alexander argues, can be grounded in the cosmological process. "Within the all embracing stuff of Space-Time, the universe exhibits an emergence in Time of successive levels of finite existences, each with its characteristic empirical quality. The highest of these empirical qualities known to us is mind or consciousness. Deity is the next higher empirical quality to the highest we know; and . . . at any level of existence there is a next higher empirical quality which stands towards the lower quality as deity stands towards mind." There are strong similarities between Alexander's idea of direct experience and Spinoza's notion of *scientia intuitiva,* James's radical empiricism and Whitehead's speculative reason: all point toward the kind of religious experience in the wilderness that the biblical sages and John Muir repeatedly enjoyed. "That the universe is pregnant with such a quality we are speculatively assured. What that quality is we cannot know; for we can neither enjoy nor still less contemplate it. *Our human altars still are raised to the unknown God.*" Yet through religious experience itself, Alexander contends, we have a "direct experience" of something beyond ourselves, "of something higher than ourselves which we call God."[62]

Deity or God, however, provides only an impetus for evolutionary change; there is no divine determinism in Alexander's cosmology.[63] The concept of God then necessarily assumes a changed meaning within an organismic philosophy, and this for at least two reasons. First, no entity—including Deity—exists apart from the nexus of relations that determine its reality. Second, God is no longer an autonomous designer outside the cosmic machine but is bound with all other things in a continuing process of creation. Thus God for Alexander is not *before* all creation but *with* all creation. In one sense Deity-God for Alexander answers a fundamental question: Why does the cosmos exist when by all apparent reason it could just as easily not exist? Alexander's view of deity is consistent with creative evolution, and opposes any notion of a cosmic teleology, since to assume that deity has one grand purpose is to fall into contradiction. As Charles Hartshorne argues, "An absolutely controlling purpose would be the sole purpose, and could not have as its aim the creation of other purposes. If there be even two purposes, two decisions, then the conjunction of these two into a total reality must in some aspect be undecided, unintended, a matter of chance. Since a 'solitary purpose' is meaningless or pointless, chance is inevitable, granted purpose." Here we have both a cosmos of actuality (real existents) and potentiality (ideals). It follows, according to Hartshorne, that God is not the creator but also the created.

> A God who eternally knew all that the fulfillment of his purpose would bring could have no need of that fulfillment or of purpose. Complete knowledge is complete possession: it is just because a man does not know in detail what "knowing his friends better" would be like that he has the purpose to come to know them better. As Bergson and Peirce were among the first to see, even a world-purpose must be indeterminate as to details. For one thing, an absolute and inexorable purpose, supposing this meant anything, would deny individuality, self-activity, hence reality, to the lesser individuals, the creatures.[64]

Such a position categorically brackets the intense anthropocentrism that has characterized the Modern Age. Summarily stated, the natural world cannot be either logically or empirically thought of as existing for no reason save to serve human ends: the cosmos has no such single purpose. *Humankind, a part of cosmic process, must stand in awe of that sacrality which envelops (God as body) and transcends (the restlessness of time)*. Further, humankind can here enjoy fellowship (Spinoza's summmum bonum) with deity (though not in an anthropocentric fashion, since we are not the goal of evolutionary process).

ACT 5: Getting Back to the Garden

Assuming that a postmodern hierophany is at least possible and that Postmodernism will entail some old-new image of the human project as set in a sacred place, a fundamental question remains. Once expelled from the Garden, can Adam and Eve ever return, even when redirected to its location? In stating this question we have come full circle. Perhaps what is required is a new image of nature as the Garden, not the eco-machine. Frederick Ferré suggests that "the image of the Garden, then, bids to replace the religious world model of the Machine in postmodern consciousness, if holistic ecology becomes the paradigmatic science of our future."[65] But beyond images, is there any cause to hope that postmodern reason might help us choose between alternative futures? What is the human prospect? And how are we to choose among alternatives? Have we caught the glimmer of some possibility of an old-new way of being? of a perennial philosophy that leads beyond Modernism to the Postmodern Age? of a recovery of some sense of absolute value? of a postmodern idea of wilderness?

Perhaps the sternest test of a postmodern idea of wilderness lies in the is-ought, fact-value, science-ethic schisms. We have argued that the modern mind can show us no way beyond environmental crisis. The panoply of modernistic ideas of wilderness do not address the question of why we are doing what we do to the environment. From the beginning of the scientific revolution the value question has hovered over the Modern Age. Although Descartes had no reservations about the ends to which the power of science was to be put, Bacon was less sanguine, for he understood that force did not in its own right exalt nature. During the twentieth century the problem of values has only intensified, while skepticism that science might contribute to the selection of guiding purposes has also increased.[66] The need to heal the two-culture split, as C. P. Snow named this fissure, has long been apparent, but the modern mind has philosophically undercut the possibility of any relation between science and ethics. Yet both Einstein and Schrödinger have recognized the inescapable reality that scientific knowledge finds meaning only within cultural context.

Enter here the postmodern mind, where the assumed bifurcation between an ideal world of human intentionality—the oughts of ethics—and a natural world of brute facticity—the facts of science—is denied. The natural world provides a real context to enframe human action, defining both limits (at least in any meaningful human time-frame) and potentialities. The existence of biologically organized complexity implies directed evolution through transformation of high-energy, low-entropy matter-energy.[67] Mutatis mutandis, the human project can be understood only as the result of a similar evolutionary process that grounds yet transcends human purpose. *Cogito quia vivo* the postmodernist insists, thereby dispelling the illusion of both the eternal Christian soul and the disembodied Cartesian ego. The means-ends continuum transcends the dualistic impasse between disembodied souls seeking transcendental ends and a natural world of brute facticity.

Leopold's arguments, for example, are clearly those of a thinker who has transcended the is-ought fallacy and accepted the reality of evolution. Leopold is the first ecologist to see the full implications of the Darwinian paradigm for determining human behavior, realizing that the Darwinian revolution undercuts an Abrahamic concept of land and the Cartesian dream that Homo sapiens can master and possess nature. Consequently, Leopold argued that advanced industrial culture must refashion its traditional decision-making matrix—one dominated entirely by the unquestioned aims of the Modern Age—and adopt a biocentrically informed decision-making matrix, that is, an ecology-based land ethic. In a fashion sure to engender its rejection by the modern mind, the land ethic combined science, history, and philosophy. The land ethic was grounded in ecological science because it factually presupposed a systems-level understanding of biotic communities; in this sense nature's way serves as an alternative to the ideology of Modernism, for the human animal is compelled by the verdict of science to consider the reality of its membership in both global and regional biotic communities. Further, the land ethic presupposed historical judgment, the possibility of meaningful changes in human consciousness, and the potential for an expansion of ethics beyond an Abrahamic (anthropocentric) concept of the land to include wild nature (analogous to the expansion that gave the masses political and economic rights within liberal democratic society). Finally, the land ethic presupposed the philosophical judgment that human beings were obliged to adopt as an ideal (the ought) a standard of behavior that transcended the manifest deficiencies (the is) of contemporary culture. The philosophical rationale for the land ethic might be summarized as follows: evolutionary potential exists (open future consistent with the stream of influence); ethical choice is an informed choice (an idea fundamental to the classical foundations of Western culture); and reflective thought underlies choice (direction of evolutionary potential), thereby inextricably fusing (teleonomically, not teleologically) is and ought.[68] So viewed, the land ethic is a remarkable anticipation of the judgment rendered by Ilya Prigogine some thirty years later. "We can no longer accept the old a priori distinction between scientific and ethical values. This was possible at a time when the external world and our internal world appeared to conflict, to be nearly orthogonal. Today we know that time is a construction and therefore carries an ethical responsibility."[69] We are the children of Creation, and we now know that our actions irreversibly ripple throughout the life-world.

Final Curtain: Wilderness as the Source

By whom impelled soars forth mind projected?
By whom enjoined goes forth the earliest breathing?
By whom impelled this speech do people utter?
The eye, the ear—what God, pray, them enjoineth?
It is conceived by him by whom It is not conceived of.
He by whom It is conceived of, knows It not.
It is not understood by those who [say they] understand It.
It is understood by those who [say they] understand It not.
—Kena Upanishad

Our study of the idea of wilderness has followed a long and sinuous path, and we now approach the end of our journey, having discovered that the idea of wilderness has been caught up in a never-ending process of change. Paleolithic people, living in the hunting-gathering phase, believed themselves bound up with the Magna Mater, the Great Mother who held her children—all plants and animals—to her nurturing bosom. The totems of the Paleolithic mind symbolized this idea of organic unity between humankind and wild nature. Yet in our Paleolithic coming to self-consciousness lay the potential to conceal that primordial bond between the elements of Creation, for humankind was now aware—through the reality of self-consciousness—of a difference between itself and the plants and animals. Although the Paleolithic mind shows no sign of believing in an absolute separation from the natural world, the very existence of totemism implies some sense of alienation. With the Neolithic revolution the end of totemism, as a universal practice, was inevitable.

The how of the Neolithic revolution is relatively clear, as is the resultant influence of the agricultural turn upon the Paleolithic idea of wilderness as the Great Mother. As the Western world settled deeply into agriculture, the wilderness increasingly became a threat to civil society; from the wilderness came barbarians to pillage and loot, beasts to prey on livestock, and pests to ruin the harvest. Yet humankind was aware, if dimly, of a Fall, and dreamed of a return to the Garden, to an Eden free of the travails of agriculture. With the rise of logocentrism in Attica, the concealment of the *source* that underlies existence was complete, and the rationalization of agriculture a foregone conclusion. Yet even for the classic mind, in what is best interpreted as a primitive survival of the Paleolithic mind, nature remained animate, for both plants and animals were considered to cause themselves to move. Pagan animism, however, was dispelled by Judeo-Christianity and the birth of supernaturalism.

With the rise of the Holy Roman Empire the vestiges of organic totemism and pagan nature worship were swept away. In that peculiar inversion of being which is the West, the source became phantasmagorical and illusory, and God and Heaven became reality. Adam and Eve had fallen and could only be saved by the supernatural. The Judeo-Christian worldview was one of such force and power that—as Clarence Glacken has so brilliantly shown—it ruled the world for nearly two millennia, virtually a perfect rationalization of agriculture. The scientific revolution little altered the fundamental impress of Judeo-Christianity. No doubt, classical science played havoc with and destroyed certain cherished articles of faith, such as geocentrism. Science also promised to help make good on that ancient Neolithic project to rise above nature. As Bacon foresaw, science was power, and in conjunction with the ideology of capitalism and liberal democracy, the alchemy of Modernism transformed the Western world. The Modern Age, though unmistakably a new form of cultural existence, was yet founded on Judeo-Christian and Greek articles of faith: that God had made a orderly and clocklike world, that time had a beginning and an end, and that Homo sapiens was the culmination of God's creation. Modern science, reflecting its social context, also presupposed a God who had created a world perfect, a rational world that humankind could know and control. Through the alchemy of Modernism something beyond eternal salvation was introduced into Western culture, for the modern mind foresaw the possibility of realizing the biblical injunction to rule over the fallen earth and create the New Jerusalem.

Although the marriage of Faith and Reason, epitomized by Bacon, was to end in failure, the alchemy of Modernism was potent. The natural world was increasingly thought of as mere matter-in-motion. As science assumed cognitive hegemony in the West, vanquishing Faith to the sleepy and overtly anti-intellectual backwaters of religious fundamentalism, the effects of the machine metaphor on Homo sapiens's self-conceptualization, including even personality, and on the organization of society, were profound. As any number of observers have reported, human beings are increasingly alienated from an *It world* and from one another, and modern life becomes increasingly robotic. And, most crucially, the image of nature as an ecomachine has edged the Western world ever closer to ecological apocalypse. So inescapable is the reality of environmental disaster that even the mass media, those bold purveyors of conventional wisdom, have seized on it.[70]

Today a postmodern idea of wilderness, a profoundly evolutionary perspective on cosmic process, is faintly visible on the horizon. In its starkest terms the question is whether the human species, now engulfing the planet and spreading into the near reaches of the solar system, is a failed experiment or a viable project. Lacking any power of prophecy, and surely wishing to avoid wearing Cassandra's mantle, we cannot answer this question. We can be sure that an uncertain future lies ahead. We live in a universe where, Prigogine contends, "the security of stable, permanent rules seems gone forever. We are living in a dangerous and uncertain world that inspires no blind confidence, but perhaps only the same feeling of qualified hope that some Talmudic texts appear to have attributed to the God of Genesis."[71] Time's arrow moves in one direction only, and we are part of that evolutionary movement. A postmodern idea of wilderness as the source lies near the cutting edge of a conscious reconciliation with the origin of all things physical, biological, and cultural. Perhaps we can believe with Erazim Kohák that "it is as dwellers in time that humans find their place in nature; it is as bearers of eternity that they find their justification."[72]

Flying in the face of reason, let us imagine ourselves suddenly awakening with the red face of humankind, living as the archaic bush people of Africa or as the indigenous people of the Amazon's emerald world, seemingly in harmony with nature.[73] But is a world devoid of Bach and Wordsworth, the Bible and the *Tao te Ching,* Plato and Shakespeare, Einstein and Schrödinger, a world with only the singing sounds of running water, the wind, the birds, a better world? Would the good earth be better off without poetry, music, art, religion, science, philosophy, and all those other achievements of the human spirit that seem to distinguish us from the rest of Creation? And what would be the consequences for wild nature if the human species failed? Can a cosmos devoid of consciousness to contemplate itself be a cosmos? Would Jeffers's noble rocks be noble in a world without sentience to perceive the transhuman magnificence of things? There is a real question as to whether we can become people of Indigen wisdom who dare to dream of an old-new way of being, who think like a mountain. Can we face the reality of our own mortality, that seat of our painful and longstanding *chronic* insecurity, and then dare to believe that every day is a resurrection and that God's Creation continues anew? The idea of wilderness may be, as Roderick Nash contends, nothing more than a romantic anachronism, oblivious to the reality of holes in the ozone and the greenhouse effect. Perhaps we had best lay aside our lingering memories of the Paleolithic mind and be on about the business of taming the environment.

I have proposed, with more than a little trepidation, a cosmic creation story, and this story can be interpreted as one that might reinvest human sensibility with some sense of an enveloping and therefore transcending and sacred cosmic context. *Do we dare think that we are nature watching nature?* For if we are only the product of natural process, then there is nothing to watch since consciousness is but an epiphenomenon or, worse, totally subjective. Yet if nature is simply a fabrication of the knowing mind, then we are just watching ourselves. Even after these many pages of inquiry there is more than a little question, particularly for the late modern mind, as to just where we presently stand. Indeed, this question is acute, for we profess to be within the hermeneutic circle. We have become conscious of the reality that Homo sapiens is—qua sapiens—language. Language bears our culture, sustains our religions, carries our thoughts, and writes our science and poetry. We assert that we are Homo sapiens, forgetting the reality that language speaks reason, that language intermediates between ourselves and nature. "Language constitutes," Ricoeur writes, "at both the biological and human levels, the very archetype of a teleological system."[74] Thus language deceives us, for its implicit teleological structure is confused with (as Alexander so accurately noted) the constitution of the world. *But we must not forget, even for a moment, that we are not the end or raison d'etre of evolutionary process but merely a coordinate interface.* We must refocus attention on language in its symbolizing function, for with the Paleolithic mind's coming to self-consciousness, humankind unknowingly severed the organic link with the Magna Mater, with the cosmic womb that gave us birth.

With that umbilicus severed, first art and then language was placed between human consciousness and nature. Indeed, art is language, and in its initial manifestation artistic creation is asserted as real.[75] Can we doubt that the Paleolithic mind reenacted the birth of cosmos in those magnificent subterranean amphitheaters? An explicit chronology and account of the relations between language and art are both irrelevant and beyond our purposes here, for there was likely a "simultaneous constitution of technology, language and sociality."[76] By standing within the hermeneutic circle we somehow engage ourselves in a self-conscious quest to escape the strictures of language (and therefore of culture) and reestablish contact with the ground (bios, Ursprung) that lies beneath our feet.

"But what," asks the modernist, "is this hermeneutical circle? Can such be relevant to our inquiry into the idea of wilderness?" Surely we now know, after these thousands of years of culture, the value of nature and our relation to it, for it is the environment, a limitless cornucopia of resources, that sustains us. Have we not caught that meaning within our scientific, political, and economical web of language? Have we not through the power of science and technology, and the humanizing potential of liberal democracy, become master and possessor of nature? But the question begged here—and understandably, for we are all enframed in time—is an awareness of the primordial question of language. Can it be that the malaise of modern society is grounded in our self-alienation from nature and the Magna Mater? We now know that there are no resources apart from *the source*—evolutionary process, the cosmic wilderness. Our use of the word *resource* so affects our sensibilities that wild nature disappears, shrouded by a linguistic curtain of meaning defined solely as use-value.[77] And yet there are those to whom Hermes has spoken: these are the thinking poets and poetic thinkers. They have stood within the hermeneutic circle, and then passed through environment (the ecomachine) to the green world on its other side.

All nature will fable, Thoreau tells us, if we will but let it speak. We must forget our conventional wisdom, for this is a positive ignorance, and return to nature. We have been weaned early from her breast, and we are not as wise as the day we were born. But our Mother will speak to us, if we will listen. Her words yet have earth clinging to their roots; her statements are grounded in granitic truth. Such fables are revealed, however, only to a person of Indigen wisdom, who seeks no more than a sympathy with intelligence—a negative knowledge, because its meaning goes beyond the web of belief.

John Muir, too, stood within the hermeneutic circle. His words describe the life of a man lived inside the radical brackets of the wilderness. He felt as if God spoke to him directly in a strange but native tongue and that when God spoke it was if he were present at the birth of Creation. This was not Daniel Muir's God, not the God above nature, and not the God who offered a suddenly self-conscious creature salvation from death. No, this was a true God of creation, revealed immediately and directly to John of the Mountains, a God still at work in the continuing act of Creation. Every day was resurrection day, for from death comes life and renewal in evolutionary process.

And what is history but the eternal return to that continuing creation for a durable scale of values? asked Leopold. Humankind is an interloper, a newcomer to a splendid evolutionary process writ large across the tens of thousands of millennia. We can, if we dare loosen the strictures of convention—of the logos that obscures the reality of the bios beneath—think like a mountain, and thereby grasp that palpable reality of the source. To think like a mountain demands that we break free of our Abrahamic concept of the land. For Western culture has forgotten the source of life, the point of origin from which wells up all that is good and free and beautiful, and has turned the land into environment, into re-source. By thinking like a mountain—truly a Thoreauvian trope of gargantuan proportion—our species might rediscover its grounding in cosmic process. To promote the perception of things—the beauty, integrity, and stability of things—was enough for Leopold.

The poets lie too much! So began Jeffers's poetic odyssey. But his words were not simply self-abnegation but a proclamation from within the hermeneutic circle, for he knew that the human animal had grown a little too abstract, a little too wise. Humankind must learn to kiss and feel the earth again, to let life run down to the roots and become calm and full of ocean. Jeffers knew that a culture cultivating only itself was one bound to have a speedy limit. Homo sapiens was a small package, an insignificant mote of dust in a magnificent cosmic stream. Immersed in a logorrhea of science and religion and philosophy we have become blind to the beauty of things. Their transhuman magnificence can be seen only by the inhumanist, who through the word redirects attention from things human to the transhuman, that is, things in their audacious reality. Those things wild and free will impress themselves upon our sensibilities if we will let them.

And there is an old-new way of being, beckoning on the horizon. Turtle Island is its name. Snyder's vision seems to make even the deep ecologist a vulgar pragmatist, and yet that primordial green world beckons with subtle gestures. Tao says no words; deep and obscure is its meaning. Pasque flowers yet bloom in mountain meadows, nourished by microorganisms below and the sun above, which summons forth spring's blossoms from winter's grip. On a summer's night the Milky Way streaks majestically across the black of empty space, as Sol retreats to the other side of our world. And we, flickering embers of sentience, know that our sun and planet are small outposts in the Perseus arm of a mighty galaxy, itself only an infinitesimal part of a vast cosmic wilderness. We are, as was sung on occasion to a vast assemblage of flower children, star dust, and we've got to get ourselves back to the Garden.

Denouement

Only insofar as [reflective inquiry] . . . is not entirely bound by previous thought is it free and autonomous; only insofar as, in its development, it both maintains old relationships and establishes new relationships with its past is it rational and ordered.
—James A. Diefenbeck, *A Celebration of Subjective Thought*

Our inquiry into the idea of wilderness has been fraught with peril, beginning with a conjectural study of the Paleolithic mind and concluding in cosmological inquiry. I have attempted to trace in this book a good portion but certainly not the whole of the story that is the idea of wilderness in an age of ecology. Although books begin and end, the cosmic process that is in one way or another the subject of all inquiry does not. Postmodernism has disclosed the contingency of all human speech-writing-thought (since it is predicated upon language), and perhaps in so doing has confirmed the insight of those sages who wrote the Kena Upanishad. They confronted the cosmic question long before there were any Western categories to distract the mind. Can our belief that we are nature grown self-conscious be a useful fiction? a postmodern myth? a new beginning? a recovery of that which we have somehow lost? Is the Magna Mater, who has borne in her life all the flora and fauna, a child of cosmic process? And is Sol the Father, whose photons energized the womb of the Magna Mater, himself a child? And who are we but beings who have lost their animal innocence, grown ashamed of our nakedness and covered in garments of our own making, taking refuge in a dream world born from ideas that boil forth from our fevered imaginations. We, the spoiled children of the Great Mother, we who refuse to see, to hear and heed Her message, Her laws. Is salvation possible? Or have we so fouled this earth, so covered the green world beneath our second world, that no light can penetrate the world's midnight? Is there hope for the plant and animal people? Is there hope for us all? These are questions that must be answered by the postmodern mind, for only through that exercise of consciousness can our modern dilemma be transcended.

Notes

Chapter 1. The Idea of Wilderness

1. See Allen W. Johnson and Timothy Earle, *The Evolution of Human Societies: From Foraging Group to Agrarian State* (Stanford: Stanford University Press, 1987), 15 ff., and Mark Nathan Cohen, *The Food Crisis in Prehistory: Overpopulation and the Origins of Agriculture* (New Haven and London: Yale University Press, 1977). Population growth is clearly relevant to explaining, and may be the primary variable driving, subsistence intensification.

2. Robinson Jeffers, *The Double Axe and Other Poems: Including Eleven Suppressed Poems* (New York: Liveright, 1977), 56.

3. Compare Sigurd Olson, *Reflections from the North Country* (New York: Alfred A. Knopf, 1976).

4. Colin Fletcher, *The Complete Walker III* (New York: Alfred A. Knopf, 1986), 220.

5. John Muir, *Our National Parks* (Boston: Houghton Mifflin, 1901), 3. A relevant cross-cultural comparison lies in the fact that Amerindigens (see below, n. 12) working in cities will drive thousands of miles over a weekend just to spend a few hours on a reservation. But for the Amerindigen, in distinction from Anglo-Caucasians, the wilderness is a sacred place.

6. The characterization of nature as feminine is deliberate, and this chapter will presumably explain why. I avoid sexist language in my own writing and believe that such an effort is intellectually, if not ethically, obligatory, although we cannot here argue those cases. In citing writers from other times and places, when people were oblivious to the male bias of standard English, I have let their use of false generics stand. Although I sometimes correct sexist usages in contemporary texts, I cannot change, for example, Thoreau's usages without taking liberties that I am not prepared to assume.

7. Compare Joseph L. Sax, *Mountains without Handrails: Reflections on the National Parks* (Ann Arbor: University of Michigan Press, 1980).

8. While such skeptics as Anna Bramwell equate wilderness rhetoric with primitivism, some misplaced and in any case impossible desire to return to an archaic past, others see in the language of the wilderness a renewing potential that transcends the manifest insufficiencies of the modern age. See Anna Bramwell, *Ecology in the Twentieth Century: A History* (New Haven and London: Yale University Press, 1989). See also Hans Peter Duerr, *Dreamtime: Concerning the Boundary between Wilderness and Civilization,* trans. Felicitas Goodman (New York: Basil Blackwell, 1987); E. O. Wilson, ed., *Biodiversity* (Washington, D.C.: National Academy Press, 1988); Michael E. Soulé, *Conservation Biology: The Science of Scarcity and Diversity* (Sunderland, Mass.: Sinauer, 1986); and Gary Snyder, *Turtle Island* (New York: New Directions, 1974), for a small but representative array of arguments—spanning history, biology, ecology, philosophy, and poetry—that a restorative wilderness hermeneutic is essential.

9. There was no consensus on what the park was to be. The initial rationale was to keep the land from falling into the hands of profit seekers. Only later did the notion of preserving the wilderness for future generations emerge.

10. The term *wilderness* denotes different ecosystems—including grasslands, hardwood and coniferous forests, mountains, and deserts—identified by such characteristics as having little or no economic value and consequently unhumanized or developed; also an unsettled or unpopulated region suited only to beasts; and a rugged, primitive area that lacks the amenities of civilization. The adjective *wild* connotes undisciplined, unruly, even barbaric. Wilderness areas are often viewed as wasteland, barren, uninhabitable, desert, or otherwise distinguished from land suited to human development in the name of economic progress and civilization. The oldest Indo-European root is *welt*, also *uelt* (c. 6000 B.C.E.), meaning forest or wildwood. See Roderick Nash, *Wilderness and the American Mind,* 3d ed. (New Haven and London: Yale University Press, 1982), 1–7, for an interesting discussion of difficulties in defining wilderness since it "is so heavily freighted with meaning of a personal, symbolic, and changing kind" (1). Indo-European etymologies are misleading since terms with similar meanings were in use long before the Old English *wild-deor-ness,* or place of wild beasts. For example, the Hebrew word *midbar* (coming from the Semitic rather than Indo-European language family), used throughout the Bible, translates in virtually all conventional connotations as our own "wilderness." See Deut. 8.15 for *midbar* as a hostile, fearsome place inhabited by dangerous animals. Compare Isa. 21.13–15 for wilderness as a place of refuge, and Exod. 15.22–17.7 for a sense of wilderness as a place that civilized people avoid because of its barren nature. *Midbar* also connotes zones of ecological transition be-

tween desert and more fruitful areas and oases, or between unsettled and populated areas, as in the Transjordan Plateau (Num. 21.13–18).

11. See Joseph M. Petulla, *American Environmental History: The Exploitation and Conservation of Natural Resources* (San Francisco: Boyd and Fraser, 1977), for an overview of a voluminous literature. See also W. Elliot Brownlee, *The Dynamics of Ascent: A History of the American Economy* (New York: Alfred A. Knopf, 1974), for an overview of American economic history. *Dynamics of Ascent* assumes the given political economy as its interpretive framework, thus seeing transformation of wilderness as economic success. *Environmental History* presents an alternative interpretation of the same process. Comparison of Petulla's and Brownlee's accounts illustrates how ideology inevitably colors historical narrative.

12. Christopher Columbus thought he had found India when he set foot in the New World, and thus called the indigenous peoples "Indians," a sobriquet with which they have been saddled ever since. The term *Amerindigen* avoids this unfortunate connotation. The Indo-European root for native is *gen*—to give birth, a form recognizable in such modern English words as regenerate, indigenous, genesis, and progeny. For discussions of the impact of civilized people on aboriginal societies see Dee Brown, *Bury My Heart at Wounded Knee: An Indian History of the American West* (New York: Holt, Rinehart and Winston, 1971); Paul Shepard, *The Tender Carnivore and the Sacred Game* (New York: Charles Scribner's Sons, 1973); Marvin Harris, *Cows, Pigs, Wars, and Witches: The Riddles of Culture* (New York: Vintage, 1975); Frederick W. Turner, *Man against Geography: The Western Spirit against the Wilderness* (New Brunswick, N.J.: Rutgers University Press, 1983); and Peter Matthiessen, *Indian Country* (New York: Viking, 1979).

13. The best account of this process remains Nash's *Wilderness and the American Mind*. A complete listing of relevant literature is impossible; Nash's bibliographical notes are as complete as any.

14. A historical study pushed to the limit need confront both universal—as in José Ortega y Gasset, *An Interpretation of Universal History*, trans. Mildred Adams (New York: W. W. Norton, 1973)—and cosmological implications, as in Teilhard de Chardin, *The Phenomenon of Man*, trans. Bernard Wall (New York: Harper and Row, 1965). Such universal and cosmological studies are fraught with methodological and substantive peril, highly suspect in an age of reduction and analysis.

15. See Peter J. Wilson, *The Domestication of the Human Species* (New Haven and London: Yale University Press, 1988), and Paul Shepard, "A Post-Historic Primitivism," in Max Oelschlaeger, ed., *The Wilderness Condition: Essays on Environment and Civilization* (San Francisco: Sierra Club Books, 1992). Simply stated, "social scientists see other soci-

eties through an implicit, comparative lens, their own society" (Wilson, x). Shepard's work is essential reading for anyone attempting to understand the deep past.

16. The metaphor comes from Duerr (e.g., *Dreamtime*, 125). Although Duerr is European, the metaphor is apropos of America in light of the relentless advance of agriculture across the Western landscape. The farmers arrived only a little later than the ranchers, who by then had largely routed the Amerindigens. So-called barbed wire changed the West, a fact recorded by historians and lamented by novelists and poets.

17. A perusal of relevant literature sustains the point. See Hobbes's *Leviathan* for a classic example. *Wilderness and the American Mind* also restates this orthodoxy.

18. Similarly, the modern mind finds almost incomprehensible any idea that native Americans, such as the Lakota Sioux and Zuni, do *not* want to integrate into mainstream American society (euphemistically called "assimilation" by anthropologists).

19. Contemporaneous field research on foragers, especially of an ecological nature, was stimulated by Lee's work on the !Kung San. See Richard B. Lee and Irven DeVore, eds., *Man the Hunter* (New York: Aldine de Gruyter, 1968). Many scholars have contributed directly or indirectly to the recovery of archaic culture, including Claude Lévi-Strauss, *The Savage Mind* (Chicago: University of Chicago Press, 1966); Stanley Diamond, *In Search of the Primitive: A Critique of Civilization* (London: Transaction Books, 1987); Marshall Sahlins, *Stone Age Economics* (New York: Aldine de Gruyter, 1972); José Ortega y Gasset, *Meditations on Hunting*, trans. Howard B. Wescott (New York: Charles Scribner's Sons, 1972); Joseph Campbell, *The Masks of God: Primitive Mythology* (New York: Penguin, 1977); Gary Snyder, *The Old Ways* (San Francisco: City Lights, 1977); and Shepard, *Tender Carnivore*. Collectively, such thinkers perhaps lead the way toward a new paradigm for the study of prehistoric people.

20. Herbert N. Schneidau, *The Sacred Discontent: The Bible and Western Tradition* (Baton Rouge: Louisiana State University Press, 1976), 103. We shall explore Schneidau's arguments in chap. 2.

21. I owe this felicitous appellation to Paul Shepard.

22. The new evolutionary synthesis, sometimes called *circumscription theory*, recognizes three fundamental interacting components in cultural evolution: human individuals (themselves presupposing the human genetic inheritance), a natural environment, and culture. "The environment presents the opportunities and the limitations: the ecological context within which individuals must find sustenance and avoid life-threatening hazards. The culture is the technology, the organization, and the knowledge

that help individuals in their quest for survival" (Johnson and Earle, *Evolution of Human Societies,* 3–4).

23. Compare, e.g., Kim Hill and A. Magdalena Hurtado, "Hunter-Gatherers of the New World," *American Scientist* 77 (September–October 1989): 437.

24. Compare Sherwood L. Washburn and C. S. Lancaster, "The Evolution of Hunting," in Lee and DeVore, *Man the Hunter,* 296, n. 4.

25. The argument is that normal ontogeny requires socialization in a natural context. See Paul Shepard, *Thinking Animals: Animals and the Development of Human Intelligence* (New York: Viking, 1978); Konrad Lorenz, *Studies in Animal and Human Behavior,* 2 vols. (Cambridge: Harvard University Press, 1970, 1971); and Dolores LaChapelle, *Sacred Land, Sacred Sex—Rapture of the Deep: Concerning Deep Ecology and Celebrating Life* (Silverton, Colo.: Finn Hill Arts, 1988), esp. 54–71.

26. See Duerr, *Dreamtime.* Even anthropologists characteristically avoid such a view.

27. See R. G. Collingwood, *The Idea of History* (London: Oxford University Press, 1956). Collingwood's study is essential, but later students of historical consciousness, such as Herbert Schneidau, fill in many details that the *Idea of History* overlooks. Schneidau argues that the sense of history that virtually defines the West originates in the *sacred discontent,* that is, the Hebraic demythologizing of mythic consciousness.

28. See Neil Evernden, *The Natural Alien: Humankind and Environment* (Toronto: University of Toronto Press, 1985); Schneidau, *Sacred Discontent;* and Holmes Rolston III, *Philosophy Gone Wild: Essays in Environmental Ethics* (Buffalo: Prometheus Books, 1986) for insightful discussions. See also Shepard, "Post-Historic Primitivism."

29. Duerr, *Dreamtime,* 126.

30. Gary Snyder, "The Etiquette of Freedom," *Sierra* 74 (September–October 1989): 75.

31. Paul Shepard, *Nature and Madness* (San Francisco: Sierra Club Books, 1982), 125.

32. Duerr, *Dreamtime,* 125.

33. See Shepard, *Thinking Animals.*

34. Duerr, *Dreamtime,* 130.

35. The term is Eric Gould's, and is roughly a postmodern equivalent to the modern term *truth.* See Gould, *Mythic Intentions in Modern Literature* (Princeton: Princeton University Press, 1981), 3–14. See also William C. Doty, *Mythography: The Study of Myths and Rituals* (Birmingham: University of Alabama Press, 1986), 232–48, for a cogent account of myth and the hermeneutic circle, and Richard Rorty, *Contingency, Irony, and Solidarity* (New York: Cambridge University Press, 1989), for an insight-

ful account of the contingency of language. Viewed ironically, "truth" is always associated with textuality, including interpretations derived from scientific texts, which ostensibly lay out the dimensions of truth that is "out there," objective, rational, beyond subjectivity and human history. Doty points out that the intellectual today is confronted by "the vast importance of texts' *intra*-textuality—and hence their relativity, with the fact that meanings are *given* to texts *by the critic* who initiates the interpretive gestures by seeking to discover what is there; different critical postures produce different meanings" (234). And, apropos of our study, the upshot of Rorty's argument is that any "rational-irrational distinction is less useful than it once appeared" (48). A critical vocabulary, Rorty continues, that "revolves around notions like 'rational,' 'criteria,' 'argument' and 'foundation' and 'absolute' is badly suited to describe the relation between the old and the new" (49).

36. Gould, *Mythic Intentions*, 6.
37. Leszek Kolakowski, *The Presence of Myth*, trans. Adam Czerniawski (Chicago: University of Chicago Press, 1989), 29.
38. Joseph Campbell, *The Hero with a Thousand Faces* (Princeton: Princeton University Press, 1949), 3. See also Doty, *Mythography;* Lee W. Gibbs and W. Taylor Stevenson, eds., *Myth and the Crisis of Historical Consciousness* (Missoula, Mont.: Scholars Press, 1975); Henry A. Murray, ed., *Myth and Mythmaking* (Boston: Beacon, 1959); and Alan M. Olson, *Myth, Symbol, and Reality* (Notre Dame, Ind.: University of Notre Dame Press, 1980).
39. Gould, *Mythic Intentions*, 6.
40. Schneidau, *Sacred Discontent*, 51.
41. Gould, *Mythic Intentions*, 6.
42. Albert Cooke, *Myth and Language* (Bloomington: Indiana University Press, 1980), cited in Doty, *Mythography,* 11.
43. Lévi-Strauss, *Savage Mind*, 16.
44. See Shepard, *Nature and Madness*, 56–57, for an able summary of these dramatically different views of life. See also Schneidau, *Sacred Discontent*, esp. 50–103, "The Mythological Consciousness." See chaps. 2 and 3, below, for an account of the emergence and articulation of historic consciousness.
45. Joseph Campbell, *Mythologies of the Great Hunt*, pt. 2 of *The Way of the Animal Powers*, vol. 1 of *Historical Atlas of World Mythology* (New York: Harper and Row, 1988), xxiii. The crucial issue here is one of evidence; but evidence exists only from a particular point of view. What the student of the deep past recognizes as evidence does not exist for the modern mind.
46. We are not here committing the *argumentum ad ignorantium;* our con-

jecture is plausible since cultural myopia is ubiquitous even among modern human beings, and since aboriginal people characteristically think of themselves as living a natural way of life in harmony with rather than distinct from creation. Further, virtually all the evidence indicates that Paleolithic people had no conception of time (or history) analogous to our own. Time was for them cyclical, and past, present, and future were indistinguishable.

47. Schneidau, *Sacred Discontent*, 58.

48. Evidence confirming the existence of a transpolar hunter mythology is nearly overwhelming. The works of Joseph Campbell marshal a wide array of data that bear on the issue, including evidence of the West-to-East dispersal of the mythology of the Great Hunt; the migration of Paleolithic hunters to North America along temporary land bridges (c. 25000 B.C.E.) and the subsequent similarities of belief; and interpretations of Paleolithic painting, rock art, and funerary rituals. But no summary can replace the reader's own perusal of Campbell's work. See Campbell, *Mythologies of the Primitive Hunters and Gatherers*, pt. 1 of *The Way of the Animal Powers*, vol. 1 of *Historical Atlas of World Mythology* (New York: Harper and Row, 1988), 26ff., and *Mythologies of the Great Hunt*. See also his *Primitive Mythology*, esp. 286–354.

49. Compare Campbell, *Primitive Mythology*, 339ff.

50. Snyder, *Turtle Island*, 5. Paul Shepard and Barry Sanders, *The Sacred Paw: The Bear in Nature, Myth, and Literature* (New York: Viking Penguin, 1985), is near definitive. See chap. 8, below, for further discussion of poetic language in its ontogenetic role.

51. See Karl W. Luckert, *The Navajo Hunter Tradition* (Tucson: University of Arizona Press, 1975), 133; E. E. Evans-Pritchard, *Theories of Primitive Religion* (Oxford: Oxford University Press, 1965); John J. Collins, *Primitive Religion* (Totowa, N.J.: Littlefield, Adams, 1978); and Ninian Smart, "The Study and Classification of Religions," *Encyclopedia Britannica*, 15th ed. (1985), 26:548–68, for useful discussions of totemism. In her insightful treatment of totemism, LaChapelle points out that it "does not involve some special magical plant or animal, in other words a 'substance'; but, in its essence deals with the relationships of humans both to nature, deep inside our own brain/body and outside of us, in nature itself. It's all the same nature; *the boundary* we insist on drawing between our human self and the rest of nature is something we inflict on the whole by means of our narrow 'merely human' [civilized] part of the brain" (*Sacred Land*, 71, emphasis added). See also Duerr, *Dreamtime*.

52. Shepard, *Tender Carnivore*, 203.

53. Shepard, *Tender Carnivore*, 132.

54. The spread of the human species across the earth's surface is beyond the

scope of this study. Obviously, such technological changes as the mastery of fire, construction of temporary shelter, and development of garments facilitated dispersal.

55. Shepard, *Tender Carnivore,* 204.

56. Presumably there were conditions where an individual might become lost or separated from the tribe. Such an experience could have been life threatening and in any case was likely frightening. See Martin Buber, *I and Thou,* trans. Walter Kaufmann (New York: Charles Scribner's Sons, 1970). Buber advances an interesting observation on the language of archaic peoples. "The nuclei of . . . [their] language, their sentence-words—primal pre-grammatical forms that eventually split into the multiplicity of different kinds of words—generally designate the wholeness of a relation. We say, 'far away'; the Zulu has a sentence-word instead that means: where one cries, 'mother, I am lost. . . .' In this wholeness persons are still embedded like reliefs without achieving the fully rounded independence of nouns or pronouns. What counts is not these products of analysis and reflection but the genuine original unity, the lived relationship" (69–70). Following Buber's lead, we may conjecture that the modern mind's sense of alienation from nature is grounded at least in part in the rise of modern and therefore object language. As our study proceeds (see chaps. 5, 8, and 9, below) we shall focus now and again on these pivotal questions of language and cognition. See also Robert Bunge, *An American Urphilosophie: An American Philosophy BP (Before Pragmatism)* (Lanham, Md.: University Press of America, 1984), esp. chap. 7, "The Grid of Language," concerning the problems of language not only generally, but particularly in relation to the task of understanding archaic cultures.

57. Sahlins, *Stone Age Economics,* 33.

58. Sahlins, *Stone Age Economics,* 37–38.

59. Life expectancy must be distinguished from lifespan. Ignoring the philosophical question of just how facts are to be decided, the skeptic must bear in mind that statistical studies which show, for example, that life expectancy has increased considerably in the twentieth century, are not causally relevant to the question of the genetically determined potential for longevity.

60. See also René Dubos, "Environmental Determinants of Human Life," in David C. Glass, ed., *Environmental Influences* (New York: Rockefeller University Press, 1966); Dubos, *So Human an Animal* (New York: Charles Scribner's Sons, 1968), esp. 146–60; and Philip Handler, ed., *Biology and the Future of Man* (New York: Oxford University Press, 1970), esp. chap. 19, "Environmental Health."

61. Claude Lévi-Strauss, "The Concept of Primitiveness," in Lee and DeVore, *Man the Hunter,* 351.

62. Compare Claude Lévi-Strauss, *Myth and Meaning* (New York: Schocken, 1979).

63. Lévi-Strauss, *Savage Mind,* 13. Lévi-Strauss's work is not sui generis in its analysis of scientific thought viewed as a response to the world. What is unique is his combination of anthropological data with structuralism to outline the "savage mind."

64. The Indo-European root for mother is *ma-ma-,* a vocalization made by suckling infants; similar imitative sounds are found in other language families. The relevance of sexual intercourse to reproduction, and thus the male's role in perpetuating life, was apparently unknown until c. 2500 B.C.E. Motherhood was perhaps the central mystery of life.

65. Few modernists appreciate this aboriginal sense of a female presence in nature. To the Lakota the Maká Iná is there, a pervading presence throughout the living world, a bountiful mother who provides everything they need. Robert Bunge argues in "Community: Key to Survival," *Contemporary Philosophy* 12 (Winter 1988), that for them, and for Amerindigens generally, existence is inconceivable apart from these bonds, for the Great Mother provides all. For the Lakota "the soil of . . . [their] hereditary home was . . . [humankind's] highest heaven and to be earthbound [their] greatest joy. It was impossible to get too close to this nurturing mother; people loved to walk barefoot and sit or lie upon a grassy plot to soak up thereby the healing power of the land. The serpent was considered the wisest creature by many native peoples because every part of him from head to tail was in contact with the ground and hence . . . privy to the earth's innermost secrets and power. Indians never could understand why white people propped themselves up and away from this therapeutic contact of the source of life by sitting on wooden chairs" (30).

66. Such an assertion appears to modernists as "wistful primitivism." However, consistent with the argument of this book, the aim is not to go back to nature but to advance from where we are, aided in that project by insights into the deep past.

67. Insofar as such studies as Arnold Toynbee's *Study of History* are cogent, there is no reason to suspect that modern culture will be an exception. See D. C. Somervell, *A Study of History: Arnold J. Toynbee* (Oxford: Oxford University Press, 1946), for a useful abridgment. It is difficult to imagine that any culture could be an exception to evolutionary process.

68. See Campbell, *Mythologies of the Great Hunt,* esp. 147ff. Many variations on this theme are preserved in the rites of persisting archaic cultures. Bunge notes that certain Sioux reenact the bear rituals, placing the skull and bones "on an elevated scaffold out of the reach of predators" so that the bear will return again and game will not become scarce. Women among the Lakota Sioux prize a nut that grows only in a thorny bush, sure to lacerate any human hand. But field mice gather the nuts freely

and secrete them in their burrows. The women gather some of the nuts
from the burrow, leaving other foodstuffs in their place, thus maintaining balance and order in the cycle of nature ("Community," 31). Navajo
hunters reenact an almost timeless rite at the shrine of the reclining lions
(Bandelier National Monument), saying prayers and piling antlers around
stone figures to ensure that the order of the cosmos is not disturbed by
the hunt.

69. Compare among many, Shepard, *Tender Carnivore,* and Sahlins, *Stone
Age Economics.*

70. Surviving archaic peoples have been pushed onto marginal habitat by the
spread of Western culture and agriculture, thus making them more vulnerable to hunger. Similarly, native populations have often been decimated
by diseases introduced through contact (however fleeting) with civilized
people.

71. There is reason (given the pervasive geographical distribution of Paleolithic Venus figurines) to think of the Magna Mater as a more ancient
metaphor than that of the Earth Mother, and thus to distinguish the
Great Mother of the Paleolithic from the Earth Mother of the Neolithic.
Whereas the Magna Mater mythology suggests a nurturing, even biocentric relation between nature and humanity, rather than the homocentric relation of the later agrarian mind, the Paleolithic idea of nature as
feminine undoubtedly contains the seed of the Neolithic Earth Mother
metaphor. Paul Shepard associates the Great Mother with the agrarian
rather than hunting-gathering mind and interprets the concept as part
of the perversion of a natural hunting way of life by later agriculturists.
"Motherhood, which had a symbolic place in human religion, was mon-
strously exaggerated in the farmer's preoccupation with fecundity. . . .
Farming put upon human females the job of emulating the barnyard animals, then of becoming baby machines. The mystique and rationale used
to enforce and justify this subversion penetrated the center of all peasant religions, where the Great Mother was elevated, not for her essential
feminine traits, but as the breeder of men and food" (*Tender Carnivore,*
244). Robert Graves argues that almost all Neolithic Europe "had a remarkably homogeneous system of religious ideas, based on worship of the
many-titled Mother-goddess, who was also known in Syria and Libya"
(*The Greek Myths,* rev. ed., vol. 1 [New York: Viking Penguin, 1960],
13). Graves also contends that this matricentric belief system endured
largely intact until the concept of fatherhood was introduced into religious thought. See chap. 2, below, and compare Marija Gimbutas, *The
Gods and Goddesses of Old Europe, 7000 to 3500 B.C.: Myths, Legends,
and Cult Images* (Berkeley: University of California Press, 1974).

72. See Karl J. Narr, "Paleolithic Religion," trans. M. O'Connell, in Mircea
Eliade, ed., *The Encyclopedia of Religion,* vol. 11 (New York: MacMil-

lan, 1987). He counsels us to avoid the temptation of imposing "a single general explanation on everything. Nonetheless, it also seems clear that animals and shapes with animal attributes [the animal masters] . . . , and a female principle [the Magna Mater] . . . often played a part in the mental and spiritual world of the Paleolithic and fit in with the peculiar character of a world of gatherers and specialized hunters" (157).

73. Joseph Campbell profiles two mythic systems existing side by side throughout the era of the Great Hunt. The mythology of the cave paintings was largely male engendered and concerned with the mysteries of the game, whereas the rock art mythology was essentially feminine and directed more to the mysteries of life and death. This distinction leads to the inevitable question of the respective roles of the male and female, and further questions concerning the possibility of diverse Paleolithic ideas of wilderness. Campbell believes that the cave paintings and rites reflected the experienced reality of life and death on the hunting fields, whereas the rock art reflected the domestic hearth and the experienced realities of life and death through procreation and birth. He also distinguishes the painter's art from that of the sculptor's, and the abstract images of the animal master paintings from the concrete statuary representing the female body. "The painter's art, translating into two-dimensional forms optical experiences of three, was, like the art of the hunt, to which it was applied, an intensely outward-directed exercise of the analytical mind, whereas the sculptural approach and regard were in the way rather of an acclamation and metakinetic interpretation of the forms as they were, in being" (*Mythologies of the Great Hunt*, xxi). The debate over the role of women in the Paleolithic lies beyond the scope of our inquiry. But two observations are perhaps appropriate. First, regardless of arguments about sex roles in the genetic and cultural articulation of our species, either male or female alone is an abstraction from biological reality. Second, though some have argued that environmental crisis is rooted in male characteristics, such a theory must be seen as a useful simplification. See below, esp. chaps. 2 and 9, for further discussion of ecofeminism.

74. This hypothesis finds some support in the belief systems of contemporary aborigines, such as the Lakota Sioux. The Lakota word *Wakán* is used to characterize the whole process of life and death as holy. The Lakota religion, Bunge argues, clearly contrasts to the supernaturalism of the Modern era, for "nothing could be better than *Maká Iná* (Mother Earth), even with all its perils and insecurity," since existence in and of itself is holy or sacred ("Community," 32).

75. See Clifford Geertz, "Religion," in Arthur C. Lehmann and James E. Myers, eds., *Magic, Witchcraft, and Religion: An Anthropological Study of the Supernatural*, 2d ed. (Mountain View, Calif.: Mayfield, 1989).

76. Compare Narr, "Paleolithic Religion," 151.

77. See Mircea Eliade, *The Sacred and the Profane: The Nature of Religion,* trans. Willard R. Trask (New York: Harcourt Brace Jovanovich, 1959), 17.

78. Narr, "Paleolithic Religion," 151. See also Roy A. Rappaport, *Ecology, Meaning, and Religion* (Richmond, Va.: North Atlantic Books, 1970). Rappaport argues that any divorce between biological-ecological inquiry and that attempted by philosophy, hermeneutics, psychology, and so on is misguided.

79. See John W. Bennett, *The Ecological Transition: Cultural Anthropology and Human Adaptation* (New York: Pergamon, 1976), for insightful discussion of the interrelation of ecological and anthropological inquiry.

80. Even for the devout Judeo-Christian the world is profane, given over to the blind operation of matter-in-motion.

81. Eliade, *Sacred and Profane,* 14. Eliade's assertion must be qualified, since aborigines who exemplify the attitude of Homo religiosus remain.

82. Eliade, *Sacred and Profane,* 15.

83. Eliade, *Sacred and Profane,* 116, 117. See also Bunge, *Urphilosophie,* for parallel insights into the Lakota Sioux.

84. Narr, "Paleolithic Religion," 159.

85. The first period is the Aurignacio-Perigordian (c. 14000–13500 B.C.E.) age, which includes the famous cave of Lascaux and a number of voluptuous female figurines (the so-called Venuses). The second period is the Soiutreo-Magdalenian (c. 14000–9500 B.C.E.), and it includes the murals at Rouffignac and Niaux (compare Campbell, *Mythologies of the Primitive Hunters,* 58ff.). Abbé Henri Breuil and André Leroi-Gourhan led the way in demolishing the modern prejudice that cave art is merely a puerile and isomorphic representation of animals. A fine introduction to Paleolithic cave art is Mario Ruspoli, *The Cave of Lascaux: The Final Photographs,* trans. Sebastian Wormell (New York: Henry M. Abrams, 1987).

86. Grahame Clarke, *World Prehistory in New Perspective,* 3d ed. (Cambridge: Cambridge University Press, 1977), 39.

87. Here we enter the domain of philosophical psychology. An interesting starting point for such inquiry is R. G. Collingwood, *Speculum Mentis, or the Map of Knowledge* (Oxford: Oxford University Press, 1924). Collingwood's phenomenology of consciousness bears directly on the analyses that Lévi-Strauss makes of magic and science or that Joseph Campbell does apropos of myth and science. See also R. G. Collingwood, *The New Leviathan, or Man, Society, Civilization, and Barbarism* (London: Oxford University Press, 1942), and Collingwood, *The Principles of Art* (New York: Oxford University Press, 1958).

88. Cited in Campbell, *Mythologies of the Great Hunt,* xvi.

89. Lucy R. Lippard, *Overlay: Contemporary Art and the Art of Prehistory* (New York: Pantheon, 1983), 41. Campbell also sees the Venus statuary

as more concrete than the painting. But he differs in giving a more spiritual than material interpretation to Paleolithic art generally. He believes that the overwhelming beauty of prehistoric art comes from its three dominant themes: *integritas,* or wholeness, *consonantia,* or harmony, and *claritas,* or radiance. These marks of the aesthetic consciousness confirm "the why" of cave art: the painting and statuary are not crude imitations of the world but represent what is known or believed to be true of reality. Thus the meaning or "connotation [of cave art] is simultaneously of the human and celestial as the one event, the micro- and macro-cosmic mystery as of equivalent dignity and import" (*Mythologies of the Great Hunt,* xxi).

90. Campbell, *Mythologies of the Great Hunt,* xv.

91. Narr, "Paleolithic Religion," 155.

92. See Shepard, *Tender Carnivore,* 163, 169. See also Duerr, *Dreamtime,* chap. 3, "The Vagina of the Earth and Venus Mountain," and chap. 9, below. Almost unquestionably the caves played a central role in rites of initiation. The role in adult life is less clear; yet almost surely, just as religiosity does not end as one becomes an adult in our society, so in Paleolithic culture.

93. Campbell, *Primitive Mythology,* 377.

94. See chap. 2, below, esp. "Greek Rationalism and the Leavening of Christianity," where the seeds of our modern conception of time were planted. The desacralization of time is central to the modern idea of progress, for if humankind views itself as living in an eternal present, then there is no way to conceive of life as getting better in every way every day.

95. Eliade, *Sacred and Profane,* 70.

96. See Charles A. Reed, ed., *Origins of Agriculture* (The Hague: Mouton, 1977), for a valuable collection of essays entertaining this question, esp. 879–953. Our focus is the Near East—those lands that lie along or near the ancient Mediterranean. Reed, among others, believes that the Near East presents the clearest picture (for many reasons) of the process of cultural change known as the agricultural revolution. Agricultural revolutions also occurred in other locales, such as China, India, and South America, implying that pre-adaptations in hunting-gathering culture made agriculture possible. We must also bear in mind that hunting-foraging endured, based on enormous herds of bison, on the American plains until near the end of the nineteenth century, and continues on the margins of civilization.

97. Sahlins, *Stone Age Economics,* 2.

98. Clarke, *World Prehistory,* 43.

99. For a general introduction see Nigel Calder, *Timescale: An Atlas of the Fourth Dimension* (New York: Viking, 1983). See also Reed, *Origins*

of Agriculture; Clarke, *World Prehistory;* and H. H. Lamb, *Climate: Present, Past and Future,* vol. 2 (New York: Methuen, 1977), for technical discussion and bibliographies.

100. Compare Reed, *Origins of Agriculture,* 879f., 899f. Initially the selection of full ripe heads was unconscious, since seed heads remaining intact are naturally maladaptive for cereal grasses. Even so, unconscious selection eventuated in the increased survival of what—viewed in terms of natural evolution—are pathological genes: that is, heads of grain that cohere until harvested. Genes that were "semilethal in the wild not only allowed but channeled cereal agriculture into paths of 'improvement' (from the human viewpoint), leading to the diversification of each kind of grain, to the spread of its cultivation beyond the normal range of the wild ancestor, and thus to the increase of its yield" (880).

101. Reed, *Origins of Agriculture,* 899.

102. Whitehead implies such a thesis in the form of a cosmological argument. See Alfred North Whitehead, *The Function of Reason* (Princeton: Princeton University Press, 1969). Whitehead contends that there is in cosmic process a countervailing inclination to the second law: a tendency in the course of events to live (life itself), to live well (the bird's nest, the beaver's dam), and finally to live better (civilization, human technology). José Ortega y Gasset suggests a similar thesis in *The Idea of Principle in Leibnitz and the Evolution of Deductive Theory,* trans. Mildred Adams (New York: W. W. Norton, 1971), where he argues that physics is the instrument of human happiness. See also among others Ervin Laszlo, *Evolution: The Grand Synthesis* (Boston: New Science Library, 1987), which is predicated throughout on the assumption of an "upward tendency" in the course of events.

103. The issue is complicated and involves the nature-nurture question. Nothing in principle precludes such change, since evolution itself presupposes the reality of time. See chap. 10, below, for further discussion of the concept of time and cultural transformation.

104. For example, Arthur Koestler, Konrad Lorenz, and Kurt Vonnegut have explored this thesis.

105. Human beings do not possess a gene that predestines them to become agriculturists; the diversity of cultural forms through time refutes such a premise.

106. Eliade, *Sacred and Profane,* 17.

107. Joseph Campbell argues in *Mythologies of the Primitive Hunters* that ritual sacrifice and cannibalism (which were not characteristic of hunting-gathering culture) were pervasive among prehistoric jungle cultures, and he attributes these differences to geography. Life in the fecund equatorial jungles was different than life on the hunting plains. "Out of the rot of fallen wood and leaves, fresh sprouts arise—from which the les-

son learned appears to have been that from death springs life, out of death, new birth; and the grim conclusion drawn was that the way to increase life is to increase death. Accordingly, there has been endemic to the entire equatorial belt of this globe what can be described only as a frenzy of sacrifice, vegetable, animal, and human . . . . Moreover, in variously modified forms, the influence of this order of primitive rites entered and inspired much of the mythology of the higher cultures, where it survives in myths and rituals of sacrifice and communion with which many of us, of whatever religious affiliation, have been long familiar" (10).

108. Many observers consider philosophy and theology as foregone conclusions, concomitant with emergence of the neocortex or new brain of species Homo sapiens. Compare, e.g., Jacquetta Hawkes, *Prehistory*, vol. 1, pt. 1 of *History of Mankind: Cultural and Scientific Development* (New York: New American Library, 1963); Günter Altner, ed., *The Human Creature: Toward an Understanding of Man* (Garden City, N.Y.: Anchor, 1974); and J. S. Weiner, *The Natural History of Man* (Garden City, N.Y.: Anchor, 1973). Weiner argues that through the dynamic interplay of biology and the environment new and favorable characters emerge, such as the neocortex, and that the natural history of our species culminates in achieving self-awareness of the human predicament. Once Homo sapiens achieved self-consciousness, then religion, philosophy, and science were inevitable.

109. There is agreement on the pivotal role of Egyptian and Sumerian culture in making the transition from prehistory to history. Compare, e.g., Samuel Noah Kramer, *History Begins at Sumer: Thirty-Nine Firsts in Man's Recorded History* (Philadelphia: University of Pennsylvania Press, 1981), and Henri Frankfort, *The Birth of Civilization in the Near East* (Garden City, N.Y.: Doubleday, 1956). For more popular accounts, compare Leonard Cottrell, "Gift of the Nile," in S. G. C. F. Brandon, ed., *Milestones of History: One Hundred Decisive Events in the History of Mankind* (New York: W. W. Norton, 1971), and Will Durant, *Our Oriental Heritage* (New York: Simon and Schuster, 1954).

110. Compare Clarence Glacken, *Traces on the Rhodian Shore: Nature and Culture in Western Thought from Ancient Times to the End of the Eighteenth Century* (Berkeley: University of California Press, 1967), 35–37, esp. n. 2, and 708.

*Chapter 2. Ancient Mediterranean Ideas
of Humankind and Nature*

1. The *OED* associates Eden with the point of origin of the human species, usually located in Mesopotamia. The Indo-European root is *gher*, garden. An edenic existence has come to be associated with a state of supreme

happiness. The Bible gives two accounts of the Fall and plays prominently
in our narrative. Although the Fall is associated with sin (engendered
through defiance of Yahweh), it has been interpreted brilliantly by such
scholars as Herbert Schneidau as representing the human achievement
of self-consciousness, not only as a species distinct from nature but as
individuals distinct from the tribe (*Sacred Discontent,* 43 ff.).

2. Compare J. D. Bernal, *The Emergence of Science,* vol. 1 of *Science in History* (Cambridge, Mass.: MIT Press, 1971), 77, 96.

3. Shepard's perspective on the ecological transition from the Paleolithic to the Neolithic is detailed in *Tender Carnivore.* He argues that agriculture is not the glorious rise of the human species above nature but the beginning of the Fall. "The ways of the hunters are beginning to show us how we are failing as human beings and as organisms in a world beset by a 'success' that hunters never wanted" (154).

4. Compare, e.g., Thorkild Jacobsen and Robert M. Adams, "Salt and Silt in Ancient Mesopotamian Agriculture," *Science,* November 21, 1958, 1251–58; John Perlin, *A Forest Journey: The Role of Wood in the Development of Civilization* (New York: W. W. Norton, 1989), 35–43; and A. Leo Oppenheim, *Ancient Mesopotamia: Portrait of a Dead Civilization* (Chicago: University of Chicago Press, 1977), 35–45.

5. The etiological matrix that explains this situation is unclear, but the division was not rooted in religion or politics; locations relatively abundant in water were, of course, more conducive to agriculture. Notwithstanding distinction of two ideal types—agriculturalists and hunter-gatherers—there were also hybrids like the seminomads.

6. See Glacken, *Traces,* esp. pt. 1: "The Ancient World," for an insightful analysis.

7. From the standpoint of a market economy, the subsistence economies of archaic people appear to be failures. Similarly, magical practices and rituals associated with the hunt appear, from the perspective of science, to be inefficient and ignorant. Lévi-Strauss has helped to dispel this mistake. For an accessible example see John Reader, *Man on Earth* (Austin: University of Texas Press, 1988), 136–39. Reader argues that magic, understood in an ecological context, can be both efficient and intelligent.

8. I use the term *idolatry* without pejorative connotation. See below, n. 62.

9. See Gimbutas, *Gods and Goddesses,* 195–96. As Merlin Stone points out, however, "No single name, symbol, image, set of rituals and beliefs, or natural element such as the sun, moon, earth, or stars can be said to represent all goddess reverence in the Near East" ("Goddess Worship in the Ancient Near East," in Robert M. Seltzer, *Religions of Antiquity* [New York: Macmillan, 1989], 63). See also chap. 1, n. 71.

10. See Henri Frankfort, H. A. Frankfort, John A. Wilson, and Thorkild

Jacobsen, *Before Philosophy: The Intellectual Adventure of Ancient Man* (Baltimore: Penguin, 1949), for an able discussion of this process.

11. Compare Thorkild Jacobsen, "Mesopotamian Religions," in Seltzer, *Religions*, 3–33. Jacobsen suggests a process of transformation from physiomorphism to anthropomorphism. Yet even when the gods took on human shapes, nonhuman forms remained as primitive survivals, although "the phenomenon subsided into a mere thing owned or managed by the deity, and the form derived from it into a mere emblem" (10).

12. See James S. Mellaart, *Çatal-Hüyük: A Neolithic Town in Anatolia* (New York: McGraw-Hill, 1967), and Ian A. Todd, *Çatal-Hüyük in Perspective* (Menlo Park, Calif.: Cummings, 1976).

13. The process of domestication of wild animals during the Neolithic age is poorly understood. Human intervention in animal breeding is evidenced by morphological transformations (such as the reduction of body size and horns), but the first steps toward domestication are unknown. See Hawkes, *Prehistory*, 376ff., for an introduction to this subject. See also Reed, *Origins of Agriculture*, 19, for a discussion of the difficulties inherent in defining the term *domesticated*.

14. Gimbutas, *Gods and Goddesses*, 237.

15. Stone, "Goddess Worship," 67.

16. Along with agriculture came diseases largely unknown to hunter-foragers. Although humankind had been acquainted with natural mortality since c. 75000 B.C.E., epidemics and the like appeared to the agriculturists as mysteries. The Egyptians perhaps surpassed all other ancient cultures in efforts to explain disease. The Sumerian version of the biblical flood is tied to their explanation of disease. They believed that the gods had created humans to support them, but as humans multiplied they made so much noise that the gods could no longer sleep. Enlil sent the flood to eradicate the human race; the gods, having grown dependent on humans, became hungry. Thereafter disease was used to control population.

17. See David Ulansey, "The Mithraic Mysteries," *Scientific American*, December 1989, 130–35, for an argument that Mithraism has more to do with the discovery of the precession of the equinoxes than continuities with older forms of thought.

18. The Indo-European roots of our modern language are a case in point. Even Proto-Indo-European is not an Ur-language, yet it stretches back to the dawn of our sense of history, c. 6000 B.C.E.

19. See Frankfort et al., *Before Philosophy*, for an able discussion of the late Neolithic mind—Egyptian and Sumerian.

20. The bull commanded veneration for several reasons, not the least of which was the countless millennia during which it was hunted, testing hunters while inspiring their admiration; the bull's evident virility, as well as its

strength and combativeness, encouraged veneration. Tribal leaders were thought to possess these same virtues.

21. See Kramer, *History Begins at Sumer.*

22. Herbert Mason, *Gilgamesh: A Verse Narrative* (New York: New American Library, 1970), 35. For a literal translation see N. K. Sandars, *The Epic of Gilgamesh: An English Version with an Introduction* (Baltimore: Penguin, 1967). Although the area is barren today, before subsistence intensification the hills and mountains of the Fertile Crescent were heavily forested (see Perlin, *Forest Journey,* 35). The Egyptians were loathe to enter the forests, as were perhaps the Sumerians, at least at first. Enkidu, Gilgamesh's companion, suggests that the forest guarded by Humbaba extended ten thousand leagues in every direction. Nonetheless, the Sumerians rapidly deforested the region, using wood for temples, houses, furniture, and fuel. Mineral salts, leached from the exposed salt-bearing sedimentary rocks, slowly salinized fertile soil. Over time, agricultural productivity dwindled. By 2000 B.C.E. Sumerian civilization collapsed, in part because no agricultural surplus existed to fuel the elite superstructure that bound society (Perlin, *Forest Journey,* 43).

23. Stone, "Goddess Worship," 66. Stone explains that the concept of divine right to the throne was ensured though a connection with the goddess of the land and was usually "ritualized in a *hieros gamos,* a sacred marriage between the man who was to be king and the priestess who represented the goddess" (66). Jacobsen notes that the actors were bedded on a marital couch, and the "rising of the king's member in the sexual congress" was believed (sympathetic magic) immediately to make the "plants and greenery shoot up" ("Mesopotamian Religions," 30).

24. See, e.g., Sir James George Frazer, *The Golden Bough: A Study in Magic and Religion,* abridged ed. (New York: Macmillan, 1950). For a critique of Frazer see Ludwig Wittgenstein, *Remarks on Frazer's* Golden Bough, trans. A. C. Miles, rev. trans. Rush Rhees (Atlantic Highlands, N.J.: Humanities Press, 1979). Wittgenstein argues that "Frazer's account of the magical and religious motions of men is unsatisfactory: it makes these notions appear as *mistakes*" (1e). The problem is that Frazer views myth through the lens of history.

25. Eliade, *Sacred and Profane,* 65.

26. See Peter L. Berger and Thomas Luckmann, *The Social Construction of Reality: A Treatise in the Sociology of Knowledge* (Garden City, N.J.: Doubleday, 1967), 125–26, apropos of the roles intellectuals play in society. Some intellectuals (e.g., deconstructionists, edifying philosophers) are not wanted by society, whereas others are. Economists and political scientists, for example, often sooth the psyche with rhetoric that reinforces the accepted worldview.

27. Compare Frankfort, *Birth of Civilization,* 56–57.

28. Frankfort, *Birth of Civilization,* 63.
29. Compare Drew A. Hyland, *The Origins of Philosophy: Its Rise in Myth and the Pre-Socratics* (New York: G. Putnam's Sons, 1973), 30.
30. See Glacken, *Traces,* 4.
31. Norman K. Gottwald, *The Tribes of Yahweh: A Sociology of the Religion of Liberated Israel, 1250–1050 B.C.E.* (Maryknoll, N.Y.: Orbis, 1979), 4, 5. On the limitations of academic specialization see also Schneidau, *Sacred Discontent,* xii.
32. I shall follow the convention of capitalizing the word *god* when referring to the deity of Judeo-Christianity; a lowercase convention is otherwise employed.
33. See Lynn White, Jr., "The Historical Roots of Our Ecologic Crisis," *Science,* March 10, 1967, 1203–7. Citations herein are from White's article as reprinted in Ian G. Barbour, ed., *Western Man and Environmental Ethics* (Reading, Mass.: Addison-Wesley, 1973). See also Nash, *Wilderness and the American Mind,* 15–20. For a careful consideration of White's thesis in larger context see William Leiss, *The Domination of Nature* (New York: George Braziller, 1972), 29ff. Clearly the Bible conditions but does not determine the modern idea of the relation of humankind to nature. Religious conservatives argue that the Bible encourages not environmental despotism but stewardship: since nature is God's creation, humankind must treat it wisely. See, e.g., Francis A. Schaeffer, *Pollution and the Death of Man: The Christian View of Ecology* (Wheaton, Ill.: Tyndale House, 1973).
34. White, "Historical Roots," 29, 24–25, 25. The term *Judaism* is misleading, since Judaism per se did not emerge until the first century B.C.E.
35. Norman K. Gottwald, *The Hebrew Bible: A Socio-Literary Introduction* (Philadelphia: Fortress, 1985), 607. See also Hans-Georg Gadamer, *Truth and Method* (New York: Crossroad, 1988), 460–98.
36. Gottwald, *Tribes,* 701, 704.
37. Compare Gottwald, *Hebrew Bible,* esp. 137–41. Within the Bible, and even within single books, are historically and philosophically distinct elements. The Bible is a many-layered historical document containing motifs from as early as the twelfth century B.C.E. to treatises as late as the second century C.E. Gottwald's discussion of alternative paradigms employed in Old Testament study and exegesis is excellent. See also Claus Westermann, *Handbook to the Old Testament,* trans. and ed. Robert H. Boyd (Minneapolis: Augsburg, 1967). Westermann argues that the Pentateuch in some senses misleads us, since the sequential order—first the primeval history, second the patriarchal history, and finally the Exodus—disguises the fact that the individuals who gave it this form "did so with utmost care and wise restraint, so as not to cover up or efface the fact that a great number of independent traditions were involved in it" (15).

38. Nevertheless, the Hebrew God was still associated with rainfall. See Jeanne Kay, "Concepts of Nature in the Hebrew Bible," *Environmental Ethics* 10 (Winter 1988): 323, and Pss. 147.15–18.

39. John Passmore, *Man's Responsibility for Nature: Ecological Problems and Western Traditions* (New York: Charles Scribner's Sons, 1974), 7. Genesis per se was obviously not available to the people of the genesis; the book was their product.

40. Compare Kay, "Concepts of Nature." Kay reads the Bible "geosophically," as she describes it—that is, in terms of Iron Age and Near Eastern perspectives themselves set in the ecological context of Canaan. Such an approach "attempts to understand a culture's geographical beliefs in its own terms, rather than through an unflattering comparison with the researcher's own ethnocentric biases" (312). By so doing Kay believes that the prevailing interpretations of the Old Testament—either the stewardship model favored by religious fundamentalists or the despot model favored by environmentalists—are displaced by interpretations consistent with the actual belief system of the tribes of Yahweh. On her reading the Bible does not sanction human arrogance in regard to nature, but only refuses to worship it as divine.

41. Compare Gottwald, *Tribes,* 293–98.

42. Compare Gottwald, *Tribes,* 401f., and Schneidau, *Sacred Discontent,* 125. An ancient treaty between the Hittites and the Ugarites mentions the territory of the 'apiru as a place where stateless people were permitted to live. Also the term Hebrew may derive from 'eber (compare Gen. 10.21–25; 11.14–15), a term referring to the person, Eber, a distant ancestor of many Semitic people. Shem (Gen. 10.21) is the father of the children of Eber, that is all Hebrews, including those who became united as the nation of Israel. Compare Herbert G. May and Bruce M. Metzger, eds., *The New Oxford Annotated Bible: Revised Standard Version* (New York: Oxford University Press, 1973), 13, n. 11.10–32.

43. Gottwald, *Hebrew Bible,* 65.

44. Schneidau, *Sacred Discontent,* 28–29, 114. As Schneidau implies, the Israelites flourished for only a short while; the Northern Kingdom of Israel fell to the Assyrians in 721 B.C.E.

45. Frankfort et al., *Before Philosophy,* 241, 237.

46. Among other New Testament references to agriculture are the following: (1) herdsmen and their livestock: Matt. 18.12, 25.33; Luke 2.8, 15.4, 15.23, 15.29; Mark 5.11; (2) herdsmen and cultivators: Matt 9.37, 13.30; (3) basic functions of the farmer: Matt. 13.24–30, 21.28; Mark 4.26–29, 12.1; Luke 2.8, 13.7, 13.19; Rom. 11.17–18, 14.2; 1 Cor. 9.7; (4) specific tasks of the farmer: Matt. 6.26, 7.19, 13.24, 13.27–28, 13.30; Luke 12.18, 13,8, 13.15, 17.7.

47. *Oxford Annotated Bible,* 5, n. 4.1–26. See also Samuel Sandmel, ed.,

The New English Bible with the Apocrypha: Oxford Study Edition (New York: Oxford University Press, 1976), 4, n. 4.1–26.

48. Moshe Weinfeld, "Israelite Religion," in Seltzer, *Religions*, 96–121, is a useful study. The problems of research into the Israelite experience are enormous—our reconstructions must be understood as provisional. But any claim that the tribes of Yahweh were true nomads is difficult to reconcile with any conception of nomads as people who eternally wander. True nomads neither possess nor own land, and they are not compelled to defend "property."

49. See Gottwald, *Tribes*, 441ff., and Schneidau, *Sacred Discontent*, 119ff.

50. Schneidau, *Sacred Discontent*, 125.

51. Jesus also characterizes himself as a shepherd, as in John 10.11–12. And the tradition is venerable, since leaders were often associated with shepherds. The pharaonic regalia itself includes the shepherd's staff.

52. Whether Abraham is a person or an eponymous figure is debated, as is dating this phase of history. At least three time frames have been proposed; the most widely accepted is the Middle Bronze Age (c. 2000–1500 B.C.E.). During this period at least three types of nomadic-pastoralist can be identified in or around the Arabian desert: the true Bedouin tribe that traveled widely with its herd of camels in unsettled areas of sparse vegetation and rainfall (less than 4 inches a year); the semi-Bedouin that herded goats and sheep in areas of ecological transition (between the semiarid desert and land suited to cultivation) bordering more extensive human settlement with rainfall of 4 to ten inches a year; and the cattle herder who found grasslands (with sufficient rainfall to sustain graze), and ceased nomadic wandering for the settled life. Compare Robert Redfield, *The Primitive World and Its Transformations* (New York: Cornell University Press, 1953).

53. *Oxford Annotated Bible*, 1.

54. Weinfeld usefully elaborates that Yahweh is known not through mythological stories but through his actions set in the context of his relation to the tribes of Yahweh or the nation of Israel. "Mythology, here defined as storytelling about gods and their life, activities, and adventures, is inconceivable" since Yahweh is conceptualized as transcendent and single ("Israelite Religion," 97).

55. The E texts can be read as representing a preagricultural religious tradition, a religion-in-the-wilderness, where nature was sacred space. J was composed c. 960–930 B.C.E. and reflects the southern view of Judea; the oral traditions of this source were stabilized perhaps as early as the tenth century B.C.E. during the reign of Solomon. E, by contrast, was composed c. 900–850 B.C.E. and reflects a northern locale (Ephraim). According to Gottwald, the Elohist source "put special emphasis on early Israel as a religiously and ethically obligated community in treaty (or covenant)

with Yahweh. In the eyes of the E traditionists the covenant community of Israel was older and more fundamental than the political dynasty of David in Jerusalem or the more recently established northern kingdom. . . . In all events, the Elohist—less awed by governmental authority than the Yahwist—was fairly explicit in presenting criteria for defining Israel that transcended and criticized the current kingdom of Judah and Israel. The E document was apparently intended as a conscious corrective to the J document" (*Hebrew Bible,* 138). The E source can be interpreted as stretching back into the mists of an oral tradition that speak of a time when God revealed himself to humans-in-the-wilderness. So viewed, it represents a primitive survival of Paleolithic religion. However, there is a fundamental difference: Elohim is not a nature god but a God above nature.

56. Schneidau, *Sacred Discontent,* 128.

57. Also of interest is the gender conversion inherent in the change from the Magna Mater metaphor to Elohim. A conjecture that the conversion of god from female to male is rooted in the transition from hunting-gathering to farming is consistent with our study. But the transformation was not instantaneous, although the "official religion" of Israel might convey that impression. Weinfeld argues that cultic practices reflecting "pagan beliefs, especially beliefs connected with a divine power of fertility that was represented by the female characteristic of the deity," long prevailed, even to the point of religious syncretism ("Israelite Religion," 98). Stone points out that there is antipathy in the Hebrew Bible between male monotheists and goddess worshipers to the point that "the religion of the goddess as Asherah or Astarte continually rivaled the religion of the Hebrew Yaveh" ("Goddess Worship," 67). Compare, e.g., Judg. 2.13, 3.7, and 1 Sam. 7.3–4, 1 Kgs. 15.13, 2 Kgs. 21.7. Clearly, however, through the domestication of animals and grains nature slowly lost its feminine mystery and became a foe to be conquered; ecofeminists have argued that the West's relentless humanizing of nature is at least in part a consequence of conceptualizing god as male. See below, n. 58, and chap. 9 for further discussion.

58. Schneidau, *Sacred Discontent,* 142. Just as the early agriculturists experienced a new phenomenal field, so the desert altered perception. As Shepard argues, "If ideas have habitats in which they originate and prosper, then the desert edge might be called the home of Western thought" (*Nature and Madness,* 47). Frankfort concurs, arguing that tribes of Yahweh understandably conceptualized human experience as taking place outside nature: that was the price of freedom from domination. "For whoever rejects the complexities and mutual dependencies of agricultural society not only gains freedom but also loses the bond with the phenomenal world." (*Before Philosophy,* 247). Therein lies the grounds for the

intense Hebraic preoccupation with history—a concept foreign to mythic consciousness. As Shepard explains, "History is a collective memory of the past which denies the telluric dimension of place. History was the only way to keep myth while holding that the desert was no more than a stage. Eventually its authoritarian, masculinist, ascetic ideology would spread into the cities themselves, defeating the feminine mysteries associated with riverine and oasis agriculture, a victory for transcendence over the natural and indigenous" (58).

59. See also Job 38.4–41, Pss. 65.5–8, 104.1–4.

60. See also Gen. 4.17, where Cain is depicted as founder of a settled agricultural community, as verses 19–22 imply.

61. The P source gave Genesis its final form. The priestly writer was particularly concerned to revitalize the Sinai covenant and the unique constitution of the religious community of Israel. Gottwald explains that "the effect of joining J and E was to affirm the national political tone of J but to permeate and leaven it with the religious and ethical qualifications of E" (*Hebrew Bible*, 140). And because the northern kingdom had been destroyed, the E source is much more poorly preserved than J.

62. Idolatry was a common practice in ancient Near Eastern religions. Set in historic context, the Old Testament is the "queer duck," unusual in that it epitomizes an *aniconic* tradition and states the prohibition against idols at several places (Exod. 20.3–5, Deut. 5.7–9). Hebrew words for idols such as *'elilim* (meaning powerless ones) and *gillulim* (meaning pellets of dung) capture some of the contempt the Hebrews held for people that worshiped idols, especially the Babylonians (see, e.g., Isa. 40.18–20).

63. See Gottwald, *Hebrew Bible*, 328.

64. Schneidau, *Sacred Discontent*, 59.

65. Compare *New English Bible*, 2, n. 28.

66. Other passages reinforce this agriculturist viewpoint. The "Parable of the Farmer" (Isa. 28.23–29) implies that Yahweh's plan is manifest in the mundane activities of tilling and harvesting, and that indeed divine purpose is apparent in the farmer's savoir faire. This passage is not atypical, since most of the activities associated with agriculture assume figurative meaning for the Israelites. Their metaphors repeatedly reveal an agrarian outlook. Isaiah 21.10 (dealing with the fall of Babylon) suggests that the Israelites, "once trodden out and winnowed on the threshing-floor" (carried off into exile), can now return to the Promised Land. Later passages in the Old Testament reinforce and amplify these themes. Generally the settled Hebraic agriculturists regarded the wilderness as accursed. Deuteronomy 8.15 and Isa. 42.15 suggest that a wrathful God will punish sinful people by bringing drought. "I will lay waste the mountains and hills, and dry up all their herbage. I will turn the rivers into islands,

and dry up the pools." By contrast, a beneficent God brings forth water into the barren wilderness (Deut. 8.7; Isa. 35.1, 6, 43.20; see also Isa. 41.18–19, 32.15, on related themes).

67. Compare Harold Bloom, *Ruin the Sacred Truths: Poetry and Belief from the Bible to the Present* (Cambridge: Harvard University Press, 1989), 3.

68. Schneidau, *Sacred Discontent*, 154, 21.

69. James Shiel, *Greek Thought and the Rise of Christianity* (New York: Barnes and Noble, 1968), 7.

70. See Paul Feyerabend, *Farewell to Reason* (New York: Verso, 1987). Feyerabend questions the "triumph" of reason with his clear analysis of Xenophanes (c. 570–475 B.C.E.); while Xenophanes is often held up as an example of reason's victory over superstition, Xenophanes' own arguments cannot stand critical scrutiny (91–95). Feyerabend concludes by observing how a logocentric attitude (i.e., the assumed superiority of Reason over mythic consciousness) "destroyed Indian cultural achievements in the USA without so much as a glance in their direction" and is the same "attitude that is now destroying non-Western cultures under the guise of 'development'" (102).

71. See Philip J. Davis and Reuben Hersh, *The Mathematical Experience* (Boston: Houghton Mifflin, 1982), 322–30; Philip J. Davis and Reuben Hersh, *Descartes' Dream: The World According to Mathematics* (Boston: Houghton Mifflin, 1987), xv, 276–77; Nicholas Georgescu-Roegen, *The Entropy Law and the Economic Process* (Cambridge: Harvard University Press, 1971), esp. 79–82; Stephen Edelston Toulmin, *The Uses of Argument* (Cambridge University Press, 1958); and Gödel's proof.

72. For a related treatment see Eugene C. Hargrove, *Foundations of Environmental Ethics* (Englewood Cliffs, N.J.: Prentice Hall, 1989), 14–47.

73. Frankfort, *Before Philosophy*, 251.

74. G. S. Kirk, J. E. Raven, and M. Schofield, *The Presocratic Philosophers: A Critical History with a Selection of Texts*, 2d ed. (Cambridge: Cambridge University Press, 1983), 202.

75. Kirk, Raven, and Schofield, *Presocratic Philosophers*, 211.

76. Frankfort, *Before Philosophy*, 256.

77. Just as the early Greeks were refugees, so this event might be seen as the outcome of war. The Athenian League was formed in 471 B.C.E. to protect Attica and the Aegean from Persian invaders; the intellectual and political hegemony of Athens coincides almost precisely with this event.

78. For Socrates' place in Western civilization see A. E. Taylor, *Socrates* (Garden City, N.Y.: Doubleday Anchor, 1953); Karl Jaspers, *Socrates, Buddha, Confucius, Jesus: The Paradigmatic Individuals,* ed. Hannah Arendt, trans. Ralph Mannheim (New York: Harcourt, Brace, 1962); and Leonard Nelson, *Socratic Method and Critical Philosophy,* trans. Thomas K. Brown III (New York: Dover, 1965).

79. Socrates specifically, and Greek rationalism generally, can be understood as an intensification of the Neolithic movement toward explicit self-consciousness and linear thinking. Julian Jaynes argues that prehistoric people heard voices and had visions (activities of the right cerebral hemisphere) and acted on the basis of these events, whereas agricultural people began to cope with the conditions of existence through logic and reason (activities of the left cerebral hemisphere). See Julian Jaynes, *The Origin of Consciousness in the Breakdown of the Bicameral Mind* (Boston: Houghton Mifflin, 1976). There are several other theories of the origin of consciousness and no absolute vantage point from which to view any of them. See Curtis Smith, *Ancestral Voices* (Englewood Cliffs, N.J.: Prentice-Hall, 1985), for a biological theory of consciousness. Smith believes that a neural capacity for language was created before the emergence of language and its concomitant, consciousness. He also argues that the Cro-Magnon people (c. 75000 B.C.E.) first had this capability. Homo neanderthalensis was, according to Smith, prelinguistic and therefore preconscious, and thus doomed to extinction. Jaynes's theory that the operation of the linear-logical brain/consciousness originates in Greek rationalism is not necessarily incompatible with Smith's, since it presupposes an underlying genetic structure.

80. For further discussion see among many Dolores LaChapelle, *Earth Wisdom* (Silverton, Colo.: Finn Hill Arts, 1984), esp. chap. 9, and Michael E. Zimmerman, "Toward a Heideggerian *Ethos* for Radical Environmentalism," *Environmental Ethics* 5 (Summer 1983).

81. Hargrove, *Foundations of Environmental Ethics,* 21.

82. See *Timaeus* 28c–29b, 69b–c.

83. Compare Glacken, *Traces,* 46, and John Dewey, *Experience and Nature,* 2d ed. (New York: Dover, 1958). Dewey argues that the artisan was believed to draw out forms latent in nature. "The actualization in an organic body of the forms that are found in things constitutes mind as the end of nature. Their immediate possession and celebration constitutes consciousness, as far as the idea of consciousness is found in Greek thought" (92). See also Hargrove, *Foundations of Environmental Ethics,* 29–30, who notes that Plato, on observing the environmental consequences of deforestation (*Critias* 111 a–d), seems unconcerned. This attitude is likely a consequence of "the metaphysical perspective that he inherited from the pre-Socratics [specifically, Parmenides and Pythagoras]: the view that the natural world was an illusion and did not exist as experienced in any fundamental sense."

84. Shepard, *Tender Carnivore,* 239–40.

85. Ernst Mayr, *The Growth of Biological Thought: Diversity, Evolution, and Inheritance* (Cambridge: Harvard University Press, 1982), 87. This near definitive intellectual history of biology is an invaluable reference for

both historians and philosophers of science. Mayr emphasizes the contrast between Plato's and Aristotle's ideas. For Plato supernatural forms explain the regularity of animate nature and the realization of complex goals, whereas for Aristotle natural entities "act according to their own properties, and . . . all phenomena of nature are processes or the manifestations of processes. And since all processes have an end, he considered the study of ends as an essential component of the study of nature" (88). Mayr also points out that Aristotle anticipates the "why" questions asked by evolutionary biologists and recognizes, if imprecisely, that biological activity and structure find meaning only in context: that is, in adaptive significance (89).

86. Mayr argues that "Aristotle's outstanding characteristic was that he searched for causes" (*Biological Thought*, 88). Aristotle's causal syllogism is perhaps the definitive classical viewpoint on change in nature. If the Aristotelian paradigm is accepted, then the syllogism does allow change in nature to be comprehended, for the pivotal middle term of an Aristotelian syllogism is a cause. (See *Posterior Analytics* 2.94a.) Properly understood, natural objects were impelled to move from a merely potential level of being (e.g., the acorn) toward some final form (e.g., the mature oak) because of their nature. In spite of the contempt the modern mind holds for the Aristotelian syllogism, this kind of explanation works effectively apropos of biological phenomena. Mayr points out, "Aristotle's *eidos* is a teleonomic principle which performed in [his] . . . thinking precisely what the genetic program of the modern biologist performs" (88). Aristotle also developed a metaphysical level of explanation for change in nature by postulating the existence of an eternal unmoved mover who set the world in motion.

87. R. G. Collingwood, *Idea of Nature* (London: Oxford University Press, 1945), 3–4, 4.

88. Compare Collingwood, *Idea of Nature*, 7–15; and Glacken, *Traces*, esp. chap. 3, "Creating a Second Nature."

89. Glacken, *Traces*, 168.

90. This last stage will be too briefly described for some, but my objectives necessitate a narrow focus. Those who have indicted Christianity as the root of our ecologic crisis may feel that I have focused on relatively insignificant details in the evolution of the Hebrew-Christian outlook on nature and have thereby obfuscated its guilt. And Christians, certainly those of evangelical or fundamentalist persuasion, will find my analysis heretical. What must be recognized is that although Christianity grows out of a substratum of belief through faith in the reality of certain historic events, particularly the virgin birth and resurrection of Jesus of Nazareth, Christian theology grows out of Greek rationalism.

91. Taylor, *Socrates*, 133.

92. See Gen. 2.7: "Then the Lord God formed a man [Heb. *'ādām*] from the dust of the ground and breathed into his nostrils the breath of life. Thus the man became a living [Heb. *chayah*] soul [Heb. *nephesh*]." The Hebrews believed that human beings were formed from dust (a theory likely based on observation of bones uncovered in ancient tombs or crypts), and that the breath of God literally brought a human to life. But all living creatures were similarly created. The term *living* in Gen. 2.7 is the same as that used to characterize living animals (Gen. 1.20), thus undercutting any idea that for the Hebrews the soul was the essence of a person as distinct from the rest of creation. We therefore have no reason to think that the Greek concept of soul as *psyche*, itself adopted by the early Christians, was rooted in or anticipated by the Hebrew conception of soul as *nephesh*. See also Pss. 104.29–30, and Job 34.14–15.

93. Even the drama of the Reformation left the soul—in its most fundamental sense—unchanged; worldly success was permitted, even psychologically encouraged through the Reformation, but the goal remained eternal salvation.

94. The Greek term *aiōn* is distinct from the terms *chronos,* usually meaning time as a quantity, as in a little more or less time, and *kairos,* usually meaning time as a quality, as in the time for action. For the Greeks the passage of the weeks and years is either a mere repetition of the cycles of existence or the striving in time (appetition) of individuals to achieve universal and therefore perfect forms beyond time.

95. Charles M. Sherover, *The Human Experience of Time: The Development of Its Philosophic Meaning* (New York: New York University Press, 1975), 1. See Paul on the new covenant (2 Cor. 3.6–15); see also Matt. 26.28, Mark 14.24, and 1 Cor. 11.25. See Paul J. Achtemeier, ed., *Harper's Bible Dictionary* (San Francisco: Harper and Row, 1985), for a succinct summary of biblical conceptions of time.

96. J. L. Russell, "Time in Christian Thought," in J. T. Fraser, ed., *The Voices of Time: A Cooperative Survey of Man's Views of Time as Expressed by the Sciences and Humanities,* 2d ed. (Amherst: University of Massachusetts Press, 1981), 62, emphasis added. See also in the Old Testament, Gen. 1.1–2, Job 38.1–13, Pss. 90.2, 102.25–26, Prov. 8.22–29, Isa. 45.12, 18, 48.13, and 65.17–25. In the New Testament, see Matt. 13.24–30, 36–43, 49–50, 24.3–35, Mark 13.3–33, Luke 21.5–33, Col. 1.16–17, Heb. 1.10–12, 2 Peter 3.3–13, and Rev. 10.5–6.

97. Paul indicated the radical nature of this new beginning in First Corinthians, for Christianity flew in the face of conventional wisdom. "For Jews demand signs and Greeks seek wisdom, but we preach Christ crucified, a stumbling block to Jews and folly to Gentiles, but to those who are called, both Jews and Greeks, Christ the power of God and the wisdom of God. For the foolishness of God is wiser than men, and the weakness of God is

stronger than men" (1 Cor. 1.22–25). Paul recognized the paradoxes that vexed the Corinthians and attempted to meet the Corinthians' doubts by pointing to a dimension beyond time as ordinarily understood.

98. Russell, "Time in Christian Thought," 65.

99. Russell, "Time in Christian Thought," 66. Basically this viewpoint enframes all modernist views of history, as epitomized by Hegel.

100. The fact that Paul was a Greek convert to Christianity is more than an accident of history, for Greek philosophy (and the Greek language, for its power and precision opened the door for theological refinement) was central to his mission. There can be little wonder that ultimately Greek-speaking Gentiles, and not Hebrews, became the bulk of the converts to Christianity—for the conceptual linchpin of the New Testament was the Greek concept of the soul.

101. See, e.g., Lev. 23.10–18: "Speak to the Israelites in these words: When you enter the land which I give you, and you reap its harvest, you shall bring the first sheaf of your harvest to the priest." Then, after the seventh sabbath following, or fifty days, "you shall present to the Lord a grain offering from the new crop. You shall bring from your homes two loaves as a special gift . . . . They are the Lord's firstfruits."

102. Letter to the Hebrews (an anonymous treatise) continues in an argumentative vein, being not only "the longest sustained argument of any book in the Bible" but also "an elaborate proof of the pre-eminence of Christianity over Judaism" (*Oxford Annotated Bible*, 1455).

103. Collingwood, *Speculum Mentis*, 139.

104. Duerr, *Dreamtime*, 116–17, is especially clear.

105. José Ortega y Gasset, *Man and Crisis*, trans. Mildred Adams (New York: W. W. Norton, 1962), 135.

106. Ortega y Gasset, *Universal History*, 280.

107. Thomas Aquinas, *Summa Theologica*, trans. Fathers of the English Dominican Province, rev. Daniel J. Sullivan, in Robert Maynard Hutchins, ed., *Great Books of the Western World*, vol. 19 (Chicago: Encyclopedia Britannica, 1952), 526.

108. Russell, "Time in Christian Thought," 64.

Chapter 3.   The Alchemy of Modernism

1. Compare Leiss, *Domination of Nature*, 36ff., on the historical association of alchemy and early modern science. Leiss argues that the "dominance of nature" became the central theme of the modern age by the end of the seventeenth century. I am indebted to an anonymous reviewer for suggesting the relevance of Leiss's analysis to my study.

2. Here the shadow of Georgescu-Roegen's *Entropy Law* falls over the claims of either socialistic or capitalistic society to have engendered ma-

terial progress. That claim is true *only* upon the assumption that maximizing the waste-creating (entropy) process defines socioeconomic advance or improvement. See also Sahlins, *Stone Age Economics,* for a deconstructive anthropological approach to the idea that Homo sapiens is born a creature of virtually unlimited economic needs.

3. See Pete Gunter, "The Big Thicket: A Case Study in Attitudes toward Environment," in Blackstone, *Philosophy and Environmental Crisis,* for discussion of the term *man infinite.* The term *Lord Man,* a complementary concept, was coined by John Muir (see chap. 6, below).

4. Roland Barthes, *Mythology,* trans. Annette Lavers (New York: Hill and Wang, 1972), 99.

5. "Periodization" is a troublesome concept, and many find questionable the notion that the Middle Ages were succeeded by a Renaissance, a reawakening of culture and the arts. There are also problems inherent in the chronology of the Renaissance—often marked as commencing with the naming of Petrarch as the poet laureate of Rome (1341)—as well as its geography or locale. The term *Renaissance* was not used until the seventeenth century.

6. Glacken, *Traces,* 175.

7. See Hargrove, *Environmental Ethics,* 46, n. 31, concerning the association of symbolism and medieval realism.

8. Peasant farming economies spread slowly from the ancient Mediterranean theater to the Aegean (c. 6000 B.C.E) and finally the Baltic (c. 4000 B.C.E.). The reason is obvious, since domesticated cereals and animals came from the indigenous wild species of the Near East. Beyond the northern limits of the European deciduous forest, subsistence foraging economies remained the rule. Also see Edgar Anderson, *Plants, Man, and Life* (Berkeley: University of California Press, 1967), for an intriguing account of the advance of agriculture, and its effects on the natural landscape. Closely studied, Anderson argues, "the history of weeds is the history of man" (15).

9. Compare Perlin, *Forest Journey,* and Glacken, *Traces,* 171–351.

10. Sherwood forest was perhaps the most famous of these, providing refuge for Robin Hood—the legendary twelfth-century figure immortalized in William Langland's *Vision of William Concerning Piers the Plowman*—and his brigands from the sheriff of Nottingham. Many commentators observe that forested and other wilderness areas have served as refuge for groups resisting an entrenched political order. They are concerned that eradication of the hinterlands would eliminate the chance of overthrowing some Orwellian Big Brother. Once established in contemporary society, such an order might never be challenged since resistors would have no place to hide.

11. Collingwood, *Speculum Mentis,* 15–38. Collingwood's analysis of the

unity of the medieval mind is restricted to art, religion, and philosophy, but logic and history justify extension to politics and economics.

12. See chap. 1, n. 35, above. Also see David Tracy, *Plurality and Ambiguity: Hermeneutics, Religion, Hope* (San Francisco: Harper and Row, 1987). The meaning of a text, including a culture's classics and its most "sacred" texts, is not fixed but necessarily changes through time. A text whose meaning did not change in response to cultural circumstance would eventually be relegated to obscurity. During the late Middle Ages the meaning of the Bible—indeed, the very definition of Judeo-Christianity—can be seen as undergoing significant reinterpretation. Bacon, for example, looked to the Bible to ground his argument that the power of science could be used to create (in effect) Heaven on Earth.

13. For an overview of economic life in the Middle Ages see Robert L. Heilbroner, *The Making of Economic Society* (Englewood Cliffs, N.J.: Prentice-Hall, 1962); Henri Pirenne, *Economic and Social History of Medieval Europe,* trans. I. E. Clegg (New York: Harcourt, Brace and World, 1937); and George Clarke Sellery, *The Renaissance: Its Nature and Origins* (Madison: University of Wisconsin Press, 1950). I necessarily ignore such issues as the influence of the enclosure system, the monetization of local economies, and the Crusades on the economic elements of the Renaissance.

14. Perlin points out that extensive and sometimes ruinous deforestation occurred throughout the Old World. The Roman Empire, for example, was heavily financed by silver from Iberia, and during four hundred years of operating the smelting furnaces an estimated five hundred million trees, nearly seven thousand square miles of forest, were consumed (*Forest Journey,* 125f.).

15. Compare Glacken, *Traces,* esp. 312–13.

16. See Duerr, *Dreamtime,* and John H. Smith, *The Death of Classical Paganism* (New York: Charles Scribner's Sons, 1976). Duerr's discussion of sorcery and witchcraft is able. Smith contends that paganism never existed as a unified body of belief or organized practice and was largely a figment of the Christian imagination.

17. The Fall has traditionally been associated with the loss of humankind's dominion over nature. Modernism, I shall argue here, attempts to restore that power of control through science. But other alternatives exist. Compare Susan Power Bratton, "The Original Desert Solitaire: Early Christian Monasticism and Wilderness," *Environmental Ethics* 10 (Spring 1988): 31–53. By going into the wilderness (now free of the entangling vines of civilization), the monk was afforded opportunity to achieve moral progress—to rise above his fallen condition and achieve a prelapsarian purity. Bratton gives several examples of benign, even harmonious, rela-

tions between monks and wild nature. Antony (c. 250 C.E.) took refuge in the wilderness and came to believe that his love of place (*agapo*) was divinely inspired. Crucially, given the later importance of the argument from design, he believed that nature revealed God's work. "My book . . . is the nature of created things, and as often as I have a mind to read the words of God, it is at my hand" (35). Paul the Hermit sought to benefit rather than dominate the beasts. Wild animals were often seen as exemplifying Christian virtues, such as honesty and fidelity. Although demons appeared in the guise of wild animals, these were not signs that the animals themselves were evil, for they were possessed by Satan; they tested the believer. Bratton also suggests the possibility that primitive survivals from Paleolithic and early Neolithic times influenced the monks outlook on nature, since "the shaman has animal familiars or can transform himself into an animal. Only a god or someone with the element of the divine can command free roaming beasts" (46). See also Susan Power Bratton, "Oaks, Wolves and Love: Celtic Monks and Northern Forests," *Journal of Forest History* 33 (January 1989): 4–20.

18. Although Albert did engage in theology and philosophy, his student, Thomas Aquinas, surpasses him in these regards. But Albert's *Summas de Creaturis* (Handbook of doctrine concerning creatures), was the definitive compendium of natural history in its time.

19. Bratton, "Desert Solitaire," 52.

20. See Guido de Ruggiero, *The History of European Liberalism*, trans. R. G. Collingwood (Oxford: Oxford University Press, 1927).

21. Compare Marsilius of Padua, *Defensor Pacis*, trans. Alan Gewirth (Toronto: University of Toronto Press, 1980).

22. The important point, Leiss suggests in relation to the idea of the dominance of nature, "is that in different ages the same conceptual form is filled with a different content. Whatever may have been the understanding of it in earlier epochs, the modern version of this conception is firmly associated with the ongoing successes in science and technology" (*Domination of Nature*, 33). Mutatis mutandis, we may assert the same of the idea of wilderness.

23. The discovery and settlement of the New World also reinvigorated European life. Christopher Columbus's voyage had immediate consequences, since people and goods, animals and plants, passed in constant stream between the Old and New Worlds. Gold and silver flowed into the coffers of European monarchs, and a little wealth fueled a desire for more. Dreams of establishing a New Jerusalem were kindled, for here were lands apparently free of the evils of Europe. The New World also caught the imagination of European intellectuals, as reflected during the Romantic period in ideas such as Rousseau's noble savage. However disastrous

for the indigenous peoples of the Americas (see chap. 1, n. 12, above), the European humanization of the New World enormously enriched Western culture and engendered a dramatic socioeconomic expansion in Europe.

24. See Ernst Troeltsch, *Protestantism and Progress: The Significance of Protestantism for the Rise of the Modern World* (Philadelphia: Fortress, 1986), and Max Weber, *The Protestant Ethic and the Spirit of Capitalism,* trans. Talcott Parsons (New York: Charles Scribner's Sons, 1958). For a related study see David R. Williams, *Wilderness Lost: The Religious Origins of the American Mind* (Cranbury, N.J.: Susquehanna University Press, 1987).

25. Robert L. Heilbroner, *The Worldly Philosophers: The Lives, Times, and Ideas of the Great Economic Thinkers,* 4th ed. (New York: Simon and Schuster, 1972), 25.

26. The repression of intellectuals was not just a feature of Italian life. See Frederick Turner, *Natural Classicism: Essays on Literature and Science* (New York: Paragon, 1985), for an interesting account of intellectual repression during the English Renaissance.

27. Kuhn draws extensively on the history of astronomy and is presupposed as a background. See Thomas S. Kuhn, *The Structure of Scientific Revolutions,* 2d ed. (Chicago: University of Chicago Press, 1970); see also I. Bernard Cohen, *Revolution in Science* (Cambridge: Harvard University Press, 1985), and A. R. Hall, *The Scientific Revolution, 1500–1800: The Formation of the Modern Scientific Attitude* (Boston: Beacon, 1956). Kepler's system remains a part of the foundation of modern astronomy because of its mathematical nature, and is therefore more important than Copernicus's work—a nonmathematical, positional rearrangement of Ptolemaic theory.

28. Some heavy sledding is involved in understanding the idea of a paradigm shift and its many consequences. We must understand intellectual history not only as this relates to tracing the evolution of the idea of wilderness but also as it relates to the philosophy of science and to such other issues as perception. See Harold I. Brown, *Perception, Theory, and Commitment: The New Philosophy of Science* (Chicago: University of Chicago Press, 1977); Richard Rorty, *Philosophy and the Mirror of Nature* (Princeton: Princeton University Press, 1979); Georgescu-Roegen, *Entropy Law;* Kuhn, *Structure of Scientific Revolutions;* and Gary Gutting, ed., *Paradigms and Revolutions: Appraisals and Applications of Thomas Kuhn's Philosophy of Science* (Notre Dame, Ind.: University of Notre Dame Press, 1980).

29. See chap. 2, n. 86, above.

30. See among others Lewis Mumford, *The Myth of the Machine: The Pentagon of Power* (New York: Harcourt Brace Jovanovich, 1964); J. D.

Bernal, *The Scientific and Industrial Revolutions,* vol. 2 of *Science in History;* and Collingwood, *Idea of Nature.*

31. Cited in Mumford, *Myth of the Machine,* 86.

32. The untenability of mechanistic-materialism remained concealed until the so-called new physics (quantum theory, the principle of indeterminacy) destroyed its ontological underpinnings. See chap. 10, below. But there was an almost immediate response to scientific materialism and mechanism, and we shall discuss these critical reactions in chap. 4.

33. Collingwood, *Idea of Nature,* 103. See also Stillman Drake, *Galileo* (New York: Oxford University Press, 1980), and Drake, "Galileo Galilei," in Paul Edwards, ed., *The Encyclopedia of Philosophy,* vol. 3 (New York: Macmillan, 1967).

34. The problematic nature of this claim is confirmed by Galileo's difficulties. As Paul Feyerabend explains in *Against Method,* rev. ed. (New York: Verso, 1988), Galileo's observations were constituted within a new and highly abstract observation language that itself called for justification (67–79). Furthermore, his observations were problematic, since his telescope presented "evidence" that controverted his own observations (89–106). See also Feyerabend, *Farewell to Reason.* Astronomers "are entirely safe when saying that a model has predictive advantages over another model, but they get into trouble when asserting that it is therefore a faithful image of reality. Or, more generally: the fact that a model works does not by itself show that reality is structured like the model" (*Farewell to Reason,* 250).

35. This is one reason why so-called big science is so enormously expensive; space telescopes and super-colliders are costly.

36. Compare Leiss, *Domination of Nature,* 76.

37. See Dewey, *Experience and Nature.* Galileo commits what Dewey calls "the philosophic fallacy," whereby the modern mind distinguishes between primary experiences and the abstractions of scientific thought, and then relegates the primary experiences to subjective oblivion—that is, labels them as noncognitive experience. Dewey grants that primary experiences are often vague but argues that they are not, therefore, unimportant, entirely subjective, and capricious. They are genuine traits of nature, and "unless there is a breach of historic and natural continuity, cognitive experience must originate within that of a non-cognitive sort." Further, Dewey contends, "it is literally impossible to exclude that context of non-cognitive but experienced subject-matter which gives what is *known* its import" (23). For a related but more complicated analysis see Alfred North Whitehead, *Science and the Modern World* (New York: Free Press, 1967), esp. chap. 5. For a near definitive but extraordinarily intricate analysis see Whitehead, *Process and Reality: Corrected*

Edition, ed. David Ray Griffin and Donald W. Sherburne (New York: Free Press, 1978), esp. chap. 2. See also Leiss, *Domination of Nature,* 135 ff. He suggests that since the scientific revolution there have been "two worlds of nature: intuited nature (*lebensweltliche Natur*) and scientific nature (*wissenschaftliche Natur*), the experienced nature of everyday life and the abstract-universal, mathematized nature of the physical sciences" (135–36).

38. Although the distinction between primary and secondary qualities is often attributed to the British empiricist John Locke, this paradigmatic fundamental is Galileo's, a position developed in his work of 1623, *Il saggiatore* (The assayer).

39. See among others Rorty, *Mirror of Nature,* esp. 357–94; Feyerabend, *Farewell to Reason,* 198–99; and Duerr, *Dreamtime,* 125–33, for critiques of this metaphysical position.

40. Ignoring the implicit substantialist ontology, such a dichotomization illustrates the misuse of language, for the emotive nuances of the term *secondary,* as compared to *primary,* subtly but undeniably influence the mind. Duerr points out that within a scientific laboratory there is a progressive " 'demythologizing' of reality" that is then accepted arbitrarily as "*naked* reality," the truth. Yet in that view of reality occurs the enormous paradox that "reality has no colour, no voice, no hearing" (*Dreamtime,* 114). So-called primary qualities are not more real than secondary qualities but are in fact phenomenal qualities (sensa) that can be measured and thereby subsumed within a framework for inquiry known as classical science. A metaphysical distinction between primary and secondary qualities, though useful, makes secondary qualities incommensurable with the assumed framework of inquiry, and therefore they become subjective.

41. Don Ihde, *Technics and Praxis* (Dordrecht: D. Reidel, 1979), 21–23.

42. See Brown, *Perception, Theory, and Commitment;* Norwood Russell Hanson, *Observation and Explanation: A Guide to Philosophy of Science* (New York: Harper and Row, 1971); and Hanson, *Patterns of Discovery: An Inquiry into the Conceptual Foundations of Science* (London: Cambridge University Press, 1969), for relevant discussion.

43. Galileo Galilei, *Il saggiatore,* cited in Collingwood, *Idea of Nature,* 102.

44. Compare Drake, "Galileo," 266. Here we can only touch on complicated issues. From a contemporary vantage point (post-*Principia Mathematica*), a position that distinguishes mathematical from syllogistical reason is untenable, as is Galileo's claim that mathematical (or geometrical) inquiry provides some absolute vantage point on nature. Mathematical rigor is essential to scientific inquiry (see, e.g., Whitehead, *Science and the Modern World*), but no defensible claim can be made that any one system of mathematical organization is absolute.

45. Compare Galileo Galilei, *Dialogues Concerning Two New Sciences,*

trans. Henry Crew and Alfonso de Salvio, in Hutchins, *Great Books,* vol. 28. Galileo emphasized the revolutionary nature of his new science by observing that "there is, in nature, perhaps nothing older than motion, concerning which the books written by philosophers are neither few nor small; nevertheless, I have discovered by experiment some properties of it which are worth knowing and which have not hitherto been either observed or demonstrated" (197).

46. Glacken, *Traces,* 376. Francis Bacon developed these distinctions (between the argument from design and final cause, and efficient cause as the vehicle for understanding natural motion) in a more detailed and creative manner.

47. See Bertolt Brecht, *Galileo,* English version by Charles Laughton (New York: Grove, 1966). Brecht's dramatic fiction, read in conjunction with Feyerabend's analysis, rounds out the reconstruction of Galileo's significance.

48. Compare Glacken, *Traces,* 461–97; see also Leiss, *Domination of Nature,* 45–71.

49. Leiss, *Domination of Nature,* 71.

50. Compare Loren Eiseley, *The Man Who Saw through Time* (New York: Charles Scribner's Sons, 1961), 14.

51. Francis Bacon, *The New Organon and Related Writings,* ed. F. H. Anderson (Indianapolis: Bobbs-Merrill, 1960), 3–4. Unless otherwise noted, pagination is from this edition.

52. Bacon, *New Organon,* 118.

53. Hans-Georg Gadamer, "On the Scope and Function of Hermeneutical Reflection," in Brice R. Wachterhauser, ed., *Hermeneutics and Modern Philosophy* (Albany: State University of New York Press, 1986), 292.

54. Eiseley, *Man Who Saw through Time,* 14.

55. Passmore, *Responsibility for Nature,* 19. Compare Leiss, *Domination of Nature.* "In [Francis] Bacon's view religion and science were engaged in a mutual effort to compensate for the damage incurred as a result of the expulsion from Paradise: 'For man by the fall fell at the same time from his state of innocency and from his dominion over creation. Both of these losses however can even in this life be in some part repaired; the former by religion and faith, the latter by arts and sciences' " (49).

56. Bacon, *New Organon,* 3, 15, 7. There is an inconsistency between Gen. 1.28, where Yahweh named the beasts, and Gen. 2.19, where he brings them before Adam "to see what he would call them; and whatever the man called every living creature, that was its name." Although Adam's naming of the animals was Bacon's favorite biblical allusion to the putative power of humankind over nature, he also cautioned that arrogance led Adam to judge (to name for himself) what was good and evil—which was the prerogative of God alone. As Leiss points out, only by separating

natural knowledge (science) from moral knowledge could Bacon alleviate suspicion that science undercut either religious authority or faith. "This clear separation of natural knowledge and moral knowledge gradually became a cardinal principle of modern thought: it echoes in the fashionable contemporary distinction between 'facts' and 'values,' according to which questions of values constitute a unique discourse outside the scope of 'scientific' knowledge" (*Domination of Nature*, 52).

57. Passmore, *Responsibility for Nature*, 19.

58. Glacken, *Traces*, 474.

59. Passmore, *Responsibility for Nature*, 18–19.

60. Eiseley, *Man Who Saw through Time*, 63. This issue is central to what is now called the two cultures, the sciences and the humanities. Bacon, with his usual acumen, was at least aware of a yawning gulf, if imprecise in his description. "Let there be therefore (and may it be for the benefit of both) two streams and two dispensations of knowledge, and in like manner two tribes or kindreds of students in philosophy—tribes not hostile or alien to each other, but bound together by mutual services; let there in short be one method for the cultivation, another for the invention, of knowledge" (*New Organon*, 36).

61. Bacon, *New Organon*, 15.

62. Sir Francis Bacon, *Advancement of Learning, Novum Organum, New Atlantis*, in Hutchins, *Great Books*, 30:48. Bacon termed the knowledge of nature as "radius directus" and the knowledge of God as "radius refractus."

63. Leiss, *Domination of Nature*, 53. See also n. 17, above.

64. The critical literature is voluminous. See among many Martin Heidegger, *The Question Concerning Technology and Other Essays*, trans. William Lovitt (New York: Harper and Row, 1977); Jacques Ellul, *The Technological Society*, trans. John Wilkinson (New York: Alfred A. Knopf, 1964); and Frederick Ferré, *Philosophy of Technology* (Englewood Cliffs, N.J.: Prentice Hall, 1988).

65. Compare Collingwood, *Idea of Nature*, 100–101. Judged solely in terms of his influence on the course of philosophy, Descartes exceeds either Bacon or Galileo in importance. As Galileo vis-à-vis modern science, so Descartes has been called the father of modern philosophy, since he virtually frames the epistemological and metaphysical issues around which it revolves.

66. Bertrand Russell, *A History of Western Philosophy* (New York: Simon and Schuster, 1945), 558.

67. Leiss, *Domination of Nature*, 21.

68. René Descartes, *Rules for the Direction of Mind, Discourse on the Method, Meditations on First Philosophy, Objections against the Medi-*

tations and Replies, The Geometry, in Hutchins, *Great Books,* 31:61, emphasis added. All trans. Elizabeth S. Haldane and G. R. T. Ross, except *The Geometry,* trans. David Eugene Smith and Marcia L. Latham.

69. Descartes, *Rules for the Direction of Mind,* 3.

70. Descartes also furthered Galileo's project to mathematize the knowledge of nature, aggressively extending the implications of mathematical inquiry for physics. Cartesian coordinate geometry (although not entirely original with Descartes) was a method of precisely describing the motion of physical objects relative to a system of coordinates (the x, y, and z axes). Such a method guaranteed that the commitment to one physics might be realized, for the motion of heavenly and earthly bodies could be quantitatively depicted in the same fashion. Physical change in the new science was no longer a matter of quality but one of demonstrable position.

71. Bernard Cohen observes in *Revolution in Science* that "Descartes's goal of reducing all animal (and human) functions to machine-like actions was perhaps his boldest innovation in the sciences." The effect was revolutionary, since "in time his reductionist principles of biology came to dominate much of modern physiology" (157). Ernst Mayr observes that perhaps no one "contributed more to the spread of the mechanistic world picture than the philosopher René Descartes" (*Biological Thought,* 97).

72. Descartes, *Rules for the Direction of Mind,* 60.

73. The mechanistic program for biology was an abject failure. Mayr argues that "like Plato before him, Descartes demonstrated by the failure of his method that one cannot solve biological problems through mathematical reasoning" (*Biological Thought,* 98). The Cartesian picture of the living world as nothing more than inanimate-matter-in-motion has "proven to be quite erroneous," a "millstone around the neck of biology, the effects of which . . . have carried through to the end of the nineteenth century" (97).

74. Among the many critiques of the insufficiencies of Cartesian dualism see Max Scheler, *Man's Place in Nature,* trans. Hans Meyerhoff (New York: Noonday, 1961); Dewey, *Experience and Nature;* and Whitehead, *Science and the Modern World.*

75. Russell, *History of Western Philosophy,* 561.

76. Scheler, *Man's Place in Nature,* 72.

77. Passmore, *Responsibility for Nature,* 21, 22–23.

78. A detailed account of similarities and differences between Newton and his contemporaries can be found in Carolyn Merchant, *The Death of Nature: Women, Ecology, and the Scientific Revolution* (New York: Harper and Row, 1980), 275 ff.

79. Compare Brown, *Perception, Theory, and Commitment,* 95, and Cohen, *Revolution in Science,* 174–75. Mayr points out that the *Principia* had

an almost immediate and pernicious effect on biology, even though a few simple experiments would have immediately refuted the mechanistic approach (*Biological Thought*, 96).

80. Sir Isaac Newton, *Mathematical Principles of Natural Philosophy,* trans. Andrew Motte, rev. Florian Cajori, in Hutchins, *Great Books,* 34:1, 1–2. Of particular interest is Newton's admission that he cannot derive all phenomena of nature by the method he proposes, while maintaining in principle the faith that such a derivation could ultimately be accomplished. Newton thus encountered the same problem that has always brought Parmenideanism to its knees: the Heraclitean flux, the moving river of life. Of course, we can envision nature as a machine functioning with clocklike regularity. But as Merchant observes, the problem is still that of "successfully abstracting the form or structure of reality from the tangled web of its physical, material, environmental context. Structures are in fact not independent of their contexts . . . but integrally tied to them" (*Death of Nature,* 230). Just as Plato, and then Descartes, so Newton himself had been forced to admit that the complexity of things in the world inhibits analysis into simple elements, however much we desire it. As our contemporary, J. B. S. Haldane observes, nature is not only queer, but queerer than it seems.

81. Ortega y Gasset, *Idea of Principle,* 40.

82. Cohen, *Revolution in Science,* 174.

83. Compare, e.g., Cohen, *Revolution in Science,* 267.

84. Heilbroner, *Economic Society,* 75.

85. Sahlins, *Stone Age Economics,* 39.

86. Adam Smith, *An Inquiry into the Nature and Causes of the Wealth of Nations,* in Hutchins, *Great Books,* 39:1. Smith's inquiry, while ostensibly Newtonian and thus an inquiry into *the causes* of the wealth of nations, rests on false premises, dubious assumptions, and logical fallacies. These include the premise that life in the state of nature was nasty, brutish, and short, the assumption that the Newtonian model for physical science was appropriate for understanding the human world, and *ad baculum* and *ad populum* fallacies. His ad baculum plays on the fear that even civilized people might resort to barbaric behavior under conditions of poverty. His ad populum trades on the premise that everyone recognizes that more is always better than less; only a fool could doubt the invidious comparison of savage and civil society. Or an anthropologist. For further discussion of underlying philosophical and anthropological issues see Georgescu-Roegen, *Entropy Law,* and Sahlins, *Stone Age Economics.*

87. In addition to armchair anthropology, Smith ignored facts of life in his own society, such as the cholera that periodically decimated the populace, and the choking poverty of eighteenth-century European society (so powerfully disclosed in William Blake's poetry: "Is this a holy thing to

see,/In a rich and fruitful land,/Babes reduced to misery,/Fed with cold and usurious hand?").

88. Smith, *Wealth of Nations*, 1.
89. Compare Bennett, *Ecological Transition*, 42–43. Only by making what Bennett terms the "cognitive-symbolic step" is environment transformed into "natural resource." On the other end of the production-consumption cycle are "economic goods," the ultimate goal for which the natural resource is destined. But these categories, too, are a cultural product. That is, economic goods and natural resources are not naturally given but culturally defined. For example, crude oil is a natural resource *only* within the context of industrial society, becoming black gold through transmutation into gasoline, plastics, fertilizers, and other petrochemicals. Thus, as Bennett observes, "the output end of the basic human ecological process has an open door, an invitation to 'blue sky' energy [matter-energy] transformation, provided that the technology is up to it" (43).
90. Georgescu-Roegen, *Entropy Law*, 18.
91. See chap. 9, below, for further discussion. Re cost-benefit analysis see *Ekistics: The Problems and Science of Human Settlements* 46 (May–June 1979); this issue is dedicated to an analysis of the inadequacies of cost-benefit analysis.
92. Compare Leiss, *Domination of Nature*, 182–83.
93. Compare Cohen, *Revolution in Science*, 146–47.
94. Merchant, *Death of Nature*, 185.
95. Merchant, *Death of Nature*, 190. Merchant offers a compelling illustration of the sculpture entitled "Nature Reveals Herself" by Louis-Ernest Barrias (191). Leiss notes that "the psychological dynamic of mastery over nature is still discernible . . . in Bacon's language . . . . [I]t displays strong overtones of aggression (including the sexual aggression connected with the feminine gender of the noun and the use of 'her' as the pronoun): 'hounding,' 'vexing,' and 'subduing' nature. This legacy and the psychological complex which inspired it is no longer visibly present in the references to the mastery of nature found in modern social theory" (*Dominance of Nature*, 60). See also chap. 2, n. 57, above, and chap. 4, n. 18, and chap. 9, below.
96. Leiss, *Domination of Nature*, 183.
97. Merchant, *Death of Nature*, 2.

Chapter 4. Wild Nature

1. See Paul Shepard, *Man in the Landscape: A Historic View of the Esthetics of Nature* (New York: Alfred A. Knopf, 1967), and Hargrove, *Environmental Ethics*, 77–107.
2. The validity of this boundary can be questioned. See Duerr, *Dreamtime*,

esp. chap. 12. Duerr argues that crossing the divide between nature simpliciter and wild nature is essential to the health of scientific inquiry.
Quantum theory, which flows out of Planck's discoveries that energy was
quantized, and that there was a least quantum (the Planck constant, h),
bears meaningfully on questioning the ontological distinction between
poetic nature and *scientific nature.* See J. Baird Callicott, "The Metaphysical Implications of Ecology," *Environmental Ethics* 8 (Winter 1986),
and Michael Zimmerman, "Quantum Theory, Intrinsic Value, and Panentheism," *Environmental Ethics* 10 (Spring 1988); see also chap. 3, n. 37,
above, and chap. 10, below.

3. Whitehead's *Science and the Modern World* remains the best introduction to the philosophical side of this paradigmatic confrontation. Merchant's *Death of Nature* is an able historical study that details the triumph of mechanistic materialism over earlier organic ideas of nature and
explores contemporary organicism. The most accessible scientific treatment for nonspecialists is Prigogine's *Order Out of Chaos,* an empirically
grounded study animated by close attention to philosophical issues (Ilya
Prigogine and Isabelle Stengers, *Order Out of Chaos: Man's New Dialogue with Nature* [New York: Bantam, 1984]). Social scientists will find
Georgescu-Roegen's *Entropy Law* a challenging but penetrating treatment apropos of economics.

4. Compare Glacken, *Traces,* chap. 8, "Physico-Theology: Deeper Understandings of the Earth as a Habitable Planet." See also Mayr, *Biological Thought,* esp. chap. 2, "The Place of Biology in the Sciences and
Its Conceptual Structure." Mayr argues that historians and philosophers
of science have displayed an "extraordinary ignorance when discussing
methods other than the experimental one" of classical science (30). In
consequence the history and philosophy of biology is poorly understood,
especially its essential differences in subject-matter and methods from the
physical sciences.

5. By the twentieth century this critical stream became a raging torrent.
This is most pointed in the works of Martin Heidegger (e.g., *Question
Concerning Technology,* and *Poetry, Language, Thought*), Ortega y Gasset (*Man and Crisis, Revolt of the Masses,* and *The Idea of Principle*),
and Hans-Georg Gadamer (*Truth and Method*). Rorty (see *Mirror of
Nature*) identifies this stream of reaction as "edifying philosophy," that
is, a philosophy that runs counter to the world in force (Modernism) and
is therefore inherently subversive. "Systematic philosophy," which has
dominated conventional wisdom, is that which reinforces the prevailing
worldview.

6. Part of the wonder of scientific method is that people of ordinary intellect, who have had no hand in creating science, can employ its methods
and produce results. Scientists often lack knowledge of the history of

science, a circumstance rooted in such factors as the so-called proliferation of knowledge and the structuring of undergraduate education around specialized tracks of study. The consequences, as Einstein, Whitehead, Georgescu-Roegen, and many others have observed, can be devastating, especially among those—such as economists—who, once removed from the study of the natural world, slavishly emulate the methods of science. The technician—scientist manqué—is the prototype of the modern educated person.

7. Kepler believed the inclination of the earth on its axis (a feature that makes the planet habitable) to be evidence of cosmic design. Newton, in contrast, explicitly denied Kepler's interpretation of the earth's inclination but found evidence of God's presence in the orderly motions of celestial bodies.

8. Compare Mayr, *Biological Thought*, 162. See also Donald Worster, *Nature's Economy: The Roots of Ecology* (San Francisco: Sierra Club, 1977), an essential text for those studying the history of ecology, and Glacken, *Traces*.

9. See John Passmore, "More, Henry," in *The Encyclopedia of Philosophy*, vol. 5. More also had a discernible influence on Newton, a fellow member of the Cambridge group, and Newton's ultimate appeal to final cause probably reflected this influence.

10. Glacken's and Worster's interpretation of Ray are somewhat at odds. Glacken interprets him as adopting an organismic model in lieu of the mechanical model, while Worster argues that Ray struck a compromise. Worster finds in Ray's adaptation of More's idea of an inner "plastic nature" a "clear anticipation of Henri Bergson's *élan vital*" (*Nature's Economy*, 43).

11. Ray, *Wisdom of God*, cited in Glacken, *Traces*, 421.

12. Glacken, *Traces*, 421. Ray's work inspired the Reverend William Derham, whose work *Physico-Theology* is, Glacken notes, in some ways "a more exhaustive and richer work" (*Traces*, 421). Natural theology died on the Continent before the end of the eighteenth century but flowered in England well into the nineteenth century through Paley and his works, *Natural Theology* (1803) and the *Bridgewater Treatises* (1832–40). Darwin's association with the natural theologians of his day had much to do with the structure of his arguments in the *Origin of Species* (Mayr, *Biological Thought*, 104f., 394ff.).

13. Worster, *Nature's Economy*, 2.

14. White was not consistent in this belief, since he argued that certain noxious pests might be eliminated by the naturalist, thus lending a hand to divine providence and benefiting nature's own humane purposes.

15. Publius Vergilius Maro, 70–19 B.C.E., was himself following in an ancient tradition of Theocritus (c. 270 B.C.E.) and Psalm 104. This line is virtu-

ally unbroken through contemporary times, with writers such as Louis Bromfield (*Malabar Farm*) and John Graves (*Hard Scrabble*) yet singing praises of the bucolic life.

16. Worster, *Nature's Economy*, 10.

17. Linnaeus, "The Oeconomy of Nature," cited in Worster, *Nature's Economy*, 36. Such expressions as "for the sake of man" and "subservient to his use" reveal both an androcentric and a homocentric orientation.

18. Worster, *Nature's Economy*, 52. See also Susan Griffin, *Woman and Nature: The Roaring Inside Her* (New York: Harper and Row, 1978). Griffin's study, in the context of this study, attempts to document the destruction of the Magna Mater mythology before the advancing front of Modernism. She argues that the subjugation of both nature and woman springs from a common patriarchal core (see esp. 3–91). The section on Linnaeus (146–47) vividly contrasts his patriarchal quest to reestablish domination of nature through naming and an aesthetic (female) view of nature.

19. Actually, as Mayr points out, such events in the second half of the eighteenth century as "the earthquake of Lisbon, the horrors of the French Revolution, and the realization of the intensity of the struggle for existence" undermined the optimistic worldview based on the argument from design (*Biological Thought*, 105). These events, having little to do with the advance of science, were more an existential than an intellectual refutation of natural theology.

20. See Loren Eiseley, *Darwin's Century: Evolution and the Men Who Discovered It* (New York: Doubleday, 1961), for an account of independently developing yet converging advances in nineteenth-century geology, paleontology, and biology. Darwin's hypothesis effectively combined these developments in an evolutionary paradigm.

21. Compare Mayr, *Biological Thought*, 402. See also Richard Dawkins, *The Blind Watchmaker: Why the Evidence of Evolution Reveals a Universe without Design* (New York: W. W. Norton, 1986).

22. The implied distinction is between classical and contemporary process-relational theology.

23. Charles Darwin, *The Origin of Species by Means of Natural Selection, The Descent of Man and Selection in Relation to Sex,* in Hutchins, *Great Books,* 49:590. Darwin wrote in his *Autobiography* that "the mystery of the beginning of all things is insoluble to us, and I for one must be content to remain an agnostic" (cited in Mayr, *Biological Thought*, 402).

24. See Glacken, *Traces,* and L. Robert Stevens, *Charles Darwin* (Boston: Twayne, 1978), 133–34.

25. Part 2 of Mayr's *Biological Thought,* entitled "Evolution," is enormously helpful in grappling with the evolutionary paradigm. He concludes that "evolutionary thinking is no longer restricted to biology, and there is no

field of human endeavor with a historical component that has not adapted evolutionary thinking and evolutionary methodology. . . . Evolutionary thinking is indispensable in any subject in which a change in the time dimension occurs" (627). The implications of the second law also bear profoundly on evolutionary thought; see Prigogine, *Order Out of Chaos*.

26. George Marsh, *The Earth as Modified by Human Action* (New York: Scribner, Armstrong, 1874), iii. This volume is an edited reprint of *Man and Nature* (1863).

27. Marsh, *Earth as Modified by Human Action*, 643–44.

28. Darwin was wide of the mark in some ways; for example, since he was ignorant of genetics, he lacked a satisfactory account of the process by which favorable variation in the struggle for survival might be passed on to succeeding generations.

29. Worster, *Nature's Economy*, 63.

30. Thomas Robert Malthus (1766–1834) has been a favorite whipping boy of contemporary pro-growth advocates. True enough, Malthus was oblivious to the short-term ability of industrial technology (particularly as applied in agriculture) to outrun population. What the anti-Malthusians forget is that nothing evades the second law of thermodynamics.

31. Glacken, *Traces*, 427. See also Mayr, *Biological Thought*, 120–22.

32. Glacken argues that "modern ecological theory, so important in our attitudes toward nature and man's interferences with it, owes its origin to the design argument: The wisdom of the Creator is self-evident, everything in the creation is interrelated, no living thing is useless, and all are related one to the other" (*Traces*, 423). There are, of course, antecedents to physico-theology.

33. Ernst Mayr, *Toward a New Philosophy of Biology: Observations of an Evolutionist* (Cambridge: Harvard University Press, 1988), 60.

34. Prigogine, *Order Out of Chaos*, 292, 291.

35. Compare Nash, *Wilderness and the American Mind*, 44f., and Evernden, *Natural Alien*, 29–34.

36. Nash, *Wilderness and the American Mind*, 47.

37. See Hargrove, *Environmental Ethics*, 48–75, for discussion of attitudes concerning land use and property.

38. Thomas Burnet, *The Sacred Theory of the Earth* (London: Centaur, 1965), 109–10. Burnet placed considerable emphasis on the importance of an "actual view" of the mountains, "for the sight of those wild, vast and indigested heaps of Stones and Earth, did so deeply strike my fancy, that I was not easie till I could give my self some tolerable account how that confusion came in Nature" (110).

39. A consistent neglect of atheism is the reality that Western culture is almost incomprehensible apart from its Judeo-Christian backdrop. See Northrop Frye, *The Great Code: The Bible and Literature* (New York: Harcourt

Brace Jovanovich, 1981). Furthermore, without the context of belief provided by Judeo-Christianity, it is unlikely that the scientific revolution could have occurred. See David C. Lindberg and Ronald L. Numbers, *God and Nature: Historical Essays on the Encounter between Christianity and Science* (Berkeley: University of California Press, 1986).

40. M. H. Abrams, *Natural Supernaturalism: Tradition and Revolution in Romantic Literature* (New York: W. W. Norton, 1971), 68. For an account of Judeo-Christian–inspired parallels between Bacon and Wordsworth, see 59–63. Bacon, as we have seen, believed that the promised millennium would come through the power of science. Wordsworth believed that the path to recovery from the Fall followed poetic imagination rather than scientific understanding.

41. See Whitehead, *Science and the Modern World;* Maurice Mandelbaum, *History, Man, and Reason: A Study in Nineteenth-Century Thought* (Baltimore: Johns Hopkins University Press, 1971); and Allan Megill, *Prophets of Extremity: Nietzsche, Heidegger, Foucault, Derrida* (Berkeley: University of California Press, 1985).

42. Whitehead, *Science and the Modern World,* 87.

43. Evernden, *Natural Alien,* 32.

44. Mandelbaum, *History, Man, and Reason,* 350.

45. Compare Megill, *Prophets of Extremity.*

46. Whitehead "appreciated the spirit of the Romantic poets," Pete Gunter explains, "because they had taught him the concept of nature cannot be divorced from aesthetic values, and that these values are for the most part immediately derived from the organic wholeness of the natural world" (Pete A. Y. Gunter and Jack R. Sibley, eds., *Process Philosophy: Basic Writings* [Washington, D.C.: University Press of America, 1978], 486). It is from the Romantic poets that Whitehead ultimately found his way to his belief that the order which exists in nature is the consequence of aesthetic order—a metaphysics of feeling.

47. To lie, for example, would be to universalize falsehood, a move that destroys any rational basis for ethical judgment. Similarly, to steal would undercut any rational basis for social order. Accordingly, Kant believed that the categorical imperative preserved both the ethical heritage of Judeo-Christianity (the golden rule) and freedom for the human soul, and thereby responsibility.

48. Immanuel Kant, *The Critique of Pure Reason, The Critique of Practical Reason and Other Ethical Treatises, The Critique of Judgement,* in Hutchins, *Great Books,* 42:360–61. See Erazim Kohák, *The Embers and the Stars: A Philosophical Inquiry into the Moral Sense of Nature* (Chicago: University of Chicago Press, 1984), 226, n. 6. Kohák points out that Kant, who personifies the "post-Galilean hypothetico-deductive approach," contradicts the verdict of his own scholarship by appealing to the

embers and stars. See also Errol E. Harris, *The Reality of Time* (Albany: State University of New York Press, 1988), 96–102. Harris argues that only because we are in time (the lived body) can we know nature. Furthermore, as Prigogine and C. F. von Weizsäcker argue, once we recognize the inescapable reality of time, then we must also recognize that the second law is intrinsically involved in accounting for the emergence of sentient order out of chaos. See C. F. von Weizsäcker, *The History of Nature*, trans. Fred D. Wieck (Chicago: University of Chicago Press, 1949).

49. Ernst Mayr and many others have recognized that there are many Kants and that the Kant of the first and second critiques is not the Kant of the third. This is not the mark of a fatal inconsistency and vacillation, but the sign of an honest intellectual who refused to sweep legitimate problems under a "paradigmatic" rug. And as Mayr suggests, "one can never understand the impact of a thinker throughout his lifetime if one does not understand the permutations of his thought" (*Biological Thought*, 831).

50. Megill, *Prophets of Extremity*, 11–12.

51. A clear expression of this aesthetic is Collingwood's *Principles of Art*. See also R. G. Collingwood, *Essays in the Philosophy of Art* (Bloomington: Indiana University Press, 1964).

52. A similar notion that the good and the beautiful are related has been articulated by Henry Nelson Wieman (among many others). Compare Henry Nelson Wieman, *The Source of Human Good* (Chicago: University of Chicago Press, 1946), 54–70.

53. Michael Moran, "Coleridge, Samuel Taylor," *Encyclopedia of Philosophy*, 2:135.

54. Coleridge was nevertheless greatly influenced by Schelling, especially by his concept of art as bridging the natural and spiritual. Schelling believed that the Absolute combined mind and matter into the One and that history was a series of stages culminating in the Absolute. Schelling's nature philosophy may be viewed in part as a response to the absolute idealism of Fichte, who saw nature as a construction of the ego. But Schelling believed that nature was real independent of the knowing subject and that this objectivity provided the content which the ego knew.

55. Samuel Taylor Coleridge, "Frost at Midnight," in Alexander W. Allison et al., eds., *The Norton Anthology of Poetry*, rev. shorter ed. (New York: W. W. Norton, 1975), 253.

56. Moran, "Coleridge," 135.

57. Whitehead, *Science and the Modern World*, 83.

58. See chap. 10, below, for discussion of the role deity might play in a postmodern wilderness philosophy.

59. William Wordsworth, *Wordsworth: Poetical Works*, ed. Thomas Hutchinson and Ernest De Selincourt, rev. ed. (London: Oxford University Press, 1969), 590, 591. Morris Abrams observes that Wordsworth's an-

nounced project "was perhaps the most remarkable, and certainly one of the most grandiose, ever undertaken by a major writer" (*Natural Supernaturalism,* 19).

60. Wordsworth, *Poetical Works,* 62.

61. Whitehead, *Science and the Modern World,* 77.

62. Wordsworth, *Poetical Works,* 590.

63. Wordsworth, *Poetical Works,* 462.

64. Whitehead, *Science and the Modern World,* 84.

65. Percy Bysshe Shelley, *Shelley: Poetical Works,* ed. T. Hutchinson and G. M. Matthews, rev. ed. (London: Oxford University Press, 1970), 261.

66. Shelley, *Poetical Works,* 264.

67. Whitehead, *Science and the Modern World,* 85.

68. Shelley, *Poetical Works,* 205.

69. Abrams, *Natural Supernaturalism,* 92.

70. Compare Stuart Hampshire, *Spinoza* (New York: Penguin, 1951). See also Paul Wienpahl, *The Radical Spinoza* (New York: New York University Press, 1979); Jon Wetlesen, *The Sage and the Way: Spinoza's Ethics of Freedom* (Oslo: Universitetsforlaget, 1968); Arne Naess, *Freedom, Emotion, and Self-Subsistence: The Structure of a Central Part of Spinoza's Ethics* (Oslo: Universitetsforlaget, 1975); and Marjorie Grene, ed., *Spinoza: A Collection of Critical Essays* (Notre Dame, Ind.: University of Notre Dame Press, 1979).

71. Compare Hampshire, *Spinoza,* 161f.

72. Compare George Sessions, "Spinoza and Jeffers on Man in Nature," *Inquiry* 20 (1977). Sessions argues that "Spinoza did not extend his *intuitiva scientiva* to a direct apprehension of the biological world, and in this sense, his conception of self-knowledge remains a reflection of Judeo-Christian anthropocentrism. But the . . . concepts are there in Spinozism for such an extension: God as Nature manifesting itself though each and every particular thing (mode); individual [humans] . . . as finite dependent modes within the infinite system of Nature, the *necessarily* limited nature of human knowledge, the structure of the universe as interdependent systems existing within wider interdependent systems, the concept of intuitive sympathetic understanding which transcends scientific knowledge, the emphasis upon the proper aims of [humans] . . . as active and free through self-enlightenment" (509).

73. Various concepts of theism, pantheism, and panentheism appear in our study. See below, esp. chaps. 6 and 10.

74. A variation on this theme views the natural world as simply a part of God, or as God's body.

75. Benedict de Spinoza, *Ethics,* in Hutchins, *Great Books,* 31:355.

76. Charles Hartshorne believes that pantheism is not defensible. Even

granted the idea of the unity of nature, he argues, there is no legitimate deduction that nature is divine. There is also an inherent problem in the idea of the unity of nature itself *if* the unity of nature is interpreted to mean the One; for if all is one, what could then possibly remain to be unified? See chap. 6, below, for further discussion.

77. Compare Hans Jonas, "Spinoza and the Theory of Organism," in Grene, *Spinoza Essays,* 263–65.

78. See George Sessions, "Western Process Metaphysics (Heraclitus, White-head, and Spinoza)," in George Sessions and Bill Devall, *Deep Ecology: Living as If Nature Mattered* (Salt Lake City: Peregrine Smith, 1985), 236–42.

79. Russell, *History of Western Philosophy,* 571.

80. Hampshire, *Spinoza,* 81.

81. Russell, *History of Western Philosophy,* 571.

82. Arthur Schopenhauer, *Schopenhauer Selections,* ed. DeWitt H. Parker (New York: Charles Scribner's Sons, 1928), 58–59.

83. In this Schopenhauer anticipated the pragmatic naturalists, beginning with William James. Schopenhauer's insights must also be recognized as remarkable anticipations of later evolutionary insights, as for example our knowledge that the neo-cortex was shaped by an active, natural environment, and that the evolution of science itself (which presupposes the neo-cortex) is in effect a manifestation of the continuing interaction between humankind and the natural environment. Above all else, the human animal thinks because it must live.

84. Schopenhauer, *Schopenhauer Selections,* 59.

85. Compare Walter H. O'Briant, "Man, Nature, and the History of Philosophy," in Blackstone, *Philosophy and Environmental Crisis,* 88.

86. We cannot here entertain any systematic study of Nietzsche's thought. His thought is relevant to our study since much of the twentieth-century critique of Modernism (Heidegger, Gadamer, Foucault, Derrida) proceeds through the door that Nietzsche opened. See Megill, *Prophets of Extremity,* 29–102, and Erich Heller, *The Importance of Nietzsche: Ten Essays* (Chicago: University of Chicago Press, 1988), esp. 141–48.

87. Mayr, *Biological Thought,* 79. Mayr also meets the critics of organicism in his *Philosophy of Biology,* arguing that any philosophy of science that hopes to be current "must do justice to the living world as well as the physical one" (v). What has been particularly nettlesome to the old guard in the philosophy of science has been the fact "most regularities encountered in the living world lack the universality of the laws of physics. Consequently, biologists nowadays make use of the word *law* only rarely" (vi). Nature, in short, is not a machine, and the human animal is not related to the biological world only externally.

88. Prigogine, *Order Out of Chaos,* 32. See also Ilya Prigogine, "Man's New Dialogue with Nature," *Perkins Journal* 36 (Summer 1983), and Prigogine, "The Meaning of Entropy," *Krisis* 5–6 (1986–87), for parallel statements.

89. Prigogine, "New Dialogue," 4.

90. Whitehead, *Science and the Modern World,* 17.

91. That Whitehead and Prigogine find inspiration in Modernism's critics perhaps lends credence to the hypothesis that they shared a commitment to organismic principles, since Whitehead and Prigogine are surely the twentieth-century's thorniest challenge to the idea of nature as nothing but matter-in-mechanical-motion. Both endorse the idea of nature as an organic, self-creating process. Whitehead's philosophy of organicism, as Prigogine observes, demonstrates "the connection between a philosophy of *relation*—no element of nature is a permanent support for changing relations; each receives its identity from its relations with others—and a philosophy of *innovating becoming*" (*Order Out of Chaos,* 95). Although postmodern organicism has been influenced both by relativity theory and quantum mechanics, and is therefore unique in part, neither is it entirely distinct from earlier organismic arguments. In spite of the formidable nature of the arguments against the modernist worldview, no one believes the battle with proponents of mechanistic materialism is over. At best the struggle has been joined. *Imperial ecology,* a biological science that presupposes the reality of a living nature, has maintained a metaphysical distinction between humankind and the web of life: the ideology of Lord Man lives on in the very midst of our late twentieth-century environmental crisis. *Resourcism* (the conservationist idea of wilderness) rules the modern world and is grounded in a slavish emulation of seventeenth-century physical models; see chap. 9, below, for further discussion.

92. Zimmerman, "Quantum Theory," 17.

93. David Bohm, "Postmodern Science and a Postmodern World," in David Ray Griffin, ed., *The Reenchantment of Science: Postmodern Proposals* (Albany: State University of New York Press, 1988), 60–61, 61. See also David Bohm, *Wholeness and the Implicate Order* (London: Routledge and Kegan Paul, 1980).

94. David Bohm, *Causality and Chance in Modern Physics* (Philadelphia: University of Pennsylvania Press, 1957), 152–53.

95. Theories of either internal or external relations have promoted dogmatizing absolutism. The most exaggerated form of the theory of external relations is to be found in the logical atomism of the early Wittgenstein. All that exists in this ideal world are logical atoms; wholes are merely collections or aggregates of parts, and membership in such a collection in no way changes the intrinsic makeup of the parts. Further, all characteristics of the whole are simply manifestations of the characteristics of the parts. But such a theory cannot explain satisfactorily the existence of even

a simple yet qualitatively rich compound like water. H_2O, for example, can indeed be reduced to its constituent elements, two hydrogen and one oxygen; yet this does not explain the phenomenon of water at even its most prosaic levels. Water naturally exists in three states, as a liquid, as a gas (vapor), and as a solid, a fact not predictable from knowledge of its two component elements. Liquid hydrogen and oxygen are normally held under pressure at temperatures far below the freezing point of water; and, while water turns into a gas at 212°F, both its components are gases throughout the range of atmospheric temperatures.

96. See Whitehead's *Science and the Modern World* and Prigogine's *Order Out of Chaos* for accessible philosophical treatments. Whitehead argues that an identifying characteristic of an organism is "that the plan of the *whole* influences the very characters of the various subordinate organisms which enter into it." Of course nothing (atom, electron, organism) is totally free, and Whitehead suggests the utility of the term *organic mechanism.* "In this theory, the molecules may blindly run in accordance with the general laws, but the molecules differ in their intrinsic characters according to the general organic plans of the situations in which they find themselves" (79–80). Furthermore, Bohm insists in *Wholeness and Order,* knowledge itself must be understood as part of organic process—indeed, as a constitutive element of reality (compare 48–66).

97. Fractal theory provides possibilities for a new kind of mathematical inquiry into natural process and for new insights into how living systems structure themselves—how order emerges out of chaos (to use Prigogine's term). And yet fractals conceal at least one implicit danger: an ever present tendency to commit the arithmomorphic fallacy, for the qualitative dimension of existence invariably eludes quantification.

Chapter 5. Henry David Thoreau

1. The standard biography of Thoreau is Walter Harding, *The Days of Henry Thoreau: A Biography* (New York: Dover, 1982). Joseph Wood Krutch, *Henry David Thoreau* (New York: William Sloane, 1948), is a useful source. See Walter Harding and Michael Meyer, *The New Thoreau Handbook* (New York: New York University Press, 1980), chap. 1, for a relatively complete accounting of the Thoreau biographies. An insightful recent intellectual biography is Robert D. Richardson, Jr., *Henry Thoreau: A Life of the Mind* (Berkeley: University of California Press, 1986). Helpful in setting Thoreau in context is F. O. Matthiessen, *American Renaissance: Art and Expression in the Age of Emerson and Whitman* (New York: Oxford University Press, 1941).

2. There are important differences between Marx and Thoreau. Marx, for example, is a collectivist, Thoreau an individualist—a stance reflected in

their discrepant views of the role of government (although the denouement of history, in the Marxian framework, closely resembles Thoreau's view that when people are ready, they shall have a government that governs least). Further, Marx believes in the doctrine of historical inevitability, as in the uprising of the proletarian masses against the bourgeoisie. Thoreau more accurately sees that the bonds of capitalism are not political but psychic, a thesis explored both in *Walden* and in his essay "Life without Principle," and that history moves more in channels of irony than destiny. Finally, Marx sees nature as an inorganic substance subject to human domination; Thoreau sees nature as a living web of life embracing humankind.

3. See Jerome Rothenberg and Diane Rothenberg, eds., *Symposium of the Whole: A Range of Discourse Toward an Ethnopoetics,* (Berkeley: University of California Press, 1983), 10; and Turner, *Natural Classicism,* 171–201.

4. Evernden, *Natural Alien,* 56.

5. Compare, e.g., Sherman Paul, *The Shores of America: Thoreau's Inward Exploration* (Chicago: University of Illinois Press, 1958).

6. Ralph Waldo Emerson, *Selected Writings of Ralph Waldo Emerson,* ed. William H. Gilman (New York: New American Library, 1965), 217, 222–23, emphasis added.

7. Recall both Kant's critique of the arguments for God's existence and his dictum that concepts without percepts are empty, percepts without concepts blind, thus implying that natural phenomena cannot in principle be reduced solely to mind.

8. All citations from the *Journal* are from Henry David Thoreau, *The Journal of Henry David Thoreau,* ed. Bradford Torrey and Francis H. Allen (Salt Lake City: Gibbs M. Smith, 1984). This reprint of the original Houghton Mifflin edition (1906) contains an introduction by Walter Harding and a botanical index prepared by Ray Angelo. See also Sharon Cameron, *Writing Nature: Henry Thoreau's Journal* (New York: Oxford University Press, 1985). She maintains that Thoreau's journal, though private, takes conceptual precedence, even over the works published during his life. Harding observes that after 1850 Thoreau "began to conceive of the journal as a work of art in itself and began to compose it for its own sake" ("Introduction," *Journal* 1:vii). Yet, he continues, "it is hard to imagine how Thoreau ever thought a work the length that his journal eventually proved to be, with more than two million words filling fourteen large printed volumes, would ever be published" (1:vii).

9. All of these essays are found in Henry David Thoreau, *Excursions and Poems,* vol. 5 of *The Writings of Henry David Thoreau* (Boston: Houghton Mifflin, 1906). Citations for "Wachusett," "Natural History," and

"A Winter Walk" are from this edition. The first edition of *The Writings* was published by Houghton Mifflin in 1893, and reprinted in 1906. Relatively complete statements of the publishing history and other biographical details of Thoreau's essays and books can be found in Harding, *Handbook.*

10. "Wachusett," 134.

11. Thoreau's poems are generally weak, and he gradually lost his early enthusiasm for writing poetry. The "Wachusett" poem had been submitted to and rejected by Margaret Fuller, editor of *The Dial* and sister of Richard Fuller, who accompanied Thoreau on his walk to Wachusett. Compare Harding, *Handbook,* 69–71. See Henry David Thoreau, *Collected Poems of Henry Thoreau,* ed. Carl Bode, enlarged ed. (Baltimore: Johns Hopkins University Press, 1970). Bode suggests that although the poems are uneven, they provide useful insights.

12. "Wachusett," 148, emphasis added. Notice the literary affectation of the English spellings of "centre" and "moulded."

13. "Natural History," 105, 106.

14. Compare Paul, *Shores of America,* 107–8.

15. See chap. 3, n. 37, above. Thoreau cannot be considered either a pragmatic naturalistic like John Dewey or a process-relational philosopher like Whitehead. But Thoreau's approach to inquiry shows a relentless effort to avoid both the reification of second-order abstractions from primary experience (the philosophic fallacy, as Dewey calls it) and the error of mistaking abstractions for concrete experience (the fallacy of misplaced concreteness, as Whitehead terms it).

16. "Natural History," 131, emphasis added. This critical approach testifies to Thoreau's genius, to his originality of insight. As Leiss argues in the *Domination of Nature,* even now our vaunted mastery of nature through science conceals from us "a host of ambiguities and unclarified premises" (101). Thoreau was intuitively aware that his fellows' preoccupation with the dominance of nature precluded them from understanding the complementary idea—the liberation of nature. Thoreau grasped the overt ideological nature of classical science and its effect on society (primarily through capitalism), perhaps by observing its effect on Emerson; he understood that Modernism was fallaciously equated with social progress and that classical science was erroneously perceived as the only valid means of understanding nature. Modernism represented, as Leiss suggests, "a decisive break with the past, an elimination of naturalistic categories, and a qualitative change in the possibilities for the satisfaction of needs" (187). Thoreau perhaps instinctively sensed—early in his life, as "Natural History" shows—that such an ideology would eventually undermine the promise of science and technology that Bacon had envi-

sioned. Thoreau was one of the first to seek nature's liberation—"that is, the liberation of human nature: a human species free to enjoy in peace the fruits of its productive intelligence" (193).

17. "Natural History," 117.
18. "A Winter Walk," 166–67, 167.
19. "A Winter Walk," 168, 171, 180–81.
20. See Frederick Garber, *Thoreau's Redemptive Imagination* (New York: New York University Press, 1977). Thoreau's imaginative departure from the path of conventional wisdom is emphasized by Garber. *Walden* and "Walking," viewed from such a perspective, are paradigmatically revolutionary statements where Thoreau effectively transcends the epistemological anomalies of classical science (e.g., secondary qualities excluded from cognition) and idealistic philosophy (e.g., wild nature reduced to categories).
21. The decision to go to Walden was Thoreau's declaration of independence from Emerson. Emerson had encouraged him to go to New York City, a step he thought essential for an erstwhile American scholar. The city literally made Thoreau ill, and while there he resolved to make a wilderness retreat. After Walden, things were never the same between them.
22. *A Week on the Concord and Merrimack Rivers* was originally published in May 1849. The revised edition was published in 1868 and was reprinted (vol. 1) in *The Writings* (1906).
23. Henry David Thoreau, *A Week on the Concord and Merrimack Rivers,* in Brooks Atkinson, ed., *Walden and Other Writings of Henry David Thoreau* (New York: Modern Library, 1937), 307.
24. *A Week,* 301.
25. *A Week,* 333.
26. See Gould, *Mythic Intentions,* esp. 6–7, for an insightful perspective on language and being that illuminates Thoreau's ultimate turn to myth. As Gould puts it, "event and meaning are never simultaneously present. We have no meaning without interpretative processes, given the perennial failure of verbal expression to be adequate to experience and to be an adequate naming of the world" (7).
27. Compare Martin Heidegger, *Poetry, Language, Thought,* trans. Albert Hofstadter (New York: Harper and Row, 1971), and Heidegger, *On the Way to Language,* trans. Peter D. Hertz (New York: Harper and Row, 1971).
28. *A Week,* 344, 356.
29. Compare José Ortega y Gasset, *What Is Philosophy?,* trans. Mildred Adams (New York: W. W. Norton, 1960).
30. Compare Geoffrey O'Brien, "Thoreau's Book of Life," *New York Review of Books,* January 15, 1987, 48.

31. The trip to Greylock, nearly five years after the river trip with his brother, was a healing experience. Thoreau had been disgraced in Concord by an unfortunate fire he caused near Fairhaven Bay.

32. This selection is routinely omitted from most contemporary abridgments of *A Week*. But William Howarth has preserved it in his delightful selections from and commentary on Thoreau. See William Howarth, ed., *Thoreau in the Mountains: Writings by Henry David Thoreau* (New York: Farrar, Straus, Giroux, 1982), 62.

33. Compare Turner, *Natural Classicism*, 187–95. Thoreau also lowers the boom on conventional religion in this book, which, as Harding suggests in the *Handbook*, contributed to its sparse sales (44).

34. Turner, *Natural Classicism*, 191.

35. See Henry David Thoreau, *Maine Woods* (New York: Harper and Row, 1987). *The Maine Woods* was originally published in 1864 (Ticknor and Fields) and was reprinted in 1892 and 1893 by Houghton Mifflin. Thoreau's original account of the trip to Ktaadn was published in 1848 in the *Union Magazine*.

36. He had been to Maine in May 1838, in search of employment as a teacher. Although frustrated in that end, he had been struck with Maine's frontierlike character. Massachusetts, with its two-hundred-year history of European settlement, was relatively a civilized locale. While at Walden, Thoreau read an account of two Harvard men who had climbed to the summit; thus inspired, he decided to attempt the excursion, attracted by the prospect of adventure and recognizing the potential to publish an account of the journey.

37. *Maine Woods*, 71, 73–74.

38. *Maine Woods*, 75.

39. *Maine Woods*, 80–82, 84.

40. *Maine Woods*, 84–85, 85–86.

41. *Maine Woods*, 93–95. Thoreau fell short of the summit, reaching only the top of the last ridge.

42. Only the melting sandbank passage in *Walden* is as powerfully written and as important in understanding Thoreau's idea of wilderness.

43. *Maine Woods*, 4.

44. Viewed as a proto-anthropologist, Thoreau accurately describes the outlines of Homo oeconomicus both here and elsewhere, as in the introductory section of *Walden*.

45. *Maine Woods*, 163–64. This analysis paralleled in insight and refinement that of the opening passage of *A Week*, where he carefully distinguished the two names for the grass-ground river.

46. Chronologically, "An Excursion to Canada" might be considered Thoreau's next wilderness writing. It was originally published as a series of

pieces entitled "A Yankee in Canada," beginning in the January 1853 issue of *Putnam's Magazine*. Thoreau opens with the observation that "what I got by going to Canada was a cold."

47. Compare J. Lyndon Shanley, *The Making of Walden* (Chicago: University of Chicago Press, 1957). *Walden* has been reprinted many times. All references herein are to Henry David Thoreau, *Walden and Other Writings by Henry David Thoreau,* ed. Joseph Wood Krutch (New York: Bantam, 1962).

48. "Walking" was not published until June 1862 but may be considered contemporaneous with *Walden*. Thoreau presented "Walking" as a public lecture several times (1851, 1852, 1856, and 1857). These lectures and the essay are rooted in ideas he explored in the *Journal* for the years 1850–52. "Walking" is fundamental Thoreau and should be considered in context with *Walden*. As Thoreau revised the essay in the last months of his life, we may consider it as making a definitive statement.

49. *Walden*, iii, 109.

50. *Walden*, 113, 172. His analysis, for example, parallels Berger and Luckmann's sociological epistemology and G. H. Mead's theory of symbolic interaction.

51. *Walden*, 113, 115, 132.

52. *Walden*, 158, 172–73.

53. *Walden*, 115–16. This notion is amplified in "Life without Principle," where Thoreau argues that the title "wise" is normally falsely applied, and in "Walking," where he deflates all conventional claims to knowledge.

54. Similarly, Marx critiqued philosophers as speculating about the world but doing nothing to change it. But Marx glorified the worker.

55. *Walden*, 176.

56. *Walden*, 178.

57. *Walden*, 183, 187, emphasis added.

58. *Walden*, 224.

59. Perhaps only Dilthey and Nietzsche, among nineteenth-century thinkers, rival Thoreau in such understanding.

60. Paul Ricoeur, "The Hermeneutics of Symbols and Philosophical Reflection," trans. Denis Savage, *International Philosophical Quarterly* 2 (May 1962): 192–93. So viewed, "Natural History" might be considered as manifesting a hermeneutic of suspicion, where the language of science and transcendentalism is revealed as a wasteland of conventionality, a prison for the human spirit that draws boundaries between civilization and the wilderness. *Walden* is relatively, though not entirely, a hermeneutic of restoration, where the borders between wilderness and civilization are crossed.

61. *Journal* 5:135.

62. Schneidau's *Sacred Discontent* goes to the heart of the matter: "Why

'myth' has been so appealing to poets . . . is obvious. . . . Myth tantalizes us with the suggestion that the world is a language which, when illumined, we can learn to read. And, of course, the treatment of nature and man and god as a continuum helps resolve the poets' form of the perennial Western philosophic dilemma of subject and object: specifically, how can the individual subject have anything valid to say about what is outside him? Even fragments of the mythological ideology can help heal this alienation. But the most revealing use of myth by poets is as disguised criticism of their own society [or mentors], for to affirm myth is to rebuke the West" (99).

63. *Walden*, 200, 204, 203, 202, 207, emphasis added.

64. *Walden*, 219, 219–20, 228, 202. Thoreau knew that some events and processes were beyond human ken and value, and contemporary ecology confirms his insight, as in our new understanding of forest fires, predators, and hurricanes. All play a vital role in nature's economy.

65. *Walden*, 222, 222–23, 226.

66. *Walden*, 227. Thoreau takes the analysis even to the level of the particular in "Baker Farm," where he found John Field and his family caught in a hand-to-mouth cycle of bondage to the soil. Thoreau observes that Field "was discontented and wasted his life into the bargain" (257).

67. *Walden*, 254.

68. *Walden*, 260.

69. *Walden*, 332, 329–30.

70. Of course, Thoreau's evolutionary insights, though confirmed in the later flow of nineteenth-century events, would not—without scientific corroboration—compel attention of the scientific community. Yet the role of imagination is largely neglected except by those who understand Kant's insights into knowledge.

71. *Walden*, 330–31. I do not read this section (327–33) as entailing any commitment to the argument from design. Clearly, Thoreau thinks of the Cosmic Artist in a way much like Whitehead's idea of God's primordial nature. But the evolutionary outlook described in *Walden*, and later in "Walking," is teleonomic rather than teleological; further, Thoreau implicitly denies the doctrine of special creation by equating the human animal with a lump of clay.

72. *Walden*, 331–32, emphasis added.

73. *Walden*, 332–33, emphasis added.

74. In his last years of life, after reading Darwin, Thoreau wrote a scientific essay entitled "The Succession of Forest Trees." Originally published in 1860, the essay synthesized material from his journal (roughly 1852–60). The essay was reprinted in *Excursions*. See also "Succession," in Henry David Thoreau, *Henry David Thoreau: The Natural History Essays* (Salt Lake City: Peregrine Smith, 1984). Typically Thoreauvian, the essay is

filled with witticisms and pithy observations of himself and his fellows. But its crux is its implementation of evolutionary principles in observing the evanescence of organic forms in and around Concord. The essay was not surpassed in ecological insight and accuracy for nearly forty years, although it took the biological community more than eighty years to recognize Thoreau's pioneering work.

75. Henry David Thoreau, "Walking," in *Excursions*, 205, 237. The reference to "English nobility" is an oblique but astute criticism of Emerson's *English Traits*, a book for which Emerson was lionized.

76. "Walking," 209, 211, 216, 217, 218. Thoreau is on slippery footing, forgetting perhaps that China—the home of the master Kung Fu Tzu, whom he so approvingly quoted in *Walden*—had long been settled. Thoreau perhaps overemphasized America as epitomizing the movement to the West: "To Americans I hardly need say,—'Westward the star of empire takes its way'" (223). Since "Walking" was often delivered as a lecture, one might see this as a stratagem designed to win assent to the argument.

77. "Walking," 224, emphasis added.

78. "Walking," 228–29, 229.

79. "Walking," 239.

80. Compare Emerson, "Thoreau," in *Selected Writings*. Emerson's point, delivered in his eulogy, was that Thoreau lacked ambition. Lacking "this, instead of engineering for all America, he was the captain of a huckleberry-party" (427). This statement would have confirmed Thoreau's worst suspicions of Emersonian transcendentalism. It was the engineering mentality —the modern mind—that then, and now, lies at the heart of cultural crisis. "Walking," if nothing else, refutes Emerson's belief in social engineering.

81. "Walking," 240, emphasis added.

82. See chap. 4, n. 25, above.

83. "Walking," 226.

84. Krutch, *Walden and Other Writings*, 353. Thoreau prepared the manuscript for publication shortly before his death, and it was published posthumously in October 1863. Versions of the essay had been presented as public lectures as early as 1854. The essay particularly appeals to those who interpret Thoreau along lines of Emersonian transcendentalism, and it is sometimes touted as Thoreau's version of Emerson's "Self-Reliance." I disagree with the notion that the essay represents his writing at the highest level or ties together all his fundamental principles.

85. Henry David Thoreau, "Life without Principle," in Krutch, *Walden and Other Writings*, 371.

86. See Henry David Thoreau, *Cape Cod*, intro. Paul Theroux (New York: Penguin, 1987). See also Harding, *Handbook*, 66.

87. *Cape Cod*, 218, 219–20.

88. John M. Dolan, "The Language of Concord's Fields," in Ray Angelo, *Botanical Index to the Journal of Henry David Thoreau* (Salt Lake City: Gibbs M. Smith, 1984), 8.
89. *Journal* 9:406, emphasis added.
90. *Journal* 11:55.
91. *Journal* 14:306–7.

Chapter 6. John Muir

1. See Stephen Fox, *John Muir and His Legacy: The American Conservation Movement* (Boston: Little, Brown, 1981), reissued as *The American Conservation Movement: John Muir and His Legacy* (Madison: University of Wisconsin Press, 1985); citations herein are from the Wisconsin edition. See also Michael P. Cohen, *The Pathless Way: John Muir and American Wilderness* (Madison: University of Wisconsin Press, 1984); and Frederick Turner, *Rediscovering America: John Muir in His Time and Our Own* (New York: Viking Penguin, 1985), reissued as a Sierra Club Books edition, 1985.
2. There are a few studies of the philosophical implications of Muir's work; see, e.g., Bill Devall, "John Muir as Deep Ecologist," *Environmental Review* (Spring 1982). To his credit, Roderick Nash recognizes Muir as an important figure in the wilderness movement, but other intellectuals (e.g., Lynn White, Jr., Paul Taylor) ignore his work despite its conceptual precedence. Wilderness practitioners (foresters, ecologists, and wildlife scientists) and preservationists have been more attentive to Muir's writings: see, e.g., John Daniel, "The Long Dance of the Trees," *Wilderness* 51 (Spring 1988): 19–34.
3. The word *biocentrism* (*bios* means life) connotes the idea that life is at the center of existence, the most basic principle of being.
4. Stephen Fox, "Author's Response," in Bill Devall, review of *John Muir and His Legacy: The American Conservation Movement*, by Stephen Fox, *Humboldt Journal of Social Relations* 9 (Fall–Winter 1981–82): 197.
5. See, e.g., John Muir, *The Wilderness World of John Muir*, ed. Edwin Way Teale (Boston: Houghton Mifflin, 1954), esp. sec. 7, "The Philosophy of John Muir." This material runs a scant thirteen pages (311–23). See also J. Baird Callicott, *In Defense of the Land Ethic: Essays in Environmental Philosophy* (Albany: State University of New York Press, 1989). Callicott argues that although Muir advocated the idea that humans had ethical responsibilities to nonhuman others, he "neither fully articulated nor fully grounded it, as Leopold did, in a supporting matrix of ideas" (223).
6. Rorty, *Mirror of Nature*, 379, 377.
7. William Frederic Badè, "Introduction," in John Muir, *A Thousand-Mile Walk to the Gulf* (Boston: Houghton Mifflin, 1916), xxi. One might com-

pare Muir's use of biblical phraseology with Nietzsche's in *Thus Spake Zarathustra*.

8. Northrop Frye, *The Educated Imagination* (Bloomington: Indiana University Press, 1964), 111.

9. The word *orthodox* comes from the Greek root *orthodoxein*, which means right or true opinion, especially as defined by traditional authority. Orthodoxy of any kind (religious, economic, political) is directed toward maintaining an established belief structure rather than facilitating its modification. Some readers interpret Muir's views on God and creation as consistent with traditional Judeo-Christian beliefs. But such interpretation hinges precariously on an argument committed to the premise that belief in God's immanence is orthodox, since Muir clearly expresses that belief.

10. Cohen, *Pathless Way*, 125.

11. Turner, *Rediscovering America*, 56–57.

12. Turner, *Rediscovering America*, 116. These two interpretations are not necessarily contradictory. Many techniques, including fasting and sleepless vigils, have been used to promote religious experiences.

13. John Muir, *Letters to a Friend: Written to Mrs. Ezra Carr, 1866–1879*, cited in Cohen, *Pathless Way*, 109. See also Turner, *Rediscovering America*, 120.

14. Cohen, *Pathless Way*, 109.

15. See Callicott, *Land Ethic*, for a useful discussion of differences between this kind of ecologically based holism and the mystical holism of some Eastern philosophies and religions. In the Hindu equation that *Atman* = *Brahman*, for example, the diverse natural world is dismissed as an illusion. "The unity of things is thus substantive and essential and the experience of it homogeneous and oceanic" (111). In distinction, an ecological perspective views the diverse world of natural things as an internally related whole, where individuals are defined in relation to that nexus of relations. Clearly, then, there are still real—qualitatively and quantitatively discriminated—things and selves. "The multiplicity of particles and of living organisms . . . retain, ultimately, their peculiar, if ephemeral, characters and identities. But they are systemically integrated and mutually defining. The wholes revealed by ecology . . . are unified, not blankly unitary; they are 'one' as organisms are one, rather than 'one' as an indivisible, homogenous, quality-less substance is one" (111).

16. John Dewey, *A Common Faith* (New Haven: Yale University Press, 1934), 80.

17. Turner, *Rediscovering America*, 71.

18. Muir, *Wilderness World*, 312.

19. Muir kept a journal throughout his life, and he mined it to produce his

books, with many passages being almost verbatim transcriptions. The journal itself is in part the product of later reflection.

20. See Cohen, *Pathless Way*, 140–42. Cohen recognizes the Thoreauvian strain in Muir, although he largely interprets Thoreau along lines of transcendental orthodoxy. Muir had read much of Thoreau's work, including "Walking" and *Maine Woods*.

21. Muir, *National Parks*, 108.

22. John Muir, *My First Summer* (Boston: Houghton Mifflin, 1911), 236.

23. Cohen, *Pathless Way*, 51.

24. Sessions and Devall, *Deep Ecology*, 47.

25. Muir's annotated copy of "Nature" is in the Yale University Library rare book room.

26. George Santayana, "The Genteel Tradition in American Philosophy," cited in Sessions and Devall, *Deep Ecology*, 47.

27. Some scholars suggest that Muir uses the term *God* so liberally in his writing to win support for his wilderness cause; this is dubious.

28. Dewey's distinction in *A Common Faith* between religion and religious experience here applies. Emerson is a religionist who experienced a crisis of faith and set out to recapture his belief system. For Muir, by contrast, wilderness was a religion and all creation was sacred. As Dewey explains, a religion "always signifies a special body of beliefs and practices having some kind of institutional organization, loose or tight. In contrast, the adjective 'religious' denotes nothing in the way of a specifiable entity, either institutional or as a system of beliefs. It does not denote anything to which one can specifically point as one can point to this and that historic religion or existing church. For it does not denote anything that can exist by itself or that can be organized into a particular and distinctive form of existence. It denotes attitudes that may be taken toward every object and every proposed end or ideal" (9–10).

29. *National Parks*, 144, 145, 147, 149.

30. The affinity of Muir's methods (his radical empiricism, intuition, and speculative thought) with such later thinkers as William James, Henri Bergson, and Alfred North Whitehead is remarkable. See John E. Smith, *The Spirit of American Philosophy* (London: Oxford University Press, 1963), esp. 54, 78, and 172–73, for similarities with James and Whitehead; see Pete A. Y. Gunter, "Bergson and a Post-Modern World," in David Ray Griffin, ed., *Process Philosophy and the Postmodern World* (Albany: State University of New York Press, 1989), for comparisons with Bergson.

31. *Wilderness World*, 318. Compare Matt. 5.8: "Blessed are the pure in heart, for they shall see God."

32. *First Summer*, 229.

33. *Wilderness World,* 314.

34. If the case that Muir is not a transcendentalist needed further buttressing, there is ample evidence. For example Muir and Emerson are almost diametrically opposed as they look on nature's landscape and see the impact of the human animal. Emerson is relatively sanguine about the human prospect, indeed prideful in what humankind has accomplished in converting nature to human ends. "The useful arts are reproductions or new combinations by the wit of man, of the same natural benefactors. . . . By the aggregate of these aids, how is the face of the world changed, from the era of Noah to that of Napoleon!" (Emerson, *Selected Writings,* 191). Muir's outlook is quite different.

35. For a clear and concise discussion of theism, panentheism, and pantheism see J. E. Barnhart, *Religion and the Challenge of Philosophy* (Totowa, N.J.: Littlefield, Adams, 1975). The term *pantheism* comes from the Greek words *pan* and *theos,* meaning that everything is God. "For a pantheist, God is the whole of reality. Nothing exists outside his own being" (152). In other words, the world *is* God. The word *panentheism* "stresses the point that the world is *in* God as a real and vital part of his being. The world is not thought of as an illusion or a mere appearance of God but as integral to his life. Yet at the same time, God's consciousness is his own and is distinguishable from the world. According to this way of thinking, the world is something analogous to the body of God" (152). Panentheism is like traditional theism in maintaining belief in a separate essence of God, particularly insofar as that essence of God is transcendent and therefore unchanging. But panentheism is unlike classical theism in two distinct ways. First, "the finite creatures within God are not simply the passive effects of God but are also *causes* having an impact on one another and consequently on or in God" (152). And second, rather than God giving all meaning to the world, for a panentheist "the *world of finite beings also provides meaning to God's life.* While he does not need you or me or any one particular world of finite realities, God nevertheless needs *some* particular world of finite entities to enrich his everlasting existence and to give it stimulus and meaning, as well as 'embodiment'" (153).

36. Some critics believe that of all the world's religions Christianity is the most selfish and egotistical, for its primary concern is individual salvation.

37. *Thousand-Mile Walk,* 1–2.

38. Turner, *Rediscovering America,* 142. Turner observes that the notion of spirit in nature is "one of the hardest heresies missionizing Christians had to extirpate, and it is somewhat startling to meet it here in the thought of one whose background was so strongly Christian" (153).

39. Passmore's attack, in *Responsibility for Nature,* on environmental philosophers is based on his belief that they are antiscientific nature mystics. This claim cannot be sustained. See also above, n. 15.

40. See Eugene Odum, *Ecology* (New York: Holt, Rinehart and Winston, 1963); and Amos Turk et al., *Environmental Science* (Philadelphia: W. B. Saunders, 1974).

41. Turner, *Rediscovering America*, 57.

42. On the importance of such a quest see among others Dolores LaChapelle, "Toward an Understanding of Psychology as the Study of the Relationship between Nature Within and Nature Without," *Contemporary Philosophy* 12 (March 1989): 10–14; Duerr, *Dreamtime*, esp. 104–24; and Shepard, *Thinking Animals*. Shepard argues that the human mind needs nonhuman others to develop. "By presenting us with related-otherness—that diversity of non-self with which we have various things in common—they further, throughout our lives, a refining and maturing knowledge of personal and human being" (249). Duerr suggests that the quest itself, the intentional crossing of the divide between wilderness and civilization, is essential to even the possibility of psychic maturation. "To get to the point of origin . . . a person needs what the Indians call 'reverence.' Humans must become *unimportant* before the other beings of nature" (110). What modernists, and some scientists and philosophers, Duerr continues, "call a 'disease of the mind' . . . [is actually] the dissolution of an analytic attitude, making it possible for an archaic mode of perception to reveal itself, which is normally kept under lock and key by cultural conditioning" (121). LaChapelle, citing Jung, argues that "we forget that we are still primates, that we still have to take into account those primitive layers of soul. . . . We all need psychic nourishment. We do not find it in the apartment house from which no green lawn, no tree in blossom can be seen. We also need a permanent connection with nature. . . . With all my heart and thought, I believe in the human need for roots" (11).

43. *Thousand-Mile Walk*, 140.

44. Here the term *animism* is chosen over *panpsychism*. Muir was not engaging mechanistic materialism per se as an explicit philosophical doctrine, but was instead articulating the impressions he had of the natural world as alive. Alternatively stated, Muir was responding empathetically to the wilderness, as characteristic of archaic people to this day, rather than viewing nature from the standpoint of Modernism. Whether we characterize Muir as animist or panpsychist, any assumed ontological separation between human beings as ensouled and nature as nothing but matter-in-motion is bracketed. Spinozism, Leibnizianism, and Whiteheadianism are all philosophical elaborations of the theme that insentient matter does not exist.

45. *First Summer*, 188.

46. Cohen, *Pathless Way*, 41.

47. John Muir, *Travels in Alaska* (Boston: Houghton Mifflin, 1979), 96.

48. *National Parks*, 325.

49. *Thousand-Mile Walk*, 136. Turner believes—based on his idea that Muir edited his journal soon after the original entries were made, perhaps in January 1868—that the *Thousand-Mile Walk* contains no "substantive changes," although "textual scholars will find a great many inconsistencies of a minor nature" (*Rediscovering America*, 373). Fox believes, by contrast, that the journal is a "more pointed" indictment than the version published in the book (*American Conservation*, 391).

50. *Thousand-Mile Walk*, 98–99, emphasis added. Here as elsewhere Muir employs terms, such as "unfallen" and "undepraved," that appear Calvinistic even while he is standing that orthodoxy on its head.

51. During this pivotal phase of his life, recounted in *First Summer* and *Thousand-Mile Walk*, Muir effects a veritable paradigmatic revolution—viewed philosophically—or undergoes a conversion experience—viewed psychologically. As both Turner and Fox clearly see and decisively establish, Muir transcended the anthropocentric Christian paradigm. According to Fox, "This was the central insight of Muir's life, the philosophical basis of his subsequent career in conservation" (*American Conservation*, 53). And, according to Turner, "Muir was stating the bedrock principle that would in time become the basis of the American environmental movement" (*Rediscovering America*, 154).

52. Charles Hartshorne, *The Divine Relativity: A Social Conception of God* (New Haven: Yale University Press, 1948), 89. Although we cannot here argue the case systematically, Hartshorne contends that nothing in the Bible precludes thinking of God pantheistically, that is, as an all-inclusive reality.

53. *Thousand-Mile Walk*, 92, 93, emphasis added.

54. *Thousand-Mile Walk*, 211, 211–12, emphasis added.

55. *First Summer*, 3–4, 15–16. See also Turner, *Rediscovering America*, 377.

56. *First Summer*, 39. This insight was foreshadowed in *Thousand-Mile Walk*, where Muir criticized the death orthodoxy imposed on town children. He also questioned the superstitions, rooted in the Old Testament view of Sheol (compare, e.g., Isaiah 5.14), that gripped the human species, for we "are haunted by imaginary glooms and ghosts of every degree. Thus death becomes fearful, and the most notable and incredible thing heard around a death-bed is, 'I fear not to die'" (70).

57. *First Summer*, 242–43.

58. Linnie Marsh Wolfe, *John of the Mountains: The Unpublished Journals of John Muir* (Madison: University of Wisconsin Press, 1979), 168–69. Muir's notion of the imperishable and unspendable wealth of the universe is analogous to Whitehead's notion of the primordial nature of God.

59. *National Parks*, 102.

60. Hartshorne sketches three possibilities in *Divine Relativity*. The pantheistic view is that "God is merely the cosmos, in all aspects inseparable

from the sum or system of dependent things or effects." The panentheistic view is that God "is both this system and something independent of it." And the theistic view is that God "is not the system, but is in all aspects independent" (90).

61. *Unpublished Journals*, 137–38, 153–54, 137, 138. The year 1873 was his most prolific for journal writing.

62. *Travels in Alaska*, 67. This passage can be read as consistent with panentheism, but on balance Muir is best read as a pantheist.

63. Barnhart, *Challenge of Philosophy*, 152–53. See also Charles Hartshorne and William L. Reese, *Philosophers Speak of God* (Chicago: University of Chicago Press, 1953), esp. 1–25, for an insightful and succinct discussion of deity and temporality. They argue that the only consistent way "to relate the supreme to awareness and to the world is to admit a temporal aspect of deity" (19). And see chap. 10, below.

64. *Travels in Alaska*, 68.

65. *Unpublished Journals*, 138, emphasis added.

66. Alasdair MacIntyre, "Pantheism," in *The Encyclopedia of Philosophy*, 6:35.

67. See Evernden, *Natural Alien*, and Kohák, *Embers and Stars*, for penetrating critiques of those who desacralize the natural world by viewing it solely as an objective phenomenon.

68. Charles Hartshorne, *A Natural Theology for Our Time* (La Salle, Ill.: Open Court, 1967), 8–9.

69. *Oxford Annotated Bible*, 2, n. 1.26–27.

70. *Thousand-Mile Walk*, 140.

71. Compare Christopher D. Stone, *Should Trees Have Standing? Toward Legal Rights for Natural Objects* (Los Angeles: William Kaufmann, 1972).

72. Rolston, *Philosophy Gone Wild*, 11. Of course, Muir was well aware that nature may speak with more than one tongue. Cohen argues correctly that "Muir was too careful a naturalist to ignore the violence in Nature" (*Pathless Way*, 164). In short, he knew that ants bit, parasites fed on the blood of other creatures, and that life itself necessitates death.

73. *First Summer*, 157–58.

74. See Robert McIntosh, *The Background of Ecology* (Cambridge: Cambridge University Press, 1985), 1–27, for discussion of problems in defining the term *ecology*.

75. Evernden, *Natural Alien*, 76.

76. *Wilderness World*, 313, 313, 320.

77. Compare Nash, *Wilderness and the American Mind*, 129, and Callicott, *Land Ethic*, 223. That Muir's ecological vision was incomplete goes with the reality of human finitude. Cohen, among the contemporary biographers, presents the most penetrating analysis of Muir's insufficiencies.

For example, although Muir in many ways rekindled a Paleolithic mode of awareness of nature, he "never managed to integrate completely the figure of Native Man into his ecological vision" as did Thoreau (*Pathless Way,* 189). Or, unlike Leopold, who entertained penetrating questions about human nature in relation to the living land, Muir "was never aware of the significant bond forged between hunter and hunted, when [the human species] . . . became a part of the flow of energy in Nature" (184). Unable to answer the nettlesome questions accompanying his contention that humankind improved by becoming part of nature's flow, he would have been "hard pressed to explain why Californian Indians had not been ennobled by their surroundings" (186).

78. The point stands only with an important qualification made by Worster in *Nature's Economy.* Ecology as a branch of biology perhaps begins with Haeckel. "But the study of ecology is much older than the name; its roots lie in earlier investigations of the 'economy of nature.' The major theme throughout the history of this science and the ideas that underlie it has been the interdependence of living things. An awareness, more philosophical than purely scientific, of this quality is what has generally been meant by the 'ecological point of view.' Thus, the question of whether ecology is primarily a science or a philosophy of interrelatedness has been a persistent identity problem. And the nature of this interdependence is a parallel issue: Is it a system of economic organization or a moral community of mutual tolerance and aid?" (378).

79. Bramwell, *Ecology in the Twentieth Century,* 45.

80. Haeckel and Muir came to different answers to these questions. Most germane to our inquiry is the fact that Haeckel still believed that progress was a law of nature. That doctrine is untenable, since nature does not define progress. The question is basically, "What constitutes progress?" The modern mind believes that society will get better and better each and every day as a matter of course. If nothing else, Muir called that naive outlook into question.

81. *First Summer,* 26, 22.

82. *Thousand-Mile Walk,* 141.

83. *First Summer,* 94–95.

84. *National Parks,* 372.

85. *National Parks,* 392, 302.

86. See Worster, *Nature's Economy,* esp. 180–84, for discussion of nineteenth-century ethical (Victorian) outlooks on nature. He points out that only a few could look at plants and animals biocentrically and that Charles Darwin towered over all others. In the *Descent of Man,* according to Worster, Darwin "attempted to demonstrate an inner moral as well as outer physical continuity among all species" (181). Even more crucially, "The evolution of moral behavior within a natural context had for

Darwin its final issue in civilization. As art and music were born of an ancient struggle for survival but have grown beyond that purely utilitarian purpose, so morality evolves toward something more than usefulness or expediency. In its last and highest stage it becomes a self-transcending sense of mercy, sympathy, and kinship with all of animate existence, including the earth itself" (182). Muir's biocentric thinking was also on the cutting edge of the evolutionary paradigm. See also Mayr, *Philosophy of Biology*, 75–91.

87. *Thousand-Mile Walk*, 138, 138–39.

88. *First Summer*, 142.

89. John Muir, "Wild Wool," in John Muir, *Wilderness Essays* (Salt Lake City: Peregrine Smith, 1980), 242.

90. *First Summer*, 160, 58.

91. Paul W. Taylor's *Respect for Nature: A Theory of Environmental Ethics* (Princeton: Princeton University Press, 1986), for example, makes no reference (bibliographic or otherwise) to Muir. Lynn White's "The Historical Roots of Our Ecologic Crisis" also neglects his work.

92. Worster, *Nature's Economy*, 184.

93. Fox, *John Muir*, 352.

94. Fox, *John Muir*, 354, 355, 354, 352.

95. The best contemporary study of the concatenation of ideology, institutions, and environmentalism is Robert C. Paehlke, *Environmentalism and the Future of Progressive Politics* (New Haven and London: Yale University Press, 1989). Paehlke, like Fox, attempts to see ideas and institutions in historical process, and he makes clear the intrinsic riskiness of this project. Paehlke's treatment is judicious and balanced, and his argument that Western culture will either rise or fall with the basic institutional framework now in place is both reassuring and frightening. Paehlke makes a cogent case for the premise that environmentalism can have a major effect in reshaping the course of events.

96. Paehlke, *Environmentalism*, 175.

97. Fox argues that of the three "historical overviews of conservation, one (by J. Leonard Bates) treats it as a democratic protest against selfish economic interests; another (by Samuel P. Hays), as an exercise in scientific management and modernization; a third (by Michael Lacey), as a reaction against Herbert Spencer in favor of an evolutionary positivism that urged human intervention in the natural world. But all three deal only with professional or utilitarian conservation" (*American Conservation*, 351).

98. Fox, *American Conservation*, 352.

99. David W. Ehrenfeld, *Conserving Life on Earth* (New York: Oxford University Press, 1972), 12.

100. The terms *conservation* and *preservation* mean different things to different people. See O. H. Frankel and Michael E. Soulé, *Conservation*

and Evolution (Cambridge: Cambridge University Press, 1981). Evolutionary biologists, for example, use the terms in different ways than do resource economists. For resource economists conservation means saving resources now for consumption later. Frankel and Soulé use conservation "to denote policies and programmes for the long-term retention of natural communities under conditions which provide the potential for continuing evolution, as against 'preservation' which provides for the maintenance of individuals or groups but not for their evolutionary change. Thus, we would state that zoos and gardens may preserve, but only nature reserves can conserve" (4). There can be no argument that one definition is right, and another wrong; what is crucial to inquiry is that we are clear on how we use the terms. Frankel and Soulé also endorse an ethical view much like Muir's, observing that "nothing but incisive action by *this* generation can save a large proportion of now-living species from extinction within the next few decades" (4).

101. John B. Cobb, Jr., "Ecology, Science, and Religion: Toward a Postmodern Worldview," in Griffin, ed., *Reenchantment of Science*, 106. Cobb identifies two specimens of postmodern thought that center on ecological thinking: deep ecology (which he contends departs "radically from the Western tradition") and a postmodern ecology (or, as he puts it, a postmodern ecological worldview). Interestingly, Cobb's panentheistic commitments lead him to attack pantheistic views of the interconnectedness of all things. My judgment is that, given rigorous definitions of pantheism, panentheism, and theism such as those proposed by Charles Hartshorne and Joe Barnhart, Cobb's view of interconnectedness might be interpreted as implying a disconnected God (i.e., supernaturalism). See chap. 10, n. 2, below, for further discussion.

102. Griffin, *Reenchantment of Science*, x, xi. Such a return is in fact not possible, as witness the almost compelling evidence that the "fall of man" was engendered by dramatic climatological changes. Drought either diminished the carrying capacity or destroyed the Paleolithic grasslands and thus the biological basis of the cynegetic economy.

103. Rorty, *Mirror of Nature*, 389.

Chapter 7. Aldo Leopold and the Age of Ecology

1. The other two books are Aldo Leopold, *Report on a Game Survey of the North Central States* (Madison, Wis.: Democrat Press for the Sporting Arms and Ammunition Manufacturer's Institute, 1931), and Luna B. Leopold, ed., *Round River: From the Journals of Aldo Leopold* (New York: Oxford University Press, 1953). See also Aldo Leopold, *The River of the Mother of God and Other Essays*, Susan L. Flader and J. Baird Callicott,

eds. (Madison: University of Wisconsin Press, 1991), for a collection of Leopold's major essays, as well as a definitive bibliography.

2. See Rorty, *Contingency, Irony, and Solidarity,* 3–22, and Hilary Lawson, *Reflexivity: The Post-modern Predicament* (LaSalle, Ill.: Open Court, 1985), esp. 9–10. Leopoldian ecology enables descriptions of nature that transcend fact-value, mind-matter dualism—dichotomies endemic to the language of classical science.

3. McIntosh's *Background of Ecology* differentiates between ecologists seeking "historical" and "ahistorical" explanations. The latter are "those who study ergodic properties which are invariant and involve no historical considerations" (6). The former recognize temporal process as a meaningful dimension of ecological inquiry. Since human actions have ecological consequences, human values and ethical choices thus fall within the foundational ecologist's purview. The imperial ecologist believes that such considerations are outside the ecologist's domain of inquiry. See also J. Baird Callicott, "Just the Facts, Ma'am," *Environmental Professional* 9 (1987): 279–88. Callicott delineates a middle ground between imperial and foundational ecology, arguing that so-called ultimate "values have been standardized by natural selection and include genuine altruism. Real-world value conflicts center on 'proximate' values—the best means to achieve our shared ultimate ends. Such conflicts thus reduce to matters of fact and the theoretical organization and interpretation of facts and are, therefore, amenable to, rational scientific solution" (279). Callicott uses Leopold to illustrate how scientific research informs ethical choice, that is, the selection of the proximate means to implement shared (objective, because biologically determined) ultimate values.

4. Aldo Leopold, *A Sand County Almanac: With Essays on Conservation from Round River* (New York: Random House, 1970), xix. Subsequent citations are to this edition. *Sand County Almanac* was originally published in 1949 by Oxford University Press, as was *Round River* in 1953. The foreword (written in 1948) published with *Sand County Almanac* is in part a response to criticism from editors at Knopf that the book lacked unity; thus, this foreword directly points to the relations between ecology and ethics, unlike the original (written in 1947) foreword, which has a personal, even autobiographical texture. See Curt Meine, "Building 'The Land Ethic,'" in J. Baird Callicott, ed., *Companion to* A Sand County Almanac: *Interpretive and Critical Essays* (Madison: University of Wisconsin Press, 1987). The 1947 foreword can be found in *Companion* (281–88).

5. McIntosh, *Background of Ecology,* 304; see also 4–9.

6. Several studies disclose differences between Leopoldian ecology—a subversive science—and classical science. Compare, e.g., Callicott, *Land*

Ethic, esp. pt. 2: "A Holistic Environmental Ethic." Of particular relevance is Callicott's close reading of Hume as providing a metaethical model that justifies Leopold's land ethic (see 121–27). On Darwin and ethics see n. 19 and n. 22, below.

7. The characterization of ecology as a subversive science originates with Paul Sears in "Ecology—A Subversive Subject," *Bioscience* 14 (July 1964). See also Paul Shepard and Daniel McKinley, eds., *The Subversive Science: Essays toward an Ecology of Man* (Boston: Houghton Mifflin, 1969). See also chap. 6, n. 100, for terminological clarification on the usages of preservation and conservation.

8. McIntosh, *Background of Ecology,* 6.

9. Here meaning that ecology means different things to different people and that meaning rests largely on the final vocabulary adopted. More generally, evolutionary inquiry remains in a preparadigmatic phase.

10. Compare McIntosh, *Background of Ecology,* 289–323.

11. Bramwell, *Ecology in the Twentieth Century,* 248.

12. Beginning in 1924 Turner and Leopold lived two houses apart in Madison, Wisconsin. Their exchanges were undoubtedly mutually beneficial.

13. See José Ortega y Gasset, *The Modern Theme,* trans. James Cleugh (New York: Harper Torchbooks, 1961), for discussion of the concept of "historic level."

14. See Susan Flader, *Thinking Like a Mountain: Aldo Leopold and the Evolution of an Ecological Attitude toward Deer, Wolves, and Forests* (Columbia: University of Missouri Press, 1974), and Curt Meine, *Aldo Leopold: His Life and Work* (Madison: University of Wisconsin Press, 1988).

15. Flader, *Thinking Like a Mountain,* 5.

16. See Curt Meine, "The Utility of Preservation and the Preservation of Utility: Leopold's Fine Line," in Oelschlaeger, *Wilderness Condition.*

17. See McIntosh, *Background of Ecology,* 66–68. Students of Leopold's life are struck by his concern for the institutionalization and professionalization of ecology, as well as the marriage of ecology with public policy issues.

18. See Callicott, "Metaphysical Implications of Ecology," in *Land Ethic,* 101–14, for a concise explication of these differences. The "new ecology," as Callicott terms it, is distinguished from classical science in that "energy seems to be a more fundamental and primitive reality than are material objects or discrete entities—elementary particles and organisms respectively" (109). And second, "it is impossible to conceive of organisms—if they are, as it were, knots in the web of life, or temporary formations or perturbations in complex flow patterns—apart from the field, the matrix of which they are modes" (110). Thus, third, internal relations are real; from an ecological perspective "relations are 'prior to' the things related,

and the systemic wholes woven from these relations are prior to their component parts. Ecosystemic wholes are logically prior to their component species because the nature of the part is determined by its relationship to the whole" (110–11). The new ecology thus has major implications for psychology and ethics. "Since individual organisms, from an ecological point of view, are less discrete objects than modes of a continuous, albeit differentiated, whole, the distinction between self and other is blurred. Hence the central problem of modern classical moral philosophy . . . — the problem of either managing or overtly overcoming egoism—is not solved by the moral psychology implicated in ecology so much as it is outflanked" (112).

19. Social Darwinism was the earliest attempt to derive an ethic from the theory of evolution, and this unfortunate chapter of history clearly impeded later efforts to explore the ethical implications of post-Darwinian naturalism. For relevant reading see Michael Ruse, *Taking Darwin Seriously: A Naturalistic Approach to Philosophy* (Oxford: Basil Blackwell, 1986), and Florian von Schilcher and Neil Tennant, *Philosophy, Evolution, and Human Nature* (Boston: Routledge and Kegan Paul, 1984).

20. Aldo Leopold, "Wilderness," n.d., Aldo Leopold Papers (University of Wisconsin Archives), cited in Meine, *Aldo Leopold*, 359.

21. E. O. Wilson, *Sociobiology: The Abridged Edition* (Cambridge: Harvard University Press, 1980), 300.

22. Mayr, *Philosophy of Biology*, 77, emphasis added. George Gaylord Simpson makes a similar point in *The Meaning of Evolution: A Study of the History of Life and Its Significance for Man*, rev. ed. (New Haven: Yale University Press, 1967). He argues that "the means to gaining right ends involve both organic evolution and cultural evolution, but human choice as to what *are* the right ends must be based on human evolution. It is futile to search for an absolute ethical criterion retroactively in what occurred before ethics themselves evolved. The best human ethical standard must be relative and particular to man and is to be sought rather in the new evolution, peculiar to man, than in the old, universal to all organisms. The old evolution was and is essentially amoral" (cited from the Bantam Books edition, 1971, 283). Joseph W. Meeker notes in his book, *The Comedy of Survival: In Search of an Environmental Ethic* (Los Angeles: Guild of Tutors Press, 1980), that the most provocative new ideas in ethics during this century have come from "an unexpected source: ecological biology" (124). Clearly, biologically oriented inquiry is relevant to questions concerning the good life. Among such lines of inquiry are sociobiology: compare, e.g., Wilson, *Sociobiology;* ethology: compare, e.g., Lorenz, *Animal and Human Behavior* (2 vols.); behavioral psychology: compare, e.g., B. F. Skinner, *Science and Human Behavior* (New York: Free Press, 1953); and human ecology: compare, e.g., Paul

Shepard, *Thinking Animals*. That such inquiry is a necessary but not sufficient basis for choice is readily apparent, both in theory and in practice.
Disputes between Third World nations seeking to develop rain forests
and industrial societies interested in protecting the ecosphere illustrate
that the appeal "human nature" as underlying "ultimate values" is not an
ethical panacea: the ultimate value of life manifests itself in many ways.
And the enormous vagueness of the sociobiologist's appeal to an "ecological steady-state," as well as an inability to sort ostensibly "obsolete"
from functional parts of human nature that have "adaptive significance,"
illustrate the theoretical limits of any appeal to human nature (see Wilson, 299–301). Interestingly, Wilson thinks that by following the guide
of evolutionary sociobiology we can enjoy a "planned society" (which
he sees as inevitable) maintaining itself in an ecological steady-state that
does not rob "man of his humanity." In contrast, Leopold believed that by
understanding the ecology of human behavior we could avoid the planned
society.

23. The limits of such resistance remain subject to inquiry. Continuing research into the questions concerning environmental stability and the destabilizing effects of human activities is important—locally, regionally,
globally. Compare, e.g., Richard A. Houghton and George M. Woodwell,
"Global Climatic Change," *Scientific American,* April 1989.

24. Aldo Leopold, "Some Fundamentals of Conservation in the Southwest"
in *River and Other Essays,* 93, 94. This essay was originally published in
Environmental Ethics 1 (Summer 1979).

25. See Susan L. Flader and J. Baird Callicott, "Introduction," in *River and
Other Essays*. They argue that ecological science at this juncture (1923)
had not yet achieved a "functional approach to the total environment"
(4). Consequently, Leopold retained in his ecological perspective certain
shibboleths, as for example the beliefs "that forest fires should always be
prevented because they set back succession" (4) and his belief that the
only good predator was a dead one.

26. Aldo Leopold, "Fundamentals of Conservation," in *River and Other
Essays,* 95.

27. Compare Flader and Callicott, "Introduction," *River and Other Essays,*
5–6.

28. Leopold sometimes used organic and mechanistic metaphors in the same
paper. Meine believes (personal communication) that Leopold alternated
between mechanistic and organismic metaphors for a practical reason,
namely, to communicate the idea of dynamic interrelatedness to people,
especially students, who were inclined to think only in mechanistic terms.
He also suggests that the philosophical inconsistency of this strategy
was clear to Leopold as early as "Fundamentals of Conservation." Callicott argues (personal communication) that Leopold was a consistent
organicist.

29. Although Leopold was dissatisfied with a mechanistic outlook on nature, he did not know precisely where to turn for help. Vitalism was an early response to mechanistic materialism (Darwin had shown that physiology alone could not account for evolution), but it gave way to new explanations based on stochastic processes. Mayr argues in *Philosophy of Biology* that "at the same time an exclusively physicalist approach to organisms was being questioned, the influence of the vitalists was also diminishing, as more and more biologists recognized that all processes in living organisms are consistent with the laws of physics and chemistry, and that differences which do exist between inanimate matter and living organisms are due not to a difference in substrate but rather to a different organization of matter in living systems" (12). In any case, Leopold's essential point was that the apparently dead earth was actually a functional or interdependent whole; he did not claim that there was any mysterious, vital force that enlivened matter.

30. An insightful treatment of the problem of natural evil can be found in Annie Dillard, *Pilgrim at Tinker Creek* (New York: Bantam, 1974), 65–67. Leopold was keenly aware of the problem, and his writing is liberally sprinkled with references to "tooth and claw."

31. Leopold gave a second argument in "Fundamentals of Conservation" for the necessity of an ethical inquiry into the ground of conservation, raising the question of just what the earth was made for and then offering an answer much like Muir's: "It is just barely possible that God himself likes to hear birds sing and see flowers grow" (96). He also looked to the Bible, and found a kindred spirit in Ezekiel, who "seems to scorn waste, pollution, and unnecessary damage as something unworthy . . . . We might even draw from his words a broader concept—that the privilege of possessing the earth entails the responsibility of passing it on, the better for our use, not only to immediate posterity, but to the Unknown Future, the nature of which it not given us to know" (94).

32. Contemporary analyses that explore the psychological ramifications of the bifurcated brain and/or the biological basis of human behavior bear on the issue. See Robert E. Ornstein, *The Psychology of Consciousness* (San Francisco: W. H. Freeman, 1972), and Gregory Bateson, *Steps to an Ecology of Mind* (New York: Chandler, 1972). Wilson argues that "self-knowledge is constrained and shaped by the emotional control centers in the hypothalamus and limbic system of the brain. These centers flood our consciousness with all the emotions—hate, love, guilt, fear, and others—that are consulted by ethical philosophers who wish to intuit the standards of good and evil. What, we are then compelled to ask, made the hypothalamus and limbic system? They evolved by natural selection. That simple biological statement must be pursued to explain ethics and ethical philosophers, if not epistemology and epistemologists, at all depths" (*Sociobiology*, 3). But such inquiry must also allow (minimally) for a

larger purview, such as that of Richard Dawkins, *The Selfish Gene* (New York: Oxford University Press, 1978). He opens evolutionary inquiry up onto the rich world of culture—texts, languages, creation stories, values. These controlling *memes,* as he terms them, change by nongenetic means, that is, "evolve in historical time in a way that looks like highly speeded up genetic evolution, but has really nothing to do with genetic evolution" (204; cf. Wilson, *Sociobiology,* 284). Dawkins also sees the possibility, as did Leopold, of defying "the selfish memes of our indoctrination. We can even discuss ways of deliberately cultivating and nurturing pure, disinterested altruism—something that has no place in nature, something that has never existed before in the whole history of the world" (215). So viewed, Leopold's land ethic grew out of a tension between his biologically based intuitive response to the natural world and his learned (culture-dwelling) behavior.

33. Aldo Leopold, "A Criticism of the Booster Spirit," in *River and Other Essays,* 103, 105. Leopold's technical works of this Southwestern period, most notably *The Watershed Handbook,* "Grass, Brush, Fire and Timber in Southern Arizona," and "A Criticism of the Booster Spirit," offer in Meine's opinion a "full, buoyant, and precise, actually better, if less lofty, expression to his evolving ideas about conservation and the quality of life" (*Aldo Leopold,* 223) than his earlier and more philosophical "Conservation in the Southwest."

34. Flader, *Thinking Like a Mountain,* 19.

35. Aldo Leopold, "Game and Wild Life Conservation," in *River and Other Essays,* 165–66.

36. Laurence R. Jahn, "Foreword," in Aldo Leopold, *Game Management* (Madison: University of Wisconsin Press, 1986), xxi. *Game Management* was originally published in 1933 by Charles Scribner's Sons. Herbert L. Stoddard was an exemplar for Leopold; the index for *Game Management* cites Stoddard's work eighty-four times, not including the reference on xxxii.

37. Compare Hargrove, *Environmental Ethics,* 151–55, for an interesting view on *Game Management.* He contends that the book was obsolete almost from the moment Leopold wrote it, since he was rapidly moving away from imperial ecology with its inherent reductionism and utilitarian orientation toward *therapeutic nihilism.* "Thwarted in his efforts to maintain ecosystem stability through active manipulation, Leopold opted [in the long run] for passive therapy, placing his faith in self-regulation as the best basis for what he came to call land or ecosystemic health" (153). Hargrove sees the conversion in Leopold's thinking as almost complete by 1936, when he read a paper at Beloit College entitled "Means and Ends in Wild Life Management." In that paper Leopold confessed that the artificial equilibria sought by wildlife managers could not replace

natural equilibria and that he would not choose to implement simulated controls even if he could.

38. *Game Management*, 403.

39. *Game Management*, 5, 391, emphasis added. Leopold, we might add, greatly admired the work of Lorenz.

40. Antihunters who assess Leopold's hunting as either inconsistent with or contradictory to his land ethic ignore the question of human nature. They also ignore the historical role that sport hunters have played in the American conservation movement. See John F. Reiger, *American Sportsmen and the Origins of Conservation* (New York: Winchester, 1975).

41. As early as 1922, in an essay entitled "The River of the Mother of God," Leopold broached considerations of human nature vis-à-vis wilderness. Foreshadowing later themes, he argued that preservation of wilderness areas (which he called "Unknown Places") was essential to both the physical and spiritual well-being of humankind. He expressed alarm that, in geographic terms, "the end of the Unknown is at hand. This fact in our environment, seemingly as fixed as the wind and the sunset, has at last reached the vanishing point. Is it to be expected that it shall be lost from human experience without something likewise being lost from human character?" (*River and Other Essays*, 124).

42. Meine, *Aldo Leopold*, 504–5.

43. *Game Management*, xxxi.

44. Compare J. Baird Callicott, "The Conceptual Foundations of the Land Ethic," in Callicott, *Companion*. Callicott argues that the land ethic is an expansion of or an addition to, but not a replacement for, other kinds of ethics.

45. Aldo Leopold, "The Conservation Ethic," in *River and Other Essays*, 182, 183.

46. "Conservation Ethic," 188.

47. Compare Meine, *Aldo Leopold*, 306. Leopold wrote a companion piece to the "Conservation Ethic" entitled "Conservation Economics," where he adopted an ecological point of view on the land. With far-reaching insight, long ahead of the economic theoreticians of his time, he saw that the well-being of a society was not adequately measured in terms of dollars, rates of economic growth, and the size of the gross national product; cultural welfare depended on the health of the land. Leopold's vision also transcended what only now has become an issue: the mistaken notion that environmental conservation and preservation engenders opposition between social classes. Leopold understood that the biological reality that underlies any sustainable, healthy culture cuts across class lines.

48. "Conservation Ethic," 192.

49. They met at a conference held at Matamek River, Quebec, July 22–31, 1931.

50. Callicott, "Conceptual Foundations," 200.

51. Worster, *Nature's Economy,* 295. Interestingly, Bramwell does not mention Tansley (or Raymond Lindeman, his theoretical successor), and Elton only briefly, in *Ecology in the Twentieth Century.* Yet she suggests that the combination of moral and cultural criticism that normative ecology offers, when combined "with the full apparatus of quantitative argument" offered by imperial ecology, explains why ecologism has become "the powerful force it is today" (4).

52. Meine, *Aldo Leopold,* 284. Meine thinks that the Eltonian model for ecology is a dynamic one, as opposed to a static model in natural history. Granted, the new ecology attempted to view biological communities as evolutionary phenomena, and this attracted Leopold. But the natural history tradition was not blind to evolution (cf. Mayr, *Philosophy of Biology,* 560–61); what natural historians like Thoreau, Muir, and Haeckel saw and rejected was the belief that qualitative change could be reduced to conceptual permanence. More generally, Mayr points out, no adequate history of evolutionary natural history has been written (143, 560). Evolutionary thought remains, in spite of all that has happened this century, in a preparadigmatic phase.

53. McIntosh, *Background of Ecology,* 93. McIntosh notes that "Leopold was much less involved than Elton in scientific ecology and more concerned with management than theory of populations. He transformed ecological concerns into problems of ethics, morality, and aesthetics as well as science, resource management, and public policy" (168). I would attribute at least part of this difference to Leopold's concern about the human impact on and the restoration of natural ecosystems—issues now addressed by conservation biology and restoration ecology.

54. Even late in life Leopold employed organismic (as in thinking like a mountain), mechanistic (as in the land mechanism), and communitarian (as in the land community) metaphors. But I agree with Callicott that it is "the holism of the land ethic, more than any other feature, [that] sets it apart from the predominant paradigm of modern moral philosophy" ("Conceptual Foundations," 197). Whatever the lingering hold of mechanism on Leopold's thinking, his normative ecology rested on a paradigmatic shift that abandoned the machine metaphor and the theory of external relations, and recognized the reality of internal relations between humankind and nature analogous to those among the elements of a living organism or community.

55. A term like *mainstream ecology* must be used with reservation. McIntosh notes that ecologists (and others) tend "to use the generic term *ecology* when they should specify some part of it" (*Background of Ecology,* 89). This is all the more important when confronting the paradigmatic fray among "ecologists" and helps us to see how differences in subject mat-

ter between Elton and Tansley led to different conceptions of method. As a terrestrial ecologist Tansley was especially interested in the interactions between biotic *and* abiotic components, and "to the combination of and interchanges between the organic and inorganic he gave the name *ecosystem*" (98).

56. McIntosh notes that the holistic tradition is antecedent to the ecosystem concept in ecology (*Background of Ecology*, 194) and that the dispute between holists and reductionists remains alive. "Perhaps the most involved, persistent, and least conclusive argument among ecological theorists is that between traditional holists, neoholists and knowing, or unknowing, reductionists" (252). Furthermore, some ecologists reject the approach modeled on physics (e.g., the hypothetico-deductive method) as definitive and argue that "ecological theory comes in many forms, including *verbal models*" (248, emphasis added).

57. Flader and Callicott, "Introduction," 7. Callicott argues (personal communication) that Raymond Lindeman's 1942 paper, "The Trophic-Dynamic Aspects of Ecology" (published in *Ecology*, 23) actually "followed through on the new physics-inspired quantifiable model" broached by Tansley. "It was Lindeman who made measurable solar energy the central object of ecological analysis and put ecology on an analytic and quantitative basis parallel to the other hard sciences."

58. Worster, *Nature's Economy*, 301.

59. See Worster, *Nature's Economy*, 289.

60. The interpretation of Leopold as an ethical ecologist is consistent with Bramwell's view of ecologism. She argues that "ecologism does not involve the web of life alone; it was used originally as co-terminous with ethology, the study of animal behaviour in its environment, and with *oekonomie*, the concept of 'economical' household management. This implies that the use and conservation of resources is a moral activity as well as an economic one; and a morality closely bound up with the survival of the group" (*Ecology in the 20th Century*, 14–15). Precisely! Leopoldian ecology is inconceivable apart from the Darwinian turn and its ethical upshot: the "biologization of ethics," as E. O. Wilson calls it (*Sociobiology*, 3).

61. Aldo Leopold, "Land Pathology," in *River and Other Essays*, 217, emphasis added.

62. "Land Pathology," 212.

63. "Land Pathology," 213–14. Callicott argues (personal communication) that this usage does not entail a commitment to mechanistic materialism. What Leopold envisions is something like a tax or other incentive to encourage wise use of the land (a subject he discussed on more than one occasion). Yet undeniably Leopold occasionally used a true machine metaphor, sometimes in the most unlikely of places. For example, in *Sand*

County Almanac, Leopold suggests that people think that "science knows what makes the community clock tick," but scientists know that they do not since "the biotic mechanism is so complex that its workings may never be fully understood" (240–41). Elsewhere in *Sand County Almanac,* e.g., 190, he mixes mechanical and organic metaphors.

64. "Land Pathology," 215, emphasis added.

65. Compare Meine, *Aldo Leopold,* 396.

66. "Land Pathology," 217.

67. Rorty, *Mirror of Nature,* 363. Callicott argues in *Land Ethic* that quantum theory forces reconsideration of any "simple, sharp distinction between fact and value (between intrinsically value-free objects and intentionally valuing subjects)" (166–67). But Leopold made no use of the new physics in his own arguments. As Hargrove implies, Leopold grew tired of viewing nature through the lens of history; Leopoldian ecology generally, and the land ethic specifically, advances a new vocabulary (or verbal model) to describe nature based on a communitarian and organismic rather than atomistic and mechanistic metaphors.

68. Aldo Leopold, "Marshland Elegy," in *Sand County Almanac,* 101, 103, 106–7, 107–8.

69. Aldo Leopold, "Conservationist in Mexico," in *River and Other Essays,* 244, 243–44.

70. Aldo Leopold, "Engineering and Conservation," in *River and Other Essays,* 253, 253, 254.

71. Aldo Leopold, "Natural History: The Forgotten Science," in *Sand County Almanac,* 208.

72. A few months earlier Charles Elton and his wife visited the Leopolds in Madison. In writing the paper Leopold was communicating Elton's message to an audience of foresters and conservationists.

73. Aldo Leopold, "A Biotic View of Land," in *River and Other Essays,* 266, 267.

74. This is an important point, for perhaps the most salient difference between organismic and mechanistic paradigms turns on the irreversibility of time. Compare Prigogine, *Order Out of Chaos;* Weizsäcker, *History of Nature;* and Georgescu-Roegen, *Entropy Law.*

75. "Biotic View of Land," 269, 269–70.

76. Meine, *Aldo Leopold,* 395.

77. Aldo Leopold, "Biotic Land Use," cited in Meine, *Aldo Leopold,* 404.

78. See McIntosh, *Background of Ecology,* and Meine, *Aldo Leopold,* 404–5, for relevant discussion. Some fifteen billion years of evolutionary history confirm that increasing diversity is the general rule. Stability, however, is another matter, since climatological, geological, and extraterrestrial factors (e.g., meteor showers) exert influence. Leopold's work (e.g., the problem of erosion in the Southwest and the deer herds of Wisconsin) gave

him ample evidence to support his conjecture that stability and diversity were tied.

79. Worster, *Nature's Economy*, 285.

80. Leopold also wrote a second paper in 1944 entitled "Conservation: In Whole or in Part?" in which he begins by restating his core concept of land as an organism—"a collective functioning of interdependent parts for the maintenance of the whole"—and offering a one-sentence definition of conservation: "Conservation is a state of health in the land" (in *River and Other Essays,* 310). Then he lowered the boom, summarizing in two short sentences almost ten thousand years of Western history. "Land, to the average citizen, is still something to be tamed, rather than something to be understood, loved, and lived with. Resources are still regarded as separate entities, indeed, as commodities, rather than as our cohabitants in the land-community" (311). He continued that the rapidity and violence of human-made changes upset native land-communities by destroying diversity. "This leads to the 'rule of thumb' which is the basic premise of ecological conservation: the land should retain as much of its original membership as is compatible with human land-use" (315).

81. Aldo Leopold, "Thinking Like a Mountain" in *Sand County Almanac,* 137.

82. See George Lakoff and Mark Johnson, *Metaphors We Live By* (Chicago: University of Chicago Press, 1980), for a cogent account of how metaphors fundamentally affect the ways in which we perceive, think, and act. This is true for science no less than economics, philosophy, and religion. Susan Flader notes that Leopold used "the expression 'thinking like a mountain' to characterize objective or ecological thinking: it should not be used as a personification" (*Thinking Like a Mountain,* 1). This contention is fine, so far as it goes. The issue, of course, is what do we mean by "objective"? See Lakoff and Johnson, 195–222, for an argument that metaphor is essential to knowledge of any objective phenomenon (as, for example, an alpine ecosystem).

83. "Thinking Like a Mountain," 137, 138–39, 141.

84. From Aldo Leopold to Bill Vogt, January 21, 1946, Leopold Papers, cited in Meine, *Aldo Leopold,* 478, emphasis added.

85. Aldo Leopold, "Fundamentals of Conservation," 94.

86. T. H. Watkins, "Editor's Note," *Wilderness* 51 (Winter 1987): 57.

87. *Sand County Almanac,* xvii.

88. *Sand County Almanac,* xviii, 251, 274, 163.

89. Compare Simpson, *Meaning of Evolution.*

90. J. Baird Callicott, "The Land Aesthetic," in Callicott, *Companion,* 163. See also Kant's *Third Critique;* Collingwood's *Principles of Art;* and Duerr's *Dreamtime.*

91. Callicott, "Conceptual Foundations," 200.

92. *Sand County Almanac,* 290.

93. Callicott, "Land Aesthetic," 169.

94. *Sand County Almanac,* 258.

95. *Sand County Almanac,* 262, 257, 279.

96. The view of poetry as rhetoric without truth value will be deconstructed in chap. 8. Callicott argues that the confusion results from Leopold's "condensed prose style," the novelty of his ethical assumptions and paradigm, and "the unsettling practical implications" of the land ethic ("Conceptual Foundations," 187).

97. See Roderick Nash, "Aldo Leopold's Intellectual Heritage," in Callicott, *Companion.* Nash, with some justification, criticizes Leopold for ignoring those who had gone before.

98. Re Hegel see Collingwood's *Idea of History;* re Darwin see Eiseley's *Darwin's Century.*

99. *Sand County Almanac,* 189.

100. Wallace Stegner, "The Legacy of Aldo Leopold," in Callicott, *Companion,* 245.

101. Peter A. Fritzell, "The Conflicts of Ecological Conscience," in Callicott, *Companion,* 129, emphasis added.

102. Fritzell, "Ecological Conscience," 142–43. Compare Bramwell, *Ecology in the Twentieth Century,* 7–8.

103. Gregory Bateson, cited in Sessions and Devall, *Deep Ecology,* 1.

104. *Sand County Almanac,* 279.

Chapter 8. The Idea of Wilderness in the Poetry of Robinson Jeffers and Gary Snyder

1. Sessions and Devall, *Deep Ecology,* 102.

2. Joseph W. Meeker, *The Comedy of Survival: In Search of an Environmental Ethic* (Los Angeles: Guild of Tutors Press, 1980; orig. publ. Charles Scribner's Sons, 1974), 25. Meeker offers the useful term *literary ecology* for such inquiry. See also Jim Cheney, "Postmodern Environmental Ethics: Ethics as Bioregional Narrative," *Environmental Ethics* 11 (Summer 1989), for an insightful discussion (from a postmodernist perspective) bearing on literary ecology.

3. See Frye, *Educated Imagination,* 56.

4. See Rothenberg and Rothenberg, *Symposium of the Whole.*

5. Loren Eiseley, *The Invisible Pyramid* (New York: Charles Scribner's Sons, 1970), 137.

6. Compare Abrams, *Natural Supernaturalism.*

7. Many critics claim that Jeffers substitutes the notion of the eternal return—simplistically, the idea that history repeats itself in a meaningless and painful cycle of life and death—for the Romantic's notion of history

as linear and progressive. Jeffers's post-Romantic view of history cannot be subsumed within the confines of the theory of eternal return, for he is a thoroughgoing evolutionist.

8. Snyder's view of history differs from Jeffers's by admitting a possibility of recapturing the premodern sensibilities that helped humans live in harmony with nature, such as the idea of nature as intrinsically feminine. Snyder believes that human beings might begin to live in an old and simultaneously new way.

9. George Sterling, cited in Alex Vardamis, "Robinson Jeffers: The Opinion of His Peers," *Robinson Jeffers Newsletter* (April 1987): 12. See also Alex A. Vardamis, *The Critical Reputation of Robinson Jeffers: A Bibliographical Study* (Camden, N.J.: Archon Books, 1972).

10. Dana Gioia, "Strong Counsel," *Nation*, January 16, 1988, 59. This essay reviews Robinson Jeffers, *Rock and Hawk: A Selection of Shorter Poems*, ed. Robert Hass (New York: Random House, 1988).

11. In Great Britain see Robinson Jeffers, *Robinson Jeffers: Selected Poems: The Centenary Edition* (Manchester: Carcanet, 1987); see also Robinson Jeffers, *Jeffers Poems in Translation*, trans. Tom Miura (Tokyo: Kokubun-Sha, 1986), and Robinson Jeffers, *Robinson Jeffers, Interjochte Erde: Gedichtem*, trans. Eva Hesse (Munich: Piper, 1987).

12. Bill Hotchkiss, "Afterword," in Jeffers, *Double Axe*, 177.

13. See William Everson, *The Excesses of God: Robinson Jeffers as a Religious Figure* (Palo Alto: Stanford University Press, 1988), and James Karman, *Robinson Jeffers: Poet of California* (San Francisco: Chronicle, 1987). Articles and chapters include Robert Brophy, "Robinson Jeffers," in *Literary History of the American West* (Fort Worth: Texas Christian University Press, 1986), 398–415, and John Elder, "The Covenant of Loss," in *Imagining the Earth: Poetry and the Vision of Nature* (Urbana: University of Illinois Press, 1985). Dissertations include David Copland, "Literature and Environment: The Inhumanist Perspective and the Poetry of Robinson Jeffers," (Ph.D. diss., University of Washington, 1984), and John Michael Yozzo, "*In Illo Tempore, Ab Origine*: Violence and Reintegration in the Poems of Robinson Jeffers," (Ph.D. diss., University of Tulsa, 1985).

14. Robert J. Brophy, ed., *The Robinson Jeffers Newsletter: A Jubilee Gathering, 1962–1988* (Los Angeles: Occidental College, 1988), xv.

15. Gioia, "Strong Counsel," 60, 62. See also Helen Vendler, "Huge Pits of Darkness, High Peaks of Light," *New Yorker*, December 26, 1988, for a generally antagonistic but interesting review of *Rock and Hawk*. The *Jubilee Gathering* also reprints Ed Abbey's letter (probably one of the last things he wrote before his death) to the editors of the *Nation*, thanking them for publishing Gioia's review. Abbey observed that Jeffers was more than a great poet, he was a great prophet. "Everything he wrote

about the corruption of empire, the death of democracy, the destruction of our planet and the absurd self-centered vanity of the human animal has come true tenfold since his time. Let justice be done—even in the literary world!" (222).

16. See Snyder's essay "Poetry, Community & Climax," in Gary Snyder, *The Real Work: Interviews and Talks, 1964–1979* (New York: New Directions, 1980), 171ff., which can be read as a regionalist poetics.

17. Robert Ian Scott, "The Great Net: The World as God in Robinson Jeffers' Poetry," *Humanist* 46 (January–February 1986): 46.

18. Jeffers's major collections of poetry include *Roan Stallion, Tamar and Other Poems, The Women at Point Sur, Cawdor and Other Poems, Dear Judas and Other Poems, Give Your Heart to the Hawks and Other Poems, Solstice and Other Poems, Such Counsels You Gave to Me and Other Poems, Be Angry at the Sun, The Double Axe and Other Poems,* and *The Beginning and the End and Other Poems.* Tim Hunt is editing a definitive collection entitled *The Collected Poetry of Robinson Jeffers,* published by Stanford University Press (one volume in print through 1988).

19. See Robert J. Brophy, *Robinson Jeffers: Myth, Ritual, and Symbol in His Narrative Poems (with Additions and Corrections)* (Camden, N.J.: Archon Books, 1976).

20. *Double Axe,* xxi.

21. *Double Axe,* 171.

22. *Double Axe,* 172. In the original preface Jeffers speaks of "a next step in human development," a notion clearly inconsistent with his inhumanism and the prevailing outlook within "The Double Axe." The preface of 1948 contains no suggestion that human history is progressive.

23. Thoreau, *Walden,* 172.

24. *Double Axe,* 174.

25. See chap. 10, below.

26. William Everson, "Foreword," *Double Axe,* xix. See also Samuel Alexander, *Space, Time, and Deity* (Gloucester: Peter Smith, 1979; orig. publ. Macmillan, 1920). Alexander argues that to place divinity outside cosmic process is to consign God to nonbeing, for there can be no being apart from process. In other words, divinity can be revealed only through relation to an other.

27. Compare Kohák, *Embers and the Stars,* 22.

28. Robinson Jeffers, *The Selected Poetry of Robinson Jeffers* (New York: Random House, 1959), 576.

29. *Selected Poetry,* 88.

30. Robert Bringhurst, "Peter and the Wolf Editions," *Robinson Jeffers Newsletter* (October 1989): 11. As Jeffers put it, "Poetry cannot speak without remembering the turns of the sun and moon, and the rhythm of the ocean" (cited in Bringhurst, 11).

31. Brophy, *Jubilee Gathering*, xi, xiv.
32. Jeffers also argued that poets lie, and was fond of quoting Nietzsche's remark about poets. " 'The poets? The poets lie too much.' I was nineteen when the phrase stuck in my mind; a dozen years passed before it worked effectively, and I decided not to tell lies in verse. Not to feign any emotion that I did not feel, not to pretend to believe in optimism or pessimism, or unreversible progress; not to say anything because it was popular, or generally accepted, or fashionable in intellectual circles, unless I myself believed it; and not to believe easily" (*Selected Poetry*, xv).
33. Robert Zaller, "Tamar's Oedipal Transcendence," in *Robinson Jeffers Newsletter* (April 1989): 14.
34. *Selected Poetry*, 559.
35. *Selected Poetry*, 614.
36. See Dewey, *A Common Faith*, for relevant discussion.
37. *Double Axe*, 142.
38. *Selected Poetry*, 594, 614.
39. *Selected Poetry*, 615.
40. Compare Cobb, "Ecology, Science, and Religion," 112.
41. The question a traditional theist asks is the one of need. The answer is that a transcendent God in heaven is categorically and empirically implausible, caught in a web of paradox and confronted by an avalanche of evolutionary facts. See Schubert M. Ogden "Prolegomena to a Christian Theology of Nature," in Jack Bemporad, ed., *A Rational Faith: Essays in Honor of Levi A. Alan* (New York: KTAV, 1977). Ogden argues that an adequate theology of nature requires not only "naturalizing man but also historicizing the rest of nature" (132). So viewed, what makes humankind distinct is not special creation, but rather understanding or sentience. As Whitehead puts it, "The mentality of mankind and the language of mankind created each other. If we like to assume the rise of language as a given fact, then it is not going too far to say souls of men are the gift from language to mankind." It follows, Whitehead continues, that "the account of the sixth day [Genesis] should be written, He gave them speech, and they became souls." See Alfred North Whitehead, *Modes of Thought* (New York: Free Press, 1968), 40–41.
42. Alfred North Whitehead, *Adventures of Ideas* (New York: Macmillan, 1954), 13.
43. Interestingly, Cobb denies the viability of a pantheistic vision such as Jeffers's on the grounds that "every individual has its own indissoluble reality, activity, and value in and for itself and not only for others" ("Ecology, Science, and Religion," 111). But Cobb appears inconsistent in asserting that "the ecological worldview holds that all the units of reality are internally related to others. All units or individuals are constituted by their relations" (108). He also claims that "there is no self who is the

subject of experience apart from the activity that is the experience in the human being" (109).

44. *Selected Poetry*, 594, ellipsis in original.
45. Robinson Jeffers, *Robinson Jeffers: Selected Poems* (New York: Vintage Books, 1965), 37.
46. *Selected Poetry*, 4, 9.
47. Brophy, *Jubilee Gathering*, xii.
48. *Double Axe*, 72.
49. Robinson Jeffers, *The Beginning and the End and Other Poems* (New York: Random House, 1963), 13, 24.
50. Brophy, *Jubilee Gathering*, 3.
51. See H. Arthur Klein, "The Poet Who Spoke of It," in Brophy, *Jubliee Gathering*.
52. *Selected Poems*, 39.
53. *Double Axe*, 148.
54. *Double Axe*, 164, 141.
55. *Selected Poems*, 9.
56. Literary ecologists will find Meeker, *Comedy of Survival*, 106–17, especially insightful. He argues that time itself is a bioesthetic structure, that only in recent decades—since the beginnings of modern ecology—have humans developed sufficient analytical skills to describe environmental integrity (order, process), and that an intuitive sense of nature's orderly process served historically to ground the poetic perception of beauty. "Greater analytical knowledge merely increases the sense of awe and wonder at the contemplation of natural and artistic systems, whether they are understood as biologists do as art critics do" (113). Meeker also contends that although judgments of fact and beauty have historically stood opposed, they are better understood as alternative descriptions of the same natural processes. The continued separation of the arts and sciences is "absurd once it is accepted that human works are elements in a world ecosphere and when it is recognized that natural processes have provided the basic forms for human thought and creativity. Ecology demonstrates the interpenetrability of people and the natural environment, an insight which is richly confirmed by the evidence of human artistic creations" (117). See also Shepard, *Man in the Landscape*.
57. *Double Axe*, 131.
58. *Selected Poems*, 3. Jeffers became intimate with stone through masonry, learning the skill by watching his home being built and later singlehandedly building an addition to it. Most of the stones used in constructing the house and tower were rolled up from the beach below, but others from various places around the world were also incorporated. See also Helen and Scott Nearing, *Living the Good Life* (New York: Schocken, 1970), who explain that their choice of building in stone was based on

the principle that "utility and beauty are qualities possessed by wholes rather than parts. If the environment permits of utility and is a thing of beauty, the building must continue the lines of that utility and fill out the exquisite balance and harmony which give rise to that beauty" (49). Jeffers would agree, since the local materials he used helped create the impression that Tor house was a part of the wild, rocky Pacific Coast.

59. Whitehead, *Process and Reality,* 340.
60. *Selected Poetry,* xviii.
61. Brophy, *Robinson Jeffers,* 219. Brophy usually characterizes Jeffers as a pantheist. Jeffers almost invariably looks at God as an all-inclusive and immanent divinity revealed to humankind through the painful process of self-discovery.
62. Brophy suggests that Jeffers's religious conversion occurred sometime around his thirtieth year (*Jubilee Gathering,* xiii–xiv).
63. *Double Axe,* 105.
64. *Double Axe,* 113.
65. *Selected Poetry,* 551.
66. *Selected Poems,* 101, 100, 107.
67. From the perspective of literary ecology a meaningful distinction can be drawn between prophetic and alternative literatures. Prophetic literature is often cast in a utopian-pastoral mode: a tradition that views civilization as coming apart at the seams yet holds out hope that by returning to more natural ways salvation might be achieved and civilization put right again. But confronted by the harsh realities of the twentieth century— in both our social and ecological order—some believe that the pastoral-prophetic tradition of protest has lost any reason to be—what is needed is an alternative literature written in perhaps a picaresque mode. In this mode humankind is, according to Meeker, shown as a natural creature, "living [in some ways] as animals live, confronting the present defensively and opportunistically, without expectations or illusions, proud of strength but accurately aware of its limitations, mistrustful but not malicious, and above all adaptive to the immediate environment" (*Comedy of Survival,* 104). In other words, the future is now. Alternative literature is not a literature of protest per se. A picaro, such as Robert Nichols, bearing witness to the decline of nature and society, and perhaps the impending collapse of Western industrial civilization, says "Let it come . . . in this instant we'll find a way out." Robert Nichols, "A Literature of Alternatives," *Mesechabe* (Spring 1989): 12. See also Dolores LaChapelle, "Living Wild," *Earth First,* August 1, 1989, and Meeker, *Comedy of Survival,* 79–104, for discussion of the pastoral and picaresque traditions in literature.
68. Sessions and Devall, *Deep Ecology,* 171. Sessions in particular has influenced me to see and read Snyder as the poet laureate of deep ecology.

See George Sessions, "Gary Snyder: Post-Modern Man," manuscript. LaChapelle suggests the term *sacred ecology* as an alternative to *spiritual ecology*. See LaChapelle, *Earth Wisdom*, 137–50.

69. Gary Snyder, *The Back Country* (New York: New Directions, 1968), 130.
70. Kazuaki Tanahashi, ed., *Moon in a Dewdrop: Writings of Zen Master Dōgen* (San Francisco: North Point Press, 1985), is an insightful guide to the philosophical dimensions of Zen.
71. See Toshihiko and Toyo Izutsu, *The Theory of Beauty in the Classical Aesthetics of Japan* (The Hague: Martinus Nijhoff, 1981), who provide a useful explanation of haiku that bears meaningfully on Snyder's poetics. In Japanese poetry "Nature-description . . . is no longer to be elaborated and tempered at the level of *omoi* [analytical, conscious thought] . . . . Rather, it is to be a pure Nature-description in the sense that it is directly linked to the external world of Nature—natural things and events—as objects to be recognized, perceived and sensed by the poet through the whole of his subjectivity" (21).
72. Compare the *Tao te Ching*, chap. 1, verse 1.
73. Dōgen, *Writings*, 99.
74. Quoted material from "G. S. Brief Biography," unpublished, dated January 1989 (personal communication).
75. Snyder, *Real Work*, 92. *Sādhanā* means purificatory action or study; for the Zen Buddhist there is no paradox in saying that "life is my *sādhanā*" since Zen is life. Alternatively, wherever there is life there is Zen.
76. Although Snyder is not a Marxist, Marxism was probably a positive influence on his thinking, providing a critical perspective on capitalistic society.
77. Snyder, "Brief Biography."
78. Snyder, "Brief Biography."
79. Snyder, *Turtle Island*, 105. Snyder's spiritual ecology cannot be reduced to any simple "back-to-the-land" formula, and he does not romanticize the peasant life or the dirt farmer. Anyone who has lived close to nature will soon learn not to idealize it.
80. Snyder's poetry books include *Turtle Island; The Back Country; Riprap and Cold Mountain Poems; Myths and Texts; Six Sections "From Mountains and Rivers Without End"; Regarding Wave; The Fudo Trilogy; Axe Handles;* and *Left Out in the Rain.* His books of prose include *Earth House Hold; The Old Ways; He Who Hunted Birds in His Father's Village: The Dimensions of a Haida Myth; The Real Work;* and *Passage through India.*
81. Snyder is presently at work on a book manuscript entitled "The Practice of the Wild," which offers fresh insights into his idea of wilderness.
82. Collected in *The Old Ways*, the article is based on a talk Snyder gave

at the Ethnopoetics conference held at the University of Wisconsin—Milwaukee in April 1975.

83. Gary Snyder, *He Who Hunted Birds in His Father's Village: The Dimensions of a Haida Myth* (Bolinas, Calif.: Grey Fox Press, 1979), xi, emphasis added.

84. Gary Snyder, *Earth House Hold: Technical Notes & Queries to Fellow Dharma Revolutionaries* (New York: New Directions, 1957), 118.

85. The term *ethnopoetics*, which emphasizes the intersection between anthropology and poetry, likely originates (1968) with Jerome Rothenberg.

86. *The Old Ways*, 42, 42–43.

87. *Earth House Hold*, 120, 121–22.

88. *Turtle Island*, 5, 6.

89. Much as heart disease is endemic to industrial society, so the ancient ones succumbed to the consequences of malnutrition in old age because sandstone grit had worn away the enamel on their molars—one reason Snyder envisions old-new ways.

90. *Turtle Island*, 3. Snyder's dedication reads "For Lois Snyder Hennessy/ My Mother," a simple act that reinforces the centrality of the female in *Turtle Island*.

91. *Turtle Island*, 3–4.

92. *Turtle Island*, 18. Snyder is best understood as having abandoned any traditional Western political economy in favor of bioregionalism.

93. *Turtle Island*, 19. See Calvin Martin, *Keepers of the Game: Indian-Animal Relationships and the Fur Trade* (Berkeley: University of California Press, 1978), for an in-depth account of Amerindigen use of fire (179f.). See also William H. Romme and Don G. Despain, "The Yellowstone Fires," *Scientific American*, October 1989, for an interesting account of the ongoing scientific debate over the role of fire in forest ecology.

94. *Turtle Island*, 19. Paleolithic and archaic people lived in relative harmony with the environment; however, the consequences of ecological ignorance were as pernicious then as now. Southwestern Indigens sometimes exhausted the fertility of the soil through intensive agriculture to support their increasing populations. Shepard's thesis that in the turn to agriculture lies the roots of environmental ruin bears directly on this issue.

95. *Turtle Island*, 24, 25.

96. See *The Old Ways*, 35.

97. *Turtle Island*, 12–13.

98. *Earth House Hold*, 124.

99. *Turtle Island*, 47.

100. See Ferré, *Philosophy of Technology*, esp. chap, 8, and Max Oelschlaeger, "The Myth of the Technological Fix," *Southwestern Journal of Philosophy* 10 (June 1979).

101. *Turtle Island,* 67, 50, 51.

102. *The Old Ways,* 35–36.

103. *Turtle Island,* 41. See n. 71, above.

104. *Turtle Island,* 77, 77.

105. *Turtle Island,* 80–81.

106. *Turtle Island,* 106.

107. L. Edwin Folsom, "Gary Snyder's Descent to Turtle Island: Searching for Fossil Love," *Western American Literature* 15 (1980): 109.

108. *Turtle Island,* 106, 104, 107, 108, 102.

109. Peter Berg is usually credited with being the first to use (1976) the term *bioregionalism.* Berg credits Raymond F. Dasmann, who had completed a study in Switzerland for the United Nations on "biotic provinces." Believing that conventional designations for the land left people out, they coined the new term *bioregion.* "A bioregion would be a place that has a continuity of watersheds, river valleys, continuity of landforms, of climate, of native plants and animals, and that had in the past, by at least some people, been defined as a home place" (Peter Berg, cited in LaChapelle, *Sacred Land,* 181). See also LaChapelle, 178–85. She contends (see esp. 182) that when the bioregional movement became politicized (in 1985, at the First North American Bioregional Conference) along conventional lines, then the original impetus—as in the Amerindigen sense of "home place"—was lost. LaChapelle insists that Snyder is one of only a few bioregional spokespeople who understands the core concept: humankind living in place and in close relation with a distinctive biotic community. See also LaChapelle, "Not Laws of Nature but *Li* (Pattern) of Nature," in Oelschlaeger, ed., *Wilderness Condition.* Here she contends that the neoconfucian concept of *li* reflects an ancient (c. 1200 C.E.) understanding that grounding in place was essential to realization of humankind's potentialities.

110. *Turtle Island,* 101.

111. *Real Work,* 85, 87.

112. *Real Work,* 139. See Paehlke, *Environmentalism and Politics,* for related reading, esp. chap. 6. Paehlke's analysis of the concepts that lie at the heart of environmental politics (e.g., decentralization, appreciation of the web of life, sustainable economics) coincides remarkably with Snyder's. Both believe that environmentally committed constituencies will play an increasingly important role in Western liberal democracies.

113. *Real Work,* 140, 140–41.

114. Gary Snyder, "The Place, the Region, and the Commons" (manuscript, 1989).

115. *Real Work,* 141, 86–87.

116. *Earth House Hold,* 131–32.

117. *The Old Ways,* 36–37.
118. *Earth House Hold,* 127.
119. Heidegger, *Poetry, Language, Thought,* 213, 146.
120. Heidegger, *Poetry, Language, Thought,* 196–97.
121. Gadamer, *Truth and Method,* 143. Compare Frye's judgment that "the Bible is clearly a major element in our own imaginative tradition, whatever we may think we believe about it" (*Great Code,* xviii).
122. Campbell, *Mythologies of the Primitive Hunters,* 10.

Chapter 9. Contemporary Wilderness Philosophy

1. Samuel P. Hays, *Beauty, Health, and Permanence: Environmental Politics in the United States, 1955–1985* (New York: Cambridge University Press, 1987), 247. Hays captures a sense of the sweep of environmental thinking across American life in chap. 16, "Environmental Society and Environmental Politics."

2. Paehlke argues in *Environmentalism and Politics* that a "green" political movement in America may be a potent force for social and economic change. See also J. F. Pilat, *Ecological Politics: The Rise of the Green Movement* (London: Sage, 1980). Pilat maintains that the greens are essentially primitivists with a self-serving agenda that leads them to oppose progress, as for example nuclear power. See Bramwell, *Ecology in the 20th Century,* for a discussion of green politics in Europe. Like Pilat, Bramwell equates environmentalism with primitivism, although her study is more penetrating. See also Craig W. Allin, *The Politics of Wilderness Conservation* (Westport, Conn.: Greenwood, 1982), for an informed discussion of the shift from a politics of wilderness exploitation to the politics of preservation. Allin came to a relatively pessimistic observation near the end of his study in late 1980. "If wilderness preservation has prospered as affluence has grown, then perhaps the 1980 election marks the end of both. . . . If this is the end of American prosperity, then we might well expect that Americans will choose to sacrifice their remaining wilderness to the necessities of economic progress" (275). Allin concluded the outcome will hinge on a philosophical choice between "two competing concepts of our place on this planet" (276). See Hays, *Beauty, Health, and Permanence,* 491–543, for a balanced look at American environmental politics since 1980.

3. See Ehrenfeld, *Conserving Life on Earth,* 3–23; Nash, *Wilderness and the American Mind,* esp. 161–80; George Sessions, "Ecocentrism, Wilderness, and Global Ecosystem Protection," in Oelschlaeger, ed., *Wilderness Condition;* Alan Drengson, "Protecting the Environment, Protecting Ourselves: Reflections on the Philosophical Dimension," in R. Bradley and

S. Duguio, eds., *Environmental Ethics,* vol. 2 (Burnaby, Canada: Simon Fraser University, Humanities Institute, 1989), for relevant discussions.

4. See Paehlke, *Environmentalism and Politics,* esp. chap. 3, "The Malthusian Dilemma Updated: Population and Resources."

5. Marsh, *Earth as Modified by Human Action,* iii.

6. Theodore Roosevelt, letter (November 1907) to the Governors of the United States, in Henry Jarrett, ed., *Perspectives on Conservation: Essays on America's Natural Resources* (Baltimore: Resources for the Future, 1958), 51.

7. Compare Petulla, *Environmental History,* 287.

8. See Samuel Eliot Morison, *The Oxford History of the American People* (New York: Oxford University Press, 1965), 889.

9. See Sax, *Mountains without Handrails,* for an illuminating discussion of wilderness-oriented recreation.

10. See Samuel P. Hays, *Conservation and the Gospel of Efficiency: The Progressive Conservation Movement, 1890–1920* (New York: Athenaeum, 1972), and Hays, *Beauty, Health, and Permanence.*

11. See Handler, *Biology and the Future of Man,* 774.

12. For a perceptive reading of the resource management approach at work in historical context see Donald Worster, *Rivers of Empire: Water, Aridity, and the Growth of the American West* (New York: Pantheon, 1985). Chapter 7 of Worster's study is essential reading for anyone trying to see beyond resourcism. Also see Mark Sagoff, *The Economy of the Earth: Philosophy, Law, and the Environment* (Cambridge: Cambridge University Press, 1988), for a wide-ranging, largely critical approach to resourcism generally and cost-benefit analysis specifically.

13. Many difficult questions are involved. Who can define the public interest, and how in a society such as ours can it be separated from private interest? What is a democracy? Although such issues are vital, they are beyond the scope of this book. For relevant reading see Grant McConnell, *Private Power and the American Democracy* (New York: Vintage, 1970); G. William Domhoff, *Who Rules America?* (Englewood Cliffs, N.J.: Prentice-Hall, 1967); Robert A. Dahl, *After the Revolution: Authority in a Good Society* (New Haven and London: Yale University Press, 1970); and David L. Hall, *Eros and Irony: A Prelude to Philosophical Anarchism* (Albany: State University of New York Press, 1982).

14. See Earl Finbar Murphy, *Governing Nature* (Chicago: Quadrangle, 1967), for an overview of the legislative policy-making and administrative decision-making process as impacting on nature.

15. Marsh, cited in Ehrenfeld, *Conserving Life on Earth,* 13.

16. See Anne LaBastille, *Beyond Black Bear Lake* (New York: W. W. Norton, 1987), for an example; she discovers the effects of acid rain even at the remote reaches of her cabin.

17. Bramwell, *Ecology in the 20th Century,* 22. Bramwell overlooks the

choice thrust on the modern mind by these qualitative changes. Ecologism equates with primitivism only so long as the values of Modernism are held as absolute presuppositions. A virtue of studies like Hays's or Paehlke's is recognizing that environmentalism has a potentially positive role to play in sociocultural transformation. Such transformation is not necessarily a retreat to premodern forms of life, even if different from modern culture, but an informed advance effected through the political institutions of Western culture. See William D. Ruckelshaus, "Toward a Sustainable World," *Scientific American,* September 1989. He contends that American values have been green throughout the 1980s but that institutional restructuring has not occurred precisely because green values have not yet been politically efficacious.

18. Evernden, *Natural Alien,* 23, 21.
19. For a definitive critique of this ideology see Georgescu-Roegen, *Entropy Law.* Also see Max Oelschlaeger, *The Environmental Imperative: A Socio-Economic Perspective* (Washington, D.C.: University Press of America, 1977).
20. See Thorstein Veblen, *The Theory of the Leisure Class: An Economic Study of Institutions* (New York: Macmillan, 1899), for relevant discussion.
21. See Georgescu-Roegen, *Entropy Law,* and Max Oelschlaeger, "Cost-Benefit Analysis: A Philosophical Reconsideration," *Ekistics* 46 (May–June 1979), for critiques of cost-benefit analysis.
22. Rolston, *Philosophy Gone Wild,* 207. Darwin's contemporary, Alfred R. Wallace (1823–1913), was likely the first to use the "species as pages" metaphor.
23. Evernden, *Natural Alien,* 22. Means and ends are also dichotomized by modern economics; see Georgescu-Roegen, *Entropy Law,* 18–19. See also Leiss, *Domination of Nature,* 117–19, and Meeker, *Comedy of Survival,* 133–35. Leiss adds to Evernden's observation the further point that Modernism assumes "the rationality of the scientific methodology itself . . . is 'transferred' intact, as it were, to the social process and mitigates social conflict by satisfying human wants through the intensified exploitation of nature's resources" (118–19). Meeker makes a similar point. Resourcism reflects the utilitarian faith "that human beings are perfectible and that they will grow in goodness as they are released from bondage to nature by an increasingly efficient technology. As machines perform their tasks ever more perfectly, mankind is expected to use the resulting leisure and freedom to cultivate reason, goodness, and beauty. As machines become more *mechanically* efficient, humans should grow more *ethically* efficient" (132). There is little evidence that this is so, in part because "both nature and humanity are subject to degradation and pollution by these same techniques" (133).
24. The inherent inconsistencies, if not outright contradictions, between con-

servationist and preservationist ideas of wilderness have manifested themselves in the lives of many ecologists. See Edwin P. Pister, "A Pilgrim's Progress from Group A to Group B," in Callicott, *Companion*, for an arresting account of his transformation from resourcism.

25. Merchant, *Death of Nature*, 293. Of course, species in context come and go in a virtual kaleidoscope of change without ecosystemic collapse.

26. This battle continues within contemporary biology and ecology. See Barry Commoner, *Science and Survival* (New York: Viking, 1963), 30ff.; Mayr, *Biological Thought*, 59–67; McIntosh, *Background of Ecology*, 252–56; and Andrew Brennan, *Thinking about Nature: An Investigation of Nature, Value, and Ecology* (Athens: University of Georgia Press, 1988). Brennan terms holistic thinking metaphysical ecology and his own reductionistic ecology scientific ecology (31). He apparently chooses to ignore the many arguments against the theoretical possibility of a universally commensurable scientific vocabulary.

27. Barry Commoner, *The Closing Circle: Nature, Man, and Technology* (New York: Alfred A. Knopf, 1971), 29. For more technical discussions see Bohm, *Wholeness and the Implicate Order*, and Prigogine, *Order Out of Chaos*.

28. Prigogine, *Order Out of Chaos*, 177.

29. Alexander's teleonomic perspective in *Space, Time, and Deity* has not been surpassed.

30. Compare J. E. Lovelock, *Gaia: A New Look at Life on Earth* (New York: Oxford University Press, 1987). *Gaia* translates from the Greek as Mother Earth. Lovelock also discusses (esp. chaps. 7–9) the collectivized warfare between rival groups of holists and reductionists within the biological and ecological scientific communities. See also James E. Lovelock, "Hands Up for the Gaia Hypothesis," *Nature*, March 8, 1990, 100–102.

31. For example, island ecosystems in the Pacific Ocean are fragile because of the small landmass and number of species, whereas continental landmasses and ecosystems are more impervious to rapid change.

32. Compare William Tucker, *Progress and Privilege: America in the Age of Environmentalism* (Garden City, N.Y.: Doubleday, 1982). Tucker argues that liberal environmentalists have protected more than nature: namely, the socioeconomic status quo.

33. Our goal is merely to clarify usages adequate to sustain our argument. Readers who wish to pursue the issue to its contemporary terminus may find relevant reading in Hargrove, *Environmental Ethics*, esp. 166–67; Rolston, *Philosophy Gone Wild*; Holmes Rolston III, *Environmental Ethics* (Philadelphia: Temple University Press, 1988), esp. 73–77; and Callicott, *Land Ethic*, esp. 101–14. We might categorize Hargrove, Rolston, and Callicott as environmental ethicists who advance arguments for the moral considerability of nonhuman others (both living

and nonliving) on anthropocentric, biocentric, and ecocentric grounds respectively. Briefly, Hargrove argues that anthropocentric arguments and human values remain vital to preservationists, since otherwise the protection of nonliving things (like caves) is dependent on trickle-down biocentric arguments. Rolston argues that "anthropocentric biocentrism" (e.g., Hargrove's position) draws an illicit dividing line between the human and nonhuman and that humans ought to follow nature's (the living biological world's) ways. Callicott, in distinction from both Hargrove and Rolston, argues from one central fact—"we are enfolded, involved, and engaged within the living, terrestrial environment" (101)—to a radically revised ontological-metaphysical perspective underlying an ecocentric outlook. Hence, nature becomes a structured, differentiated whole in process, and human egoism gives way to aesthetic and ethical relationalism. Callicott might argue against Hargrove that he begs the question by assuming the existence of valuing human subjects independent of natural process; and he might argue against Rolston that his biocentric appeal to "nature's way" rests on an ontological (rather than historical or evolutionary) distinction between the human and nonhuman.

34. Compare Teilhard de Chardin, *Phenomenon of Man*, 33. I am not entirely unsympathetic to Teilhard's arguments, as for example his contention that the true physics is one that will include Homo sapiens in a coherent picture of the world (36).

35. Smuts, *Holism and Evolution*, in Gunter and Sibley, *Process Philosophy*, 234.

36. Hurricanes, however destructive of human property, are ecologically beneficial to tidal estuaries and saltwater bays.

37. See Rolston, *Philosophy Gone Wild*, 121. A clear outline of a biocentric idea of wilderness can be found in Taylor's *Respect for Nature*, 99–168.

38. Coevolutionists, such as Frederick Turner, argue that the successful restoration of Wisconsin prairie reveals the potential to heal the earth. This contention faces at least four objections. First, the example underlying the generalization is an abstraction divorced from any ecosystemic context. Second, the argument begs questions of energy and capital and other issues involving the second law. Third, any claim that restored prairie is "the same" or equivalent to a natural prairie strains the imagination; where, for example, are the indigenous species that once roamed that prairie, the carnivores and herbivores, and what of micro-organic life? Finally, even granting that Wisconsin prairie can be restored, neither a logical method nor empirical data justifies concluding that such restoration is globally feasible.

39. Passmore attacks biocentrists in *Man's Responsibility* (1974), but the argument extends to ecocentrism. John Passmore has since abandoned this position. He now claims that "we do need a 'new metaphysics' which

is genuinely not anthropocentric. . . . The working out of such a meta-physics is, in my judgement, the most important task which lies ahead of philosophy . . . [since] the emergence of new moral attitude to nature is bound up . . . with the emergence of a more realistic philosophy of nature. This is the only adequate foundation for effective environmental concern" ("Attitudes toward Nature," cited in Devall and Sessions, *Deep Ecology*, 52).

40. Rolston, *Philosophy Gone Wild*, 33.

41. Duerr, *Dreamtime*, 128.

42. William James, *Pragmatism* (Indianapolis, Ind.: Hackett, 1981), 110, 111.

43. There are a number of other problems, including the pathetic fallacy, which we shall not discuss here.

44. Leopold, *Sand County Almanac*, 262.

45. See Callicott, "Hume's Is/Ought Dichotomy and the Relation of Ecology to Leopold's Land Ethic," in Callicott, *Land Ethic*, 117–27, for a de-fense of the land ethic against such charges. Callicott argues that Hume provides a metaethical model that justifies Leopold's ethical claims. "If Hume's analysis is essentially correct, ecology and the environmental sci-ences can thus directly change our values: what we value, not how we value. . . . [E]cology changes our values by changing our concepts of the world and of ourselves in relation to the world. It reveals new relations among objects which, once revealed, stir our ancient centers of moral feeling" (127).

46. Taylor, *Respect for Nature*, 51. Leopold's argument does not go from fact (is) to value (ought) but rather from a present system of oughts with (empirically confirmed) pernicious environmental effects to a new system of oughts that conjecturally and arguably avoids adverse ecological con-sequences. Rolston's *Philosophy Gone Wild* and *Environmental Ethics*, and Callicott's *Defense of the Land Ethic*, help clarify the is-ought issue; see also Wayne C. Booth, *Modern Dogma and the Rhetoric of Assent* (Chicago: University of Chicago Press, 1974), esp. chap. 1 and appendix B, for a critique of the fact-value split.

47. Neither (1) or (2) can be avoided. For example, the principle of indeter-minacy alone sustains the first claim, and Gödel's theorem the second. See also Rorty, *Contingency, Irony, and Solidarity*.

48. See also Callicott, *Land Ethic*, 157–74, for a defense of a land ethic via an ecological perspective informed by quantum theory; and see chap. 7, n. 67, above, and chap. 10. below.

49. Ecocentrists sometimes extend their arguments to include animal rights, often in ways similar to Albert Schweitzer's notion of the reverence for life. See Peter Singer, ed., *In Defense of Animals* (New York: Harper and Row, 1985); see also James Serpell, *In the Company of Animals: A Study of Human-Animal Relationships* (Oxford: Basil Blackwell, 1986).

50. Rolston, *Philosophy Gone Wild*, 157.

51. Compare George Sessions, "The Deep Ecology Movement: A Review," *Environmental Review* (Summer 1987); Devall and Sessions, *Deep Ecology;* Michael Tobias, ed., *Deep Ecology* (San Diego: Avant, 1985); and Arne Naess, "The Deep Ecology Movement," *Inquiry 88* (Oslo, 1973).

52. Warwick Fox, "Deep Ecology: A New Philosophy of Our Time?" *Ecologist* 14 (1984), cited in Devall and Sessions, *Deep Ecology,* 66.

53. Sessions, "Ecological Consciousness and Paradigm Change," in Tobias, *Deep Ecology,* 39.

54. Some deep ecologists might question the desirability of any paradigmatic structure, since living *within* nature entails different values according to place. See, e.g., LaChapelle, "Not Laws of Nature but *Li.*"

55. Arne Naess, "The Basics of Deep Ecology," *Resurgence* (January–February 1988): 6.

56. Sessions, "Deep Ecology Movement," 117.

57. See Arne Naess, *Ecology, Community, and Lifestyle: Outline of an Ecosophy,* trans. and rev. ed. by David Rothenberg (New York: Cambridge University Press, 1989), based on the original work by Naess, *Okologi, Samfunn, Og Livsstil* (1976).

58. David Rothenberg argues that value questions cannot be eluded by deep ecology. He points out that while some deep ecologists have eschewed the question of an environmental axiology (he mentions Warwick Fox by name), their language reveals a value-laden orientation. See David Rothenberg, "Introduction: Ecosophy T—From Intuition to System," in Naess, *Ecology, Community, and Lifestyle,* 19–20.

59. Compare Lawson, *Reflexivity.*

60. See Sessions, "Western Process Metaphysics," 236. In "Deep Ecology Movement," however, Sessions is more favorably disposed toward process philosophy (109). No deep ecologist has systematically read the Whiteheadian corpus for its ecological insights. Such a reading might begin with Whitehead's arguments in *Science and the Modern World,* 109–12.

61. Griffin, *Reenchantment of Science,* x. The deep ecologist's methodological predicament is virtually inescapable, since an ecological perspective requires a doctrine of internal relations, and that doctrine is inconsistent with privileged truth claims.

62. Compare Cobb, "Ecology, Science, and Religion," 106ff. The fundamental issue is whether humanism can be reconciled with an ecological paradigm. See David Ehrenfeld, *The Arrogance of Humanism* (New York: Oxford University Press, 1978). The paradox of humanism, Ehrenfeld maintains, is that it is a religion of humanity where, hidden behind the screen of modern reason, Homo sapiens becomes a veritable God unto itself.

63. Anthony Lejeune, "Green, Green, Their World Is Green," *Denton Record Chronicle,* October 25, 1989, 16A. Lejeune is the London correspondent for the *National Review.*

64. The "speculative knowledge" of a Whitehead, the "radical empiricism" of a James, and the "true empiricism" of a Bergson are not mystical states of consciousness.

65. Compare Murray Bookchin, "Marxism as Bourgeois Sociology," in *Toward an Ecological Society* (Montreal: Black Rose, 1980). For a more recent critique of Marxism by a social ecologist see John P. Clark, "Marx's Inorganic Body," *Environmental Ethics* 11 (Fall 1989). Clark argues that although there are a few ecologically sensitive passages in Marx, the literature is dualistic and anthropocentric, viewing nature as little more than a valueless *materia prima* upon which humankind imposes form, and thus value. See also Leiss, *Domination of Nature,* 179–80, who points out that Marxism and capitalism are—under the surface—more similar than dissimilar in their outlook on nature. More generally, Marxism appears to most critics as both existentially (as witness the recent events in the Eastern bloc) and theoretically moribund, an economic reflection (as is capitalism) of the underlying metaphysics and epistemology of Modernism, redolent with anthropocentrism (since all that counts is human telos), logocentrism (since the categories of human history exhaust the universe of meaning), and ethnocentrism (since revolutionary Western people will save the world).

66. See Murray Bookchin, "As If People Mattered," *Nation,* October 10, 1988, 294. See also Murray Bookchin, "The Crisis in the Ecology Movement," *Green Perspectives: Newsletter of the Green Program Project,* May 1988, in which he restates his case with amplifying detail. For a succinct statement of Bookchin's platform for social ecology see Murray Bookchin, "Toward a Philosophy of Nature—The Bases for an Ecological Ethics," in Tobias, *Deep Ecology.* For a short list of his many publications see Robyn Eckersley, "Divining Evolution: The Ecological Ethics of Murray Bookchin," *Environmental Ethics* 11 (Summer 1989): 100, n. 2.

67. See Kirkpatrick Sale, "Deep Ecology and Its Critics," *Nation,* May 14, 1988.

68. George Sessions, personal communication. See also Ehrenfeld, *Arrogance of Humanism,* 53–54, for criticism of Bookchin's social ecology.

69. Eckersley, "Divining Evolution," 111.

70. Charles Sanders Peirce, *Philosophical Writings of Peirce,* ed. Justus Buchler (New York: Dover, 1955), 54.

71. Compare, e.g., Martin W. Holdgate, "Planning for Our Common Future: Options for Action," *Environment* 31 (October 1989).

72. Devall and Sessions discuss five ecotopian visions in chap. 9 of *Deep Ecology,* drawing on the work of Loren Eiseley, Baker Brownell, Aldous Huxley, Paul Shepard, and Gary Snyder. See also Ernest Callenbach, *Ecotopia: The Notebooks and Reports of William Weston* (Berkeley: Banyan Tree, 1975), for an imaginative vision of an ecotopian future.

73. Sessions and Devall, *Deep Ecology,* 1.

74. Devall and Sessions imply in *Deep Ecology* that many other women, such as Mary Hunter Austin (1868–1934), might be considered as eco-feminists. However, if we define ecofeminism as a combination of the post–World War II environmental and feminist movements, then Austin cannot be included, despite her abilities as a naturalist.

75. Table 8 is neither definitive nor exhaustive. By using these criteria our study can at least begin to encompass relevant arguments of the entire feminist continuum, including post-Christian goddess feminists as well as such radical feminists as Mary Daly. Where Daly, for example, traces ecological malaise to "phallo-technic society" and "patriarchal myth and language," this book has emphasized (for example) the Neolithic and scientific revolutions. But these perspectives are neither a priori inconsistent nor contradictory and in fact overlap at certain points. See Mary Daly, *Gyn/Ecology: The Metaethics of Radical Feminism* (Boston: Beacon, 1978).

76. Merchant, *Death of Nature,* xv.

77. Thoreau, "Walking," 237.

78. Merchant, *Death of Nature,* xv.

79. LaChapelle, *Earth Wisdom,* 33.

80. Merchant, "Feminism and Ecology," in Sessions and Devall, *Deep Ecology,* 229.

81. See Daly, *Gyn/Ecology.* She argues that "in Western society both 'tight' women ('dried-up old maids') and 'loose' women ('dirty whores') are sexually *wrong* by male standards. For in fact female sexuality—as an expression of female be-ing—is essentially wrong by androcratic, heterosexist standards" (160).

82. Daly, *Gyn/Ecology,* 9.

83. See Doty, *Mythography,* esp. chap. 3, for a penetrating discussion of the functions of ritual, and Rothenberg and Rothenberg, *Symposium of the Whole.*

84. Dolores LaChapelle, "Ritual Is Essential," in Sessions and Devall, *Deep Ecology,* 247, 250. See also LaChapelle, "Understanding Psychology,"

85. Merchant, *Death of Nature,* 2, emphasis added.

86. See Elinor Gadon, *The Once and Future Goddess: A Symbol for Our Time* (San Francisco: Harper and Row, 1989), esp. part two, for an account of the patriarchal appropriation of the Mother Goddess. There is little doubt that, as Gadon puts it, "in Sumer and all the ancient Near East, the Goddess's powers and values were co-opted to serve the state" (142). Compare Gimbutas, *Gods and Goddesses of Old Europe.*

87. Rosemary Radford Ruether, *Sexism and God-Talk: Toward a Feminist Theology* (Boston: Beacon, 1983), 93, 54.

88. Ruether, *Sexism and God-Talk,* 265. On witchcraft and wild nature

see Duerr, *Dreamtime,* esp. chaps. 1, 2. See also Emily Dickinson, ed. Thomas H. Johnson, *The Complete Poems of Emily Dickinson* (Boston: Little, Brown, 1960), 656. "Witchcraft was hung, in History,/But History and I/Find all the Witchcraft that we need/Around us, every Day—." The work of Emily Dickinson is interpreted by Susette Graham as a rich vein of nineteenth-century ecofeminism. See Deborah Dooley, Susette Graham, and Jane Koenen, "Ways of Knowing, Ways of Being: A Feminist Approach to Wilderness in Idea and Word," *Contemporary Philosophy* 12 (September–October 1989).

89. Ruether, *Sexism and God-Talk,* 265–66.

90. Zimmerman, "Feminism, Deep Ecology, and Environmental Ethics," 42, 34, 40–41, 41. See also Riane Eisler, *The Chalice and the Blade: Our History, Our Future* (San Francisco: Harper and Row, 1987), for an interesting inquiry into the structure of a partnership society (gylany) that escapes patriarchy and matriarchy.

91. Merchant, "Feminism and Ecology," 231.

92. See Nash, Bramwell, and many others who seem to agree on this point. Although a number of communes exist that practice the principles of deep ecology, most legislative and administrative action that has led to wilderness preservation has been inspired by preservationist principles.

93. "Profoundly" here implies accepting and following the implications of evolution—biologically, ecologically, and philosophically.

94. Among many see Diamond, *In Search of the Primitive,* and Feyerabend, *Against Method.* Diamond argues that anthropology can help in the escape from the repressive categories of Modernism "precisely because we are so civilized and so in need of a deeper vision of man. It is in this way anthropology can become a revolutionary discipline, though it may often seem the most remote and eccentric of inquiries" (123). Feyerabend writes that he is "against ideologies that use the name of science for cultural murder" (4). So understood, *Against Method* is an epistemology of liberation, both for wild nature and the *indigenas* of the world.

95. Irrelevant since becoming bears etiologically on both the human and the natural worlds; fallacious because any argument that either explicitly or implicitly denies evolution is unsound (i.e., assumes false premises).

96. See Peirce, *Philosophical Writings,* 18ff.

97. Evernden, *Natural Alien,* 124, emphasis added.

98. Thoreau, "Walking," 232.

99. Rorty, *Mirror of Nature,* 389.

100. Compare Rorty, *Contingency, Irony, and Solidarity,* 189ff. I emphasize that Rorty does *not* make such an extension himself; further, his work has been critiqued by ecologically minded postmodernists. In "Ethics as Bioregional Narrative," Cheney charges that Rorty's deconstruction

of totalizing narratives (in *Mirror of Nature*) retains a hidden dualism between language and the world (since language becomes free floating, that is, free of the world), and leaves the Cartesian ego in place, free to create whatever world it might choose. While this *may* be a valid criticism of Rorty's position in *Mirror of Nature,* his more recent work in *Contingency, Irony, and Solidarity* avoids this problem. Rorty clearly deconstructs the Cartesian self; he opens the door to recognition of non-human others through his discussion of cruelty and pain; and he forces us to recognize that all action is action in context—both cultural and natural.

Chapter 10. Cosomos and Wilderness

1. Compare Doty, *Mythography,* 233.
2. See Loyal D. Rue, *Amythia: Crisis in the Natural History of Western Culture* (Tuscaloosa: University of Alabama Press, 1989). Rue argues for the ideal of a third covenant grounded in an evolutionary creation story. Yet, even granted the possibility of a third covenant, the question is, as Schubert Ogden puts it, "whether the essential claims of the Christian witness of faith can be expressed in [such] terms" ("Theology of Nature," 135). Leiss appears skeptical in the *Domination of Nature,* since the fundamentally Baconian cast of Modernism precludes (in his opinion) the re-integration of humankind and nature consistent with Judeo-Christianity. Modernism, he writes, "conceived as the possession of power *over* nature by the human species as a whole, is an idea which makes sense only in relation to the absolute separation of spirit (God) and nature in Judaeo-Christian theology—and thus is an idea which cannot be secularized without losing its internal harmony" (188). Gottwald is a bit more hopeful. He argues in *Tribes of Yahweh* that "all forms of religious faith and practice that fail to grasp and to act upon their connection with and dependence upon the cultural-material evolution of humankind are doomed to irrationality and irrelevance, whatever diversionary consolation they offer at the moment" (709). Gottwald emphasizes that the religious symbolism for a postmodern project "will have to grow out of an accurate scientific understanding of the actual material conditions we face" (706).
3. Compare Thoreau, "Walking"; Heidegger, *Poetry, Language, Thought,* esp. "The Thinker as Poet"; and Kohák, *Embers and the Stars.*
4. Jacques Monod, *Chance and Necessity: An Essay on the Natural Philosophy of Modern Biology,* trans. Austryn Wainhouse (New York: Vintage, 1972), 177. Monod draws conclusions apropos of acting on an ethic of knowledge which are moot.
5. Albert Einstein, *Ideas and Opinions,* trans. Sonja Bargmann (New York:

Bonanza, 1954), 42; see also Einstein, *Albert Einstein: The Man and His Theories,* ed. Hilaire Cuny, trans. Mervyn Savill (Greenwich, Conn.: Fawcett, 1966), 111.

6. Erwin Schrödinger, *What Is Life? and Other Scientific Essays* (New York: Doubleday, 1956), 127.

7. Carl Friedrich von Weizsäcker, *The Ambivalence of Progress: Essays on Historical Anthropology* (New York: Paragon, 1988), 20. Originally published as *Der Garten des Menschlichen* (Munich: Carl Hanser Verlag, 1977).

8. Erwin Schrödinger, "Are There Quantum Jumps?" *British Journal for the Philosophy of Science* 3 (1952), cited in Prigogine, *Order Out of Chaos,* 18.

9. Whitehead, *Science and the Modern World,* 47.

10. Among others see David Ray Griffin, ed., *Physics and the Ultimate Significance of Time: Bohm, Prigogine, and Process Philosophy* (Albany: State University of New York Press, 1986); Errol E. Harris, *The Reality of Time* (Albany: State University of New York Press, 1988); Fraser, *Voices of Time;* and Sherover, *Experience of Time.*

11. Compare Cobb, "Ecology, Science, and Religion," 112.

12. Compare Prigogine, *Order Out of Chaos,* and Prigogine, *From Being to Becoming: Time and Complexity in the Physical Sciences* (New York: W. H. Freeman, 1980), 19–45.

13. Eiseley, *Darwin's Century,* 347. See Bruce J. West, *An Essay on the Importance of Being Nonlinear,* vol. 62 of *Lecture Notes in Biomathematics,* ed. S. Levin (New York: Springer-Verlag, 1985), for an insightful and rigorous mathematical treatment of these issues.

14. Compare Prigogine, *Order Out of Chaos,* 14–16, and *Being and Becoming,* xi–xix. Prigogine notes that although the second law radically departs from the mechanistic worldview of modern physics, and is therefore not deducible from dynamics, it is compatible. That is, although nonequilibrium thermodynamics is consistent with the descriptions of dynamic systems made possible by Galileo and Newton, it also introduces dramatically new elements, which elude classical science, into the world picture. Most elementarily, and dramatically, "irreversible processes have an immense constructive importance: life would not be possible without them" (*Order Out of Chaos,* 125). Bruce West argues that there are times when a nonlinear view of natural phenomena is preferable to a linear perspective. "One consequence of the linear world view is the *principle of superposition* which qualitatively states that a complex event can be segmented into a number of simple components in order to understand the components separately and then recombined back into an organized whole that can be understood in terms of the properties of the compo-

nents. Nonlinear interactions preclude the recombining of the constitutive elements back into such an organized whole" (*Importance of Being Nonlinear*, 65).

15. Prigogine, *Order Out of Chaos*, 225. As a minimum any alternative *scientific* description must be in principle be falsifiable; those descriptions which have been falsified are no longer an acceptable part of a scientific worldview. Scientific hypotheses are proposed descriptions subject to further inquiry.

16. Prigogine, *Order Out of Chaos*, xxvii, 19, 3, xxix.

17. See David Ray Griffin, "Introduction: Time and the Fallacy of Misplaced Concreteness," in Griffin, *Physics and Time*, 29.

18. Ilya Prigogine, "Irreversibility and Space-Time Structure," in Griffin, *Physics and Time*, 232.

19. Prigogine, *Order Out of Chaos*, 225.

20. Compare Kuhn, *Structure of Scientific Revolutions*; Rorty, *Mirror of Nature* and *Contingency, Irony and Solidarity*; and Feyerabend, *Farewell to Reason* and *Against Method*.

21. Lawson, *Reflexivity*, 10.

22. Davis and Hersh, *Descartes' Dream*, xv, emphasis deleted, 277. This premise finds confirmation in the opinion of many of the deepest thinkers of Western culture, including Georgescu-Roegen (see *Entropy Law*, especially his warning about the arithmomorphic fallacy), and Whitehead, who in spite of his deep affinity with mathematical thought realized its limitations.

23. Marjorie Grene, "The Paradoxes of Historicity," in Wachterhauser, *Hermeneutics and Modern Philosophy*, 182.

24. See Brian Swimme, "The Cosmic Creation Story," in Griffin, *Reenchantment of Science*, 53. See also Jacques Merleau-Ponty and Bruno Morando, *The Rebirth of Cosmology*, trans. Helen Weaver (New York: Alfred A. Knopf, 1976), who warn against thinking of any cosmology as a finished or adequate account. The specialist in nuclear physics, astrophysics, cosmology, and related disciplines will find the discussion irrelevant to their research but not, I hope, jejune. I write essentially for the nonspecialist. I have presupposed that the preponderance of the evidence bears favorably on the case for an evolutionary cosmology, and I believe that the cosmic creation story presented in chap. 10 is consistent with the advancing front of postmodern cosmology. See A. K. Raychaudhuri, *Theoretical Cosmology* (Oxford: Clarendon, 1979); Milton K. Munitz, ed., *Theories of the Universe: From Babylonian Myth to Modern Science* (New York: Free Press, 1957); and John D. Barrow and Frank J. Tipler, *Anthropic Cosmological Principle* (New York: Oxford University Press, 1986).

25. See Jay M. Pasachoff and Marc L. Kutner, *University Astronomy* (Phila-

delphia: W. B. Saunders, 1978); see also Adrian Webster, "The Cosmic Background Radiation," in Owen Gingerich, ed., *Cosmology + 1* (San Francisco: W. H. Freeman, 1977).

26. See Bart J. Bok and Priscilla F. Bok, *The Milky Way,* 5th ed. (Cambridge: Harvard University Press, 1981), for an accessible introduction to galactic evolution.

27. For an accessible introduction to H-R diagrams see Pasachoff and Kutner, *University Astronomy,* and Robert Burnham, Jr., *Andromeda-Cetus,* vol. 1 of *Burnham's Celestial Handbook: An Observer's Guide to the Universe Beyond the Solar System* (New York: Dover, 1978).

28. See Handler, *Biology and the Future of Man;* Simpson, *Meaning of Evolution;* A. G. Cairns-Smith, *Seven Clues to the Origin of Life: A Scientific Detective Story* (Cambridge: Cambridge University Press, 1985); and Loren Eiseley, *The Immense Journey* (New York: Vintage, 1959), for complementary although different naturalistic accounts of the origin of life on earth. I am also indebted to J. A. Diefenbeck for sharing his "Philosophy of Organism" in manuscript and to Frederick Turner for allowing me to read his epic poem, "Genesis," in manuscript.

29. Handler, *Biology and the Future of Man,* 165. The grounds for a useful distinction between modern and postmodern perspectives (both scientific and philosophic) perhaps lies here. The modernist believes that life can be entirely explained in terms of the principles of material existence; if so, then efficient causation reigns cosmologically, and the cosmos is a deterministic system capable of complete elucidation. The claim that the emergence of life is a historic event entails the reality of evolution: namely, the appearance of a novel kind (the organic) that cannot in principle be reduced to the inorganic. That is, the effects do not reside in and cannot be predicted from the initial conditions even though such circumstances are necessary conditions. Matter, for example, carbon, is a necessary but not sufficient condition for life. Synergetic phenomena are a manifestation of true novelty rather than invariant repetitions of pre-established regularities. Many difficult scientific and philosophic issues are involved here, not only at the level of the biological (the emergence of the organic from the inorganic) but also at the level of the psychological (the emergence of the self-conscious neocortex).

30. Eiseley, *Immense Journey,* 12.

31. Compare John 1.1–5 and Gen. 1.1–5. As a minimum we need to distinguish the notion that words function ontogenetically from the idea that words function cosmogenetically. These are two distinct ideas, although they appear to converge on the anthropic cosmological principle. The ontogenetic function of language reflects the reality that we are culture-making, culture-dwelling animals. So viewed, John 1.1–5 sheds light on the origin of our Western belief system but yields little cosmological in-

sight. Our social reality includes cosmology, which is a highly refined language, a system of theoretical constructs tied to observations of the world.

32. See, e.g., Jean Charon, *Cosmology: Theories of the Universe*, trans. Patrick Moore (New York: McGraw-Hill, 1970).

33. Robert Jastrow, *God and the Astronomers* (New York: Warner, 1980), 105–6.

34. Paul Davies, *God and the New Physics* (New York: Simon and Schuster, 1984), 223.

35. Schubert M. Ogden, "Christliche Theologie und die neue Religiosität," in Rainer Volp, ed., *Chancen der Religion* (Gütersloh: Gütersloher Verlagshaus Gerd Mohn, 1975), 159–60. See also Ogden, "Theology of Nature."

36. J. T. Fraser, *Time: The Familiar Stranger* (Amherst: University of Massachusetts Press, 1987), 356.

37. Kurt Vonnegut, Jr., *Cat's Cradle* (New York: Dell, 1970), 124.

38. The evidence is here overwhelming, although the claim that the first Mousterian skeleton discovered at La Ferrassie gave evidence of deliberate burial initially met opposition. But within only a few years subsequent discoveries confirmed to the satisfaction of prehistorians the widespread practice of funerary rituals in not only the upper but the middle Paleolithic strata.

39. Compare Campbell, *Mythologies of the Primitive Hunters*, 25.

40. Loren Eiseley, *Immense Journey*, 125.

41. Fraser, *Time: The Familiar Stranger*, 355, 355–56.

42. Compare Virginia Trimble, "Cosmology: Man's Place in the Universe," *American Scientist* 65 (January–February 1977). Trimble perhaps goes too far in claiming, however facetiously, that once evolution has proceeded to the point of the genetic mechanism, "then the entire mechanism of Darwinian selection and mutations takes over, and the evolution from a primeval slime mold to a local politician seems practically inevitable. We therefore expect that life will eventually become intelligent life in many cases" (84). Even Hartshorne, evolutionary pantheist that he is, believes that the human species surprised God. In retrospect, we can see that evolution has worked as it has; but we cannot conclude that Homo sapiens was an inevitable outcome. Trimble aptly draws an analogy between human intelligence and a waterfall. Consider, she urges, "a water molecule, whose structure, energy levels, and so forth can be calculated with some precision by the methods of quantum mechanics. But nothing in that calculation would ever lead us to predict waterfalls. The waterfall is a result of very many particles interacting in ways we cannot, in practice, predict or calculate" (86). More fundamentally, once we take time seriously, the future, though conditioned by the past, remains open. Unlimited chance would equate to chaos, but directed evolution eventuates in novel outcomes: emergent order out of chaos.

43. The weak anthropic cosmological principle (WAP), according to Barrow and Tipler, is that "the observed values of all physical and cosmological quantities [the speed of light, the gravitational constant, Planck's constant, and the electric charge of the proton and neutron] are not equally probable but they take on values restricted by the requirement that there exist sites where carbon-based life can evolve and by the requirement that the Universe be old enough for it to have already done so" (*Anthropic Cosmological Principle,* 16). Perhaps the anthropic principle leads to the hypothesis that since the universe thinks, it is. There are, however, disputes over this doctrine, including the charge that the WAP is a dressed-up argument from design (92f.). Here we must take care and not fall prey to either a hidden teleology or the pathetic fallacy or philosophical idealism, for in asserting that the universe thinks we allude strictly and only to the self-organization of nonequilibrium systems. Following upon this conjecture, as Collingwood suggests, just as no one can understand natural science unless he understands history, so "no one can answer the question what nature is unless he knows what history is" (*Idea of Nature,* 177).

44. Compare Weizsäcker, *History of Nature,* 8–9.

45. Henry Nelson Wieman, *The Source of Human Good,* in Gunter and Sibley, *Process Philosophy,* 379.

46. Compare esp. chap. 4 in *History of Nature.*

47. Mayr, *Philosophy of Biology,* 237.

48. Charles Darwin, *Autobiography,* cited in Mayr, *Philosophy of Biology,* 239. See also Richard Dawkins, *The Blind Watchmaker: Why the Evidence of Evolution Reveals a Universe without Design* (New York: W. W. Norton, 1987).

49. Eliade, *Sacred and Profane,* 203.

50. Compare Schaeffer, *Christian View of Ecology,* for a tortured attempt to reconcile evangelical Christianity with ecology. Schaeffer's fundamental difficulty is that he does not meaningfully address the question of time. His God is a supernatural creator who fashioned humankind to rule the earth. Therefore, Schaeffer concludes, "we treat it with respect because God made it. When an orthodox, evangelical Christian mistreats or is insensible to nature, *at that point* he is more wrong than the hippie who has no real basis for his feeling for nature and yet senses that man and nature should have a relationship beyond that of spoiler and spoiled" (76). Distinctions must be drawn between Schaeffer's and other Christian-based approaches to ecological issues, such as Ogden's.

51. Loren Wilkinson, ed., *Earthkeeping: Christian Stewardship of Natural Resources* (Grand Rapids, Mich.: William B. Eerdmans, 1980), 197.

52. Wilkinson, *Earthkeeping,* 199, emphasis added. See n. 2, above.

53. Jack Weir, "Species Extinction and the Concho Water Snake: A Case

Study in Environmental Ethics," *Contemporary Philosophy* 12 (January 1989): 8.

54. No discussion of the conservationist idea of wilderness is required here since (see chap. 9) we have argued that resourcism is not a viable platform for the future of life on earth.

55. Paehlke, *Environmentalism and Politics,* 283.

56. Much that has been done to save wildlife and lands and to provide environmental safeguards has been accomplished through the effort of such individuals as John Muir and Aldo Leopold. But at no time has any challenge to the prevailing cultural paradigm (Modernism) enjoyed widespread support.

57. Sessions, "Spinoza and Jeffers on Man in Nature," *Inquiry* 20 (1977): 492. This article has been overlooked by those advancing the cause of the so-called ecological worldview, as distinct from deep ecology.

58. Kohák, *Embers and the Stars,* 182. Although I agree with Kohák's affirmation of the possibility of hierophany in the wilderness, and although his inquiry has influenced my own, I disagree with his conclusion that personalism is a necessary alternative to materialism. See Rue, *Amythia,* for an alternative.

59. Compare Sessions, "Spinoza and Jeffers," and O'Briant, "Man, Nature and the History of Philosophy." See also David Ray Griffin, *God and Religion in the Postmodern World: Essays in Postmodern Theology* (Albany: State University of New York Press, 1989), for a useful discussion of Spinoza's pantheism, and Jonas, "Spinoza and the Theory of Organism," for a discussion of affinities between Spinoza and ecological or systems theoretical thought.

60. Henri Bergson, *Creative Evolution,* trans. Arthur Mitchell (New York: Modern Library, 1944), 140.

61. For useful overviews see Barrow and Tipler, *Anthropic Cosmological Principle.*

62. Alexander, *Space, Time, and Deity,* 2: 345, 347 (emphasis added), 352.

63. Although both Whitehead and Alexander ground deity-God in evolutionary process, Whitehead seems tender-minded (to use William James's distinction) relative to Alexander's tough-minded approach to the question of deity. Yet Whitehead is not so tender-minded as perhaps David Griffin makes him out in *Religion in the Postmodern World,* where the argument that Whiteheadian philosophy enables naturalistic theism is advanced; neither is Alexander as tough-minded as Collingwood argues in *Idea of Nature.*

64. Charles Hartshorne, *The Logic of Perfection and Other Essays in Neoclassical Metaphysics* (LaSalle, Ill.: Open Court, 1962), 214, 205–6. Also in Gunter and Sibley, *Process Philosophy,* 293, 287.

65. Frederick Ferré, "Religious World Modeling and Postmodern Science," in Griffin, *Reenchantment of Science,* 95. Joseph Meeker is less sanguine, arguing that "the attempt to achieve the values of the garden—nourishment, beauty, peacefulness, and stability—leads inevitably to disappointment in a perverse and competitive world" (*Comedy of Survival,* 103).

66. Weizsäcker's *History of Nature* (1949) predates Snow's study by nearly ten years, and J. Bronowski's *Science and Human Values* (1956) also goes to the heart of the issues Snow addressed in his Rede Lectures (1959). In the past two decades the need for a "scientific humanism" has been argued by a number of scientists. In 1970, for example, the Nobel Prize–winning French biologist Jacques Monod argued that the ethic of knowledge is the only value system consistent with the complexities of twentieth-century life. That same year the National Academy of Science published *Biology and the Future of Man,* a collective study that reached much the same conclusion by a different route. And more recently *Science* (1977) published Eugene Odum's article "The Emergence of Ecology as a New Integrative Discipline," in which Odum argued that ecology might yield knowledge commensurate with the complexity of culture's large-scale, long-term problems, integrating economic and environmental values more effectively. Prigogine's work also bears meaningfully on the two-culture fissure.

67. A teleological explanation assumes the existence of a final cause or goal toward which natural process moves and is therefore inconsistent with natural selection. A teleonomic explanation eschews final cause in favor of the notion of directed evolution. The goal-directedness of teleonomic systems, such as the Rio Gavilan, comes not from final cause but from the irreversibility of thermodynamic process. Teleomatic systems are nonliving systems, and thus can be adequately explained by natural laws (Newton's laws of motion). But the future of any teleonomic system remains open in principle, since time is real and irreversible. Goal-directedness, such as the integrity or stability of natural systems, is not a consequence of design but the emergence of order out of chaos. See Prigogine, *Order Out of Chaos,* and Mayr, *Philosophy of Biology.*

68. Such a position itself is a corollary to a postmodernist paradigm which assumes that (1) time is real and irreversible, (2) process is evolutionary (i.e., emergent novelty is real and moves toward increasingly organized complexity), and (3) inquiry is process revealing itself (i.e., rational process is an actual constituent of reality).

69. Prigogine, *Order Out of Chaos,* 312.

70. *Time* magazine made the environment its 1988 Man of the Year; also see the December 1988 issue of *National Geographic.* The mass media have made both the rending of the ozone layer over both poles and the greenhouse effect almost household words; in consequence, public opinion has

been galvanized in a pro-environment direction. More than one pundit has suggested that the environment is back. Regrettably, that very fact confirms the longstanding lack of serious discussion and understanding of the grounds of ecological malaise: humankind still prays for and invests in the quest for a technological fix for "environmental" crisis.

71. Prigogine, *Order Out of Chaos,* 313.
72. Kohák, *Embers and the Stars,* 103.
73. The Red Face of Humankind is today more of an ideal type than an empirical actuality, for there are few if any places on earth where archaic culture survives in a pristine state. More often than not, as many anthropologists point out, whenever archaic peoples have encountered Western civilization they have been dispatched into oblivion almost instantly. Whatever its romantic appeal, the reality of archaic life is another matter. Gary Snyder has made a particularly objective assessment, since the archaic life is not a bed of roses or an unproblematic mode of existence. What appeals primarily to our imagination is a Paleolithic awareness of being one with nature, a sense that we have lost.
74. Paul Ricoeur, *Main Trends in Philosophy* (New York: Holmes and Meier, 1979), 242 (orig. publ. as *Main Trends of Research in the Social and Human Sciences—Part II,* chaps. 7 and 8).
75. Compare Collingwood, *Speculum Mentis,* 108–53.
76. Ricoeur, *Main Trends in Philsophy,* 242.
77. Compare Rolston, *Philosophy Gone Wild.*

Index

Abbey, Ed, 433n15

Abraham, 45–46, 49, 52, 375n52

Abrams, Morris, 112, 121, 398n40, 399n59, 432n6

Adam: as first man, 51–52; and the Fall, 102, 111; and Eve and Garden of Eden, 344, 348

Age of ecology, 34, 132, 205, 208, 234, 242, 290, 314

Agricultural revolution: and social stratification, 21; domestication of cereals and animals, 24–25, 28–29, 33–34, 48, 200, 313, 371n13; contributing factors, 25–27, 32, 370n5; effect on fertility and population, 26–27, 355n1; conceptual changes accompanying, 28–29, 41; spread in Near East, 32; ecological consequences of, 32–34; and emergence of civilization, 36; effect on Western civilization, 43–44, 183, 347–48; spread in ancient Mediterranean, 45–46; influence on Greek thought, 58–59; Judeo-Christianity as climax of, 61–62; as continuing in Middle Ages, 70–73; influence on goddess worship, 376n57; mentioned, 367n96

Agriculture: mentioned, 15, 46, 52, 54, 80, 95, 111, 183, 209, 212, 249, 262, 287, 293, 327

Albert the Great, 72–73

Alexander, Samuel, 192, 343–44, 350, 434n26, 444n29

Anderson, Edgar, 383n8

Androcentrism: in Emerson, 135; ecofeminist critique of, 310–15

Animals, wild, 28, 33, 52, 148, 188, 209. *See also* Wildlife

Animism: in Sumerian and Egyptian thought, 37; and Judeo-Christianity, 43; in Greek thought, 60; and physicotheology, 101–2; and Spinoza, 124; and Muir, 184–86; in the present, 347

Anthropocentrism: as anthropocentric viewpoint, 21, 43, 73, 81, 84, 108, 135, 173, 177, 180, 197, 219, 235, 248, 286–88, 292, 297–98, 305, 307, 316, 321, 330, 344, 346; roots in Old Testament, 52; influence of Christianity on, 52, 65, 185–86; in Greek rationalism, 57–58, 60; as a consequence of Modernism, 69, 344; definition of, 292–95

Anthropomorphism: as an Egyptian and Sumerian outlook, 41; ridiculed by Xenophanes, 56; critiqued by Tansley, 224; critiqued by Sessions, 341

Aquinas, Thomas, 33, 66–67, 76, 385n18

Arcadian ecology: and arcadian ecologists, 98; as response to Modernism, 100; defined, 103–4; as contributing to ecology, 109; influence on Thoreau,

Arcadian ecology (*cont.*)
132; in Leopold's thought, 206, 208,
214, 216, 226, 231, 234–35
Archaic culture, 16, 21, 26, 154
Argument from design, 72, 100, 102,
106, 109, 138, 196, 337, 397n32
Aristotle, 33, 41, 53–54, 59–60, 73, 79,
299, 306, 379n85, 380n86
Art: Paleolithic, 6, 18, 20, 22–24; medi-
eval and Renaissance, 71, 73; and
Leopold, 207; and language, 279, 332,
349–50; and Coleridge, 399n54; and
Darwin, 418n86; and Meeker, 436n56.
See also Cave art
Artisan, the: in Greek thought, 41, 58,
379n83
Atheism, 101, 397n39

Bacon, Francis: as new Renaissance
person, 80–88, 393n95, 405n16; in
relation to Descartes, 88–90, 108,
110, 135, 195–96, 210, 217; in Judeo-
Christian context, 389nn46,55,56,
390n62, 398n40, 451n2; and the two
cultures, 390n60; mentioned, 76, 92–
93, 105–6, 111, 119, 122, 127, 139, 158,
207, 221, 226, 229, 242, 256, 327,
345, 348
Barnhart, Joe, 191, 414n35, 420n101
Bateson, Gregory, 242, 425n32, 432n103
Beauty: of things, 2, 237, 245–48, 252,
257–60, 279–80, 352; as naturally
existing, 17, 99, 115, 118, 137, 164, 171,
174–76, 180–82, 188–89, 197, 200,
229, 235, 297–98; as emotional or
subjective, 23, 58, 120–21, 148, 157,
204, 251, 272, 332; in medieval art,
71; in land ethic, 206, 210, 235, 238,
241; its role in conservation, 226; as
endangered by industrialism, 234; as
value to be preserved, 292, 294; in

deep ecology, 303; in Paleolithic art,
366n89
Bennett, John W., 281, 366n79, 393n89.
See also Ecological transition, the
Berger, Peter, 372n26, 408n50
Bergson, Henri, 323, 342, 344, 395n10,
413n30, 448n64, 457n60
Bible, the: and research, 42, 373n37,
375n55; and interpretation, 43,
374n40, 376n57, 377nn61,66, 384n12;
Hebrew Bible, 45–47, 49, 52, 61–62,
102; its influence on objectivity, 53;
in Middle Ages, 71, 73; and physico-
theology, 102–3; in Spinoza, 123; in
Emerson, 135–36; in Muir, 176, 179–
80, 189, 192–93; in Jeffers, 250; and
evolutionary cosmology, 331, 349; on
wilderness, 356n10, 373n33; on the
Fall, 369n1; on time, 381n95, 381n96;
its cultural role, 397n39, 441n121;
on pantheism, 416n52; in Leopold,
425n31. *See also* Old Testament
Big Bang, the, 255, 328–29
Biocentrism, 185, 193, 200, 315, 444n33;
as biocentric outlook, 73, 169, 192,
206, 208, 235, 364n71, 418n86,
445n37; as biocentric theology, 177,
182, 186; defined, 292–94, 411n3;
criticism of, 445n39. *See also* Ecocentrism
Bioregionalism, 276, 308, 317, 439n92,
440n109
Bloom, Harold, 52, 378n67
Bohm, David, 130, 402n93, 403n96,
444n27, 452n10
Boltzmann, Ludwig, 324
Bookchin, Murray, 307–8, 448n66
Boundary (or line), between wilderness
and civilization, 2, 4–5, 7, 82, 94, 98,
132, 139, 145, 151, 160, 178, 219, 255,
287, 361n51, 393n2, 408n60, 415n42.
See also Civilization

Bramwell, Anna, 196, 208, 231, 262, 286, 356n8, 428n51, 429n60, 432n102, 441n2, 442n17, 450n92

Bratton, Susan, 69, 72, 384n17

Brophy, R. J., 246, 249, 255, 258–59, 433nn13,14, 434n19, 437n61

Brown, Harold I., 386n28, 388n42, 391n79

Brownell, Baker, 308

Buddhism, 250, 267. *See also* Zen

Bunge, Robert, 362n56, 363n65, 365n74, 366n83

Burnet, Thomas, 111–12, 122, 397n38

Callicott, J. Baird, 213, 223, 236–37, 393n2, 411n5, 412n15, 417n77, 420n1, 421n3, 422n18, 424n25, 427n44, 428n54, 429nn57,63, 430n67, 432n96, 443n24, 444n33, 446n45

Calvinism, 87, 177

Campbell, Joseph, 10–11, 21, 23, 280, 358n19, 360n45, 361n48, 363n68, 365n73, 366n89, 368n107, 455n39

Capitalism, 69, 91–92, 95–96, 171, 198, 222, 261, 348, 403n2, 405n16, 448n65

Causation: efficient cause, 80, 96, 98, 100–102, 104, 109, 123, 125, 206; final cause, 80, 96, 98, 100, 104, 109, 135, 389n46, 395n9; efficient causation, 99, 106, 195, 332, 454n29; causal laws, 125–27, 129; and Aristotle, 380n86; and Smith, 392n86; and God, 414n35; and explanation, 458n67

Cave art: in relation to mythology, 22; role of women and men in, 22, 366n89; interpretation of, 22–23; in ecological context, 22–23, 367n92; in Snyder, 270; time frame and sites, 366n85

Channing, Ellery, 145, 168

Christianity: mystical dimensions of, 21; and patristic fathers, 32–33; as dualistic, 43; and time, 49, 62–64; and Yahwism, 53; and Greek Rationalism, 60–67, 380n90; and stewardship, 103, 108, 338; mentioned, 264, 267. *See also* Judeo-Christianity

Circumscription theory, 24, 27, 358n22

Civilization: as distinct from wilderness, 1, 5, 7–8, 28; as triumph over nature, 2, 4, 19, 39, 41, 65–66, 68, 110, 119, 316; in nineteenth century, 3; as obscuring deep past, 5, 16; as based on archaic culture, 11; poverty as consequence of, 14; compared to archaic culture, 14–17; as absent from Paleolithic mind, 23–24; and agricultural revolution, 30, 60, 95, 183; and writing, 36, 243–44; in ancient Mediterranean, 36–37, 41; as rejected by Yahwists, 47–50, 52–53; Greco-Roman, 53–54; Socrates' role in, 56–57, 60; and Christianity, 66. *See also* Boundary (or line), between wilderness and civilization

Civilization, outlook on: Bacon's, 81–82; Rousseau's, 111; Thoreau's, 132, 139, 143–46, 151–52, 154, 164, 168, 170, 247, 310, 334; Muir's, 177–78, 183, 195; antimodernist, 201; Leopold's, 219–22, 234; Jeffers's, 258; Snyder's, 262, 267, 270, 272, 275–76; postmodern, 285; modern, 285, 340; resource management, 287–88, 316; deep ecological, 306; hermeneutical, 319

Clausius, Rudolf, 1, 128, 237, 239, 250, 286, 321, 323–24

Clements, F. E., 213, 224

Cobb, John B., Jr., 203, 420n101, 435n43, 447n62, 452n11

Cohen, I. Bernard, 386n27, 391n71

Cohen, Michael P., 172, 175–76, 179, 185, 413n20

Coleridge, Samuel Taylor, 115–18, 120–21

Collingwood, R. G., 60, 65, 359n27, 366n87, 380nn87,88, 383n11, 387n33, 390n65, 399n51, 431n90, 432n98, 456n43, 457n63, 459n75

Commoner, Barry, 290, 300, 444nn26,27

Community: natural, 13, 223; biotic, 183, 206, 238, 295–96, 298; of life, 189, 193, 196, 198–200, 206, 232, 237, 264; as model, 223; the land, 232, 234, 236, 241

Consciousness: mythic, 10–12, 37, 42, 49, 54; historical, 28, 37, 46; transcendental, 135, 138; postmodern, 262, 270, 345; as reflexive, 317

Consciousness, self-: as specifically human, 6, 22, 56, 62, 66, 117, 139, 149–51, 248, 251, 310, 317, 330, 332, 346–47, 350; as developmental, 22, 149, 151, 171, 320, 353; cave art as evidence of, 22–23; and nature, 134, 149, 350

Conservation: nineteenth-century, 3; and Muir, 172–73, 175, 201–3, 416n51; movement, 201–2, 209, 222, 234, 236, 284, 302; radical amateur tradition in, 201–3; holistic, 202; and Leopold, 208–10, 212–14, 216, 218–19, 221–24, 226, 228–32, 234, 236, 425n31, 426n33, 427n47, 428n53, 431n80; progressive, 209, 212, 236; views of, 419n97; defined, 419n100; and hunters, 427n40. See also Deep ecology; Ecocentrism; Ecofeminism; Preservationism; Resource conservation; Resourcism

Copernicus, Nicholas, 76, 120, 255; Copernican revolution, 179, 207

Cosmology, 8, 20, 164, 305, 324, 327, 331, 343, 357n14, 368n102, 453n24, 454nn29,31, 456n43; cosmic process,
3, 244, 248, 250, 254, 257, 260, 271, 295, 325, 328, 330, 334, 336, 343–44, 348, 352–53, 434n26; cosmic context, 10, 175, 350; cosmic evolution, 129, 328; cosmic creation, 161, 328, 332, 349, 395n7; cosmic vision, 175; cosmic synergism, 321

Cosmos, 2, 4, 6, 10, 19–20, 28, 40, 100, 112, 121, 129, 155, 162, 171–72, 176, 179, 184, 188, 192, 194, 199, 252, 269, 310, 314, 318, 320, 327, 331–32, 334–36, 338–40, 343–44, 349–50, 363n68, 416n60

Cowles, H. C., 213

Creationism. See Special Creation

Daly, Mary, 311, 449nn75,81

Darwin, Charles: and second scientific revolution, 1, 106–9, 237, 239, 286, 321, 324; *Origin of Species*, 27, 103, 106–7, 163, 282; and evolutionary perspective, 27, 128, 250, 282, 323, 337, 456n48; compared to Aristotle, 59; and rhetoric, 82; and physico-theology, 98, 395n12; and Thoreau, 133, 149, 162, 167, 171, 409n74; Darwinian paradigm, 200, 346, 396n20; and Leopold, 211, 425n29; and Jeffers, 255; and biocentrism, 293, 418n86, 421n6; and social Darwinism, 299, 423n19. See also Evolution

Davies, Paul, 331

Davis, Philip J. See Hersh, Reuben

Dawkins, Richard, 396n21, 425n32, 456n48

Death: in Paleolithic, 12, 14; life and death as natural cycle, 17–18, 24, 42, 49, 55, 178, 189, 191, 208, 253, 269, 273, 329; in Egypt, 38–40; in Christianity, 62–64, 313; in Wordsworth, 120; and natural evil, 214; in Jeffers, 250, 253, 255–56, 259, 260; in Snyder,

266, 269, 273–74; of industrial society, 301; as self-conscious awareness, 332–33, 351

Deep ecology: as idea of wilderness, 3, 301–9; defined, 208; and Leopold, 242; and Snyder, 261, 281; in cultural context, 317, 450n92; and postmodernism, 420n101, 457n57; and value questions, 447n58; and Whitehead, 447n60

Democracy, 68, 96, 257, 275, 281, 348, 351, 419n97, 440n112; democratic life, ix, 217, 442n13; basic principles of, 74; and Jeffers, 433n15

Demythology: Hebraic, 42, 45, 57; in Western culture, 54, 68–69, 76; Greek, 56–57, 60

Descartes, René: as dualist, 85–88, 127, 207, 345, 390n65, 391n74; and power of science, 122, 125, 200; and animals, 124, 391n71; Descartes's dream, 225, 378n71, 392n86, 453n22; and scientific method, 391n70; and biology, 391n73; mentioned, 76, 90, 97, 101, 106, 225, 323, 342

Devall, Bill, 261, 308, 401n78, 411n2. *See also* Sessions, George

DeVore, Irven, 358n19, 359n24, 362n61

Dewey, John, 174, 177, 299, 379n83, 387n37, 391n74, 405n15, 412n16, 413n28, 435n36

Diamond, Stanley, 306, 358n19, 450n94

Diefenbeck, James A., 352, 454n28

Domination of nature: absence in old stone age, 17–18; origin in new stone age, 28–29, 31–32; in Greek rationalism, 59–60; Judeo-Christian roots, 67; in social ecology, 307; mentioned, 229, 292. *See also* Bacon, Francis; Liberation of nature

Doty, William G., 359n35, 449n83, 451n1

Dualism, 57, 88, 99, 101, 114, 116–18, 125, 127, 158, 203, 206, 244, 299, 313, 316, 324, 342, 421n2; humankind as apart from nature, 42, 78, 126, 173, 190–91, 206; science-ethics, 56, 213, 227, 239, 345; fact-value, 85, 206, 227, 237, 299, 345; mind-matter, 88, 99, 101, 119, 125; subject-object, 203, 237; means-ends, 345; is-ought, 345–46

Duerr, Hans Peter, 8–9, 297, 356n8, 358n16, 359n26, 367n92, 384n16, 388n40, 393n2, 415n42, 449n88

Eckersley, Robyn, 307, 448n66

Ecocentrism: as ecocentric outlook, 171, 300–302, 304–5; defined, 292–96; arguments against, 296–300; and deep ecology, 301; and ecofeminism, 309; in cultural context, 316–17; and postmodern wilderness philosophy, 320

Ecofeminism, 309–15, 317, 365n73, 376n57, 449nn74,88

Ecological transition, the, 30, 35–36, 38, 42, 73

Ecology: global, 2; and physico-theology, 99–101; and Marsh, 109; and organicism, 131; and Thoreau, 135, 171; and Muir, 194–96, 202; and Leopold, 205–14, 219, 223–25, 227, 229–31, 233–35, 237–42; normative, 206, 225, 240; shallow, 208, 210, 292, 302, 309; new, 223–24; and Jeffers, 253–54; spiritual, 261–62, 269–70, 274–75, 310; and Snyder, 262, 265, 267, 269–70, 274–75; sacred, 265, 437n68; foundational, 282, 286, 296, 301–2, 317; and resourcism, 286, 288–89; first law of, 290; and preservationism, 290, 292; and ecocentrism, 295–96, 298, 300; and ecofeminism, 314; in cultural context, 317, 327, 345–46. *See also* Age

Ecology (*cont.*)
of ecology; Arcadian ecology; Deep
ecology

Economics: and progress, 25, 69, 194,
217; in Middle Ages, 71, 383n11,
384n13; in Renaissance, 74; and expansion, 75, 216; and Smith, 91–92;
human economy, 92, 104, 217, 218;
and growth, 92–93, 201, 240, 280,
283, 338; and alchemy, 93–94; and
Bentham, 127; and Thoreau, 171;
and ecology, 205, 418n78, 429n60,
458n66; and Leopold, 208, 211–13,
234, 427n47; economic issues, 212;
and resourcism, 287; and ecocentrism,
300; and deep ecology, 301, 303, 309;
and ecofeminism, 314, 336; and conservation, 419n97, 440n112, 441n2,
444n32; and metaphor, 431n82; as
dualistic, 443n23. *See also* Georgescu-
Roegen, Nicholas; History, economic;
Homo oeconomicus; Nature's economy

Eden, Garden of, 22, 31, 50–51, 60, 83,
111, 183, 199, 333, 347, 369n1

Ehrenfeld, David, 202, 238, 419n99,
441n3, 447n62, 448n68

Einstein, Albert, 15, 239, 263, 322, 328,
345, 349, 394n6, 451n5

Eiseley, Loren, 82, 84, 323, 330, 333,
389n50, 396n20, 432n98, 448n72,
454n28

Eliade, Mircea, 19–20, 24, 27, 40, 94,
337, 366n81

Elohim, 45–46, 50, 62, 375n55, 376n57

Elton, Charles, 223–24, 231, 428nn51–
53, 55, 430n72

Emerson, Ralph Waldo: and Coleridge,
116; "Nature," 134–36, 148, 157, 170,
179–80; mentioned, 294. *See also*
Muir, John; Thoreau, Henry David

Endangered species, 4, 240, 296, 320,
340; and Endangered Species Act
(1973), 194, 218, 247, 289–90

Environment: degradation of, 32, 108–
9, 131, 209, 312; and deforestation,
70, 150, 197, 212, 372n22, 379n83,
384n14; erosion of, 213, 370n4,
430n78; exploitation of, 226; and
extinction of species, 419n100, 456n53

Environmental crisis: explanation of, 43–
44, 61, 197, 212, 340; and Snyder, 261;
and ecohumanism, 339; and modern
mind, 345

Environmental ethics, 292, 339, 340,
425n31. *See also* Deep ecology; Ecocentrism; Ecofeminism; Preservationism; Resourcism

Environmental movement, the, 203,
276, 309, 320, 340; as environmentalism, 318

Evernden, Neil, 113, 134, 194, 202,
286, 288–89, 300, 318, 321, 338, 340,
359n28, 417n67, 443n23

Evolution: evolutionary paradigm, x,
107, 110, 130, 211, 250, 322, 396n20,
396n25, 418n86; in thought or consciousness, 2, 4, 30, 54, 62, 65, 277,
304, 317–18, 380n90, 386n28; evolutionary perspective, 5, 149, 192, 348;
in culture, 7, 24, 26, 34, 42–44, 48,
358n22, 363n67, 423n22; in intelligence, 13; evolutionary theory, 101,
126, 326; evolutionary hypothesis,
106, 330; evolutionary process, 109,
124, 155, 162, 206, 239, 241, 259,
284, 290, 294, 296–97, 301, 305, 316,
327, 330, 332, 335, 343–45, 350–51;
and Spinoza, 125; and postmodern
thought, 128–30, 322–23, 325, 328–
30, 334–36, 338, 341, 343–46; and
Thoreau, 133, 137, 149, 162–63, 165,

167; evolutionary insight, 133, 168, 185; evolutionary epistemology, 166, 211; evolutionary pantheism, 173, 181; evolutionary metaphysics, 192, 368nn102,103, 454n29; evolutionary outlook, 193; and Muir, 200, 203; and Leopold, 209, 211, 218, 221, 229, 231, 239, 241; and Jeffers, 254–55; and Glacken, 286; in nature, 290–91, 368n100; and ecocentrism, 295; creative evolution, 335–36, 338, 341, 343–44; and Aristotle, 379n85. *See also* Bergson, Henri; Darwin, Charles; Heraclitus; Prigogine, Ilya; Whitehead, Alfred North

Experience, religious, 28, 176, 250, 265, 335, 341, 343; wilderness, 9, 118, 166; primary, 88, 139, 157, 271; conversion, 177, 188

Fall, the, 50–51, 61, 63–64, 66–67, 83, 89–90, 103, 333, 369n1, 370n3, 384n17, 389n55, 398n40

Ferré, Frederick, 345, 458n65

Feyerabend, Paul, 325, 378n70, 387n34, 388n38, 389n47, 450n94

Flader, Susan L., 210, 213, 216, 232, 420n1, 422n14, 424n25, 431n82

Fox, Steven, 201–2, 411n1, 416n51, 419n97

Fox, Warwick, 301, 447n52

Francis of Assisi, 72–73

Frankfort, Henri, 47, 55–56, 369n109, 370n10, 376n58

Fraser, J. T., 332–33, 381n96, 455n36

Fritzell, Peter A., 240–41

Frye, Northrop, 174, 397n39, 412n8

Gadamer, Hans-Georg, 82, 279, 373n35, 389n53, 394n5, 401n86

Gadon, Elinov, 449n86

Gaia, 291, 444n30. *See also* Magna Mater

Galileo, Galilei: and new physics, 77–81, 387nn34,37, 388nn38,44,45,47, 452n14; mentioned, 6, 76, 86, 89, 94, 98, 106, 120, 323

Garber, Frederick, 133, 406n20

Georgescu-Roegen, Nicholas, 94, 378n71, 382n2, 386n28, 392n86, 394nn3,6, 430n74, 443n21, 453n22

Gimbutas, Marija, 35, 364n71, 449n86

Glacken, Clarence, x, 30, 58, 61, 70, 80, 83, 103, 109, 286, 348, 369n110, 370n6, 394n4, 395n10

God: and myth, 9; as transcendent, 21, 45, 50–51, 331; garden of, 31; as incarnate, 35, 40, 181–82, 190, 192; as woman, 35, 376n57; and Judeo-Christianity, 42–43, 45–47, 49–52, 61–67, 95, 313, 322–23; in Plato, 58; God's divine plan, 64, 71, 77; medieval conceptions of, 70–75; and Scientific Revolution, 77, 80, 82–83, 87; and Romanticism, 99, 111–12, 114, 116–18; and physico-theology, 100–103, 105; and Darwinism, 106–7, 109; and Spinoza, 122–25, 305; and Leibniz, 127; and philosophical idealism, 130–31; and Emerson, 135–36, 139, 150, 158, 179–80; and Thoreau, 141, 149, 153, 161, 171; and Muir, 174–77, 180–82, 185–87, 189–93, 196, 199, 204; and poetry, 243, 279; and Jeffers, 245–46, 248–53, 255, 257–60; as living, 249; and Snyder, 272; in postmodern context, 330–33, 336–38, 341–44, 348–49, 351. *See also* Argument from design; Magna Mater

Goethe, Johann, 123–24, 263

Gottwald, Norman, 42, 44, 51, 373n37, 374n42, 377n61, 451n2

Gould, Eric, 9–10, 359n35, 406n26

Graves, John, 281, 395n15

Greek rationalism, 33, 53–54, 60–61, 64–65, 77, 322

Grene, Marjorie, 319, 326, 400n70, 453n23

Griffin, David, 203, 413n30, 420n102, 453n17, 457n59

Griffin, Susan, 396n18

Gunter, Pete, 383n3, 398n46, 413n30

Haeckel, Ernst von, 196, 418nn78,80, 428n52

Hampshire, Stuart, 125, 400n70

Hanson, Norwood, 114, 388n42

Harding, Walter, 168, 403n1, 404n8, 405n11, 407n33

Hargrove, Eugene C., 378n72, 379n83, 383n7, 393n1, 397n37, 426n37, 430n67, 444n33

Harris, Errol, 398n48

Hartshorne, Charles, 186, 192, 253, 306, 344, 400n76, 416nn52,60, 417n63, 420n101, 455n42

Hays, Samuel P., 281, 419n97, 441nn1,2, 442nn10,17

Heidegger, Martin, ix, 82, 143, 243, 278–79, 303–5, 319, 341, 390n64, 394n5, 401n86, 406n27, 451n3

Heilbroner, Robert L., 91, 384n13

Heisenberg, Werner, 324

Heraclitus, 55–56, 90, 130, 257, 323; Heraclitean process, 55, 119, 124–25, 164, 189, 257, 259, 325, 334, 392n80

Hermeneutics, x, 156; hermeneutic circle, 43, 285, 316, 318–19, 326, 350–52; hermeneutical insight, 143; and Judeo-Christianity, 384n12

Hersh, Reuben, 326, 378n71, 453n22

History, economic: as colored by ideology, 357n11, 382n2, 393n89

Hobbes, Thomas, 74, 81, 92, 97, 111

Homo neanderthalensis, 62, 332–33, 379n79

Homo oeconomicus, 25, 71, 94, 119, 159, 198, 249, 286, 338, 407n44

Homo religiosus, 19–20, 24, 40, 180, 198, 249, 259, 286, 337, 366n81

Humanization of the land, 1, 3, 8, 31, 44, 49, 68, 73, 108, 209, 218, 313, 316, 322, 327, 350. *See also* Boundary (or line), between wilderness and civilization

Hume, David, 125, 421n6, 446n45

Idea of history, 7, 31, 239, 359n27. *See also* Consciousness: historical; Judeo-Christianity: and historical consciousness

Idea of nature, 1, 30, 56–57, 59–60, 77, 81, 85–86, 98–99, 104, 107–9, 113, 125–31, 138, 158, 174, 194, 305, 312, 321, 338, 364n71, 402n91, 433n8. *See also* Mechanism; Organicism

Idea of wilderness: introduction to, x, 1–6; Paleolithic, 7, 12–13, 16, 30, 61, 347; postmodern, 20, 56, 128, 235, 286, 317, 319, 345, 348–49; history of, 30, 33, 54; ancient Mediterranean, 32–33; Yahwistic, 42, 53; Judeo-Christian, 61; early Christian, 66–70; medieval, 70; Renaissance, 73–75; effect of science on, 76; effect of Modernism on, 95; Romantic, 110; in Shelley, 121; American, 133; interpretation of, 385n22, 386n28; mentioned, 407n42, 438n81, 445n37. *See also* Deep ecology; Ecocentrism; Ecofeminism; Jeffers, Robinson; Leopold, Aldo; Muir, John; Preservationism; Resourcism; Snyder, Gary; Thoreau, Henry David

Idolatry, animal, 33–37, 47, 52, 56

Imagination, 134, 178; the aesthetic turn, 111, 113, 117; Thoreau's, 141; ecological, 237; land aesthetic, 236–

37; wilderness aesthetic, 237; Kant's aesthetic, 237, 409n70

Indians, American, 4, 209, 215, 271, 357n12, 363n65, 378n70, 415n42, 417n77, 439n93; and Thoreau, 139–46, 152, 154–55, 157, 159, 165–66, 170

Indigen wisdom, 232, 273, 276, 280, 349, 351

Industrial Revolution, 69–70, 77, 88, 91, 93, 127

Inhumanism, 245–50, 256, 259–60, 280, 301, 434n22; as perspective, 252–53, 255, 257–59, 280, 352

Intuition, 96, 112, 182, 213, 306, 448n64; as immediate experience, 57, 139, 163, 184; as *scientia intuitiva*, 123, 343; as immediate awareness, 143, 195; as radical empiricism, 343

James, William, 164, 171, 297, 343, 401n83, 413n30, 448n64, 457n63

Jastrow, Robert, 331

Jeffers, Robinson, 2, 243–61, 263, 274, 279–80, 301, 303, 349, 352; and stone masonry, 255, 257–58, 436n58; and eternal return, 432n7; and Snyder, 433n8, 434n16; as prophet, 433n15; and theology, 435nn41,43

Jesus Christ, 62–65, 251–52, 255

Judeo-Christianity: conventional critiques by environmentalists, 42–44; and historical consciousness, 45, 49, 244; as consummating ancient Mediterranean ideas of wilderness, 61–67; its mythology, 76; and Galileo, 80; and Bacon, 82–83, 398n40, 451n2; as desacralizing nature, 95, 160, 347; and idea of progress, 97; and physico-theology, 99–103; and evolutionary theory, 106–8; and Romantics, 112, 117; and Kant, 117; and Goethe, 124; and Spinoza, 124, 400n72; and

Thoreau, 145, 155, 158; and Emerson, 167; and Muir, 173–74, 177, 180, 183, 185–86, 191–92, 196, 199, 201, 412n9; and Leopold, 235–36; and Jeffers, 245, 250, 253, 256–59; and resourcism, 286–87; as androcentric, 313; in the present, 322, 340, 345, 348. *See also* Christianity

Kant, Immanuel, 99, 113–17, 119, 125, 136, 207, 236–37, 263, 398n48, 399n49, 404n7, 409n70

Kohák, Erazim, 341, 349, 398n48, 417n67, 451n3, 457n58

Kolakowski, Leszek, 10

Krutch, Joseph Wood, 142, 168, 403n1

Kuhn, T. S., 301, 325, 386n27, 453n20

LaChapelle, Dolores, 309–12, 359n25, 361n51, 379n80, 415n42, 437n67, 437n68, 440n109, 447n54, 449n84

Land ethic, 205–8, 210–11, 215, 218, 221, 223, 225, 230, 234–35, 237–41, 298–99, 304, 346. *See also* Leopold, Aldo

Language: and myth, 9–11, 406n26, 408n62; Paleolithic or archaic, 11, 61, 362n56, 379n79; nature's, 79, 156–57, 160, 187, 288, 443n22; Bacon's, 82; and evolution, 109, 425n32; Thoreau's, 142–43, 151, 156–58, 160, 167, 408n60; Muir's, 175, 187, 192; Leopold's, 217, 223–24, 226, 231, 424n28, 428n54, 429n63, 430n67; and Modernism, 243, 297, 317–18; and wilderness poets, 244, 279, 361n50; and Jeffers, 249; descriptive, 279, 299, 387n34, 388n40, 421n2; prescriptive, 293, 322, 447n58; and ecofeminism, 310–11, 393n95, 449n75; and postmodernism, 319, 324–26, 330, 332–33, 336, 350–51, 353, 359n35,

Language (*cont.*)

450n100; and sexism, 355n6; and wilderness rhetoric, 356n8; Indo-European roots of, 371n18; Greek, 382n100; and verbal models, 429n56; and metaphor, 431n82; and Whitehead, 435n41; and cosmology, 454n31. *See also* Gadamer, Hans-Georg; Heidegger, Martin; Hermeneutics; Rorty, Richard

Lao Tzu, 251–52

Lee, Richard B. *See* DeVore, Irven

Leibniz, G. W., 79, 127, 342–43; Leibnizianism, 415n44

Leiss, William, 80, 85–86, 211, 373n33, 382n1, 385n22, 387n37, 389n55, 405n16, 443n23, 448n65, 451n2

Leopold, Aldo: and Judeo-Christianity, 43, 220, 235–36; and Thoreau, 171, 205, 207, 214–15, 220, 232–33, 235–37; and Muir, 194–95, 205, 212–14, 232, 235–36, 411n5, 417n77; on resource and wildlife management, 205, 208–10, 216, 218–21, 229, 232, 234–35; and forestry, 205, 209–16, 220, 229; and idea of wilderness, 205, 210, 218, 234–35, 239, 241; and biocentric view, 206, 208, 235; and beauty, 206, 210, 226, 229, 234–35, 237–38, 240–41; and wildness, 207, 228, 233; and Darwinian thought, 209, 211, 237, 239–41, 422n18, 423n19, 423n22; and ecological conscience, 218, 237; and ecological imagination, 236–37; in contemporary context, 282, 286, 291, 293, 298–301, 303–5, 346, 351–52; mentioned, ix, 19, 132, 280. *See also* Ecocentrism; Land ethic

Lévi-Strauss, Claude, 1, 11, 15, 358n19, 363n63, 366n87, 370n7

Liberation of nature, 405n16

Lindeman, Raymond, 428n51, 429n57

Linnaeus, 104–6, 109, 225

Lippard, Lucy, 22, 366n89

Literary ecology, 244, 432n2, 436n56, 437n67

Lorenz, Konrad, 359n25, 368n104, 423n22, 427n39

Luckmann, Thomas. *See* Berger, Peter

McIntosh, Robert P., 205, 207–8, 223, 231, 417n74, 422n17, 428nn53,55, 430n78, 444n26

Magna Mater, 2, 17–18, 20, 23–24, 27–30, 34, 50, 60–61, 139, 269, 271, 273–74, 310, 347, 350–51, 353, 364nn71,72, 376n57, 396n18. *See also* Mother Earth

Malthus, Thomas Robert, 109, 282, 337, 397n30

Mandelbaum, Maurice, 113

Marsh, George P., 103, 106–8, 209, 282, 285, 337

Marx, Karl, 128, 133, 160, 171, 201, 277, 403n2, 408n54, 448n65

Mathematics, 33, 79, 89–90, 139, 158, 326, 378n71, 386n27, 387n37, 388n44, 391nn70,73, 403n97, 452n13, 453n22

Matter-in-motion, 24, 69, 77, 80, 88, 90, 94–95, 99, 101, 103, 110, 112, 115, 120–22, 126, 147, 182, 188, 206, 218, 299, 321, 331–32, 348. *See also* Mechanism

Mayr, Ernst, 59, 109, 128, 211, 337, 379n85, 380n86, 391n73, 394n4, 395n8, 396nn19,25, 399n49, 401n87, 418n86, 425n29, 428n52, 444n26, 458n67

Mechanism (as paradigm): and Descartes, 76, 87–88, 391nn71,73; and God, 77; in contrast to organismic paradigm, 77, 95–96, 98, 110, 129–31, 230, 394n3, 395n10, 430n74; and Newtonian mechanics, 89–90, 391n79;

and Smith, 92, 94; and machine metaphor, 97, 102, 124, 195, 202, 223,
323, 348; and alchemy of Modernism,
97–98; critical responses to, 98–99,
101–2, 387n32, 402n91, 452n14;
and imperial ecology, 103, 105; and
ecology, 109–10; and Romanticism,
112–13, 116, 118–19, 244; and Spinoza, 123–25; and British empiricism,
127; adverse effect on society, 128–29;
and Thoreau, 132, 140; and Muir, 174,
182, 184, 200, 415n44; and Leopold,
206–7, 211–12, 223–25, 227, 229–30,
232–33, 237, 241, 424n28, 425n29,
428n54, 429n63; and Snyder, 274; and
historical process, 285; and ecology,
290–91; and ecofeminism, 312; and
preservationism, 316; and classical
physics, 323–24; and environmental
ethics, 339; and space-time, 430n74,
455n42. *See also* Matter-in-motion;
Nature: as ecomachine; Organicism;
Paradigm: mechanistic
Meeker, Joseph, 243, 423n22, 436n56,
437n67, 443n23, 458n65
Megill, Allan, 115, 401n86
Meine, Curt, 221, 223, 227, 231–32,
424n28, 426n33, 428n52
Merchant, Carolyn, 94–95, 289, 309–
10, 312, 315, 391n78, 392n80, 393n95,
394n3, 444n25
Mill, J. S., 125, 127
Mind, the: savage, 1, 59, 65; Neolithic,
3, 21, 29, 37; modern, 5–6, 10–11, 15–
16, 19, 21, 24–25, 36, 40, 77, 119, 253,
257, 259, 278, 285–86, 295, 299, 301,
308, 317–18, 321, 326, 331–32, 335,
338–41, 345–46, 348, 350; Paleolithic,
9, 11–13, 16–20, 22, 24, 27, 37, 39, 42,
44–45, 50, 55–57, 60, 62, 65, 116, 122,
142, 150, 161, 174, 178, 184, 187, 200,
271, 274, 317, 333, 335, 347, 349–50;

352; archaic, 66, 311; medieval, 70–72;
postmodern, 285, 317, 331, 334, 341,
345, 353
Modern age, 7, 19, 22, 82, 85, 90, 221,
256, 272, 299, 327, 331, 337–38, 344–
46, 348
Modernism: as mythic, 9; defined, 68,
97, 202; alchemy of, 68–69, 95, 231,
286, 340, 348; and classical science,
70, 78, 321–23; and Bacon, 81; and
Smith, 91, 94; as ideological, 95, 198,
202, 318; its consequences, 96, 243,
321; critical responses to, 97–132;
and Thoreau, 133, 145, 151–53, 168,
171; and Muir, 174, 187, 191–92, 195,
203; and conservation, 209; and Leopold, 217, 223, 225, 227, 230–31,
234, 237, 240, 242, 346; and evolutionary science, 211, 324–25; and
wilderness poetry, 244; and Jeffers,
248; and Snyder, 268, 272, 274; and
postmodernism, 285–86, 317, 320, 331,
338, 345; and resourcism, 286, 316;
and ecocentrism, 291, 294, 299, 301;
and deep ecology, 301–2, 305, 309,
317; and ecofeminism, 310, 313, 317;
mentioned, 77
Modern worldview, 154, 247
Monod, Jacques, 322, 451n4, 458n66
More, Henry, 101–2
Mother Earth, 148, 262, 271–72,
274, 285, 287, 310–11. *See also*
Magna Mater
Mother goddess, 23, 244, 310–11
Muir, Daniel, 180, 183, 192, 351
Muir, John: and Thoreau, 150, 172–73,
175, 177–79, 182–83, 187–88, 191,
195–96, 201, 203; evolutionary pantheism of, 173, 176–77, 181, 185–86,
190–92, 194, 196, 202, 414n35; and
Emerson, 173, 178–82, 186–87, 192,
414n34; and evolution, 173, 179, 181,

Muir, John (*cont.*)
185, 190, 192–94, 200, 203; his idea of
wilderness, 173–74, 177–79, 182, 203,
351, 416n51; and Leopold, 212–14,
235–36, 425n31; and Snyder, 261, 276,
280; and deep ecology, 301, 303, 306,
411n2; and Old Testament, 416n56;
mentioned, x, 2–4, 19, 132, 210, 282,
295, 343, 383n3, 428n52, 457n56
Murphy, Earl Finbar, 284
Myth: modern, 9, 244; of Great Hunt,
15, 18, 20, 23, 32, 36–37, 59, 270;
creation, 20, 40, 313, 321, 330–34;
in Sumeria and Egypt, 36, 40–41;
shepherd-farmer, 48–49; in Greek
thought, 54, 56; and Thoreau, 142,
406n26, 408n62; wilderness, 151, 157,
160; and Haeckel, 196; and Jeffers,
258; and Snyder, 261–62, 264–66,
268, 274; phallic, 311, 449n75; postmodern, 341, 353. *See also* Consciousness: mythic; Demythology; Language

Naess, Arne, 208, 303–4, 306
Narr, Karl J., 19, 21, 364n72
Nash, Roderick, x, 43, 110, 195, 201,
309, 327, 349, 356n10, 357n13, 373n33,
397n35, 411n2, 417n77, 432n97,
450n92
National Environmental Policy Act
(1969), 218
Natural history, 4–6, 12, 103–4, 137–41,
187, 207, 210, 216, 220, 223–24, 228,
230–32, 242, 290, 334, 338, 369n108,
385n18, 428n52
Nature: in its order of operation, 20,
56, 59; unity of, 103, 107, 109, 113,
122–23; as ecomachine, 107, 286–88,
291–92, 305, 332, 345, 348, 351. *See
also* Mechanism; Organicism
Nature's economy, 7, 104, 165, 200, 208,
218, 234, 409n64

Neolithic revolution, 25–27, 29–30, 45,
61, 91, 183, 286, 340, 347, 449n75
Newton, Isaac, 76–77, 79, 89–90, 92,
97–98, 100–101, 106, 120, 124, 154,
342, 391n78, 392n80, 395n7, 452n14;
Newtonian paradigm, 90, 97, 139, 174,
290, 301; Newton's laws, 92, 101, 185,
468n67; Newtonian-Cartesian outlook, 113–14, 118–19, 121, 123, 126,
136, 157, 184, 188, 195, 318, 322–324
Nietzsche, Friedrich, 100, 128, 133, 250,
254, 401n86, 408n59, 411n7, 435n32

O'Briant, Walter, 342, 401n85
O'Brien, Geoffrey, 143
Odum, Eugene, 131, 458n66
Oelschlaeger, Max, 357n15, 439n100,
443n21
Ogden, Schubert, 331, 451n2, 456n50
Old-new ways, 7, 266, 269, 276, 326,
344–45, 349, 352, 439n89
Old Testament, 41–42, 45–46, 62–64,
89, 102, 250; on idolatry, 377n62; as
typifying agriculture, 377n66
Organicism, 110, 124, 129–31, 196;
nature as alive, 12, 16, 59; nature as
organism, 77. *See also* Mechanism:
in contrast to organismic paradigm;
Relations, internal
Ortega y Gasset, José, 66, 90, 143, 223,
357n14, 358n19, 368n102, 394n5,
422n13
Ouspensky, P. D., 213–14

Paehlke, Robert, 202, 340, 419n95,
440n112, 442n17
Paleolithic mind. *See* Mind
Panentheism, 123, 186, 190, 192
Pantheism, 123–24, 173, 176–77, 181,
185–86, 190–92, 194, 196, 202,
400n76, 414n35, 420n101, 457n59
Paradigm: shift, 6, 76, 386n28, 406n20,

416n51; mechanistic, 77, 97, 129, 388n38, 394n3, 430n74; ecological, 196, 314, 428n54, 447n62, 447n54; wilderness, 182, 189, 192, 202–3, 320; and deep past, 358n19; and Bible study, 373n37; Aristotelian, 380n86; Kantian, 399n49; Thoreauvian, 406n20; Leopoldian, 428n55, 432n96; postmodern, 458n68. *See also* Evolution: evolutionary paradigm; Kuhn, T. S.; Mechanism; Organicism; Scientific Revolution

Parmenides, 55–57, 90, 124–25, 323, 326, 379n83; Parmenidean outlook, 57, 77, 88, 90, 113–15, 124, 131, 322, 324–26, 334, 343

Passmore, John, 46, 82–84, 88, 238, 296–97, 445n39

Patriarchy, 315, 396n18, 449n75, 450n90. *See also* Ecofeminism

Paul, Saint, 33, 63–65, 67, 187, 193

Peirce, Charles S., 164, 171, 308, 318, 344

Pinchot, Gifford, 201, 209, 282

Plato, 15, 41, 53–54, 57–59, 65, 73, 170, 349, 379n83, 391n73, 392n80

Posthistoric primitivism, 5, 7–9, 11, 25, 54, 64, 309; deep past, 5–8, 12, 22, 37, 58, 61–62; lens of history, 6–7, 9, 19, 21, 25, 42–43, 54; modernist fallacy, 16

Postmodernism, 203, 285, 305, 308, 317–18, 344, 353; reason, 240, 345; wilderness philosophy, 320; worldview, 133, 324. *See also* Consciousness: postmodern; Mind: postmodern

Preservationism, 282, 286, 289–92, 295, 297, 300–301, 308, 315–17. *See also* Conservation

Preservation, wilderness, 2–4, 8, 172, 205, 216, 218, 220, 232, 234, 320. *See also* Wildness

Prigogine, Ilya, 110, 128, 131, 211, 290,

324–25, 327, 341, 346, 349, 394n3, 396n25, 398n48, 402n91, 430n74, 452n14, 458n67

Primitive, the: and civilization, 1, 134, 161, 319; and human nature, 7; and art, 22; in Thoreau, 139, 146, 152, 161, 166; in Snyder, 266–67

Primitive people, 9, 183, 200, 219, 272, 277, 280

Primitive religion. *See* Religion

Primitive survivals, 37, 50, 54, 62, 347

Primitive worldview, 331

Primitivism, 5, 7–9, 11, 25, 54, 64, 111, 208, 262, 285, 309. *See also* Posthistoric primitivism

Quantum theory, 324, 387n32, 393n2, 402n91, 430n67, 446n48, 455n42

Radical environmentalism. *See* Deep ecology

Ray, John, 100–106, 109, 111, 122, 337

Reed, Charles, 26, 367n96, 368n100, 371n13

Relations, external, 118, 124, 129–31, 227, 237

Relations, internal: theory of, 129–31, 227, 314; as interrelationships, 136, 142, 149, 169, 203, 206, 219. *See also* Web of life

Religion: Paleolithic, 18–19, 21, 45; interpretation of, 18–20, 42–44; Neolithic, 19, 32, 34–36; nature religion, 51, 72, 102; in Greece, 54, 56; in Middle Ages, 71; and Reformation, 75; and Bacon, 84; and Descartes, 86–87; and Kant, 114, 117, 398n47; and Spinoza, 122; and Comte, 127; and Thoreau, 139; and Muir, 172, 174; religious conversion, 174, 177, 180, 186; and antimodernism, 201; and Leopold, 212; and Jeffers, 247, 250–51, 255;

Religion (*cont.*)

and Snyder, 261–62, 264; and resourcism, 286; and deep ecology,
304; and postmodernism, 325, 335–
36, 338–39, 340–41, 349–50, 352. *See
also* Christianity; Homo religiosus;
Judeo-Christianity; Tribes of Yahweh

Resource conservation, 3, 202–3, 283–
84, 286, 288, 302, 308–9

Resource management, 208, 210, 232,
282–85

Resourcism, 203, 210, 281–89, 291–
93, 297, 300–301, 308, 315–17, 339,
402n91, 442n12, 443nn23,24, 457n54

Ricoeur, Paul, 157, 319, 350, 408n60

Rolston, Holmes, III, 194, 238, 288, 295–
96, 300, 359n28, 444n33, 446n46,
459n77

Roosevelt, Theodore, 209, 282

Rorty, Richard, 174, 204, 227, 319,
325, 359n35, 386n28, 388n39, 394n5,
421n2, 446n47, 450n100

Rothenberg, Jerome, 134, 144, 439n85

Rousseau, Jean-Jacques, 93, 110–11, 267,
385n23

Rue, Loyal, 451n2, 457n58

Ruether, Rosemary, 309, 313–14

Russell, Bertrand, 86, 88, 124–25

Sacred, the: and place, 23, 40, 165,
344; and sacrality of existence, 36,
160, 173–74, 176–77, 180, 248, 271,
336, 339, 341, 344. *See also* Homo
religiosus; Time

Sagoff, Mark, 442n12

Sahlins, Marshal, 14, 92, 306, 358n19,
364n69, 382n2, 392n86

Sale, Kirkpatrick, 307

Santayana, George, 180

Sax, Joseph, 2, 442n9

Scheler, Max, 88, 391n74

Schneidau, Herbert, 6, 10, 47–48, 50–53,
68, 76, 358n20, 359n27, 369n1, 373n31,
374n42

Schopenhauer, Arthur, 100, 113, 125–28,
133, 136, 254

Schrödinger, Erwin, 206, 322, 345, 349

Science: power of, 11, 82, 85, 87, 97, 103,
202, 226, 228, 256, 345, 350; modern
(classical), 15–16, 43, 77, 99, 109–
10, 122, 124, 128–29, 196, 206–8,
211, 239, 250, 255, 259, 291, 322–24,
326, 331, 348; scientific instruments,
78, 98, 127, 139; scientism, 78, 203,
285; scientific method, 80–81, 85–
86, 236; scientific nature, 97, 113, 115,
118, 122, 125, 127; normal, 98, 301–2;
postmodern, 107, 124, 324; scientific
worldview, 171, 324; revolutionary
science, 240. *See also* Paradigm

Scientific Revolution, 1, 69, 76, 78, 80,
89, 94–96, 100, 106, 128, 237, 250,
286, 312–13, 321–22, 325, 341–42, 345,
348; new science, 79, 86, 102, 113, 223;
new physics, 90, 106, 389n45; new
biology, 106; and dualism, 387n37;
and Judeo-Christianity, 397n39; mentioned, 449n75

Sessions, George, 124, 179, 195, 238, 261,
301–2, 305, 307–8, 340–42, 400n72,
401n78, 437n68, 441n3, 447n60,
449n74, 457n57

Shelley, Percy Bysshe, 98–99, 115, 120–
21

Shepard, Paul, 8, 13, 31, 58, 208, 306,
308, 357n15, 358n19, 359n25, 360n44,
361n50, 364n71, 367n92, 376n58,
393n1, 415n42, 422n7, 423n22,
436n56, 439n94, 448n72

Sherover, Charles, 63

Sierra Club, 3, 172, 205

Simpson, George G., 423n22, 431n89, 454n28

Singer, Peter, 446n49

Smith, Adam, 76, 90–95, 97, 111, 151, 153, 160, 217, 287, 392n86

Snow, C. P., 345

Snyder, Gary, 8, 12, 243–45, 261–80, 301, 303, 310, 314, 352, 356n8, 358n19, 433n8, 448n72, 459n73

Socrates, 54, 56–57, 87, 180, 378n78

Special creation, 106–7, 109, 191, 199, 337; creationism, 193–94

Spinoza, Benedict, 99, 113, 121–27, 301, 303, 305, 342–44, 400n72, 457nn57,59

Stegner, Wallace, 240

Stengers, Isabelle. *See* Prigogine, Ilya

Stevens, L. Robert, 396n24

Stone, C. D., 194

Stone, Merlin, 36, 370n9, 372n23, 376n57

Supernaturalism, 33, 108, 117, 177, 192, 347

Tansley, A. G., 223–25, 428nn51,55, 429n57

Tao, the, 262, 272, 349, 352

Taylor, A. E., 378n78

Taylor, Paul W., 238, 299, 411n2, 419n91, 445n37

Teilhard de Chardin, Pierre, 290, 294, 357n14, 445n34

Thales, 54–55

Theism, 123, 177, 181, 191, 203, 338; male monotheism, 313; and deity, 341. *See also* Pantheism

Thermodynamics, nonequilibrium, 99, 295–96; second law of, 128, 255, 288, 291, 323, 335–36, 343, 397n30, 452n14; entropy, 131, 382n2

Theroux, Paul, 168

Thoreau, Henry David: in contemporary context, 1–4; and Emerson, 132–40, 148–50, 154–56, 163, 165–67, 170–71, 406n21, 410nn75,80,84, 413n20; and evolution, 133, 137, 149, 162–63, 165, 167; idea of wilderness, 136, 142, 144–45, 149, 161, 171, 173, 407n42; art form, 141, 151, 170; and language, 142–43, 151, 156–58, 160, 167, 318, 355n6, 406n26, 408nn60,62; and Muir, 175, 177–79, 182–83, 187, 191, 196, 201, 203, 417n77; and Leopold, 205, 210, 214–15, 220, 232–33, 235; and Jeffers, 247; and Snyder, 261, 276, 280; evolutionary outlook of, 294, 330, 334, 351, 409nn70,71,74, 428n52; and Marx, 403n2, 408n54; *Journal*, 137, 145, 168, 169–70, 404n8; his poetry, 405n11; mentioned, ix–x, 19, 132, 301, 310, 321

Time: as eternal mythical present, 12, 24, 42, 65, 142, 155, 157, 198, 249, 360n46; as sacred, 23, 24, 40; in Judeo-Christianity, 33, 63–66, 367n94, 381n96, 456n50; space-time, 114, 323, 335, 343; in Thoreau, 154–55; as eternal return, 254, 351; in Greek thought, 381n94; as irreversible, 398n48, 430n74, 458nn67,68; as bioesthetic structure, 436n56. *See also* Evolution; Homo religiosus; Judeo-Christianity

Totemism, 12–13, 15, 21, 34–36, 50, 59, 347, 361n51; in Thoreau, 161; in Snyder, 270

Tracy, David, 384n12

Transcendentalism, 133, 135–36, 142, 144, 149, 151, 158, 160, 166, 168, 171–73, 175, 178–81, 210, 294, 334; transcendental universals, 141, 143

Tribes of Yahweh, 41–42, 44, 46–47, 50, 374n40, 375n48, 376n58
Troeltsch, Ernst, 386n24
Turner, Frederick, 134, 144, 386n26, 445n38, 454n28
Turner, Frederick Jackson, 3, 209, 275, 422n12
Turner, Frederick W., 176, 183–84, 357n12, 411n1, 412n12, 414n38, 416n49

Utilitarianism, 108, 116, 127, 238, 287, 419n97, 426n37, 443n23

Value, intrinsic, 2, 89, 94, 97, 105, 199, 208–10, 231, 234, 238, 287, 293–95, 297, 300, 303, 305; recreational, 5; of myth, 11; in stone age, 14, 20; comparative, 21, 36, 166, 219, 235; and Judeo-Christianity, 33, 48, 64, 80, 112, 124, 338; use-value, 88, 150, 154, 159–60, 202, 217, 293, 316, 351; lack of natural, 94, 174, 194, 236, 316; market, 96, 168; instrumental, 105, 208, 233, 288, 293, 300–301; and Kant, 114, 117–18; heuristic, 131; religious, 174; in antimodernism, 201; and postmodernism, 203; recovery of, 207, 215, 217, 334–36; ultimate, 228, 340–41, 345; unexamined, 232, 299, 345; cultural, 238, 285; and Jeffers, 246–47, 250, 253, 257, 260, 280; and Snyder, 277; source of, 295–96, 338; and deep ecology, 301–3, 305–6; and environmentalism, 318, 340; and science, 322, 326, 346; economic, 356n10. *See also* Dualism
Veblen, Thorstein, 201, 443n20
Virgil, 104, 137, 143, 147, 156
Vonnegut, Kurt, 332–33, 368n104

Weber, Max, 386n24

Web of life, 2, 8–9, 73, 109, 181, 184, 193, 197, 225, 238, 276, 282, 293, 300, 402n91, 403n2, 422n18, 429n60, 440n112. *See also* Relations, internal
Weir, Jack, 456n53
Weizsäcker, C. F. von, 322, 398n48, 430n74, 456n44
West, Bruce, 452n13, 452n14
White, Gilbert: as arcadian ecologist, 104–7; mentioned, 109, 123, 169, 173, 214, 232
White, Lynn, Jr., 43, 373n33, 411n2, 419n91
Whitehead, Alfred North, 97, 112–13, 118, 120–21, 128–29, 192, 196, 253, 258, 290, 298, 322, 343, 368n102, 387n37, 394n6, 398n46, 402n91, 403n96, 405n15, 409n71, 413n30, 416n58, 435n41, 447n60, 448n64, 453n22, 457n63
Wieman, Henry Nelson, 335, 399n52
Wild lands, 2–3, 209, 289, 327
Wildlife, 72, 205, 216–18, 281, 288, 292–93, 303
Wild nature: idea of, 1, 3–4, 32, 61, 77, 81, 93–94, 97, 104–5, 109, 111, 124, 127–28, 136, 150, 160, 173, 177, 179–81, 183, 186, 205, 209–10, 213–14, 221, 228, 232–33, 235, 268, 278, 280, 282, 287, 294, 297–98, 300, 302–3, 313, 316, 346–47, 351; and contemplation, 2, 118, 140, 143, 151, 156–59, 164, 170–71, 175–77, 188, 191–92, 213, 241, 303, 321, 330; and recreation, 5; and culture, 8, 24, 275; and agriculture, 28–29, 35, 58, 62; and Hebrews, 49; and Modernism, 68–70, 74, 243; in Middle Ages, 72; as distinct from civilization, 82, 88, 219, 237–38, 244, 261, 339; as essential, 134, 327; in contemporary context, 201, 217, 239, 292, 349; mentioned, 145, 245, 270, 284

Wilderness: religion, 45, 49–50; theology, 173, 176–77, 181–82, 186, 190,
192; and nature worship, 313, 348
Wilderness Society, 205, 232
Wildness: as essential, 2, 3, 285, 321;
as preservation of the world, 2, 165,
171, 207, 285, 321, 334; and human
beingness, 7–9; and Thoreau, 147,
151, 160–61, 164–65, 167; and Muir,
200, 207; and Leopold, 228, 233; and
Jeffers, 254
Wilson, E. O., 211, 356n8, 423n22,
425n32, 429n60

Wittgenstein, Ludwig, 320, 372n24,
402n95
Wordsworth, William, 98, 113, 115,
118–21, 250, 349, 398n40, 399n59
Worster, Donald, 101, 103–5, 109, 200,
208, 223–24, 231–32, 234, 242, 290,
395nn8,10, 418nn78,26, 442n12

Zen, 185, 262, 264, 271–72, 438nn70,75.
See also Buddhism
Zimmerman, Michael, 129, 315